ASPEN PUBLISHERS

Rigos Bar Review Series™

Multistate Bar Exam (MBE) Review

Review

Volume 1: Contracts and UCC Article 2, Torts, and Real Property and Future Interests
(Course 5311)

Wolters Kluwer
Law & Business

AUSTIN   BOSTON   CHICAGO   NEW YORK   THE NETHERLANDS

James J. Rigos
230 Skinner Building
1326 Fifth Avenue
Seattle, WA 98101
Telephone: (206) 624-0716
Fax: (206) 624-0731
rigos@rigos.net

To contact Aspen Publishers' Customer Care, e-mail customer.care@ aspenpublishers.com, call 1-800-234-1660, fax 1-800-901-9075, or mail correspondence to:

Aspen Publishers
Attn: Order Department
PO Box 990
Frederick, MD 21705

Printed in the United States of America.

1 2 3 4 5 6 7 8 9 0

ISBN 978-0-7355-7333-8

This book is intended as a general review of a legal subject. It is not intended as a source for advice for the solution of legal matters or problems. For advice on legal matters, the reader should consult an attorney.

Magic Memory Outlines® is a registered trademark owned by Rigos Professional Education Programs, Ltd.

Editorial Direction

James J. Rigos is an Attorney-CPA, a graduate of Boston University Law School, and Editor-in-Chief of the creating team of this Bar Review Series, owner of Rigos Professional Education Programs, Ltd., and an author for Aspen Publishers. He has written and lectured for professional associations and for Bar- and CPA-exam review programs for over a quarter of a century. For many years he has served as a national Director of the American Association of Attorney-CPAs. He has also created a series of CLE and CPE courses focusing on professional ethics.

Acknowledgments

This work product was substantially enriched because of the robust encouragement and editorial involvement of many thoughtful individuals. Aaron Rocke, Sidney Tribe, Tracy Duany, Jason Stonefeld, Tom Smith, Bryan Brown, Kevin Stemp, Gina Lowe, Matt Conrad, Joanna Roth, Steve Johnson, and Carolyn Plant made significant drafting contributions. Law School Professors Janet Ainsworth, Jim Bond, Mark Chinen, David DeWolf, Sam Donaldson, Christian Halliburton, Gregory Hicks, and Karl Tegland made important suggestions on substantive improvements and reviewed the Rigos Bar Review Series textbooks. A special thanks to our past students for their many suggestions of substantive improvement and creative new learning aids. All their recommendations and successes are a part of every page of this Rigos Bar Review Series. The direction and guidance of Steve Errick's team (especially Melody Davies, Carol McGeehan, and Barbara Lasoff) from Aspen Publishers made this all possible.

RIGOS BAR REVIEW SERIES

MULTISTATE BAR EXAM REVIEW (MBE)

Table of Contents

This Rigos Bar Review Series Multistate Bar Exam (MBE) Volume 1 of the two part series contains the following subjects and contents:

Rigos Bar Review Series Multistate Bar Exam (MBE) Volume 2 of the two part series contains the following subjects:

RIGOS BAR REVIEW SERIES
Other Products in the Series

MULTISTATE ESSAY EXAM (MEE) REVIEW

- Succinct explanations of the most frequently-tested legal principles **provide you only the information needed to answer MEE essays**.
- **Strategies for issue-spotting and techniques for analysis** help build your confidence as you go.
- **Identifies "tips" and "traps" often encountered on the MEE**, to help you avoid common mistakes and pitfalls.
- Introductory chapter on exam strategies **tells you exactly what to expect at the exam**, advises you how to prepare, and takes the mystery out of the MEE.
- Acronyms assist you in memorizing legal elements and perfecting your approach to the essays.
- All topics are presented in an **easy-to-read, outline format**.

MULTISTATE PERFORMANCE TEST (MPT) REVIEW

- Provides **detailed instructions on the best approach to use in answering** the types of MPT questions on the exam.
- Organized so there is **an entire chapter devoted to each popular MPT-format question**.
- Includes a flowchart illustrating the frequency of MPT tasks that show up on the exam.
- Identification of common pitfalls and traps **helps familiarize you with the typical distracters used by the examiners**.
- **Seven simulated exam questions, categorized by topic with full sample answers** provided help you gauge your progress and reinforce MPT practice.
- Explanations are compact, yet **comprehensive enough to give you confidence that you have learned all the important information you need** to pass the exam.

MULTISTATE PROFESSIONAL RESPONSIBILITY EXAM (MPRE) REVIEW

- Topics are presented in an **easy-to-read outline format, allowing you to find quickly what you need** and providing a more focused approach to studying.
- Content is extensive, yet not overwhelming, and **supplies you with only the information you need to know to pass the MPRE**.
- Focuses on the finer distinctions of the rules in order to **help you eliminate possible wrong answers on the exam**.
- **Hundreds of sample questions**, organized by subject, offer extensive MPRE practice, as well as full answer rationales.
- **A mock 2-hour/60 question practice exam helps you simulate a real MPRE test-taking experience**.
- Acronyms provide a **framework for memorization of issues and rules**.

Ask your bookstore about **Rigos Bar Review Series** products from Aspen Publishers or visit us online at *http://lawschool.aspenpublishers.com.*

Multistate Bar Exam (MBE) Review

Review

Volume 1: Contracts and UCC Article 2, Torts, and Real Property and Future Interests (Course 5311)

RIGOS BAR REVIEW SERIES

MULTISTATE BAR EXAM REVIEW (MBE)

PREFACE

Table of Contents

RIGOS BAR REVIEW SERIES

MULTISTATE BAR EXAM REVIEW (MBE)

PREFACE

I. INTRODUCTION

Welcome. This introduction is an overview of the Rigos Bar Review Series Multistate Bar Exam (MBE) Review. It describes the MBE process including how the exam questions are created and graded. The question characteristics and related suggested approach tips are covered. Also detailed is our recommended organized preparation program you should follow to ensure that you score high on the MBE at the first sitting. The information in this preface is important. It should be thoroughly studied and understood before you start your Rigos Bar Review Series MBE review program. Refer back frequently.

Candidates in jurisdictions that administer the Multistate Essay Exam should use the *Rigos Bar Review Series Multistate Essay Exam Review — MEE* in conjunction with this MBE program. Our MEE course contains practice essay questions to supplement the text contained in this program.

A. <u>Successful Rigos Candidates' Comments</u>

"I chose the Rigos Bar Review program because it seemed to offer a focused approach to passing the bar, and I am happy to say that it provided just that. The materials and the practice questions taught me what I needed to know and how to use what I had learned. There were no surprises on the exam. I was able to answer the questions quickly and confidently." – G. Pisarski, Esq.

"I felt that the course content and structure were superb, and that the concise nature of the materials kept me focused on what was important for the exam, rather than sending me on some theoretical wild goose chase through lengthy legal quagmires." – R. Hulshoff, Esq.

"While the outlines are brief, they are nothing less than outstanding in their coverage. The Magic Memory Outlines® are so good that my friends who had enrolled in other review courses used them to distill the information down to a manageable size." – J. Berryman, Esq.

"The amount of material was manageable. Where the other courses' outlines seemed overwhelming, the Rigos Bar Review presented an amount of information for each subject that could be approached and conquered in a short period of time. The acronyms were a life-saver for approaching the commercial code and contract subjects. They provided a framework for dealing with the issues and rules. The information on grading gave me a realistic expectation of the exam. Your course made the whole process seem much less intimidating." – R. Church, Esq.

"The Magic Memory Outlines® were very helpful. I recommended the Rigos Bar Review to the other firm associates even before I found out I had passed the bar. The combination of superior passing rate and panic free study materials makes this the clear choice in review courses. I would highly recommend the Rigos Bar Review Series to every law student preparing for the bar." – N. Montstream, Esq.

"Concise material that doesn't create information overload. The material is organized in a fashion that is focused, sensible, and understandable. It focuses on the fine line distinctions which are so frequently tested on the MBE" – G. Cook, Esq.

"The Rigos Bar Review seamless process was incredibly effective and I went into the bar exam confident that I would pass." – J. Piza, Esq.

B. Focused, Positive Mental Attitude

What the mind can conceive, dedicated hard work can achieve. You must believe you can and will pass the bar exam and become a successful attorney at law.

1. Join the Winning Team: The Rigos professional review courses have over 100,000 professional alumni who have used our structured programs to pass their professional entrance exams. Therefore, your objective of passing the MBE at the first sitting is very attainable.

2. Success-Focused Program: Exam confidence is the result of a well-organized and well-executed preparation program. Students following the complete Rigos Bar Review Series seamless program are geared for exam success.

C. MBE Exam in General

The MBE is a testing product of the National Conference of Bar Examiners (NCBE). The MBE takes one full day of testing and is scheduled for the last Wednesday in February and July. It is required in all but a handful of states. Over 60,000 students a year sit for the MBE. The student must complete two sets of 100 multiple-choice questions in morning and afternoon sessions of three hours each. Both the actual MBE test booklets and this Rigos Bar Review Series text are printed in 12-point type.

II. QUESTION DETAILS

The MBE has 200 four-stemmed multiple-choice questions, 100 in each morning and afternoon set. The subjects of Contracts and Torts have 34 questions each. The other four subjects (Criminal Law and Procedure, Constitutional Law, Evidence, and Property) have 33 questions each. The exam tests the six subjects in random order.

A. Question Source

1. Organization: The NCBE has six MBE Drafting Committees monitoring the six MBE subjects tested. There are five people per committee with broad representation from law school professors, professional bar examiners, and practicing attorneys.

2. New Questions: The NCBE creates new questions on an ongoing basis to refresh the test bank of potential questions and promote breadth of topic coverage. Law school professors and practitioners are a fertile source for new questions. Proposed new questions are subject to multiple reviews by Committee members to ensure they are well drafted, accurate, unambiguous, and fairly test the subjects.

3. Broad Input: Each participating state bar association may submit comments to the Committee prior to acceptance of a new question. A thorough review of all questions is made prior to printing each final published exam.

B. Grading System

1. Scoring: Every right answer you choose is worth one point regardless of the question's degree of difficulty. There is no penalty for wrong choices. The average raw score is about 125 to 130 out of 200.

a. Scaled for Difficulty: The final number of right answers reported for a particular exam depends upon that exam's overall difficulty. The NCBE has a scaled ("equating" is their descriptive term) difficulty system, so the final score awarded to students is comparable from exam to exam. The additional scaling points typically run between 10 and 20 points. Thus, the final equated score averages around 135 to 140.

b. Ensure Consistency: The examiners' analysis of answers and the scaling system is intended to correct the effect of any bad questions on a particular exam. This ensures grading consistency and comparisons from exam to exam.

2. State Passing Rate: Each jurisdiction decides how to combine the MBE scaled score with their own state specific testing. Nationally, about 60% of the students receive a "passing" scaled score, although this percentage varies from state to state (for a breakdown go to http://www.ncbex.org/uploads/user_docrepos/BEMaystatsweb_01.pdf). In states that permit students from non-ABA-approved law schools to sit, the pass rate may be significantly lower.

a. State Rules Vary: Most states combine the MBE and essay scores using various formulas and weights. Some allow a waiver on the essays if you achieve a certain MBE score. A few accept MBE scores from other jurisdictions.

b. Particular State: For details of the passing statistics and particular grading method used in your jurisdiction, you should check with your individual state bar association. Go to www.abanet.org/barserv/stlobar.html for an online listing of state-by-state bar exam information.

C. Question Approach

1. Focus: The fundamental legal principles of the America Law Institutes's (ALI's) Restatements of Law are the testing focus. Statutes and local or minority case law positions are not usually tested. The MBE questions concentrate on analysis and the detailed black letter law rules, not the usual broad concepts found in law school or bar exam essay questions.

2. Call of the Question: The facts of a question provide the foundation to test the applicable legal rule.

a. Facts Lead to Requirements: The facts are presented in either single or multiple paragraph format. Over the past few years the fact patterns have become longer, creating more time pressure. The facts lead to a requirement sentence containing a "call of the question." The correct answer is the one alternative which is the most directly responsive to the call of the question.

b. Requirement Position: The student is usually required to take either the position of a judge (decide the likely outcome) or an advocate (best or worst argument). A few questions call for the candidate to choose the most effective structuring of a transaction or legal problem. You may also be asked to give a client an opinion on the best course of action. The reasoning is more important than the likely outcome.

3. Candidate Approach: About one-third of the exam questions are quite difficult.

a. Systematic Approach: A systematic approach to correct answer selection helps. An enlightened guessing system is also useful (see detailed suggestions below). Detailed analysis of all four alternatives is necessary; instinctive answers are often wrong because fine-line distinctions are everywhere on the MBE.

b. Tricks Abound: There is usually some merit in each of the four alternatives, but some small factual difference or nuance of the determinative legal rule makes one alternative a more compelling answer. The examiners work hard to make the red herrings and distracters seem quite attractive.

D. Subjects Tested

There are six substantive subjects tested on the MBE. The NCBE does issue content specification outlines with rough percentage distributions. We have summarized the topic coverage as follows:

1. Contracts and UCC Article 2: Expect over two-thirds of the testing to be under the common law "SIR" topics (services, intangibles, and real estate). The questions will also cover various provisions of UCC Article 2 sale of goods, especially where there is a different or expanded treatment under the UCC as compared to the common law. The majority of the testing focus is on the formation elements (especially offer and acceptance issues, defects in meeting of the minds, and statute of frauds compliance), performance (especially reasons for non-performance), and remedies. Many MBE authorities believe that the contract questions test both deeper and broader that the other five subjects.

2. Torts: Expect up to half of the questions in this common law topic to cover various aspects of negligence in some detail. Up to one-quarter of the questions may be on claims asserted under strict liability and product liability theories. The remaining questions are spread over the other tort topics fairly evenly. The emphasis is on the elements of the tort action that P must prove to make a prima facie case and the various defenses that may be asserted by D.

3. Property and Future Interests: These are common law topics. Future interests are about one-quarter of the subject testing and may involve quite difficult questions. Acquisition of property by deed or adverse possession is heavily tested. Easements, conveyances and recording are also frequent topics. Restrictive covenants have reasonable coverage and landlord-tenant issues receive some attention. Testamentary devises and rights in personal property are lightly tested.

4. Evidence: Almost all the testing in this subject is from the Federal Rules of Evidence (FRE). The usual call of the question is to analyze the reasons why a particular item of evidence is admissible or inadmissible under the facts presented in the question. Admissibility of evidence and hearsay evidence constitute two-thirds of the testing. The focus is most frequently on the particular rules that exclude or limit admissibility.

5. Constitutional Law: The emphasis is on the US Federal Constitution's effect on the actions and powers of the three branches of federal government: the Executive, Legislative, and Judicial. In addition, the constitutional limits establishing what a state may or must do in enforcing their laws is tested. Approximately half the questions test individual rights with the candidate usually required to determine whether a statute is valid or invalid.

6. Criminal Law and Procedure: The testing concentrates on the basic common law criminal rules, although some questions focus on the modern majority rules of statutory modifications. Criminal procedure questions emphasize US constitutional limitations on the states' ability to introduce evidence to convict a criminal defendant. The emphasis is on the controlling standards and appropriate procedural requirements the states must meet in the prosecution process.

III. MBE QUESTION CHARACTERISTICS

A. Comments and Pitfalls

The following question approach tips are extremely important. Tests show that avoiding the MBE question pitfalls may add up to 10% more right choices on uncertain questions. The exam tests not only your knowledge of the black letter law but also your MBE question analytical skills, which can only be developed through practice.

1. Format: All the MBE questions are multiple-choice with four alternatives. All levels of difficulty are represented and there is no pattern to the sequence.

2. Preferred Answer Objective: Look for the best alternative. Often one pair of answers concludes that A will prevail while the other concludes that B will prevail. The rationale supporting the conclusion thus becomes the determining factor.

a. Objective: This may mean the most nearly correct or conversely, the least incorrect answer. There is often some truth in each alternative; the best alternative must be the most completely correct and it must relate to the facts. Look for the fact(s) in the question that make one alternative more compelling than the others. Appreciate the difference between the command adverbs "may" and "shall"/"must."

b. Problems: Typically, two of the four alternatives are the same or very close in outcome, and both may sound accurate. An alternative may reach the right conclusion for the wrong reason or for a reason less compelling than another alternative's rationale. Watch out also for incomplete definitions of the determinative rules of law, particularly legal rules that have more than one requirement, but only one requirement is stated in the question.

3. Negatives: A few questions have negatives in the facts, the call, or the alternatives. This means that the correct choice is the worst, least helpful, least likely, or most false alternative. The candidate must reason very carefully through the alternatives and reverse the normal frame of reference. The "true-false" approach discussed in item 4 below is often quite helpful in dealing with negatives. If looking for the negative, the false or incorrect alternative is the best choice.

4. Try a True-False Approach: For some questions it may help to use a true-false analysis for each of the four alternatives. This is where you evaluate each answer option by asking the question, "Is this statement true or false?" The true-false approach is especially useful for questions having a negative call. Ideally you will end up with a 3-1 split; the odd one out is usually the right answer.

5. Absolutes: Be on the alert for sweeping exclusionary words such as "all," "always," "none," "never," "under no circumstances," or "solely." An alternative containing such words is so broad that it is unlikely to be correct. Ask yourself "is there any exception?" The more narrowly stated, inclusive alternative, is usually preferable to an "open door" option.

6. Nonsense Theory: Occasionally the MBE will include answer options containing a nonsense principle, concept, or theory such as "res gestae" or "doctrine of changed circumstances." A good rule of thumb is that such an alternative is wrong unless you have seen the theory in the Rigos Bar Review Series texts.

7. Be Selective: More facts or law may be given in the question than is necessary.

a. Distracters: Red herrings are often present in the facts. The examiners are very clever in creating attractive factual distracters. They are designed to support logic that leads to one of the wrong alternatives.

b. Detail May Be Coding: Also look for seemingly meaningless detail because such a reference may provide a necessary fact required for the application of a controlling legal rule. An example is a transaction between a wholesaler and a retailer; they are both considered "merchants" and this is necessary to the applicability of some UCC provisions. If dates or dollar amounts are given, they are usually necessary for the correct conclusion.

8. Analyze Modifiers in the Alternatives: Many answer alternatives begin with the conclusion (e.g., "P will prevail," "P will not prevail," or "D's defense will be effective"). This is then followed by a conditional or limiting modifying word ("because," "since," "if," "only if," or "unless") and a statement of a supporting legal reasoning or rationale. Picture the below three element skeleton.

✳ **Conclusion | Conditional or Limiting Modifier | Supporting Reasoning or Rationale**

a. "Because," "Since," or "As": These conditional requirement modifiers indicate the following rationale is usually the reasoning necessary to satisfy the legal conclusion.

(1) Example: "Alice prevails because she validly accepted thus creating a contract that is binding on the offeror." "Alice prevails" is the conclusion, "because" is the conditional modifier, and "she validly . . . offeror" is the legal rationale.

(2) Reasoning Requirements: The reasoning must be consistent with the facts given in the question. The reasoning must also resolve the central legal issue in the question.

b. "If" and "Only If": This limiting modifier indicates the following rationale need only be possible under the facts; it is not required to be totally consistent, as in "because" or "since" questions.

(1) Example: "Baker prevails if (or "only if") she reasonably relied." "Baker prevails" is the conclusion, "if (or only if)" is the conditional modifier, and "she reasonably relied" is the legal rationale.

(2) Reasoning Requirement: The "if" modifier can – and usually does – go beyond the given question facts to create a more compelling factual argument to support the legal conclusion. "Only if" is similar except it creates an exclusive condition that must be satisfied. An "if" or "only if" modifier also requires you to reason through the other three alternatives to be sure there is not a better "if" or "only if" argument.

c. "Unless": This conditional modifier usually has a rationale following that addresses more of the required legal reasoning than the other modifiers.

(1) Example: "Carol prevails unless she had actual, constructive, or inquiry notice of the encumbrance." "Carol prevails" is the conclusion, "unless" is the conditional modifier, and "she had actual, constructive, or inquiry notice of the encumbrance" is the legal rationale.

(2) Reasoning Requirement: This "unless" reasoning must be necessary for the application of the controlling principles of law. If there is any other reason or way that the result can occur, an "unless" alternative is incorrect. Again, you should reason through all the other alternatives to be sure there is not a better argument.

9. Remember our Default Rules: Some topics in some MBE subjects are very challenging. Examples are future interests in property and some UCC topics like remedies in sales contracts. The time necessary to analyze and answer these questions may not be efficient and often there remains a high degree of uncertainty even after the effort. By eliminating wrong answers you can usually reduce the choice to two alternatives and use the following default rules. They provide a logical basis for an educated guess.

a. Longest Alternative: Everything else being equal, the longer alternative is slightly more likely to be the correct answer than a shorter alternative. A correct answer must usually contain all the required information and reasoning of the governing black letter law necessary for the best choice. A fragmented alternative is less attractive. This concept favors the more detailed alternative; this is usually the one with the most technical words and specific terminology.

b. Precision: Everything else being equal, the more precise the alternative the better. Vagueness is never encouraged in the law. The three incorrect alternatives in such a question will contain distracters to create confusion.

c. Easier to Prove: An answer choice that the facts suggest is easier to prove is preferred to one that has more complicated legal requirements.

d. Opposite Answer: If only two of the four alternatives are opposite (e.g., P wins because … as contrasted to … P loses because …), one of the two opposites is likely to be the best answer to the question. This technique may also be applied if a similar rationale supports opposite answer outcomes (e.g., P wins because … as contrasted to … D wins because …).

e. Another Legal Subject: An alternative that includes another legal subject is usually wrong. Only infrequently do questions crossover between subjects and almost never is the alternative that refers to the other subject the correct answer.

f. Eliminating Wrong Answers: It may be helpful to understand that there are three common reasons that an MBE answer choice is wrong:

(1) Legal Rule Misstatement: The statement of the rule may be wrong or, more frequently on the MBE, is an incomplete statement of the legal principle.

(2) Factual Misstatement: The facts required to support the alternative may not be stated in the question fact pattern at all. The alternative's facts may also go clearly and impermissibly beyond what is given in the question. In a few instances, the facts of the alternative directly contradict the facts in the question. Read the question carefully.

(3) Legal or Factual Irrelevancy: The law or facts in the answer may be accurate as stated but do not focus on the central determinant concern of the question. Again, the central determinant concern usually involves an element of law that P must prove to establish a prima facie case thus avoiding a summary judgment of dismissal or directed verdict.

B. Approach to MBE Questions

Parts of this section refers to practicing exam-type questions on paper. If you want to use the CD-ROM feature, make sure you also review the instructions in Section V infra.

1. Stay Within Time Allocation:

a. Pace Yourself: Carefully manage your time as you proceed through the questions. The trend is towards longer fact patterns but you should answer every question. There are 100 question in each of the two 180-minute (3 hour) sessions. This is an average of 1.8 minutes per question. You need to work up to this pace.

b. Time Management: Start working questions with a 3 minute maximum (or 10 in 30 minutes). One third of the way through your study period drop to 150 seconds each, the next third to 120 seconds each, the final third to 108 seconds each.

c. Procedure: It is important to work as quickly as possible without sacrificing thoroughness and accuracy. Read intensely and analyze the fact pattern carefully because you only have time to read it once. If a particular question is giving you difficulty, either skip it or make your best educated guess and mark it in the margin.

2. Series Questions:
Many of the MBE questions include a common fact pattern followed by a series of 2 to 4 related questions. On a time-per-question basis, analyzing the facts in these questions is usually more efficient than single questions. Still, if you find them too taxing, perhaps skip the series question for subjects in which you feel weak the first time through. If you do skip some of the series questions, make sure you also skip blackening those bubbles on the MBE answer sheet.

3. Analyze Facts and Law:
You need to analyze both the facts and the law. Try to understand the precise facts of the question separately from the four alternative choices

presented below. The facts in the question are always developed chronologically. As you read the facts, circle all the people's names in the question book; every new person adds another potential legal relationship and set of claims. Analyze the facts carefully; selecting a wrong answer usually occurs because the candidate failed to appreciate the consequence of a significant fact. For some of the most complicated questions it may be helpful to quickly create a chronological skeleton diagram of the events.

4. Go Through Questions Twice: Initially, go through all the questions in order. Time is so precious it is usually a mistake to not do every question in order the first time through. Still, some candidates use a two-step approach.

a. First Time Through: The first time through, every question should be put into one of three categories. You can do this with notes to yourself in the margins, on a separate sheet of paper, or in your head.

(1) Sure of Subject: If you are reasonably competent in the subject, answer all the subject's questions and move on. This applies even if you are not sure of the exact details of the issue being tested. Circle your alternative choice – A, B, C, or D – on the question sheets.

(2) No Clue? Skip It: If you have great difficulty with a question's subject or if the particular question would take too long, skip it. Do not get frustrated by the skipped questions or spend more than 10 seconds before deciding to skip.

(3) Unsure? Take Your Best Shot: If you have some idea, but are unsure which alternative is the best answer, make your best educated guess. After you eliminate the wrong alternatives, you will usually be down to two choices. If you have spent more than 20 seconds on the question you must commit, there is just not enough time to waste on second-guessing. Answer the question and mark the margin, come back later and check the answer.

b. Second Time Through: After you have gone through all 100 questions once, look at the time left and count the skipped questions. Calculate the time per question you have left. Keep on your new time schedule. You must answer every question.

(1) Do Skipped Questions First: The second time through, work the skipped questions first. Do not exceed the average remaining time. Do not get hung up; some of the series questions intentionally have very long and complicated fact patterns. If still unsure after a reasonable intellectual effort, use the default rules discussed above.

(2) Review Marked Questions Last: After the skipped questions are completed, turn to questions you marked in the question book to determine if you see anything new. The questions you have worked may have jogged your memory. If the uncertainty is still present, go with your first judgment; it is probably your best shot at the correct answer.

5. Answer Sheets are Critical: Attention to detail here is critical. A mistake in marking the right number on the official bubble answer sheet can be fatal. Always circle your answer choice on the examination book just before you mark the answer sheet so you have a cross-check. Every 20 questions (36 minutes on average) you should consciously cross-check the numbering on both documents to be sure you did not make a transposition error. This is especially necessary if you have skipped answering some of the questions the first time.

IV. RECOMMENDED MBE PREPARATION PROGRAM

A. Substantial Effort Necessary

A large time commitment is necessary to achieve MBE success. The details of the rules tested take time to absorb and synthesize into your own Magic Memory Outlines®. This knowledge must then be directed towards the MBE multiple-choice method of testing.

1. Disassemble Book: Carefully take the book apart at the perforated line a few pages at a time and place everything in a three-ring binder. This will allow you to study more efficiently by spreading out the various parts of your book for easy reference.

2. You Must Work Questions: Familiarization with the examiner's fine-line distinctions and various tricks is best mastered by working hundreds of MBE-patterned questions. This Rigos Bar Review Series text contains a compendium of over 1,700 questions of varying degrees of easy, average, and hard difficulty. Overall our questions are more complex and contain more tricks than the MBE so that you may find the actual exam questions seem somewhat superficial. The focus is on the most frequently asked topics on the MBE.

3. Time Commitment: The total necessary preparation time depends upon how long ago you studied the subjects in law school and how efficient you are in the MBE learning process.

    a. Time Variables: Our successful students report an average of 20 to 40 hours per chapter or about 200 hours average in total. Some get by with less time, but for others it takes a greater effort.

    b. Do It Right: It is a mistake to underestimate the necessary effort required to pass the MBE. This is a very competitive exercise and you never know when you cross the passing line. The prudent approach is to aim for a healthy margin of safety.

4. Schedule and Calendars: A well-organized effort is necessary. Use our weekly calendars to schedule out all the necessary time. Work backward from the MBE exam date.

5. Three-Hour Time Blocks: Get used to studying in three-hour solid blocks of time without a break. You may have to work up to this. On the final page of this Preface, you will find an overall seven-week planning sheet and a week-by-week calendar.

B. Six Element Success Program

The Rigos Bar Review Series MBE Review is most effective when used in a structured learning environment. A multi-step approach works best because the student is exposed to the substantive law and question nuances from many different viewpoints. The result is a complete preparation program and a seamless process that leaves nothing to chance. The total integrated preparation effort is more effective than the sum of the individual parts.

1. Preview Text Chapter-by-Chapter: Start by reading all the pages of this text in one sitting to acquaint yourself with the MBE subjects upon which the exam questions are based. Then go through every chapter individually in much detail. Be sure to allocate sufficient time for the important four learning steps described below. Your Rigos Review covers only what is tested on the MBE, not the broader coverage found in some law school courses or other bar review courses.

2. Detailed Study of Chapter: Study each chapter's text slowly and carefully. You must know the black letter law thoroughly. Pay particular attention to the MBE Tips that point out areas of testing concentration or technique suggestions. Highlighted in the text and tips are important facts or legal rules upon which the fine-line distinction answers frequently turn.

3. Preparing Your Own Magic Memory Outline®: This is essential to success.

a. Summarize Your Knowledge: You need to prepare a summary of every chapter in your own words. This is best accomplished using the Magic Memory Outlines® that are printed both in the book and on the CD-ROM software templates. The words in the Outline correspond to the bold headings in the text.

b. Capture the Essence: Your job is to summarize the text by capturing the essence of the rule and entering your summarized wording into your own outlines. Aim for concise yet comprehensive statements of the rule. Focus on the required technical elements of the legal principles. Integrate any helpful "learning question" information into your outline.

c. Memorize Your Outlines: After you have completed your own Magic Memory Outline® for the whole chapter, read it over carefully once or twice. You need to commit your Magic Memory Outline® to rote memory. Every week between your Outlines preparations and the actual MBE exam read over your Magic Memory Outlines® at least once.

4. Work Chapter's Questions:

a. Work Questions: Next, work the practice questions at the end of the chapter. These questions are not necessarily in the same order as the topics in the chapter, but the Chapter's Question Maps will serve as a cross-reference. The questions preceded by a bold F at the right refer to final exam questions. A few questions contain alternatives from rules in subsequent chapters. Lay the question sheets alongside the answer sheets to save having to flip back and forth. It is usually worthwhile to review the answer rationales since they reinforce the relevant fine-line distinctions tested within that rule of law.

b. CD-ROM Option: The same book questions are also on the CD-ROM so you can also use the software to work the questions in order. On the CD-ROM Question Map software, a question pertaining to that topic will pop up if you click on the question.

c. Do a Few At a Time: Work the chapter questions in small bites. Make sure you stop after a few questions to check the answer rationales while the facts are still fresh in your active memory. Some students refer to the answer rationales after every question.

d. Learn From Mistakes: The objective is to learn from your mistakes by reviewing the answer rationales while you still remember the details of the question. It is good to miss a few; they will help you become familiar with the MBE nuances, tricks and fine-line distinctions. Put a red star alongside (or if you're working on the CD-ROM, note on a sheet of paper) every question you missed. Missed questions should be worked again just prior to taking the actual MBE.

5. Take the Practice Exam: Volume 2 contains a simulated MBE exam. There are 200 questions in random order broken down into two groups of 100 each. While many of the questions in the text are intentionally easier or more difficult, the Final Exam has approximately the same overall difficulty as the actual MBE.

a. Solid Block of Time: It is best to create actual exam conditions. Time yourself and work as quickly as you can without sacrificing accuracy.

b. Answer Corrections: The answers do not follow the individual questions. Correct all your answers after you complete the full exam.

(1) Learn From Your Mistakes: When you refer to the answer rationales, be sure to understand why you picked the wrong choice. The fine-line distinctions are critical. Again, it is usually worthwhile to review the answer rationales to all of the four alternatives because they reinforce the details of the relevant issue. More than one answer rationale may be identical if the alternatives are incorrect for the same reason.

(2) Mark Mistakes: Again, put a red star in the margin alongside every question you missed and work them again the day right before sitting for the actual MBE. If you are using the software, make note of the questions you missed on a sheet of paper.

6. Update and Memorize Magic Memory Outlines®: As you work the end of the chapter and the practice exam questions, you may want to supplement and update your Magic Memory Outlines®. Key determinative facts have a tendency to repeat themselves on the MBE even though the scene of the questions may be superficially different. Your self-prepared Magic Memory Outlines® should be committed to memory by reading them over many times.

C. Other Study Tips

1. Keep Working Questions: You should continue to work practice MBE questions by mixing topics from different chapters. Make your own exams with the Rigos Bar Review Series CD-ROM software. You may work 5, 10, 20, or 100 random questions at a time. When you have a few spare minutes try working a number of short exams. Review every learning, chapter, and practice exam question you missed in your preparation process shortly before sitting for the actual exam (these questions should have a red star alongside them). Learn from your mistakes.

2. Study Time Blocks: Concentration during your study time is critical. We recommend you build your studying block time to a full three hours. This will not be easy at first but the Rigos Bar Review Series CD-ROM "make your own exam" software will help. This will build up your stamina and concentration intensity so that you don't have to take breaks during the actual exam.

D. Additional Rigos Tools and Assistance

If you are also using our MEE volume, we have an additional service that overlaps with this MBE text coverage. This three-pronged assistance program is available for an additional charge. Go to www.rigos.net for registration.

1. Help Desk: If you have substantive legal questions about the text and/or practice questions, send them to our experts at rigoshelpdesk@gmail.com. Please put the subject of your questions in the email subject line, such as "Contract question." You can ask more than one question in an email, but please keep the questions to one subject, such as contracts. So one email with two contract questions would be fine.

2. Submitting Essays for Grading: You should email your essay answer as an email attachment to rigosgrading@gmail.com. Please send only one essay per email, as each question is being graded by a different grader. Do not send anything but essays to this email address. The graders are all former Rigos students who know the substance of our texts, details of our "seamless process," and the Bar exam grading system very well. Put the essay name in the email subject line so the correct grader will pick up your essay. Please identify your essays with your last name. An example is a student named John Smith and the essay named Able v. Baker would be labeled Smith-Able and Baker.doc.

3. Mentoring: After we grade five essays, a former successful Rigos student will contact you to discuss your progress. While the grader will focus on your presentation style and legal content, feel free to ask questions about other concerns of your Bar exam preparation.

V.   HOW TO USE THE RIGOS BAR REVIEW SERIES CD-ROM SOFTWARE

There are many ways to work the questions contained on this software. You can mix and match the techniques below. With 1700 questions, you won't soon run out of new challenges.

A. Straight Through

You can also work practice questions from one subject at a time in order.

1. How It Works: The questions will appear one at a time beginning with Learning Question Number 1 for that chapter. You can work questions in order, just as you would in the text, until you want to stop. They are designed to reinforce the textual study.

2. How to Use It: Go to the main page and click the chapter you want to work (for example, Chapter 1, Contracts). The questions will appear in the same order as in the text, and you can work them from beginning to end. If you are reading the text material you can use this software feature to work through the Learning Questions in order. Read the fact pattern and call of the question thoroughly, and then click on your selection, "A," "B," "C," or "D." When you make your answer selection, a window will open and indicate whether your choice was correct or incorrect and why.

B. Final Exam

1. How It Works: The Final Exam is a mock MBE with the same number of questions, difficulty range, and time constraints as the actual MBE. It is timed at 180 minutes per 100-question set. It is designed to be your final review of what you have learned as well as a practice run for the MBE. It should give you confidence when you go in for the real MBE.

2. How to Use It: When you are ready, go to the main page and click "Chapter 7, Final Exam." The final exam contains 200 questions, 100 for the morning set and 100 for the afternoon. It is timed at 180 minutes for each set. Work the a.m. exam straight through without stopping. Take a one hour break, and then work the p.m. set. Unlike your practice sessions, the correct answers will not be revealed until you have completed the whole exam.

C. Make Your Own Exam

This feature allows you to create organized practice sessions in sets of 5, 10, 20, or a specified number of questions of your own choosing with the click of a mouse.

1. How It Works: The questions appear in random order from all of the six MBE topics. You should review all of the answer rationales to gain a depth of subject understanding. You can use this feature as many times in a row as you wish, and you will constantly get new questions. You should be working many questions without stopping, to build stamina.

2. How to Use It: To use this feature, simply click the "Make Your Own Exam" button on the main page. Choose the number of questions that you want to work: click "5," "10," "20," or type any whole number into the white box and click "X." The questions will come on the screen one at a time. Read the fact pattern and call of the question thoroughly, and then click on your selection, "A," "B," "C," or "D." When you make your answer selection, a window will show whether your choice was correct or incorrect and why. If you find it helpful, you can read all four answer rationales to gain a more thorough understanding of the subject.

VI. EXAM SITE TIPS

A. Be Punctual

1. Consider a Convenient Hotel: If you live far away or have transportation problems, consider booking a hotel room near the exam site. Many authorities advise staying alone so there are no distractions. It is best to walk from your hotel room to the exam site; this avoids all the uncertainties and stress of traffic, bus, train, or subway travel.

2. Arrive Early: Don't be rushed on the morning of the exam. Arrive early on exam day at the exam-site before the scheduled starting time. Avoid hurrying or arriving late because it is disconcerting and may adversely affect your composure. Check in at the registrar's desk. Look over the facilities and restroom locations.

3. Improve Morning Performance: If you are usually a late riser, practice getting up early every morning for a week before the exam. First thing in the morning, do one or two dozen questions from varied subjects to get into the test-taking mental routine as you start the day. Use the "Make Your Own Exam" feature on the Rigos Bar Review Series CD-ROM software.

B. What to Bring With You

1. Admission Card: Candidates should bring to the exam site the written instructions and the admission card provided by the state bar testing authority. Also bring two pieces of backup identification bearing your signature and picture, preferably a driver's license. Take an accurate watch to both morning and afternoon exams.

2. Comfort and Practicality: Dress comfortably in the clothes that make you feel the best. You can bring a cushion to soften the chairs if you like. Some candidates who are easily distracted bring earplugs. If you are going to use earplugs in the actual exam, use them while working questions during the preparation period.

3. Snacks: Food and beverages are not usually allowed in the exam room. Do not consume a large meal or massive liquids just before the exam. Restroom breaks are possible but cost you valuable time and break your concentration. Time is very precious in this exercise. Your studying should have expanded your ability to sit and concentrate for three-hour blocks. Go for foods that provide energy and are easy to digest (raisins, peanuts, apples, oranges, bananas, energy bars), but that do not give you a letdown or make you feel tired.

C. Focus Only On the MBE

1. Preserve Your Mental Energy: Get a full night's sleep before you take the exam. Fight to keep mentally sharp and intense for the full two three hour sessions. If you find your mental intensity weakening in the last hour, pause, close your eyes and take four deep breaths.

2. Concentrate on the Task: Imagine you and the exam booklet are in a glass box. During the 180 minutes in each MBE session, the only thing that you should think about is making your best effort on this exam. Personal problems should be left outside the exam room. Use the time management techniques you have learned and practiced in the course.

D. Be Confident

1. Relax: Consciously attempt to relax; deep, slow breathing will facilitate this mental state. Don't listen to the pre-exam chatter of the other nervous candidates. You do not want their test anxiety to affect you. It is too late to add anything to your knowledge and this distraction will only confuse and drain you. It is better not to talk to anyone. If the other candidates are bothering you, take a little walk away from them to relax.

2. Confidence and Poise: Get psyched up to make the MBE your finest intellectual effort. Approach the exam with mental confidence and poise. Think of the MBE as a game that you are going to win. Don't get discouraged by early difficult questions. Think of them as opportunities to use your keenly developed MBE analytical skills. Work quickly without sacrificing accuracy. Many of your competitors have not followed a thorough review program and are there "for practice." Rigos Bar Review Series® candidates are there to pass.

3. Contemplate the Moment: Just before the examiner says "Start your exam," contemplate the moment. Close your eyes and picture the bar admission ceremony in which you will be sworn in. For lawyers, this is our professional rite of passage and you will only do it once. Prepare yourself mentally to go for every grading point and make a commitment not to leave either session early. The most important race of your professional life has just begun.

E. Go the Distance

Fight to the end of both exam sessions. Don't leave any questions unanswered. The difference between a passing and failing score can get down to one or two extra correct questions. Only the inexperienced or the foolish leave any exam session early.

VII. CONCLUSION

This MBE exam is very passable. The Rigos Bar Review Series seamless preparation program works well for those candidates willing to work well at it. There is simply no short cut to planning and following a thorough complete preparation program. Plan to spend the necessary time and distribute all six subjects over at least seven (7) weeks until the exam using the planning calendars on the next page. This allows you to break the effort down into manageable modules. Leave time at the end for the practice exam and a final review of your Magic Memory Outlines®. Plan your success program and stay on schedule week-by-week.

After you get your results, please complete and fax or mail in the student evaluation at the end of this book. It will help us to improve our course for other students, and we may publish your ideas and thoughts. Good luck on the MBE and in your legal career.

James J. Rigos
Editor-in-Chief
Seattle, Washington

CHAPTER 1

CONTRACTS

AND UCC SALES

ARTICLE 2

RIGOS BAR REVIEW SERIES

MULTISTATE BAR EXAM REVIEW (MBE)

CHAPTER 1

CONTRACTS AND UCC SALES ARTICLE 2

Table of Contents

RIGOS BAR REVIEW SERIES

MULTISTATE BAR EXAM REVIEW (MBE)

CHAPTER 1

CONTRACTS AND UCC SALES ARTICLE 2

I. INTRODUCTION

Contract questions can arise on the Multistate Bar Exam (MBE) under the common law, including court decisions and the American Law Institute's (ALI) Restatement, or under the Uniform Commercial Code (UCC) Article 2. Contract issues are also occasionally present in constitutional law, property transactions, or tort subjects.

A. MBE Exam Coverage

1. Weight and Format: 34 of the 200 MBE questions test contract subjects. All questions have a four-stemmed multiple-choice format. Two, three, and four-string questions flowing from a common fact pattern are frequent. About 50% of the MBE testing covers offer, acceptance, and defenses to formation. Parol evidence rule, remedies, and excusable non-performance are also frequently tested.

2. Testing Areas: Most of the MBE contracts testing is under the common law. UCC Article 2 questions are approximately 25% of the subject coverage. The UCC is integrated with the common law in this Rigos Bar Review Series MBE review text. Special attention is given to areas where there is a different or expanded rule under the UCC.

3. Requirements: Question requirements focus on the two parties Plaintiff (P) and Defendant (D). Typical is "Will P's claim for breach of contract prevail?" and the alternatives provide two sets of related reasoning to support both the conclusions – yes or no. Another type of question is "What is P or D's best/worst argument/theory for recovery/defense?" Questions may ask which factual alternative would have the most or least influence on the case's outcome. The most difficult questions present alternatives with conditional or limiting modifying words leading to a focused rationale. (See the detailed question characteristics in the preface.)

B. Approach

Unlike many subjects tested on the MBE, there is no one recommended approach to contract questions. Most of the questions focus on only one topic such as the four requirements necessary for the application of the firm offer rule. Circle the names of the parties as you read and analyze the facts; they are the parties P and D in the claims and/or counterclaims. Parties' negotiation words stated in quotation marks always have a legal significance.

1. Conclusion and Conditional Modifiers: The answer conclusion (prevail or not prevail) is less important than the best reasoning to support your choice. The modifiers "because," "since," "if," "only if," and "unless" focus on the best rationale for the conclusion. See the preface for significant detail on MBE question characteristics and default rules.

2. Preferred Result: Read the facts of the question very carefully. Everything else being equal, the odds on the MBE favor the answer alternative concluding that an enforceable contract exists.

C. Overall Common Law Memory Ladder Acronym

Your overall memory ladder acronym for contract law is **OACLLS VIPR TAD**.

- **O**ffer by offeror expressing intent to be bound that is not yet revoked or rejected
- **A**cceptance by offeree through a return promise or performance
- **C**onsideration – benefit to promisor or detriment to promisee
- **L**egal capacity of contracting parties – not 3 Is of **i**nfancy, **i**nsanity, or **i**ntoxication
- **L**egal subject matter and not against public policy
- **S**tatute of frauds compliance – writing signed by D – if a **MOULS** contract

- **V**oid or voidable circumstances – **MUFFED**
- **I**nterpretation of contract – **II PACC**
- **P**erformance and breach
- **R**emedies – **MRS DAISI**

- **T**hird party beneficiary – creditor or donee
- **A**ssignment of Rights by promisee
- **D**elegation of Duties by obligor

OACLLS represents the formation elements that are necessary for an enforceable contract.

D. Common Law v. UCC Distinction

Contract questions frequently require a distinction between the common law and the UCC. The MBE heavily tests the issues where there is an expanded treatment or different result under the UCC as opposed to the common law. If the UCC is silent on a particular issue, the common law rule of the state applies. The UCC section numbers are listed for a reference source; it is not necessary to memorize the UCC section numbers.

> **MBE Tip:** Your substantive Contracts text that follows usually begins the analysis of a particular legal topic by discussing the common law rule as applied in the majority of states. If the UCC demands or suggests either a different or expanded treatment, that treatment and analysis immediately follows. If there is no such UCC designation, assume the common law rule applies to the UCC.

1. UCC Standard of Reasonableness: The UCC was created to provide a more practical way for buyers and sellers of goods to regulate transactions. It alleviates some of the rigidity and harshness of the common law by requiring less precision in contracting. [UCC 1.203] The UCC imposes a general standard of reasonableness and good faith on all the contracting parties. For merchants, this standard is raised to honesty in fact and adherence to reasonable commercial standards of fair dealing in the trade. [UCC 2.103]

2. Application:

a. **Common Law – SIR:** The common law "**SIR**" rules apply to contracts involving **s**ervices, **i**ntangibles, and **r**eal estate. **S**ervices include personal (employee's work), professional (attorney's advice), and construction (builder's construction). **I**ntangibles include software, patents, trademarks, copyrights, accounts receivable, legal claims, and money. **R**eal estate includes contracts for the sale, purchase, or encumbrance of land.

b. **Goods:** Article 2 of the UCC rules apply to contracts for the sale of new or used "goods" that are movable. Goods also include fruit on trees, crops, timber, and minerals that can be severed from the real property without harm. [UCC 2.105] The common law supplements a goods contract where the UCC rules do not displace it.

c. **Distinction:** This distinction can be subtle: a contract for the sale of a book is a UCC contract. In comparison, a contract to bind or repair the same book is a personal service contract and thus classified under the common law.

d. **Mixed Contract:** If both "goods" and "services" are included in the same contract, the "predominant purpose" test is applied. The UCC rules control if the predominant purpose for which the parties contracted was the sale of goods. This is a question of intention not necessarily the relative prices of the goods and services covered by the contract.

e. **Examples:** A contract to purchase a computer with a service agreement is likely under the UCC. Construction contracts are also heavily tested. An agreement to lay a foundation for a building would include the cement, the re-bars, and the labor (both goods and services). The common law of contracts would control both the inadequate performance of the contractor and a defect in materials under the "predominant purpose" test. Some states have adopted the "gravamen test" which allows UCC warranty protection for hybrid contracts if the goods themselves caused the injury.

3. **UCC Default Provisions:** The UCC controls contracts for goods and, if a provision is in conflict, supersedes the common law. A UCC default provision also fills in the blanks with "gap filling" terms where the contracting parties have not specified the treatment of an item or term. If the parties have not addressed the particular term in their agreement, the UCC rule controls. The court can fill in all open items, except quantity.

4. **Duty to Communicate:** The UCC may impose an affirmative duty to communicate on one or both of the parties under certain circumstances.

5. **Merchant v. Casual Party:** The UCC has special provisions that may apply if one or both of the parties is a "merchant." A merchant is one who deals in goods of that type or holds himself out as an expert having special knowledge and skill in those goods. Wholesalers and retailers are usually merchants. A merchant is distinguished from a casual party or individual consumer. A merchant, such as a car dealer, is to be held to a higher standard of conduct than would a casual private party selling the same automobile. [UCC 2.104]

6. **Application by Analogy:** The court may always apply the UCC by analogy to a common law topic. UCC authorized matters such as those requiring good faith, reasonableness, and a duty to mitigate damages may therefore be imposed by a court upon the parties in a common law **SIR** contract.

> **MBE Tip:** Start your analysis by determining which law – the common or UCC – governs the contract. The predominant purpose controls. If the conclusion is the common law, remember that the court may apply an appropriate UCC rule or treatment by analogy.

E. Express or Implied

1. Express Contract: An express bargained for exchange is formed by written or oral language.

2. Implied Contract: An implied contract is exhibited by the actions of the parties even though an agreement is not explicitly made. Implied contracts may be enforceable such as the receipt, inspection, and acceptance of goods without objection.

a. Implied in Fact: An implied-in-fact contract is made by circumstantial implication showing mutual intention (patient accepts a doctor's services without objection but did not agree on the exact fee).

b. Implied in Law: An implied in law contract arises from implied obligations. It is a method to impose justice and avoid unjust enrichment (plumber fixes a burst or leaking pipe without the homeowner's knowledge). This doctrine is also called "in quasi-contract" or "quantum merit" and allows recovery of the reasonable value of the services performed.

F. Acceptance by Promise or Act

1. Bilateral: If the original promisor's offer is seeking a return promise for acceptance ("I promise to pay you $1,000 if you promise me you will prepare my estate plan documents"), the contract is bilateral. Mutuality of obligation applies because both parties are both a promisor of an obligation and a promisee of a right. In theory, breach of either promise is actionable independently of the status of the other promise. The court may create a constructive condition of performance as a prerequisite to bringing suit for non-performance of the other promise.

2. Unilateral: If acceptance is demanded in the form of a requested action (I promise to pay you $1,000 if you prepare my estate plan or ship the goods), the contract is unilateral. If it is uncertain whether the contract is bilateral or unilateral, the objective intent of the parties controls. Reward offers always seek performance and thus are unilateral contracts.

> **MBE Tip:** Vague wording in the offer – as to whether the requested acceptance may be rendered by a mere promise or requires actual performance – suggest consideration of a unilateral contract.

G. Executory Contracts

An executory contract is where there is not yet full performance. If wholly executory, only promises have been given, and there has been no performance by either contracting party.

1. Partially Executed: Partial executory means there has been some performance by at least one party. It may also mean that one side has completely performed while the other party has only promised.

2. Fully Executed: The contract is fully executed when both parties have completely performed and no obligations remain.

H. Divisible Contracts

A divisible contract is capable of being separated into multiple portions, performance of each being independently enforceable. This allows a court to enforce the performed part of a executed contract and require the breaching party to pay an equivalent percentage amount. Employment contracts are usually considered divisible even if the agreement specifies only a lump sum. Divisibility may apply even though performance of a subsequent portion does not conform to the contract's specification.

MBE Tip: Interpreting a contract as divisible is a way a court can avoid a total contractual forfeiture.

STOP! Go to page 113 and work Learning Questions 1 to 7.

II.   OFFER

A person who makes an offer is called an offeror, and the person to whom it is addressed is called an offeree. An offer is usually in the form of a promise. A valid offer must include present contractual willingness and intent to be bound, certainty and definitiveness of all essential terms, and communication to the offeree. Upon receipt of the offer, a power of acceptance is created in the offeree. If the offeree exercises this power, a contract is formed.

A. Definiteness

The common law requires that an offer be unambiguous, certain, and definite on all material terms. The offeror's manifest actions must be sufficiently definite so as to indicate a clear intention and willingness to enter into a present binding contract. ("I am thinking about selling at $1,000" or "would you paint my house for $5,000" are only pre-offer forms of negotiations.)

1. Objective Test: Courts apply an objective test to determine an offeree's acceptance intention. The question is how would a reasonable offeree have interpreted the offeror's apparent expressions? "Are you still interested in purchasing this item?" leaves doubt whether the party intended to be bound. The more definite the offeror's apparent intent to be bound, the more likely the expressed communication will be characterized as a valid offer. The offeror's claim that she did not intend to be bound is not necessarily controlling.

2. Invitations to Deal and Mere Inquiry: The offer must rise above mere puffing, jest, or an invitation / solicitation to a potential buyer to submit offers or bids. Examples include "I am looking for a buyer willing to pay $1,000 for this car." Look also for a mere inquiry such as "will $1,000 buy this car?" Similarly an "agreement to agree in the future" does not manifest a present intention to be bound.

3. Advertisements: A general advertisement, price list, or product availability quote does not usually rise to the level of a formal offer. The more specific and detailed the proposed terms (i.e. buyer, price, quantity) in the advertisement. the more likely it evidences the intent to create the power of acceptance in the buyer and thus be judged to constitute a valid offer.

> **MBE Tip:** To qualify as an offer, the communication must create the power of acceptance in the offeree. Even if the acceptance seems quite definite, there can be no contract if the offer is too indefinite.

B. Open Items

The treatment of terms not addressed in an offer depends upon whether the court can determine what the parties intended.

1. Common Law: Under the traditional common law, essential terms include the parties, subject matter, price, quantity, and time of performance. A contract to purchase land must contain an adequate description of the property and the price.

2. UCC Missing Term Treatment: The UCC recognizes that the actions and conduct of the parties may establish an agreement even though some terms may be left open. UCC authorized or default terms may be used to fill in the gaps (missing term in the agreement) if there is a reasonable basis for giving an appropriate remedy. If the price is missing, the court may impose a reasonable market price.

a. CPU Order of Imposing Terms: The court looks to three evidential sources in priority order to determine what term to impose. First, the course of performance in the existing contract if there was prior performance. Second, any past course of dealings in prior contracts between the parties. Third, usage of trade in the industry.

b. Result: The UCC's "gap filling" function fosters the formation of a greater number of sales contracts resulting from negotiations than would result under the common law. [UCC 2.204]

> **MBE Tip:** Wherever you spot a UCC missing term in the question, look for a dual issue involving agreement formation and open items. The CPU (Central Processing Unit) "course of performance," "past course of dealings," and "usage of trade," are exceptions to the Parol Evidence Rule and the judge may use them to determine what is a "reasonable" UCC term to impose in the circumstances.

C. Revocability

Offers are generally revocable (can be withdrawn) at will by the offeror prior to acceptance. Revocations are effective when received by the offeree. If a public offer (such as a reward), an effective revocation must be made with a comparable degree of publicity.

1. Common Law: A naked promise to hold open an offer is not enforceable under the common law; the offer is revocable at will. Revocation may be made by the offeree learning of any act or statement that is inconsistent with a continuing intent to enter into a contract.

2. Option With Consideration (Option Contract): An exception applies in the case of an option contract. An option is an irrevocable promise supported by independent consideration flowing to the offeror. For example, a buyer of land offers to pay $10 if the seller will hold open the offered price for the land for one week. The consideration creates an option contract that is irrevocable for the specified period of time. Rejections and/or counteroffers on the underlying contract do not terminate an option contract.

3. UCC Firm Offer: A "firm offer" is a signed writing by a merchant that gives explicit assurances that the offer will be held open. Be sure that the offeror engages in commercial sales of the goods in question and is not a mere collector or casual seller. The firm offer rule applies only to merchant offerors. [UCC 2.205]

a. Irrevocability: A firm offer may not be revoked or withdrawn for the stated period of time up to three months. This rule applies even if consideration is lacking. If no time period is specified, a firm offer is irrevocable for a reasonable period of time. If the firm offer is for four months, the offeror regains the power to revoke during the final month.

b. Rejection and Subsequent Acceptance: An offeree's rejection of a "firm offer" does not terminate the offer, unlike the common law. Under the UCC "firm offer" rule, an offeree's acceptance subsequent to rejection may produce a valid contract.

D. Termination

Open offers are terminated after a reasonable time period has passed. The offeror may also terminate an offer prior to an acceptance by the offeree.

1. Usual Situations: The offeror can expressly revoke or withdraw the offer unless it constitutes an irrevocable option. An offer is also considered revoked by implication if the offeree learns that the item was sold to another buyer or the offeror acts in a manner inconsistent with maintaining an open offer. If an effective time period is stated in an offer, then that offer is terminated when the time period expires. A stated time period begins to run on the date the offer is received by the offeree. An offer is terminated by operation of law if there is death or insanity of the offeror, the subject matter of the offer becomes illegal, or the subject matter is destroyed.

2. Refusal or Rejection: The receipt of an offeree's unequivocal refusal or rejection will also terminate an offer such as "I refuse to accept" or "I reject your offer." Depending on the language, such a communication may also create a counteroffer which proposes a different substitute bargain that can be accepted by the original offeror. For example, "I accept your offer only if you agree to pay in advance." In that case, the parties change position.

E. Contractor and Subcontractor Rules

Special rules apply to a general contractor's solicitation of bids from subcontractors.

1. Bids by Subcontractors: Bids by subcontractors are usually treated as irrevocable offers for a reasonable time until the general contractor's prime bid is awarded or rejected. This is an application of the doctrine of promissory estoppel (see below).

2. Contract Formation: A contract does not exist until the general contractor accepts the subcontractor's bid or offer.

3. Low or Suspect Bids: The general contractor may not rely on a low subcontractor bid if the offered price is unreasonably below the other bids. Similarly, the subcontractor may not be required to perform if the general contractor has reason to believe that there might have been a mistake in the submitted bid. (See Mistakes discussion below.)

> **STOP!** Go to page 114 and work Learning Questions 8 to 12.

III. ACCEPTANCE

> **MBE Tip:** Regardless of how strong the responsive communication appears to be, a bargained for exchange agreement can only result if the acceptance is made in response to a valid offer.

A. In General

The intended offeree has the power to accept an open offer that has not been revoked or terminated. The acceptance creates a bargained for exchange resulting in a contract. In a bilateral contract, acceptance may be a mere unequivocal promise to be bound to the terms of the offer. Acceptance of a unilateral contract requires performance of the act requested by the offeror. In the MBE questions, performance often constitutes implied acceptance such as the goods being delivered, inspected and accepted without objection.

1. Intended Offeree: Offers are not assignable and the power of acceptance is thus personal to the offeree. Acceptance must be made by the party to whom the offer was directed. Reward offers are intended to be accepted by any member of the public.

2. Terms: The MBE frequently poses a fact pattern where the given term in controversy is absent in the offer, stated to the contrary in the acceptance, or absent in both.

a. Stipulated in Offer: If the offer stipulates details of the method, manner, means of communication, price, or timeliness of acceptance, such terms are binding.

b. Stipulated in Acceptance: If the offer does not stipulate a particular term or method of acceptance, look to see if the acceptance contains the same particular term. If so, the original offeree becomes the new offeror of a counteroffer under the common law.

c. In Neither Offer nor Acceptance: If neither communication contains the term and there is a reasonable basis for finding a contract, the court may provide a missing term under the UCC. A reasonable price may thus be imposed. [UCC 2.204 and 2.305]

> **MBE Tip:** The offeror is the master of the terms in her bargain; such terms are generally binding on the offeree. This concept is frequently tested on the exam.

3. Knowledge Necessary: Acceptance by the offeree must be made with knowledge of the offer. Unknown reward offers are frequent on the MBE. Crossing offers or performance without knowledge of an offer does not create a contract.

4. Objective Standard: Whether an offeree's actions constitute sufficient acceptance (i.e., intention to be bound) is measured by a reasonable person standard. This is the outward manifestation of assent. An acknowledgement by the offeree that the offer was made or a "thank you" is insufficient. "I would like to do business with you" is less certain.

5. Silence: Under the common law, silence is not usually unilaterally imposed as constituting acceptance.

    a. Exception: An exception exists if the parties expressly or through their past course of dealings intend silence to constitute acceptance of an open offer. The custom of a trade or industry may also recognize silence as acceptance. In these situations, there may be a duty to speak to avoid contract formation.

    b. Conduct: Conduct may create an implied contract even though there was not an express agreement. Frequently on the MBE, the parties performed without ever formally agreeing to the contract's terms; the court will enforce such a contract.

    c. Unsolicited Items: Unordered newspapers, periodicals, and other unsolicited goods or services offered to a party are deemed gifts in many states. The receiver has no duty to return or pay for such items received in many states.

6. Counteroffer: A response to an offer that specifies different terms is known as a counteroffer. Such a response is a rejection of the original offer and the extension of a new offer in its place. For example, one party offers to buy a good at $40. If the other party responds, "I will sell it for $50." This is not an acceptance but rather a rejection and a counteroffer. The original offeror could then accept at $50.

B. Unilateral Contract

A unilateral offer requires acceptance in the form of performance of the act requested within the specified time limit. A promise to perform is not acceptance. Acceptance of a unilateral offer requires complete performance by the offeree unless other terms are agreed. Even the shipment of non-conforming goods may constitute a seller's acceptance (and a simultaneous breach) thereby allowing the other party a contractual claim for damages.

1. Offer Revocation: It would be inequitable to allow the offeror to revoke after the offeree has made a substantial beginning of performance.

    a. Common Law: Substantial part performance by the offeree is considered sufficient under the common law of most states to prohibit an offeror's revocation.

    b. Restatement: The Restatement goes one step further. Mere beginning of performance is sufficient to create an option to complete which temporarily suspends the offeror's power to revoke. Under some circumstances, even mere preparations to perform may constitute justifiable reliance sufficient to make the offeror's promise irrevocable.

2. UCC Bilateral Acceptance: An ambiguous UCC offer looking to (but not expressly demanding as a condition of the offer) the current shipment of the goods may be accepted by either an actual shipment or a promise to ship. Note that this provision may convert a unilateral offer into a bilateral contract. To eliminate the possibility of an acceptance by promise, the offeror should explicitly state that a mere promise to ship the goods is not sufficient to constitute acceptance. [UCC 2.206(1)]

3. UCC Notification Necessary: The offeree must notify the offeror she is beginning performance to bar the offeror's right to revoke. The beginning of performance without notification is ineffective to create acceptance under the UCC. [UCC 2.206(2)]

4. Promise To Complete: An offerree's mere beginning performance may create an implied promise to complete thereby providing the offeror a cause of action for breach.

5. Reward Offers: A frequent MBE question is an advertisement offering a public reward. The offeree must be aware of the reward offer at the time of performance. Read the conditions of the reward offer very carefully; are all conditions met? An exception is a bounty offer. Knowledge is not necessary to collect a bounty in many states.

MBE Tip: Multiple aspects of unilateral offers are frequently tested. A unilateral contract requires the offeree's performance to create the required acceptance, while a bilateral contract only requires a promise indicating an intent to be bound. Even if bilateral, a court may find a contract by interpreting the offeree's action of performance as an acceptance.

C. Output and Requirement Contracts

A contract that measures the quantity by the total output of a seller or the total requirements of a buyer is enforceable. This is the only exception to the rule that a UCC contract must state the quantity. [UCC 2.306]

1. Mechanism: Such a contract means that the total quantity is the actual output of the seller or the actual requirements of the buyer as may occur in good faith. Be on the alert for an illusory promise such as, "I will buy as much as I will order." A quantity may not be tendered or demanded if it is unreasonably disproportionate to a stated estimate, or to prior output requirement amounts but reasonable growth in quantity may be allowed.

2. Responsibilities of Parties: An output or requirement exclusive dealings contract imposes an obligation on the seller to use her best efforts to supply the goods and on the buyer to use best efforts to promote the product. The UCC section comments state that the seller under such a contract is expected to refrain from supplying another dealer or agent within the exclusive territory, if such is specified.

D. Sales by Auction

At auction, the bid is the offer and the fall of the hammer the acceptance which completes the sale. A bid may be withdrawn until the fall of the hammer. An auction sale is "with reserve" unless the goods are stated in explicit terms to be put up "without reserve." While auctions are usually used for goods, real property may also be sold at auction.

1. With Reserve: "With reserve" means the auctioneer retains the right to withdraw the goods before completion of the auction. The auctioneer does not have to accept the highest bid until the reserve price is met. Similarly the bidder may withdraw a bid before the fall of the hammer. A retraction by one bidder does not revive the prior bid.

2. Without Reserve: "Without reserve" means the auctioneer has made an irrevocable offer to sell the goods to the highest bidder. Once the bidding starts, the auctioneer must accept the highest bid even if this amount is less than the seller desired. An individual bid may be withdrawn until the fall of the hammer. A retraction by one bidder does not revive the previous bid. [UCC 2.328]

E. Conditional or Additional Items

1. Common Law: A valid acceptance must be unequivocal, unconditional, and a "mirror image" of the offer under the common law. A reply that adds qualifications, conditions, or additional terms is not an acceptance. Such a communication is usually treated as a rejection and counteroffer that vests in the offeror the power to accept the counteroffer.

2. Mere Inquiry: A mere inquiry about further or different terms or a request for clarification is neither acceptance nor rejection. This may be treated as crossing offers. Examples include "Interesting offer, will you accept $1,000," "I can pay $1,500," or "I would be willing to pay $1,250." The original offer stays open and a second offer may be created.

3. Request for Additional Terms: A grumbling acceptance that "requests" minor additional terms can still be a valid acceptance unless the additional terms are an express condition of the acceptance. "I accept; will you please pay an extra $2,000?" A contract is formed at the original price and the $2,000 is treated as a proposal for an addition to the contract.

> **MBE Tip:** The MBE frequently tests the fine-line distinction between an offeree's mere inquiry/request for additional terms as opposed to a rejection and a counteroffer.

4. Acceptance With a Demand for Different Terms: A common law response that affirmatively accepts the offer but specifies different terms is treated as an acceptance with a demand for different terms. For example, one party offers to repair a car for $40 and the other party responds, "I accept but will only pay $35," or "I accept subject to the condition of being able to secure financing to buy the land." Under the common law, these are treated as rejections that terminate the original offer and may create a counteroffer.

> **MBE Tip:** The exact wording of the acceptance is quite important. Almost any response by the offeree creates a counteroffer. If there is a subsequent communication by the offeror addressing the specific communication, it may be deemed an acceptance. Read each stem of each question carefully so that you are sure whether the "final controlling" offer is made by the original offeror or offeree.

5. UCC Treatment: The UCC rejects the literal "mirror-image" acceptance rule. Unless the offer specifies to the contrary (such as a statement that "only an ironclad response may constitute acceptance of the terms of this offer"), an expression of acceptance in any manner and by any medium is adequate to create the contract. [UCC 2.206 and 2.207]

a. Minor Additional Terms: The UCC allows an acceptance with proposed consistent minor additional terms. Look for "add-on" terms not specified in the offer. Acceptable new minor terms include setting reasonable delivery dates, imposing credit terms and interest on overdue invoices, or limiting the right to reject goods within trade tolerance.

(1) Non-Merchant Party: Unless both parties are merchants, the additional terms are treated as mere proposals that the offeror must expressly approve. [UCC 2.207]

(2) Merchant to Merchant: Between merchants, the minor new additional terms become a part of the contract unless the offer expressly precluded any new terms. To avoid the additional terms, the original merchant offeror must notify the offeree of their objection to their inclusion within a reasonable period of time. If either party is not a merchant or the additional terms materially alter the original bargain, explicit assent to the additional terms by the offeror is required.

b. Materially Alter Bargain: The UCC comments give examples of clauses that materially alter the bargain of the original agreement. The concern is that material new terms may result in surprise or hardship if incorporated without the other party's express awareness. [UCC 2.207]

(1) Examples: Included are arbitration clauses, provisions negating standard warranties, clauses reserving to the seller the right to cancel upon a buyer's failure to pay an invoice when due, and clauses requiring that complaints and/or rejections be made within a time period materially shorter than customary or reasonable. These terms are not minor and thus are excluded from the automatic inclusion rule.

(2) Treatment: An acceptance containing such terms would still create a contract with the new material terms treated as proposals for addition. Affirmative agreement by the offeror to the inclusion of the new proposed terms would be necessary.

MBE Tip: Additional terms in an acceptance are heavily tested on the MBE. Determine first if the contract is for a common law topic or "goods" and if there are "add-on" terms in the acceptance. Second, are both parties merchants? If so, any additional terms are binding unless **MOP** – they **m**aterially change the essence of the bargain, **o**bjected to by the offeror, or such additional terms were **p**recluded in the offer. If either party is not a merchant, there may still be a contract, but the offeror must agree to the additional terms.

F. Conflicting Terms

1. Common Law: Where the offer and acceptance differ on a particular term, the common law rule is that a non-conforming acceptance is deemed to be a counteroffer. This leads to a "battle of the forms" as the parties' roles change. Acceptance of the last counteroffer may be by performance of the other party. The terms of the last communication usually prevail under the "master of the bargain" – "last shot" rule.

2. UCC: The UCC addresses the "battle of the forms" by assuming both parties object to the other's treatment of the term. The conflicting terms in both the offer and acceptance are to be disregarded (or "knocked out") and do not become a part of the contract. The contract to be imposed consists of the terms upon which both parties have expressly agreed plus any applicable UCC "gap filling" provisions. The exception is an increase in quantity; the offeror's quantity maximum always controls. [UCC 2.207]

MBE Tip: Conflicting terms, such as different performance dates or treatment of risk of loss, are heavily tested on the MBE. Frequently, neither party explicitly accepted the other's term, but there was performance. Unlike additional terms, both parties do not have to be merchants.

G. Effective Date

The effective date of all communications is usually the date of receipt of the communication by the other party.

1. Revocation by Offeror: If the offeror revokes or withdraws the offer prior to acceptance, there is no contract since the offer is no longer open. Under the common law, revocability is generally at will, unless consideration was paid to the offeror. Revocations are effective on receipt by the offeree.

2. Mailbox Rule: The common law "mailbox rule" applies where parties are communicating their negotiations non-instantaneously. If the terms of the offer require that acceptance is effective only on receipt, the mailbox rule is not available to the offeree. Acceptance would only then be effective on receipt by the offeror.

    a. Acceptance is Effective On Dispatch: The rule allows acceptance upon dispatch as long as the offeree uses authorized means of communicating the acceptance. This includes the same means as the offeror used or faster. For example, a letter offer authorizes acceptance by letter, telegraph, fax, e-mail, or messenger.

    b. Offeror's Revocation or Unawareness: The mailbox rule might result in a valid acceptance (and thus a contract) even if the offeror had sent a previous revocation or was unaware of the acceptance. Because there is a contract on dispatch, the parties are theoretically bound even if the acceptance is lost in transmission to the offeror.

    c. Unauthorized Means/Options: If an unauthorized slower medium of communication is used, the acceptance is only effective upon receipt. Also, the exercise of an option (irrevocable offer supported by consideration) is only effective when received by the offeror. Finally, if the acceptance was misaddressed, was absent postage, etc., the mailbox rule does not apply.

> **MBE Tip:** The mailbox rule and situations where it doesn't apply – acceptance of an option, slower means, misaddress by the offeree, or a communication using means precluded in the offer – are heavily tested on the MBE.

3. Rejection Exception: An exception to the mailbox rule applies on the MBE occasionally if the offeree first rejects and then subsequently attempts to accept. In such a case, the effective date of acceptance goes back to the general rule: the date of receipt by the offeror. The effectiveness of the acceptance would depend on which arrived first, the rejection or the subsequent acceptance.

> **MBE Tip:** For there to be a valid acceptance, there must be an open offer. If the prior rejection reaches the offeror, it terminates the offer. Thus a question factual tip that this provision is being tested is that the rejection was delayed or lost in transmission to the offeror. This is necessary so that the subsequent acceptance reaches the offeror before the rejection.

4. UCC Treatment: The mailbox rule also applies to acceptances under the UCC. The statute liberalizes the common law treatment by requiring that acceptance must only be made in a reasonable manner and by any reasonable medium. Under the UCC, this may be slower than the offer such as a letter acceptance in response to an offer made by e-mail, telegraph, or telephoned offer. [UCC 2.206]

5. 3-Day Cooling-Off Rule: The Federal Trade Commission (FTC) allows a consumer a three-day period to cancel a contract. To qualify for this cancellation right, the goods must cost $25 or more and be purchased in the consumer's home or at a location other than the merchant's main place of business. The salesman must inform the consumer of the cancellation right at the time of the sale. [16 CFR 429]

H. Approach to Offer-Acceptance Cross Problem

Offer/acceptance cross problems are often tested on the MBE. These arise when offers, acceptances, or revocations "miss each other" in their transmission.

1. Skeleton for Analysis: To sort out the various communications and keep the relevant dates straight, you might want to consider the following skeleton:

PARTY   COMMUNICATION   SENT   RECEIVED   EFFECTIVE

2. Example: In a June 1 letter, A offered to sell land to B without dictating any required details about effective acceptance. B received the offer on June 2. On June 2, B sent a rejection by mail, but A never received it. On June 3, A revoked her offer by letter. On June 4, B sent an acceptance letter that was received by A on June 6. On June 5, A's revocation letter was received by B. Did a contract result?

PARTY	COMMUNICATION	SENT	RECEIVED	EFFECTIVE
A	Offer	6/1	6/2	6/2
B	Rejection	6/2		
B	Acceptance	6/4	6/6	6/6
A	Revocation	6/3	6/5	6/5

Answer: No. B's attempted rejection of 6/2 operated to terminate the use of the mailbox rule. If the rejection had been received by A, the offer would have terminated. Therefore, a subsequent acceptance can only be effective upon receipt by the offeror. Acceptance on 6/6 is too late because A's revocation was effective on 6/5.

> **MBE Tip:** Every MBE exam has multiple contract formation questions containing various offer and acceptance issues. You must understand every detail of the topics just covered.

I. Formation Overall Checklist

A good overall MBE contract checklist has three analytical steps. First, look to the offer – were any acceptance terms specifically dictated by the offeror? If so, such terms are binding on the offeree. Second, analyze the wording of the purported acceptance. Was this communication an acceptance, a mere inquiry, an acceptance requesting changes, or an effective rejection such as an acceptance with a demand for different terms? Third, if an acceptance, what was the effective date? Remember the mailbox rule for an acceptance.

> **STOP!** Go to page 115 and work Learning Questions 13 to 21.

IV. CONSIDERATION

The nuances of consideration are heavily tested on the MBE. The general rule is that the legal obligation of a promise is not enforceable unless it is made in a bargained-for exchange. Consideration provides the "quid pro quo" (something for something) to bind the parties to their naked promises.

A. In General

1. Legal Sufficiency: Consideration must be bargained for and sufficient.

a. Benefit/Detriment Test: "Bargained for" is satisfied if the act, forebearance, or return promise results in a benefit to the promisor or a detriment to the promisee. The promisee may incur a future detriment by agreeing to something that one is not legally obliged to do. An example is agreeing to quit smoking or forbear in filing suit. Being hired for a new job, a pay raise, or a promotion given to an existing employee may provide the consideration for an employee's promise not to compete.

b. Unilateral Contract: In a unilateral contract, the consideration detriment may be the offeree's performance.

2. Mutuality: The parties' exchange does not have to be of equal value, but mutuality of consideration is necessary. Mutual promises of commitment by both parties or a contemporary exchange are usually sufficient.

3. Non-Qualifying Conditions:

a. Past Consideration: This is where a transfer of value occurs before the other party makes the promise such as, "In consideration of your past employment services, I promise to pay $100,000." The general rule is that past consideration is no consideration.

b. Moral Obligation: A few courts may invoke the doctrine of "moral obligation" to support that portion of a new written promise where valuable consideration once existed and was innocently surrendered. Examples included a promisee's formerly valid claim barred by the statute of limitations. Also tested on the MBE is a creditor-promisee's non-objection to a bankruptcy based upon the promisor's written statement they would later pay the discharged debt; this may be enforced.

4. Gifts: An executory promise to make a gift lacks consideration because it is not a bargained-for exchange. The donee has lost nothing except the receipt of a prospective future gift. If, in comparison, the gift promisor requires completion of a condition by the donee, the bargain element is met. A completed gift (delivery and acceptance) intended to create a property right is irrevocable.

5. Illusory Promises: Be alert on the MBE for an illusory promise that does not create a legal detrimental obligation, such as, "I promise to pay a bonus to be determined by the parties in the future." Also illusory and tested is a promisor's statement of non-commitment such as, "I will perform if it suits me," or an option revocable at will.

6. Aleatory Contracts: This is where performance of one party's obligation is conditional upon some uncertain future event outside the party's control. The duties in an aleatory contract are independent and each party may sue the other for breach even though the P is also in breach. An example is a promise by an insurance company in a policy to pay a claim if a pre-defined loss event occurs. The insurance proceeds must be paid unless the policy owner has received notice that the policy has been affirmatively canceled; mere non-payment of the premium is insufficient to void the coverage.

MBE Tip: Past consideration, gifts, and illusory promises are frequently tested on the MBE.

B. Pre-Existing Duty Rule

The pre-existing duty rule is a defense to a contractual recovery where a new promise (or modification of the old) is given for the same act a party has already promised to perform.

1. Exam Questions: Typical questions include a contractor extracting a homeowner's promise to pay an additional amount for completion of the same original contract. Another frequent fact pattern to look for on the MBE is a buyer who makes a new promise to pay an additional sum demanded by a seller to avoid the seller's threat to breach. These are to be treated as either a modification or an accord and require consideration.

2. Consideration Exception: This may apply if there is an honest dispute about the adequacy of performance or the amount which is properly owed (amount is "unliquidated.") If the contractor agrees to complete the job a month before the prior performance date, there is consideration (detriment to the promisee). This consideration will support enforceability of the homeowner's promise to pay the extra sum to the contractor.

MBE Tip: The pre-existing duty rule and modifications / accords of existing contracts (see below) are tested on every MBE.

C. Partial Payment Rule

This rule applies where a partial payment of a debt is tendered with "payment in full" written on the check and the claimant is aware of the condition of the tender.

1. Unliquidated Dispute: If a good faith dispute exists about the amount due, the debt is "unliquidated." The tendered sum must represent a genuine compromise – not merely a token offer.

2. Acceptance: If the payee accepts the tendered amount as full payment, this acceptance discharges the balance of the debt and the check maker is also barred from suing on the claim. If the payee crosses out a "paid in full" notation or adds "all rights reserved" and deposits the check, the debt is still discharged and the payee will be deemed to have accepted the tendered sum as payment in full in most states. [UCC 3.311]

MBE Tip: The partial payment rule is often combined with accord and satisfaction – see below.

D. Surrendering a Legal Claim

If a party promises not to pursue a legal claim that he/she believes in good faith to be valid in return for another party's promise to pay money, there is a detriment to the promisee.

Even if the claim is actually legally invalid, consideration is still present if the holder of the claim reasonably believed that the claim was well founded and enforceable.

E. Promissory Estoppel

The doctrine of promissory estoppel may validate a donative promise in the absence of a bargained for exchange supported by contemporaneous consideration. The lack of consideration is not fatal if the promisee has reasonably changed her position in reliance on the promise. The Restatement confirms that consideration is implied by law to avoid injustice resulting from detrimental reliance as evidenced by the promisee's action or forbearance.

1. Foreseeable Reliance Required: Detrimental reliance by the promisee must be reasonably foreseeable by the promisor to induce action or forbearance.

2. Damage Measure: Reliance interest is the usual measure of damage under a promissory estoppel theory of recovery – see Remedies section below.

3. Examples: This includes pledges made to a charity or church. Another frequent MBE topic is where an employee stays on the job because of a promise to provide a pension or other retirement benefits. Also asked is where the employee moved across the country to accept a promised promotion. The employee could enforce the employer's promise made with the intention of inducing the employee's action if the reliance was reasonable.

MBE Tip: Every MBE tests consideration in surrendering a legal claim, "moral obligation," or promissory estoppel. Remember estoppel is only a substitute for consideration otherwise lacking. Often the consideration in the question is a detriment to the promisee.

F. UCC Modifications

UCC contract modifications made in good faith do not require consideration to be binding. [UCC 2.209]

1. Additional Amount Promise: A modification occurs where a buyer has promised to pay a higher price for the same goods. Often this occurs after extra costs have been incurred by a seller and the contract is still executory.

2. In Good Faith Required: In the case of a merchant, "in good faith" is defined as "honesty in fact in the transaction and the observance of reasonable commercial standards of fair dealing in the trade." An frequent MBE example is where a manufacturer's input and/or production costs have increased and the buyer agrees to pay the increase. Compare this to a seller seeking a buyer's promise to pay an extra amount because another customer offered to pay more. The UCC does not define "good faith" for a casual seller. [UCC 2.103(1)(b)]

MBE Tip: Contract modifications are a frequent MBE topic. Under the UCC, a modification does not require consideration if made "in good faith." The common law's pre-existing duty rule would normally preclude recovery for such modifications.

G. Third Party Beneficiaries

Third party beneficiaries are non-contracting parties who may receive enforceable rights even though they lack privity of contract. If they meet certain legal requirements, they are allowed to "boot strap" onto the consideration provided by the promisee. (See discussion of the third party beneficiaries below.)

The trilogy of Offer, Acceptance, and Consideration are collectively referred to as "mutual assent" or a "bargained for exchange." All three are necessary to form a contract.

V. LEGAL CAPACITY – 3 Is

A. General Rule

The contracting parties must have full legal capacity. Three groups – infants, the insane, and the intoxicated – generally lack capacity.

1. Incapacity as a Defense: These groups may assert incapacity as a defense to a contract enforcement action.

2. Voidable Unless Ratified: With the exception of certain contracts by infants (minors), contracts made by parties lacking capacity are voidable unless ratified. Incapacitated parties may enforce the contract or escape from it. The creditor may not unilaterally escape the contract obligation.

B. Infants

1. Basic Rule: Infants' (under 18 years old in most states) contracts for luxuries (supplied in the past or executory in the future) may be disaffirmed by infants or their guardian at their option. An infant remains liable for the fair value of past "necessaries" contracts not provided by his parents. Examples of necessaries include agreements to purchase food, shelter, clothing, medical care, insurance, and similar basic items. Cars and motorcycles are not necessaries.

2. Election to Disaffirm: After reaching the age of majority, the infant has a reasonable time period to make an election to avoid/disaffirm or to ratify/affirm the entire contract. Ratification will be implied by conduct if the infant brings suit to enforce the contract. In many states, a lack of disaffirmance within a reasonably prompt period of time after reaching the age of majority is deemed to constitute ratification.

3. Infant's Suit for Rescission: Where the infant chooses to disaffirm the contract, he must return the remainder of the luxury item(s) to the other contractual party. In addition, any rescission of money paid by the infant will be offset by the reasonable value of the benefit received.

4. Creditor's Possible Recoveries: If the child is over 14, it may be possible to recover against an infant who materially misrepresents his age via an action for fraud, restitution, or in-quasi-contract. (See Remedies below.) Parents are not usually liable for an infant's contracts.

MBE Tip: Infancy of one of the contracting parties is a favorite twist to throw into a MBE question. Look for an under 18 year-old actor. Remember that this capacity defense applies to all types of contracts, but excludes past necessaries. Only the infant has the election to avoid the agreement (not the creditor) when they reach the age of majority and the creditor has potential equitable recoveries as an alternative to a contract recovery.

C. Insanity

Insanity, senility, extreme mental retardation, or other neurological disorders may be contract capacity defenses.

1. Judicial Determination Required: A controlling court must have declared that the party did not have sufficient capacity to understand the contract. This usually involves a competency hearing in which there is a detailed evaluation of the party's capacity. Unadjudicated incompetents, informal incapacity opinions, and showings of mental imbalance, neurosis, or other similar conditions without a judicial determination are usually insufficient unless the other contracting party had reason to know of the mental incapacity.

2. Burden of Persuasion: The burden of establishing mental incompetence is on the party claiming insanity.

D. Intoxication

Intoxicated individuals may lack formation capacity if so intoxicated that they were not aware of the legal consequences of their act. On the exam usually the other party had knowledge of the situation and took advantage of the capacity impairment.

1. Required Standard: Cognitive capacity requires a reasonable understanding of the nature, terms, and legal consequences of the transaction at the time of contract execution. The fact that the D would not have entered into the contract if they had been sober is not controlling. The test is whether the intoxicated individual was able to understand the nature, terms, and legal consequences flowing from entering into the agreement.

2. Awareness: On the MBE, the other party is often aware of the intoxication and resulting incapacity. One caveat is that this defense is only successful in extreme cases.

E. Agency Liability

An agent disclosing his or her principal and agency capacity is not usually personally liable to a third party for breach of the principal contract.

1. Agency Authority: The principal is usually liable for contract responsibilities created by an agent on behalf of the principal if the agent had authority to enter into the contract. This requires the principal to bestow upon the agent express, implied, or apparent authority to enter a legal agreement creating the responsibility in question.

2. Agent Personal Liability: Under a few circumstances, the agent may be personally liable to the contracting third party.

a. Non- or Mis- Disclosure: This applies if the agent fails to disclose to a third party that the principal lacks capacity (infant or insane principal) or misrepresents the scope of her authority (unauthorized contract).

b. Personal Involvement: The agent is also liable if she represented that she was dealing for her own account, affirmatively stated that there was no undisclosed principal, or she guaranteed the contract. Examples include a del credere sales agent who guarantees payment of her customer's accounts.

> **STOP!** Go to page 117 and work Learning Questions 22 to 28.

VI. LEGAL SUBJECT MATTER

The subject matter of the contract must not be illegal or violate public policy. If illegal, the contract is unenforceable and void. The court will leave the parties as it finds them.

A. Violation of Law

Violation of statutory laws includes a contract to commit a crime or tort. Performing professional (legal, accounting, architecture, real estate broker, and similar) services without a state license is also illegal. No fee is collectable even if the service was satisfactory.

1. Exception for Beneficiaries: If the licensing statute violated was regulatory in nature and intended to protect the public, including one of the contracting parties, the contract would be enforceable by that party. An example is a contractor required to register and obtain a state license. The customer can recover damages for breach of contract even though the contractor failed to comply with the registration law.

2. Not "In Pari Delicto": If the parties are not "in pari delicto" (equally culpable) because one has much more fault, the contract may be enforced by the more innocent party.

3. Divisible Contract: This may apply if the contract's primary purpose is not illegal, but the contract contains an illegal provision. If the contract is divisible into two or more equivalent parts, the court may sever the illegal portion and enforce the remainder.

4. Subsequent Illegality: If the statute creating the illegality was enacted after the offer, but before acceptance, the offer terminates. If passed after acceptance, the contract is discharged because of impossibility of legal performance. (See below, Supervening Illegality under Excusable Nonperformance for details.)

B. Violation of Public Policy

Agreements which violate public policy may also be held unenforceable. Such contracts include the topics discussed below. The court has discretion to strike only the offensive portion of the agreement and leave the remainder of the contract in effect. Also possible is a court decision to hold the entire contract unenforceable as against public policy if the oppressive portion goes to the heart of the agreement.

1. Restraint of Trade: Contracts restraining trade and contracts requiring antitrust activities are specifically prohibited by statute in almost all states. An agreement to fix prices, allocate markets, and other anti-competitive actions including some corporate mergers and acquisitions would qualify. Also included may be extremely unfair business practices.

2. Non-Competition Employment Agreement: Non-competition agreements in employment contracts require consideration and if unreasonably broad may also be against public policy.

a. Consideration Required: There must be some valid independent consideration to support the employee's promise because such prohibitions may restrict a person's ability to earn a living. This may be a benefit to the promisee such as receiving a salary increase.

b. SAT – Reasonable Subject, Area, and Time: Courts dislike employment-related non-competition agreements. Therefore courts enforce such restraints only to the extent necessary to protect the employer. Non-competes must be reasonable as to the subject matter (type of work and contacts) covered, the geographic area, and the durational time period.

> **MBE Tip:** Look for an employer demanding existing employees sign a non-compete or lose their job. This is not sufficient consideration. Are the SAT terms unreasonable?

3. Business Sale: If associated with a business sale or trade secret disclosure, the normal presumption is that the non-compete restraint is reasonable. This is usually imposed to protect the business buyer and any purchased goodwill.

4. Tortious Interference: If the agreement promotes or encourages tortious interference with a third party, the court may decline to enforce the restraint.

5. Exculpatory Clauses: Exculpatory clauses purport to relieve a contracting party from liability resulting from his own negligence or breach of contract. If the public interest is involved, exculpatory clauses are usually against public policy. An example is an attorney's representation agreement that includes a clause relieving the law firm of liability for failing to exercise due care.

VII. STATUTE OF FRAUDS – MOULS

> **MBE Tip:** Unless the MBE question expressly states that the agreement was written and signed, consider the statute of frauds (SOF) as a defense to contract formation. Look for a telephone call, in-person negotiations, or the words "stated," "offered," "agreed," etc., where it is not clear whether a writing was involved.

The Statute of Frauds (SOF) in most states requires a writing signed by the party to be charged (the D or her authorized agent) for certain types of important contracts. If required by the subject of the contract, the writing requirement may not be waived by the parties. Oral contracts are unenforceable under the rule unless an exception applies.

Only the signature of the party against whom enforcement is sought (the D) is required to validate the contract. Thus the contract may not be enforced against a party who did not sign it. The five instances in which a writing is usually required under the statute of frauds in most states are abbreviated by the acronym **MOULS**.

A. Marriage Including Property Transfer

If marriage was the consideration for a promise regarding a property transfer, the marriage contract must be written. This would include prenuptial and community property agreements. An exception is a mutual promise to marry without any reference to a property transfer, which may be oral.

B. Over One Year

The statute applies – so a writing is necessary – if the contract performance duty is expressly required by the agreement term to extend more than one year from the date of execution. This concept is frequently tested on the MBE, usually in an employment agreement (but may also apply to a UCC contract over one year). This may be complicated by:

1. Immediate Beginning: Watch for a contract with exactly a one year term beginning immediately. This would not require a writing.

2. Later Beginning: A contract for one year beginning tomorrow must be written, as it is over one year.

3. Indefinite Term: An oral contract not stating a specified term is usually excluded from the operation of the statute. Thus an employment contract for life ("as long as you live") or without a time limit (an "at-will contract") can be oral because the employee could die, quit, or be fired for cause within a year. The fact that performance of the oral and/or unsigned contract later extends over a year does not affect its enforceability under the SOF.

4. Executed Portion Enforceable: One party's performance takes the performed portion of the contract out of the SOF application. Therefore, a normal employment contract will be enforceable for the executed time period which the employee worked; the future executory portion would remain unenforceable.

> **MBE Tip:** Often the facts in the question apply to an employment contract where the performance of the project for which an employee was hired is expected to take over a year. This is a distracter because only if the employment term is expressly over a year does there have to be a writing.

C. UCC If $500 US or More – PAWS Exceptions

UCC sales contracts for $500 or more in US dollars or modifications raising the new contract amount to $500 or more must be written. Similarly an oral modification to a contract over $500 is not enforceable even if the change is not over $500. The writing threshold for a lease contract for goods is $1,000. Exceptions also apply to **PAWS** situations as follows:

1. Part Performance: Oral contracts are enforceable for the executed portion of a contract already performed. This would apply if the seller delivered part of the order, the buyer inspected them for conformity, and thereafter accepted that portion of the goods. Even if there was not a written agreement for the whole contract, this performed portion would be enforced.

2. Admission: An oral agreement is also enforceable if the D admits it exists.

3. Written Merchant-to-Merchant Confirmations: Written confirmations between merchants sufficient to bind the sender that are not objected to in writing within 10 days also satisfy the writing requirement. The memorandum must reasonably identify both the goods in question and the two contracting parties. Both parties are bound by a written merchant-to-merchant confirmation.

4. Specially Manufactured Goods: Oral contracts for goods specially manufactured for that particular buyer may be enforced without a writing. The goods must not be suitable for sale to others in the ordinary course of the seller's business. This exception applies even if the specially manufactured goods amount is $500 or more.

5. Quantity Required: A UCC contract is not generally enforceable beyond the quantity of goods specified in the agreement. Output and requirement contracts for $500 or more must thus be written (see below).

6. "Some" Writing Sufficient: The UCC section's official comments relax the common law writing requirements of being signed by the party to be charged. Any written authentication which identifies the party against whom performance is sought will suffice. The actual signature of the D is not necessary if there was an intent to authenticate the writing such as initials. An unsigned company letterhead or e-mail from the D containing a name and address may thus be a sufficient writing under the UCC. As under the common law, the contract may be enforceable against only one party.

7. Party to be Charged: Only the "party to be charged" must have signed a writing under the SOF. If A did not sign a writing, but B did, A may sue B, but B may not sue A. If A sues B and B asserts a counterclaim for breach, then A's "admission" in his pleading will make the contract enforceable against him, but only up to the quantity of goods she has placed at issue.

MBE Tip: While only an "authorization" is required for a UCC contract, a signature is required for a merchant's "firm offer." This creates an irrevocable offer without consideration.

D. Land Sale or Lease

All land transaction contracts must be written, state the price, and be signed by at least the seller. The full legal description of the land is also required. Lease agreements of real property for over one year must also be in writing and signed by the lessor in most states.

1. Included Agreements: The SOF includes conveyancing deeds and liability encumbrances relating to real property. Also included are contracts for land-based resources such as timber, minerals, oil, and related resources. Contracts for crops are not included (unless over $500). Any agreement authorizing or employing an agent or broker to sell or purchase real estate for compensation must be written ("equal dignity rule"). All modifications to such agreements must also be written.

2. Land Possessor Exception: An oral real property conveyance contract may be enforced if a land possessor makes a down payment, takes possession, and performs substantial improvements to the property. Paying property taxes is also strong evidence of ownership. The possessor must be clearly evidence more ownership characteristics than a mere tenant.

E. Suretyship Promises

A writing signed by the party to be charged is required for suretyship undertakings. Included in this category are a promise to guarantee the debts or default of another and a promise by a personal representative to answer personally for a decedent's or an estate's debts. Examples of suretyship include a loan guarantee, a bonding company in a construction project, or a fidelity insurance bond securing the honest performance by an employee.

> **MBE Tip:** Be sure the promisor is undertaking in a secondary capacity a liability obligation of another and not a primary obligation of the promisor's own responsibility. "Ship the goods to my child and I will pay for it" is a primary promise and the SOF does not apply. An oral agreement to stand for a primary liability at the transaction date is enforceable. A secondary liability would be "I will pay if my child does not." This promise must be written.

1. Contract Issues: The suretyship contract is formed when a surety makes a promise to either the creditor or debtor. Consideration issues may be present on the MBE.

a. Consideration – Promise to Creditor: If the surety promise is made to the creditor as a part of the transaction process, the required consideration is the goods delivered or the loan extended to the debtor (a detriment to the promisee). Consideration in the form of a detriment to the promisee is also present if the creditor extends the due date on the loan. Another example is the creditor expressly forbearing to bring suit on a delinquent loan in exchange for the surety's promise.

b. Consideration – Promise to Debtor: If the surety promise is made to the debtor after the obligation was created, there must be consideration in the form of a benefit to the promisor-surety. This follows because there is no detriment to the promisee-debtor; the debtor receives a benefit from the surety's participation.

> **MBE Tip:** The fine-line distinction of the consideration differences depending upon the direction of the guarantee promise (to creditor or debtor) is frequently tested on the MBE.

2. SOF Exception: The general rule is that a writing signed by the surety is required.

a. Main Purpose Rule: If the main purpose of the surety's undertaking is intended to substantially benefit their own economic interest, an oral promise of guarantee may be enforceable. Consideration for the guarantee promise is the benefit to the surety.

b. Examples: Examples of exceptions to the Statute of Frauds include a promisor who was a pre-existing creditor of the debtor who would receive the proceeds of the bank loan. A parent corporation's guarantee of the debts of a subsidiary would qualify. A parent orally guaranteeing the obligation of their son or daughter for necessaries (loan for law school tuition) has also been asked on the MBE. In contrast, an oral promise to pay the debt of a friend is not usually enforceable.

3. Antecedent Debt Promise: The majority of jurisdictions do not require that consideration is necessary to support a new promise to pay all or a part of a debt barred by the statute of limitations (SOL) if the new promise is in writing and signed by the debtor.

> **MBE Tip:** A guarantor's oral undertaking for his own economic advantage is frequently tested on the MBE.

F. Private Statute of Frauds

1. Common Law: Most jurisdictions enforce a contract provision requiring written modifications and/or prohibiting subsequent oral modifications of written common law contracts. Modifications must be written and signed by both parties.

2. UCC: The UCC agrees that a contract provision requiring all modification must be written is to be enforced. However the UCC would allow ineffective attempts at oral modifications to be considered as evidence of waiver of the "written modifications only" provision. [UCC 2.209]

G. Other Statute of Frauds Exceptions

1. Divisibility: If the SOF applies and there is no writing, determine if the contract could be interpreted as divisible. Part performance by a seller may take the executed portion out of the SOF analysis. This would require an equivalent percentage payment amount.

2. Estoppel: The Restatement specifies that promissory estoppel may, in extreme cases, negate the need for a writing (see above discussion). Similarly, estoppel may apply if the D represented no writing was necessary or that she would sign a written agreement later. ("My word is my bond and I will sign when we put it in writing.") If a party suffered great damages in reliance on an oral agreement in which the D was unjustifiably enriched, estoppel may be asserted.

MBE Tip: SOF issues are included in many MBE questions. If your analysis concludes there is a SOF violation, look for promissory estoppel or part performance which may validate the performed portion of the contract.

H. Alternative Remedies

Even if the SOF is violated, the P might still recover compensation through a tort recovery theory or a quasi-contract suit to avoid unjust enrichment. See Remedies below.

STOP!   Go to page 119 and work Learning Questions 29 to 34.

VIII. VOID OR VOIDABLE CIRCUMSTANCES – MUFFED

Illegal contracts and contracts violating the SOF are "void" as a matter of law and have no legal force or effect. A motion to dismiss on the pleadings may be brought on the basis P cannot make out a prima facie **OACLLS** case.

A contract can be merely "voidable" rather than void where a party has the power to avoid the legal relations. Examples include the parties not reaching a true "meeting of the minds" or one of the parties lacking capacity. There is still a contract, but the aggrieved party could avoid performance by petitioning a court to declare the agreement void. This is equivalent to rescission, which restores the parties to their previous position without an award for damages.

A. Mistakes

Mistakes occur when a party's basic assumption about some significant aspect of the exchange is not in accordance with the truth. Mistakes are frequently characterized as unilateral or mutual. The usual remedy for mistakes which are excused is rescission.

1. Unilateral: Only one party was mistaken. This includes a party who misunderstands the legal consequences of an agreement or the facts upon which the contract was based. Often the MBE questions raise this issue when a contractor makes a mechanical calculation mistake in preparing the price of a construction bid. Another example is one party who thinks the subject of the contract is worth much more than the true market value.

      a. General Rule is Enforceable: A unilateral mistake by one party is not grounds for avoidance so the general rule is that the contractor bears the risk. This requires performance according to the contract terms even if the contractor suffers a loss.

      b. Exception Excusing Performance: The mistaken party may be granted relief by asserting an affirmative defense if the other party had:

            (1) Knowledge: Actual or constructive knowledge of the mistake or failed to correct a known basic mistake significantly affecting the other party.

            (2) Aided in Mistake: Substantially contributed to a significant mistake such as failure to disclose a significant hidden defect. At some point, the non-disclosure may become so significant as to be characterized as fraudulent concealment.

MBE Tip: Frequently the question contains facts indicating the property owner had some idea that the contractor's bid price was unrealistically low. Also frequent is where the workman who had contracted to do the repairs was unaware that there was a hidden defect in the property. If the owner knew of the defect creating the mistake and did not make disclosure, there may be a viable defense for the workman.

---

      2. Mutual: Both parties were mistaken about a significant fact material to the contract. Mutual mistakes of minor consequence are legally irrelevant. Further, courts are more likely to consider the issue of mistake if the contract is still executory. If performance is fully executed, the court will more likely decline to intervene.

      a. Mutual Mistake of Value: A mutual mistake of value is not usually grounds for rescission. (Both parties believed the item had no value and it was actually very valuable.)

      b. Mutual Mistake of Fact: A mutual mistake of fact is grounds for avoidance if the factual dispute is so material that it is clear there was no true meeting of the minds. For example, the parties disagree on which item was purchased or whether the painting sold to the buyer was an original work of art or merely an inexpensive copy.

      c. Mixed Value and Fact. If the mutual mistake is of both value and fact, the courts interpret it as a factual mistake allowing avoidance. An example is a contract to purchase land that both parties thought contained oil, but the land was dry. Whether there was oil in the land or not is a question of fact, but it still affects the land's value.

B. Unconscionability

"Unconscionable" contracts under both the common law and the UCC are too unfair, oppressive, one-sided, or harsh to be enforceable. This is a question of law for the court but is only rarely found in the commercial contracting context. In a consumer sales contract, the court may either strike only the unconscionable portion or rescind the whole contract.

1. Characteristics: The facts must shock the conscience of the court and be beyond all reasonable standards of fair dealing.

a. Two Requirements: In most jurisdictions, there are two requirements for unconscionability to constitute a viable contract defense. First, an unfair bargaining process – an absence of meaningful choice under the circumstances (procedural unconscionability) is necessary. The second element is that there must be an oppressive harshness in the outcome (substantive unconscionability) such as a grossly excessive price.

b. Adhesion Contract: Such a fact pattern may arise in a standard form contract which was presented by the superior party on a take-it or leave-it non-negotiable basis. Examples include a disclaimer in small print on the back of a boilerplate lease imposed by a landlord on a tenant, or a sales contract prepared by a merchant negating all warranties or disclaiming liability to consumers for even gross negligence. [UCC 2.302]

2. UCC Treatment:

a. Good Faith Required: The UCC requires good faith by all contracting parties. Confession of judgment clauses in a sales contract may be declared unconscionable.

b. Personal Injury in Consumer Goods: A limitation on consequential damages resulting from personal injury in consumer goods contracts is "prima facie" unconscionable. This shifts the burden to the seller to show the limitation is fair and equitable. The Code will normally allow a limitation of damages where the loss is commercial. [UCC 2.719(3)] The presumption does not apply in a commercial transaction.

MBE Tip: The unconscionability defense on the MBE is usually obvious; look for an extreme situation involving a merchant taking advantage of a consumer by using an adhesion contract which contains terms that are patently unfair.

C. Fraud

Fraud or misrepresentation may be an affirmative defense and grounds to rescind a contract. Fraud may be in the execution or inducement. This is a heavily tested MBE topic.

1. Fraud In the Execution: Fraud in the execution (or fraud in the factum under UCC Article 3 Commercial Paper) goes to the instrument itself and creates a void transaction. This type of fraud is possible if an innocent party was tricked into unknowingly signing a document that was later changed into a complete contract by the other party. An example would be the buyer's signature on what they thought was a delivery receipt which was later added to and thereby changed into a promissory note.

2. Fraud In the Inducement: Fraud in the inducement or misrepresentation in the contract formation stage may make the contract voidable. The required **FIRD** elements are:

a. False Statement of a Material Fact: A fact must rise above opinion or puffing. Compare "this car gets 30 miles per gallon" to "this car is a great buy."

b. Intention to Deceive the P: "Scienter" or the intention to deceive must be present.

c. Reliance on the D's False Statement: The P must reasonably rely on the D's misrepresentation in entering into the contract.

d. Damages: The benefit of the bargain is the usual measure of damages.

3. Fraudulent Concealment: An omission or nondisclosure of a material fact or hidden defect may be grounds for rescission of the contract if significant damages results therefrom. Active concealment by one party may override an unilateral mistake by the other party. (See Torts chapter for more detail covering fraud.)

MBE Tip: Fraud by the D – execution, inducement, or concealment – is present as an affirmative defense to performance in many MBE contract questions.

D. Fiduciary's Undue Influence

A "fiduciary" is a person who occupies a position of special confidence and trust towards another. There is usually a disparity in business experience, education, or age between the fiduciary and the beneficiary. The abused party is often particularly susceptible to overreaching because of their trusting reliance on the fiduciary. Included in this category are an attorney, CPA, corporate director, guardian, trustee, and personal representative of an estate.

1. Undivided Loyalty Required: Such a relationship imposes on the fiduciary a high degree of undivided loyalty, obedience, good faith, and due care. Conflicts of interest and business transactions with clients are suspect and closely scrutinized. Breach of fiduciary duty may be asserted as a defense in a contract enforcement action. All relevant facts must be disclosed or a fiduciary is liable.

2. Unfair Persuasion: Undue influence involves unfair persuasion. This is a question for the trier of fact. Such a contract defense may be used where a fiduciary abuses a position of trust. If an attorney exerts undue influence over an elderly client by entering into an unfair transaction with the client, the contract may be voidable by the elderly client. The fiduciary has the burden of proving the transaction was fair and at arm's length.

3. Constructive Trust: This may arise if a fiduciary acquires legal title to property owned by a beneficiary through undue influence, fraud, theft, or extreme duress.

MBE Tip: Almost any question that involves a business transaction between a professional and a layperson, especially if the professional is a lawyer, merits consideration of fiduciary duties and the defense of undue influence.

E. Estoppel

The doctrine may be asserted as a defense to a contract enforcement action. It differs from promissory estoppel in that the false statement is one of fact rather than a promise.

1. Equitable Estoppel: Here, the P deliberately did or said something that created a justifiable belief by the other party that a right would not be enforced in the future. That statement is inconsistent with the lawsuit the P is now asserting against the D. An example would be if P wrote to D stating that she would not enforce a contract and D justifiably relied upon the statement. Later the P brings suit on the same contract (see Accord and Satisfaction below).

2. Judicial Estoppel: This defense applies if the P previously gave sworn testimony in a court proceeding that is inconsistent with the position they are taking in a subsequent legal proceeding. An example is a D's denial of a fact in opposing a summary judgment motion that is inconsistent with her admission in a prior deposition.

F. Duress

The defense of duress applies where a contracting party is coerced into contract consent (or to modify a previous contract) because of an improper threat overcoming free will.

1. Exam Situations: Examples include impending physical threat such as holding a gun to the head of a person or threatening imprisonment unless the other party signs a contract. Also tested is the unjustified threat of pursuing a criminal prosecution. The victim must show that the improper threat or pressure would have induced a reasonably prudent person to assent to the contract against their will. Such a contract is voidable by the victim. However, a threat of civil litigation is not usually sufficient.

2. Economic Duress: A few extreme cases have recognized the doctrine of economic duress where the necessities were immediately needed and could not be obtained from another source. The D usually created the desperate situation or actively intermeddled in the market to make the situation worse. Doubling the price of insulin by the sole source of supply in an isolated market is an example.

IX. INTERPRETATION OF CONTRACT – II PACC

A. Intentions of Parties Control

The objective intentions of the parties control the interpretation of the contract terms. Normally the language of the contract is the guiding interpretation principle the court will follow.

B. Incorporation by Reference

Incorporation by reference may be present if the agreement refers to another document. The document referred to must be identified with reasonable certainty. If the treatment of a given item in the two documents is different, the most recent agreement generally controls.

C. Parol Evidence Rule – DUCAS Exceptions

The parol evidence rule (PER) attempts to finalize a written agreement.

1. General Concept: Application of the PER is a question of law for the judge. The rule excludes from evidence at trial the terms of any prior or contemporaneous extrinsic discussions or agreements that contradict the terms of the final written "integrated" contract.

a. Integration: An "integrated" contract is intended by the parties as a final expression of their entire agreement concerning the included terms. A "merger clause," such as this is the "final" or "total agreement," may be effective to raise the PER. The MBE may use fuzzy language to describe the degree of integration.

b. Partial or Total: A few MBE questions distinguish between a "partial integration" and a "total integration." The former – a partial integration – was not intended as the complete agreement of the parties so consistent extrinsic verbal terms and understandings may be introduced into evidence. In some jurisdictions, the latter – a total integration – may not be supplemented by evidence of any prior discussions or agreements.

c. Unaffected Extrinsic Terms: Unstated consistent terms and recitals of fact may usually be introduced from extrinsic evidence. Beyond this, the general PER rule of exclusion is subject to the following **DUCAS** exceptions, which are heavily tested.

2. Defect in Formation: Defects in formation rendering the contract void or voidable may be introduced by extrinsic evidence. Examples include fraud in the inducement, mutual mistake, failure of consideration, duress, illegality, or lack of capacity by one of the contracting parties. This includes preliminary false representations made by one party (usually a sales agent) that contradict the terms of the final written agreement which the buyer signed.

3. UCC Trade and Dealings: If the subject of the contract is goods, three categories of extrinsic evidence helpful in clarifying contract intent or supplementing or qualifying terms may be introduced. [UCC 2.202] The **CPU** order of priority is:

a. Course of Performance: The parties' earlier course of performance in the present contract is usually considered to be the best evidence to clarify uncertainty. If the contract provides for a schedule of repeat performances, consistency may be inferred and imposed in the current dispute. [UCC 2.208]

b Past Course of Dealings: The past course of dealings between the parties illustrates how the undecided term was handled in previous contracts. Previous conduct may also establish a particular meaning to, supplement and/or qualify terms of the final agreement. [UCC 1.205]

c. Usage of Trade: Evidence indicating a regularly accepted practice or method used in the industry or trade may be introduced. The trade practice must be such as to justify an expectation that it will be observed in this contract. [UCC 1.205]

4. Condition Precedent: If the parties agree elsewhere that the contract was not to become effective until a certain condition occurs, evidence of the non-occurrence of the condition may be introduced.

5. Ambiguity Interpretation: Evidence of extrinsic negotiations may be admitted to define, interpret, or clarify an ambiguous term within the written integrated agreement. The term term at issue must be susceptible of more than one meaning or interpretation to qualify as "ambiguous."

6. Subsequent Modifications: Subsequent contract modifications and acts of the parties that arise after the written integrated agreement and change one or more of its terms may be introduced. Under the common law, consideration is required for a modification.

> **MBE Tip:** The parol evidence rule is a favorite exam issue. Three **ICE** questions exist: (1) Is the final agreement "**i**ntegrated?" [If not integrated, the PER does not apply and the extrinsic evidence comes in.] (2) Is the **c**ontested term covered in the contract? [If not; it is admissible.] (3) If so, is there a **DUCAS e**xception? [If so, the extrinsic evidences comes in.]

D. Ambiguity

Ambiguous words or terms are susceptible of more than one meaning. This is a question of law for the court. A latent ambiguity is where the contract appeared clear at formation, but subsequent facts show a term to be ambiguous. The most basic rule is that a term has the ordinary, usual, and popular meaning unless a contrary intent is clearly demonstrated.

1. Construction: Ambiguous terms are usually to be construed against the party who drafted the agreement since the creator of the confusion had the power to use more exact language in the document. A latent ambiguity is enforced in favor of the unaware party if the other party was aware of the ambiguity.

> **MBE Tip:** This construction rule may be combined with the ambiguity exception to the PER, discussed above.

2. Contradictory Terms: A contract may contain more than one statement of the same term in conflicting expressions.

a. Narrative-Time Conflict:

(1) Rule: Generally speaking, handwritten terms prevail over typed terms; typed terms prevail over the terms of a standard form printed agreement. This is because the rule as applied is that the parties' most recent expression of the term controls.

(2) Example: Consider a different expression of the same term is an optometrist's printed contract which stated a price of "$40.00 for eyeglasses." The secretary typed in wording to change the description to "$40.00 for eyeglasses per eye." At the time the patient picked up the eyeglasses, the parties added writing to the description producing "$40.00 for eyeglasses per eye excluding eyeglass frames." The handwritten term controls.

b. Amount Designation Conflict: If a number depicted in numerals conflicts with one written by words, the word designation controls. An example is a check designated in numerals as "$8,000" but written in words as "eighty thousand." The correct amount of the check would be treated as $80,000. The $72,000 material alteration would be disregarded by the court absent compelling evidence of a contrary intent.

E. Controlling Statute

If the agreement does not address a particular item or matter and there is a controlling statute (such as the UCC, Uniform Partnership Act, Model Business Corporations Act, etc.), the statutory provision fills in the gaps. An example would be a contract that does not specify risk of loss in shipment. The applicable UCC rule covering risk of loss would apply.

F. Conflict of Laws

The controlling procedural or substantive rules of law may vary from state to state, or between counties, or between cities. Where parties reside in different jurisdictions with conflicting laws, a reasonably related contract designation controls. [UCC 1.105(1)]

1. Substantial Relationship Required: There must be a substantial relationship to the jurisdiction specified to qualify the contract designation.

2. Most Significant Relationship: Absent a valid contract designation, the courts look to the forum with the most significant relationship with the contract parties, subject, and performance. This is a balancing test.

3. Examples: In a sale of property, usually look to the location of the property; in a sale of goods, the place of delivery is often applied. For a personal service contract, the place of performance usually controls.

4. Forum Selection Designation: If the contract specifies the forum in which suit must be brought, it is usually enforceable. The parties by agreement may usually consent to personal jurisdiction in a court that lacks a significant relationship to the parties even in another state. A party seeking to invalidate a forum designation has the burden to establish that the designated forum is very unfair or unreasonable.

> **STOP!** Go to page 120 and work Learning Questions 35 to 41.

X. UCC SALES OF GOODS PROVISIONS

A. Shipment/Delivery/Payment Terms

Almost all of the UCC "default" provisions only apply if the parties do not expressly address the term by agreeing to specific contractual terms to the contrary.

1. Payment, Price, and Delivery: Unless otherwise agreed, payment is usually due at the time and place of delivery of conforming goods. [UCC 2.310] Payment by check is usually sufficient. If the seller demands payment in legal tender, she must give an extension of time reasonably necessary for the buyer to procure the cash. [UCC 2.511]

a. COD and Acceptance: COD always means collect on delivery. [UCC 2.310] All goods must be tendered in a single delivery and payment is then due. [UCC 2.307]

b. Non-Conforming Goods Accepted: The buyer must pay at the contract rate for any goods accepted. This means that even if the goods are defective, they must be paid for, although the buyer has a right to deduct reasonable damages from the price so long as he gives the seller notice of his intent to do so. [UCC 2.717]

c. Open Price Term: A contract may be enforceable even if the price is not settled unless the parties intended to be bound only if the price was agreed. The price to be imposed is a reasonable price at the time of delivery. [UCC 2.305]

d. Place of Delivery: The place for delivery is the seller's place of business (or residence if no place of business). The seller must give the buyer whatever notification is reasonably necessary to enable the buyer to take delivery. [UCC 2.308]

MBE Tip: The facts may specify who bears shipping costs by stating terms such as the below; if not, the court will look to the three CPU factors for this determination.

---

2. Free on Board (FOB): FOB vessel or vehicle means the seller bears the expense of putting the goods in possession of the carrier and loading.

a. FOB – Place of Destination: In an FOB place of destination contract, the freight charges are paid by the seller. The seller bears the risk of loss until the goods are tendered to the buyer at the designated destination location.

b. FOB – Place of Shipment: In an FOB seller's place of business shipment point contract, FOB loading dock, or if FOB is stated but no location is specified, the buyer pays freight. The seller pays for and is liable for damages in loading to the carrier, but the buyer bears the risk of loss thereafter. [UCC 2.319(1)]

3. Free Alongside (FAS): FAS means that the seller, at her own expense, must deliver goods free alongside the carrier at a named port and tender a receipt for the goods. If properly delivered to the carrier, risk of loss shifts to the buyer who must arrange and pay for loading the goods on board. [UCC 2.319(2)]

4. Cost, Insurance, and Freight (CIF): CIF means that the seller's price includes in a lump sum all the cost, insurance, and freight to the buyer's destination. The seller delivers the goods to the carrier and pays for the insurance and freight. Delivery to the carrier shifts risk of loss to the buyer who must seek any remedy against the carrier or insurer. At this point the seller is released from the risk of loss. The seller then forwards the ownership documents to the buyer, who must pay on tender of the documents. [UCC 2.320]

5. Ex-Ship: The seller must deliver the goods free of carriage liens to the buyer at the named port of destination and pay for vessel unloading. Risk of loss then passes to the buyer. [UCC 2.322]

6. No Arrival/No Sale: "No arrival/no sale" or "to arrive" in a destination contract excuses the seller from liability if the nondelivery resulted solely from hazards of transportation. [UCC 2.324]

MBE Tip: Past MBE questions have focused on the allocation of risk of loss between the seller and buyer where the goods are in the process of being transferred.

B. Title and Risk of Loss

1. General Rule:

a. Parties Agree: The parties may agree to when title passes as long as it is after the goods are in existence and have been identified in the contract.

b. General Provisions: Under the common law, risk of loss transfers with title. Under the UCC, title passes when the seller has completed performance of delivery. Risk of loss for goods thus generally shifts to the buyer upon receipt and acceptance of conforming goods. The parties may vary from this rule and agree as to who will bear the risk of loss in a particular situation.

c. No Agreement: If the parties do not specify otherwise, the general rule is that the breaching party retains risk of loss until the other party has insurance coverage.

d. Non-Conforming Delivery: If a tender or delivery of goods so fails to conform to the contract as to give the buyer a right of rejection, the title and risk of loss remain with the seller until the breach is cured. Similarly, if the buyer accepts and later rightfully revokes acceptance, the risk of loss shifts back to the seller. [UCC 2.510]

2. "Tender" of Delivery: The seller must tender delivery to the buyer. Delivery is to be in one lot unless agreed to the contrary. [UCC 2.307] If the seller's tender of delivery is refused by the buyer and the goods are subsequently destroyed while remaining on the seller's premises, the status of the seller becomes important. [UCC 2.503]

a. Non-Merchant Seller: Risk of loss passes to the buyer upon a non-merchant (casual) seller's mere tender of delivery of conforming goods.

b. Merchant Seller: If the seller is a merchant, risk of loss only passes upon actual receipt by the buyer; mere tender of delivery is insufficient. Usually this means the merchant bears the risk of loss because risk stays with possession of the goods at the seller's place of business. [UCC 2.509(3)]

MBE Tip: In addition to title, the above two provisions – risk of loss when there is a buyer's right of rejection and tender refusal – are the most likely testing areas on the MBE.

---

3. Destination and Shipment Contracts: If the seller is obligated to ship to a particular destination, risk of loss passes when delivery of the goods is tendered at that destination. If the seller is obligated to ship the goods to the buyer but no particular destination is specified, risk of loss passes when the goods are delivered to the carrier. The seller must promptly notify the buyer of the shipment. [UCC 2.504]

4. Documents of Title: Documents of title are instruments constituting ownership of the goods such as a warehouse receipt. Unless otherwise agreed, the buyer must pay against a tender of the documents of title if goods are in the possession of a warehouseman or bailee. Risk of loss passes to the buyer at the time when he/she accepted negotiation of the document. [UCC 2.509(2)]

5. Power to Transfer: A purchaser of goods acquires all rights that her transferor had. A person with voidable title has the power to transfer good title to a good faith purchaser for value even though the goods were delivered in exchange for a check that was later dishonored. In comparison, a thief can never transfer good title to stolen goods. Entrusting goods to a merchant who deals in those kinds of goods usually gives the merchant the power to transfer all rights to a buyer in the ordinary course of business. [UCC 2.403]

6. Conditional Sales: These rules cover situations where the buyer has the right to return conforming delivered goods to the seller. The question is whether the buyer's creditors may levy on such goods that are on the buyer's premises. A wholesaler providing a retailer with inventory is an example.

a. Sale or Return: A "sale or return" applies if the goods are primarily for resale. This arrangement allows a retailer buyer who cannot resell the goods to his customers to return them to the wholesaler at her own risk and expense. Title and risk of loss pass to the retailer upon receipt of the goods. This allows the retailer's creditors to levy on the goods before the wholesaler is paid.

b. Sale on Approval: A "sale on approval" applies if the goods are primarily for the buyer's use. Title and risk of loss are retained by the seller so that the goods are not subject to claims of the retailer's creditors. The buyer must formally approve or accept the goods before the title and risk of loss transfer to the buyer. The buyer's acceptance may be inferred by the refusal to return the goods within a reasonable time period. Returns are at the seller's risk and expense.

c. Ambiguous Terms: Reasonable doubts as to the nature of the transaction are to be resolved in favor of the general creditors of the retailer. This "sale or return" conclusion is appropriate because the wholesaler can always perfect its security interest through a proper recording of the financing statement. [UCC 2.326 and 2.327]

7. Consignments: Consignment is selling the goods of others. They are to be treated as a "sale or return" so that the buyer's creditors can levy on the goods. However, the buyer's creditors lose their rights if the consignor obtains an Article 9 security interest, a conspicuous sign on the retailer's premises states that the goods are subject to a consignor's interest, or the consignee's creditors know he is engaged in the consignment business. The uncertainty associated with the latter two methods usually prompts consignors to comply with Article 9's perfection rules by recording a financing statement. [UCC 2.326]

8. Insurable Interest: A buyer is allowed to assert an insurable interest prior to receiving title or risk of loss. Buyers may thus insure their interest in goods they do not yet physically control. [UCC 2.501]

a. Existing Goods: A buyer's insurable interest arises when a contract is entered into for existing identified goods.

b. Future Goods: For goods to be delivered in the future, a buyer's insurable interest comes into existence when they are shipped, marked, segregated, or otherwise identified as relating to the buyer's particular order. If the goods are to be manufactured, they must be at a point where they are distinguishable from the seller's other inventory.

c. Seller's Insurable Interest: The seller retains an insurable interest as long as he has title to, or any security interest in, the goods. An insurable interest in proceeds derived from the disposition of collateral is allowed if such collateral was subject to an insurable interest. [UCC 9.102(64)(E)]

XI. LIABILITY OF A UCC GOODS SELLER

A. In General

A purchaser or consumer has three legal causes of action for personal injury and property damage that can be used to pursue a seller or remote manufacturer of goods: strict liability, negligence, and warranty. The UCC creates liability to a goods seller under warranty theories of recovery and the MBE testing is focused on these topics.

> **MBE Tip:** Warranty liability theory of recovery always applies to business economic losses such as a business purchasing goods that do not conform to the contract specifications. If the question involves physical injuries of a consumer, analyze the claim under a tort liability theory. See further details in Torts.

B. Express Warranties

Express warranties include all of a seller's affirmations of fact and promises, which become a part of the basis of the bargain. The buyer must have relied thereupon, but it is not always necessary that the seller intended to create a warranty. The warranty may include a sample, blueprint, technical specification, and perhaps an advertisement. However, such affirmations must rise above mere opinion, puffing, or preliminary bargaining. [UCC 2.313]

C. Implied Warranties

In addition to any seller's affirmations, the UCC imposes certain implied warranties. These are implied warranties of absolute liability and do not turn upon negligence of the D. It does not matter if the seller had no knowledge of the defect or was not careless in his behavior. Sales (and contract) warranty liability is no fault. Under the "gravamen test," warranty recoveries will almost always be available to the injured party if the injury was caused by the good.

1. Merchantability: The UCC imposes an implied requirement on merchant sellers that their goods must be merchantable. Merchantability means pass without objection in the trade, be of fair and average quality, and fit for the ordinary purposes for which such goods are used. The container, packaging, and labeling of the goods must also meet this standard. Usage of trade will normally establish this standard. [UCC 2.314] If the buyer inspects the goods before entering into the contract, there is no implied warranty as to defects which should have been detected. There is also no warranty that livestock are free from sickness or disease. [UCC 2.316]

2. Fitness for a Particular Purpose: This applies if the buyer is relying upon the seller to use his/her expertise in selecting the most appropriate item for the buyer's particular purpose. The seller must have reason to know that the buyer is relying upon the advice in selecting a suitable good for the purpose. A writing is not required. This provision also applies to non-merchant sellers. [UCC 2.315]

3. Title and Against Infringement: This imposes on the seller the requirements of good title, the right to transfer, and that the item is free from undisclosed security interests, liens, encumbrances, or claims of which the buyer lacked knowledge. If a merchant seller, the goods must not infringe on any third party's patent or copyright. This last restriction does not apply if a buyer gives the seller the specifications for custom ordered goods. [UCC 2.312]

D. Limitations

Sellers can attempt to escape warranty liability by including limitations or exclusions in the sales contract.

1. Policy of the Law: The policy of the law is generally against limitations or exclusions of liability. Any ambiguity in such attempted language in the sales document is to be construed against the seller.

2. Dollar Limitation, Repair, or Replace: Limitations include a ceiling on the recoverable dollar amount resulting from a breach, return and refund, or the repair, or replacement of non-conforming goods. Such limitations may be enforced as the buyer's sole remedy if the contract states that such is the exclusive remedy. However, there must be a fair quantum of remedy for breach, the agreement cannot fail of its essential purpose, and any restriction cannot deprive the buyer of the substantial value of the bargain. [UCC 2.719]

E. Exclusions and Disclaimers – 5 Cs Test

Bargained-for exclusions – where the seller is attempting to disclaim total liability – are allowed with some limitations. In most states they are subject to a two step analysis. The first analytical step is whether the exclusion language meets every exclusionary element of the **5 Cs** test:

1. Clear: The language must be clearly written so a reasonable buyer would understand that there is no remedy. Any ambiguity will be construed against the seller.

2. Conspicuous: The writing must be obvious so that a reasonable buyer should have seen the exclusion. Small print or language hidden in the middle of a long convoluted paragraph is not conspicuous.

3. Conscionable: The exclusion must be bargained for in good faith and not unexpected. Standardized adhesion contracts without explicit negotiations are suspect.

a. Effect: If the disclaimer is unconscionable, the court may limit its application or void the contract in total. The UCC recognizes that most consumers have no ability to bargain and therefore no influence over what terms merchants and manufacturers include in their standard sales contracts. [UCC 2.302]

b. Personal Injury: Personal injury limitations in the case of consumer goods are "prima facie" unconscionable. This provision has the effect of shifting the burden of proof to the seller to show that the exclusion was in fact fair. This restriction will not normally apply to a commercial transaction between merchants in an arm's length situation. [UCC 2.719(3)]

4. Consistent: The exclusion cannot attempt to override express warranties previously made in the same document. The UCC 2.316 comment specifies that this consistency requirement was added to deal with clauses purporting to exclude liability from "all warranties, express or implied" or similar. This requirement makes it virtually impossible to disclaim responsibility for an express warranty.

5. Consumer Purchaser: Disclaimers by a merchant must set forth with particularity the qualities and characteristics not warranted if the purchase is for personal, family, or household use. [UCC 2.316(4)]

6. Second Step - Special Words: The second analytical step is whether the exclusionary language meets one of the enumerated tests that UCC 2.316 has authorized and the courts have historically allowed.

a. Merchantability: The statute states the implied warranty of merchantability may be disclaimed or excluded by the use of certain words. Examples include "as is," "with all faults," "not merchantable," or other language in which the buyer assumes the entire quality risk. Note that such disclaimers cannot negate express warranties. There is no requirement the merchantability disclaimer be written, but where it is written, it must be conspicuous.

b. Fitness for a Particular Purpose: Sellers may be allowed to exclude the implied warranty of fitness for a particular purpose with a disclaimer which is written and conspicuous. "There are no warranties which extend beyond the description on the face hereof" qualifies. Remember the consistency requirement of your 5 Cs. [UCC 2.316(2)]

c. Title and Against Infringement: This implied warranty is very difficult for a merchant to exclude. General disclaimers are not allowed. Detailed disclosure language or facts such that the buyer knew that the title was contested or that the seller was only conveying whatever interest he had without claim of title may qualify. [UCC 2.312(3)]

MBE Tip: Strict product liability in tort has superseded most of the above warranty protection for personal injury and consumer property damages. Business economic damages remain under the contract warranty analysis.

F. Privity – Vertical and Horizontal

The UCC extends third party beneficiary status to family or household members and guests (horizontal privity) and allows such persons to sue anyone in the distribution chain from retailer to manufacturer (vertical privity). With regard to vertical privity, case law is mixed as to the right of remote buyers to sue anyone other than the immediate seller for breach of implied warranties. The warranties run to such groups under the concept of horizontal privity because it is reasonable to expect that persons other than the immediate buyer would use, consume, or be affected by the good. Injured Ps are deemed to be within the foreseeable zone of danger. A seller may not exclude or limit this section, which expands Ps' standing despite the traditional requirement of privity. [UCC 2.318]

G. Magnuson-Moss Act

The 1975 Magnuson-Moss Act requires detailed information about any specific warranty made by a seller for a consumer product sold in interstate commerce. [15 U.S.C. § 2301-2312]

1. Full or Limited Warranty: The warranty must be designated as "full" or "limited." If "full," the implied warranty of merchantability cannot be limited. Further, an assignee of the purchaser may enforce the warranty even if beyond the privity scope of UCC 2.318. If the warranty fails to meet any of the Act's requirements, it must be clearly and conspicuously labeled "limited."

2. Anti-Lemon Provisions: The "anti-lemon" provisions apply to a "repair-or-replace" warranty limitation provision. The consumer must be allowed the choice of replacement or a complete refund (rescission) if the product is a "lemon" that cannot be repaired after repeated attempts.

3. Federal Trade Commission Enforces: The Federal Trade Commission is charged with the responsibility of enforcing the Act. A civil action is possible including class action status if there are at least 100 claimants.

STOP! Go to page 122 and work Learning Questions 42 to 50.

XII. PERFORMANCE AND BREACH

> **MBE Tip:** Performance and Breach are extensively tested on the MBE. Pay particular attention to issues of Excusable Nonperformance, Nonperformance with an Accord (and potential Satisfaction) or "modification remedy" and Breach.

There are five varieties of performance.

A. Full Satisfactory Performance

Full satisfactory performance with all conditions satisfied discharges the contracting parties. There are three types of conditions under which some defined event will trigger, limit, or extinguish an absolute duty to perform. The important distinction is the condition's timing.

1. Condition Precedent: A condition precedent must occur (or be excused by the court or other party) before the promisor's duty to perform matures. An example is an offer to buy a parcel of property that is contingent upon the buyer arranging financing. The condition may also be the performance of one side in a unilateral contract (if you produce a buyer for my property, I will pay you a commission). The condition precedent is securing a ready, willing, and able buyer. The condition precedent may also require approval by the other contracting party or a third party. The courts will review the denial of such approval using one of two standards:

a. Objective Standard: An objective (reasonable person) test is adopted if the approval involves a mechanical utility or operational fitness. An example is an architect who must certify project completion before the owner's duty to pay the contractor matures. The question is whether a reasonable architect would have rejected the contractor's performance considering the plans and construction circumstances.

b. Subjective Standard: A subjective standard is applied if performance approval involves personal taste or fancy. An example is a customer who reserves the right to be personally satisfied with the performance of an artist hired to paint a portrait of a family. The fact that other reasonable people might be satisfied with the portrait is not binding upon the buyer-obligee, assuming no bad faith.

c. Time of the Essence: A slight delay in performance completion does not usually constitute a material breach unless late performance would critically defeat the contract purpose. In comparison, an express "time is of the essence" condition will usually be enforced if damages result from late performance. If so specified in the contract, any delay is usually a major breach suspending the non-breaching party's duty to perform.

> **MBE Tip:** Look for an express condition. The promise is followed by the words "if," "provided," "on condition that," or "unless." The MBE also tests "time of the essence."

---

2. Condition Concurrent: Conditions concurrent are promises in the contract which must be performed simultaneously by both parties or at about the same time.

a. Examples: An example is a property seller tendering the deed under the condition that the buyer provides payment at the same time. Another example is delivery of goods in lots with payment within ten days of each delivery. If the buyer does not pay on time, she has breached the concurrent condition. This allows the seller to stop ongoing contractual performance, such as halting the next shipment, without being in breach.

b. Constructive: If the parties so intended or it is necessary to achieve fairness by imposing equity, a court may also imply a "constructive condition concurrent" even if not expressly stated. While each promise in a bilateral contract is usually separately enforceable, a court may constructively condition one promise as dependant on completion of the other. An example is the insured's duty to timely pay insurance premiums to recover for a loss.

3. Condition Subsequent: A condition subsequent is a pre-defined uncertain future event that operates to discharge the performance duty of one or both of the parties. An example is a long-term premise lease contract containing a termination provision if the premises are used for the sale of liquor.

4. Condition Frustration and Excuse:

a. Prevention: A party may not avoid a conditional responsibility maturing into a contractual duty by wrongfully preventing or hindering the occurrence of the condition.

b. Excused/Waiver: A condition may be expressly excused or impliedly waived. This is a voluntary relinquishment of a legal right by one of the contracting parties. A waiver may not usually be withdrawn after the other party has acted in justifiable reliance.

MBE Tip: Conditions precedent and concurrent are tested on many MBE exams. Often a condition precedent is associated with the offer or acceptance and thus affects whether the contract was formed. Less frequently, the condition is concurrent (involving both parties) or subsequent thus terminating performance. Look also for a condition waiver.

B. Substantial Performance

The common law rejects the UCC's "perfect tender" rule. Substantial performance avoids a total forfeiture. It applies where there was not technically full performance, but the defect was minor, bad faith was not present, and the substantial benefit was received.

1. Basic Test: The basic test is whether the breach was material or minor. The doctrine is designed to prevent a total forfeiture from minor breach. The failure to adhere to the letter of the contract must be insignificant to the overall performance.

2. Damage Reduction: The damages flowing from the defect are deducted from the contract price. An example is a building contractor using a different brand of pipe than that specified on the drawings or in the written specifications. The owner must show that the deficiency has less value because it is more than cosmetic.

3. In Quasi-Contract: Even if the breach is material there may still be a recovery by the breaching party to avoid unjust enrichment of the other.

> **MBE Tip:** Substantial performance is heavily tested. On the MBE, performance of services and home building contracts often fail to adhere to all the detailed technical conditions specified in the contract. Was the breach major or minor?

C. Excusable Nonperformance – CIISSU

Excusable nonperformance discharges the contractual duty where performance has become objectively impossible or unduly burdensome, not merely more difficult or expensive. The occurrence of commercial impracticability must have been reasonably unforeseeable at the contract formation date. The resulting discharge of the promisor's contract executory duties may be total, partial, or merely temporary. This may also be called frustration of purpose and applies to six situations on the MBE, abbreviated by the acronym **CIISSU**.

> **MBE Tip:** Make sure neither party agreed to assume the particular risk or caused the impossibility. This might override the below situations creating a performance excuse.

1. Cooperation Lacking or Hindrance: A party may not provide necessary cooperation or hinder contract completion. This may discharge the other party's performance duty and create the right to sue for damages. Note that a court could also hold such action or inaction as a breach of an express or implied condition against wrongful prevention.

2. Illegality After Formation: Illegality will result from legislation subsequent to the contract formation that makes the performance of the agreement legally impossible. Supervening illegality discharges the contract.

3. Incapacity: The incapacity or death of a specific personal service contractor may excuse performance of the related personal service contract. An example is if an artist dies prior to the completion of a personal portrait. In such a case the contract is excused. This results because the artist's bargained-for unique talents are no longer available. Distinguish this personal impracticality from a contractor able to hire substitute employees.

> **MBE Tip:** This excuse applies only to personal services contracts, where only one party is capable of fulfilling the terms of the contract. Watch for service contracts that any other employee or contractor could complete (like washing the windows of a house). Incapacity of the obligor will not excuse performance on such contracts.

4. Source of Supply Impossible: This applies where the designated source of supply is destroyed through no fault of the promisor. The contract must specify the particular source of the item for this provision to excuse breach. If the source is not specified, the seller must purchase goods at market to meet her contract performance duty.

5. Subject Matter Destroyed: This is also called frustration of purpose. The unique subject matter of the performance is destroyed through no fault of the contracting parties.

a. Executory Contracts: This applies before performance. If a used car is stolen after a contract to sell it is executed, the future performance is now impossible. If the seller could easily obtain replacement units to fulfill the contract delivery responsibility, destruction of the primary units may not excuse performance.

b. Partially Executed Contractor's Rule: Frequently on the MBE a fire or earthquake destroys a structure before the contractor has completed construction. If a new structure being constructed is destroyed, the risk of loss usually stays with the contractor until substantial completion and therefore no in quasi-contract recovery is awarded. If the contract is only to repair an existing structure, the contract is excused because of frustration of purpose and the contractor may recover in quasi-contract for the value of the work delivered to the owner until the destruction date.

6. UCC Failure of a Presupposed Condition: Commercial impracticability or Force Majeure may excuse the future performance duty under the UCC. The UCC states that a failure of a presupposed condition is not a breach. The non-occurrence of the supervening condition or event must have been a reasonable basic assumption upon which the contract was made. The key requirement is that the condition was not reasonably foreseeable on the agreement date. Compliance with a government regulation or order also triggers this provision. [UCC 2.615]

a. Examples: Unforeseeable conditions that qualify include fire, outbreak of war, terrorist attack, embargo, crop failure because of fire or unexpected drought, power outage, or earthquake. Normal weather variations, a mere cost increase or foreseeable increased difficulty are not usually sufficient to terminate the contract's rights and duties. In addition, the performance obligation may merely be temporarily suspended; if performance once again becomes possible, the duty may again revive and become enforceable.

b. Part Performance: If part performance is still possible after the failure of the presupposed condition, the UCC requires the seller to allocate among customers in a fair and reasonable manner. Buyers must be notified "seasonably" or promptly of the expected allocation quota amounts and delayed delivery date. [UCC 2.615]

c. Buyer's Option: The buyer is given the option of agreeing to the available quota offered. In the alternative, she may terminate the agreement if the prospective deficiency substantially impairs the value of the whole contract. [UCC 2.616]

MBE Tip: CIISSU excusable nonperformance is heavily tested on the MBE. Incapacity and the failure of a presupposed condition are frequent. The more foreseeable the condition, the less likely that performance will be excused. Parties discharged by impossibility may usually recover in quasi-contract for the value of the benefit conferred.

D. Insecurity and Assurance of Performance

1. UCC Provision: The UCC provides for a statutory right to assurances if a party has reasonable grounds to question the other party's ability or willingness to perform the executory portion of a contract. This includes a delegation of the performance duty. [UCC 2.201] Upon receipt of a written demand, the other contracting party must submit a response giving written assurance of performance to the insecure party.

2. Consequence of Non-Compliance: Failure to respond adequately within a reasonable time not exceeding 30 days allows the requesting party to treat the contract as repudiated.

a. Insecure Party Rights: Until the insecure party receives assurances, they may suspend performance without being in breach if such suspension is commercially reasonable. In addition, the UCC provides that an insecure seller may stop delivery of goods in transit upon discovery that the buyer is insolvent [UCC 2.705].

b. COD Basis: The buyer is then entitled to the goods only on a COD basis. [UCC 2.609]

3. Communication Purpose: Because the exact required response of the assurance is not specified, the UCC merely intends to promote communications between the parties.

4. Exam Fact Patterns: Exam questions have included a report from a trustworthy source that the seller will not or cannot perform, an express anticipatory repudiation by the seller, receiving new of the buyer's insolvency, the seller's delivery of non-conforming goods in the first installment of a multi-lot contract, or the buyer's failure to pay for the first lot. Acceptance of one lot of non-conforming goods or accepting late payment does not prejudice the aggrieved party's right to demand adequate assurances of compliance for future lots and other performance requirements.

E. Nonperformance – But

In some situations there may be nonperformance, but the parties agree to modify or end the contractual liability through one of the following:

1. Accord and Satisfaction: Accord and satisfaction is where the parties compromise by agreeing to modify performance from that specified in the original contract. This applies if the obligation is unliquidated in amount or the amount in controversy is in dispute. Frequently, a lesser amount of money is offered by the debtor to the creditor to resolve the dispute. If the offer is accepted by the other party, it creates an accord.

a. New Agreement: The executory accord is the new substitute agreement and the necessary consideration is the detriment of forbearance to sue on the original disputed contract. The satisfaction is performance of the new agreement. The satisfaction discharges both the obligation of the executory accord and the original contract.

b. Non-Performance of Accord: If the executory accord is not performed, the obligee has dual remedies. She may sue on either the original obligation (if the statute of limitations has not expired) or on the accord agreement.

2. Novation: A novation is a new contract wherein a new party is substituted in place of one of the original parties. A novation is distinguished from an assignment because a novation must includes the express release of the original obligor. To be bound, the new party must affirmatively promise to assume the contract obligation.

3. Cancellation: Cancellation is the rescission of the contract by mutual agreement of the parties. This terminates all executory rights/duties and discharges both parties.

4. Waiver: One party may affirmatively excuse a condition of performance required by the other party or relinquish the right to sue for breach.

a. Not Both Parties: If both parties are involved in the change of position, the most likely characterization would be a modification or accord rather than a waiver.

b. Details: A waiver may result from an express promise or may be inferred from the circumstances. Non-material conditions precedent to a contract obligation are often waived by one or both parties on the MBE. A waiver may be retracted prior to the due date for the condition's fulfillment if the other party has not acted in detrimental reliance on the waiver.

5. Release or Promise Not to Sue: A mutual release is effective to terminate the contract relationship. In most jurisdictions a release must be supported by consideration.

a. Joint Obligor: A release by the obligee of one joint obligor releases the others from breach unless an express reservation of rights is made in the release.

b. Mere Negative Covenant: However, a release must be distinguished from a mere promise not to sue one joint obligor. Such a promise does not affect the liability of the other obligors. ("I release you" as opposed to "I promise not to sue you.")

6. Modification, Accord, and Waiver Analysis:

	Modification	Accord	Waiver
Time	Usually executory	Usually executed	Usually executed by one party
Parties Change	Both	Both	One party only
Consideration	Yes	Yes	No, so revocable
Original Terms	Terminated	Reserved if not satisfied	Terminated, if condition not material

F. Breach

Performance that is not substantial, is not excused, and in which the parties did not agree to an accord and satisfaction, novation, cancellation, or release is breach of contract. Under the

UCC, a seller's good faith shipment of nonconforming goods as an accommodation is nonetheless a breach.

1. Performance Presently Due: Breach can be failure to perform a duty presently due.

2. Anticipatory Repudiation: This expressly occurs when the D has indicated that she will not render prospective performance required in the future that substantially impairs the whole of the contract. The expression of intention to breach in the future must be objectively unequivocal, unambiguous, and go beyond performance uncertainty. Similarly, doing an act that demonstrates prospective inability to perform may qualify as implied anticipatory repudiation.

a. Non-Repudiating Party: The non-repudiating party is entitled to not only suspend her performance, but also to cancel the contract and immediately sue for damages. The aggrieved party may also wait until the performance date to determine if the D will revoke the repudiation. [UCC 2.610]

b. Retraction Before Change: If the D retracts the repudiation before the P has materially changed position, there is no breach and the contract is reinstated. [UCC 2.611]

c. UCC Assurance of Performance: Anticipatory repudiation will create the right to submit a written demand for an adequate assurance of performance under the UCC. The repudiating party must respond in writing within 30 days. A non-response is treated as anticipatory repudiation [UCC 2.609]

MBE Tip: Anticipatory repudiation is heavily tested especially where the statement is equivocal or merely expresses some doubt about the willingness or ability to perform

---

3. Divisibility of Contract:

a. Common Law: To avoid an entire forfeiture, a court may interpret a contract as having multiple divisible portions rather than one entirety. An equivalent payment is required for the performed portion. An example would be the partial painting or siding of a house that was destroyed by fire through no fault of the worker. Another example is the death of an employee after one day during a week-long employment contract. One-fifth equivalent payment would be required.

b. UCC Contracts: Unless intended to the contrary, a single delivery is assumed under the UCC. If delivery is made in separate lots, the contract price may be apportioned. The UCC will usually enforce whatever quantity was delivered, accepted, and paid for. A court may also interpret a UCC contract as divisible to avoid forfeiture of the whole. [UCC 2.307] This recovery is similar to substantial performance for contractors.

4. Installment Contract: If the delivery of separate lots is required or authorized in the contract, the buyer may reject any installment that is non-conforming. A non-conforming installment must be accepted if the seller gives adequate assurance that he/she intends to cure. If the non-conforming installment is not cured and it substantially impairs the value of the whole contract, the entire contract is breached. [UCC 2.612]

5. Minor (Nonmaterial) Breach:

a. Question of Fact: Breach of a performance duty is material or total if it goes to the essence of the entire contract or undermines the basis of the bargain. This allows the non-breaching party to cancel his or her own future executory performance under the contract. Ultimately the materiality of the breach is a question of fact. If the breach is only a minor deviation and does not affect a material benefit (nonmaterial), the non-breaching party must continue performance and has a claim for damages.

b. Example: Usually a slight time delay is considered minor. Suppose an employee is hired for six months at a lump sum price of $30,000 payable upon completion. The employee performs adequately for four months. In month five, the employee gets sick, but returns to work in month six. While the employer may claim this was a material breach that eliminates all his responsibility for the whole contract, a court would probably hold that the breach was minor so the employer's duty to pay the $30,000 is not suspended. The employer would still be entitled to recover for the one month damages.

> **STOP!** Go to page 124 and work Learning Questions 51 to 60.

XIII. REMEDIES – MRS DAISI

The P must specify in her legal complaint the remedy (or remedies) she wants the court to award or order. Most of these remedies are not mutually exclusive and can be pled in the alternative. The memory ladder acronym is **MRS DAISI**.

> **MBE Tip:** Consider all available **MRS DAISI** remedies which appear feasible in the situation and then focus upon the details most appropriate to the P in the question.

A. Money Damages

Money damages are the preferred remedy under the common law. They may include the following categories:

1. Liquidated Damages: A common law or UCC contract may contain stipulated provisions liquidating the damages from a future breach. An example is $20,000 per day for late completion of an office building contract where it is difficult to accurately calculate the prospective damages which might occur in the future.

a. Enforceability:

(1) Relationship to Actual Damages: To qualify, the liquidated sum must either be a reasonable forecast of damages at the contract formation or have a reasonable relationship to the actual damages at the time of the breach.

(2) Sole Remedy: If either of these standards is met, the liquidated sum may be allowed and imposed as the sole and exclusive remedy for the damages that the liquidation provision covers. Damages resulting from some other source and specific performance may also be allowed in addition to the liquidated damage award.

b. Penalty Interpretation: The court may conclude that the liquidated damages are so large as to constitute a penalty. This determination would usually be based upon a finding of significant disparity with the actual damages. The liquidated damage provision will be disregarded and P is then limited to recovering actual damages. [UCC 2.718(1)]

> **MBE Tip:** Liquidated damages must bear a reasonable relationship to the anticipated damages either at the time the contract was made or in light of the actual losses incurred from the breach. Watch for situations where the contract liquidation provision covers only late performance and there were only minimal other damages that resulted from the breach.

---

2. Compensatory Damages: If so large as to constitute a penalty, a liquidation damage clause may be disregarded. P is then entitled to recover compensatory or expectation damages.

a. Tort Actions: For torts, the required compensation attempts to put the P in the same financial position she was in prior to the tort.

b. Contract Actions: For breach of contract, the innocent party should realize the expectation of the benefit of the bargain. The benefit of the bargain is designed to compensate the P in an amount that would have resulted if the D had not breached the contract.

c. Special Contractor Rules: Frequently on the exam is a fact pattern where the contractor has begun but not yet completed the construction project.

(1) Owner's Breach: The owner may repudiate the balance of the contract and wrongfully terminate the builder. The contractor is allowed to collect the full contract price less the costs of the necessary components they would have incurred to complete the project.

(2) Contractor's Breach: The other possibility is that the contractor walks off the job without sufficient reason. The owner may collect the difference between the contract price and the costs of hiring another contractor to complete the project. Any amount paid the contractor is treated as a credit. Any net recovery to the contractor would be in quasi-contract since the contractor as the breaching party was not entitled to enforce the contract.

3. Reliance Interest: The Restatement allows this remedy where the contract fails such as a **MOULS** contract which was not written or promissory estoppel. The reliance interest attempts to return the relying party to their pre-promise financial position as a consolation to the expectation interest. Another situation is where in quasi-contract recovery will not avoid injustice. P is entitled to recover any out-of-pocket costs incurred in reliance on the expectation that the D would perform the contract.

> **MBE Tip:** Frequently on the MBE the injured party is entitled to recover the out-of-pocket costs incurred in reliance on the expectation that the D would perform the contract.

---

4. Punitive Damages: Punitive or exemplary damages are intended to punish the D for reprehensible conduct and deter such behavior in the future. Punitive damages are not awarded in most jurisdictions for simple breach of a common law or UCC contract. An exception exists for a fiduciary breaching a contract or where punitive damages are authorized by statute. Such statutes tend to be focused on protecting consumers. Occasionally punitive damages are authorized in the contract itself.

5. Emotional Distress: Recovery for emotional distress (or outrage) is not allowed under contract law unless it was foreseeable to D that serious physical or emotional injury would result from the breach of contract. Examples include breach of a contract to marry or a contracting bailee's loss of a cherished possession such as a family history book. Also asked on the MBE was a breach of contract to deliver a message to children regarding their mother's serious illness so they can see her before her death.

6. Nominal Damages: This applies where a breach of a valid contract occurred but P can not prove actual damages; $1.00 may be awarded.

7. Interest Award: Interest is usually recoverable on contracts involving liquidated damages since the amount is capable of being computed with exactness. An example is a collection suit on a promissory note. The theory is that the P would have had the use of the money had the D not breached the payment responsibility. Pre-judgment interest on the damages awarded is not usually allowed in tort. Tort interest would begin to accrue as of the judgment date.

8. Recovery Limitations: There are two limits on the recoverability of "general" or "special-consequential" monetary damages. Recovery of damages may also be limited in the contract by agreement of the parties.

a. Foreseeable: At the contract formation date, D must have been able to reasonably foresee that the resulting damages would occur as a probable consequence of the breach. *Hadley v. Baxendale.* This is an objective standard. If damages are unforeseeable as of the contract date, recovery may be denied.

b. Certainty: The P must also establish with certainty both the amount of the actual loss and the fact that the damages would have been avoided but for the breach. An example is a claim for lost profits made by a new business with no prior history of profitability; such damages may be too uncertain and speculative. If P cannot prove actual damages with sufficient certainty, only nominal damages will usually be awarded.

c. Contractual Damage Limitations:

(1) In General: Consequential damages may usually be limited or excluded in the contract. Examples include such terms as "repair or replace" in a commercial contract or limited to a certain dollar ceiling such as $1,000 maximum for a lost suitcase on an airplane. The UCC will not allow a remedy limitation that fails its essential purpose. [UCC 2.719(2)] This is a question of law for the court.

(2) Deposit Retention: If a buyer breaches, a seller may always retain up to the smaller of 20% of the contract or $500 of the buyer's payment of deposit. [UCC 2.718]

(3) Unconscionability: A limitation of damages in commercial transactions is usually allowed unless unconscionable. An example of unconscionability is limiting personal injury liability in a goods contract for consumer use. [UCC 2.719(3)]

9. UCC Remedies: The UCC analyzes remedies in terms of which party breached the contract.

a. Seller's Remedies: An aggrieved seller (such as where a buyer refuses to accept a timely conforming tender of performance or fails to furnish an agreed letter of credit) has certain remedies.

(1) Right To Cure: If a tender of performance is rejected because the goods fail to conform, the buyer must state the particular defect. [UCC 2.605] The seller has the right to "cure" a defect before the contract performance date. The seller must promptly ("seasonably") notify the buyer of the intention to cure. [UCC 2.508]

(2) Basic Damage Measure: Upon the buyer's breach, the seller may stop goods in transit and demand COD for any future shipment.

(a) Cancellation and Sue: The seller may also cancel the contract and/or sue for damages. The measure is the difference between the contract price and the market price at the time and place of tender. The amount received upon resale of the goods to another party determines the market price. [UCC 2.703 and 2.708]

(b) Resale Details: An aggrieved seller resale of the goods may be either public or private and the buyer must be notified of the sale. All aspects of the resale must be in good faith and commercially reasonable. [UCC 2.703] A person buying in good faith at the resale takes free and clear of any rights of the original buyer. [UCC 2.706]

(3) Incidental Damages: Incidental damages are costs incurred by the seller in a reasonable attempt to avoid loss. These may include the goods' storage, insurance, commissions, and costs of resale incurred to mitigate damages. Notice that consequential damages are not available to the seller. [UCC 2.710]

(4) Goods In Production: Goods in production may be sold as scrap or completed if commercially reasonable. The UCC defines this as a decision where the marginal revenue from production completion exceeds the related marginal costs. [UCC 2.704]

(5) Lost Profit Remedy: Sellers routinely sell the same good at the same price to all buyers. Thus the market price is usually the same as the contract price. If the buyer breaches, the seller is to be awarded the lost profit. This is the net amount that the seller would have realized had the buyer not breached the contract and includes an amount for reasonable overhead. The profit remedy does not pile up damages because the seller could have made two sales rather than one. An example is a buyer repudiating a contract to purchase a car that the dealer sells to another customer at the same price. The damages are the lost profit. [UCC 2.708]

(6) Buyer's Insolvency: If the seller discovers the buyer is insolvent, the seller may stop delivery or refuse to make delivery except for cash. [UCC 2.705] A seller may also reclaim goods from an insolvent buyer who purchased on credit as an alternative to seeking damages. This right applies up to 10 days after delivery. There is no time limit to reclamation if the buyer (in writing) misrepresents solvency within three months of delivery or pays for the goods with a dishonored check. Reclamation is an exclusive remedy. No other damages are possible. [UCC 2.702]

b. Buyer's Remedies: If the seller fails to deliver, delivers non-conforming goods timely, or delivers late, the aggrieved buyer has a choice of multiple remedies. A buyer may accept all, reject all, or accept any commercial unit and reject the rest of non-conforming goods. [UCC 2.601] The buyer must make an effective rejection to avoid acceptance. [UCC 2.606] A rejection must be made within a reasonable time of receipt and communicated to the seller. The details of any alleged non-conformity must be specified. [UCC 2.607]

MBE Tip: The buyer's remedies are tested more heavily on the MBE than the seller's. A "perfect tender" is required. "Cover" damage details are the biggest issue tested, but incidental and consequential damages are also frequently present.

---

(1) "Perfect Tender" Rule: The "perfect tender" rule specifies that a non-conforming shipment sent as an accommodation is nonetheless a breach. A buyer's right to reject arises if the goods "fail in any respect to conform to the contract." A buyer may accept none, all, or any commercially reasonable portion of such a non-conforming shipment. [UCC 2.601] Any rejection must be seasonably communicated to the seller. [UCC 2.602]

MBE Tip: A seller's non-conforming shipment under a unilateral contact may constitute both an acceptance and a breach. If such a shipment is sent before the scheduled delivery date, some courts would interpret it as a new offer by the seller.

---

(2) Inspection Right: A buyer has a reasonable right to inspect the goods before payment or acceptance. While COD may require payment before inspection, this is not acceptance. If non-conforming, the price may be recovered. [UCC 2.513]

(3) "Cover" Damages: Upon breach or repudiation by a seller, a buyer may immediately "cover" his or her requirements by purchasing equivalent substitute goods from another supplier. The cover price must be commercially reasonable. The buyer's damage amount is the difference between the contract price and the market "cover" price as of the time the buyer learned of the breach.

(4) Other Buyer's Damages: In addition to this basic measure, the buyer is entitled to incidental and consequential damages less any expenses saved by the breach.

(a) Incidental Damages: Incidental damages are the buyer's mitigation costs flowing from the breach. This would included care and custody of rightfully rejected goods and the reasonable expenses of effecting cover. [UCC 2.715(1)]

(b) Consequential Damages: Consequential damages protect the buyer's expectancy interest. This is the buyer's economic advantage that would have resulted from the contract had there not been a breach. The seller must have had reason to know (foreseeability) that such consequential damages would result from the breach. An example is the profit that the buyer would have realized on resale. Consequential damages may usually be limited or excluded unless unconscionable. [UCC 2.715(2)]

(5) Market Price Remedy: If the buyer cannot or does not cover, the remedy is the difference between the market price and the contract price on the date the buyer learned of the breach. This may be before the contractual date specified for performance. Incidental and consequential damages are also recoverable. [UCC 2.713(2)]

(6) Anticipatory Repudiation: After a seller's anticipatory repudiation, the buyer's damage award is the cover cost less the contract price. This is to be determined when the buyer learned of the repudiation. This provision will bar damages attributable to later price increases occurring before the buyer actually covers; there is no windfall. If, in comparison, the market price goes down between the repudiation date and the time the buyer covers by buying substitute goods, the lower price controls. [UCC 2.713]

(7) Specific Performance: A buyer is allowed specific performance or replevin under the UCC only if the goods are unique or under "other proper circumstances." Usually three conditions must be met. [UCC 2.716]

(a) Unable to Cover: The buyer must be unable to cover;

(b) Identified to Contract: The goods must have been identified in the contract; and

(c) Not Transferred to BFP: The goods cannot have been transferred to a bona fide purchaser (BFP). It is not likely that all three of these conditions will be met and thus the UCC does not favor specific performance as a buyer's remedy when the seller breaches.

(8) Rejection: The buyer may reject the seller's tender of non-conforming goods.

(a) Buyer's Option: If the goods fail in any respect to conform to the contract, the buyer may reject the entire amount or accept some units and reject the rest. Partial acceptance is permitted and a buyer accepting non-conforming goods does not lose any remedy otherwise available. [UCC 2.601]

(b) Particularized Defect: Affirmative action by the buyer is necessary to avoid acceptance. Effective rejection requires the buyer to give the seller notice of the particular defect within a reasonable period of time of receipt to allow a cure. [UCC 2.602] If the defect in tender could have been cured by the seller, a buyer who merely rejects without specific objections loses the ability to justify rejection or establish breach. [UCC 2.605]

(9) Revocation of Acceptance: A discovery of substantial hidden defects subsequent to acceptance may justify a rejection. A revocation of acceptance becomes effective only when the buyer notifies the seller. This right must be exercised within a reasonable period of time after discovery of the particular non-conforming defect and before the condition of the goods has substantially changed. [UCC 2.608]

10. Damage Mitigation: The non-breaching party has a duty to mitigate or minimize the monetary losses caused by the breach. Some states call this the doctrine of avoidable consequences. It operates to reduce the damages of the aggrieved party. Damages, losses, and related costs that could have been reasonably avoided are not recoverable. The Code distinguishes required mitigation depending on which party is aggrieved.

a. Common Law: Often tested is a terminated employee who must have made a reasonable effort to find other employment. The employer has the duty to show that the replacement position the former employee refused was of comparable nature and pay.

b. UCC Seller's Duty: If the buyer breaches, the seller's sale at market must be commercially reasonable and at the highest possible price. [UCC 2.706]

c. UCC Buyer's Duty: The UCC distinguishes between two types of buyers.

(1) Non-Merchant: A casual buyer may have taken physical possession of goods before a rightful rejection. Upon rejection, the seller must be notified. The buyer also has a duty to hold the goods with reasonable care for the seller's disposition. The non-merchant buyer has no further obligation to the seller. [UCC 2.602]

(2) Merchant: A merchant buyer with possession of a seller's non-conforming goods must notify the seller and follow any reasonable instructions of the seller. This includes returning the goods if requested. If no instructions are received from the seller and the goods are perishable (crops) or will decline speedily in value, the buyer must make a reasonable effort to sell them for the seller's account. [UCC 2.603(1)] The buyer is entitled to the proceeds of the sale for prior payments made to the seller and expenses of the sale including a selling commission of up to 10% of the gross proceeds. [UCC 2.603(2)]

(3) Security Interest in Goods: A buyer has a security interest in goods in their possession for payments made to the seller. This is to be increased by costs of inspection, care, and custody. These charges have a priority from the proceeds of any disposition sale the buyer decides to undertake. [UCC 2.711]

MBE Tip: Any mention in an MBE question of reasonable steps made (or not made) to reduce loss available to the parties after breach raise the mitigation issue.

---

11. Litigation Expenses: Litigation expenses include court costs, attorney fees, expenses incurred in the discovery process, transcript charges, and expert witnesses' fees. Under the U.S. system, a prevailing party's may recover litigation expenses from the loser only if authorized by contract, a controlling statute, or court rule.

MBE Tip: While money damages are only one of the possible **MRS DAISI** remedies, they are the most likely to be tested on the MBE.

STOP! Go to page 126 and work Learning Questions 61 to 67.

B. Rescission/Reformation/Replevin/Restitution

Equity has developed a number of possible remedies that do not involve money damages. Equitable remedies may be necessary since liquidating the damages to a monetary figure may be too speculative, may not resolve the dispute or may not adequately measure the detriment suffered by the P. He who seeks an equitable remedy must act equitably and have clean hands.

1. Rescission or a Complete Undoing: Rescission is a complete undoing that places both parties in their pre-contract positions and discharges all duties. This is a frequent remedy for formation defects, mutual mistake, fraud in the inducement, and excusable nonperformance of an executory contract.

2. Reformation or Changing the Contract: A court may order reformation of a contract to conform to the parties' original true intent. Reformation changes only the mistaken or offensive portion of the agreement while leaving the remainder of the contract in place. An example is when the parties orally agreed to a price of $150, but the written price was $510 because of a typographical error in the final contract that was not noticed by the buyer when signing.

3. Restitution: This remedy includes two types:

a. Value to D: This applies where the P has not fully performed such as where D wrongfully repudiates the contract before a P contractor is allowed to complete performance. P's restitution interest is measured as the value bestowed on the D because of the P's performance. The value of the enrichment to the D is not limited to the contract price as in expectation or reliance measures of recovery. It also applies even if P would actually have lost money had they completed the contract.

MBE Tip: Most contractor questions are resolved using the damage calculation rules under XIII.A.2.c. Apply the value to D measurement if the question contains the word "restitution."

---

b. Economic Crime: This restitution remedy may also be used to compensate a victim of an economic crime. An embezzler may be ordered to make restitution to the business from which the funds were wrongfully taken.

4. Replevin of Stolen Goods: Replevin is an action brought to recover possession of goods unlawfully taken from the true owner. A replevin bond may be required to indemnify the officer who recovers the goods from suit or liability. The bond may also cover damages that may be incurred by the person from whose custody the goods were wrongfully taken.

C. Specific Performance

Specific performance is a frequent buyer's remedy under the common law. Specific performance is less likely to be granted under the UCC. UCC 2.716 provides that absent special circumstances, specific performance is only awarded if the goods are unique, have been identified to the contract, and have not been transferred to a bona fide purchaser (BFP).

1. Performance Order: The court can order the breaching party to complete her performance as promised in the contract. Failure to obey the order may lead to contempt of court.

2. Remedy Availability: Specific performance is usually only available if (1) liquidated or compensatory money damages are inadequate, or (2) the subject of the contract is a unique item, such as a valuable painting, an antique automobile, or a parcel of land. The seller could be ordered to tender a marketable property deed to the escrow agent at closing.

3. Non-Availability: Specific performance is not generally available to enforce a personal service contract such as an employment contract or legal representation engagement by an attorney. Courts would have difficulty in enforcing an order requiring involuntary servitude by an employee or forcing an employer to accept an unwelcome employee. There are also constitutional considerations. (See the Constitutional Law chapter.) Specific performance may not be used to enforce a promise to make payment, satisfy a judgment, or convey an asset no longer in the possession of the breaching party.

D. Declaratory Judgment

One or both parties may seek a judicial declaration covering all or some provision of a contract before or after a breach has occurred.

1. Includes: This may be a determination of the meaning of an ambiguous term or that there was a mutual mistake. Another example is a declaration that the contract lacks a required formation element such as a failure of consideration or illegality.

2. Requirements: There must be a justiciable controversy and the judicial declaration must not prejudice the rights of persons not parties to the proceeding.

E. Accounting

The remedy of accounting applies where the court determines not only the basic liability issues, but also determines the proper judgment amount. An example is a trial resulting in an order of contribution in a partnership dissolution case or the royalties due on a patent infringement case.

F. Injunctions

Injunctions and restraining orders are court orders to stop an action, such as infringing upon a patent, trespassing, or logging land. Injunctions will not be issued to prevent breach of contract, but may be sought in a personal service contract to prohibit the D from performing for anyone other than the P. If the D continues the prohibited action after an injunction has been issued, he or she can be held in contempt of court, fined, or even jailed.

1. Temporary Restraining Order: A temporary restraining order (TRO) is issued after the lawsuit has been filed. The purpose of the order is to provide immediate protection for a person or property. In some circumstances, prior notice of the motion to the opposing party is not required. An example is a TRO issued by a court preventing an estranged ex-husband from having any contact with his former wife and children.

2. Preliminary Injunction: A preliminary injunction is issued prior to a trial which determines the merits of the underlying dispute. There must be a showing of probability of eventual success and/or irreparable injury. This is usually designed to maintain the status quo until there is a proper judicial resolution of the ultimate controversy.

3. Permanent Injunction: A permanent injunction is issued after the court conducts a full trial on the merits. The permanent injunctive provision may become part of the final resolution ordered to conclude the underlying dispute.

G. Statute of Limitations

The statute of limitations (SOL) bars actions at law unless a lawsuit is commenced within the time period specified in the contract or dictated by the controlling state statute. The law favors a prompt resolution of disputes.

1. Common Law: Under the common law, the parties may usually stipulate in the contract the length of time the cause of action remains alive. Absent an agreement, the applicable jurisdiction's SOL rules control.

2. Contract Rule: Statutes in most states specify that the non-breaching party has six years to file a complaint arising out of a written agreement. Two or three years is usual for an oral agreement. The time period is triggered and begins to run against the P on the date the contract is breached.

3. Tort Rule: There are different statutes of limitations for torts based on the type of tort and how it occurred.

    a. 3 Years: Most states allow three years for many tort actions.

    b. 2 Years: If the tort is short-lived such as assault, battery, false imprisonment, libel or slander, many states allow only two years to bring an action.

    c. Trigger Date: This period is triggered on the date the tort was committed.

    d. Discovery Rule: This tort rule may be extended to the date the P actually discovered or, in the exercise of reasonable diligence, should have discovered the tort.

4. UCC Treatment: An action arising from the sale of goods must be commenced within four years after the cause of action has accrued.

    a. Date of Breach Triggers: This is when the breach occurs, even if the aggrieved party initially lacked knowledge of it. (The tort discovery rule does not apply.)

    b. Parties May Modify: The parties may agree to reduce the period to not less than one year but may not extend it beyond four years. [UCC 2.725]

5. Tolled (Suspended) Time Period: The statute may be tolled (suspended) by D's absence from the jurisdiction, particularly when the absence is related to an attempt to evade service. Also tolling the outer limit of the time period is the disability of the P, such as infancy, temporary insanity, or coma.

6. Laches: Traditionally the SOL does not apply to equitable actions. The time period in which to bring the claim is governed by the doctrine of laches. A party asserting laches must prove that the P unreasonably delayed commencement of the lawsuit after acquiring knowledge of all material facts constituting a cause of action. If this doctrine is applied, it is usually because the delay has unfairly prejudiced the D.

MBE Tip: Dates in the question usually raise a SOL issue. The SOL for a common law contract is triggered upon breach; not the discovery rule of torts. Under the UCC, the statute is triggered upon accrual even if the aggrieved party lacked knowledge of the breach at that time. Look for a delayed discovery of breach of a common law contract.

H. In Quasi-Contract

The remedy of in quasi-contract or "in quantum meruit" seeks the fair market value of goods or services performed where there was no contract or the contract has failed at law. This may be distinguished from restitution where there is a valid contract that was not completed. In quasi-contract is also called an implied-in-law contract.

1. Purpose: The purpose is to promote fairness and avoid unjust enrichment where there is no enforceable contract at law. D knowingly received a benefit from P who had a reasonable expectation of compensation.

2. Recovery Amount: The amount of the recovery is the value of the benefit which has unjustly enriched D. As in restitution; this may be less (or even more) than the actual contract price.

3. Examples: MBE fact patterns include an agreement violating the SOF, an infant purchasing luxury goods, a doctor rendering emergency medical treatment to an unconscious patient, or an innocent P mistakenly providing a valuable service to the wrong party.

4. Laches: The SOL does not apply to in quasi-contract equitable actions. The time period in which to bring the equitable claim is governed by the doctrine of laches. See above detailed discussion.

> **MBE Tip:** If for any reason your analysis concludes there is no contract, always consider in quasi-contract. There must be an unjustified benefit to D and D usually had knowledge that the material or service was being provided by P with an expectation of receiving payment.

> **STOP!** Go to page 128 and work Learning Questions 68 to 71.

XIV. THIRD PARTY BENEFICIARIES

The general rule is that privity of contract is necessary to provide P with standing to sue and thus enforce contractual rights. Third parties may not usually enforce such rights.

A. General Concepts

1. Intention to Bestow Rights: The contracting parties must clearly intend and specify in the contract that a designated third person will receive unqualified rights or benefits from the future contract performance. Such a designated person can directly enforce those rights against the promisor.

2. Primary Contract Contemplation: An intended beneficiary is created at the same time as the primary contract. The promisor must have had the specific third party "in contemplation" when she made the original promise. If the promissory interest is shifted to a third party after the contract formation date, it is more likely to be characterized as an assignment.

3. Legal Rights: One contracting party may agree in the contract to pay to a third party an executory obligation otherwise due the other contracting party.

a. Beneficiary's Rights: An intended beneficiary has the right to sue the promisor directly.

b. Promisor's Defenses: A suit by the beneficiary against the promisor is subject to any defense the promisor could assert had she been sued directly by the promisee. The promisor's counterclaim against the beneficiary may offset the claim, but not result in a positive judgment. The promisor also cannot raise defenses or offsets that the beneficiary and the promisee may have against each other.

4. Rights "Vest": The original parties to the contract can modify or even rescind the benefiting promise prior to the beneficiary's rights "vesting."

a. Requirements: In some jurisdictions, "vesting" of rights requires the beneficiary to manifest assent to the assignment promise or at least know the rights have been bestowed. Some jurisdictions also require the beneficiary to make some movement to indicate affirmative reliance upon the rights she has received from the contract in question. An intended beneficiary commencing a lawsuit to enforce performance of the benefiting promise constitutes vesting in all jurisdictions. The Restatement would accept any of these three means to constitute vesting.

b. Example: An example of vesting is a designated beneficiary of a promise to convey a house. The beneficiary, based on the promise, cancels a pre-existing contract to buy a different house and move to the locale. Once the rights have vested in the beneficiary, any modification requires the beneficiary's consent.

B. Creditor Beneficiary

The contract specifies that the promisor satisfy a pre-existing obligation which the promisee owes to a named third party. An example is an attorney's client who agrees to pay the promised legal fee to a specific bank to which the attorney had previously owed money. The third party (bank) may sue both the promisor (client) and/or the promisee (attorney).

C. Donee Beneficiary

A third party donee beneficiary receives the contract right assignment gratuitously from the promisee. An example is a favorite niece receiving the promise of a gift from her donor uncle of an amount due him from a third party. A donee beneficiary can only sue the promisor (third party who owes the money). There is a lack of consideration to support the donee suing the donor-promisee (favorite uncle who made the gift). Since the right was gratuitously bestowed, the donor has the right to revoke prior to performance.

D. Incidental Beneficiary

An incidental beneficiary is not intended by the contracting parties to receive benefits. An example is a wholesaler who will be paid by the retailer-debtor after the bank makes the loan to the retailer. An incidental beneficiary has no legally enforceable rights.

XV. ASSIGNMENT OF RIGHTS

Assignment and delegation involve the introduction of new parties after the original contract has been created between the promisor and the promisee. The new party may receive (through assignment from the promisee) a pre-existing contractual right or agree to perform (through delegation from the obligor) a pre-existing contractual duty. Unless indicated to the contrary, UCC 2.210(5) states that an "assignment of the contract" usually includes both an assignment of rights and a delegation of duties.

A. General Concept

Assignment of contractual rights differs from third party beneficiaries in that there was no pre-existing debt or gift, or if there was, the promisor was not aware of it. An example is a creditor who is owed money and assigns that payment right to her bank for collection.

1. Time Created: After the contract formation, the promisee transfers her present rights to the assignee with her intent to extinguish the assignor's rights. The promisor must be notified of the assignment before she is legally bound to pay the assignee rather than the original promisee – now the assignor. The assignment usually extinguishes the assignor's ability to enforce the same contractual right.

2. Limitations on Assignability:

a. Common Law: Assignability is the general rule. Non-assignable rights include a mere offer or the right to receive the personal services of another. Insurance coverage rights are not assignable, but the right to pursue a matured claim is. Payment expected to arise under a future contract not yet in existence is also not assignable. Look for a mere possible future contract payment right which may later arise only if a contract is created in the future. This is to be distinguished from an assignment of a right to future payment expected to arise out of an existing contract. The latter contract has vested rights which may be assigned.

b. UCC: Unless otherwise agreed, all UCC rights of either the seller or buyer are assignable unless the burden or risk on the other party would materially increase. This includes most requirements and output contracts unless the assignee will substantially vary the quantity. Any such assignment which delegates performance creates reasonable grounds for demanding assurances. [UCC 2.210(5)] If the assignee does not adequately respond within 30 days, the demanding party may treat the contract as repudiated. [UCC 2.609(4)]

3. Oral Assignments: Oral assignments are enforceable unless it affected an interest in land, goods over $500, or wage assignments.

4. Revocability: While an assignment does not require consideration, a non-written gratuitous assignment may be revoked. A written assignment or one made with consideration is usually irrevocable. Consideration may be given by the assignee to the assignor or the assignee may foreseeably rely on the assignment agreement to her detriment.

5. Effect of Notice: If notice of assignment is not given to the promisor, she can continue to render performance to the promisee. After notice, the rights of the assignee vest. The promisor must then pay the assignee and any modification of the promise in question requires approval by the assignee.

6. Promisor's Defenses: The assignee of the right(s) can sue the promisor directly, but again the suit is subject to all defenses and counterclaims which the promisor could have asserted against the promisee. The promisor may also set off against the assignee any other amount due her from the promisee.

> **MBE Tip:** Many MBE questions involve the promisor paying the promisee rather than the assignee. Was there notice of the assignment given to the promisor?

B. Holder-In-Due-Course

Article 3 of the UCC provides an exception to an assignee qualifying as a holder in due course (HDC) of a negotiable instrument (NI). [UCC 3.302] A HDC's rights to sue the promisor are not subject to defenses that are personal to the promisee, such as fraud in the inducement or a failure of consideration. [UCC 3.305]

C. Prohibition on Assignment

1. Common Law: A specific provision in the contract that prohibits the promisee from assigning her rights has traditionally been enforceable under the common law.

a. Modern View: The Restatement would not enforce a prohibition on assignment of the right to receive payment of money if the assignor has fully performed their obligations. Similarly, the right to sue for damages arising from breach of contract may always be assigned despite agreement to the contrary.

b. Assignee's Rights: An innocent assignee for value without knowledge of the assignment prohibition could enforce the contractual rights assigned. This follows even though the assignment might give the obligor an action for breach against the assignor.

2. Legal Prohibition and Future Rights: Usually state statutory restrictions prohibit assignments of alimony and child support payments. Wage assignments are usually limited in amount. Rights not yet in existence such as payment from an expected contract not yet signed are usually not assignable. Similarly the right to receive payment from an executory (unperformed) personal service contract is not assignable.

3. UCC Treatment: The UCC clarifies this uncertainty. The contracting parties do not have the right to prohibit an assignment of rights which are no longer executory. Examples include a right to payment of an account or transfer of a security interest in collateral. Thus a prohibition on "assignment of the contract" under the UCC is to be construed to bar only the delegation of the performance duties. [UCC 2.210 and 9.401]

D. Multiple Assignee Priority

The priority between multiple assignees becomes important if the assignor-creditor makes more than one assignment of the same contract right.

1. Common Law Rule: If the assignment is irrevocable, the assignee first in time is the first in right. This usually prevails over any subsequent takers under the common law.

2. UCC Treatment: The first assignee to "perfect" prevails. Usually this means the first assignee to file the UCC financing statement. [UCC 9.322]

3. Waiver of Defense Clause: The buyer may agree not to assert defenses against an assignee which could have been raised against the assignor. This contract waiver is not effective in a consumer contract. In addition the waiver clause may not be asserted against real defenses such as incapacity, illegality, fraud in the inducement, or duress. [UCC 9.304]

MBE Tip: Many MBE questions bring in subsequent participants operating under an assignment of rights (and/or delegation of duties). Issues may arise if the contract prohibits assignment, the promisor refuses to pay the assignee, or there were multiple assignees trying to enforce the same original contract right.

XVI. DELEGATION OF DUTIES

A. General Concept

The original obligor delegates the performance duty due the obligee to a third party delegatee who affirmatively promises to so perform. An example is a delegation by an obligor-manufacturer of the responsibility to make goods to another manufacturer who agrees to perform the contract. Delegated performance must be accepted by the obligee-buyer except in the three fact situations specified below.

B. Prohibition on Delegation

Where delegation is prohibited by the contract, the duty is non-delegable under the common law. Unlike the treatment of the assignment of a contractual right, the UCC allows the contracting parties to agree to prohibit delegation of a performance duty. [UCC 2.210(1)] Acceptance without complaint by the obligee may constitute waiver of a delegation prohibition.

C. Personal Skill of Obligor

If the performance duty involves the personal service or skill of the obligor, it is non-delegable unless the obligee consents.

1. Non-Delegable Examples: An example would be a personal service contract such as hiring an artist or attorney. Frequently asked is an owner contracting with a well-known specialty builder to complete a custom-designed home. Output or requirement contracts are also often non-delegable absent the permission of the other contracting party.

2. Objectively Determinable: If a contractor was building standardized widgets or multiple similar patterned tract homes, satisfactory performance might be sufficiently objectively determinable. Under these circumstances the obligee would be required to accept delegated performance by another contractor.

D. Material Risk or Burden Imposed

The third situation where delegation is prohibited is where the obligee is forced to accept a material increase in burden or risk. If the risk of non-performance can be shown to be much higher or the obligee is burdened by new conditions, the duty may be non-delegable. An example is an insurance contract.

E. Right to Assurances

Any delegation of the performance duty may be anticipatory repudiation. [UCC 2.609] This may create reasonable grounds for insecurity and provide the insecure party the right to demand assurances. [UCC 2.210(5)] Until such assurances are received, the insecure party may suspend their own performance if commercially reasonable. If adequate assurances are not received within 30 days, the non-response is treated as anticipatory repudiation. The obligee may also waive the right to object to the delegation; the absence of a request for assurances may so imply.

F. Delegatee Liability to Obligee

The delegatee who accepts the delegation through an express assumption may become liable to the original obligee if performance is inadequate. The obligee (customer) is an intended third party beneficiary of the delegator-delegatee contract containing the delegatee's assumption and new promise to perform. Thus the original obligee can pursue the new party.

G. Delegator Liability to Obligee

The delegator also remains liable to the obligee unless a novation or release is executed by the obligee. Recall that a novation completely substitutes the delegatee for the delegator. A mere acknowledgement or consent by the obligee to accept delegated performance does not rise to the level of an express release of the delegator.

MBE Tip: Did the obligee have a substantial interest in having the original obligor-delegator perform? Many questions involve an obligee accepting a duty delegation. Often the subsequent delegatee does not perform on a satisfactory level. The delegatee becomes liable to the obligee and (absent a novation or release) the delegator remains liable.

STOP!   Go to page 129 and work Learning Questions 72 to 76.

XVII. OVERALL MEMORY LADDER – OACLLS VIPR TAD

- **O**ffer by offeror expressing intent to be bound that is not yet revoked or rejected
- **A**cceptance by offeree through a return promise or performance
- **C**onsideration – benefit to promisor or detriment to promisee
- **L**egal capacity of contracting parties – not 3 Is of **i**nfancy, **i**nsanity, or **i**ntoxication
- **L**egal subject matter and not against public policy
- **S**tatute of frauds compliance – writing signed by D – if a **MOULS** contract

- **V**oid or voidable circumstances – **MUFFED**
- **I**nterpretation of contract – **II PACC**
- **P**erformance and breach
- **R**emedies – **MRS DAISI**

- **T**hird party beneficiary – creditor or donee
- **A**ssignment of Rights by promisee
- **D**elegation of Duties by obligor

XVIII. FINAL CHAPTER REVIEW INSTRUCTIONS

1. Completing the Chapter: Now that you have completed your study of the chapter's substantive text and the related Learning Questions, you need to button up this chapter. This includes your preparing your Magic Memory Outlines® and working all of the subject's practice questions.

2. Preparing Your Own Magic Memory Outline®: This is essential to your MBE success. We recommend that you use our software template in this process. Do not underestimate the learning and memory effectiveness derived from condensing the text chapter into your succinct summaries using your own words. This exercise is covered in much more detail in the preface and on the CD-ROM.

    a. Summarize Knowledge: You need to prepare a summary of the chapter in your own words. This is best accomplished using the Rigos Bar Review Series Magic Memory Outlines® software. The words in the outline correspond to the bold headings in the text.

    b. Capture the Essence: Your job is to summarize the substance of the text by capturing the essence of the rule and entering your summarized wording into your own outlines. Go to the text coverage and craft your own tight, concise, but yet comprehensive statements of the law. Take pride in your skills as an author; this is the best outline you have ever created.

    c. Focus: Focus your attention and wording on the required technical elements necessary to prove the relevant legal principles and fine-line distinctions. Integrate any helpful "learning question" information into your outline.

3. Memorize Outline: After you have completed your own Magic Memory Outline® for the whole chapter, read it over carefully once or twice. They are the best book ever written. Refer back to your Outlines frequently.

4. Work Old Questions: The next step is to work all the final questions of each chapter. These vary in degree of difficulty, but the ones towards the end tend to concentrate on fact patterns and issues at the most difficult testing level. Consider using the Question Map on the CD-ROM. Click on the questions under the subject and topic you have just studied. This allows you to cross relate the subjects and related MBE testing.

    a. Question Details: Again, it is usually worthwhile to review the explanatory answer rationales as they reinforce the relevant principles of law. If you are still unsure of the controlling rule, refer back to the related portion of the text. This will help you to appreciate the fine-line distinctions on which the MBE questions turn.

    b. Do a Few Questions At a Time: Work the final chapter questions in sequence. Make sure you stop after no more than a few to check the answer rationales. Do this frequently so that the facts of the individual question are still in active memory.

    c. Work Them All: We have tried to pick questions with an average or higher probability of reappearing on the MBE. You should at least read all the questions and ponder their answers. Every question and answer has some marginal learning and/or reinforcement value. On the MBE you will recognize many of the actual MBE questions as very similar to the ones in your Rigos Bar Review Series review books.

    d. Learn From Mistakes: The objective is to learn from your mistakes by reviewing the explanatory rationales while you still remember the factual and legal details of the question. It is good to miss a few; they will help you become familiar with the MBE fine-line distinctions. The examiners' use of distracters, tricks, and red herrings is repetitive.

    e. Flag Errors: Put a red star in the margin of the book along side every question you missed. Missed questions should be worked again the day right before the MBE. Do not make the same mistakes on the exam.

    f. Essays: Candidates in jurisdictions that administer the Multistate Essay Exam should refer to the *Rigos Bar Review Series Multistate Essay Exam Review — MEE* for practice essay questions.

5. Practice Exam: After you complete the last chapter, you should take the 200 item practice exam. There is detailed information covering this simulated MBE test in both the preface and at the beginning of the exam in Volume 2. This is important because you need to build your concentrated attention time span. You also need to get intellectually used to jumping between unrelated topics and subjects.

6. Make Your Own Exam: The Rigos Bar Review Series software allows you to pick 5, 10, 20 or 100 questions at random from all six MBE subjects. This is an important feature because you must become comfortable with switching intellectual gears between different subjects. If you are not an early riser and/or get going slowly when you get up, try working 10 or 20 questions using the "Make Your Own Exam" software the first thing every morning.

7. Update Your Magic Memory Outline®: The fine-line distinctions in the question and answer rationales will improve your understanding of how the MBE tests the law. Consider updating your Magic Memory Outline® while the question testing environment is still fresh in your mind.

8. Next Chapter: It is now time to go to the beginning of the next subject. Begin by previewing the chapter. Scan the typical coverage.

RIGOS BAR REVIEW SERIES

MULTISTATE BAR EXAM REVIEW (MBE)

CHAPTER 1

CONTRACTS AND UCC SALES ARTICLE 2

Magic Memory Outlines®

RIGOS BAR REVIEW SERIES

MULTISTATE BAR EXAM REVIEW (MBE)

CHAPTER 1

CONTRACTS AND UCC SALES ARTICLE 2

Question Distribution Map

> Numbers immediately following the topic are the chapter question numbers. The **boldface** numbers preceded by "F" are the final exam question numbers. For example, for the topic "I. D. 2. d. Mixed Contract" below, questions 2 and 144 are in the chapter questions on pages 1-113 and 1-147, respectively; question **F138** is in the final exam on page 7-483 of Volume 2.

MEE Candidates: If your jurisdiction administers the Multistate Essay Exam in addition to the MBE, please refer to the *Rigos Bar Review Series Multistate Essay Exam Review — MEE* for practice essay questions and sample answers covering contracts and UCC Article 2 sales.

RIGOS BAR REVIEW SERIES

MULTISTATE BAR EXAM REVIEW (MBE)

CHAPTER 1

CONTRACTS AND UCC SALES ARTICLE 2

Questions

Learning Questions

1. The most likely contract to be classified under the Uniform Commercial Code (UCC) is a contract for
  - (A) An attorney's advice on an estate plan.
  - (B) Crops and timber to be severed from the property later.
  - (C) The purchase of a commercial property building.
  - (D) The sale of an intangible asset.

2. Connie Computer decided to purchase a new keyboard and mouse for $50 to use with her laptop computer to use during law school. When she went into Computer Retailer Inc., the salesperson also sold her a 5-year service agreement for $500 for a total price of $550. Nine months later, the laptop stopped working and Computer Retailer refused to perform on their service agreement. If Connie sues Computer Retailer, the trial court will likely find for
  - (A) Connie, under the common law because the predominate purpose for which the parties contracted was the sale of goods.
  - (B) Connie, under UCC Article 2 because the predominate reason for entering into the contract was for the service portion of the contract.
  - (C) Connie, under UCC Article 2 because the predominate purpose of the agreement was for the service agreement portion of the contract.
  - (D) Computer Retailer, if the court determines that the predominate purpose of the agreement is

determined by intent and not the relative dollars assigned to the computer and the service agreement.

3. Wendy Wholesaler sold merchandise to Roberta Retailer. A dispute has arisen between the parties and Roberta is trying to prove that Wendy is a "merchant" as opposed to a "casual party." The least important factor indicating the status of a "merchant" under UCC Article 2 is that Wendy
  - (A) Is a wholesaler rather than a retailer.
  - (B) Deals in the goods sold to Roberta.
  - (C) Holds herself out as an expert in the goods sold to Roberta.
  - (D) Sells under 10 units a year to Roberta.

4. Where a client accepts the services of an attorney without an agreement concerning the amount of the fee, there is
  - (A) An implied-in-fact contract.
  - (B) An implied-in-law contract.
  - (C) An express contract.
  - (D) No contract.

5. Sarah Student was a third-year law student who had just purchased the Rigos Multistate Bar Review MBE Review program. She was studying in the law library and decided to take a short refreshment break. When she returned to her study desk ten minutes later, her Rigos Multistate Bar Review was gone. She ran into the student lounge and announced, "I will pay $20 to anyone who identifies the dirty bum who took my Rigos Multistate Bar Review MBE Review books." Donna

Doubtful saw Terry Thief pick up Sarah's Rigos Multistate Bar Review books, but did not believe Sarah would actually pay her the $20, if she made the identification. Thus, Donna went up to Sarah and said, "I know the identity of the thief and promise to tell you, but I want the $20 in advance." The effect of Donna's statement is to

    (A) Create a unilateral contract.
    (B) Create a bilateral contract.
    (C) Create no contract.
    (D) Create a contract which is defeasible unless Donna makes the required disclosure within a reasonable period of time.

6. There may be a substantial time period between contract formation and final completion of performance. Concerning these executory contracts, which of the following is the least correct?

    (A) A wholly executory contract is where only promises have been exchanged and there has been no performance by either party.
    (B) A partially executed contract means that one party has completed performance while the other party has only promised.
    (C) An executed contract exists when both parties have fully performed and no obligations remain.
    (D) A partially executed contract means that at least one party has begun performance.

7. Charlie Contractor entered into a contract with Nancy Non-cooperative to remodel a bathroom and kitchen in Nancy's home. The contract assigned $10,000 to the bathroom and $15,000 to the kitchen with the $25,000 total due when all the remodeling was complete. Charlie completed the bathroom, but refused to begin the kitchen because Nancy did not cooperate in allowing him access to the house. If Charlie sues Nancy, the likely outcome is for

    (A) Charlie in an amount of $25,000 since he alleges that Nancy breached the contract.

    (B) Charlie in an amount of $12,500 since he completed the bathroom construction.
    (C) Charlie in an amount of $10,000 if the court finds the contract divisible and the $10,000 is an equivalent amount for the completed portion of the agreement.
    (D) Nancy since Charlie will not complete the contract, he is not entitled to any compensation.

8. Jack and Jill began to negotiate for the transfer of a business. Their negotiations continued for some time. Jack is asserting that Jill made a promise containing an offer which he accepted with a return promise. Jill asserts that the agreement was not what she intended. In determining whether a contract has been created, the courts look primarily at

    (A) The fairness to the parties.
    (B) The objective intent of the parties.
    (C) The subjective intent of the parties.
    (D) The subjective intent of the offeror.

9. Which of the following offers for the sale of widgets is not enforceable if the seller changes his mind prior to acceptance?

    (A) A merchant tells buyer in writing she will sell the widget for $35,000 and that the offer will be irrevocable for ten days.
    (B) A merchant writes buyer offering to sell the widget for $35,000.
    (C) A merchant telegraphs buyer offering to sell the widget for $35,000 and promises to hold the offer open for ten days.
    (D) A merchant writes buyer offering to sell the widget for $35,000 and stating that the offer will be irrevocable for ten days if buyer will pay $1.00. Buyer pays.

10. In order to have an irrevocable offer under the UCC Article 2, the offer must

    (A) Be made by a merchant to a merchant.

(B) Be contained in a signed writing which gives assurance that the offer will be held open.

(C) State the period of time for which it is irrevocable.

(D) Not be contained in a form supplied by the offeror.

11. James makes a written offer to Fred for the sale of land for $100,000. In this offer, James states, "This offer will not be revocable for a ten-day period of time." The offer was signed on April 1, mailed to Fred on April 3 and received by Fred on April 5th. Which of the following is true?

(A) Fred's unqualified acceptance on April 10 will not create a contract.

(B) Fred's acceptance on April 5 will not create a contract if James dies on April 4.

(C) Fred stating on April 5, "I accept your offer, but will pay only $90,000" creates a contract.

(D) Fred's unqualified acceptance on April 15 will not create a contract.

12. A merchant's irrevocable written offer (firm offer) under Article 2 of the UCC to sell goods

(A) Must be separately signed if the offeree supplies a form contract containing the offer.

(B) Is valid for three months.

(C) Is nonassignable.

(D) Can not exceed a three-month duration even if consideration is given.

13. Water Works had a long-standing policy of offering employees $100 for suggestions actually used. Due to inflation and a decline in the quantity and quality of suggestions received, Water Works decided to increase the award to $500. Several suggestions were under consideration at that time. Two days prior to the public announcement of the increase to $500, a suggestion by Farber was accepted and put into use. Farber is seeking to collect $500. Farber is entitled to

(A) $500 because Water Works had decided to pay that amount.

(B) $500 because the suggestion submitted will be used during the period that Water Works indicated it would pay $500.

(C) $100 in accordance with the original offer.

(D) Nothing if Water Works chooses not to pay since the offer was gratuitous.

14. Betty Buyer wanted to buy an antique Volvo automobile owned by Sarah Seller who had previously expressed some interest in selling the car. Betty wrote Sarah a signed letter on April 1 stating "I will buy your Volvo for $10,000 cash upon your bringing the vehicle to my home before April 5. This offer is not subject to countermand." On April 2 Sarah received the letter and wrote back a signed letter to Betty stating "I accept your offer and promise to deliver the Volvo to you as you request." Unfortunately, the Postal Authority delayed delivery of Sarah's letter for 10 days. In the mean time, Betty grew tired of not hearing from Sarah and purchased another car. When she learned that Betty would not complete the transfer, Sarah sued for breach of contract. The court will likely hold that

(A) The mailing of the April 2nd letter did not prevent a subsequent effective revocation by Betty.

(B) The April 2nd letter bound both parties to a bilateral contract when received.

(C) The April 2nd letter bound both parties to a unilateral contract.

(D) The April 2nd letter was effective to form a contract on April 12th, when the offeror received it.

15. Fernandez is planning to attend an auction of the assets of Cross & Black, one of his major competitors who is liquidating. In the conduct of the auction, which of the following rules applies?

(A) Such a sale is without reserve unless the goods are explicitly put up with reserve.

(B) A bidder may retract his bid at any time until the fall of the hammer.

(C) The retraction of a bid by a bidder revives the previous bid.

(D) If the auction is without reserve, the auctioneer can withdraw the article at any time prior to the fall of the hammer.

16. Base Electric Co. has entered an agreement to buy its actual requirements of copper wiring for six months from the Seymour Metal Wire Company and Seymour Metal has agreed to sell all the copper wiring Base will require for six months. The agreement between the two companies is

(A) Unenforceable because it is too indefinite as to quantity.

(B) Unenforceable because it lacks mutuality of obligation.

(C) Unenforceable because of lack of consideration.

(D) Valid and enforceable.

17. A contractor and home owner were bargaining on the price for the construction of a new home. The contractor proposed a number of offers for construction to the home owner including one for $100,000. Which of the following communications would not terminate the offer so that a subsequent acceptance could be effective

(A) The home owner asks the contractor if they would be willing to build the house for $95,000.

(B) The contractor contacts the home owner and states that the offer is withdrawn.

(C) The contractor dies before the home owner accepts but the contractor's son intends to continue the business.

(D) The home owner states "I accept your offer but the price is to be $97,000.

18. Calvin Poultry Co. offered to sell Chickenshop 20,000 pounds of chicken at 40 cents per pound under specified delivery terms. Chickenshop accepted the offer as follows:

"We accept your offer for 20,000 pounds of chicken at 40 cents per pound per city scale weight certificate."

Which of the following is correct?

(A) A contract was formed on Calvin's terms.

(B) Chickenshop's reply constitutes a conditional acceptance, but not a counteroffer.

(C) Chickenshop's reply constitutes a counteroffer and no contract was formed.

(D) A contract was formed on Chickenshop's terms.

19. Rainmaking Lawfirm regularly purchased its office supplies from catalogs. Marty Manager saw an advertising catalog from Priceco offering 10,000 envelopes for $1,000 CIF. He immediately sent a purchase order which stated "our law firm accepts your $1,000 offer for 10,000 envelopes for $1,000 CIF." Priceco then sent Rainmaking an order confirmation which stated "Envelope order acceptance conditional upon a loading charge of $50 per thousand envelopes. If the parties disagree on the proper contract relationship, a court would likely rule:

(A) A contract at $1,000 because the offer terms CIF means cost, insurance and freight including all loading charges.

(B) A contract at $1,500 because the loading charges are to be included.

(C) No contract because the order confirmation was a counteroffer which was not accepted.

(D) No contract because the purchase order was the offer and, under the mirror image rule, can not be deviated from.

20. On October 1, Arthur mailed to Madison an offer to sell a tract of land located in Summerville for $13,000. Acceptance was to be not later than October 10. Madison posted his acceptance on the

3rd of October. The acceptance arrived on October 7. On October 4, Arthur sold the tract in question to Larson and mailed to Madison notice of the sale. That letter arrived on the 6th of October, but after Madison had dispatched his letter of acceptance. Which of the following is correct?

(A) There was a valid acceptance of the Arthur offer on the day Madison posted his acceptance.

(B) Arthur's offer was effectively revoked by the sale of the tract of land to Larson on the 4th of October.

(C) Arthur could not revoke the offer to sell the land until after October 10.

(D) Madison's acceptance was not valid since he was deemed to have notice of revocation prior to the acceptance.

21. Berg offered to sell a parcel of land to Jones for $75,000 cash. The offer was in writing on March 1 and made by sending an e-mail to Jones' web site. Jones responded by mailing a letter on March 10 which stated "I accept but would like to request that I can pay $25,000 in three equal installments over the next three years." Berg received the letter on March 15. A contract was

(A) Formed on March 10.

(B) Formed on March 15.

(C) Not formed because Jones' addition of the three year payment request was a condition that Berg had to agree should be included.

(D) Not formed because the addition of the three year request was, in effect, a rejection.

22. Lee Motors sold an oral option to Hall, Inc., for $50. The option was to purchase at cost any late model used automobiles received by Lee as trade-ins on new cars for the next 100 days. Hall paid the $50 in cash and promptly sent Lee a signed memorandum which correctly described the agreement and its terms. Lee did not respond until after 30 days had elapsed and it had

discovered it had made a very bad bargain. Therefore, it notified Hall that it would no longer perform under the terms of the option, which it alleged was invalid, and it enclosed a check for $50 to Hall's order. Which of the following is correct?

(A) The oral option is invalid for lack of consideration.

(B) The Statute of Frauds can be validly asserted by Lee to avoid liability.

(C) Lee has entered into a valid contract with Hall.

(D) Options for a duration of more than three months are unenforceable.

23. Bunker's son, Michael, was seeking an account executive position with Harrison, Inc., the largest brokerage firm in the United States. Michael was very independent and wished no interference by his father. The firm, after several weeks of deliberation, decided to hire Michael. They made him an offer on April 12, and Michael readily accepted. Bunker feared that his son would not be hired. Unaware of the fact that his son had been hired, Bunker mailed a letter to Harrison on April 13 in which he promised to give the brokerage firm $50,000 in commission business if the firm would hire his son. The letter was duly received by Harrison and they wish to enforce it against Bunker. Which of the following is correct?

(A) Harrison will prevail since the promise is contained in a signed writing.

(B) Harrison will not be able to enforce the contract against Bunker.

(C) Harrison will prevail based upon promissory estoppel.

(D) The preexisting legal duty rule applies and makes the employment promise unenforceable.

24. Which of the following will be legally binding despite lack of consideration?

(A) An employer's promise to make a cash payment to a deceased employee's family in recognition of the employee's many years of service.

(B) A promise to donate money to a charity on which the charity relied in incurring large expenditures.

(C) A modification of a signed contract to purchase a parcel of land.

(D) A merchant's oral promise to keep an offer open for 60 days.

25. In which of the following situations would an oral agreement without any consideration be binding under UCC Article 2?

(A) A renunciation of a claim or right arising out of an alleged breach.

(B) An oral firm offer by a merchant to sell or buy goods which gives assurance that it will be held open.

(C) An agreement which is a large requirements contract.

(D) An agreement which modifies an existing sales contract.

26. Egan, a 17 year old minor, contracted with Baker to purchase Baker's used computer for $400. The computer was purchased for Egan's personal use. The agreement provided that Egan would pay $200 down on delivery and $200 thirty days later. Egan took delivery and paid the $200 down payment. Twenty days later, the computer was damaged seriously as a result of Egan's negligence. Five days after the damage occurred and one day after Egan reached the age of majority, Egan attempted to disaffirm the contract with Baker. Egan will

(A) Be able to disaffirm despite the fact that Egan was not a minor at the time of disaffirmation.

(B) Be able to disaffirm only if Egan does so in writing.

(C) Not be able to disaffirm because Egan had failed to pay the balance of the purchase price.

(D) Not be able to disaffirm because the computer was damaged as a result of Egan's negligence.

27. Michelle Minor, a 17-year-old mature appearing female, entered into a $10,000 contract with Mary Motorcycle, an adult, to purchase a Hardly Demon motorcycle. Mary delivered the motorcycle to Michelle who paid the $10,000 and used the motorcycle for three months. The thrill wore off and Michelle returned the motorcycle to Mary and demanded the $10,000 back in rescission. Assuming the reasonable rental value of the motorcycle was $200 a month, Michelle will recover

(A) $10,000 because the contract is voidable by the infant.

(B) $10,000 because Mary may disaffirm the contract.

(C) $9,400 because the minor's recovery should be offset by the reasonable value of the benefit received.

(D) $9,400 because the absence of a contract means the court must apply the detriment to the party with capacity in determining damages.

28. Paul Principal decided to buy a sailboat. He felt that it was necessary to investigate comparable boats with different nautical options. Paul was leaving on a trip and he authorized Alice Agent to do the necessary research and purchase the appropriate boat. Alice conducted research and finally decided to purchase a $5,000 Choy Lee 26 foot sloop from Splendid Sailboats Unlimited. She signed the sales contract with Splendid as "Paul Principal by his agent, Alice Agent." When Paul returned from his trip he refused to accept the sailboat or pay the $5,000 to Splendid. Splendid sued Paul and Alice. The likely outcome of the suit is that

(A) Splendid will prevail against Alice only if Paul refuses to accept the sailboat.

(B) Splendid will prevail against Paul because the purchase was in writing.

(C) Splendid will not prevail against Alice even if she guaranteed the payment of the sailboat purchase contract.

(D) Splendid will not prevail against Alice if she misrepresented the scope of her authority to purchase the sailboat.

29. West, a California lawyer, incorrectly represented to Zimmer that he was admitted to practice law in Kansas. There is a Kansas statute that regulates attorneys and requires all attorneys to be admitted in the state and properly licensed. Zimmer signed a contract agreeing to pay West a fee for handling a personal injury matter in Kansas. West did not sign the contract. West secured a large settlement but Zimmer refused to pay West the agreed upon fee. If West sued Zimmer for nonpayment of the fee, Zimmer would be

(A) Liable to West only for the value of services rendered.

(B) Liable to West for the full fee.

(C) Not liable to West for any amount because West did not sign the contract.

(D) Not liable to West for any amount because West violated the Kansas bar admission and licensing requirements.

30. The Uniform Commercial Code Section 2.201 Statute of Frauds

(A) Codified common law rules of fraud.

(B) Requires that all formal contracts be in writing and signed by the parties to the contract.

(C) Does not apply if the parties waive its application in the contract.

(D) Sometimes results in a contract being enforceable by only one party.

31. Duval Manufacturing Industries, Inc., orally engaged Harris as one of its district sales managers for an 18-month period commencing April 1. Harris commenced work on that date and performed his duties in a highly competent manner for several months. On October 1, the company gave Harris a notice of termination as of November 1, citing a downturn in the market for its products. Harris sues seeking either specific performance or damages for breach of contract. Duval pleads the Statute of

Frauds and/or a justified dismissal due to the economic situation. What is the probable outcome of the lawsuit?

(A) Harris will prevail because he has partially performed under the terms of the contract.

(B) Harris will lose because his termination was caused by unforeseeable economic factors beyond Duval's control.

(C) Harris will lose because such a contract must be in writing and signed by a proper agent of Duval.

(D) Harris will prevail because the Statute of Frauds does not apply to contracts such as his.

32. Doral, Inc., wished to obtain an adequate supply of lumber for its factory extension which was to be constructed in the spring. It contacted Ace Lumber Company and obtained a 75-day written option (firm offer) to buy its estimated needs for the building. Doral supplied a form contract which included the option. The price of lumber has risen drastically and Ace wishes to avoid its obligation. Which of the following is Ace's (seller's) best defense against Doral's assertion that Ace is legally bound by the option?

(A) Such an option is invalid if its duration is for more than two months.

(B) The option is not supported by any consideration on Doral's part.

(C) Doral is not a merchant.

(D) The promise of irrevocability was contained in a form supplied by Doral and was not separately signed by Ace.

33. Ace and Baker both signed a memorandum that stated that Ace agreed to sell and Baker agreed to purchase a tract of land. The contract specified that the transaction should be closed and conveyance made and accepted "by tender of general warranty deed conveying a good and marketable title" on a date specified. The memorandum signed by the parties contains all of the elements deemed essential and necessary to satisfy the Statute of Frauds applicable to the transaction, except there was omission of a recitation of the purchase price agreed upon.

Ace has refused to perform the contract, and in an action by Baker for specific performance, Ace relies upon the Statute of Frauds as a defense. If Baker offers evidence, in addition to the written memorandum, that the parties discussed and agreed upon a purchase price of $35,000 just prior to signing, Baker should

- (A) Succeed, because the law implies that the parties contracted for the reasonable market value of the land, although the price to be paid may not necessarily be that orally agreed upon.
- (B) Fail, because the evidence does not show that the price agreed upon is in fact the reasonable market value of the land.
- (C) Succeed, because Ace is estopped from denying that such agreed price is a fair and equitable one, which will be implied by law as a term of the written memorandum.
- (D) Fail, because the price agreed upon is an essential element of the contract and must be in writing.

34. Deborah Debtor took out a loan at Friendly Finance to start a small retail specialty shop. She had no credit history so her friend Samuel Surety offered to guarantee the repayment in the event Deborah defaulted. Unfortunately, Deborah's new shop was unable to generate the volume of revenue she had hoped it would.

The shop's working capital position grew progressively worse and Deborah was pressed by the more aggressive creditors. Finally she found it necessary to seek relief from her creditors by filing a bankruptcy petition. If Friendly Finance brings suit against Samuel on his guarantee, Samuel's worst defense is that:

- (A) He did not receive any consideration for his promise that he made to Deborah.
- (B) An agreement he entered into with Deborah contained a right of indemnification/ reimbursement so the responsibility remains with Deborah.
- (C) The loan was never made to Deborah.
- (D) His undertaking was only oral.

35. Smith, an executive of Apex Corporation, became emotionally involved with Jones. At the urging of Jones, and fearing that Jones would sever their relationship, Smith reluctantly signed a contract that was grossly unfair to Apex. Apex's best basis to rescind the contract would be

- (A) Lack of express authority.
- (B) Duress.
- (C) Undue influence.
- (D) Lack of consideration.

36. Sarah Sailor owned two sailboats, a 32 footer and a 37 footer. Bill Buyer has seen the 37 footer sailboat but not the smaller sailboat. Sarah offered in writing to sell "my sailboat" to Bill for $15,000 cash. Bill accepted and paid Sarah the $15,000 cash.

The next day, Sarah delivered the sailboat to Bill who rejected the tender since it was not the sailboat he thought he was buying. Sarah refused to return Bill's $15,000 payment and insisted that Bill take the smaller sailboat. The best facts supporting Bill's argument to seek relief would be

- (A) Express fraud by Sarah.
- (B) A latent ambiguity was known by Sarah but not by Bill.
- (C) There was a mutual mistake.
- (D) Bill's subjective intent should control requiring reformation of the contract subject.

37. An unsophisticated elderly patient in a hospital needed insulin immediately to treat her diabetes. The hospital forced her to sign a contract relinquishing any right to sue for physical injuries that might develop from using the prescribed medicine. Also, the contract price for the insulin was three times higher than the price available in public drug stores. The insulin was defective causing her death. If her personal representative sues the hospital and it defends on the basis of the insulin contract relinquishment, the likely result is

(A) The court (judge) would likely hold the contract relinquishment unconscionable.

(B) The jury would likely hold the contract relinquishment unconscionable.

(C) Dismissal because the estate can only prove procedural unconscionability not substantive unconscionability.

(D) Dismissal because the estate can only prove substantive unconscionability not procedural unconscionability.

Questions 38 and 39 are based on the following:

Forward Fred was an associate in a prominent law firm who had just been promoted to partner. Along with a large salary increase, the senior partner told Fred that it was time he began to do some "rainmaking" for the firm. Fred considered moving to a bigger home in a better area in order to meet business owners.

Fred wrote a firm's client named Charlie Client a letter stating he had sold his house and offering to sell him "all his household stuff for $50,000 that had cost over $100,000 and was now worth over $200,000. This is the parties final agreement." Client believed this included the two antique automobiles stored in the basement, which Fred had previously orally referred to as "part of our household stuff." Client also believed the cost and current market valuations Fred stated, because Client had been a firm customer for many years and respected all

the attorneys he had met from the firm.

Client mailed a letter to Fred that stated "I accept, can I pay $5,000 a month for 10 months?" Later Client learned that the household furnishings cost Fred only $40,000 and they were worth much less than that figure on the date Fred made the offer. Fred is also refusing to include the two antique automobiles in the sale. Fred is insistent that Client comply with his agreement and has threatened to file a lawsuit.

38. Client's worst defense to Fred's suit would be:

(A) Fred was a fiduciary and should be held to a very high standard of disclosures when dealing with a firm's client.

(B) There was no contract because "household stuff" is a latent ambiguity precluding a true meeting of the minds.

(C) Fred committed a fraud in the inducement.

(D) Fred never agreed or disagreed with the terms of paying over 10 months at $5,000 per month so there is no contract.

39. Assume for this question only that a contract exists between Fred and Client. Will Client be able to introduce evidence (assuming it is relevant) that Fred previously referred to the two antique automobiles as "part of our household stuff"?

(A) Yes, because facts involving fraud in the inducement is an exception to the parol evidence rule.

(B) Yes, because there is an ambiguity in the contract term.

(C) Yes, because the offered evidence only contradicts a recital of facts and not an essential contract term.

(D) No, because the contract stated it was "the parties final agreement" which imposes the parol evidence rule of exclusion on prior inconsistent statements.

40. Elrod is attempting to introduce oral evidence in court to explain or modify the written contract he made with Weaver. Weaver has pleaded the parol evidence rule. In which of the following circumstances will Elrod not be able to introduce the oral evidence?

(A) The modification asserted was made several days after the written contract had been executed.

(B) The contract indicates that it was intended as the "entire contract" between the parties, and the point is covered in detail.

(C) There was a mutual mistake of fact by the parties regarding the subject matter of the contract.

(D) The contract contains an ambiguity on the point at issue.

41. West sent a letter to Baker on October 18 offering to sell a specified tract of land for $70,000. The offer stated that it would expire on November 1. Baker sent a letter on October 25, indicating the price was too high but that he would be willing to pay $62,500. On the morning of October 26, upon learning that a comparable property had sold for $72,500, Baker telegraphed West and made an unconditional acceptance of the offer at $70,000. West indicated that the price was now $73,000. Baker's letter offering $62,500 arrived the afternoon of the October 26. Under the circumstances,

(A) West's letter was a firm offer as defined under the Uniform Commercial Code.

(B) Baker validly accepted on the morning of October 26.

(C) There is no contract since Baker's acceptance was not in a signed writing.

(D) The parol evidence rule will preclude Baker from contradicting his written statements with oral testimony containing terms contrary to his letter of October 25.

42. Rowe Corp. purchased goods from Stair Co. that were shipped C.O.D. Under Article 2 of the UCC, which of the following rights does Rowe have?

(A) The right to inspect the goods before paying.

(B) The right to possession of the goods before paying.

(C) The right to reject nonconforming goods.

(D) The right to delay payment for a reasonable period of time.

Questions 43 and 44 are based on the following:

Mighty Manufacturing orders two large production line machines for use in their assembly line from Mega Equipment. The machines were received in a large crate at Might's receiving dock with no visible defect apparent on the outside of the crate. The receiving clerk signed an "Acceptance of Delivery" form. Mighty paid Mega the full price 30 days after delivery.

43. One machine was moved to the assembly line area. It took five weeks for Mighty to reconfigure the assembly line so the new equipment would perform. As soon as the new equipment was installed, it was clear there were serious defects in the new equipment. Mighty notified Mega of the defect and requested Mega pick up the equipment. The night before Mega was to pick up the equipment, a fire destroyed the Mighty Manufacturing assembly line area. If Mighty's insurance is insufficient to cover the machine loss, the balance of the loss should be borne by

(A) Mighty, because the machine was on their premises.

(B) Mega, because the machine was defective.

(C) Mega, if it was reasonable for Mighty to have waited five weeks before notifying Mega of the defect.

(D) Mighty, because payment for the goods usually constitutes acceptance.

44. The second piece of equipment was likewise left in its crate in Mighty's receiving area when the fire destroyed the adjoining building containing the manufacturing line. Mighty decided it did not want the second machine. It thus shipped it back to Mega and prepaid all freight and demanded its cash back. Upon receipt, Mega had the machine inspected by a neutral industrial engineer, who determined the machine perfectly conformed to the contract specifications. Mega notified Mighty the machine was perfect and that they were holding them to their contract. One week later an unexpected earthquake occurred destroying the warehouse where Mega was storing the machine. If Mega's insurance is insufficient to cover the machine loss, the balance of the loss should be borne by

(A) Mega because the machine was on their premises.

(B) Mighty because they repudiated or revoked their acceptance.

(C) Mighty because they paid for the machines and this constitutes acceptance.

(D) Mega because they produced the machine in question.

45. Which of the following factors result(s) in a UCC Article 2 express warranty with respect to a sale of goods?

I. The seller's description of the goods as part of the basis of the bargain.

II. The seller selects goods knowing the buyer's intended use.

(A) I only.

(B) II only.

(C) Both I and II.

(D) Neither I nor II.

46. The UCC Article 2 implies a warranty of merchantability to protect buyers of goods. To be subject to this warranty the goods need not be

(A) Fit for all of the purposes for which the buyer intends to use the goods.

(B) Adequately packaged and labeled.

(C) Sold by a merchant.

(D) In conformity with any promises or affirmations of fact made on the container or label.

47. Which of the following conditions must be met for a UCC Article 2 implied warranty of fitness for a particular purpose to arise in connection with a sale of goods?

I. The warranty must be in writing.

II. The seller must know that the buyer was relying on the seller in selecting the goods.

(A) I only.

(B) II only.

(C) Both I and II.

(D) Neither I nor II.

48. The UCC Article 2 provides for a warranty against infringement. Its primary purpose is to protect the buyer of goods from infringement of the rights of third parties. This warranty

(A) Only applies if the sale is between merchants.

(B) Must be expressly stated in the contract or the Statute of Frauds will prevent its enforceability.

(C) Does not apply to the seller if the buyer furnishes specifications which result in an infringement.

(D) Can not be disclaimed.

49. In general, UCC Article 2 disclaimers of implied warranty protection are

(A) Permitted if they are explicit and understandable and the buyer is aware of their existence.

(B) Not binding on remote purchasers with notice thereof.

(C) Void because they are against public policy.

(D) Invalid unless in writing and signed by the buyer.

50. Under the UCC Sales Article 2, an action for breach of the implied warranty of merchantability by a party who sustains personal injuries may be successful against the seller of the product only when

(A) The seller is a merchant of the product involved.

(B) An action based on negligence can also be successfully maintained.

(C) The injured party is in privity of contract with the seller.

(D) An action based on strict liability in tort can also be successfully maintained.

51. Murphy contracted with a builder to construct a new home and specified in the contract that an architect must approve the house before payment was due. The builder substantially completed the house but could not agree with the architect as to certain remaining items. Murphy's wife engaged a well-known local artist to render an oil painting of the family. Murphy's wife rejected the painting because she felt it was not done well and did not depict the family in the proper manner. The builder and the painter filed individual lawsuits against Murphy and his wife. The lawsuits alleged both the architect and Murphy's wife improperly refused to accept performance. Under the circumstances

(A) Murphy and his wife will lose both lawsuits if the Ps can prove that a reasonable architect would have accepted the home, and the painting was a reasonable likeness of the family that would be accepted by most people.

(B) The builder will prevail if it can show a reasonable architect would have accepted the builder's performance.

(C) The artist will prevail if he can demonstrate in court that nine out of ten witnesses who are also associates of the family would have accepted the painting as reasonably similar to their mental image of the family.

(D) The court will adopt an objective standard to determine whether the architect's and Murphy's wife's refusal was reasonable.

52. Wilcox mailed Norris an unsigned contract for the purchase of a tract of real property. The contract represented the oral understanding of the parties as to the purchase price, closing date, type of deed, and other details. It called for payment in full either by cash or certified check at the closing. Norris signed the contract, but added above his signature the following:

> This contract is subject to my (Norris) being able to obtain conventional financing of at least $100,000 at 9% or less interest for a payment period of not less than 25 years.

Which of the following is correct?

(A) The parties had already made an enforceable contract prior to Wilcox's mailing of the formalized contract.

(B) Norris would not be liable on the contract under the circumstances even if he had not added the "conventional financing" language since Wilcox had not signed it.

(C) By adding the "conventional financing" language above his signature, Norris created a condition precedent to his contractual obligation and made a counteroffer.

(D) The addition of the "conventional financing" language has no legal effect upon the contractual relationship of the parties since it was an implied condition in any event.

53. Magnum, Inc. contracted with Kent Construction Company to construct four small dwellings according to specifications provided by Magnum. To save money, Kent deliberately substituted 2 x 4s for the more expensive 2 x 6s called for in the plans in all places where the 2 x 4s would not be readily detected. Magnum's inspection revealed the contract variance and Magnum is now withholding the final payment on the contract. The contract was for $100,000, and the final payment would have been

$25,000. Damages were estimated to be $15,000. In a lawsuit for the balance due, Kent will

(A) Prevail on the contract, less damages of $15,000, because it has substantially performed.
(B) Prevail because the damages in question were not substantial in relation to the contract amount.
(C) Lose because the law unqualifiedly requires literal performance of such contracts.
(D) Lose all rights under the contract because it has intentionally breached it.

54. Acme Manufacturing Co.'s warehouse experienced a severe earthquake. This destroyed some of the goods in production which had been contracted for a buyer named Baker, Inc. Baker

(A) Can sue for damages because Acme breached the contract.
(B) Is entitled to notice from Acme if part performance is still possible.
(C) Does not have the option to accept a partial shipment of the goods.
(D) Must accept a partial shipment of the goods.

55. Stand Glue Corp. offered to sell Macal, Inc., all of the glue it would need in the manufacture of its furniture for one year at the rate of $25 per barrel, F.O.B. seller's city. Macal accepted Stand's offer. Four months later, due to inflation, Stand wrote to Macal advising Macal that Stand could no longer supply the glue at $25 per barrel, but offering to fulfill the contract at $28 per barrel instead. Macal, in need of the glue, sent Stand a letter agreeing to pay the price increase. Macal is

(A) Legally obligated to pay only $25 per barrel under the contract with Stand.
(B) Legally obligated to pay $28 per barrel under the contract with Stand.
(C) Not legally obligated to purchase any glue. Stand has breached the contract.

(D) Legally obligated to pay $28 per barrel due to the fact inflation represents an unforeseen hardship.

56. Charlie Crawford owns Crawford's Vineyards. He entered into firm sale agreements to sell 200 tons of Sirhan wine grapes to Hogue Winery on January 15 and 100 tons to St. Michelle Winery on February 15. The contract specified that all the grapes were to come only from Crawford's vineyard. A very unusual mid-summer rain and thunderstorm occurred. There was lightning generated in the storm and it started a field fire in the vineyard where Crawford grew the Sirhan wine grapes. The fire destroyed all but 30 tons of Crawford's Sirhan wine grapes.

Crawford then contacted Hogue and St. Michelle and offered to replace the Sirhan grapes with Merlot grapes at a reduced price. He also offered to deliver to Hogue 20 tons and to St. Michelle 10 tons of the Sirhan grapes. Hogue demanded all the 30 tons because they purchased first. Crawford gave him the 20-ton allocation and Hogue purchased his other 180 tons from another grower at a price that was $24,000 higher than the price he had negotiated with Crawford. If Hogue brings suit against Crawford, Crawford's worse defense is:

(A) The cause of the shortage was beyond his control.
(B) His pro-rata allocation between Hogue and St. Michelle was reasonable.
(C) He should not be held liable because he offered a substitute grape at no extra price.
(D) Neither he nor Hogue foresaw that a fire would occur in the grape fields.

57. Dick Debtor owed Carol Creditor $15,000 which was the disputed amount of a construction job billing balance. After negotiations between the parties' attorneys, the parties agreed to settle the dispute for $10,000. Debtor was to pay Creditor the $10,000 amount within one year. Six months later Dick changed attorneys and the new attorney felt that Debtor had no fault in the underlying dispute and should pay nothing. Dick made it very clear to Carol that he was not going to pay the $10,000 in six months when it was due. Carol has come to you seeking advice. Your opinion should include that Carol

(A) Must write the receivable off in total.
(B) May not litigate for the underlying $15,000 dispute since she is limited to the $10,000 compromise.
(C) May sue for the $10,000 compromise or the original $15,000 if the statute of limitation is still open on the underlying claim.
(D) Must wait for six months to see if Dick changes his mind and pays the $10,000.

58. Alpha and Beta entered into a written agreement to sell and purchase real property. After they had signed the agreement but before closing, they got into an argument. Alpha decided the price was too low, Beta decided the price was too high, and they both decided to cancel the contract. Later Beta changed his mind and decided he would pay what Alpha wanted for the property. He contacted Alpha who refused to sell to him at any price. If Beta brings suit against Alpha for specific performance, Alpha's best defense is that

(A) Beta did not give consideration for the original agreement.
(B) Beta did not retract his waiver before any detrimental reliance by Alpha.
(C) The contract was not subject to a novation agreement.
(D) The contract had been discharged through rescission.

59. Under the Sales Article 2 of the UCC, which of the following rights is (are) available to the buyer when a seller commits an anticipatory breach of contract?

	Demand assurance of performance	Cancel the contract	Collect punitive damages
(A)	Yes	Yes	Yes
(B)	Yes	Yes	No
(C)	Yes	No	Yes
(D)	No	Yes	Yes

60. Under the Sales Article 2 of the UCC, which of the following events will release the buyer from all its obligations under a sales contract?

(A) Destruction of the goods after risk of loss passed to the buyer.
(B) Impracticability of delivery under the terms of the contract.
(C) Anticipatory repudiation by the buyer that is retracted before the seller cancels the contract.
(D) Refusal of the seller to give written assurance of performance when reasonably demanded by the buyer.

61. The Balboa Custom Furniture Company sells fine custom furniture. It has been encountering difficulties lately with some customers who have breached their contracts either after the furniture they have selected has been customized to their order, the fabric they have selected has been cut, or the selected fabric has actually been installed on the piece of furniture purchased. The company therefore wishes to resort to a liquidated damages clause in its sales contract to encourage performance or provide an acceptable amount of damages. Regarding Balboa's contemplated resort to a liquidated damages clause, which of the following is correct?

(A) Balboa may not use a liquidated damages clause since it is a merchant and is the preparer of the contract.
(B) Balboa can simply take a very large deposit which will be forfeited if performance by a customer is not made for any reason.
(C) The amount of the liquidated damages stipulated in the contract must be reasonable in light of the

anticipated or actual harm caused by the breach.

(D) Even if Balboa uses a liquidated damages clause in its sales contract, it will nevertheless have to establish that the liquidated damages claimed did not exceed actual damages by more than 10%.

62. Harry Homeowner decided to purchase an underground watering system for his lawn and garden. In December he signed a $5,000 contract with Wendy Waterhouse which included installing the underground watering system and all labor and materials. The project was to begin three months hence on March 1st and Wendy scheduled her workers to complete Harry's project. On February 1st, Harry decided to do the work himself and called Wendy telling her that the contract was off. Wendy told Harry that she intended to hold him to the agreement. She then began to buy the plastic piping, nozzle heads and faucets necessary to complete the job. On March 1st, Wendy showed up at Harry's house to begin the work, but Harry refused to allow her access to the property. Wendy spent $1,000 on the plastic piping and $500 on the nozzle heads and faucets. She expected to realize a profit of $2,500 on the job. If Wendy brings suit against Harry for breach of contract, she will likely recover:

(A) $5,000 because this is the agreed upon price of the contract that Harry intentionally breached.

(B) $2,500 in expectation damages.

(C) $1,500 in restitution damages.

(D) $3,500 consisting of $2,500 in expectation damages and $1,500 in restitution damages.

63. Brown ordered 100 cases of Delicious Brand peas at list price from Smith Wholesaler stating "prompt shipment." Upon receipt of Brown's order, Smith immediately sent Brown an acceptance which was received by Brown. The acceptance indicated that shipment would be made within ten days. On the tenth day Smith discovered that all of its supply of

Delicious Brand peas had been sold. Instead it shipped 100 cases of Lovely Brand peas, stating clearly on the invoice that the shipment was sent only as an accommodation. Which of the following is correct?

(A) Smith's shipment of Lovely Brand peas is a counteroffer, thus no contract exists between Brown and Smith.

(B) Smith's note of accommodation cancels the contract between Smith and Brown.

(C) Brown's order is a unilateral offer, and can only be accepted by Smith's immediate shipment of the goods ordered.

(D) Smith's shipment of Lovely Brand peas constitutes a breach of contract.

64. Brown & Company entered into a written agreement to sell 2,500 widgets to a large distributor in Seattle. When the date for performance arrived, Brown called the buyer and stated it could not deliver as per the agreement. The buyer could not find substitute goods and therefore lost a large contract with an airplane manufacturing company. The buyer could recover

(A) The reasonable value of the time spent working on the Brown purchase and all attorney fees.

(B) All incidental damages which developed because of the seller's breach.

(C) Consequential damages only if the agreement specified that in the event of breach both parties are allowed to collect lost profits.

(D) All incidental and consequential damages which flow from Brown's breach.

65. Pretty Production Co. entered into a contract to sell an antique oriental carpet to Bountiful Buyer for $20,000. One month before the designated delivery date, Pretty contacted Bountiful and told them they needed to charge an extra $5,000 or Bountiful "should look elsewhere for a carpet." Bountiful has found two similarly colored oriental carpets that were approximately the same size; one cost $15,000 but was of lower quality, and the other $40,000 although it was of a much higher quality than the one they expected to purchase from Pretty. Which of the following statements is true about Bountiful's remedies?

(A) They must wait for the one month to see if Pretty changes their mind and will deliver the original carpet.

(B) They may cover their requirements by buying the $40,000 carpet.

(C) They must cover their requirement by buying the $15,000 carpet.

(D) They may be allowed an order of specific performance.

66. Pacific Gas Company was a retailer of natural gas for homeowners and businesses. In 2003, Pacific signed a 5-year requirement contract with Mega Gas Producers, a company which piped natural gas from the central plains of Canada. In early 2005, Mega informed Pacific that due to a significant price increase they were experiencing from the drillers, it could no longer afford to supply gas to Pacific unless they paid a surcharge of 20%. There were other suppliers that then offered to sell gas to Pacific. Pacific responded to Mega's repudiation by filing a lawsuit against Mega seeking an order of specific performance. Concerning the order of specific performance, the court will likely decide for

(A) Pacific unless they are able to cover their requirement from another source.

(B) Mega because the gas was available on the spot market and therefore the goods are not unique.

(C) Mega unless Pacific's commercial feasibility of replacement was low.

(D) Pacific if the factors resulting from the supply cut-off satisfied the "other proper circumstances" test.

67. Ace & Co. entered into a written contract to purchase 35 computer manuals from Lamb & Co. Ace was located in Seattle and Lamb in Boston, but the manuals were to be shipped from New York. Lamb hid the defective manuals in the bottom of the boxes. Upon receipt of the manuals, Ace only inspected the top manual and signed an acknowledgment of delivery. Nine days later it discovered that all the other manuals had been misprinted. Ace bought 35 manuals from another source to fulfill their contract with their buyer. Under the circumstances, Ace is not entitled to the following remedy

(A) To revoke the acceptance because of the discovery of material defects subsequent to acceptance.

(B) Specific performance because Ace has effectively covered.

(C) The difference between the contract price and the cover price together with incidental and consequential damages flowing from the breach.

(D) Profit on the sale it would have made to its customer had its purchase from Lamb been as per the contract.

68. Marvin contracted to purchase goods from Ling. Subsequently, Marvin breached the contract and Ling is seeking to recover the contract price. Ling can recover the price if

(A) Ling does not seek to recover any damages in addition to the price.

(B) The goods have been destroyed and Ling's insurance coverage is inadequate, regardless of risk of loss.

(C) Ling has identified the goods to the contract and the circumstances indicate that a reasonable effort to resell the goods at a reasonable price would be to no avail.

(D) Marvin anticipatorily repudiated the contract and specific performance is not available.

69. Generous George was the owner of a glass sculpture shop. He was in an automobile accident and Helpful Harry assisted him by pulling him out of the

flaming automobile. Helpful accompanied George to the hospital and a discussion developed there about one of his glass sculptures named Emeritus. Harry had always admired the Emeritus which he knew to be worth over $5,000. He told George "I love the Emeritus but can not afford it because I only have $500." George said he would sell to Harry at that price; Harry gave him his check for $500. Unbeknown to either George or Harry, the Emeritus had been sold by one of Generous' salesmen earlier that afternoon to Betty, a bona fide purchaser for value. If Harry requests specific performance of the Emeritus from George, the likely outcome is:

(A) Denied because George's promise was 90% a gift which can be revoked at will.

(B) Denied because specific performance against George is no longer possible.

(C) Ordered because the accident assistance is additional consideration.

(D) Ordered because there was a bargained-for-exchange of promises even if the consideration was unequal.

70. Wally Waterworks contracted with Harriet Homeowner to install an underground watering system at her new home. Subsequently Wally found that he had booked too many orders after Harriet's. Wally was therefore unable to complete some of the jobs he had contracted for including Harriet's. Harriet was furious because some of the new trees and plants she had planted died without the water. She investigated and learned that while Wally was refusing to do her watering system, he was doing one for Nancy Next. If Harriet files suit against Wally

I. She will be able to collect punitive damages.

II. She will not be able to collect punitive damages.

III. She will be able to obtain an injunction prohibiting Wally from working on Nancy's watering system.

IV. She will not be able to obtain an injunction prohibiting Wally from working on Nancy's watering system.

(A) I and III are correct.

(B) I and IV are correct.

(C) II and III are correct

(D) II and IV are correct.

71. Carol Consumer hired Albert Attorney to prepare a will for her. Under state law only admitted attorneys are allowed to prepare wills. Albert did not tell Carol that he had failed the bar examination and had not been admitted to the local State Bar Association. The completed will was accepted and paid for by Carol. Carol passed away eight years later and her personal representative discovered that the will did not contain a disclaimer provision which would have allowed her heirs to avoid a large part of the federal estate tax. If Carol's personal representative brings a civil professional malpractice suit against Albert, the best defense he can assert is:

(A) Carol never paid him for preparing the will.

(B) Carol knew and appreciated that a disclaimer clause was not included.

(C) The contract was illegal since it violated the state law requiring the drafter to be admitted to the local bar association to practice law.

(D) The suit is not timely because the malpractice statute of limitations in the state was three years and it has run.

72. Wilson sold his factory to Glenn. As part of the contract, Glenn assumed the existing mortgage on the property that was held by Security Bank. Regarding the rights and duties of the parties, which of the following is correct?

(A) The promise by Glenn need not be in writing to be enforceable by Security.

(B) Security is a creditor beneficiary of Glenn's promise and can recover against him personally in the event of default.

(C) Security is a mere incidental beneficiary since it was not a party to the assignment.

(D) Wilson has no further liability to Security.

Questions 73 – 75 are based on the following:

Gloria Gardener completed a spring gardening contract with Harriet Homeowner which included pruning all the fruit trees in her backyard. The contract was for $500, payable ten days after completion, and stated "no rights herein can be assigned." Gloria had an expectation that Harriet would hire her to do the summer lawn mowing, edging, and gardening functions for $1,000. Gloria also sold some lawn furniture to Harriet for $2,000 which was to be paid in one month. This lawn equipment contract also specified "no right herein can be assigned."

73. Gloria became short on cash and approached Friendly Finance for a loan. Friendly insisted that Gloria assign the three contractual rights to Friendly in return for advancing her a loan of $3,000. Friendly was to collect the full $3,500 from Harriet with the $500 to cover interest, collections costs, and an assignment fee. Gloria did not tell Friendly that the contracts prohibited the assignment of rights. If Harriet refuses to pay Friendly and Friendly brings suit, Harriet will likely have to pay Friendly

(A) -0- because all the contracts stated no rights could be assigned.

(B) $500 representing the amount due on the spring gardening contract.

(C) $2,500 for the spring gardening contract and the contract for the lawn equipment.

(D) $3,500 representing the full face amount on all three contracts.

74. The legal effect of the contract covenant not to assign the $2,000 from the sale of the lawn equipment is

(A) Enforceable because the agreement so states.

(B) Not enforceable because it appears to be against public interest.

(C) Not enforceable because the lawn equipment was transferred from Gloria to Harriet.

(D) Enforceable because Friendly was a third party beneficiary of the Gloria and Harriet contract.

75. The legal effect of the prohibition against assignment of the expected $1,000 summer lawn mowing, edging, and gardening contract payment was

(A) Not enforceable because it is a future contract.

(B) Enforceable by Friendly

(C) Enforceable by Friendly but Harriet has a breach of contract claim against Gloria.

(D) Not enforceable only if Friendly knew of the assignment prohibition.

76. A common law duty is delegable even though the

(A) Contract provides that the duty is nondelegable.

(B) Duty delegated is the payment of money and the delegatee is less credit worthy than the delegator.

(C) Delegation will result in a material variance in performance by the delegatee.

(D) Duty to be performed involves the personal skill of the obligor.

Contracts and UCC Sales Practice Questions

77. Harper is opening a small retailing business in Hometown, USA. To announce her grand opening, Harper places an advertisement in the newspaper quoting sales prices on certain inventory items. The advertisement did not contain specific words of commitment. Many local residents come in and make purchases. Harper's grand opening is such a huge success that she is unable to totally satisfy the demand of the customers. Which of the following correctly applies to the situation?

(A) Harper has made an offer to the people reading the advertisement.
(B) Harper has made a contract with the people reading the advertisement.
(C) Harper has made an invitation seeking offers.
(D) Any customer who demands the goods advertised and tenders the money is entitled to them at that price.

78. Maurice sent Schmit Company a telegram offering to sell him a one-acre tract of commercial property located adjacent to Schmit's warehouse for $8,000. Maurice stated that Schmit had three days to consider the offer and in the meantime the offer would be irrevocable. The next day, Maurice received a better offer from another party, and he telephoned Schmit informing him that he was revoking the offer. The offer was

(A) Irrevocable for three days upon receipt by Schmit.
(B) Effectively revoked by telephone.
(C) Never valid, since the Statute of Frauds applies.
(D) Not effectively revoked because Maurice did not use the same means of communication.

79. Nichols wrote Dilk and offered to sell Dilk a building and land for $50,000. The offer stated it would expire 30 days from July 1. Nichols changed his mind and does not wish to be bound by his offer. If a legal dispute arises between the parties regarding whether there has been a valid acceptance of the offer, which of the following is correct?

(A) The offer will not expire prior to the 30 days even if Nichols sells the property to a third person and notifies Dilk.

(B) If Dilk categorically rejects the offer on July 10, Dilk can not validly accept within the remaining stated period of time.
(C) If Dilk phoned Nichols on August 1 and unequivocally accepted the offer, it would create a contract, provided he had no notice of withdrawal of the offer.
(D) The offer can not be legally withdrawn for the stated period of time.

80. Martin sent Dobbs the following offer by mail:

> I offer you 150 fantastic television sets, model J-1, at $65 per set, F.O.B. your truck at my warehouse, terms 2/10, net/30. I am closing out this model, hence the substantial discount. Accept all or none.
> (signed) Martin

Dobbs immediately wired back:

> I accept your offer re: the fantastic television sets, but will use Blue Express Company for the pickup, at my expense of course. In addition, if possible, could you have the shipment ready by Tuesday at 10:00 AM because of the holidays?
> (signed) Dobbs

Based on the above correspondence, what is the status of Dobb's acceptance?

(A) It is valid upon dispatch despite the fact it states both additional and different terms than those contained in the offer.
(B) It is valid but will not be effective until received by Martin.
(C) It represents a counteroffer which will become a valid acceptance if not rejected by Martin within ten days.

(D) It is not a valid acceptance because it states both additional and different terms than those contained in the offer.

81. Starbest Corporation sent Crane Company an offer by a telegram to buy twenty tons of coffee. The Starbest telegram indicated that the offer would expire in ten days. The telegram was sent on February 1 and received on February 2 by Crane. On February 8, Starbest telephoned Crane and indicated it was withdrawing the offer. Crane telegraphed an acceptance on the 11th of February. Which of the following is correct?

(A) Starbest's withdrawal of the offer was ineffective because it was not in writing.

(B) The offer was an irrevocable offer, but Crane's acceptance was too late.

(C) No contract arose since Starbest effectively revoked the offer on February 8.

(D) Since Crane used the same means of communication, acceptance was both timely and effective.

82. Luxor wrote Harmon offering to sell Harmon Luxor's real estate business for $200,000. Harmon sent a telegram accepting the offer at $190,000. Later, learning that several other parties were interested in purchasing the business, Harmon telephoned Luxor and made an unqualified acceptance on Luxor's terms. The telegraph arrived an hour after the phone call. Under the circumstances

(A) Harmon's telegram effectively terminated the offer.

(B) Harmon's oral acceptance is voidable, because real estate is involved.

(C) The offer was revoked as a result of Harmon's learning that others were interested in purchasing the business.

(D) Harmon has made a valid contract at $200,000.

83. On October 1, Baker, a wholesaler, sent Clark, a retailer, a written signed offer to sell 200 pinking shears at $9 each. The terms were F.O.B. Baker's warehouse, net 30, late payment subject to a 12% per annum interest charge. The offer indicated that it must be accepted no later than October 10, that acceptance would be effective upon receipt, and that the terms were not to be varied by the offeree. Clark sent a telegram which arrived on October 6, and accepted the offer expressly subject to a change of the payment terms to 2/10, net/30. Baker phoned Clark on October 7 rejecting the change of payment terms. Clark then indicated it would accept the October 1 offer in all respects, and expected delivery within 10 days. Baker did not acknowledge Clark's oral acceptance of the original offer. Which of the following is a correct statement?

(A) Baker's original offer is a firm offer, hence irrevocable.

(B) There is no contract since Clark's modifications effectively rejected the October 1 offer, and Baker never accepted either of Clark's proposals.

(C) Clark actually created a contract on October 6, since the modifications were merely proposals and did not preclude acceptance.

(D) The statute of frauds would preclude the formation of a contract in any event.

84. Montrose sent Bilbo a written offer to sell his tract of land located in Majorsville for $50,000. The parties were engaged in a separate dispute. The offer stated that it would be irrevocable for 30 days if Bilbo would promise to refrain from suing Montrose during this time. Bilbo promptly delivered a promise not to sue during the term of the offer and to forego suit if she accepted the offer. Montrose subsequently decided that the possible suit by Bilbo was groundless and therefore phoned Bilbo and revoked the offer ten days after making it. Bilbo mailed an acceptance on the 30th day. Montrose did not reply. Under the circumstances,

(A) Montrose's offer was supported by consideration, and was irrevocable when accepted.

(B) Bilbo's promise was accepted by Montrose by his silence.

(C) Montrose's revocation, not being in writing, was invalid.

(D) Montrose's written offer would be irrevocable even without consideration.

85. Marglow Supplies Inc., mailed a letter to Wilson Distributors on September 15, offering a three year franchise dealership. The offer stated the terms in detail and at the bottom stated that the offer would not be withdrawn prior to October 1 of the same year. Which of the following is correct?

(A) The statute of frauds would not apply to the proposed contract.

(B) The offer is an irrevocable option which can not be withdrawn prior to October 1.

(C) The offer can not be assigned to another party by Wilson if Wilson chooses not to accept.

(D) A letter of acceptance from Wilson to Marglow sent on October 1 which was received on October 2 would not create a valid contract.

86. Under Article 2 of the UCC, when a signed written offer has been made by a merchant without specifying a means of acceptance but providing that the offer will only remain open for ten days, which of the following statements represent(s) a valid acceptance of the offer?

I.   An acceptance sent by regular mail the day before the ten-day period expires that reaches the offeror on the eleventh day.

II. An acceptance faxed the day before the ten-day period expires that follows a rejection received by the offeror two days previously.

III. An acceptance made on the seventh day when the offeror sold the item to a third party on the fourth day.

(A) I only.

(B) II only.

(C) Both I and II.

(D) I, II, and III.

87. Filmore purchased a Miracle color television set from Allison Appliances, an authorized dealer, for $499. The written contract contained the usual one-year warranty as to parts and labor as long as the set was returned to the manufacturer or one of its authorized dealers. The contract also contained a disclaimer of any express warranty protection, other than that which was included in the contract. It further provided that the contract represented the entire agreement and understanding of the parties. Filmore claims that during the bargaining process Surry, Allison's agent, orally promised to service the set at Filmore's residence if anything went wrong within the year. Allison has offered to repair the set if it is brought to the service department, but denies any liability under the alleged oral express agreement. Which of the following would be the best defense for Allison to rely upon in the event Filmore sues?

(A) The Statute of Frauds.

(B) The parol evidence rule only if the contract was integrated.

(C) The fact that all warranty protection was disclaimed other than the express warranty contained in the contract.

(D) The fact that Surry, Allison's agent, did not have express authority to make such a promise.

88. Madison advertised for the submission of bids on the construction of a parking lot. Kilroy submitted a bid of $112,000. There were nine other bids. Kilroy's bid was $45,000 less than the next lowest bid. The discrepancy was due to the omission of a $46,000 item on the part of Kilroy's staff. Madison accepted the bid and demands either performance or damages from Kilroy. Kilroy is

(A) Bound by the acceptance at $112,000.

(B) Not bound by the acceptance but only if Madison actually knew a mistake had been made.

(C) Not bound by the acceptance if the mistake should have been known by Madison.

(D) Not bound by the bid submitted because there was no subjective meeting of the minds.

89. Paul filed a $20,000 fire loss claim with the Williams Fire Insurance Company. Dickerson, Williams' adjuster, called Paul on the phone and invited him to come to his hotel room to settle the claim. Upon Paul's entry to the room, Dickerson locked the door and placed the key in his pocket. He then accused Paul of having set the building on fire and of having been involved in several previous suspicious fire claims. Dickerson concluded by telling Paul that unless he signed a release in exchange for $500, he would personally see to it that Paul was criminally prosecuted by the company for arson. Visibly shaken by all this, Paul signed the release. Paul has subsequently repudiated the release he signed. The release is not binding because of

(A) Fraud.

(B) Lack of consideration.

(C) Undue influence.

(D) Duress.

90. Walton owed $10,000 to Grant. Grant assigned his claim against Walton to the Line Finance Company for value on October 15. On October 25, Hayes assigned his matured claim for $2,000 against Grant to Walton for value. On October 30, Line notified Walton of the assignment to them of the $10,000 debt owed by Walton to Grant. Line has demanded payment in full. Insofar as the rights of the various parties are concerned

(A) Walton has the right of a $2,000 set-off against the debt which he owed Grant.

(B) Walton must pay Line in full, but has the right to obtain a $2,000 reimbursement from Grant.

(C) Line is a creditor beneficiary of the debt owed by Walton.

(D) The claimed set-off of the Hayes claim for $2,000 is invalid since it is for an amount which is less than the principal debt.

91. Fennell and McLeod entered into a binding contract whereby McLeod was to perform routine construction services according to Fennell's blueprints. McLeod delegated the contract to Conerly. After the delegation

(A) Fennell can bring suit under the doctrine of anticipatory breach.

(B) McLeod extinguishes all his rights and duties under the contract.

(C) McLeod extinguishes all his rights but is not relieved of his duties under the contract.

(D) McLeod still has all his rights but is relieved of his duties under the contract.

92. Megabank U.S. has historically made a year-to-year loan to Fred and Sally who operate a small convenience store. A large discount store opened across the street from Fred and Sally's store, which caused them to lose business and pay some of the loan payments late. Megabank has requested that the borrowers obtain a guarantee if they want to renew the loan for the next year. As a favor, Sally's father orally promised Fred and Sally he would become jointly liable and pay one-third of Megabank's loan if they defaulted again. If Megabank sues Sally's father on his guarantee, the strongest legal defense that he can assert is

(A) The promise was oral and thus violates the Statute of Frauds.

(B) There was no consideration to support the father's promise.

(C) The principle of promissory estoppel is not met.

(D) The bank did not first pursue Fred and Sally.

93. Archie Architect in New York contracted with Donna Developer to design the architectural plans for a twenty-story office building in New Jersey. The architectural firm drafted a contract that contained a clause stating "any and all claims of any type resulting from performance under this contract must be formally asserted within one year from the date of occurrence." The state statute of limitations in New York for a written contract is six (6) years, while the same statute in New Jersey is four (4) years. Five years after the office building had been completed, the parties were still disagreeing about the final balance due on the architectural contract and the architect filed suit. If Donna brings suit and seeks a declaratory judgment, the court is most likely to hold the applicable statute of limitations should be

(A) One year.
(B) Four years.
(C) Five years.
(D) Six years.

Questions 94 – 96 are based on the following:

Ace owned the Wild and Crazy nightclub in mid-town Manhattan, New York. In June, Ace contracted in writing with Hot Tunes Band to provide the club with live dance music for the month of December. This was a popular band with a very in demand singer named Lead Man. Ace immediately began to advertising their appearance. Hot Tunes called Ace in November and informed him that the lead singer had suffered a heart attack and that therefore they might be unable to perform. Ace objected strenuously and stated he had advertised the band and Lead Man extensively, sold a number of tickets, and would sue the band if they didn't perform as per their contract. Hot Tunes stated they could get another singer, but Ace insisted that Lead Man perform. One week before the band was to begin playing, Ace called to check on Lead Man's condition. He was informed Lead Man had died and it was too late to hire a replacement singer.

94. If the club performance dates come and Ace hires a different band and brings suit

against Hot Tunes, the best defense that Hot Tunes can assert is

(A) Ace was unreasonable in refusing to accept a substitute singer.
(B) Excusable nonperformance.
(C) Ace failed to mitigate damages.
(D) The breach was only minor and thus Ace should be allowed only nominal damages.

95. In the above question, the first communication from the band that Hot Tunes' lead singer had suffered a heart attack

(A) Was an anticipatory repudiation, but the offer to substitute another singer is a retraction.
(B) Was only a minor breach because another singer could perform.
(C) Was an anticipatory repudiation that requires Ace to demand an adequate assurance of performance from Hot Tunes.
(D) Was not an anticipatory repudiation because the prospective lack of performance was uncertain.

96. In the above question assume that Lead Man recovered fully before the engagement date and that he and the Hot Tunes band stated that they would still refuse to perform in Ace's club on the scheduled date. If Ace wants to pursue a judicial remedy he should sue and seek

(A) Specific performance and request an order requiring the Ds to perform.
(B) The reliance interest.
(C) An in quasi-contract recovery.
(D) Compensatory damages.

Questions 97 and 98 are based on the following:

At a popular ski resort named Sugar Mountain, a snowboarder named Nancy Negligent, went over a jump and hit a skier, Carl Careful, in the head. Carl was rendered unconscious by the blow. 30 seconds later Don Doctor, a local radiologist, skied by. One of the Ski Patrol members on the scene, Susan Safety, knew Don Doctor and asked him if he would examine Carl before the Ski Patrol loaded him on the rescue sled to transport him to the main lodge in the valley.

Don examined Carl and determined he was suffering from extreme shock, that a vertebra in his neck was fractured and that the sled trip to the lodge could irreparably damage his vertebra and spinal cord. Based upon Don Doctor's advice, Susan skied down to the lodge and called for a helicopter. Two hours later, it arrived and transported Carl and Don to the local hospital. Don was unable to return to the ski area that day. Later he sent a bill to Carl for $3,000 representing 6 hours of his professional medical service at his standard billing rate of $500 per hour.

97. Carl Careful's best defense against having to pay Don Doctor's claim for fees is
- **(A)** There was no contract since neither he nor anyone else on his behalf had consented to the medical assistance.
- **(B)** He did not receive any benefit because the surgery was not performed by Don Doctor, but rather the hospital.
- **(C)** Don Doctor did not have a reasonable expectation of being compensated for his medical advice.
- **(D)** He had not requested the medical assistance.

98. Assume the doctor is entitled to a recovery of his fees in the skiing accident discussed in the previous question. If Don Doctor does not file suit against Carl Careful until 1,100 days after the accident and the state statute of limitations for tort actions at issue is 3 years, the best defense Carl can raise is
- **(A)** Carl Careful was unconscious for over 10 days and thus the statute of limitations was tolled.
- **(B)** Rendering medical assistance in such circumstances benefits the public interest and thus the statute of limitations should not apply.
- **(C)** Laches.

- **(D)** The statute of limitations for an oral contract is 4 years in the state where the professional services were rendered.

99. Linda Landlord owned a small rental house that was in need of repairs. She entered into an oral contract with Robert Rental to sell him the house for $59,000 cash. Robert relied upon this representation and borrowed the purchase money from his parents. Robert paid the $59,000 to Linda, moved into the house, and began to make improvements and paid the property taxes. Linda developed seller's remorse six months later, refunded the money, and demanded Robert leave the house. If Robert sues Linda for specific performance of the house transfer, Linda's best defense is
- **(A)** The statute of frauds requires a writing signed by the seller.
- **(B)** Whatever improvements Robert made were not substantial.
- **(C)** She returned the $59,000 to Robert Rental.
- **(D)** The house was a rental unit and Robert was just a tenant.

Questions 100 – 102 are based on the following:

Richard Rescuer saw a child hanging from a cliff. Realizing the child could fall to her death, Richard scaled the cliff and brought the child down. Richard then put a demand on the child's parents to pay him $10,000 or he would sue them and their child. The child's mother signed a promissory note in which she promised to pay Richard Rescuer $10,000 "in consideration of him agreeing not to sue me, my husband, or my child and for saving my child's life." The mother later had second thoughts about paying the $10,000.

100. What additional facts would best reinforce Richard Rescuer's claim to the $10,000?
- **(A)** Rescuer paid $1 for the promissory note.

(B) Rescuer believed he had a legitimate legal claim for the $10,000 compensation when the promissory note was signed.

(C) The promissory note recited there was "valuable consideration."

(D) Rescuer would not have gone to the assistance of the child unless compensated.

101. Does Richard Rescuer saving the child alone constitute sufficient consideration for the $10,000 promise?

(A) No, because the value of the act is too uncertain.

(B) Yes, because the child and her parents became morally obligated to the rescuer.

(C) Yes, because the child and her parents substantially benefited from the rescue.

(D) No, because neither the child nor her parents requested Rescuer to save the child.

102. Under which of the following theories of recovery would Richard Rescuer most likely prevail?

(A) The child's mother is bound by promissory estoppel.

(B) The $10,000 promise is a form of novation.

(C) The parties have entered into an executory accord to settle a disputed claim.

(D) The child should pay restitution because she received substantial benefits.

Questions 103 – 106 are based on the following:

Mary Manufacturer and Tony Trucker entered into a written contract on January 1st in which Mary agreed to build 100 trucks for Tony over the next 10 months. The price was to be $100,000 per truck and the manufacturing schedule was that 10 trucks per month were to be completed. The contract stated in part "it is expressly agreed

that Tony would be under no payment obligation under this agreement unless 10 trucks are completed no later than June 30th." 5 trucks meeting the specifications were completed and tendered to Tony by the contractor on June 30th. The remaining 5 trucks were completed and tendered on September 1st

103. The provision in the contract contained within the quotation marks is

(A) Neither a promise nor a condition.

(B) A promise but not a condition.

(C) A condition but not a promise

(D) Both a promise and a condition.

104. In a collection action by Mary, which of the following defenses by Tony would best resist a motion for a directed verdict?

(A) Mary had not substantially performed as of June 30th.

(B) The market value of the completed trucks had decreased by 10% between the time the contract was executed and June 30th.

(C) Time was of the essence in the contract.

(D) A flood had destroyed Tony's main place of business.

105. The above contract is

(A) Entire.

(B) Divisible.

(C) Neither divisible nor entire.

(D) Partially divisible and partly entire.

106. The shipment of 5 trucks instead of 10 was

(A) Not a breach but rather an accommodation.

(B) A breach of the whole contract.

(C) Grounds for Tony to refuse to pay.

(D) Grounds for Tony to request assurances of performance for the remainder of the order.

Questions 107 – 110 are based on the following:

Everyone Passes the Bar Exam Law School is located in California. The Law School Dean has heard rumors that some students had found a preliminary draft copy of the final professional responsibility exam in the garbage. Alumni have also complained recently that this form of cheating has discredited the reputation of the law school. To deal with this problem, the Dean on April 1st posted a written notice on the student lounge bulletin board that stated "The law school offers a $1,000 reward to any student who provides the law school administration with convincing evidence of cheating by a fellow student."

Sally Snitch decided to try and collect the reward. She wrote a letter to the Dean that identified Chris Cheater as one of the culprits. After she had posted her letter on April 10th but before receipt by the Dean, the faculty met. They reasoned that the faculty member who did not shred the preliminary examination draft was negligent and that this should not be a disciplinary offense. They met with the Dean who agreed with their position. Accordingly, a new written notice was posted on April 15th that stated "after reflection the dean and faculty have concluded that the $1,000 reward must be withdrawn."

107. If the first posting was seen by most of the students
- (A) The first posting was merely a preliminary invitation because no particular offeree was specified.
- (B) The first posting was a preliminary invitation to deal analogous to a general newspaper advertisement for goods, which is not usually considered to be an offer.
- (C) The first posting was a valid offer and created a power of acceptance.
- (D) The first posting was a mere promise to make a future conditional gift of money.

108. In the above question, the first posting proposed a
- (A) Unilateral contract only.
- (B) Unilateral contract, which ripened into a bilateral contract when the acceptance was mailed.
- (C) Bilateral contract only.
- (D) Bilateral contract or unilateral contract depending upon the offeree's option.

109. In the above question, the first posting was
- (A) Not enforceable on public policy grounds because it would require one student to snitch on another student.
- (B) Enforceable by Susan's personal representative if she dies prematurely before the student in question is disciplined.
- (C) Not enforceable because Susan was under a pre-existing duty to report a fellow student who cheats in law school.
- (D) Enforceable under the principle of promissory estoppel.

110. In the above question, the second posting on April 15th
- (A) Was too late to avoid paying Susan.
- (B) Effectively revoked the April 1st offer.
- (C) Effectively revoked the April 1st offer if Susan saw it before her written communication was received by the law school.
- (D) Effectively revoked the April 1st offer if Susan's communication was lost in the mail and never received by the law school.

111. Betty Brown was negotiating to buy a piece of property owned by Sarah Smith. Smith wrote Brown on December 1st offering the property for $100,000. Brown felt the price was too high and wrote Smith a letter on December 10th that stated. "I reject your offer but will pay you $80,000 for the property." Due to the fault of Brown's agent, the letter was never delivered. Brown later realized that the property was worth the full asking price and sent a second letter to Smith on December 15th in which she agreed to buy the property for the full $100,000. Smith received the letter on December 20th. Regarding the negotiations

- **(A)** A contract was formed on December 10th.
- **(B)** A contract was formed on December 15th.
- **(C)** A contract was formed on December 20th.
- **(D)** No contract was formed because Brown rejected the offer.

Questions 112 and 113 are based on the following:

Paul Painter and Harry Homeowner agreed in writing that Paul would prepare and paint the wood exterior of Harry's whole home for $5,000 and that the work would be completed in 30 days. There was a clause in the agreement that stated "late performance will result in a charge of $100 per day." Paul was delayed and it took 90 days to finally complete the painting. In addition to the late performance, Harry objected in good faith that some of the wood had not been properly prepared prior to painting. Harry refused to pay Paul anything.

Paul grew increasingly insistent that Harry pay him and threatened to hire a lawyer to sue if payment was not forthcoming. Based upon this, Harry sent Paul a check for $4,000 The check stated "Payment in full covering the contested painting contract." Paul cashed the check without comment or reserving any rights. Two months later, he had his attorney bring suit against Harry for the $1,000 deficiency.

112. The $100 per day late charge
- **(A)** Will automatically be enforced because it was bargained for.
- **(B)** Will be enforced only if Harry can prove that he incurred damages of the same amount.

- **(C)** Will not be enforced if such amount is not related to the anticipated or actual damages.
- **(D)** Will not be enforced unless the contract was substantially performed.

113. In the lawsuit seeking the $1,000 deficiency
- **(A)** Paul will not prevail because he cashed the check without reserving rights or otherwise objecting.
- **(B)** Harry will prevail if he can show the $1,000 cash reduction bears a reasonable relationship to the defect in Paul's painting.
- **(C)** Paul will prevail because he has substantially performed.
- **(D)** Harry will prevail because Paul has not substantially performed.

Questions 114 – 116 are based on the following:

Paul Purchaser orally agreed to purchase real property from Larry Landowner for $65,000. Larry asked Paul if he would pay Bill Beneficiary $30,000 to satisfy a prior debt he owed. Paul agreed. Unfortunately, the lawyer who drafted the purchase and sale agreement specified the $65,000 land sale price and description of the property but neglected to include the provision of the $30,000 payment to Bill. Neither Paul nor Larry read the agreement before they signed it.

114. The most important factor in deciding if Bill should prevail against Paul for $30,000 would be whether
- **(A)** Paul was negligent in failing to read the written contract before signing it.
- **(B)** Larry was negligent in failing to read the written contract before signing it.
- **(C)** The Paul Purchaser to Larry Landowner agreement was a complete integration.
- **(D)** Bill was an actual party to the contract.

115. If Bill sues Paul to collect the $30,000 which of the following is (are) correct?

I.   Paul could successfully raise the statute of frauds as a defense because the Larry to Paul agreement was for the sale of land.
II. Paul could successfully raise the statute of frauds as a defense because the Larry to Paul payment agreement was a contract to answer for the debts of another.
(A) I only.
(B) II only.
(C) Both I and II.
(D) Neither I or II.

116. If Bill sues Paul to collect the $30,000, which of the following would best serve Paul as a defense if proved:
(A) Whatever action on the underlying debt Bill may have had against Larry was barred by the statute of limitations prior to the agreement for the property sale.
(B) Before Bill became aware of Paul's agreement with Larry, Paul and Larry agreed that Paul would not pay anything to Bill.
(C) There was no consideration to support the prior agreement of Larry to pay Bill
(D) Before he sued Paul, Bill had not notified either Larry or Paul that he had accepted the agreement they had entered into to retire his debt.

Questions 117 – 119 are based on the following:

Charlie Client hired Laurie Lawyer to prepare an estate plan, a will, and a trust for his family. The written agreement was for $5,000 total to be paid at the end of the engagement. The agreement specified that Laurie would not be liable if she failed to exercise due care or complete the engagement. After Laurie began to draft the will and trust documents, she and Charlie got into a dispute about the operations of the trust and the identity and powers of the trustee. Laurie decided it would be better if she assigned the engagement to another lawyer. Without informing Charlie, Laurie assigned the rest of the engagement to Nathan Newbie who agreed to complete the engagement.

117. Assume that when Charlie learned of the assignment, he informed Nathan he did not want him to continue. Charlie also brought suit against Laurie and requested the court to require Laurie to complete the will and family trust. Will the court grant this request for specific performance?
(A) No, because Laurie effectively delegated her remaining contractual duties to Nathan.
(B) No, because the court will not order specific performance.
(C) Yes, because Laurie has already completed over half the work.
(D) Yes, because Laurie's skill and services are unique.

118. If Charlie brings suit against Laurie for damages
(A) Laurie will prevail because Charlie is partly responsible for the dispute.
(B) Charlie will prevail because Nathan did not assume the primary liability.
(C) Laurie will prevail because the clause in the contract relieves her of any liability.
(D) Charlie will prevail because the clause in the contract relieving Laurie of any liability is exculpatory and not enforceable.

119. Nathan finally completed the estate plan and will but it was quite late and he charged a much larger fee than Charlie had expected to pay. Charlie refused to pay. In addition, the IRS audited the plan and disallowed it. If Charlie brings suit against Nathan,
(A) Charlie will prevail over Nathan on a third party beneficiary theory.

(B) Charlie will prevail over Nathan only if he has privity of contract with Nathan.

(C) Nathan will prevail over Charlie because he is sheltered under the clause relieving Laurie of any liability.

(D) Nathan will prevail over Charlie because Charlie did not pay him.

120.   Jackie Jones was 16 and one-half years of age when she entered into a written two-year contract for the lease of a luxury apartment. The state statute specified the age of majority at 18. At the time Jackie also lived at home with her parents and wanted to use the apartment as a place to meet her lover. Her parents were unaware of the lease. After one year, she broke off the relationship with her lover. She then told the landlord her true age and quit paying the rent. The landlord then requested that Jackie's parents make payment; they refused to pay anything. The landlord then brought suit against both Jackie and her parents for breach of the lease contract. The contract case would be decided against

(A) Both Jackie and her parents.

(B) Jackie only.

(C) Jackie's parents only.

(D) Neither Jackie nor her parents.

Questions 121 – 124 are based on the following:

Fred Farmer owned and actively worked two separate fruit orchards. One 5,000-acre farm was used to grow apples and the other 5,000-acre farm was used to grow grapes. The grapes were sold to wine and juice producers and the grape orchard was more valuable than the apple farm. Wendy Winemaker was an attorney who makes wine as a hobby once a year. She buys all her wine grapes from Fred every fall. In the summer, Wendy visited the wine orchard but Fred was not there. During Fred's annual trip to the city to sell his crops, Fred mentioned to Wendy that he was growing tired of fruit farming and thus was thinking about selling his fruit farm.

Wendy had always wanted to buy a grape orchard of her own and asked if Fred would give her an option for the purchase of the fruit farm so she could attempt to raise the money. Fred was reluctant to tie up his properties but at Wendy's urging he signed an agreement she drew which stated "I hereby agree to sell my fruit farm to Wendy for $500,000. This offer will expire 60 days from date and seller has the right to withdraw it at any time." Wendy orally promised to give Fred $500 for signing and said she would forward him her check covering the option fee when she returned to her home.

Two days after signing the Wendy agreement, Fred's neighbor Bob, who was a real estate broker, called him on the phone. Bob said that he had a customer that was interested in purchasing the fruit farms. Fred said he would sell the grape farm for $750,000 and/or the apple farm for $500,000. Bob said that he would charge a 5% brokerage commission if he could provide a satisfactory buyer. Fred did not reply nor did he mention the previous agreement he had entered into with Wendy.

Later that same day, Bob produced a written offer for both farms at Fred's full asking prices. The buyers had previously made direct offers to Fred. Fred accepted the new offer but refused to sell unless the buyers dealt directly with him without Bob's involvement. The buyers really wanted the farms and agreed. Fred then called Wendy and told her what had occurred. Wendy was very upset because she had just raised the $500,000 she intended to use to buy the grape farm. Wendy refused to send the $500 option fee to Fred.

121.   If Wendy sues Fred, a court would be most likely to hold

(A) The subject of the Fred to Wendy contract was the grape fruit farm.

(B) The subject of the Fred to Wendy contract was the apple fruit farm.

(C) There was no Fred to Wendy contract because no meeting of the minds.

(D) Ambiguity should be construed against Wendy since she drafted the agreement.

122. In the above question, if Fred sues Wendy to receive the $500 option fee what facts will Fred have to allege and prove?

I. That there was a contemporaneous oral agreement.
II. Wendy received a revocable-at-will option to buy the fruit farm.
III. The option was not paid for.

(A) I, II, and III.
(B) I and II but not III.
(C) II and III but not I.
(D) III but not I or II.

123. Wendy's best defense against the suit would be

(A) Fred sold the grape farm to another.
(B) She had an exclusive right to purchase the grape farm for 60 days.
(C) The promise given by Fred was illusory.
(D) Promissory estoppel.

124. If the neighboring broker Bob sues Fred for the 5% brokerage commission, which of the following would provide Fred a viable defense?

I. Fred did not accept the broker's offer.
II. The buyers in question had already contacted Fred and thus no bargained-for consideration supported any alleged express or implied promise to pay a commission.
III. The statute of frauds is violated.

(A) I and II only.
(B) II and III only.
(C) I and III only.
(D) I, II, and III.

125. Alice Attorney prepared a will and estate plan for Carol Client. She delivered the legal documents to Carol on 12/15/X1.

On 12/15/X2 Carol was audited by the Internal Revenue Service and it asserted a large tax deficiency against her because Alice had prepared the will and estate plan in a negligent manner. Alice left the state for 2 years from 12/15/X3 until 12/15/X5. On 12/15/X7 Carol filed suit against Alice for malpractice. The state statute of limitations specifies a three-year period of time for negligence. Carol's suit was

(A) Filed timely because the statute of limitations was tolled and only triggered on discovery.
(B) Not filed timely because it was six years after the will and estate plan were delivered
(C) Filed timely because there is no statute of limitations applicable to clients bringing a malpractice suit against an attorney.
(D) Not filed timely because it was five years after the IRS asserted the tax deficiency.

Questions 126 and 127 are based on the following:

Harry Hotrod-Homeowner contracted with Mike Mechanic to replace the motor in his antique automobile for $2,500 cash due upon completion of the installation. He had purchased an expensive racing motor to soup-up the car and hoped to create his own street hot rod. He also contracted with Sarah Sider to install aluminum siding on his existing home. The siding price was $3,000 cash payable in three equal installments of $1,000 each. The first installment was due at the signing of the contract, the second half way through the job, and the final third due upon completion of the job. Before the engine work began, the antique automobile was stolen. Harry bought a different antique automobile and demanded that Mike install the racing motor in it. Mike refused.

Sarah began siding the house and was 80% of the way completed when a fire burned the house to the ground. The fire had been set by juvenile delinquents from the neighborhood;

the fire department was unable to get there in time. At the time of the fire, Harry had paid Sarah $2,000 of the $3,000 contract price.

126. If litigation develops between Harry and Mike over the racing motor installation in either Harry's new or old automobile, the likely outcome is
- (A) Harry will be entitled to an order of specific performance, which would require Mike to install the racing motor in the new automobile.
- (B) Harry will be entitled to money damages if the cost to hire another mechanic to install the racing motor exceeds the cost at which Mike agreed to make the installation.
- (C) Mike does not have to install the racing motor in the new automobile and is not liable for damages for failing to install the racing motor in the first automobile.
- (D) Mike either has to install the racing motor in the new automobile or is liable for failing to install the racing motor in the first automobile.

127. If litigation develops between Harry and Sarah over the siding contract, the likely outcome is:
- (A) Harry is entitled to a return of the $2,000 he paid Sarah.
- (B) Harry is entitled to a return of $500 since both parties share equally if the subject matter is destroyed.
- (C) Sarah is entitled to the last $1,000 under the contract since she was not responsible for the fire.
- (D) Sarah is entitled to be paid $400 more from Harry under the contract.

128. David Debtor approached Bountiful Bank and requested a loan to start a new business selling books over the Internet. The loan officer issued a written "preliminary loan commitment" based upon the splendid business plan David had submitted. David was very excited and with the bank's knowledge began to hire Java and C++ programmers. One month later, the loan

officer learned that all of David's experience was in store-based retail book sales; not sales over the Internet. He wrote David telling him the Bank had decided against making the loan. If David Debtor brings suit against Bountiful Bank, David's recovery would likely:
- (A) Be denied because the final loan documents had not been executed before the bank changed their mind about making the business loan.
- (B) Include the profit the business would have made for a reasonable period of time to be determined by expert testimony.
- (C) Be limited to David's out-of-pocket expenses.
- (D) Include both David's out-of-pocket expenses and the profit the business would have made for a reasonable period of time to be determined by expert testimony.

129. Bob Breeder bred golden retrievers. He ran an advertisement in a local newspaper under the category of "Pets For Sale." Patty Petowner saw the newspaper advertisement and called Bob on the phone to get his address. She then went to his house and looked at the golden retriever pups. Bob said that he would sell one of the four pups for $400 cash but that the sale had to take place in the next 10 days. Patty went to other breeders and looked at a number of other pups after she left Bob's. Five days later, she called Bob and said she wanted to purchase one of the pups. Bob only had one left at that time and had promised it to his mother. Rather than explain this to Patty, he just said that all the golden retriever pups had been sold. Patty found out from a neighbor that Bob still had one pup left and she brought a lawsuit to either recover monetary damages or secure an order of specific performance. The court will likely
- (A) Grant the request for an order of specific performance because Bob was untruthful.
- (B) Allow the award of money damages so that Bob can give the last pup to his mother.

(C) Deny Patty any recovery because Bob's promise was a mere invitation to deal.

(D) Deny Patty any recovery because Bob terminated the offer.

130. Alice Actress contracted to direct and star in a Broadway play in New York. The financiers were very hopeful the play would be a big hit and that they could syndicate the theme for a television series. Alice signed a $600,000 agreement paying her $50,000 per month for a minimum of 12 months acting and directing. The first two payments of $100,000 were given to her at signing. Three months later when she was owed $450,000 for the last nine months she assigned her rights to Albert Assignee as consideration for the purchase of his home. She then assigned the same right to her favorite nephew as a gift. Subsequently she assigned the same rights to First National Bank as additional collateral for a loan she owed the Bank from a previous year. All three assignees are requesting the financiers pay them the $450,000 executory balance on the Alice contract. As between the parties which of the following most accurately describes their respective rights?

(A) Albert Assignee has a priority because this was the first assignment the promisee made.

(B) First National Bank has a priority because the date they made the loan predates both Alice's gift to Alice's nephew and her home purchase.

(C) All three assignees will share the funds in an amount their obligation bears to the total of the three obligations.

(D) None of the three assignees will have any claim to the funds due Alice from the financiers of the Broadway play.

Questions 131 and 132 are based on the following:

In Everycity, USA, a number of prominent local attorneys decided to start a law school. They approached a very hard working and well-published law school professor at the Ivy League Law School and orally inquired if she would be interested in becoming the Dean if the American Bar Association approved the law school's accreditation application. Dorothy Dean-to-be said yes and accepted their offer of employment to be the new Dean.

131. The promise by the organizers of the law school is:

(A) Fully enforceable without any conditions.

(B) Not enforceable because the promise is illusory.

(C) Not enforceable because there is no valid consideration given by both parties.

(D) Enforceable as a conditional promise.

132. In the above fact pattern, assume the American Bar Association approved the Law School. However during the accreditation process, one member of the accrediting committee recommended an experienced Dean that she knew was looking for a new law school. The organizers reviewed the experienced Dean's credentials and publications. They concluded that in an overall review, the new applicant was substantially superior to Dorothy Dean-to-be. They thus hired the new candidate and informed Dorothy Dean-to-be that they were sorry but that they had changed their minds. If Dorothy brings suit against the organizers and the new law school, their best defense is:

(A) The Statute of Frauds.

(B) The promise did not become final until the American Bar Association approved or disapproved the new law school and then the organizers had discretion to accept or not accept her as the Dean.

(C) Dorothy Dean-to-be did not detrimentally rely upon the organizer's promise by giving her current law school notice of her resignation.

(D) Dorothy Dean-to-be was a career law school professor; she was thus a merchant in these matters, and as such she impliedly warranted her credentials were merchantable and would be accepted by everyone.

Questions 133 – 135 are based on the following:

Larry Landlord owned a retail shopping center in which Teresa Tenant wanted to establish a yogurt shop. Her plan was to market the yogurt heavily among the other tenants in the shopping center. Teresa did not believe there was enough demand in the shopping center to support two yogurt outlets. In their negotiations, she and Larry orally agreed that Teresa would have an exclusive right to sell yogurt in the shopping center. Unfortunately Larry forgot to include the exclusive sales provision in the written lease which contained a merger and integration clause. Teresa signed the lease without reading it and she assumed that Larry had included the exclusive provision condition.

Teresa opened her yogurt shop, which was an immediate success. The shop proved to be quite profitable. Six months later, Larry rented an adjacent space to a fast food restaurant named McDaisey. McDaisey began selling a yogurt dessert to go for a price considerably below the price Teresa was charging. This caused a significant drop in the business of Teresa's yogurt shop; the previously profitable operation turned into a break-even situation.

133. If Teresa asserts a claim for damages against Larry, the oral agreement concerning the exclusive right given Teresa to sell yogurt in the shopping center:
- **(A)** Would be excluded by the parol evidence rule.
- **(B)** Would be excluded by the merger and integration clause.
- **(C)** Would be excluded because the negotiations occurred before the lease was signed.
- **(D)** Would not be excluded.

134. If Larry can introduce evidence that Teresa agreed that McDaisey's could sell a yogurt desert to go, Larry's attorney would argue that:
- **(A)** A waiver of the condition has occurred.
- **(B)** A cancellation of the condition has occurred.
- **(C)** A release of the condition has occurred.
- **(D)** A repudiation of the condition has occurred.

135. If Teresa desires to continue operating the yogurt shop under the exclusive agreement, she would request:
- **(A)** Reformation.
- **(B)** Reformation and damages.
- **(C)** Rescission.
- **(D)** Rescission and damages.

Question 136 and 137 are based on the following:

Bertha Basketball was a very successful personal injury attorney who received a multi-million dollar fee after winning a big case. She decided to purchase a basketball team, but her CPA convinced her the risk was very high and that a lease agreement would minimize this risk. The lease contract she entered into with Slippery Seller to purchase the Othello Ordinary Boomers Basketball team contained a provision that if the team did not win at least half their games in the next season, the lease would terminate.

After Bertha assumed management of the Boomers team, she began to make improvements including firing the existing coach and hiring a winning coach named Wally Winner. The Wally contract provided for a penalty of $500 per game that the team lost if Wally quit before the end of the season. Wally coached for 4 weeks and won 10 out of the first 12 games but got into frequent disagreements with Bertha. Wally then left to coach another team and Bertha hired another coach to complete the season. The new coach was not proficient enough to sustain the winning momentum and the team began to lose. With one game left to go the win-loss record was 24-24. Unfortunately, the Othello Boomers lost their last game of the season.

136. If Bertha sues Wally for the penalty sum of $1,000, the likely outcome is
  (A) For Wally because penalties are not enforceable.
  (B) For Bertha because penalties are enforceable.
  (C) For Wally because Bertha can show no actual damages.
  (D) For Bertha because Wally intentionally breached the contract.

137. If Bertha sues Slippery Seller seeking to terminate the lease, the likely outcome is
  (A) For Slippery, because if Bertha would have been nicer to Wally he would have stayed and the team would have won over half their games.
  (B) For Bertha, because the condition subsequent occurred.
  (C) For Slippery, because Bertha's liquidated damage provision was her sole remedy.
  (D) For Bertha, because having the same coach complete the basketball season was an implied condition of the lease contract.

Questions 138 – 140 are based on the following:

In Miami there was a rash of armed robberies conducted by a gang. The robberies resulted in injuries to bank guards and large monetary losses. A syndicate of private commercial banks hired an expert ex-FBI investigator named Frank Forensic to apprehend the criminals. Frank was paid $1,000 per week.

Two months later, the robberies were becoming more frequent and beginning to adversely affect tourism. The city government began to be pressured and placed a series of prominent newspaper advertisements offering a $50,000 reward for information leading to the arrest and conviction of the gang. One month later, Frank's effort finally paid off and he identified the gang leader. He then reported the information to the police where he learned of the reward. Frank's reporting led to arrests and convictions of many of the gang, but the city refused to pay him the $50,000 reward.

138. If Frank sues the city and the City wins the lawsuit, the best reason would likely be
  (A) Frank was under a pre-existing duty to perform and thus there was no consideration to support the promise.
  (B) Frank was compensated by the bankers and it would be inequitable and against public policy to allow him to be compensated twice for the same performance.
  (C) Frank failed to communicate his acceptance to the offerror before performance.
  (D) Frank did not know of the reward at the time of his performance.

139. If Frank wins his suit against the City, the best reason would likely be
  (A) City's $50,000 advertisement was in essence a bounty so contract formalities were not necessary.
  (B) The City realized substantial benefit from Frank's efforts and therefore an in quasi contract recovery should be imposed.
  (C) To not reward Frank would discourage citizens from assisting the City in the future.
  (D) Frank's compensation from the private bankers was only $12,000, which was significantly below the $50,000 City reward.

140. Assume for this question only that Frank read the newspaper advertisement that referred to the $50,000 reward. Assume also that the following week, the City government had a number of complaints from the public that City resources should not be used to subsidize commercial banks. Based upon this criticism they revoked the offer by including the revocation in two public service announcements on a local radio station, which Frank did not hear. The best statement of the status of the offer's revocation is

(A) The offer was revoked.

(B) The revocation was ineffective because it did not use the same or comparable publicity as the offer.

(C) A public service announcement is effective because the City is a governmental unit.

(D) The revocation was ineffective because it did not use exactly the same means of communication as the offer.

141. Debbie Dwelling wanted to sell her home and decided to run an advertisement in the local newspaper. Her neighbor, Nancy Nextdoor, had always wanted to buy Debbie's home. Nancy, without being aware of the pending advertisement signed and posted a letter offering to pay Debbie $100,000 for the house. The next day Debbie wrote Nancy stating that she had the house for sale for $100,000. Was a valid contract formed between Debbie and Nancy?

(A) No, because the statute of frauds requires that both parties to a property transaction must sign the same writing.

(B) No, because there were two crossing offers and no acceptance; thus there was no mutual assent.

(C) Yes, because Nancy's letter constituted acceptance of the offer contained within the newspaper advertisement.

(D) Yes, because Debbie's letter constituted acceptance of the offer contained within Nancy's letter.

Questions 142 – 144 are based on the following:

Paula Painter and Harriet Homeowner entered into a written agreement in which Paula agreed to paint the exterior of Harriet's home for $8,000 payable at $2,000 per side. The contract stated it was the parties' final integrated agreement and could only be amended in a writing signed by both parties. When Paula had painted three sides of the house and had been paid $6,000, she informed Harriet that a shortage of painters made it impossible for her to complete the job for the final $2,000 and that it would cost an additional $500. Harriet, believing it would be impossible to get another painter to do only one side of her home, agreed to pay the extra $500. After the house painting was completed, Harriet paid the $2,000 but refused to pay the $500 on the basis there was no consideration for the promise and that it violated the parol evidence rule.

142. Paula is least likely to recover the additional $500 if she attempts to show that the parties intended to

(A) Ensure completion of the original contract.

(B) Establish new duties for Paula.

(C) Rescind the original agreement.

(D) Enter into a novation.

143. Will Harriet's defense of the parol evidence rule prevail?

(A) Yes, because the oral agreement changed an essential term of the original painting contract.

(B) No, because the oral promise was subsequent to the integrated agreement.

(C) Yes, because the subsequent oral promise was not in writing.

(D) No, because the painting contract was divisible.

144. Paula's worst argument to collect the additional $500 would be based on the fact

(A) Harriet could have hired another painter to complete the job so there was no economic duress.

(B) The main reason the parties entered into the contract was for the paint rather than the labor.

(C) Paula would not have completed the job if she had known Harriet would not pay the $500.

(D) When Harriet made the promise to pay the $500 she was aware that Paula would hire new employees in reliance on the promise.

145. Acme Manufacturing purchased manufacturing equipment from National Equipment. They took physical possession of the goods on December 1st. On January 2nd they discovered the goods did not conform to the contract specifications and therefore sent National Equipment notice that they were formally rejecting the goods. The buyer must

(A) Do nothing if it is not a merchant.

(B) Hold the goods for a reasonable time sufficient to permit the seller to remove them.

(C) Reship the goods to the seller at the seller's expense.

(D) Reship the goods to the seller at his (the buyer's) expense.

146. Joseph Manufacturing Inc. received an order from Raulings Supply Company for certain valves it manufactured. The order demanded immediate shipment. Which of the following is a correct method of acceptance?

(A) Joseph can accept only by prompt shipment since this was the unambiguous manner indicated in the order.

(B) The order is construed as an offer to enter into either a unilateral or bilateral contract and Joseph may accept by a promise of or actual prompt shipment.

(C) If Joseph promptly ships the goods, Raulings must be notified within a reasonable time.

(D) Joseph may accept by mail, but he must make prompt shipment.

147. Magna Drug Company developed and patented a new cancer drug named "Anti-Cancer." Magna's first customer was Everystreet Drug Stores. Everystreet and Magna signed a written agreement to purchase and sell "all the amount of Anti-Cancer pills that Everystreet Drug Stores will require for the next two years at a price of $250.00 per 100 pills. Magna agrees to produce a minimum of 2,000 pills per month. Any modification to this agreement must be in writing."

One year later, demand for Anti-Cancer took off and Magna had many more customers than it could supply. Magna called Everystreet and stated that they were raising the price to $300 per 100 pills. Everystreet orally agreed to pay the higher price for its next order of 400 pills. Magna shipped the pills and an invoice for $1,200. Everystreet remitted its check for $1,000. If Magna sues for the $200 balance, the most helpful defense Everystreet can assert is

(A) UCC Article 2 requires that the modification be written and signed by Magna.

(B) The Parol Evidence Rule will not allow admission of the modifications.

(C) The modification of the price will fail because it was not supported by consideration.

(D) The modification was void because the Statute of Frauds applies to goods sales contracts exceeding $500.

148. Certain oral contracts fall outside the Statute of Frauds. An example would be an oral contract between

(A) A creditor and a friend of the debtor, providing for the friend's guaranty of the debt in exchange for the creditor's binding extension of time for payment of the debt.

(B) A landlord and a tenant for the lease of land for ten years.

(C) A school board and a teacher entered into on January 1st, for nine months of service to begin on September 1st.

(D) A retail seller of television sets and a buyer of a TV set for $399 C.O.D.

149. Harriet Homeowner commissioned Wanda Windowmaker to redo two large windows in the living room of her home. The job involved removing the wooden window frames and putting custom made stained glass in the frames. Harriet agreed to pay $750 for both windows, but Harriet was not obligated to pay if not satisfied with the windows. As Wanda was installing the windows, Harriet decided she did not like the design. Although the windows were built in a workmanlike manner, Harriet rejected them. If Wanda brings suit for the $750, the best defense Harriet could raise is

(A) The offer for the two windows was unilateral.

(B) The contract was for over $500 and not in writing as required by the statute of frauds.

(C) The windows might be saleable to another buyer who wanted that type of stained glass windows.

(D) The condition precedent of Harriet's satisfaction was not met.

Questions 150 and 151 are based on the following:

Roger Ready was a young law student sitting for the bar exam. To encourage Roger to study harder for the exam, Roger's favorite Uncle Harry promised to give Roger $200,000 the day after he sat for the bar. Pretty Porsche, Inc., sold expensive sports cars. Roger went into Pretty Porsche's showroom and ordered a brand new model "Super Car" for $90,000, paying $10,000 down with the balance due on delivery. Pretty Porsche ordered the Porsche as soon as Roger placed the order. Roger also ordered a custom made stereo system from

Good Sound, Inc., for $30,000. Good Sound ordered the stereo system components and began the assembly process as soon as Roger placed the order. Roger subsequently got mono and had to drop out of his bar review class. His Uncle Harry told Roger the $200,000 gift would not be forthcoming.

150. Roger called Pretty and told them he was canceling the order and would like his $10,000 deposit back. Pretty refused to make a refund so Roger filed a lawsuit for restitution. Pretty filed a counterclaim. Pretty's wholesale purchase cost for the "Super Car" model was $65,000 and it accurately allocated $4,000 per car for related overhead expenses. While Pretty was able to sell the car to another car buyer at full price, they did have to pay an additional $6,000 commission to facilitate the sale to the other buyer. The court should decide the lawsuit by awarding

(A) For Roger in an amount of the $10,000 he paid Pretty because the seller should not make a double profit.

(B) For Roger in a net amount of $9,500 calculated as the $10,000 he paid as a deposit less $500 deposit which is deemed forfeited on the buyer's repudiation.

(C) For Pretty in a net amount of $15,000.

(D) For Pretty in a net amount of $25,000.

151. Roger also called Good Sound, Inc., informing them he lacked the money to pay for the $30,000 stereo system they were assembling and thus was canceling the order. Good Sound is a client of your law firm and immediately asked you for advice. Good Sound has spent $12,000 on raw materials, which it could sell immediately for parts for $10,000. It could also complete the production process, which would cost $15,000 additional. They have asked you whether they can complete the production and still look to Roger to collect all their damages. Your answer is

(A) Yes, because the seller is the aggrieved party and thus entitled to all damages from the breach.
(B) No, if the proceeds from the sale of the completed system are less than $25,000.
(C) No, but Sound is entitled to a judgment against Roger for $12,000 reliance interest.
(D) No, but Sound is entitled to a judgment against Roger for $12,000 reliance interest and $1.00 for nominal damages.

152.   Barbara Murphy was a purchasing agent for a hydrorail shipping company who desired to purchase a crane that could lift 10-ton containers. She explained these requirements to the salesman in the showroom of the regional crane distributor. The salesman recommended a particular model that would satisfy Murphy's purpose. Murphy signed the sales contract that did not mention the purpose for which the crane was going to be used. Subsequently, the crane broke in lifting a 7-ton container. Under the circumstances:
(A) Murphy cannot recover against the seller because the representation was not in writing.
(B) The seller will prevail because the parol evidence rule will prohibit introduction of any prior or contemporaneous statements that contradict the terms of the final written agreement.
(C) Murphy will prevail under an implied warranty theory only if she can prove the seller knew of the reliance.
(D) Murphy could not collect if the seller was a non-merchant/casual seller.

153.   Ace Auto Sales, Inc., sold Williams a secondhand car for $9,000. One day Williams parked the car in a shopping center parking lot. When Williams returned to the car, Montrose and several policemen were waiting. It turned out that the car had been stolen from Montrose who was rightfully claiming ownership. Williams subsequently returned the car to Montrose. Williams seeks recourse against Ace Auto Sales who had sold him the car with the usual disclaimer of warranty. Which of the following is correct?
(A) Since Ace Auto Sales' contract of sale disclaimed "any and all warranties" arising in connection with its sale to Williams, Williams must bear the loss.
(B) Since Ace Auto and Williams were both innocent of any wrongdoing in connection with the theft of the auto, the loss will rest upon the party ultimately in possession.
(C) Had Williams litigated the question of Montrose's ownership to the auto, he would have won since possession is nine-tenths of the law.
(D) Ace Auto will bear the loss since a warranty of title in Williams' favor arose upon the sale of the auto.

154.   Gold sold Sable ten fur coats. The contract contained no specific provision regarding title warranties. It did, however, contain a provision that indicated the coats were sold "with all faults and defects." Two of the coats sold to Sable had been stolen and were reclaimed by the rightful owner. Which of the following is a correct statement?
(A) The implied warranty of title is eliminated by the parol evidence rule.
(B) The contract automatically contained a warranty that the title conveyed is good and can only be excluded by specific language.
(C) Since there was no express title warranty, Sable assumed the risk.
(D) The disclaimer "with all faults and defects" effectively negates any and all warranties.

155.   Webster purchased a drill press for $475 from Martinson Hardware, Inc. The press has proved to be defective and Webster wishes to rescind the purchase based upon a

breach of implied warranty. Which of the following will preclude Webster's recovery from Martinson?

(A) The press sold to Webster was a demonstration model and sold at a substantial discount; hence, Webster received no implied warranties.

(B) Webster examined the press carefully, but in regard to the defects, they were hidden and a reasonable examination would not have revealed them.

(C) Martinson informed Webster that they were closing out the model at a loss due to certain product deficiencies and that the drill press was sold "with all faults."

(D) The fact that it was the negligence of the manufacturer which caused the trouble and that the defect could not have been discovered by Martinson without actually taking the press apart.

Questions 156 and 157 are based on the following:

Connie Contractor agreed to build a deluxe custom garden for Harry Homeowner for a flat price of $5,000. Connie began to craft the garden areas and plant as per their preliminary plan. Harry wanted an active hand in the project and kept changing the layout and preliminary plans. Connie became progressively more discouraged and told Harry he should make a final decision on the plan and leave her and the workers alone. Harry refused and Connie became so emotionally distraught that she could not complete the work with Harry's continual interference. At the time she left the job she had not substantially performed, but an appraiser said her work was valued at $4,000. Harry had paid Connie $2,500. Harry hired Mary Mellow to complete the garden at a cost of $2,000.

156. If Harry sues Connie for breach of contract, the likely outcome of the suit is that Harry will

(A) Prevail because Connie breached the contract when she pulled off the garden job.

(B) Not prevail because his involvement was the cause of the incapacity of the personal service contractor.

(C) Not prevail because he breached an implied condition of cooperation.

(D) Prevail because the total job cost him more than the $5,000 contractual amount.

157. If Connie sues Harry, the likely outcome is that

(A) Not prevail since she breached the contract and failed to render substantial performance.

(B) Prevail for emotional distress or outrage.

(C) Prevail for only a nominal amount since what she had been paid plus what Harry paid the new contractor exceeded the original contract price.

(D) Prevail for $1,500.

158. Hack Company owned 100 tires, which it deposited in a public warehouse on April 25th, receiving a negotiable warehouse receipt in its name. Hack sold the tires to Fast Freight Co. On which of the following dates did the risk of loss transfer from Hack to Fast?

(A) May 1st – Fast signed a contract to buy the tires from Hack for $15,000. Delivery was to be at the warehouse.

(B) May 2nd – Fast paid for the tires.

(C) May 3rd – Hack negotiated the warehouse receipt to Fast.

(D) May 4th – Fast received delivery of the tires at the warehouse.

159. In deciding a controversy involving the question of who has the risk of loss in goods, the court will look primarily to

(A) The intent of the parties manifested in the contract.

(B) The shipping terms used by the parties.

(C) Whether title has passed.

(D) The insurance coverage of the parties.

160. Stan Seller was selling goods to Bryan Buyer with the goods to be transported by ship. The goods had been properly left on the dock alongside the vessel to be used for shipping the goods to the buyer. The crane used to load the goods from the dock to the ship was old and in need of repair. A new and inexperienced crane operator picked up too heavy a load too quickly. This resulted in the crane breaking and the goods falling in the water. As between the seller and the buyer, the liability for the loss will be on

(A) The seller, if the shipment terms are FAS shipping point.

(B) The buyer, who bears the risk and expense.

(C) The seller and buyer, each will be 50% responsible for the loss.

(D) Neither the seller nor the buyer, since the crane breaking was an unforeseeable event excusing contract performance.

161. A sailboat dealer was negotiating to buy two sailboats. The first was being sold by a yacht manufacturer and the second by a private seller. The dealer/buyer was contacted by both sellers and told that both boats were ready to be picked up in the early afternoon. The buyer decided that it would be more convenient to pick them up the next morning. A storm destroyed both sailboats later that evening. Assuming no insurance coverage, the risk of loss would be

(A) Borne by both the buyer and seller on a 50/50 basis.

(B) Borne by both sellers because they had physical control over the boats.

(C) Borne by the private seller and the dealer/buyer.

(D) Borne by the yacht manufacturer and the dealer/buyer.

162. A wholesaler wants to provide his retailer with inventory on credit but has learned that the customer is in financial trouble. One of his salesmen reported that the retailer may have lien creditors and judgment creditors who could levy on the inventory. Under the circumstances, the wholesaler might be best advised to

(A) Ship the goods on a "sale or return" basis.

(B) Make sure the retailer signs an agreement that he will not give the inventory to third parties until he has paid for the goods.

(C) Ship the goods on a "sale on approval" basis.

(D) File a financing statement within 20 days of the retailer receiving the goods.

163. Gibbeon Manufacturing shipped 300 designer navy blue blazers to Custom Clothing Emporium. The blazers arrived on Friday, earlier than Custom had anticipated and on an exceptionally busy day for its receiving department. They were perfunctorily examined and sent to a nearby warehouse for storage until needed. On Monday of the following week, upon closer examination, it was discovered that the quality of the linings of the blazers was inferior to that specified in the sales contract. Which of the following is correct insofar as Custom's rights are concerned?

(A) Custom can reject the blazers upon subsequent discovery of the defects unless the goods have substantially changed.

(B) Custom must retain the blazers since it accepted them and had an opportunity to inspect them upon delivery.

(C) Custom's only course of action is rescission.

(D) Custom had no rights if the linings were of merchantable quality.

164. A dispute has arisen between two merchants over the question of who has the risk of loss in a given sales transaction. The contract does not specifically cover the point. The goods were shipped to the buyer who rightfully rejected them. Which of the following factors will be the most important factor in resolving their dispute?

(A) Who has title to the goods.
(B) The shipping terms.
(C) The credit terms.
(D) The fact that a breach has occurred.

165. Barstow Hardware Company received an order for $850 of assorted hardware from Flanagan & Company. The shipping terms were F.O.B. Mannix Freight Line, seller's place of business, 2/10, net/30. Barstow packed and crated the hardware for shipment and it was loaded upon Mannix Freight's truck. While the goods were in transit to Flanagan, Barstow learned that Flanagan was insolvent in the equity sense (unable to pay its debts in the ordinary course of business).

Barstow wrote Flanagan asking them for assurances they could pay on time. Receiving no answer for a month, Barstow promptly wired Mannix Freight's office in Pueblo, Colorado, and instructed them to stop shipment of the goods to Flanagan and to store them and await for further instructions. Mannix complied with these instructions. Regarding the rights, duties, and liabilities of the parties, which of the following is correct?
(A) Barstow's stoppage in transit was improper if Flanagan's assets exceeded its liabilities.
(B) Flanagan is entitled to the hardware if it pays cash.
(C) Once Barstow correctly learned of Flanagan's insolvency, it had no further duty or obligation to Flanagan.
(D) The fact that Flanagan became insolvent in no way affects the rights, duties, and obligations of the parties.

166. Dey ordered 100 cases of Fancy Brand carrots at list price from Ned Wholesaler. Immediately upon receipt of Dey's order, Ned sent Dey an acceptance which was received by Dey. The acceptance indicated that shipment would be made within seven days. On the seventh day Ned discovered that all of its supply of Fancy Brand carrots had been sold. Instead it shipped 100 cases of Rabbit Brand, stating clearly on the invoice that the shipment was sent only as an accommodation. Which of the following is correct?
(A) Ned's note of accommodation cancels the contract between Ned and Dey.
(B) Dey's order is a unilateral offer, and can only be accepted by Ned's shipment of the goods ordered.
(C) Ned's shipment of Rabbit Brand constitutes a breach of contract.
(D) Ned's shipment of Rabbit Brand is a counteroffer, thus no contract exists between Dey and Ned.

167. Dodd Company sold Barney & Company 10,000 ball-point pens. The shipment, upon inspection, was found to be nonconforming and Barney rejected the pens. Barney purchased the pens elsewhere at $525 over the contract price. The Dodd sales contract contained a clause that purported to reduce the statute of limitations provision of the Uniform Commercial Code to one year. Barney has done nothing about the breach except return the pens and demand payment of the $525 damages. Dodd has totally ignored Barney's claim. The statute of limitations
(A) Is four years according to the Uniform Commercial Code and can not be reduced by the original agreement.
(B) Will totally bar recovery unless suit is commenced within the time specified in the contract.
(C) May be extended by the parties but not beyond five years.
(D) Can not be reduced by the parties to a period less than two years.

168. On February 15th, Mazur Corp. contracted to sell 1,000 bushels of wheat to Good Bread, Inc. at $6.00 per bushel with delivery to be made on June 23rd. On June 1st, Good advised Mazur that it would not accept or pay for the wheat. On June 2nd, Mazur sold the wheat to another customer at the market price of $5.00 per bushel. Mazur had advised Good that it intended to resell the wheat. Which of the following statements is correct?

(A) Mazur can successfully sue Good for the difference between the resale price and the contract price.

(B) Mazur can resell the wheat only after June 23rd.

(C) Good can retract its anticipatory breach at any time before June 23rd.

(D) Good can successfully sue Mazur for specific performance.

169. Smith contracted in writing to sell Peters a used personal computer for $600. The contract did not specifically address the time for payment, place of delivery, or Peters' right to inspect the computer. Which of the following statements is correct?

(A) Smith is obligated to deliver the computer to Peters' home.

(B) Peters is entitled to inspect the computer before paying for it.

(C) Peters may not pay for the computer using a personal check unless Smith agrees.

(D) Smith is not entitled to payment until 30 days after Peters receives the computer.

170. Under the UCC Sales Article 2, which of the following statements is correct concerning a contract involving a merchant seller and a non-merchant buyer?

(A) Whether the UCC Sales Article 2 is applicable does not depend on the price of the goods involved.

(B) Only the seller is obligated to perform the contract in good faith.

(C) The contract will be either a sale or return or sale on approval contract.

(D) The contract may not involve the sale of personal property with a price of more than $500.

171. Larch Corp. manufactured and sold Mr. and Mrs. Oak a stove. The sale documents included a disclaimer of warranty for personal injury. The stove was defective. It exploded causing serious injuries and death to Oak's spouse. Larch was notified one

week after the explosion. Under the UCC Sales Article 2, which of the following statements concerning Larch's liability for personal injury and death to Oak's spouse would be correct?

(A) Larch cannot be liable because of a lack of privity with Oak's spouse.

(B) Larch will not be liable because of a failure to give proper notice.

(C) Larch will be liable because the disclaimer was not a disclaimer of all liability.

(D) Larch will be liable because liability for personal injury cannot be disclaimed.

172. Quick Corp. agreed to purchase 200 typewriters from Union Suppliers, Inc. Union is a wholesaler of appliances and Quick is an appliance retailer. The contract required Union to ship the typewriters to Quick by common carrier, "F.O.B. Union Suppliers, Inc. Loading Dock." Which of the parties bears the risk of loss during shipment?

(A) Union, because the risk of loss passes only when Quick receives the typewriters.

(B) Union, because both parties are merchants.

(C) Quick, because title to the typewriters passed to Quick at the time of shipment.

(D) Quick, because the risk of loss passes when the typewriters are delivered to the carrier.

173. On January 1st Barbara Buyer and Sarah Seller entered into a written contract to buy and sell 300 units of widgets on February 28th at $5.00 per unit. On January 15th the market price rose to $6.00 per unit. On February 1st the market price rose to $7.00 per unit. Sarah then wrote to Barbara and stated, "I am not going to deliver the widgets due on February 28th." Barbara wrote back to Sarah and stated "I know you have repudiated your contract but hope you will reconsider before the due date of February 28th." Sarah refused to reconsider and Barbara finally purchased substitute goods at $9.00 per unit on February 28th. If Barbara brings suit on March 10th when the price was $8.00 per unit, which of the following would constitute the market price of the widgets for purposes of computing damages would be

(A) $5.00 per unit as of the contract date.

(B) $7.00 per unit as of the contract repudiation date.

(C) $8.00 per unit if Sarah did not respond to Barbara's request for her to reconsider the repudiation.

(D) $9.00 per unit as of the date the buyer purchased substitute equivalent goods.

174.   Under the Sales Article 2 of the UCC, which of the following statements is correct?

(A) The obligations of the parties to the contract must be performed in good faith.

(B) Merchants and non-merchants are treated alike.

(C) The contract must involve the sale of goods for a price of more than $500.

(D) None of the provisions of the UCC may be disclaimed by agreement.

175.   Roberta Right decided to purchase inventory from Walter Wholesaler. Walter demanded that Roberta make a deposit payment of one-half of any order. Roberta ordered $2,000 of inventory and included her check for $1,000 in the mailed purchase order. It was not possible to deliver the goods. Assuming neither party is interested in claiming damages against the other, to what refund amount is Roberta entitled?

(A) $1,000 if the Roberta is categorized as a consumer.

(B) $600 regardless of the merchant status of a Roberta or Walter.

(C) $500 because the UCC specifies that this is the maximum deposit amount due to the buyer.

(D) Zero if both parties are deemed to be merchants.

Questions 176 and 177 are based on the following:

Larry Lessee was in the pizza restaurant business. He had a number of stores in the metropolitan area and desired to locate a new store in a mall being built by David Developer. David and Larry entered into a lease agreement for 5 years for 4,000 square feet of space in the new wing of the mall. Larry hired an architect to design the planned pizza restaurant and paid $10,000 for the plans. Larry also hired a new restaurant manager to supervise the pizza restaurant. Just before the mall was to open David changed his mind and decided to lease the space to another pizza operator.

176.   If Larry Lessee seeks an order of specific performance against David Developer, the likely outcome is that the order should

(A) Issue because the subject of the contract was unique.

(B) Not issue if there were other shopping malls in the neighborhood with space available for a pizza restaurant.

(C) Not issue because a court will not issue an order a party not to breach a contract.

(D) Issue because the lease agreement is not a personal service contract.

177.   Not only did David Developer refuse to allow Larry Lessee to open his pizza restaurant, but two months later he also rented space to two other competitive pizza restaurants. Given this level of competition in the area, Larry decided to terminate his search for a location in the neighborhood. In addition to the $10,000 fee paid the architect, he paid the new manager $3,000 a month for two months. His CPA calculated that $12,000 profits would have been earned in the next four months before the other two restaurants opened. If Larry sues David for damages, he will likely recover

(A) -0- because the restaurant never began operations.

(B) $10,000 unless the architectural plans could be used in another location.

(C) $16,000 unless the new manager was overpaid or should be working in one of Larry's other restaurants.

(D) $28,000 if the loss of future profits are established with reasonable certainty.

178. An owner of goods has put them up for auction. The terms of the auction are "with reserve." This implies

(A) The auctioneer must accept the highest bid even if less than the seller desires.

(B) That the goods may be converted to "without reserve" during the auction.

(C) A bid is irrevocable once made.

(D) The goods may be withdrawn before the completion of the auction.

Questions 179 and 180 are based on the following:

Apple Farms entered into an agreement with Cider Bottling in which Cider Bottling agreed to buy all of the apples it needed for its next year's bottling operation. Apple Farms for its part agreed to sell all the output from its fall harvest that Cider Bottling would need to keep its bottling plant at full capacity through the end of the next year. One month before the apples were to be harvested, Mega Growers, Inc. approached Cider Bottling and offered to sell them their apples for 10% less than Apple Farm's agreed upon price. Cider Bottling agreed to buy at least some of their requirements from Mega.

179. The Apple Farm to Cider Bottling agreement was a

(A) A requirement, output, and exclusive dealings contract.

(B) A requirement and output contract.

(C) A requirement contract.

(D) An output contract.

180. Apple Farm is very upset about Cider Bottling's plan to purchase some of their requirements from Mega Growers. They have come to your law office and asked about their remedies. Apple believes that they could sell their output elsewhere but at a substantially lower price due to the fact that most of the bottlers have already made their purchase agreements. They would like you to seek an injunction to block Mega from selling to Cider Bottling. Your legal advice to Apple Farm is

(A) The injunction will issue because the Apple Farm to Cider Bottling contract predated the Mega to Cider agreement.

(B) The injunction will issue because performance of the Mega to Cider agreement will breach the Apple Farm to Cider Bottling contract.

(C) The injunction will be denied because Apple Farm can sell their crop to another buyer.

(D) The injunction will be denied because Apple Farms can sue for damages later.

Questions 181 – 183 are based on the following:

Bill Heavengates developed a software Internet-portal platform, which he felt had great potential. He approached a large computer manufacturer, Big Blue Inc., to see if they would be willing to purchase 10,000 units of the software and provide financing in advance for the detailed development and manufacturing. Big Blue was very interested in the arrangement and the parties signed a memorandum. The memorandum stated a delivery date of May 1st for 10,000 units at a total price of $110,000 with payments of $25,000 on January 1st, $25,000 on February 1st, $25,000 on March 1st and $35,000 on April 1st.

Big Blue paid $25,000 on both January 1st and February 1st. On February 15, Bill wrote Big Blue a letter that stated "the Beta test of the software is behind schedule and we may be unable to deliver to you the order until

June or July." On February 25th, Bill wrote a second letter stating "the 'Beta test now looks much better and we expect to be able to deliver the software on April 10th. Based on this news, Big Blue paid the $25,000 March 1st payment on time. On March 10th, Bill wrote a third letter stating "the software program had just been inadvertently bugged by a programmer's mistake and delivery would be delayed – perhaps as late as next year."

181. Which of the following best describes the legal relationship between Bill Heavengates and Big Blue as of February 20th?

(A) Bill has not breached the contract because the date of performance is not yet due.

(B) Bill has anticipatorily repudiated the contract and is subject to an immediate lawsuit for breach.

(C) Big Blue does not have to make the March 1st $25,000 payment and can demand Bill furnish them written assurances he will deliver on May 1st.

(D) Big Blue may seek an order enjoining Bill from breaching the agreement and/or seek an order of specific performance.

182. Which of the following statements least accurately describes the legal situation between Bill Heavengates and Big Blue as of March 12th.

(A) Big Blue may permit Bill a reasonable period of time to complete performance and then bring an action to recover the $75,000 paid.

(B) Big Blue must allow Bill a reasonable period to retract the repudiation or complete the performance.

(C) Big Blue may immediately purchase their software from another vendor.

(D) Big Blue may wait and see if Bill Heavengates will be able to find the bug.

183. Assume that in the above question, Bill Heavengates' February 15th communication constituted a valid repudiation. Big Blue looked for substitute equivalent software and decided Moon's $120,000 software would fulfill their requirements but decided not to purchase the software immediately. Two months later they purchased Moon's software, but the Moon price had increased to $125,000. In addition Big Blue incurred costs of locating the cover goods of $10,000 and paid a customer a late delivery penalty of $7,500 because of Bill Heavengate's breach. Big Blue will recover from Bill Heavengate

(A) $32,500
(B) $17,500
(C) $20,000
(D) $27,500

184. Charlie Supplier operated a hardware store and also a small contracting operation. He entered into a contract with Henry Homeowner to build a garage and with Betty Buyer to sell her enough lumber so she could build a second garden shed identical to one she built last year. Charlie's form specified prices of $5,000 and $800 for the two contracts, respectively. Henry's purchase order specified $4,000 and Betty's form specified $600. All the parties would like the contract to be at their price. The industry average price for the garden shed lumber was $650. Betty Buyer had paid $625 for the same lumber from Henry for her first garden shed last year. Henry completed the garage and delivered the lumber for the garden shed; both buyers were satisfied with the quality but still disagree with Henry on the prices they should have to pay. What price will a court likely assign to the two contracts?

	Garage	Garden Shed
(A)	$5,000	$625
(B)	$5,000	$800
(C)	$4,000	$600
(D)	$4,000	$650

Questions 185 – 187 are based on the following:

Sam Seller and Betty Buyer entered into a $1,000 contract for the sale of a large color television. The agreement called for shipment terms of "ex-Ship" and that assignment of this contract is prohibited unless the parties both consent in writing. Sam also asked Betty if she knew a good shipper and she reported that a local common carrier, Speedy Shipping Co. had done a good job for them in the past.

Without informing Sam, Betty then assigned "all my rights and obligations under the contract" to Alice Assignee. The television was loaded on a vessel owned by Speedy and Sam paid them $100 for the shipment charges. Unfortunately, the Speedy vessel was destroyed in an explosion during an unexpected massive vessel traffic accident at the destination port through no fault of Speedy. Delivery to Betty of the television was thus not made.

185. If Betty brings a breach of contract suit against Sam, the court should hold for
   (A) Sam, because Betty designated the vessel to transport the goods.
   (B) Sam, because the television had been delivered to Speedy in good working order
   (C) Betty, because the carrier is to be deemed to be the agent of the seller if the shipment terms are "ex-ship."
   (D) Betty, because the goods were not delivered to Betty.

186. If Alice brings suit against Betty, Alice should recover
   (A) $1,000 which was the price of the television.
   (B) The difference between the contract price and the price necessary to purchase an equivalent television.
   (C) Nothing since the television was never delivered.
   (D) Nothing because assignment of the television contract without written

consent was specifically excluded in the original contract.

187. If Sam wants to avoid liability to both Betty and Alice, his worst defense is
   (A) The explosion was unforeseeable.
   (B) Betty had the risk of loss.
   (C) A reasonable basic assumption of the contract was that such an explosion would not occur.
   (D) Betty designated the vessel to be used for the shipment and thus is partially responsible for the loss.

188. Mary Merchant sells fireplaces primarily to individual consumers and households. The sales contract that the company requires purchasers to sign contains a clause waiving the remedies available for breach of warranty. If the purchaser uses the company's time payment plan, they must sign a confession of judgment. Carl Consumer purchased a fireplace and elected to pay the price over time. Merchant installed the fireplace. Ten days later the stove exploded killing both Carl and his wife. Carl's personal representative brought suit against Mary Merchant for wrongful death and Merchant counterclaimed for the balance due on the account based upon the confession of judgment Carl signed. In this lawsuit

I.   Mary will likely prevail because Carl signed the confession of judgment.
II. Carl's personal representative will likely prevail in the wrongful death action because the court will not enforce the contract clause waiving remedies in the event of breach.
III. The UCC will not allow the seller, Mary, to exclude liability for personal injuries to consumers resulting from the sale of goods.
IV. The court will allow Carl's personal representative to recover, but not the personal representative of his wife because the wife did not purchase the fireplace.
   (A) All four above statements are correct.

(B) I, II, and III above are correct.

(C) II and III above are correct.

(D) III and IV above are correct.

Questions 189 and 190 are based on the following:

Betty Banana Farms was a fruit grower who contracted to sell 2,000 crates of "grade prime" ripe bananas to Food Stores Inc. Delivery was to be made on or before August 15th. On July 15th, Food Stores received 2,000 crates from Betty. The head of the Food Store's fruit department inspected the shipment and sent an e-mail to Betty stating "these bananas are not yet ripe so we are rejecting them as nonconforming." When she received the e-mail, Betty wrote Food Stores and said "sorry but will send the ripe ones hopefully in the next two weeks. Please refrigerate the perishable bananas so they do not spoil." On August 10th, Food Stores received the "grade prime" ripe bananas from Betty and rejected them because they had found a cheaper source. The bananas delivered on July 15th sat on the receiving dock and spoiled.

189. If Betty brings suit to collect for the bananas delivered on August 10th, she will

(A) Not prevail because the July 15th shipment did not conform to the contract.

(B) Prevail because she delivered the "grade prime ripe" bananas on August 10th.

(C) Not prevail even if the August 10th shipment conformed because she breached the contract on July 15th.

(D) Prevail because Food Stores should have returned the first shipment.

190. Betty was unable to resell the bananas delivered to Food Stores on July 15th. Food Store had not refrigerated them and they had spoiled by August 10th when Betty learned of the situation. Food Stores has declined any responsibility because the bananas did not conform to their purchase order. If Betty brings suit, she will

(A) Not prevail because the July 15th contract did not conform to the contract.

(B) Not prevail because a buyer has no responsibility to store a seller's goods unless the seller sends the expected costs in advance.

(C) Prevail because a buyer of perishable goods must take reasonable steps to prevent spoilage loss if the seller requests.

(D) Prevail because she sent conforming goods later.

Questions 191 – 193 are based on the following:

Wally Wholesaler and Roberta Retailer were negotiating to sell and purchase 10 large cranes. Roberta's purchase order was for 10 cranes at $500,000 per unit payable in 30 days. Wally's invoice was also for 10 cranes at $500,000 per unit, but contained a clause disclaiming "any and all responsibility for the warranty of merchantability." The invoice also stated ". . . the buyer's sole remedy for damages is limited to the seller replacing or repairing any defective cranes." Roberta paid the invoice on a timely basis and did not comment on the disclaiming and damage limitation clauses. Two of the cranes proved defective.

191. Under the above facts:

(A) Roberta has a claim against Wally because the merchantability disclaimer did not become a part of the contract.

(B) Roberta has a claim against Wally because the disclaimer was unconscionable.

(C) Roberta does not have a claim against Wally because she failed to object to the disclaimer within a reasonable period of time.

(D) Roberta does not have a claim against Wally because the disclaimer was enforceable.

192. Two of the 10 cranes were purchased for the particular purpose of loading large containers from a railroad-head dock onto container vessels. This requirement was unknown to Wally. The two cranes in question collapsed while loading full containers of expensive hi-tech test equipment bound for Alaska. The containers fell into the water, rendering most of the cargo valueless. If Roberta brings suit against Wally, Wally's best defense to this lawsuit is:

(A) He did not specifically state in writing that the cranes would work for that loading function.

(B) He was not aware that Roberta was relying on his advice.

(C) He was not a merchant in selling those cranes since he only sold a few of them.

(D) Roberta was a merchant and, as such, she had a duty to make her own detailed investigation

193. Roberta is very upset about the seller's attempt to limit liability to repairing or replacing the defective cranes. She asks you to file a lawsuit and attempt to get a court to issue a declaratory judgment striking the limitation. Under these circumstances, a court is likely to hold:

(A) The limitation is enforceable because the buyer should have objected.

(B) The limitation is enforceable because the buyer has a remedy.

(C) The limitation is unenforceable because it is unconscionable.

(D) The limitation is unenforceable because the provision was not expressly agreed to as the sole and exclusive remedy.

Questions 194 and 195 are based on the following:

Megabuck Motors Manufacturing was trying to sell their remaining 3,000 Nedsel model automobiles. On September 1st, Megabuck sent Debra Dealer, a retail auto dealer, a letter that stated "We offer to sell you 100 Nedsels for $12,000 each; this offer will not be revoked." Megabuck experienced rapid sales of Nedsels in September and on October 1st, sent a second letter to Debra stating "our previous offer is hereby revoked." On October 15th, Debra wrote Megabuck and stated "I accept your offer, please send 20 Nedsels. Our check for $240,000 is enclosed."

194. If Megabuck refuses to ship the cars and Debra brings suit, the likely outcome is:

(A) For Megabuck because they revoked the offer before acceptance.

(B) For Megabuck because they received no consideration that would render the offer irrevocable.

(C) For Debra because the offer made by Megabuck was irrevocable for 3 months.

(D) For Debra because it appears the acceptance was made within a reasonable time

195. If Megabuck objects to shipping an order of 20 Nedsels rather than a full lot of 100, a court will

(A) Find for Megabuck and impose 100 units on Debra.

(B) Find for Debra and impose 20 units on Megabucks.

(C) Permit the parties to introduce evidence of past course of dealings and usage of trade to determine if the contract is divisible.

(D) Determine that there was not a valid meeting of the minds so no contract resulted from the communications.

Questions 196 – 199 are based on the following:

Don Distributor sells auto parts to a network of local gas stations, garages and automobile repair shops. Don purchases his parts from a number of wholesale distributors at many different prices, discounts and payment terms: Albert Automobile Manufacturing is one of Don's suppliers. Don offered to buy all their next year's requirements of spark plugs from Albert; Albert agreed to fulfill their order. The agreement was memorialized in a written memorandum identifying both parties and the spark plugs, but it was not signed. The memorandum also did not state the unit price, quantity, place of delivery, or terms of payment.

196. If the parties disagree on whether they are bound one to the other for future purchases of spark plugs, a court will likely hold:

(A) No liability because the statute of frauds requires a writing signed by the parties and there were no signatures.

(B) No liability because the important terms of price, quantity and place of delivery were not specifically stated in the memorandum between the parties.

(C) Liability because the buyer is under a good faith purchase requirement.

(D) Liability because the past performance of the parties eliminates the necessity for a written agreement.

197. Don's customers often come into his store to buy and pick up their automobile parts, including sparkplugs. Many of the customers would prefer that the parts be delivered to their place of business by the wholesaler. Under the Albert to Don contract, the place of delivery would be:

(A) Subject to negotiation between Albert and Don's customers.

(B) Albert's place of business.

(C) Don's place of business.

(D) Don's customers place of business if they so request.

198. The market pricing for various brands of sparkplugs varies, but Don usually realizes a price from his customers of 40% mark-up over his cost. Don gives some customers a discount and other customers pay his "list" price. Under the Albert to Don contract, the price for sparkplugs would be:

(A) Subject to negotiations between Albert and Don.

(B) A reasonable price at the time that Don orders the sparkplugs in question.

(C) A reasonable price when the sparkplugs are delivered.

(D) At a price of 40% less than Don sold the sparkplugs to his customers.

199. Manufacturing representatives in this industry typically give terms of 2% discount if paid within 10 days net 30 to their established customers. If Albert and Don disagree about discount and payment length terms, a court would likely impose:

(A) 2% discount if paid within 10 days net 30 from the date of order.

(B) 2% discount if paid within 10 days net 30 from the date of delivery.

(C) Net 30 since Don is an established and reliable customer of Albert.

(D) 100% cash due upon delivery.

Questions 200 and 201 are based on the following:

Insolvent Incorporated is a large older corporation that sold circuit boards to main frame computer manufacturers for many years. Bill Heavengates started a software company that reduced the demand for the circuit boards and Insolvent began to get further and further behind in meeting their trade payables. Sarah Supplier furnished Insolvent with plastic on 45-day open account for their circuit boards. On January 1st, Insolvent owed Sarah over $100,000 that was over 90 days delinquent.

On January 13th, the Vice President of Sales told Sarah he had heard from a reliable trade source that Insolvent was about to declare bankruptcy. Sarah had delivered $6,000 worth of plastic to Insolvent on January 1st, and another $5,000 on January 12th. Another $4,000 was in transit to Insolvent and scheduled to be delivered on January 15th. On January 20th, Insolvent declared bankruptcy.

200. Regarding Sarah's $4,000 delivery of plastic that is in transit and expected to be delivered on January 15th:

(A) Sarah must deliver the goods to Insolvent as per their original contract.

(B) Sarah may not stop the goods in transit.

(C) Sarah can demand cash on delivery.

(D) Sarah may only demand cash if Insolvent agrees to a change in their credit terms.

201. Regarding Sarah's delivery of plastic to Insolvent on January 1st and 12th:

(A) Sarah has to put in a claim with the Insolvent's bankruptcy trustee as an unsecured creditor.

(B) Sarah can reclaim all the goods she delivered within 20 days of the Insolvent's bankruptcy.

(C) Sarah can reclaim all the goods she delivered within 10 days of the Insolvent's bankruptcy.

(D) Sarah can reclaim the goods and sue the bankrupt estate for incidental damages.

202. Ace Co. entered into a contract with Jennifer Jones in which Ace agreed to manufacture and deliver 1,000 computers to Jones in 20 days. Jones paid $25,000 with the order and immediately added the 1,000 computers to her casualty insurance policy. Ace began the production process the next week. Two weeks later a fire destroyed Ace's warehouse in which the computers were stored. Jennifer Jones

(A) Must sue Ace to recover the $25,000.

(B) Lacked an insurable interest in the computers since she did not have possession of the goods.

(C) Had an insurable interest in the computers as of the day she and Ace signed the sales contract and paid the $25,000.

(D) Cannot prohibit the insurance company from pursuing Ace after it pays the loss through subrogation.

Questions 203 – 205 are based on the following:

Rebecca Retailer operates a computer software retail store in a regional mall. Microhard's Doors 2003 software platform has proven a big seller in the store. Rebecca was restocking her inventory and referred to her wholesale software catalog from Microhard. The catalog price per unit of Doors 2003 platform software is $29.00. On July 4th, Rebecca placed an order for a dozen Doors 2003 via e-mail to Microhard stating "ship at once a dozen units of Doors 2003 software at $29.00 each."

On July 10th Microhard mailed an order acknowledgment to Rebecca which stated "The dozen Doors 2003 software platforms at $32.00 each will be shipped on July 25th." Rebecca received the Microhard correspondence on July 13th and did not respond. On July 22nd, Rebecca discovered that Orange Company offered an equivalent software platform for $29.00 and called Microhard to cancel her order. On July 25th, Microhard shipped the dozen Doors 2003 software platforms to Rebecca, which she received on July 28th.

203. If Microhard brings suit against Rebecca to enforce the sale of the dozen Doors 2003 software units, a court would likely hold for

(A) Microhard because the acknowledgment and promise to ship was acceptance.

(B) Microhard because Rebecca's July 22nd phone call is proof she knew there was a contract.

(C) Rebecca because she did not agree to the higher price so there was no contract.

(D) Rebecca because she canceled the order before it was shipped so there was no contract.

204. Assuming a contract resulted from the above communications, it was effective on

(A) July 10th, the day that Microhard sent their order acknowledgment to Rebecca.

(B) July 13th, the day that Rebecca received Microhard's order acknowledgment.

(C) July 25th, the day that the goods were shipped.

(D) July 28th, the day that the goods were received.

205. Assuming a contract by performance resulted from the above communications, the price per unit would probably be:

(A) $32.00 because this was the price specified by the seller.

(B) $32.00 because Rebecca knew this was the Microhard price when she received the software.

(C) $29.00 because this was the price specified by the buyer.

(D) $29.00 because this was the market price.

Questions 206 – 208 are based on the following:

Betsy Buyer agreed to buy custom-made widgets from Mary Manufacturer at a price of $1,000 each. The written agreement called for Mary to deliver to Betsy 60 widgets at a rate of three each to be delivered on the 10th day of each month for 20 months. Betsy agreed to pay $3,000 for each shipment with payment to be received by Mary on or before the 30th of the same month of the delivery.

206. For this question only, assume Betsy accepted the first installment of three widgets which was delivered timely before the 10th of the month. However, Betsy was short cash during this period and did not make the payment due on the 30th. The legal consequence of the non-payment is:

(A) Breach of a condition subsequent.

(B) Breach of a condition concurrent.

(C) Breach the whole contract.

(D) Breach of one installment only and Mary is required to deliver the future monthly installments on credit.

207. For this question only, assume Betsy accepted and paid for the first three months of widget shipments on time. At the beginning of the fourth month, Mary contacted Betsy and explained that another buyer, Helen Higher, was willing to offer a higher price for the widgets she had in inventory and that therefore Mary would not ship any widgets to Betsy in the future. If Betsy wants to require Mary to deliver the widgets to her for the remainder of the contract, will a court issue an order of specific performance?

(A) Yes because Betsy relied to her detriment on Mary's performance

(B) Yes because the widgets appear to be unique and they are in the seller's inventory.

(C) No because they may be transferred to a bona fide purchaser.

(D) No because the remedy of specific performance is not available under the UCC.

208. For this question only, assume that Mary has been ordered to or agreed to continue shipping to Betsy. Betsy receives one shipment containing one defective unit that does not conform to the contract specifications. She called the seller to complain. Mary offered to immediately repair the defective unit. Betsy said no thanks, that she had had enough of doing business with Mary, and was canceling the contract. Mary has lost her other buyer and sues to enforce the contract. Will Betsy be able to cancel the contract?

(A) Yes, because a buyer under the UCC is entitled to a perfect tender of conforming goods.

(B) Yes, because Mary previously refused to perform under the contract.

(C) No, because Mary has a right to cure the defect.

(D) No, because Betsy did not submit written notice of breach and contract cancellation.

Questions 209 and 210 are based on the following:

Harry Homeowner hired Allen Architect to design a custom built home on a steep bank of a hill for his retirement. After the plans were complete, Harry solicited construction bids from a number of contractors. Cheapest Contractor submitted the low bid of $250,000. The plans upon which the bid was made did not reveal that there was water in the hill and much of the bank consisted of sand. Had Cheapest Contractor known of the defects, they would have bid substantially more, probably about $400,000. In addition, a provision in the construction contract stated that the architect had to approve the contractor's work before the owner had to make progress payment to the contractor. Finally, the agreement stated that any dispute was subject to mandatory arbitration.

209. The contract was signed and awarded to Cheapest Contractor. Cheapest then sent their construction foreman out to the land to begin to plan the construction details. The foreman discovered the water in the hill and sand bank upon his physical inspection. Cheapest immediately realized that their construction cost was going to be substantially higher than they estimated based on the plans. Cheapest Contractor's best argument to require Harry Homeowner to renegotiate the agreement price is

(A) Cheapest had no duty to inspect the actual building site before submitting their bid.

(B) Harry Homeowner had a duty to make express disclosure that there were serious defects in the land that would increase the costs of construction.

(C) The defects in the land were hidden.

(D) The bid was made in good faith, the mistake was not intentional, and thus should be excused.

210. The parties entered into arbitration on the above issue. The arbitrator heard the arguments of both sides and physically inspected the property. The arbitrator decided that there was fault on both sides and that the contract price should be raised to $350,000. Harry Homeowner was outraged at the arbitrator's decision; he secretly instructed Allen Architect not to certify the work by the contractor. Pursuant to his instruction, Allen Architect refused to issue a certificate of compliance even though the home was in substantial compliance with the plans. The legal effect of this action is

(A) The homeowner has waived the condition precedent of architect certification.

(B) The Contractor is excused from performance because the homeowner would not cooperate.

(C) The Homeowner's scheme to prevent the occurrence of the condition precedent matured the payment responsibility into a contractual duty.

(D) None, because the architect's refusal to certify is measured by a subjective good faith standard.

211. Oscar Owner has a single-family rental house that is in a prime redevelopment area. Oscar gave Fred Flipper a $10,000 option to purchase the house for $500,000. The option did not prohibit assignment. Fred subsequently gave an option to Dave Developer for $25,000 to purchase the property for $650,000. Dave gave Fred formal notice that he was exercising his option and Fred paid the $500,000 to Oscar. Oscar transferred title to Fred. Fred then notified Dave he had title and was ready to close. Dave decided that $650,000 was too much money and refused to tender the money into escrow. Fred filed an action for specific performance against Dave and Dave counter claimed for the $25,000 option fee. The court will likely

(A) Grant Dave a $25,000 judgment against Fred.

(B) Grant Fred the right to keep the $25,000 option fee.

(C) Grant Fred a $150,000 judgment against Dave.

(D) Grant Fred specific performance.

212.   Brandy Boater owned an antique Chris Craft motorboat that she had kept in perfect condition. She had a friend named Ellen Envious who had for years liked the boat and on numerous occasions tried to get Brandy to sell it to her. Brandy always said no to the offers.

The two friends were out in the motorboat when Ellen announced it was her birthday. Brandy went below and returned with two bottles of very high quality Merlot wine from Crawford Vineyard.   The friends consumed both bottles that afternoon. As the afternoon progressed the subject of the motorboat came up.   Brandy finally said "since it is your birthday and you are such a good friend I will sell my Chris Craft to you for $400." Ellen immediately said "I accept" and they opened a third bottle and toasted their deal.

The next morning Brandy woke up with a hangover when Ellen came to her door with $400 cash. Brandy refused to convey the boat title to Ellen and Ellen sued for specific performance.   Brandy's best defense is that

(A) The contract should have been written because it involves goods.

(B) She would not have agreed to sell the boat had she been sober.

(C) When she agreed to sell the boat to Ellen she was so drunk that she was not aware of the legal consequences of her act.

(D) She intended to make a gift to Ellen and gifts are revocable at will prior to the transfer of the title for cash.

213.   Gary Gamer purchased a computer from Electronic Warehouse Inc. Which of the below facts would be most favorable to Gary if he sought to rescind the purchase?

(A) Gary and the store clerk orally agreed to the sale of the computer for a price of $750.

(B) Gary purchased the computer one month before his 18th birthday and 14 months later wants to disaffirm the contract.

(C) The computer Gary picked out was defective; Electronic Warehouse offered to repair the computer but Gary refused to specify the particular defect and demands rescission.

(D) Gary paid for the computer and was given a box that when he unpacked it at home contained a printer unit made by the same manufacturer.

Questions 214 and 215 are based on the following:

Paula Painter and Betty Beautiful entered into a contract in which Paula agreed to paint a large oil portrait of Betty. The contract stated that "Paula guarantees that Betty will be satisfied with the oil painting."

214.   Assume that Betty refused to make herself available for sittings so that Paula could complete the oil painting. Which of the below is least accurate

(A) Paula had an implied obligation to cooperate with Betty's busy schedule.

(B) Betty's cooperation with Paula was an implied condition of the contract.

(C) Betty assumed the risk of Paula not cooperating.

(D) If Betty refuses to cooperate, Paula would be excused from performance and could file a lawsuit for breach of contract.

215.   Assume that Betty did cooperate with Paula and the painting was completed. While Betty's family was very happy with the painting, Betty herself did not believe it to be an appropriate likeness of her best image. She thus rejected the painting and refused to pay. If Paula Painter brings suit on the contract, which of the following is least helpful to the likelihood of Paula's recovery?

(A) Paula's painting was not an accurate reproduction of Betty's appearance.
(B) Betty never looked at the finished painting.
(C) Betty's dissatisfaction with Paula's painting was not genuine.
(D) Betty refused to accept Paula's painting because a personality conflict arose between Betty and Paula.

Questions 216 and 217 are based on the following:

Mary Manufacturer's offer was to sell 1,000 widgets to Robert Retailer for $100,000 cash two years hence. Payment terms were specified to be in 30 days after delivery. Robert stated that he would agree to pay the $100,000 60 days after delivery. Neither party agreed to the other's payment length term even though Mary shipped the goods, which Robert accepted. Both parties' communications contained the statement "this contract may only be modified in writing."

216. If the parties file a motion for a declaratory judgment the court would probably hold the required payment time term to be determined as of

(A) The time of delivery to Robert.
(B) 60 days later since the offeree is entitled to the "last shot."
(C) 45 days later since this is the middle ground between the two payment term lengths.
(D) 30 days later since the offeror is the master of the bargain.

217. Assume in this question that three months after the contract was executed the market price of widgets doubled. Mary thus came to Robert and told him that she could not deliver the widgets for $100,000. After some negotiations the parties orally agreed to split the loss and that the price

would be increased by 50% of the difference between the contract price and the market price at the time of delivery. The price was $300,000 as of the delivery date so Mary billed Robert at a price of $200,000. If Robert pays only $100,000 and Mary brings suit the likely outcome is to decide for

(A) Mary, if she would not have produced the widgets at the higher price if she did not believe Robert's promise to pay half the loss amount.
(B) Robert, because the original contract's prohibition against oral modification was violated.
(C) Robert, because he could have sued for damages if Mary did not perform her original contract.
(D) Mary, because the oral negotiations about the price increase waived the "written modification only" provision.

218. Betty Buyer paid $500 cash for 50 widgets upon delivery by the Wally Widget Company. Later an inspection determined the widgets did not conform to the contract and Betty contacted Wally who refused to accept a return of the widgets and refused to refund any part of the $500 Betty had paid. Betty then told Wally she was going to sell the goods herself to recover her payment. The widgets brought $750 dollars at a public sale and Betty incurred advertising costs of $100. Betty should remit to Wally

(A) -0-, because Wally breached the contract.
(B) $250.
(C) $150.
(D) $75.

219. Wally Wealthy fell in love with Betty Beautiful, who was much younger than Wally. The couple had a short but exciting relationship leading to their plans to get married. Which of the following oral promises would be enforceable

(A) Wally says, "I'll give you a million dollars if you promise to marry me."

(B) Wally and Betty mutually promise to marry each other.

(C) Betty promises to enter into a prenuptial agreement releasing any future claims against Wally's assets.

(D) Betty promises to enter into a joint tenancy property agreement that would define and allocate the postnuptial status of the two spouses' separate property.

220. Carol Celebrity was walking through a public crowd when Fred Factum asked her for her signature. Carol said "sure" and Fred gave her a pad of paper to sign and a pen. Carol signed her full name near the bottom of the page and returned the tablet to Fred. Later, Fred carefully took apart the pad of paper and typed in text above Carol's signature using wording to complete a contract to sell her home to Fred. If Fred sued Carol for specific performance of a conveyance of her home, the best defense that she can assert is

(A) Fraud in the inducement.

(B) Fraud in the execution.

(C) Illegal contract.

(D) Fraudulent concealment.

221. Unreliable Engineering promised to sell 100,000 computer chips to Harry Profit for $1 each or $100,000 on 30-day open payment term with a delivery date of June 1st. Harry received an e-mail from Unreliable on May 10th that said that due to their rapid price increase they were unequivocally repudiating the delivery scheduled for June 1st. The market price was $125,000 for the order on May 10th. Harry called Unreliable and tried to talk them into completing the order. After 15 days the negotiations broke down and Harry covered at the best price he could find of $105,000. It also cost Harry a $10,000 purchasing fee and the delay was directly responsible for losing a resale profit of $40,000. If Harry later sues

Unreliable, the likely outcome would be a judgement for Harry in an amount of

(A) $15,000.

(B) $35,000.

(C) $55,000.

(D) $75,000.

222. Victoria Volvo owned a classic 1972 Volvo model P1800 coupe. The car was in very good condition because Victoria was an elderly retired schoolteacher who garaged the vehicle at all times except every Sunday morning when she drove it to church. Her friend, Evone Envious, had always wanted the car. On March 1st, Evone was able to convince Victoria to give her a $20,000 purchase option for 30 days in return for a non-refundable payment of $1,000. On March 30th, Evone sent Victoria a letter accepting the option and included her check for $20,000. On April 1st, Victoria sold the Volvo to Betty Faith Proper for $22,000 since she had not heard from Evone. Victoria received Evone's acceptance on April 2nd. The proper ownership of the classic Volvo P1800 coupe is in

(A) Betty Faith Proper if she took for value, in good faith, and without knowledge.

(B) Evone, only if she is willing to pay $22,000.

(C) Evone at the option price of $20,000.

(D) Betty Faith Proper since Victoria sold it to her before receiving Evone's acceptance.

223. Larry Law was a first-year law student who had just completed his Contracts course. He had an undergraduate freshman girlfriend named Iola Innocent. Iola has just discovered she is pregnant and is pressing Larry to get married. Larry drafts a prenuptial agreement that addresses jointly owned property and states that if the couple gets divorced, Iola gets 100% of the parental rights over the unborn child and Larry is not responsible for any child support. This provision of the agreement violated a state child support law. Iola gave birth to a daughter. Larry and Iola later got divorced and now Larry refuses to pay anything for his share of child support. Iola is poverty stricken and a public law volunteer brings suit on her behalf against her former husband, Larry Law, who is now a well-compensated associate in a large law firm. The likely outcome is that

(A) Larry will pay nothing in child support because the court will not invalidate the whole prenuptial agreement.

(B) Larry will be ordered to pay the minimum level of child support specified under the state law.

(C) Larry will be ordered to pay the maximum level of child support specified under the state law.

(D) The court will sever the provision providing for no child support.

224. Bobbie Bookie intended to start a bookie establishment where he would take bets on fantasy football games. Winners would receive "awards" for their keen judgment in analyzing the relative skill of different football players rather than winnings from gambling. Bobbie signed a two-year lease on a storefront location from which he conducted the "judgment award" contests. During the lease negotiation, Bobbie was very candid with the lessor as to the questionable legality of the operation. This final lease document specified the rental premises were to be used only for conducting "judgment award" contests.

Bobbie opened the operation, which was an immediate success. Unfortunately, the business quickly came to the attention of the state gambling commission. The attorney general assigned to the agency issued an opinion that the "judgment award" contests were illegal gambling. A judge agreed with the state's position and issued an injunction against Bobbie's continuing operation. Without any revenue, Bobbie's "judgment award" contests folded and he quit paying the rent. If the lessor brings suit against Bobbie on the lease contract, the likely outcome is for

(A) The lessor because Bobbie refused to pay the rent.

(B) Bobbie because the landlord knew the purpose of the lease.

(C) Bobbie because the lease has been frustrated by the supervening illegality.

(D) The lessor because Bobbie could use the premises for some other purpose.

225. Carol Carpenter entered into a contract with Larry Landlord to purchase his home and repair his automobile. Carol began repairing the automobile and applied for a mortgage to purchase the property. Unfortunately, Carol had a heart attack, quit repairing Larry's car, and repudiated the responsibility to purchase Larry's home. If Larry brings suit on the contract seeking specific performance on both contractual responsibilities, the likely outcome is

	Home Purchase Responsibility	Car Repair Responsibility
(A)	Prevail	Prevail
(B)	Prevail	Not prevail
(C)	Not prevail	Prevail
(D)	Not prevail	Not prevail

226. Carol Car Collector was a serious Thunderbird antique car buyer and always on the search for Thunderbirds in good shape. She saw an advertisement in the newspaper for a 1964 Thunderbird sports coupe for $25,000 complete with a website address that was to have a picture. She downloaded the photograph, which showed an automobile with a perfect body and interior. Carol paid the $25,000 and signed a sales contract stating that the Thunderbird was used and sold "as is." When Carol went to pick up the Thunderbird, she discovered that it was a 1968 rather than a 1964 model. The 1968 model was not at all rare and worth much less than the 1964 model. If Carol brings suit against the seller, the likely outcome is for

(A) Carol, because the internet picture was of a car that had never been driven, not the actual used car she was to buy.

(B) The seller, because the buyer was aware the Thunderbird was sold "as is."

(C) The seller, unless they were negligent in not explicitly stating the picture was of a new car, not the actual car to be sold.

(D) Carol, because the "as is" disclosure was not totally effective.

227. Susan Seller mailed a letter to Bobby Buyer after Bobby called her inquiring if her antique 1932 Ford Roadster was for sale. The letter stated "I want to sell my antique Ford Roadster for above $20,000. If you are interested please contact me." Three days later Bobby sent a letter to Susan stating "I agree to pay your asking price of $20,000 for the 1932 Ford Roadster." The next day Susan sold the car to Harriet Higherprice for $25,000. If Bobby brings suit against Susan for breach of contract, the likely outcome is

(A) For Bobby since her acceptance was timely under the mail box rule.

(B) For Susan because her letter to Bobby was not an offer.

(C) For Susan because the sale to Harriott was made before Susan was aware that Bobby had accepted.

(D) For Bobby because her communication met the full price which Susan was asking for the automobile.

228. Betty Buyer purchased a new computer main processor for $400 from Sally Seller over the telephone with delivery to be made within 60 days. 40 days later, Betty received a telephone call from Sally in which Sally said she had experienced a significant cost increase and that there must be a corresponding $150 increase in the purchase price. Betty felt she had no choice but to agree to the price increase if she was to get the computer processor without undue delay. She thus reluctantly orally agreed to the $150 price increase. Two days later, Betty saw an advertisement for another

similar processor for $450 and purchased it. On the arranged delivery date, Sally delivered the originally ordered computer. Betty refused to accept delivery. If Sally sues Betty for breach of contract, the most effective defense Betty can assert is

(A) The $150 agreement raising the contract price was not written.

(B) The significant cost increase in Sally's price was a foreseeable risk of business.

(C) Sally's demand for an extra $150 was unconscionable because a similarly equipped computer processor was available for $100 less.

(D) Betty's promise to pay $550 was not supported by consideration.

229. Betty Builder contracted with Henry Homeowner to build a new house. The contract set a completion date of April 15th and called for a liquidated damage award of $200 per day for late completion because Henry wanted to move into the new house. Betty completed the house late on May 1st and Henry had to pay $900 rent at a hotel during the period April 15th to May 1st. Betty refused to turn over the occupancy of the new house on May 1st to Henry. In addition, Henry had to pay $2,000 in repairs because of Betty's poor construction. If Henry sues Betty, he will likely recover for

(A) Liquidated damages of $3,000 as the sole and exclusive remedy.

(B) Liquidated damages of $3,000 and the rent Henry paid to the hotel.

(C) Liquidated damages of $3,000, the $2,000 for repairs, and an order of specific performance.

(D) Either liquidated damages of $3,000 or the total repair cost of $2,000 and an order of specific performance.

230. Scott Sugarfield owns a large sugar cane plantation in Hawaii. He entered into a contract to provide all the sugar that Sweet Tooth Beverages would use for a two year period of time. Six months of the two-year contract have expired and Scott has shipped and Sweet Tooth has accepted six lots of

sugar. Scott receives an offer from Betty Buyer to sell his sugar cane business at a price he could not refuse. Betty completes the next month's shipment to Sweet Tooth. Sweet Tooth then sends a letter to Betty with their payment for the last shipment. The letter acknowledges their receipt of the last shipment and asks if Betty intends to continue satisfying their sugar needs. Two weeks later Sweet Tooth notifies Betty and Scott that it is canceling the sugar purchase contract. Which of the following is correct?

(A) The letter sent with the payment constituted waiver of the right to delegate the performance duty.
(B) There is no right to cancel because Betty has not refused to ship another lot of sugar.
(C) Scott remains liable.
(D) The contract is cancelable at any time by any party because the UCC requires all contracts to state a quantity.

231. Generous George was a retailer of jewelry and one of his best customers, Betty Bigbucks, owed him $10,000. George's daughter had just borne his first grandchild. On April 1st, George told Betty that she should pay the $10,000 to his daughter as a gift. George knew that his daughter was behind in paying Friendly Finance because of a prior debt. George also told the Friendly Finance agent that he was going to make this gift to his daughter. Rather than pay George or his daughter, Betty bet it all on the lottery and lost. George had other business dealings with Betty and later decided to forgive the $10,000 debt that Betty was to pay to his daughter. His daughter later learned of the arrangement and believed she should have received the $10,000. If both the daughter and Friendly sue Betty, the likely outcome is

(A) No recovery for either P.
(B) A recovery for only the daughter against Betty.
(C) A recovery for only Friendly against Betty.
(D) Recoveries for both Ps.

232. Mary Megabucks owned a large estate in Beverly Hills, California that had a deluxe swimming pool. She signed a two-year agreement with Paula Poolcleaner to clean the pool weekly at a price of $200 per month. The contract stated that "Mary agrees not to assign this contract without the prior written approval of Paula." Mary sold the estate to Betty Buyer and asked Paula to agree to an assignment of the pool-cleaning contract to the new owner, Betty. Paula refused, but Mary still assigned the cleaning contract to Betty with the home sale. Betty was not told about the assignment prohibition. Paula refused to work for Betty and Betty had to hire another pool cleaning service at twice the price. If Betty sues Paula for breach of contract, the likely outcome is that the court should find for

(A) Paula because the contract was for her personal services.
(B) Betty because Paula had no right to unreasonably withhold consent to assignment of the contract.
(C) Betty because the assignment was valid in spite of Paula's refusal to consent.
(D) Paula because the contract prohibited assignment by Mary without Paula's consent.

233. Oscar Owner decided to sell his home and to list it with Barbara Broker. The written agreement was for a three-month period. It specified that the listing price was $100,000 and the 7% commission was due if the broker produced a ready, willing, and able buyer in the three-month period. Payment was due at closing. Barbara interested one of her clients named Sharp Bargainer in purchasing Oscar's home. Sharp offered $95,000 complete with earnest money of $10,000. Oscar accepted the offer, but Sharp later changed his mind and forfeited the earnest money. Subsequently, Oscar sold the house himself to a third party for $95,000. Barbara Broker insists that Oscar sue Sharp for specific performance. If Oscar refuses and Barbara sues Oscar for her commission, she will likely recover

(A) -0-
(B) $6,650 or 7% of $95,000.
(C) $7,000 or 7% of $100,000.
(D) $7,350 or 7% of $105,000.

Questions 234 and 235 are based on the following:

Go Public Inc wanted to take their corporation public in an initial public offering (IPO). They hired Big Influence Law Firm to assist them in the process. Ike Influence was a senior partner of the law firm and had been the lead person in several IPOs. Go Public's president, Ernest Entrepreneur met with the law firm to negotiate the contract. He was told there would be a charge of $400,000 to file the IPO documents with the Security and Exchange Commission (SEC) and that Ike Influence receives $500,000 for every offering he is personally involved in. In addition, the law firm demanded 1% of the offering security proceeds if the offering raised at least $50 million.

The law firm then sent a written "engagement proposal" to Go Public Inc specifying their fee to be "$400,000, $500,000 for Ike Influence if you want his involvement and 1% of the proceeds." Ernest Entrepreneur signed the document on behalf of the corporation. The offering raised $40 million and Big Influence Law Firm sent a bill for $1,300,000 to Go Public. The charges were broken down as "basic IPO fee of $400,000; Ike Influence fee of $500,000; and 1% of the offering proceeds of $400,000. Go Public refused to pay and Big Influence Law Firm sued and asserts the parol evidence rule to keep all the oral negotiations out of evidence.

234. During the trial, Ernest Entrepreneur tried to testify that the $400,000 fee for the 1% of the offering proceeds was not due since it did not raise at least $50 million. Based upon Big Influence's timely objection, this testimony should be

(A) Excluded unless it is considered to be evidence of a past course of dealings between the parties.
(B) Admitted because the condition precedent does not contradict a term in the final integrated agreement.
(C) Admitted if the court decides the parties may have had different understandings of the terms of the final agreement.
(D) Excluded unless it is considered to be consistent with customs and usage of trade within the legal profession.

235. During the trial, Ike Influence tried to testify that the $500,000 for his personal involvement was intended to be in addition to the law firm's $400,000 IPO fee, not in lieu of. Go Public's timely objection to this testimony should be

(A) Denied under the condition precedent exception to the parol evidence rule.
(B) Sustained under the parol evidence rule.
(C) Sustained unless the matter is considered to be consistent with customs and usage of trade within the legal profession.
(D) Denied if the wording used in the final written agreement is susceptible of more than one interpretation.

236. Ernest Entrepreneur desired to purchase a seminar business named Everyone is Successful and the office building in which it was located. The business was owned by Sally Seller who signed an agreement prepared by Ernest stating, "I agree to sell my business and building for $500,000 and acknowledge having received a check for $100,000 as a down payment. Ernest later responded by letter stating the description of the property. The letter also specified the place and time of the closing of the sale – the following Friday at 10:00 am at the courthouse. Ernest also added the bold wording to the letter stating, "Time is of the essence in this agreement." The wording added by Ernest is

(A) Unenforceable against Sally Seller if the original agreement did not contain the condition.
(B) Enforceable against Sally Seller because the original agreement failed to contain the condition.
(C) Unenforceable against Sally Seller because of a Statute of Frauds violation.
(D) Unenforceable against Sally Seller because Sally did not respond in writing to Ernest's letter containing the time of the essence condition.

237. Sally Seller wanted to sell a piece of property and employed Betty Broker to assist her. They entered into a written agreement in which Sally authorized Betty to sign the closing documents on her behalf. Paula Purchaser saw the "For Sale" sign on the property and orally authorized her friend Alice Agent to sign the closing documents. Betty and Alice met and both signed all the closing documents indicating they were both agents for their respective principals. Paula later decided not to purchase the property. If Sally Seller sues Paula Purchaser, she will likely

(A) Succeed since the land sales contract was in writing.
(B) Not succeed since she did not sign the contract with Paula herself.
(C) Not succeed since Paula's agency contract with Alice was not written.
(D) Succeed since Sally's agency contract is in writing.

238. Park Place Inc. owned a very old structure that was originally a large Victorian era house. Over the years, the structure had been sub-divided into numerous small apartments. The electrical system in the building was very old and Park Place decided to rewire the building. They hired Elise Electrician to do the work for a flat price of $10,000 due upon completion of the whole electrical job. Elise made a substantial beginning of the rewiring job when the area experienced an unexpected earthquake. Due to the age of the building, it collapsed. At the time, Elise had completed half the electrical job, which increased the value of the building by $4,000, but had expended $6,000 in costs. If Park Place refuses to pay and Elise brings suit, the likely recovery is

(A) Nothing since the contractor completing the job was a condition precedent to payment.
(B) $4,000 in restitution to avoid Park Place's unjust enrichment.
(C) $5,000 since she had completed half the work.
(D) $6,000 since Elise is entitled to be reimbursed her out-of-pocket costs.

239. Elmer Employee worked as an at-will employee for Heavy Handed Employer Inc. a leading seller of widgets. Recently, the Vice President of Sales quit and went to work for a major local competitor. The Vice President was successful in convincing many of Heavy Handed's customers to transfer their accounts to his new employer. This had an adverse affect on the revenues and profits of Heavy Handed. In response, Heavy Handed required all employees to sign non-compete agreements that precluded working for a competitor who sells widgets in the same state for two years after termination. Elmer signed based upon his supervisor's demand. Four years later, Elmer was terminated for cause. He is now applying for work at Heavy Handed's major local competitor who also sells widgets. If Heavy Handed files a lawsuit seeking an injunction to block Elmer working for this competitor, Elmer's best defense is the argument that

(A) The subject area – all widget sales – is too broad.
(B) The geographical area – the whole state – is too broad.
(C) The time period of the restriction – two years – is unreasonable in length.
(D) A bargained for exchange was not present.

240. Ecological Sensitive Motor Company produced and sold at retail a new

electric automobile. Two of their early customers were National Steel Company, Inc., and Nalph Rader who was a very involved environmentalist. Ecological's standard warranty form stated that their liability was limited to repairing or replacing any defects in the automobile. Both purchasers signed the contract. Unfortunately, the first models did not run well even though Ecological made numerous attempts to repair the vehicles. Both purchasers ultimately decide the vehicles were "lemons" and have asked your opinion whether there was grounds for getting their money back from Ecological. Your advice to the buyers regarding their chances for rescission should be encouraging for

(A) Both National Steel Company and Nalph Rader.
(B) National Steel Company but not Nalph Rader.
(C) Nalph Rader but not National Steel Company.
(D) Neither National Steel Company nor Nalph Rader.

241. Paul Claimant threatens to sue Iola Innocent for breach of an employment contract seeking $10,000 damages. Iola felt that the lawsuit had no merit, but discussed the defense with Larry Lawyer who demanded a non-refundable retainer of $5,000 to defend the case. Iola did not pay the $5,000 immediately and ran into Paul later in the day at the local Starbucks Coffee store. She apologized to Paul who stated, "Maybe I overreacted and I will not enforce the agreement if you publicly apologize. Iola publicly apologized and in relief, told Paul that she had decided to use the $10,000 to purchase a cruise in the Bahamas. Three months later, Iola returned to her home and was served with a summons and complaint initiated by Paul based upon the alleged breach of the employment contract. The court will likely hold for

(A) Paul because his statement that he would not enforce the contract is a pre-lawsuit settlement negotiation which is not binding.

(B) Iola because Paul is estopped due to Iola purchasing the cruise ticket.
(C) Iola because the doctrine of promissory estoppel is met.
(D) Paul because he received no consideration for his promise.

242. Ike Insane was an 84-year-old man who has lived alone for 25 years since his wife died. He had become less and less able to care for himself, conduct his own affairs, and conduct reasonable business transactions. Ike began suffering memory lapses, losing things, paying some of his bills twice, and other erratic behavior. This increasingly worried his 53-year old son, Ernest.

Ike decided to sell his home so he could move into an assisted living complex. He refused to let his son Ernest help him make the arrangements. Ike himself advertised the house at 60% of its then fair value based on an appraisal he had commissioned 10 years ago. Sharp Buyer saw the ad, realized it was a "steal price," went directly to Ike's home, prepared a deed, and got Ike to sign it. When Ernest learned of the low price of the transaction, he hired your law firm to contest the transaction. The most helpful fact, if true, to rescind the transaction is that

(A) Ike was 84 years old and senile.
(B) Sharp can not meet his burden of showing the price was at market.
(C) Sharp knew at the contract date that Ike lacked cognitive capacity.
(D) Ike can introduce testimony from a psychiatrist stating that although it could not be stated conclusively that Ike was mentally incompetent, this could be asserted as a matter of medical probability.

243. Harry Hotroder had a souped-up 1940 Ford Coupe with a Chevrolet Corvette motor. While he was dragging on Main Street in Pleasant Town, he hit Ursula Uninvolved's car, which she had just parked on the street. Ursula was personally injured and received a $5,000 bill from Happy Hospital. Harry's insurance company, Fly-

by-Night Insurance settled with Ursula for $20,000 of which $5,000 was assigned to Ursula's personal injury and $15,000 to her car's damage. Happy Hospital assigned their $5,000 receivable to Bountiful Bank. Bountiful notified Fly-by-Night Insurance that they had received an assignment of the receivable Ursula owed to Happy Hospital. Subsequently, it was discovered that Harry was actually an irresponsible minor. If Happy Hospital and Bountiful Bank bring collection action against Fly-by-Night Insurance Company, the likely outcome is

(A) For Fly-by-Night Insurance because Harry Hotroder was a minor so the liability policy contract was not enforceable.

(B) Either Happy Hospital or Bountiful Bank could recover as assignee or subassignee because Harry Hotroder's minority did not vitiate the insurance policy contract.

(C) Neither Happy Hospital nor Bountiful Bank could recover because Ursula Uninvolved was a third-party beneficiary of a liability policy and their rights can be no greater than the assignor's.

(D) Neither Happy Hospital nor Bountiful Bank could recover unless Fly-by-Night Insurance Company waived Harry Hotroder's minority.

244. Ambrose telephoned Miller Adding Machine Company and ordered 1,000 pocket calculators at $4.05 each. Ambrose agreed to pay 10% immediately and the balance within ten days after receipt of the entire shipment. Ambrose forwarded a check for $405.00 and Miller shipped 500 calculators the next day, intending to ship the balance by the end of the week. Ambrose decided that the contract was a bad bargain and repudiated it, asserting the Statute of Frauds. Miller sued Ambrose. Which of the following will allow Miller to prevail despite the Statute of Frauds?

(A) The contract is not within the requirements of the statute.

(B) Ambrose paid 10% down.

(C) Miller shipped 500 of the calculators.

(D) Ambrose admitted in court that it made the contract in question.

245. Unreliable Supplier entered into a contract with Bobbie Buyer for 100 widgets at $15.00 each. One month before the contract designated delivery date, Unreliable called Bobbie and stated they would not perform. As of that date, the market price of an equivalent widget was $20.00. Bobbie pleaded with Unreliable in the hope they would change their minds. One month later on the originally scheduled delivery date, Bobbie concluded she needed to cover and purchased substitute equivalent goods. Which of the following is correct?

(A) Bobbie will recover $500 if the price she purchased the substitute widgets at was $17.00.

(B) Bobbie will recover $700 if the price she purchased the substitute widgets at was $22.00.

(C) Bobbie will recover $500 if the price she purchased the substitute widgets at was $25.00.

(D) Bobbie will recover nothing unless she covered by buying substitute equivalent goods since they were available on the open market.

246. Paul Promisor entered into a contract with Alex Assignor in which Paul promised to pay $5,000 and Alex promised to deliver goods on a net 30 day basis. Two days after Paul received the goods, Alex decided to assign the right to receive the $5,000 as a gift to his favorite niece, Alice Assignee. Alice was elated and told her uncle that she was contracting to buy a car with the $5,000. Alex later changed his mind and instructed Paul not to pay Alice. If a lawsuit is filed for a declaratory judgment, the court is likely to hold for

(A) Alex, who may revoke at will prior to Paul receiving notice of the assignment.

(B) Alice, even if she did not give consideration for the assignment.

(C) Alice, if she foreseeably relied on the assignment to her detriment.

(D) Alex, because he received no consideration for the gratuitous assignment.

247. Harriet Homeowner wanted to build a house on her property. She requested bids from three general contractors. Geneva General Contractor decided to bid on Harriet's project and contacted Connie Carpenter, a subcontractor, to bid on doing all the carpentry work for the project. Connie's bid was $75,000 and based upon that amount, Geneva bid $220,000 for all of Harriet's project. Connie was sent a copy of the bid. Two days later, Connie repudiated her $75,000 bid to Geneva. Three days later, Harriet awarded the $220,000 contract to Geneva. Geneva was forced to hire Rebecca Replacement for $85,000 to do the carpentry work on Harriet's project. If Geneva brings suit against Connie, the plaintiff's best argument is

(A) When Geneva used Connie's bid in calculating their bid to Harriet, an option contract was created.

(B) Geneva gave Connie consideration.

(C) Connie made an offer which Geneva accepted when it submitted the bid to Harriet.

(D) Connie's bid was irrevocable for a reasonable period of time because both the general and subcontractor are merchants in bidding on construction projects.

248. Henry Homeowner decided to build a custom designed house for his family. Henry hired Arthur Architect to design and prepare the building plans for the house. He then contracted with Charlie Contractor to build the house. The contract between Henry and Charlie contained a provision that required Arthur to issue a certificate of completion as a prerequisite to payment being made by Henry to Charlie. If Arthur refuses in bad faith to issue the certificate of completion and Charlie brings suit, the court will likely

(A) Enter judgment against Arthur in favor of Charlie.

(B) Enter an order of specific performance requiring Arthur to execute the certificate of completion.

(C) Require Charlie to proceed for reformation of the Henry to Charlie contract to strike the condition requiring a certificate of completion.

(D) None of the above.

249. Great Expectations, Inc., is a growing dot com business that had not yet turned profitable. The company was able to borrow $1,000,000 from Bigbucks Bank on a one-year secured promissory note. One year later when the promissory note came due, Great Expectations did not have the funds and Bigbucks threatened to foreclose on the assets under their security agreement. Ernest Young, CPA, was the chief financial officer of Great Expectations. His father-in-law, George Gratitude, wanted to help out. He called the loan officer at Bigbucks Bank and orally stated that if the Bank would forbear from any action against Great Expectations for one year, he would personally see that the loan was paid. The Bank agreed and wrote everyone a letter stating that they would forbear for a year. Notwithstanding their promise, the next month the Bank filed a foreclosure and collection action against Great Expectations and George Gratitude. The court would likely hold George was

(A) Liable because of the main purpose rule exception.

(B) Not liable because George was never under a duty as a surety.

(C) Not liable because Bigbucks Bank filed a foreclosure and collection action before the year had expired.

(D) Liable because the Bank's promise in writing is binding upon an oral surety.

250. Peter Professor was a tenured professor at Easy Way Law School. He was under contract with the school at a rate of $10,000 per month. In the summer, the law school experienced a substantial decline in enrollment for fall semester. To get the budget back into balance, the law school cut back on library hours and laid off some support staff. Peter's September payroll check was reduced to $9,000. Peter endorsed the back of the check and deposited it into his bank. Later, he inquired of the law school payroll department as to when he was going to receive the $1,000 balance. The law school's worst argument why they should not have to pay the $1,000 deficiency is

(A) Peter knew all the law school expenses were being reduced.

(B) All the other staff members received a reduced salary.

(C) On the back of the paycheck was the statement "tendered in full payment of this month's salary."

(D) Part payment of an unliquidated claim constitutes sufficient consideration for the discharge of the entire claim.

251. Albert and Baker signed a contract for the sale and purchase of Blueacre. Albert agreed to provide a statutory warranty deed to the property at closing and Baker promised to provide a $100,000 check at closing. Albert went to the closing but a problem developed in clearing the title so he did not produce a deed. Baker refused to give Albert the $100,000 check he had in his possession. If Albert brings an action to compel Baker to perform his promise, the court will likely hold for

(A) Albert since the court will create a constructive condition concurrent on Baker.

(B) Baker since the promises were bilateral and independently enforceable.

(C) Baker since the court will create a constructive condition concurrent on Albert.

(D) Albert if he can prove that producing the deed was impossible thus discharging his promise in the contract.

252. Fred Firebug entered into a contract with Paynoclaims Insurance Co. for a homeowner's policy on his personal residence. The policy covered up to $300,000 of damage to the house from whatever source. The premium was $200 per month due no later than the tenth of the month. On October 20th, 2005, the house experienced a fire caused by a faulty electrical appliance. Unfortunately, Fred had not paid the $200 premium due October 10th, 2005. Paynoclaims Insurance denied the fire loss claim of Fred because the premium was not paid timely. If Fred sues Paynoclaims for the fire loss, his best theory of recovery is that

(A) Fred did not receive notice that the policy coverage had been cancelled.

(B) Paynoclaims Insurance was under an independent duty to pay for the fire loss.

(C) Although he failed to make the insurance premium payment, there was a bargained for exchange.

(D) Paynoclaims Insurance's duty to pay a claim was not expressly conditioned on Fred's duty to pay the premiums.

253. Elmer Employee applied for a supervisory position at Floor Mart after working for L Mart, a national competitor. Both companies were large national retail discounters. In the employment contract Elmer was required to sign as a condition of being hired, Elmer agreed not to compete with Floor Mart for five years for a national retailer. The agreement also stated that Elmer agreed that if he would author an "independent letter" stating that Floor Mart was a better place to work than L Mart. Finally, he agreed not to work in the retail business in a marketing position for a year. Floor Mart fired Elmer 11 ½ months after his hiring and is insisting he sign the letter against L Mart, which he now believes would be inaccurate and potentially libelous. If Floor Mart files suit to enforce the terms of Elmer's employment agreement, the court will likely hold that

I. The competition time restriction of five years appears unreasonable and thus is to be disregarded.
II. There was no consideration given to create a binding contract in the first place.
III. The one year restriction on working in a marketing position violates public policy.
IV. The requirement to author an "independent letter" against L Mart is enforceable.
V. The requirement of non-employment by a competitive national retailer may be reasonable and enforceable.

True	False
(A) I, II, and V.	III and IV.
(B) II and IV.	I, III, and V.
(C) I, II, and IV.	III and V.
(D) I and V.	II, III, and IV.

254. Ed Employee was under a written two-year binding employment agreement as a store manager supervising 200 employees. The employer, Ceiling Mart in Chicago, terminated Ed because he complained to the federal government about the company's illegal labor actions. The employer retaliated by wrongfully terminating Ed with 18 months left on the contract. Ceiling Mart would have paid Ed $27,000 which is 18 months at the contracted salary of $1,500 per month. Ceiling Mart hired a private detective who gave testimony at trial that Ed had refused to accept alternative employment during the 18 months he would have been employed by Ceiling Mart as follows:

I. A local counter sales job at $600 per month.
II. A traveling auditor's position at $1,000 per month.
III. A store manager's position in Los Angeles at $1,500 per month.

The likely dollar amount judgment to be entered against Ceiling Mart in favor of Ed is

(A) -0-
(B) $9,000.
(C) $12,600.

(D) $27,000.

255. Profitisall, Inc., opened a dry cleaning and laundry business. In an attempt to lower their employee expense, the company began to hire immigrant children. A 15-year-old girl named Nancy Newcomer signed an employment agreement to work up to 60 hours a week at $4.00 per hour. Both the state and federal minimum wage laws were $5.05 per hour at the time. Nancy was aware the agreed terms violated the law, but she needed the money to support her family. Six months later, Profitisall fired Nancy and has refused to pay her the last two weeks wages due of $480.00. If Nancy sues Profitisall, the likely outcome will be a judgment for

	$480 not paid	$1,092 deficiency from minimum wage
(A) Yes	Yes	
(B) Yes	No	
(C) No	Yes	
(D) No	No	

256. Computer Lease LLC leased 300 small to medium size network computers to law firms. Lindows was a major software operating system used on all the computers. Computer Lease heard that Lindows was coming out with a new system called Ulast. Computer Lease thus approached Paula Programmer and explained that they needed her to update the software of all 300 computers at a price of $100 each beginning in 30 days. Paula said, "I need to charge $150 each." Later, she said, "I would really like to have your business." Computer Lease said, "We will see you in a month."

One month later, Computer Lease had 100 of the computers delivered to Paula's office. Paula said, "I'm sorry, but I just contracted to update computers by Fell, Inc., and I am now too busy to do yours."

Computer Lease brings a suit against Paula. Which of the below statements, if true, would be the most helpful to Computer Lease in its lawsuit.

(A) Computer Lease relied upon Paula's promise to upgrade in delivering the computers to Paula's office.

(B) At the time they offered the contract to Paula, Computer Lease had another upgrade offer at $100 which was not available one month later.

(C) Paula's statement, "I would really like to have your business," constituted sufficient acceptance intention.

(D) When Paula said, "I am now too busy," Computer Lease offered to pay $120 per computer and tendered a check for $12,000.

257. Loretta Landlord owned a commercial building in a commercial strip surrounded by a residential community. One of the largest spaces was rented on a month-to-month basis at $500 per month by a dance troop which held performances in the facility. The director of the troop got a real job offer at an off-Broadway production in Times Square and left. The troop was unable to find another director so it folded.

Sally Sleazy learned of the closure and decided the location would be perfect for a topless strip joint. Sally rented the space from Loretta under a two-year lease at $1,000 per month without disclosing her intended use of the space. One month after the strip joint opened, the county commissioners passed a new law prohibiting topless strip joints in that neighborhood. Sally told Loretta the new law made her business impossible so she was leaving. If Loretta sued Sally for breach of the lease contract, the likely outcome is a judgment for

(A) Sally because the law made performance of the lease contract impossible.

(B) Loretta because the new law was passed after the lease was executed.

(C) Loretta only if she did not know of the use Sally intended for the space.

(D) Sally because the lease contract was discharged under impossibility of performance.

Questions 258 and 259 are based on the following:

Roberta Retailer operated a retail computer store in Everycity, U.S.A. She purchased her inventory of computers from a wide variety of manufacturers, usually based upon catalogs left by sales representatives. One manufacturer, Southern Sales Company, had sent Roberta a catalog containing a tear-out order form. The written order form specified that a 2% discount was given for orders of over 5 computers if paid within 10 days. Roberta decided to buy 6 computers and on December 1st, she hand wrote on the order form, "Send 6 computers and I will pay in 30 days after deducting the 2% discount." Barbara mailed the order form which was received by Southern on December 3rd. On December 5th, the six computers were trucked to Roberta. On December 7th, Southern billed Roberta in the "final sales invoice" which stated, "We shipped pursuant to your request, but if you do not pay within 10 days, the 2% discount does not apply." This was received by Roberta on December 9th. On December 31st, Roberta paid the bill after deducting the 2% discount.

258. A contract for the sale and purchase of the six computers was formed on December

(A) 1st when Roberta signed and mailed the order form to Southern.

(B) 3rd when the order form was received by Southern.

(C) 5th when Southern trucked the computers to Roberta.

(D) 7th when Southern billed the "final sales invoice" to Roberta.

259. If Southern received the discounted check and brings suit against Roberta for the discount, the likely outcome would be for

(A) Southern if Roberta knew the order form specified that the 2% discount required payment within 10 days.

(B) Roberta because Southern accepted the offer of 30 days payment with the discount.

(C) Roberta only if she had received the 2% discount for payment in the past.

(D) Southern because Roberta's agreement to purchase was on Southern's order form.

Questions 260 and 261 are based on the following:

The East Legal Publishing Company is owned by a non-American foreign corporation. In order to improve their image and disguise their foreign ownership, East started an essay contest promotion targeting first year American law students. The essay subject was "why I want to attend an American law school" and the prize was a full tuition scholarship for the second and third years of law school. Nancy Needy won the contest and was awarded the scholarship.

Nancy's favorite Uncle Harry, an attorney, was very proud of his niece and her scholarship achievements. Harry hoped Nancy would complete her J.D. degree and go onto graduate school and earn an LL.M. He knew that to be admitted to a quality LL.M. program would require a high grade point average and class standing in the J.D. program. Therefore, Harry told Nancy, "I will give you $500 for every A that you earn in the last two years of your J.D. program. In addition, if you are admitted to a quality LL.M. graduate program, I will pay all your tuition."

Nancy was very encouraged and earned eight As in her second and third year. In addition, she was accepted into a top 10 quality LL.M. graduate program. During the winter of her third year in the J.D. program, Nancy's Uncle Harry died. Nancy's cousin, Sharon Stingy, was appointed executrix and refused to pay Nancy for the five As she had earned in her third year. Sharon also informed Nancy the estate would not pay for the LL.M. tuition.

260. If Nancy asserts a $2,500 claim against the estate for the five As she earned

in her third year of law school, the likely outcome is for

(A) Nancy because her essay won the East contest.

(B) The estate because Nancy was otherwise legally required to use her best efforts in law school.

(C) The estate because Uncle Harry died before Nancy earned the As in question.

(D) Nancy if she made extra efforts in her attempt to earn As prior to Uncle Harry's death.

261. If Nancy asserts a claim against the estate for the tuition costs of her LL.M. program, the most effective defense against the claim is

(A) Harry's promise was a mere gift lacking consideration.

(B) The contract was not in writing.

(C) The contract was divisible.

(D) Harry's offer to pay the LL.M. program tuition terminated on his death.

262. Bigger Bucks law firm organized a summer intern program for 2L law students. Some of those who performed well during this internship trial period were offered full time positions as associates upon their graduation. Roger Ready participated in the summer internship program and performed very well. That fall, Roger and Bigger Bucks signed an associate employment contract that was to begin in September of the next year after he passed the bar exam. On July 15th, a recruiter from Navy JAG contacted Bigger Bucks. The recruiter indicated that Roger had enlisted in Navy JAG. This news came as a surprise to Bigger Bucks, but they immediately offered the associate position to Sharon Second who immediately accepted at the same salary offered to Roger. Unfortunately, Roger failed the final Navy physical and was thus rejected. On September 1st, Roger reported for work at Bigger Bucks law firm. The senior partner told him that he was not going to start work there. If Roger files a lawsuit for breach of contract against Bigger Bucks, the likely outcome is for

(A) Roger because he did not tell Bigger Bucks that he had accepted other employment and/or would not be starting with the law firm.

(B) Bigger Bucks because Roger's enlistment in Navy JAG was an express anticipatory repudiation of his contract with Bigger Bucks.

(C) Bigger Bucks because they hired Sharon Second as an associate in reliance on the reasonable belief that Roger would be unable to perform as agreed.

(D) Roger because he was ready, willing, and able to perform as agreed on September 1st.

263. Farmer Fred owned a 20-acre potato farm located in a mid-west jurisdiction. Fred was advancing in age and none of his children had expressed an interest in potato farming. He discussed this with his banker who agreed that a farm sale might be the best alternative. Banker also mentioned his brother was interested in purchasing potato farms. Fred met with Banker's brother and they agreed on a sale and purchase of the farm at $250,000. Banker and his brother were aware the state legislature was seriously considering authorizing funding for an interstate highway off-ramp near the farm, and that the county commissioners were considering rezoning the area from farming to commercial use. Fred was unaware of both possibilities and neither Banker nor his brother informed him of either.

Within a month of the sale and purchase of Fred's farm, the legislature authorized funding for the interstate off-ramp and the county rezoned the farm property to commercial use. The value of the land increased to $1,500,000 immediately. If Farmer Fred sues for rescission of the purchase-sale agreement, the likely outcome is for

(A) Fred, if the Banker and his brother was aware that the legislature and county actions made the farm worth substantially more that the contract price.

(B) Banker's brother, unless a reasonable person in Farmer Fred's position would have become aware that the farm was worth substantially more than $250,000 at the contract date.

(C) Banker's brother, only if both he and Farmer Fred were mistaken about the value of the farm at the contract date.

(D) Fred, but the appropriate remedy is to have the court reform the contract to reflect a value of $1,500,000.

Questions 264 and 265 are based on the following:

Oscar Owner owned Greenacre Farm in fee simple having inherited the family farm property from his parents. Oscar's children moved to the city and decided not to continue the farm. Oscar thus decided he should sell the property. He contacted a licensed real estate sales broker named Brian Broker on December 26th, 2004 and signed an agreement specifying Brian had an exclusive right to sell Greenacre for two months at a price of $250,000. The contract specified Brian was to be paid a 5% commission upon transfer of title to a buyer whom Brian produced. Brian advertised and showed Greenacre to Paula Purchaser who offered to pay full price for the property if Oscar delivered evidence of clear title. Oscar commissioned Grand Title Insurance company which researched the chain of title and issued a title policy to Oscar with no unusual exceptions.

Oscar's daughter, Denise, learned of the contemplated transaction with Paula. She had second thoughts about the family farm being sold to an outsider. She therefore pressured her father not to complete the sale to Paula.

After waiting for one month, Paula notified Oscar that she was going to purchase another farm because of Oscar's failure to deliver Greenacre's abstract of title. Oscar then contracted to sell Greenacre Farm to Denise for $200,000 on February 20th, 2005 with closing to be held on March 10th, 2005. Two days later Denise passed away without closing the transaction. Oscar decided to keep Greenacre.

264. If Brian brings suit to collect the 5% commission on the aborted sale of Greenacre to Paula, the most effective argument to prevail would be
- (A) Oscar's refusal to deliver the abstract of title frustrated the purpose of the contract between Oscar and Brian.
- (B) Brian's efforts produced a buyer who was ready, willing, and able to purchase Greenacre.
- (C) Oscar and Paula entered into a sale and purchase contract for Greenacre as a result of Brian's efforts.
- (D) Paula would have taken title to Greenacre had it not been for the willful breach of contract by Oscar.

265. If Brian brings suit to collect the 5% commission on the sale of Greenacre to Denise, the most effective argument to defeat the commission claim would be
- (A) As a result of Denise's death, transfer of title did not take place.
- (B) Brian did not produce Denise as a potential buyer.
- (C) The price of the purchase by Denise was $200,000 not $250,000.
- (D) The closing was scheduled for March 10th, 2005 which was more than two months from the listing date.

Questions 266 – 267 are based on the following:

Penny Public was a 3L student in law school. One of her non-law school friends lived in a run-down apartment house that was owned by a slum landlord. The building was continually rendered uninhabitable because the landlord failed to make basic repairs. Because the landlord failed to pay utility bills the tenants experienced utility service disruptions. Penny volunteered to prepare a complaint on behalf of all the tenants. At a meeting one of the tenants asked, "What will you charge for this?" Penny answered, "I'm not doing this for money."

Penny graduated from law school but the law firm she was hoping would employ her withdrew its employment offer after she failed the bar exam. The tenants' lawsuit was successful and resulted in a large cash judgment in favor of the tenants. Penny then told the tenants she should receive one-third of the recovery from the case. Many tenants disagreed. Penny said that she would bring suit if she did not receive some fee. The tenants agreed in a written vote to give Penny 1/6, provided she would not bring her suit.

266. Assume that the tenants change their minds and refuse to pay Penny 1/6 of the judgment amount. If Penny brings a collection lawsuit and prevails, the most likely reason would be:
- (A) A judgment for the tenants would result in the unjust enrichment of the tenants at Penny's expense.
- (B) The tenants' agreement with Penny was a compromise.
- (C) The document that the tenants executed was an offer for a unilateral contract, which Penny accepted by not bringing her prior lawsuit.
- (D) The tenants are estopped from denying the validity of the agreement to pay 1/6.

267. Independent of your answer above, assume that Penny brings suit against the tenants for the reasonable value of her services, instead of the 1/6 share specified in the prior agreement. The court will likely hold for:
- (A) The tenants, because Penny is bound to accept 1/6 even though

the tenants have repudiated their promise.

(B) Penny, under a theory of quantum meruit.

(C) Penny, if the jurisdiction has a "Good Samaritan" statute.

(D) The tenants, since Penny said, "I'm not doing this for money."

268. Article 2 of the Uniform Commercial Code

(A) Applies to the purchase and sale of a live golden retriever dog by one consumer from another consumer.

(B) Applies only if one of the parties to the live golden retriever purchase and sale was a merchant.

(C) Does not apply to a live golden retriever purchase and sale because a dog is a living thing, and thus does not meet the definition of a "good" under the UCC.

(D) Does not apply to a contract for the purchase and sale of the first pup of a specified golden retriever dog unless that pup is alive at the contract date.

269. Pat Promisor was at a deserted beach with her two children. At the beach, signs were posted stating, "Surfing is not allowed." Pat's son, a 12-year-old boy, was surfing on a large piece of plywood. A large wave caught the boy and the board and threw them ten feet into the air and into the shallow waters of the beach. The boy hit his head on a rock. This rendered the boy unconscious, and the undertow began to pull him out to sea. Pat saw all of this occur and screamed four times, "Please, anyone, save my son from drowning!" Robin Rescuer heard Pat's scream, dove into the surf, and pulled Pat's son to safety. Pat refused to pay Robin for her services. If Robin brings a lawsuit for compensation on a theory of promissory estoppel, Pat's most effective argument in her defense is:

(A) There was no consideration for Pat's promise.

(B) Pat's cries for help did not imply a promise of payment and Rescuer

was unreasonable in inferring any such right.

(C) Rescuer was a mere volunteer without any right to compensation.

(D) The value of her son's life is too speculative to support a recovery of the value received.

270. Well Computer, Inc. manufactures computers for business and personal use. Well sold directly to both consumers and retailers. Roberta Retailer had secured a purchase order for ten super-deluxe Well computers from one of its customers, to be delivered no later than December 31st. In return, Roberta ordered ten super-deluxe computers from Well, subject to delivery on or before December 30th. Well ran short of the super-deluxe model. Two of the ten computers sent as an accommodation were the model just below super-deluxe. Roberta received all ten computers on December 30th. Upon receipt of the ten computers, which of the following correctly states Roberta's rights against Well?

I.   Reject the entire 10 computers.

II. Accept the entire 10 computers.

III. Accept the eight conforming computers and reject the 2 non-conforming computers.

IV. Sue Well for damages.

(A) I or II only.

(B) I, II, or III only.

(C) II or III and IV.

(D) I or II or III and IV.

271. Greta Guarantor had a friend, Diane Debtor, who was a third year law student. Diane was short of cash and had exhausted all her student loans. Greta went to another friend, Carol Creditor and said "my friend Diane needs $30,000 to complete her final year of law school. Will you lend it to her for two years?" Carol responded, "I would like to help out, but Diane has no way to pay me back." Greta answered, "Well, okay, but why don't you lend the money to me but give it to Diane." Carol said, "That's fine." The next day Carol mailed to Diane a check for $30,000 payable to Diane's order. Two years came and went, and Carol had not received her repayment. After making a demand on both Greta and Diane, Carol filed suit against both defendants. If Greta brings a motion to dismiss herself as a defendant on the basis that there was not a written agreement between her and Carol, the likely outcome is that the motion would be

(A) Denied, if Carol's statement "That's fine" was an acceptance of Greta's promise to pay Diane's debt to Carol.

(B) Granted, because the $30,000 that Carol lent to Diane exceeded $500.

(C) Granted, if Greta's statement "Well, okay, but why don't you lend the money to me but give it to Diane" was a promise to guarantee Diane's debt to Carol.

(D) Denied, if Carol's check was a written negotiable instrument that memorialized the debt.

272. Ramona Restauranteur hired Connie Contractor to build a custom-designed restaurant. The written contract price was $400,000 to be paid in full at substantial completion of the contract, which was expected to take 4 months. Ramona began construction and appeared to be on schedule. Ramona unexpectedly received a $4 million inheritance and decided to retire. She then told Connie to stop work. Connie had spent $300,000 for labor and materials on the building and estimated that there was another $50,000 of costs to completion. Ramona offered to reimburse Connie the $300,000 she had spent but no more. The market interest rate at the time was 12% annually. Connie sued Ramona and it took one year to get the case to trial. Due to a healthy local economy, the value of the partially completed building increased to $375,000 during that year. At trial the court will likely enter a judgment for

(A) $350,000

(B) $375,000

(C) $392,000

(D) $400,000

273. Oscar Owner retained Always Building, a contractor, to build a $200,000 home for him and his family. The contract was written and contained a covenant specifying, "Both parties agree not to assign any rights under this contract." Oscar did agree to pay $50,000 of the $200,000 directly to Big Bucks Bond because Always was previously indebted to Big Bucks for that amount. Subsequently, Big Bucks assigned the $50,000 right to Second Bank. Big Bucks had a subsequent disagreement with Always and brought suit against Oscar for the $50,000 amount. The most effective argument Oscar can make in defense of claim is

(A) All assignments were illegal because they were specifically prohibited in the contract.

(B) Big Bucks made a valid assignment of their rights under the contract.

(C) Big Bucks was not a party to the Oscar-Always contract and is thus an incidental beneficiary with no enforceable rights.

(D) Oscar believes that Always' performance was inadequate.

274. Sharon Shopping Center owned a strip mall containing a tenant operating a non-profit legal clinic. Rent for the clinic's space was $10,000 per month. The legal clinic was nearing the end of its lease term and the director began to look for a new location with lower rent. The clinic found a substitute location at a rent of $8,000 per month. When Sharon learned that her tenant might not renew, she orally offered the clinic a six-month right to renew at $8,000 per month. Without telling Sharon, the legal clinic then told all their employees that they were not moving and spent $5,000 on a designer's plans to renovate the existing space.

At the last moment Sharon found a tenant willing to pay $15,000 per month for the space, and initiated an eviction action against the legal clinic. The legal clinic in return counterclaimed seeking an order of specific performance or damages. The court will likely find for

(A) The legal clinic, because it relied to its detriment on the six-month right to renew promised by Sharon.

(B) Sharon, because creating the plans to renovate the office in the future does not constitute a present detriment.

(C) Sharon, unless the legal clinic provided consideration for the option.

(D) The legal clinic, because an option may not be revoked during the specified time period, and the six-months' rent constituted consideration.

Questions 275 and 276 are based on the following:

The U.S. government was trying to equip a newly formed brigade of specialty troops to fight in the desert. To do so, it began negotiating with Harry Hummer to purchase 100 super Hummer tanks according to the government's specifications. The tanks had to operate in the desert at high temperatures for prolonged periods. Hummer's normal $15,000 Hummer tanks could not meet the specifications. Hummer told the government buyer on the phone that the cost of the vehicles would be $20,000 each or $2,000,000 payable 60 days after delivery. Delivery was expected to be made on December 25th.

Two weeks later on August 1st after securing other bids, the government lawyer telephoned Hummer and accepted the offer. The following day the buyer mailed a memorandum to Hummer that stated "please be advised that instead of paying 60 days after delivery, we will take a 10% cash discount and pay on delivery." Hummer received the memorandum on August 5th but did not respond until September 1st. In a fax dated September 1st, Hummer stated "It seems to me that we do not have a valid contract at all, so I am going to sell the specially-made vehicles to a Jordanian businessman."

275. Assume that the U.S. government brings a lawsuit against Hummer for breach of contract and Hummer defends on the basis that the statute of frauds has been violated. The court will likely find for

(A) The U.S., because Hummer failed to respond to the U.S. memorandum within a reasonable period of time.

(B) Hummer, because the sale to the Jordanian businessman is strong evidence that the goods are saleable to others in the ordinary course of business, and the contract exceeded $500.

(C) Hummer, because the U.S. memorandum was not sufficient to indicate that a contract was formed.

(D) The U.S., because their memorandum must be treated as a mere proposal for change.

276. Assume that Hummer admits he entered into the U.S. contract for the sale at $2,000,000. The U.S. then insists upon performance at a price of $1,800,000 payable on delivery. If performance is timely rendered by Hummer, the court will likely hold the transaction price to be

(A) $1,800,000 because Hummer did not specifically object to the 10% discount within a reasonable period of time.

(B) $1,800,000 because Hummer's performance is deemed to constitute acceptance under the "master of the bargain" and "last-shot" formation rule.

(C) $2,000,000 because the reduction to $1,800,000 is likely to be interpreted as a request for additional terms that was not agreed to.

(D) $2,000,000 because the discount term in the U.S.'s memorandum materially altered the terms of Hummer's offer.

277. Cablevision operated a cable television station in Pleasant Town USA offering television and internet connection services to businesses and personal homes. Cablevision purchased their installation cable in standard 6, 12, 20 and 15 foot lengths. On January 1st, Cablevision placed an order for 10,000 6-foot cables with Cabblesupplier Inc. On February 1st the cables were delivered in huge reels to Cablevision on 30 day open account. On February 15th, the first of the Cabblesupplier's cables were used on an installation job. Here it was discovered that the 6-foot cables were only 5 feet in length, and not the 6-foot variety as ordered. The workman informed the purchasing agent that same week leading to the purchasing agent preparing a memorandum of nonconformity. Before it was mailed to Cabblesupplier the memorandum had to be reviewed by the Operational Vice President. Somewhere in the chain of command the memorandum was lost and not sent to Cabblesupplier. If Cabblesupplier brings suit on April 1st for the amount due under the invoice and Cablevision defends upon the basis that the cable delivered did not conform to the contract, the court will likely hold for

(A) Cablevision, unless 15 days was an unreasonable time to delay discovery of the non-conformity.

(B) Cablesupplier because a merchant purchaser is not entitled to claim revocation of acceptance if a reasonable inspection at the time of receipt would have discovered the defect.

(C) Cabblesupplier, because the buyer Cablevision failed to inform them that the 6-foot cables ordered were only 5 feet in length.

(D) Cablevision because the 5-foot cable did not conform to the contract and a perfect tender is required.

Questions 278 and 279 are based on the following:

Terri Tenant signed a six-year lease with Louise Landlord for a retail space in Louise's strip mall. The lease contract did not address the question of whether a new party could receive an assignment. Terri started a pizza restaurant called Pizza Place which was very successful. Three years later Terri sold the Pizza Place to Betty Buyer and signed a three-year non-compete agreement prohibiting her operating a restaurant operation within a one mile radius. Terri then sent a written memorandum to Louise's specifying that Betty will be paying the rent in the future. Betty took over operation of the restaurant and began to pay the rent to Louise. Two years later, Terri began a Mexican restaurant within a mile of the Pizza Place. Betty was unable to compete, her business declined, and she vacated Louise's strip mall and ceased paying rent.

278. If Betty sues Terri for violation of the non-compete covenant the court will likely hold for

(A) Betty unless the restriction was unreasonable as to prohibitions on subject matter, geographic area or time period.

(B) Terri because the covenant did not specifically prohibit opening a Mexican restaurant.

(C) Terri if Betty drafted the restaurant sales agreement because ambiguity is to be construed against the drafting party.

(D) Betty if the non-compete covenant was bargained for.

279. If Louise Landlord sues Terri Tenant for the unpaid balance of the rent due under the lease contract the most effective argument in defense would be

(A) Louise's acceptance of the rent from Betty without objection was an implied consent to Terri's assignment to Betty.

(B) The lease document did not specifically prohibit the assignment of the balance of the contract obligations.

(C) Louise's accepting rent from Betty resulted in an effective novation.

(D) Louise's accepting rent from Betty resulted in an accord and satisfaction.

Questions 280 and 281 are based on the following:

Alice Accountant operated a medium-size CPA firm in Middletown, USA. Her husband David Downer was a third year law student whose class standing was very low. Alice was commissioned by a large law firm to do an audit of their financial statements and assist them in a significant litigation support engagement. She offered to take a 10% discount on the her accounting work if the law firm would hire her husband David. In a subsequent written agreement for her work there was no mention of the law firm hiring David although the senior partner told Alice they would bring him on for the next year as a new associate beginning immediately.

Alice subsequently told David of the one year employment agreement. David quit his job as a bartender in a local bar and went to work for the law firm. Eight months later Alice and David divorced and she informed the law firm she was waiving the requirement of David's employment. The law firm immediately discharged David.

280. David brought suit against the law firm for the balance of the compensation due under the one-year employment agreement. The court will likely decide the dispute by finding for

(A) The law firm because David gave nothing in return for the law firm's employment promise.

(B) David if he can show damages.

(C) David only if the promise of employment was in writing.

(D) The law firm because the firm and Alice rescinded their contract by mutual acceptance.

281. Assume that David brings suit against Alice for the damages he suffered from being terminated by the law firm. Alice defends upon the basis that she received no consideration for promising David that the law firm would employ him for a year. The most effective argument David could raise in rebuttal would be that

(A) Alice made an irrevocable assignment to David of her right under her contract with the law firm.

(B) Love and mutual respect is sufficient consideration to support promises between spouses.

(C) The law firm's promise to hire David was given in return for reduction of Alice's fees.

(D) The promise of employment was obtained as a gift from Alice to David.

282. Wild Wendy was the daughter of Paul and Paula from Spokane, Washington. She moved to New York City immediately after graduating from Pow Dunk College. Her parents kept hoping she would return to Spokane. To facilitate such a decision by their daughter, Paul and Paula orally promised to give Wild a single family residence they owned in Spokane. Wild made plans to return to Spokane and immediately cancelled a contract she had made to purchase a flat on the upper east side of Manhattan. Paul and Paula changed their mind about making the gift to Wild after she hooked up with her boyfriend, Wildman, whom Paul and Paula did not like. If Wild brings suit against Paul and Paula seeking specific performance of title to the Spokane residence, which of the following would be the most effective defense.

(A) The movement from New York City to Spokane was not consideration for Paul and Paula's promise to give the house to Wild.

(B) The contract for the transfer of property was not in writing.

(C) The relinquishment of the contract to purchase the flat on the Upper East Side was not adequate consideration.

(D) This was a mere gift promise that remains revocable prior to performance.

Questions 283 and 284 are based on the following:

Cheap Gas Inc. was a retail multi-location gas station company in Los Angeles, California. In order to centralize and stabilize their retail gasoline supply they entered into an agreement with a gasoline wholesaler named Mega Oil, Inc. The contract specified that Mega would furnish Cheap Gas with gasoline at a price to be determined by a formula based in part upon the marketprice of crude oil. For a two year period of time, Cheap Gas agreed to purchase all their gasoline requirements from Mega and no other source. Before the end of every month Cheap was to advise Mega of the quantity they needed for the next month. Mega would deliver that quantity over the month in three lots with payment due within 10 days of each delivery. There was no provision in the agreement relating to either party's ability to assign or delegate.

The agreement worked well for three months. Cheap advised Mega of their needs every month, Mega delivered timely and Cheap paid within 10 days of delivery. Mega then merged into Summa Gas & Oil Inc. owned by foreign interests. The next month Summa delivered to Cheap the same quantity of gasoline that they had ordered the previous month.

Within a week of receipt, Cheap paid the invoice it had received from Summa. In the same envelope Cheap's President inserted a letter he had written which demanded assurances that Summa would be able and willing to meet Cheap's need for gasoline in the future. 40 days later, not having heard from Summa, Cheap wrote to the Presidents of both Summa and Mega and stated that Cheap was canceling the contract.

283. If Summa files a breach of contract lawsuit against Cheap for failure to continue their gasoline purchases the court will likely hold in favor of

(A) Summa unless there is evidence presented that Summa would not properly perform the original Cheap-Mega contract.

(B) Cheap because Summa did not respond to the assurance request made by Cheap.

(C) Cheap because requirement contracts for necessities are not assignable unless the buyer consents in advance.

(D) Summa because Cheap did not order the gasoline for the next month following the assurance request.

284. If Cheap Gas files a lawsuit against the other party in the original contract, Mega, the court would likely hold in favor of

(A) Cheap Gas

(B) Mega unless its assignment of rights to Summa also included a delegation of duties.

(C) Mega because Cheap implicitly agreed to the delegation of duty to Mega by accepting delivery and demanding assurances from Summa.

(D) Cheap Gas only if they promptly objected to the delegation.

285. Susan Summer was driving through the Cascade Mountains in Washington State during the end of her cross country journey from Boston to Seattle. Alongside the road was a picture-perfect lake with a small island in the middle. Susan had an uncontrollable urge to go for a swim. She parked her car, put on her bathing suit and dove in. About half-way out to the Island she had a bad leg cramp. Penny Passerby saw Susan in the lake and heard her scream for help. She voluntarily and quickly swam out, pulled Susan back to shore and drove her to a hospital that was 20 miles away. The attending doctor told both women that Susan could have possibly drowned if not for Penny's quick rescue. Susan then made out a writing stating, "I hereby promise to pay you Penny $25,000 in return for you saving my life." Penny made plans to use the money to buy a new car. Two months later Penny contacted Susan demanding the $25,000 and Susan stated that she had changed her mind. If Penny brings suit which of the below would be the most effective argument to support her claim.

(A) Penny detrimentally relied upon Susan's promise.

(B) Susan's promise to pay the $25,000 was written.

(C) Penny's rescue of Susan resulted in a contract in quantum merit or implied-in-fact.

(D) Susan's promise to pay the $25,000 was supported by the moral obligation created when a person's life is saved.

Questions 286-288 are based on the following:

Sandra Stampcollecter was an enthusiastic stamp collector who specialized in rare early Colonial American mint issued stamps. Sandra authorized Debra Dealer, a well-known stamp dealer, to purchase a King George 1 pence stamp which had been issued in 1775. Her written directive to Debra on December 25th was "buy up to 5 of the mint stamp issue and I do not care about the price."

On January 1st, Debra wrote a letter to Sandra stating "I have found two mint King George 1 pence stamps in very good condition. The seller wants $65,000 each for the two stamps, which is considerably less than the market value according to the American Stamp Collector's Bluebook valuation. Are you still interested at this price? If so, please let me know if this price is acceptable to you."

Sandra received the writing from Debra on January 5th. On January 6th she sent an e-mail stating "Yes, $130,000 is a fair price if the two King George 1 pence stamps are in top condition." Sandra's e-mail server, operated by a third party, malfunctioned and the e-mail was not sent to Debra. On January 15th, not having received any communication from Sandra, Debra e-mailed another retail stamp collector named Betty Betterbuyer. She offered to sell the two King George 1 pence stamps to her for $140,000. "If interested at this price please write me a response as soon as possible."

Betty received the e-mail from Debra on January 16th and immediately returned an e-mail stating, "I accept your offer to sell the two King Georges 1 pence stamps for $140,000, Betty."

Betty had previously heard that Sandra was trying to buy mint King George edition stamps. She called Sandra on January 17th on the phone and told her she had purchased two mint stamps from Debra and would sell them to Sandra for $150,000.

On January 18th Sandra's e-mail server, operated by a third party, was fixed by a repair person. The server immediately sent out all the e-mails in the outbox which included the delayed January 5th e-mail to Debra. She then delivered the stamps to Betty.

286.   If Sandra sues Debra and the court determined that Debra's January 1st letter to Sandra was not a valid offer the most likely reason would be because the writing

(A) Did not specify terms of payment of the $130,000.

(B) Did not specify a manner of acceptance.

(C) Did not manifest an intention to be bound.

(D) Was an acceptance of the offer contained in Sandra's December 25th writing.

287. If Sandra sues Debra and the court determines that Debra's January 1st letter was a valid offer, was a contract formed between Sandra and Debra?

    (A) Yes if sending an e-mail was a reasonable manner for Sandra to accept Debra's offer.

    (B) No because an offer sent by mail may be accepted only by mail.

    (C) No if Debra had changed her mind about the prize prior to January 1st.

    (D) Yes since Sandra as a merchant dealing in rare stamps was required to act in good faith.

288. Assume that no contract resulted from the Sandra to Debra negotiations. Was there a contract that resulted from the Debra to Betty communications?

    (A) No, unless there was a past course of dealings between Debra and Betty.

    (B) Yes, because after receiving the January 16th e-mail Debra delivered the stamps to Betty.

    (C) Yes, only if the January 16th e-mail from Betty to Debra is properly characterized as an offer.

    (D) No, if January 15th e-mail from Debra to Betty did not manifest the intent to be bound.

289. Oscar Owner operated a successful Thai food restaurant in Pleasantville, New York. His cousin, Clark Kent lived in Localview, Kansas and learned of Oscar's restaurant. Clark called Oscar and asked if the restaurant was for sale. Oscar said yes and sent Clark a video showing the restaurant and the restaurant's financial statements. Based upon this information Clark agreed to purchase Oscar's restaurant at a set price to be paid in cash upon taking over the restaurant. Clark told Oscar he would sell his home in Kansas and move with his family to Pleasantville. When Clark arrived in Pleasantville, Oscar informed him that he had changed his mind and now planned to keep the restaurant. If Clark sues Oscar for breach of contract the court will likely hold for

    (A) Clark because he detrimentally relied upon Oscar's promise to sell him the restaurant.

    (B) Oscar because Clark did not pay for the restaurant.

    (C) Oscar because his family affections for Clark is not sufficient consideration to support the promise to sell the restaurant.

    (D) Clark under a theory of bargained-for exchange.

290. Carol Collector inherited a 100 year old oil painting of a well-known local artist. Her friend, Eva Envious, had wanted to obtain the painting for years because it would be a perfect match for her family room. Carol refused to sell the painting on numerous occasions. On April 15th Eva again asked Carol if she would sell the painting. Carol replied, "I'd consider selling to you but I have no idea what the painting is worth." Eva said she would commission appraisals to determine the value, if Carol would promise to seriously consider selling the painting for whatever they found to be the proper price.

On April 20th Carol and Eva executed a document stating "Carol hereby agrees to sell to Eva the antique painting for a price to be agreed upon after the appraisals are complete." Eva had three appraisals prepared producing values of $3,000, $4,000 and $5,000. When Eva demanded that Carol go forward with the transaction she refused. If Eva sues Carol seeking specific performance, the court will likely hold for

    (A) Eva but impose a price on the transaction which the judge determines to be reasonable.

    (B) Carol because the alleged contract does not manifest an intent to be bound.

    (C) Carol because specific performance will not be imposed since damages are adequate.

    (D) Eva if she is willing to pay the full $5,000 for the painting.

291. Sammy Slippery owned a outdoor clothing manufacturing company and hired a Certified Public Accountant (CPA) to upgrade their computer and accounting systems for a reasonable fee. The written agreement specified that "Sammy retains the right to end this CPA's contract before completion if a quicker substitute computer program becomes available."

Sammy did not pay the billings of the CPA firm. After many months the CPA firm finally decided to bring a contract collection lawsuit against Sammy. In deciding the contract collection action, the court will likely hold for

(A) The CPA firm because the contract is not illusory.
(B) Sammy because the right to cancel made the contract illusory.
(C) Sammy because the "reasonable fee" protection rendered the contract too uncertain to be enforced.
(D) The CPA firm under a promissory estoppel theory because they detrimentally relied.

292. Gerry Gambler operated a race track for thoroughbred horses. The revenue came both from spectators at the races and gamblers that put down bets on particular horses for particular races. Gerry tried to attract the best known thoroughbreds she could book because attendance and bets both increased in races having a big name horse participating. Gerry contracted with an owner of Racerstar, a stallion that ran very fast, for four races the weekend of July 4th and 5th. Gerry featured Racerstar in photographic layouts that were heavily advertised.

On July 1st Racerstar's owner contacted Gerry and explained that Racerstar had come down with a mysterious attack of horicitisis. Apparently the attendant veterinarian believed that the disease of horicitisis was very contagious. The owner offered to substitute three other horses in the place of Racerstar. Gerry was very upset that the

track's July 4th and 5th weekend would not include Racerstar's participation. If Gerry sues for breach of contract the remedy will be

(A) Nothing because of the defense of impossibility.
(B) Compensatory damages including any profits lost because Racerstar did not run in the July 4th and 5th races and such services may not be performed by others.
(C) Specific performance because Racerstar is unique and still able to enter the races.
(D) Nothing, because damages resulting from one more or less horse in the race are too uncertain to be awarded.

Questions 293-294 are based on the following:

Jack Jerk was a practical joker who seemed to enjoy playing practical jokes on others. He was vacationing at a mountain side resort in the Grand Tetton nation park. He was in the hotel cocktail lounge and after a few drinks met Sarah Sucker. 10 minutes later Jack loudly said "Sarah, I will pay you $3,000 if you climb to the top of the mountain within three days." Sarah said, "sure, I'll do it tomorrow morning." They exchanged cell phone numbers.

Sarah immediately went to the local climbing equipment store and purchased the necessary climbing gear. At first light the next morning Sarah began her climb which she estimated would take 10 hours. At around 10:00 a.m. the next morning Jack woke up and realized what he had said to Sarah in the cocktail lounge. He called Sarah who was then about one-third of the way up the mountain and said, "I was only joking, you can come back down."

293. Regarding the legal rights Sarah has against Jack,

(A) Sarah will prevail for $1,000 because she has performed one third of the required performance.

(B) Jack will owe nothing because the promise was made as a joke.

(C) Jack will owe $3,000 because the communications will be deemed to have created a bilateral contract to protect the offeree's performance.

(D) Sarah will prevail because the offer became irrevocable when she bought the climbing equipment and began the climb.

294. Sarah calls you as her attorney on her cell phone immediately after she received the call from Jack. She explained the details of the offer Jack made yesterday in the cocktail lounge, the following actions she had taken and that she was now one-third up the mountain. Which of the below is the most likely legal advice you would render to Sarah.

(A) She does not need to complete the climb to collect the $1,000 if she detrimentally relied on Jack's offer.

(B) She does not need to complete the climb to collect the $3,000 if she detrimentally relied on Jack's offer.

(C) She needs to complete the climb in order to qualify for compensatory damages.

(D) She is entitled to punitive damages because of Jack's outrageous reprehensible conduct in addition to compensatory damage of $1,000 if she stops or $3,000 if she completes the climb.

295. Roberta Retailer operated a retail store specializing in selling industrial vacuum cleaners. She looked at an on-line catalog from Super Vacuum Cleaner Manufacturing Co. containing a wide variety of their vacuums. Roberta completed the on-line order form for 10 model AB at $50 each. The catalog stated that this model would vacuum 5 pounds per minute. In the miscellaneous section of the order form Roberta typed the words "this order for prompt shipment with delivery no later than July 1st and preferably earlier."

Roberta's server transmitted the e-mail on June 5th and it was received the same day by Super. On June 10th, Super's sale manager authorized an order confirmation form to Roberta which states, "we are out of stock in model AB but are shipping you 10 model BCs as an accommodation." Roberta did not respond to the e-mail.

On June 15th a truck appeared at Roberta's business. The truck driver wanted to unload the 10 Super vacuums. Roberta said, "just a minute while I inspect the vacuums." Seeing that they were model BC instead of model AB, Roberta said, "I refuse to accept this shipment and you should return the vacuums to Super." As of June 16th the status of the agreement was that

(A) The contract was formed on June 10th when Super's sales manager accepted Roberta's order.

(B) No contract was formed and neither Roberta nor Super have any liability to each other.

(C) The contract was formed when Super shipped the goods and Roberta breached the contract upon her refusal to accept the vacuums.

(D) The contract was formed when Super shipped the goods and Super committed a material breach when they shipped non-conforming goods.

296. Assume for this question that Super received the 10 model BC vacuums returned by Roberta and put them back in inventory. Roberta purchased 10 vacuums from another manufacturer on June 20th. On June 29th, Super production department completed the manufacture of 100 model AB vacuums. The sale manager sent e-mail to Roberta stating "we have completed the manufacture of your order for 10 model AB vacuums and they will be delivered tomorrow morning."

On the morning of June 30th the 10 vacuum model AB arrived. The tendered vacuums conformed in all respects. Roberta again refused to accept the 10 tendered AB vacuums because she had already fulfilled her need from another source. If Super brings suit against Roberta for breach of contract the best defense Roberta can assert is

    (A) Super committed a material breach of contract when it knowingly shipped non-conforming goods on June 10th and thus Roberta may treat the contract as rescinded and purchase her requirements elsewhere.

    (B) Roberta's purchase of the 10 vacuums from another seller was anticipatory repudiation which automatically terminated Super's right to cure the non-conforming tender before the specified deadline.

    (C) Roberta's rejection of the non-conforming vacuums effectively revoked the original offer and thus the June 29th shipment was to be treated as a new offer that Roberta did not accept.

    (D) Super's June 29th e-mail to Roberta that they intended to cure the prior tender of non-conforming goods was not seasonable.

297. Betty operated a large tavern in Everytown on real property she had inherited from her parents. She married Paul Pure who was a recovering alcoholic. Paul was opposed to the sale of liquor in any way. Betty thus sold the business to Laura Lush and signed a 20-year lease giving Laura a right to purchase the property for $100,000. 19 years later the City passed a new ordinance making the sale of liquor in the City illegal with an effective date six months hence. The land had increased in value to $250,000 and Laura immediately gave notice to Betty and Paul that she intended to exercise the option to purchase.

Betty and Paul refused to convey the property because they planned to evict Laura when the use became illegal and regain the property. The resulting delay in the controversy went beyond six months. If Laura files suit the likely result would be for

    (A) Laura if she prays for specific performance.

    (B) Betty and Paul under the doctrine of supervening illegality because the sale of liquor on the property is illegal.

    (C) Betty and Paul under the doctrine of "changed circumstances."

    (D) Laura, but only for monetary damages because the land use is now illegal.

Questions 298-299 are based on the following:

Helen Healthcare operated a large carrot juice factory that was very popular with customers of health food stores. She contracted with Carl Carrotgrower, a carrot farmer, to provide her with all the raw carrots she would require for the next four years at an annual price equal to that of the previous year. Helen was required to specify the number of tons she would require in the next year by December 1st of the current year. Helen had been in business for five years and her purchase of carrots had been increasing about 20% per year. The prior year, Helen had purchased 100 tons of carrots.

298. Helen ordered and used 120 tons of carrots from Carol in the first year of the agreement. In the fall of the next year, a government agency concluded that drinking carrot juice substantially reduced the chances of getting cancer. Demand for carrots and carrot juice increased immediately and prices for carrots increased by 100%. Helen's customers increased their orders for the next year and on December 1st Helen informed Carol that her requirement for the next year would be 300 tons. The legal situation concerning Carol's requirement to provide Helen with carrots in the next year is that

    (A) Carol will not have to supply any carrots to Helen because it would be unconscionable to force Carol to sell her farm products at 50% below market value.

(B) Carol will have to supply 144 tons of carrots to Helen.

(C) Carol must supply 300 tons of carrots to Helen since the agreement provided she would supply all of Helen's requirement.

(D) Carol must supply 300 tons of carrots to Helen since the increased demand for Helen's product did not arise from any actions on her part such as a building a second store.

299. Assume for this question only that Carol must supply Helen's full requirements. Carol was very unhappy with Helen's position that they had to provide her 300 tons at last year's lower price. The factory's total annual production capacity was only 350 tons and to be forced to sell at a low price meant they would suffer losses. Carol tried to renegotiate the agreement with Helen but Helen refused to make any changes. Carol's attorney reviewed the contract carefully and concluded that there was not an express requirement that prohibited Carol going out of business. Carol thus converted half her farm land to asparagus growing and refused to enter any agreement with any one customer of carrots. She offered and Helen accepted the entire output of 175 tons of carrots from the farmland that remained. Helen then brought suit for breach of contract. The court will likely hold for

(A) Carol because the seller is a requirement contract may always elect to withdraw in whole or part from the market.

(B) Helen because the seller's partial withdrawal from the market was motivated by bad faith.

(C) Helen only if her requirements were commercially reasonable.

(D) Carol because the seller in a requirement contract may reduce the output provided the buyer if it requires incurring a loss qualifying as commercially impractical.

Questions 300 – 301 are based on the following:

Rosalind Retailer operated a retail car lot which sold automobiles to the general public. She frequently purchased used cars from Wanda Wholesaler who specialized in selling repossessed cars. Some were sold at auction and some were sold through individual negotiations. Wholesaler's purchasing agent set a flash price which was the dollar amount expected at the auction. If an offer was received before the auction date at least 10% above the expected auction flash price Wanda would sell to the offeror.

300. Rosalind spotted an antique Porsche sports car model A27 of Wanda's that was scheduled for auction with a flash price of $20,000. Rosalind had a lawyer that she knew would pay over $30,000 for the car and she also believed that the auction price would go above $25,000. She then talked to Wanda's representative after looking at the Porsche and said she would pay $22,500 for the cars. Since this figure was more that 10% higher than the auction price Wanda began the negotiation process. They went back and forth on the price and finally reached an agreement at $25,000.

Wanda then confirmed the $25,000 agreement with a written memorandum stating "this will confirm that you have purchased the 1969 Porsche model A27 for a price of $25,000 to be delivered when we receive your check within the next 30 days." Unfortunately Rosalind's customer did not want the car and she could not find another buyer at a price above $25,000 so she did not respond to Wanda. The 30-day period expired and Wanda put a demand on Rosalind to pay the $25,000. Rosalind refused. Wanda brought a lawsuit and Rosalind asserted as a defense the statute of frauds. The court will likely hold for

(A) Rosalind, because she is the party being charged and she did not sign anything.

(B) Wanda, because she suffered a detriment by not scheduling the

Porsche for auction that is sufficient consideration to bind Rosalind.

(C) Wanda, because the memorandum she signed was sufficient to bind the purchaser.

(D) Rosalind, because she was not a merchant since she did not intend to put the Porsche car into inventory.

301. Assume for this question that Rosalind did not purchase the Porsche and Wanda decided to put the car up for auction. None of Wanda's literature specified whether the auction was to be conducted "with or without reserve." At the beginning of the bidding the auctioneer stated "the reserve price is $20,000." Ethyl Eager and Paula Porschefan both attended the auction with a keen interest in purchasing the Porsche model A27.

The auctioneer asked for an "opening" bid of $15,000 and Ethyl raised her hand. Paula went up to $17,000, Ethyl to $21,000, Paula to $23,000 and Ethyl to $25,000. There were no other bids. After Ethyl's $25,000 bid was made, the auctioneer talked for two minutes and tried to get a higher bid. Ethyl had second thoughts and shouted out "I withdraw my bid" before the drop of the hammer. The auctioneer then dropped the hammer and said sold to Ethyl for $25,000. If Ethyl refuses to accept and pay for the car and Wanda brings suit the court will likely hold for

(A) Wendy against Ethyl for $25,000 because the reserve price of $20,000 was exceeded.

(B) Wendy against Paula upon her $23,000 bid since the reserve price was exceeded.

(C) Against Wendy because the auction had a reserve price and the bidders are likewise not required to commit unless they so choose.

(D) Against Wendy.

302. Debbie Debtor was a very talented but insolvent painter who borrowed $10,000

from Connie Creditor as an unsecured business debt. Unfortunately, the loan from Connie was not sufficient to carry Debbie's business over the cash shortage position. Debbie found it necessary to seek relief from the demands of her creditors by filing bankruptcy. Debbie had made some incorrect statements to Connie to induce her to make the $10,000 loan. To convince her to not object to the bankruptcy, Debbie promised in a writing to paint an oil painting of Connie's family in the future. Connie agreed. The claim of Connie against Debbie for $10,000 was discharged with all the other creditors although as an unsecured creditor she was paid $2,000.

Two years after the bankruptcy had been finalized Connie asked Debbie to start the oil painting of her family. More than six years had run since the discharged loan had been made. Debbie then did the family oil painting that everyone was satisfied with. Two months after receiving the painting. Connie received a bill from Debbie for $20,000 for the painting. Both parties agreed that $20,000 was a fair value for the painting. When Connie called Debbie she said that her attorney had told her that her promise to do the painting was unenforceable. If Connie brings an action seeking a judgment against Debbie the court would likely find for

(A) For Debbie for $20,000 because past consideration is no consideration.

(B) For Connie, because no amount is due.

(C) Against Connie holding that $12,000 is due.

(D) For Debbie for $8,000.

Questions 303 – 304 are based on the following:

Oscar Owner was a property developer who owned a 40 acre tract of property which was subdivided into 80 one-half acre lots. Oscar contracted with Betty Builder, a general contractor who specialized in building tract homes. The contract stated that "the cost of

$125,000 per home will be paid upon completion of each of the 80 homes as determined by Alice Architect."

Betty worked on 40 homes of which 30 had been completed, approved by Alice Architect and payment made by Oscar. The 10 uncompleted homes were 80% complete when a fire destroyed all 40 homes. In addition, Betty's construction equipment on the site was destroyed by the fire. Oscar received a letter from Betty that stated "all my construction equipment was destroyed in the fire on your property so I cannot complete the remaining houses. Please send me the $1,250,000 for the 10 houses I worked on which you have not paid for."

Betty waited for 30 days and then went out to Oscar's office to try to collect. When Oscar was accosted he stated, "I am sorry, but if you will not build the remaining 40 homes at the agreed price I will not pay for the 10 destroyed in the fire."

303. For this question only assume that Oscar was unable to find another contractor that would build the 40 remaining homes at $125,000 per home. Therefore, he filed a lawsuit against Betty seeking specific performance to compel her to build the 40 remaining homes. The court will likely hold for

(A) Betty because specific performance does not apply to personal service contracts.
(B) Oscar because the destruction of Betty's construction equipment will not excuse performance.
(C) Oscar only if he did not expressly assume the risk of a contract condition such as an unexpected fire.
(D) Betty because the fire was a frustration of purpose that excuses performance.

304. For this question only, assume that Betty counter claimed against Oscar seeking compensation for her work on the 10 homes destroyed in the fire on Oscar's property.

Betty had expended $650,000 in costs in building the 10 homes and the 10 homes had a fair market value to Oscar of $750,000 before the fire. The court will likely award Betty

(A) -0-
(B) $650,000
(C) $750,000
(D) $1,250,000

Questions 305 – 306 are based on the following:

Bertha Builder was a general contractor who specialized in the construction of custom designed homes. She was commissioned to construct a $500,000 personal residence for Priscilla Perfect. Priscilla had a full set of construction plans and specifications prepared by an architect that Bertha agreed to follow.

The construction of Priscilla's house began but soon into the contract it was clear that Bertha and Priscilla had personality conflicts. The two parties would blow up over small points in determining whether Bertha's performance met the plan specifications. In addition there was substantial inflation in both the costs of material and the price of the finished new homes in the locale. This conflict went from bad to worse and resulted in Bertha and Priscilla hardly talking to each other. The straw that broke the camels back was that Bertha used copper bathroom fixtures in the master bathroom rather than the chrome fixtures specified on the architects drawing. At this point the contract was 80% complete; Bertha had incurred $300,000 of costs and Priscilla had paid $250,000 but the costs to complete were $300,000. The completed home was expected to be worth $600,000.

305. Assume for this question only that Priscilla wrongfully terminates Bertha and bars her and her workers from coming back onto the construction job. If Bertha brings suit for breach of contract the likely judgment against Priscilla will be

(A) -0-
(B) $50,000
(C) $175,000
(D) $250,000

306. Assume for this question only that Bertha finally had enough of Priscilla's constant complaining and decided to quit. She told Priscilla, "you can take this house and shove it, I hope it ends up as weird as you." If Priscilla brings suit for breach of contract the likely judgment against Bertha will be

(A) -0-
(B) $50,000
(C) $150,000
(D) $175,000

Questions 307 – 309 are based on the following:

Denise Dance had always wanted to master the art of fine ballroom dancing. Her husband, Charlie Clumsy, did not like dancing at all. Charlie died and Denise, after a respectable mourning period, decided she wanted to pursue her dream of becoming a first-class ballroom dancer. She contacted the Melissa Murray Dance Company and signed the following dance contract:

> "I hereby sign up for Melissa Murray's special one-year dance lesson program at two one-hour classes a week for the next year (104 dance class hours.) This contract costs $1,040 in total. The cost is due in advance and all fees are nonrefundable. If the total enrollment cost exceeds $1,000 one-third is due on signing of this agreement, one third payable four months later and the final third shall be due eight months later."

Denise began the dance lessons at Melissa Murray Dance Company and religiously attended classes for three months. As she was walking down the exterior stairs at the end of one of her dance sessions she stumbled on a step and fell. Denise went to the hospital and the Doctor concluded her left ankle was sprained. The Doctor further ordered Denise to stay off her left foot including suspending her dance lessons until the swelling went down and the strength in her ankle improved.

The next month Denise received the second billing from Melissa Murray Dance Company for $346.66. She wrote a note on the bill stating, "I may not be attending any further classes because of the injury to my ankle and I do not feel obligated to make any additional payments." This note and the unpaid billing was returned to Melissa Murray Dance Company by U.S. mail.

307. If this note was received by Melissa Murray Dance Company which of the below accurately states the legal effect of the situation.

I. Denise may retract her repudiation if she does so before Melissa initiates a legal collector against her.
II. Melissa Murray Dance Company has the legal right to stop Denise from attending any further classes.
III. Melissa Murray Dance Company has the right to sue Denise immediately for breach of contract.

(A) I only
(B) II only
(C) I and II
(D) I, II and III

308. Melissa Murray received the note and second unpaid billing from Denise Dancer. Which of the below most correctly describes Denise's duty to pay the second installment of $346.66.

(A) It would be excused because of impossibility of performance.
(B) It would be excused because the essential purpose of the contract was frustrated.
(C) It would not be excused because the contract specified that all fees are non refundable.
(D) It would not be excused because the covenant to make the second

and third installment payments are enforceable as condition precedent.

309. For this question only assume that Denise's ankle condition improved after two weeks and she decided to rejoin Melissa Murray dance lessons. At the end of the first day that she rejoined the class after her ankle sprain Melissa approached Denise and said that she now needed to pay the second payment. Denise complained that she had not attended the last two weeks of the class and was short cash since she had been off work. Melissa felt sorry for Denise and agreed she could attend class for 10 days. 12 days later Melissa informed Denise in writing that she could not attend any more classes until payment was received. Is Melissa's position excluding Denise legally justified?

(A) Yes, because Denise's failure to make the installment payment on time constitutes anticipatory repudiation.

(B) No, because by allowing Denise to attend classes there was a waiver on the right to collect the balance of the fee.

(C) Yes, because there was no consideration to extinguish the duty to pay the balance of the installment payments.

(D) No, because allowing Denise to attend classes created an implied contract that deferred the second and third payments until the end of the dance lessons.

310. A disagreement has developed between executives in one of your corporate clients about the legal distinctions between a modification, accord and waiver. Which of the following is true?

I. A modification is more likely in a contract that is totally executory.

II. All three require consideration.

III. In an accord and a waiver the original promise remains alive until the new substituted promise or performance is completed.

(A) I

(B) I and II

(C) II and III

(D) I, II and III

311. Betty Beneficiary took out a $100,000 whole life insurance policy with Old Reliable Insurance naming her children as beneficiaries. The insurance policy contract stated that Betty promised to pay a monthly premium of $100 while Old Reliable promised to pay $100,000 if Betty died of a cause other than suicide. Betty's job was later outsourced to India and she found herself in financial difficulty and began to pay many of her bills late. Six months later, Betty was in an automobile accident and died two days later. When her children put in a claim with Old Reliable Insurance it was rejected on the basis that Betty was two months behind in paying the premiums at the time of her death. If Betty's beneficiaries bring suit against Old Reliable Insurance their best argument is

(A) Betty did not receive notice of delinquency and policy cancellation from Old Reliable.

(B) Old Reliable was under an independent duty to pay the policy face value designation if Betty died.

(C) Old Reliable's duty to pay was not expressly conditioned on Betty's duty to pay the premiums timely.

(D) There was a bargained for exchange even though Betty failed to pay the last two month's premiums and thus the recovery should be $99,800.

Questions 312 – 313 are based on the following:

Alice Author, a law school professor had written three non-fiction books focusing on the political rights of law students. Her publisher, Non-American Publishing, was paying her royalties on these three books. Non-American Publishing management began to receive pressure to drop Alice's books because the sales were decreasing and many law school administrators were upset with her central thesis that to eliminate law school grades and class rank would increase the quality of the legal educational experience.

Nonetheless, Alice began her fourth book, "Law Students Rights Are At Risk." When she had completed the second draft of the manuscript, she ran out of money. Barbara Banker agreed to loan Alice $100,000. The loan was collateralized by a written assignment of one-half the royalties from both the contract Alice had with Non-American and a contract for the new fourth book which Alice hoped to negotiate with a different publisher named Ludicrous Law School Books. When the royalty checks on the first three books were received from Non-American, Alice began to endorse them over to Barbara.

Six months later Alice had completed her new book. When the law school Dean learned of the new book under contract, he fired Alice on the basis of insubordination. Three days later Alice had a heart attack and died. The local newspapers' publicity about the unusual reason for her firing was extensive and her book sales rocketed. Ludicrous Law School Books signed a publishing agreement with the Executor of Alice's estate.

312. Barbara learned about the Ludicrous Law School Books publishing agreement. Ludicrous refused to pay the royalties attributable to the new book to Barbara. If she brings suit against the Executor, Barbara will likely

  (A) Win because her written assignment of the fourth book royalties predated the Executor's involvement.
  (B) Lose because the contract right in question was not assignable.
  (C) Lose because the right of assignment is automatically revoked on the death of the assignor.

  (D) Win, because she made the $100,000 loan to Alice.

313. Upon Alice's death, Non-American began directing the royalty checks on the first three books to the Executor. Barbara objected and showed both Non-American and the Executor the written assignment she had previously received from Alice. Six months went by and Non-American and the Executor refused to allow Barbara the royalties on the first three books. If she brings suit against Non-American Publishing, Barbara will likely

  (A) Win because she was a third party beneficiary.
  (B) Lose, because it was only after Alice's death that Non-American and the Executor learned of the assignment.
  (C) Lose because under these circumstances an assignment of future rights is not enforceable.
  (D) Win because under these circumstances an assignment of future rights is enforceable.

314. Sharon Shopper was a very alert customer who spent most of her spare time carefully scrutinizing advertisements for good buys which were on sale. She spotted an advertisement for Lucky Store in the local evening newspaper that stated:

> "A real diamond necklace which is easily worth $250.00 will be sold for $9.95 on Saturday, April 15th. First come first serve."

Sharon went down to the Lucky Store on Friday night and camped out. When the doors opened at 9:00 a.m. Sharon rushed in and demanded the diamond necklace for $9.95. The salesperson refused to sell the necklace for $9.95 stating that the advertisement was a mistake and the true sales price of the necklace was $99.50. If Sharon brings suit against Lucky Store for specific performance at a price of $9.95 the court will likely hold for

(A) Lucky Store because there was a mistake made in the advertisement.

(B) Sharon because her acceptance created a bilateral contract.

(C) Sharon because her acceptance created a unilateral contract.

(D) Lucky Store, only if Sharon's actions were insufficient to constitute promissory estoppel.

315. Olivia Owner owned a residential lot in Pleasanttown. She decided to develop the property by building a high-end residence for resale. Olivia negotiated with a general contractor named Connie Contractor to perform the construction of a home for the new property. Olivia stated in a letter to Connie "I will pay you $250,000 after you excavate the ground for the basement, frame the structure, and put a full roof on the new home as specified in the construction plans from Alice Architect."

Connie Contractor sent an e-mail in response to Olivia stating, "when should I start on your project?" The next week Connie's workers began digging the basement. It took 20 days to complete the basement and during this time period Connie's wealthy Uncle Harry died leaving Connie an inheritance of $10 million dollars. Connie received more money than she had ever dreamed of and decided to immediately retire. She so informed Olivia and stopped work. If Olivia objects and brings suit against Connie for breach of contract the court will likely hold for

(A) Olivia because the partial performance by Connie necessarily implied a promise to complete the whole contract.

(B) Connie because her response which stated, "when should I start" was not an express acceptance.

(C) Connie because the acceptance of a unilateral contract completes performance.

(D) Olivia because the doctrines of equitable and/or promissory estoppel requires the whole

contract be recognized and enforced.

Questions 316 – 317 are based on the following:

Victoria Vineyard was a widower who specialized in growing merlot grape for sale to amateur winemakers. She had two children who assisted her in cultivating the fields and harvesting the crops. Victoria signed a written contract with Wanda Winemaker to deliver two tons of merlot wine grapes on or before August 20th, 2005. Wanda was the President of the Merlot Club of New York and every year scheduled a wine stomp at which the members consumed much of last season's product and stomped the grapes for the next season's wine output. Unfortunately on August 15th both of Victoria's children became sick with summeritis and were unable to pick the wine grapes.

Victoria called Wanda on August 16th and informed her that because of the pickers' sickness she might not be able to deliver timely on August 20th. Victoria further stated she was trying to find other pickers. Wanda said, "That's OK because the stomp event is not for two more weeks so I can wait, however, I will still hold you liable for any losses we incur because of your failure to deliver." When Wanda did not receive the grapes on August 23rd, she began to get quite nervous because the club was expecting a big crowd for the stomp. She then sent an e-mail to Victoria stating "we must receive the grapes by August 28th."

316. Assume for this question only that Victoria delivers the grapes late in the afternoon of August 28th and that after inspection Wanda accepts them. If Wanda later brings a breach of contract claim because of the late delivery the court will likely hold for

(A) Victoria because the sickness of her children constituted incapacity so temporary impracticality excused performance.

(B) Victoria because Wanda's statement, "That's OK," and subsequent acceptance after inspection constituted a waiver of timely performance.

(C) Wanda because her statements to Victoria did not constitute a waiver for breach of contract.

(D) Wanda because her waiver, if any, did not have adequate consideration.

317. Assume for this question only that Victoria was unable to deliver the wine grapes by August 28th. If this is the situation and Wanda decides to purchase the grapes elsewhere, will Wanda be entitled to cancel the contract.

(A) Yes, if both parties to the contract are classified as merchants.

(B) Yes, provided that a five-day notice gave Victoria a reasonable time period in which to perform.

(C) No, because Wanda's August 16th statement was in effect a waiver of any condition of timely delivery.

(D) No, because Victoria's August 16th statement did not promise to deliver by any particular date.

318. Iota Infant was a 17-year-old high school student when she decided to purchase a new Ford Mustang. She went into a car dealership owned by Alice Autosforsale and entered into a purchase agreement for a prime Mustang priced at $26,000 with monthly payments of $500. Iota made four payments of $500 and then stopped paying because she lost her part time after school job. Alice badgered Iota to pay her bill and threatened to sue her if she did not resume payments. The day after her 18th birthday, Iota wrote Alice and stated, "While the balance on the contract is now $24,000 the car is only worth $12,000 which I am willing to pay when I get a job." If Iota does not pay for six months and Alice brings suit for collection, which of the below is the best argument Alice can make to support a recovery.

(A) The $12,000 promise created a moral obligation so the lack of consideration is not fatal.

(B) The promise Iota made on her birthday ratified the $24,000 balance due on the contract.

(C) Iota has secured a job so she can now pay the $12,000 moral obligation.

(D) The Ford Mustang should be characterized as a necessity.

319. Ethyl Homentertainer Extra-Ordinaire contracted with Grenda Gardener to provide daily flower arrangements for her monthly home entertainment tea and bridge parties. The agreement was for 24 months at $20 per month and both parties signed an agreement which stated "any change to this contract must be written." The contract proceeded and each month Grenda would appear with a suitable flower bouquet and Ethyl would pay her twenty dollars in cash. 15 months into the agreement the market price of daisy flowers skyrocketed. Grenda telephoned Ethyl and told her that she had to raise the price to $25 per month. Ethyl agreed to the increase but insisted she be allowed to pay at the end of the nine months left on the agreement. At the end of the nine months, Ethyl refused to pay more than $180. If suit is brought, which of the below is the court most likely to find

(A) The statute of frauds does not apply to the original contract because it was under $500.

(B) The contract modification from $20 to $25 per month was not enforceable because it was not supported by new consideration.

(C) The modification from $20 to $25 per month was not enforceable because it was not written.

(D) The oral modification is conclusive evidence that the parties waived the "written modifications only" provision.

Questions 320 – 321 are based on the following:

Alice owned a small mini-car. She borrowed Betty's pickup truck to move some of her personal belongings and promised to return the truck within a reasonable period of time. Alice completed the move, but found she enjoyed driving the larger vehicle. She kept Alice's truck and decided to return the truck only when Betty made demand. The truck had a fair market value of $10,000.

Three weeks later, Betty met with Connie who was a friend of both Alice and Betty. Betty disclosed to Connie that she had not yet received the pickup truck back from Alice. Connie disclosed to Betty that she owed Alice $10,000 but did not have the money to repay the loan. Betty felt sorry for her friend Connie and told Connie that she would make arrangements to satisfy the $10,000 loan Connie owed Alice.

One week later, Betty met with Alice. She attempted to convince Alice to trade the pickup truck for the $10,000 debt, but Alice said no that she really wanted the money. Alice did agree in writing to accept a promissory note executed by Betty for $10,000 with payment terms of $500 per month. The writing also recited that Alice promised to return the pickup truck to Betty. While the agreement was signed by both parties, Alice made no statement that she would release or forbear to sue the original debtor, Connie.

One week later, Alice returned the pickup truck to Betty. For three months, Betty paid $500 per month to Alice. During this time period, Alice did not bring suit against Connie. Betty then developed personal financial problems and expressly repudiated her payment agreement. Alice then initiated a breach of contract claim against Betty.

320. Assume that the statute of limitations on Alice's original $10,000 claim against Connie expired a week before Alice filed the breach of contract claim against Betty. The best defense that Betty can assert to avoid liability on the written payment contract is

(A) At the time Betty and Alice signed the agreement, Connie had a duty to repay the $10,000 and because this was not extinguished or waived by Alice, consideration was lacking.

(B) The written agreement between Betty and Alice was illusory because of the gross imbalance between the value of the promises exchanged.

(C) Alice's forbearing to sue Connie does not constitute consideration because she did not expressly agree to forbear in the contract with Betty.

(D) Alice had a pre-existing responsibility to return Betty's pickup truck at the time of the Alice-Betty agreement so there was no consideration to support Betty's promise.

321. Assume that the statute of limitations on Alice's original $10,000 claim against Connie expired one week after the written contract between Alice and Betty. Which of the below is Alice's strongest argument that Betty is liable?

(A) Betty's payment of $1,500 to Alice is a waiver of any formation defect and a ratification of the liability.

(B) Betty's payment of $1,500 to Alice manifested serious intention to be bound thus serving as an effective substitute for consideration.

(C) Betty's written promise and Alice's reliance thereon created a valid legal claim by Alice against Betty based upon the doctrine of promissory estoppel.

(D) The suretyship obligation was written and therefore legally enforceable.

Questions 322 and 323 are based on the following:

Frank Forever had worked for Magnum Industries as a welder for fifteen years. In an attempt to reduce employee turnover and reward long service, the Company put a bonus system in effect. All employees with over 10 years of service were issued the following two-part certificate of award. The top portion was prepared by the Company and the bottom half beneficiary designation completed by the employee.

> "As a reward for your faithful service, Magnum Industries will pay $10,000 upon your death, if you remain in our employ, to the individual you designate below."

> /s/ Magnum Industries

> "I hereby accept this certificate of award and designate my daughter Betty as beneficiary."

> /s/ Frank Forever

Frank did not tell his daughter of the certificate of award. On January 1st, 2006, Frank was walking to his car after work and saw three thugs robbing the President of the company. He intervened and one of the thugs turned his knife on Frank, seriously cutting Frank's arm. Seeing Frank's injuries, the President was so grateful that he stated, "Frank, you will have a job with this company for life."

Two months later, Frank's arm injuries got much worse and the arm had to be amputated. Without the arm, Frank could not work as a welder, but the President kept him on the payroll.

On June 1st, 2009, Magnum revoked the certificates by mailing letters to all the employees who had received the certificates. On June 2nd, 2009, Frank died before receipt of the letter.

322. The legal contractual relationship between Frank and Magnum Industries as of January 1st, 2006 regarding the job for life was

(A) Enforceable because Frank saved the life of the President.

(B) Not enforceable because Frank's gratuitous going to the rescue was insufficient consideration to support the promise to give him a job for life.

(C) Not enforceable if Frank reasonably expected to live over one year from the date of the President's oral promise.

(D) Enforceable because Frank's non-compensated gratuitous going to the rescue was sufficient consideration to support the President's promise.

323. On June 4th, 2009, Frank's daughter Betty opened Frank's safe deposit box and discovered the certificate of award designating her as beneficiary. She contacted Magnum Industries and asked for the $10,000 award. Magnum refused to pay and Betty brought suit. The strongest argument that Magnum can assert against Betty's $10,000 claim is

(A) Privity of contract between Betty and Magnum was missing.

(B) Consideration to support the certificate of award was insufficient.

(C) Betty was unaware of the certificate of award until after Frank's death.

(D) Magnum effectively revoked the certificate of award before Frank's death.

324. Carol Creditor was owed $10,000 on account for goods she sold on January 1st, 2005 to Debbie Debtor. Debbie was short cash and did not pay timely. Carol hired a lawyer to pursue her for collection. On February 1st, 2011, Debbie stated, "I promise to pay you, Carol Creditor, $5,000 on April 1st, 2011 in full satisfaction of what I owe you." The jurisdiction in question has a statute of limitations of 6 years for collection of a written contract. If Debbie refuses to pay the $5,000 and Carol brings suit, Carol's legal position is

(A) On February 1st, 2011, Carol will be entitled to a $5,000 judgment

against Debbie if Debbie's promise was in writing and signed.
- **(B)** On April 1st, 2011, Carol will be entitled to a $5,000 judgment against Debbie if Debbie's promise was in writing and signed.
- **(C)** On February 1st, 2001, Carol will be entitled to a $10,000 judgment because the new promise reactivated the full prior debt.
- **(D)** Carol is not entitled to any judgment because there was no consideration for Debbie's February 1st, 2011 promise.

Questions 325 and 326 are based on the following:

All-American Law School hired Ethyl Exciting as an adjunct professor under a 10-month contract. Ethyl was assigned to teach a 1L course in torts that met every Tuesday and Thursday. Ethyl taught the first four classes over the first two weeks and terrified the new 1Ls by her practice of only asking questions and never giving answers. One of the 1Ls got so upset with her that Thursday that he ran up to the podium and physically attacked her. While other students pulled the attacker off Ethyl, she was injured and spent the next three days in the hospital. Ethyl's face was bandaged and she asked the doctor if she could stay home for the next week.

When she returned to her torts class after missing one week, she learned that the law school administration had replaced her with a new adjunct professor. The law school refused to reinstate Ethyl to the 1L torts class or assign her to teach another course. Ethyl brought a breach of contract lawsuit against All-American Law School.

325. The most helpful argument that would allow Ethyl to prevail is
- **(A)** The 10 month employment agreement should be divided into a series of contracts, one for each two classes taught in a week.
- **(B)** Ethyl was excused from her responsibility to teach the one

week's classes due to physical injury.
- **(C)** Ethyl refused another teaching offer for the academic year from Non-American Law School and had she gone there, the All-American student attack would not have occurred.
- **(D)** The two class absence from the All-American torts course was not a material breach.

326. Which of the facts below, if true and can be proven, provides the All-American Law School with the best defense?
- **(A)** The new adjunct professor was the only substitute torts professor available and she demanded the full balance of the 10-month contract.
- **(B)** The new adjunct professor is a better teacher than Ethyl and the 1Ls preferred her to Ethyl.
- **(C)** Ethyl was offered a job in the law school library at the same salary she earned as an adjunct torts professor.
- **(D)** Ethyl was offered a writing instructor's position at the law school for the balance of her contract at one-third less salary than she would have earned teaching the torts course.

Questions 327 and 328 are based on the following:

Harriet Homeowner needed to have her personal residence painted and began to negotiate with commercial house painters for the job. She entered into an agreement on April 1st with Betty Bestpainter to prepare and paint her whole house for $12,000. Betty was so much in demand that two weeks after the agreement was formed, she called Harriet and informed her that it would be August 1st before she could start. This worried Harriet because she wanted to be sure the job would be completed before the fall rains came.

On April 30th, Harriet received a phone call from Greta Goodpainter inquiring if the painting job was still open. Harriet said, "Yes, and if you paint my whole house, I can pay $9,000 and I promise that this offer will not be withdrawn or revoked until May 30th." Greta had no knowledge of the prior contract with Betty. Harriet then went on a one-month vacation.

right to revoke the offer before May 30th.

327. The legal consequence of the statement "this offer will not be withdrawn or revoked until May 30th" is

(A) It prevents Harriet from withdrawing or revoking the offer before May 30th.

(B) It does not affect Harriet's right to withdraw or revoke.

(C) It has no legal affect because Harriet was already bound in contract with Betty.

(D) It provides Greta with an option that could be assigned to a third party with Harriet's approval.

328. On May 10th, Greta dispatched her painting crew to Harriet's house to begin the preparation and painting. By May 20th, the crew had cleaned and sanded all the wood on the house and by May 30th, they completed one-fourth of the actual painting. On June 1st, Harriet returned from vacation. She went to the job site and informed Greta, "I am sorry, but I have decided to revoke and withdraw the offer I made to you on April 30th." The most accurate statement of Greta's legal position is

(A) She may complete the painting of the house and recover in full because she began the preparation and painting before June 1st.

(B) She must stop painting immediately on June 1st but will recover for the value of her work performed to date.

(C) She must stop painting immediately on June 1st but will recover a pro-rata portion of the $9,000 contract amount.

(D) She may complete the painting of the house and recover in full because Harriet did not have the

Contracts and UCC Sales
Learning Question Answer Rationales

1. **/B/** The best answer because it is the only contract of the four presented that is not from the SIR topics which fall under the common law. Goods include crops and timber that can be severed from the real property without harm. **(A)** is incorrect because an attorney's advice is a type of service, which is our S in SIR. **(C)** is incorrect because a contract for property falls under the real estate category, which is our R in SIR. **(D)** is incorrect because a contract for an intangible asset falls under the intangible category, which is our I in SIR.

2. **/C/** This correct alternative has the most compelling factual argument to support the legal conclusion. Despite the fact that Connie originally went to the store to buy the keyboard and mouse, the predominate purpose of the contract (in terms of dollar amount) is the service agreement. **(A)** is incorrect because it does not fit the facts and the rationale is faulty. The predominate dollar purpose is for the personal service contract ($500 for service v $50 for goods). Even if the predominate purpose were for goods, (A) would still be incorrect because a goods contract falls under the UCC, not the

common law. **(B)** is not the best answer because the rationale does not support the conclusion. When the predominate purpose is service, then the common law applies, not the UCC. **(D)** is not the best answer; the "if" modifier makes a somewhat compelling but mushy argument. The Court would not likely apply the reasoning asserted – there is a clear answer in the UCC. Furthermore, Computer Retailer is not likely to prevail on these facts.

3. **/A/** The least important factor in determining if a seller is a merchant would be if they sold at wholesale or at retail. Either a wholesaler or a retailer could be classified as a casual seller. **(B)** is incorrect because a seller who "deals in the goods" is one of the merchant characteristics listed in UCC 2.104. **(C)** is incorrect because a seller who "holds herself out as an expert having special knowledge and skill in the goods" is one of the merchant characteristics listed in UCC 2.104. **(D)** is not the best answer because the number of units sold in a given year is not controlling as to whether the seller is a merchant or casual seller. It could be that 10 units a year would not be a sufficient quantity to qualify as dealing in those goods.

4. **/A/** The contract would be implied in the fact that the client accepts the services of the attorney. **(B)** is incorrect because the law would not necessarily imply a contract. **(C)** is incorrect because there is no express contract under these facts. **(D)** is incorrect because there is an implied-in-fact contract.

5. **/C/** The offeror, Sarah, was bargaining for a unilateral contract in which acceptance is only rendered by performance of the act requested. **(A)** is incorrect because the offeree did not perform the requested act. **(B)** is incorrect because the offeror was not bargaining for acceptance by a return promise. **(D)** is incorrect; while the offer may become irrevocable if Donna's statement is deemed to be a beginning of performance, it does not create a legal contract until acceptance.

6. **/B/** This is the least correct alternative since a partially executed contract is possible where both parties have partially performed. This is a negative question; often the best approach in such questions is to use a true-false approach. The odd-man out is the correct answer. **(A)** is true and therefore incorrect. **(C)** is true and therefore incorrect. **(D)** is true and therefore incorrect.

7. **/C/** The best answer since it is correct and states a rationale that is consistent with the law and the facts given in the question. The contract appears divisible since performance of one portion does not affect the other and payment equivalent to performance is possible. **(A)** is not the best answer since the P's allegation of D's breach is not controlling. **(B)** is incorrect because the contractor did complete a divisible portion of the contract but the dollar amount is wrong. **(D)** is incorrect because if the contract is deemed divisible, the P will collect an equivalent amount of the whole contract.

8. **/B/** When interpreting a bilateral contract, the court attempts to ascertain the objective intent of the parties. **(A)** is incorrect because fairness is not usually an issue unless the contract is unconscionable or patently unequal. **(C)** is incorrect because the subjective intent is of less importance than the objective test. **(D)** is not the best answer because the offeror's communications are to be evaluated objectively; how would a reasonable person interpret the offeror's expressions is the test.

9. **/B/** A mere offer to sell without any promise that the offer is to be held open is revocable at will of the seller. **(A)** is incorrect because under Article 2 of the UCC this written statements by a merchant would constitute a "firm offer" which would be irrevocable for the time stated up to 90 days. **(C)** is incorrect because under the UCC this written statements by a merchant would constitute a "firm offer" which would be irrevocable for the time stated up to 90 days. **(D)** is incorrect because, upon the receipt of consideration, the offer is transformed into an option contract which would be irrevocable for the stated time even if in excess of 90 days.

10. **/B/** A concise statement of UCC Article 2's "firm offer" rule. **(A)** is incorrect because only the offeror must be a merchant. **(C)** is incorrect because the UCC will impose a "reasonable" period of irrevocability

on the offeror. **(D)** is incorrect because who supplies the form is not relevant to the application of the rule.

11. /**B**/ The death of the offeror terminates an open offer. **(A)** is incorrect because such an acceptance would be effective to create a contract. **(C)** is incorrect because this purported "acceptance" is treated as a rejection and a counter offer. **(D)** is incorrect; a time period stated in the offer begins to run on the date the offer is received by the offeree so an acceptance on April 15 would be timely.

12. /**A**/ If the other party provides the contract, the merchant must separately sign the agreement to constitute a firm offer under UCC 2.205. **(B)** is not the best answer because a firm offer is valid for the offeror's stated time which may be less than three months. **(C)** is incorrect because contracted rights may always be assigned under the UCC. **(D)** is incorrect because consideration would convert the firm offer into an option contract.

13. /**C**/ Acceptance must be with knowledge of the offer. **(A)** is incorrect because the award is limited to $100, the amount known to the offeree as of the date of acceptance. **(B)** is incorrect because the award is limited to $100, the amount known to the offeree as of the date of acceptance. **(D)** is incorrect because the award is limited to $100, the amount known to the offeree as of the date of acceptance.

14. /**A**/ The offer clearly was seeking performance for acceptance and not a mere promise to perform; as a result, there was no acceptance

regardless of when it may be effective. Therefore, the revocation by action of the seller was effective since a prior valid acceptance had not been made. **(B)** is incorrect because the April 2 letter did no constitute a valid acceptance. **(C)** is incorrect because the April 2 letter did not create a contract. **(D)** is incorrect because the April 2 letter did not constitute an acceptance, no matter what the effective date might have been.

15. /**B**/ Acceptance is at the fall of the hammer and thus a bidder may retract his offer prior to that time. **(A)** is incorrect because the presumption is that auctioned goods are put up with reserve. **(C)** is incorrect because the previous bid is no longer effective once a new higher bid is accepted. **(D)** is incorrect because only if the auction is with reserve does the auctioneer have the right to withdraw the goods prior to acceptance.

16. /**D**/ This is a contract falling under UCC 2.306. Requirement contracts are valid and enforceable without specifying quantity as long as there is a reasonable basis for giving an appropriate remedy. A reasonable quantity would be imposed. **(A)** is incorrect because such a requirements contract is enforceable without quantity. **(B)** is incorrect because such a requirements contract is enforceable and involves mutuality of obligation. **(C)** is incorrect because such a requirements contract is enforceable and consideration is present due to the exchange of promises.

17. /**A**/ The answer is correct because this appears to be a mere inquiry by the offeree which has no effect on the

offer; therefore a subsequent acceptance could be still be effective. **(B)** is incorrect because the offeror can revoke an open offer thus terminating the offeree's power of acceptance. **(C)** is incorrect because the death of the offeror terminates an open offer. **(D)** is incorrect because an offeree's purported acceptance with different terms is a rejection which terminates an open offer.

18. **/D/** The UCC allows acceptance with minor additional consistent terms. Because the "per city scale weight certificate" is minor and not inconsistent with Calvin's offer and Calvin did not object, the inclusion of same does not defeat the effectiveness of the acceptance and is not to be treated as a counteroffer. **(A)** is incorrect because between merchants such additional terms become a part of the contract unless the offeror notifies the offeree of an objection to the inclusion of the additional terms in the agreement. **(B)** is incorrect because the reply is not a conditional acceptance. **(C)** is incorrect because the reply is not a counter offer.

19. **/C/** The advertising catalog is not an offer but only an invitation to deal. The offer was the "purchase order" and Priceco's "order confirmation" was an attempted acceptance with an express condition that contradicted the offer terms. Thus it should be interpreted as a counteroffer and since the counteroffer was not accepted by the original offeror, Rainmaking Lawfirm, no contract was formed. **(A)** is incorrect because there was no contract. **(B)** is incorrect because there was no contract. **(D)** is not the best answer because this probably would be interpreted as different

terms to which both parties are assumed to object. The change also adds $500 or 50% to the price which is a material change so inclusion through a seller's non-objection does not seem likely.

20. **/A/** There was a valid Arthur-Madison contract because the effective date of the acceptance was upon dispatch while the effective date of revocation was on receipt which was later. **(B)** is incorrect because revocations are only effective upon receipt. **(C)** is incorrect because there is generally no restriction on the offeror's ability to revoke. **(D)** is incorrect because acceptance occurred prior to revocation.

21. **/B/** Under the traditional common law, mailbox treatment for acceptance requires that "as fast or faster" means be used to communicate the acceptance. Here the mailed response was slower than the e-mailed offer so the acceptance can only be effective on receipt. Therefore the acceptance is effective on March 15, when Berg received it. **(A)** is not the best answer because the mailbox rule dictates that acceptance must be by means "as fast or faster" than the means used to communicate the offer. Since Jones replied by letter, the mailbox rule does not apply to his acceptance. **(C)** is incorrect because the request for the payment terms was not a condition of the acceptance – only a mere request which the offeror could reject. **(D)** is incorrect because an acceptance may contain a request for additional terms, as long as the acceptance is a mirror image of the offer.

22. **/C/** The option period was for 100 days and cannot be revoked for that period. **(A)** is incorrect because the

$50 paid was the consideration. **(B)** is incorrect because a writing would only be required if the option length was one year or longer. **(D)** is incorrect because there are no restrictions on the option length.

23. **/B/** Because Harrison had already incurred the legal detriment, there was no consideration for Bunker's promise. Past consideration is no consideration. **(A)** is incorrect because there is no contract under these circumstances. **(C)** is incorrect because there is no contract under these circumstances. **(D)** is not the best answer because the pre-existing duty would only apply between Harrison and Michael.

24. **/B/** The doctrine of promissory estoppel applies to eliminate the necessity that the donor of a charitable pledge receive consideration to support the promise. The law implies the necessary consideration. **(A)** is incorrect because this promise would be unenforceable unless supported by consideration. **(C)** is incorrect because a modification under the common law always requires consideration. **(D)** is incorrect because the UCC's firm offer rule (which would enforce such a promise for up to 90 days without consideration) only applies if the promise is written.

25. **/D/** UCC 2.209 states that a modification to a goods contract made in good faith requires no consideration. If over $500, a writing would be required. **(A)** is incorrect because a renunciation of a claim or right arising out of an alleged breach constitutes valid consideration; there would be a detriment to the promisee. **(B)** is incorrect because a firm offer

requires a writing. **(C)** is not the best answer because a "large" requirement contract would probably exceed $500 and thus would require a writing under the statute of frauds.

26. **/A/** Disaffirmance can only be effective within a reasonable time period after reaching the age of majority. **(B)** is incorrect because there is not a requirement that the disaffirmation be written. **(C)** is incorrect because disaffirmance does not require payment. **(D)** is not the best answer because while Baker may be able to sue Egan for damages resulting from the negligence, this does not limit Egan's ability to disaffirm contracts entered into before the age of majority.

27. **/C/** The best answer because while an infant's contracts are voidable at the infant's option, equitable liability in an amount of the benefit to the infant may be imposed. This would seem to be the reasonable value of the benefit received. **(A)** is not the best answer; while the rationale is correct – the contract is voidable by the infant – the conclusion of $10,000 is incorrect. **(B)** is incorrect; only the infant can disaffirm the contract. **(D)** is not the best answer because the standard is the benefit to the infant not the detriment to the other contracting party.

28. **/B/** The best answer since it provides a logical rationale to support the conclusion and is a correct statement of the UCC statute of frauds rule. **(A)** is incorrect because the agency capacity was disclosed and an agent does not impliedly guarantee that a principal will perform. **(C)** is an incorrect statement since an agent has

potential personal liability if they guarantee the performance of the principal. **(D)** is incorrect because an agent has potential personal liability if they misrepresent the scope of their authority.

29. **/D/** The contract was illegal and thus unenforceable because West was not admitted to the Kansas bar nor properly licensed under state law. **(A)** is incorrect because no portion of an illegal contract may usually be enforced unless the contract is divisible. **(B)** is incorrect because no portion of an illegal contract may usually be enforced unless the contract is divisible. **(C)** is incorrect because the statute of frauds only requires the signature of the party to be charged, Zimmer.

30. **/D/** The signatory is the only party against whom the contract may be enforced. The nonsignatory party may still assert the statute as a defense. **(A)** is incorrect because a tortious common law fraud action is not related to the statute of frauds. **(B)** is incorrect because only MOULS contracts fall within the statute. **(C)** is incorrect because the statute of frauds is a legal procedural principle that in most states cannot be overridden by agreement.

31. **/C/** Contracts with a performance duty extending more than one year require a writing to be enforceable. **(A)** is incorrect because partial performance takes only the performed portion out of the statute's application. **(B)** is not the best answer because this is not one of our CIISSU situations where the law would excuse performance. **(D)** is incorrect because Harris will lose.

32. **/D/** An authentication of the party to be charged is required by the statute of frauds. Lacking even Ace's authentication, UCC Article 2 would dictate the contract is not enforceable against Ace. **(A)** is incorrect because the firm offer rule extends the revocability period to three months. **(B)** is incorrect because Doral's commitment to buy is sufficient to constitute consideration. **(C)** is incorrect because the issue of whether Doral is a merchant is not relevant.

33. **/D/** A contract for the sale and purchase of land falls under the common law and must state the price and a sufficient description of the property. **(A)** is incorrect because the common law land contract requires the price term be stated. Absent an admission by Ace, a price would not be imposed. **(B)** is not the best answer because a reasonable price would not be imposed under the common law even though it might under the UCC's "gap-filler" provisions. **(C)** is incorrect because neither estoppel nor implied in law will excuse the missing term of price in a common law land contract.

34. **/B/** An agreement between the surety and the debtor is not binding on and does not limit the creditor. While this may allow Samuel to collect from Deborah any sums he may have to pay Friendly, it does not stop the creditor from pursuing the surety directly. **(A)** could be a good defense because consideration for the surety's promise may be either a benefit to the promisor or a detriment to the promisee. Here the facts do not specify Samuel received any benefit and if the promise was made to the debtor there would be no consideration. **(C)** could be a good defense if

Samuel can prove the loan was never made to the debtor. **(D)** could be a good defense in that if Samuel's guarantee of the loan was only oral, it would violate the statute of frauds.

35. /C/ Undue influence is where a person abuses a position of authority or close relationship. **(A)** is not the best answer because Smith as an executive had express, implied, or apparent authority to bind the principal Apex. **(B)** is not the best answer because there was not an improper threat. **(D)** is not the best answer because consideration is present.

36. /B/ If one party is aware of a latent ambiguity and does not inform the other party, the contract will generally be enforced against the aware party. **(A)** is not the best answer because there was no express false statement by Sarah; at best it was nondisclosure. **(C)** is incorrect since only one party was mistaken according to these facts. **(D)** is not the best answer since the parties objective intent controls, not the subjective intent of one party. In addition, the more likely remedy in the event of different intentions would be rescission, not reformation.

37. /A/ The determination of whether a contract is unconscionable is a question of law for the court (judge) to decide. Here there appears to be both procedural (unequal bargaining power) and substantive (extreme high price and waiver of a basic right to claim damages for wrongful death) unconscionability. **(B)** is incorrect because unconscionability would be decided by the court (judge) not the jury. **(C)** is incorrect because procedural unconscionability appears present.

(D) is incorrect because substantive unconscionability appears present. Note that if the hospital sued to collect the insulin price the defense of economic duress would be available.

38. /D/ This is a mere request in the acceptance for payment terms which were not specified in the offer. The acceptance was therefore effective to create a contract. **(A)** is a good defense because Fred probably was a fiduciary since the buyer was a client of the law firm. A lawyer-fiduciary is held to a very high standard. All disclosures should have been made as if the transaction was between the client and a third party; it seems that the false statements about the true price and market value of the "household stuff" violated the fiduciary duty. **(B)** is a good defense because a latent ambiguity is where the contract appears clear at formation but subsequent facts show a term could be interpreted in more than one way. Here there would be a contract and the ambiguity would probably be interpreted against Fred because he was both an attorney and the drafting party. **(C)** is a good defense because Fred did commit fraud in the inducement by misstating the true cost and market value and Client probably relied thereupon.

39. /B/ Ambiguity of an essential term of a contract is an exception to the parol evidence rule so extrinsic evidence going to the meaning of the ambiguous term may be introduced. **(A)** is not the best answer because the facts ask the reason to allow in the evidence of the antique automobiles – not the false statements of fact about the cost and market value. **(C)** is not the best answer because the extrinsic evidence offered goes beyond a mere recital of insignificant fact. **(D)** is incorrect because this merely is a partial statement of the general rule and is subject to the DUCAS exceptions.

40. **/B/** The parol evidence rule requires the final agreement must be "integrated." **(A)** is incorrect because subsequent modifications are exceptions to the rule. **(C)** is incorrect because ambiguities are exceptions to the rule. **(D)** is incorrect because mutual mistake is an exception to the parol evidence rule.

41. **/B/** If there is a counteroffer or rejection, a subsequent acceptance is only effective upon receipt; because the $70,000 acceptance arrived at the offeror before the $62,500 counteroffer, there was a valid contract formed. **(A)** is incorrect because this was not a UCC offer, but rather a common law contract for land. **(C)** is incorrect because only the offer has to be written. **(D)** is incorrect because a subsequent modification is an exception to the parol evidence rule.

42. **/C/** The best answer because the buyer always has the right to reject nonconforming goods. **(A)** is not the best answer because the buyer may have to pay before inspection under a C.O.D. contract. However, this is not acceptance and if the goods were nonconforming, the price may be recovered by the buyer. **(B)** is incorrect because under a C.O.D. contract, possession only occurs after payment. **(D)** is incorrect because C.O.D. requires payment on delivery.

43. **/C/** The general rule is that risk of loss passes to the buyer upon acceptance. Acceptance may be revoked if the defect was hidden and it was reasonable not to discover the defect and reject the goods prior to the date. If the revocation was proper, risk of loss would shift back to the seller at that time. Therefore, to the extent Mighty's insurance did not cover the damage, the seller would be responsible for the difference if the goods were defective. **(A)** is incorrect because possession does not always control risk of loss. **(B)** is not the best answer because it is too simplistic; the question turns on risk of loss for goods that the buyer has revoked acceptance due to non- conformity because of the hidden defects. **(D)** is incorrect because payment and acceptance are not synonymous. [UCC 2.608]

44. **/B/** The buyer would bear the risk of loss because the repudiation (assuming Mighty did not accept) or revocation (assuming Mighty did accept) was wrongful since a neutral third party determined the good conformed to the contract. Therefore, the risk of loss would shift back to the buyer. **(A)** is incorrect because possession does not always control risk of loss. **(C)** is incorrect because payment neither controls risk of loss nor does it constitute acceptance, especially where the defect may be hidden. **(D)** is incorrect because the fact that Mega produced the machine does not control risk of loss where there was a transfer to the buyer.

45. **/A/** All affirmations of fact that become a part of the basis of the bargain are express warranties; this would include a seller's description of the goods. **(B)** is incorrect because the seller's selection of goods may constitute an implied warranty of

fitness for a particular purpose but not usually an express warranty. **(C)** is incorrect because the seller's selection of goods may constitute an implied warranty of fitness for a particular purpose but not usually an express warranty. **(D)** is incorrect because the seller's selection of goods may constitute an implied warranty of fitness for a particular purpose but not usually an express warranty.

46. /A/ UCC Article 2 only requires the goods to be fit for the ordinary purposes for which such goods are used. "All" is too broad and the focus is only normal usage not the particular buyer's use. **(B)** is incorrect because the merchantability implied warranty requires this provision. **(C)** is incorrect because the merchantability implied warranty requires this provision. **(D)** is incorrect because the merchantability implied warranty requires this provision.

47. /B/ To create an implied warranty of fitness for a particular purpose, the seller must know that the buyer is relying upon the advice in selecting the item. **(A)** is incorrect in that there is no requirement that the fitness for a particular purpose representation be written. **(C)** is incorrect in that there is no requirement that the fitness for a particular purpose representation be written. **(D)** is incorrect in that there is no requirement that the fitness for a particular purpose representation be written.

48. /C/ If the specifications provided by the buyer were such that the resulting good infringes on the rights of third parties the seller is not liable to the buyer. **(A)** is incorrect because the

implied warranty of title and against infringement applies even to casual sellers. **(B)** is incorrect because the warranty is implied. Unless the seller specifically states the goods are not free of infringement claims, the implied warranty of the UCC would apply. **(D)** is incorrect because if the defect is specified, the buyer may assume the risk of infringement.

49. /A/ Exclusions must be clear, conspicuous, conscionable and consistent. **(B)** is incorrect because effective disclaimers are binding if the purchaser has notice. **(C)** is incorrect because disclaimers are not automatically void. **(D)** is incorrect because only an exclusion of the implied warranty of fitness for a particular purpose must be in writing to be enforceable.

50. /A/ Only merchant sellers are subject to the implied warranty of merchantability. **(B)** is incorrect because an implied warranty action replaces the common law tort of negligence. **(C)** is incorrect because Article 2 of the UCC and Magnuson-Moss Act expand the number of potential Ps beyond the common law privity category. **(D)** is incorrect because an implied warranty action replaces the common law tort of strict liability.

51. /B/ The best answer because an objective standard would be applied in determining if the architect's decision was reasonable. **(A)** is incorrect because the fact that most people might accept the painting is not binding where the criteria is personal taste or fancy. **(C)** is not the best answer because the fact that nine out of ten of P's witnesses believe the painting to be reasonably similar to the family does not necessarily mean it is binding on the client; beauty is in the eye of the beholder. **(D)** is incorrect because a subjective standard is appropriate if performance approval is in the nature of a personal taste or fancy.

52. **/C/** This became a condition precedent to his contractual obligation and because of its materiality would probably be deemed a rejection and thus a counteroffer. **(A)** is incorrect because the statute of frauds would apply. **(B)** is incorrect because Wilcox's lack of signature would only effect his own liability and not that of Norris. **(D)** is incorrect because such language is too substantial a condition to be implied.

53. **/D/** The common law does not require The UCC Article 2's "perfect tender" under the doctrine of substantial performance. Recovery is possible for less than 100% perfect performance. The doctrine requires that the deviation not be intentional or material. **(A)** is incorrect because Kent will not prevail. **(B)** is incorrect because the issue is whether the deviation was major or minor; structural support would seem to be major. **(C)** is not the best answer because the doctrine does not require exact performance. Note that there would be a question of whether an in-quasi contract recovery would be available

54. **/B/** If part performance is still possible after failure of a presupposed condition, the seller must notify the buyer and explain the details of possible part performance. **(A)** is incorrect because the failure of a presupposed condition is not breach of contract. **(C)** is incorrect because the buyer has the option to accept

part performance. **(D)** is incorrect because the buyer is not required to accept part performance.

55. **/B/** UCC contract modifications are enforceable if made "in good faith." It appears from the facts that the UCC requirements of "honestly in fact" and the "observance of reasonable commercial standards of fair dealing in the trade" are met. Thus this modification would be enforceable under the UCC even though the common law's pre-existing duty rule would bar a recovery for the extra $3 per barrel. **(A)** is incorrect because the buyer is obligated to pay $28 per barrel. **(C)** is incorrect because Stand has not breached the contract. **(D)** is not the best answer because the facts do not make clear whether the $25 price was a reasonable basic assumption of the contract.

56. **/C/** This alternative would appear to be Crawford's worst defense. UCC 2-615 applies to contract non-performance caused by a condition "the non-occurrence of which was a basic assumption on which the contract was made." C also assumes that there is some liability and that offering a substitute grape might assist in mitigation; a failure of a UCC presupposed condition is not a breach at all. **(A)** is a viable defense because UCC 2-615 applies to contract non-performance caused by a condition "the non-occurrence of which was a basic assumption on which the contract was made." **(B)** is a viable defense because the UCC requires that if part performance is still possible, the seller must allocate among his customers in any manner that is fair and reasonable; this pro-rata allocation appears to be reasonable. **(D)** is a viable defense because UCC 2-615 applies to

contract non-performance caused by a condition "the non-occurrence of which was a basic assumption on which the contract was made."

57. /C/ The $10,000 is an executory accord arrived at in compromise to resolve the underlying disputed amount. If the debtor later repudiates the executory accord by failing to perform the satisfaction, the creditor may sue on the accord ($10,000 potential) or sue on the underlying dispute ($15,000 potential) if the statute of limitation on the original breach has not yet run. **(A)** is incorrect because Carol has two possible claims which may be asserted. **(B)** is incorrect because the failure of the debtor to satisfy the accord reactivates the underlying dispute. **(D)** is incorrect because Dick's repudiation seems unequivocal allowing the non-breaching party all the rights had there been a present breach.

58. /D/ This is a cancellation which rescinds the entire contract by mutual agreement thus discharging both parties. **(A)** is incorrect because the consideration for the original contract was in the form of bargained-for mutual promises. **(B)** is incorrect because Beta did not waive a condition; Beta agreed to rescind the entire contract. **(C)** is incorrect because a novation involves a new contract where a new party is added in lieu of an old party.

59. /B/ The unequivocal repudiation of a future performance duty is an anticipatory breach of contract. Cancellation and demand of assurance of performance by the non-breaching party are permitted, but not punitive damages. **(A)** is incorrect because punitive damages

are not usually recoverable for mere breach of contract. **(C)** is incorrect because the non-breaching party may cancel the contract. **(D)** is incorrect because the non-breaching party may demand an assurance of performance.

60. /D/ UCC 2.609 specifies that on receipt of a written demand by the buyer (based upon reasonable grounds), the seller must provide written assurance within 30 days or the buyer may suspend performance. **(A)** is incorrect because if risk of loss has passed the buyer will not be released from the contract. **(B)** is incorrect because impracticability of delivery is a vague concept without more facts and may not release the buyer from "all" obligations. **(C)** is incorrect because a retraction of anticipatory repudiation before the aggrieved party has materially changed its position is not a breach.

61. /C/ The UCC Article 2 specifies the amount of the liquidated damages stipulated in the contract must be reasonable in the light of either the anticipated or actual harm flowing from the breach. **(A)** is incorrect because either party can avail themselves of a liquidated damage provision. **(B)** is incorrect because if liquidated damages are so large as to constitute a penalty they will be struck. **(D)** is incorrect because there is no absolute percentage limitation as to the relationship between the liquidated provisions and the actual damage. The test is one of "reasonableness."

62. /B/ Wendy is entitled to be compensated in an sufficient amount to provide her the expectation damages she would have earned had she been allowed to perform the contract; expectation

damages are also referred to as compensatory damages or the benefit of the bargain. Here the facts state Wendy would have made a profit of $2,500 on completing the contract with Harry. **(A)** is incorrect because the full contract price would include some costs that Wendy did not incur. **(C)** is incorrect because restitution focuses on the beneficial effect to the non-breaching party. **(D)** is incorrect because it includes costs that Wendy incurred after she had actual knowledge that Harry had terminated the contract; such an award would allow the piling up of damages and are therefore not generally recoverable. Usually all parties must mitigate damages.

63. **/D/** The acceptance was valid because the offer did not unambiguously specify immediate shipment. There being a valid contract in effect, the shipment of nonconforming goods is breach. **(A)** is incorrect because a non-conforming shipment is not a counter offer. **(B)** is incorrect because the contract was breached, not canceled. **(C)** is incorrect because the order does not unambiguously specify acceptance can not be by a return promise; the Restatement and UCC 2.202(1) allow a prompt promise to ship unless the offeror explicitly states a mere promise to ship is not sufficient to constitute acceptance.

64. **/D/** The best and broadest answer. The UCC provides that an aggrieved buyer's remedies include "cover" (substitute equivalent goods) and incidental and consequential damages. Because "cover" was not possible, the remaining damages available are incidental and consequential. **(A)** is not the best answer because the value of the time spent and attorney fees are only one of the incidental damages available to the buyer. **(B)** is not the best answer because consequential damages – such as lost profit on the resale of the goods – are also available. **(C)** is not the best answer because this buyer's remedy does not have to be available to the seller.

65. **/D/** Specific performance is allowed under UCC 2.716 if the goods are unique and (1) the buyer is unable to cover, (2) the goods have been identified to the contract, and (3) the goods have not been transferred to a bona fide purchaser (BFP), or (4) in other proper circumstances. All three specific performance requirements seem to be met here, and the cover requirement of "substitute equivalent" goods is not met because the quality of the two carpets is substantially lower or higher than the contracted goods. **(A)** is incorrect because there is no requirement that a non-breaching party must wait to see if the anticipatory repudiation will be revoked prior to the original performance date. **(B)** is not the best answer; it seems that the additional quality and doubling of the price would imply this was a substantially superior product than the original carpet which might exceed the "substitute equivalent" rule. **(C)** is incorrect. The buyer is not required to cover by accepting inferior goods; these goods are not a reasonable equivalent to the contract goods. If the buyer decided not to pursue specific performance, the likely monetary damages would be for the difference between the contract price and the lower market price or $5,000 ($20,000 - $15,000).

66. /D/ UCC 2.716(1) specifies that "specific performance may be decreed where the goods are unique or in other proper circumstances." **(A)** is incorrect because the question is not whether Mega is responsible for damages but rather if specific performance will be ordered. **(B)** is incorrect because the goods being unique is only required if "other proper circumstances" are not present. **(C)** is incorrect because it focuses on the "unique" factor rather than "other proper circumstances."

67. /B/ Specific performance requires that the goods have been identified to the contract. This remedy is not available if the buyer has been able to effectively cover. **(A)** is a correct statement (and thus the incorrect answer) because revocation of acceptance is allowed if the defect was hidden. **(C)** is a correct statement of an aggrieved buyer's remedies. **(D)** is not the best answer because the expected profit is not the only element of damages available to an aggrieved buyer. Incidental damages are also recoverable.

68. /C/ The measure of damages is the difference between the contract price and the market price. If there is no market price, the contract price would be the measure of recovery. **(A)** is incorrect because Ling may recover incidental damages in addition to the contract price. **(B)** is not the best answer because the risk of loss rules would determine who bears the loss. **(D)** is not the best answer because specific performance is not normally a seller's remedy.

69. /B/ Regardless of any claim that Harry may have against George, the Emeritus sculpture is now in the hands of a bona fide purchaser; therefore specific performance against the seller is not possible. **(A)** is not the best answer because the question of adequacy of consideration in the contract does not go to the central question here of specific performance. In addition, revocation of any gift would not effect the possession rights of a third party bona fide purchaser. **(C)** is incorrect because Harry's assistance at the accident scene predated the exchange; past consideration is no consideration. **(D)** is incorrect because Harry's assistance at the accident scene predated the exchange; past consideration is no consideration.

70. /C/ The best answer. Punitive damages are not usually available for mere breach of contract absent egregious circumstances or willful breach of contract by a fiduciary. Injunctions and restraining orders may be sought in a personal service contract to prohibit the D from working for anyone other than the P if the D refuses to complete the contract. **(A)** is incorrect because punitive damages are not usually available for mere breach of contract absent egregious circumstances or willful breach of contract by a fiduciary. **(B)** is incorrect because punitive damages are not usually available for mere breach of contract, absent egregious circumstances or willful breach of contract by a fiduciary. Injunctions and restraining orders may be sought in a personal service contract to prohibit the D from working for anyone other than the P if the D refuses to complete the contract. **(D)** is incorrect because injunctions and restraining orders may be sought in a personal service contract to prohibit the D from working for anyone other than the P if the D refuses to complete the contract.

71. **/B/** If Carol actually knew and appreciated that the disclaimer provision had been omitted, there would seem to be a waiver that would at least allow a partial defense to the claim. **(A)** is not the best answer because this was a bilateral contract so breach of either promise is actionable; performance with due care is an implied condition of a professional service contract. **(C)** is incorrect because the statute that was violated is regulatory in nature and intended to protect the public from bar exam candidates who can not demonstrate their competency by passing the entry exam. **(D)** is incorrect because the discovery rule tolls the statute of limitations until actual or constructive discovery when the trigger date is deemed to occur; this appears to be when Carol's personal representative discovered the omission in the will.

72. **/B/** Because Security was specifically contemplated by Glenn as receiving rights, they have third party creditor beneficiary status. They also have the right to go against him personally. **(A)** is incorrect because the subject of the contract was land requiring a writing under the statute of frauds. **(C)** is incorrect because Security is a third-party creditor beneficiary. **(D)** is incorrect because Wilson remains liable.

73. **/C/** The first spring gardening contract right to $500 payment is assignable because the assignor has fully performed her duties. The third $2,000 lawn furniture contract is likewise assignable because the assignor has fully performed. In addition, it is a UCC contract because it involves the sale of goods; the UCC will not enforce a prohibition on the assignment of a contractual right. The assignment prohibition in the second expected $1,000 contract for the summer's work will be enforced because it is a future contract. While Harriet will have to pay Friendly, she may have a claim for damages resulting from the breach of the covenant not to assign. **(A)** is incorrect because it involves a wrong combination of alternatives. **(B)** is incorrect because it involves a wrong combination of alternatives. **(D)** is incorrect because it involves a wrong combination of alternatives.

74. **/C/** UCC 2-210(3) will treat a prohibition of contract rights assignment as barring only the delegation of the assignor's performance. **(A)** is incorrect because the contract for the lawn equipment had been completely performed by the assignor. **(B)** is incorrect because such a prohibition is not against public policy. **(D)** is incorrect because Friendly is not a third party beneficiary since they were not specified in the original Gloria to Harriet contract

75. **/A/** A contractual right which may come into effect in the future may not be assigned. **(B)** is incorrect because Friendly does not want to enforce the condition prohibiting assignment. **(C)** is incorrect because Friendly does not want to enforce the condition prohibiting assignment. **(D)** is not the best answer because of the word "only" which limits the non-enforceability of the assignment prohibition conclusion to knowledge by the assignee of the condition; a future contract is another reason for non-

enforceability.

76. /B/ Because the delegator remains liable, the obligee cannot show prejudice or increased risk. **(A)** is incorrect because the parties are allowed to prohibit the delegation of a duty (unlike a prohibition on an assignment which the UCC would void). **(C)** is incorrect because delegation is not allowed where a material variance in performance would result. **(D)** is incorrect because generally personal service contracts involving personal skills are not delegable.

Contracts and UCC Sales
Practice Question Answer Rationales

77. /C/ An advertisement in a newspaper not containing details and specific words of commitment is generally construed as an invitation to deal. The customer makes the offer by tendering the price and the store accepts by delivery or a promise to deliver. **(A)** is incorrect because Harper has made neither an offer nor a contract. **(B)** is incorrect because Harper has made neither an offer nor a contract. **(D)** is incorrect because there was no contract.

78. /B/ Because there was no consideration Maurice retains the power to revoke the offer. **(A)** is incorrect because under the common law, the offeror has the power to revoke the offer at will. **(C)** is incorrect because a telegraph generally qualifies as a writing for statute of frauds purposes. **(D)** is incorrect because there is no requirement the revocation must use the same means of communication as the offer.

79. /B/ Under the common law a categorical rejection by an offeree operates to terminate the offer so that a subsequent acceptance is treated as a mere counteroffer. **(A)** is incorrect because notification will terminate the offer. **(C)** is incorrect because the offeror's dictated maximum of 30 days would expire on July 31. **(D)** is incorrect because the offer would be irrevocable only if there was consideration.

80. /A/ The mailbox rule applies and the changes are minor and consistent with the terms of the offer; therefore it is a valid acceptance. **(B)** is incorrect because such an acceptance is effective upon dispatch under the mailbox rule. **(C)** is incorrect because the communication is not a counteroffer. **(D)** is incorrect because the communication is a valid acceptance.

81. /C/ This was not a firm offer in that it did not purport to hold the offer open for 10 days, but only that the offeree must accept within 10 days from the offer. **(A)** is incorrect because the offer was revocable and the revocation was effective. **(B)** is incorrect because the offer was revocable and revocation was effective. **(D)** is incorrect because the transmission means used does not determine an acceptance timeliness and effectiveness.

82. /D/ Acceptances following a rejection are effective on receipt; since the phone acceptance was received prior to the telegraph acceptance, it was effective. If the telegraphed acceptance had been received prior to the phone acceptance, the latter would have been ineffective since the $190,000 would be a rejection and a counteroffer. **(A)** is incorrect because rejections are effective on receipt. **(B)** is incorrect because only the offer must be written. **(C)** is incorrect because the mere fact that others are interested is not sufficient to revoke an offer.

83. /**B**/ The modifications were an express condition of the purported acceptance, and they were rejected by the seller. Since the offeror stated that the terms could not be varied, this is to be treated as a rejection. Thus, a subsequent acceptance cannot be effective. **(A)** is incorrect because Baker did not purport to keep the offer open. **(C)** is incorrect because there is no contract. **(D)** is incorrect because the writing requirement was complied with.

84. /**A**/ Bilbo incurred a legal detriment by foregoing her right to sue for 30 days. It is the agreement to forbear on the legal action that constitutes the necessary detriment, not the merits of the suit (assuming Bilbo believed it had merit). **(B)** is incorrect because silence is not generally acceptance. **(C)** is incorrect because the offer was irrevocable. **(D)** is incorrect because land is to be analyzed under the common law and the UCC's "firm offer" rule would not apply.

85. /**C**/ Contract offers are not generally assignable, especially where they involve a subject dependent upon the offeree's personal skill. **(A)** is incorrect because a contract for over one year requires a writing. **(B)** is incorrect because this is not an option. **(D)** is incorrect because under the mailbox rule acceptance could be effective on dispatch. This would apply because the offeror did not preclude this treatment.

86. /**D**/ This is a UCC Article 2 offer. Since it is made by a merchant, it also qualifies as a "firm offer." Since the offeror did not specify that acceptance can only be effective on receipt, the mailbox rule applies. Statement I would qualify as acceptance because the time period is measured on dispatch. Statement II would also qualify since the acceptance was dispatched timely, the means used to transmit it appears reasonable and the prior rejection does not terminate a firm offer. Statement III would also qualify because the offer was irrevocable for ten days; the offeror's revocation was not effective. **(A)** is incorrect because all three represent valid acceptance. **(B)** is incorrect because all three represent valid acceptance. **(C)** is incorrect because all three represent valid acceptance.

87. /**B**/ The parol evidence rule would preclude Filmore from entering evidence of any prior or contemporaneous agreement that contradicts the terms of the final written integrated agreement. **(A)** is incorrect because the statute of frauds would not require a writing since the price is under $500. **(C)** is incorrect because certain warranties cannot be disclaimed. **(D)** is incorrect in that the agent had at least implied or apparent authority and that is sufficient to bind the principal.

88. /**C**/ A unilateral mistake may be grounds for avoidance if the other party had actual or constructive knowledge of the error. **(A)** is incorrect because there is no contract. **(B)** is not the best answer because actual knowledge is not always required; constructive knowledge of a material mistake

may be adequate. **(D)** is incorrect because the test is one of the objective intent of the parties.

89. /D/ Duress is where an improper threat forced a person to enter into a contract. **(A)** is incorrect because fraud requires a false statement and such information is not given in the facts. **(B)** is not the best answer because the payment of $500 is some consideration. **(C)** is incorrect because undue influence usually applies to overreaching by a fiduciary.

90. /A/ The $2,000 set-off right that would be good against Grant is also good against Grant's assignee, Line. Thus the net amount of $8,000 is the maximum the assignee, Line, may assert against the debtor, Walton. **(B)** is incorrect because Walton will only have to pay $8,000. **(C)** is incorrect because Line is only an assignee since he was not in contemplation prior to the contract. **(D)** is incorrect because the full $2,000 would be allowed as a set-off.

91. /C/ The delegator remains liable with the delegatee unless Fennell enters into a novation. **(A)** is not the best answer because delegation is not necessarily a breach and the law may impose a duty to respond to a request for assurances of performance. **(B)** is incorrect because the duties are not extinguished. **(D)** is incorrect because McLeod loses his rights but remains liable for his duties.

92. /B/ Consideration requires either a benefit to the promisor or a detriment to the promisee. Sally's father did not receive an economic benefit and the promisees – Fred and Sally – did not suffer a

detriment. **(A)** is not the best answer because the statute of frauds has an exception if the promisor surety has a main purpose to benefit themselves. Arguably assisting his daughter qualifies as his main purpose so this is not the strongest legal defense. **(C)** is incorrect because the principle of promissory estoppel appears to be met in that there was reasonable detrimental reliance by Megabank. **(D)** is incorrect because the facts do not state the creditor had to first pursue the principal debtors before looking to the surety for payment.

93. /A/ Under the common law, the parties may usually stipulate in the contract the length of time the cause of action remains alive. **(B)** is incorrect because the conflict of law issue usually only applies if a reasonably related contract designation controls. **(D)** is incorrect because the conflict of law issue usually only applies if a reasonably related contract designation controls. **(C)** is a distracter because the time in which the suit was brought is the period against which the statutory period is measured, not the time the P decided to ultimately bring suit.

94. /B/ Incapacity of a personal service contractor will excuse performance. **(A)** is not the best answer because Ace contracted for the services of Lead Man and such a personal-service contract is not delegable since a materially different performance may result. **(C)** is not the best answer because mitigation of damages is required of the non-breaching party only if a contract must be performed; here performance was excused. **(D)** is not the best answer because the question of the materiality of the

breach only arises if the contract is enforceable; here it was excused.

95. **/D/** Anticipatory repudiation must be unequivocal and go beyond performance uncertainty. Here there was only a statement that Hot Tunes might not be able to perform. **(A)** is incorrect because offering to substitute a different performance does not constitute a retraction since this does not restore the original contract. **(B)** is incorrect because this would be characterized as a material breach since Lead Man was the band's very popular singer and his personal draw was the reason Ace had sold a large number of tickets. **(C)** is incorrect because this is a common law contract not UCC. Repudiation under UCC does create the right to submit a written demand for an adequate assurance of performance. This right is not a requirement however.

96. **/D/** Compensatory damages attempt to give the P the monetary benefit of the bargain; this appears to be the preferable remedy in this case. **(A)** is incorrect because a court will not usually issue an order of specific performance for the breach of a personal service contract. **(B)** is incorrect because the reliance interest applies where compensatory damages fail; here they appear adequate. **(C)** is incorrect because an in quasi contract recovery applies only where the contract fails; here there is a contract.

97. **/C/** An in quasi-contract recovery requires that the P have a reasonable expectation of compensation. Here that would be a question of fact because Don Doctor knew Susan Safety and may have participated as a mere volunteer without an expectation of payment. **(A)** is incorrect because a request for professional services is not necessary for in quasi-contract recovery. **(B)** is not the best answer. While the hospital did the surgery, Don Doctor's advice may have prevented a much more serious prognosis for the injury. **(D)** is incorrect because consent to professional services is not necessary for in quasi-contract recovery.

98. **/C/** Laches applies to limit the time period in which equitable actions such as in quasi-contract may be brought. **(A)** is incorrect because the statute of limitations applies to actions at law; in quasi-contract is an equitable action. Thus a tolling of the statute of limitations is not directly applicable. **(B)** is incorrect because the statute of limitations does not depend upon the public interest in the underlying action. **(D)** is incorrect because the contract statute of limitations period does not apply to equitable actions such as in quasi-contract. Note that the reference to the 3-year statute of limitations for tort actions is a distracter.

99. **/B/** The improvement made by the land possessor must be substantial enough to clearly show the claiming party is more than a mere tenant. **(A)** is not the best answer because the statute of frauds has an exception for an oral real property conveyance if the land possessor makes a substantial cash payment, takes possession, and makes substantial improvements. **(C)** is incorrect because the return of the money will not negate the court's ability to give equitable enforcement of the oral contract. **(D)** is not the best answer because there is not another credible explanation for the

$59,000 cash and the improvements.

100. /B/ Forbearing to exercise a legal right which the claimant reasonably believes to be valid constitutes consideration in the form of a detriment to the promisee (even if the legal right is in fact not valid). **(A)** is not the best answer because the $1 does not seem to be adequate consideration for the $10,000 promise. **(C)** is not the best answer because a mere recital of consideration is not sufficient if there is no real consideration. **(D)** is incorrect because a prior subjective unilateral intent is neither a benefit to the promisor nor a detriment to the promisee; past consideration is no consideration.

101. /D/ The rescue was not made as a consequence of a request; thus Richard Rescuer was a mere volunteer. **(A)** is incorrect because uncertainty in the value of consideration is not a basis for invalidating an obligation based thereupon. **(B)** is incorrect because moral obligation is not usually a substitute for consideration. **(C)** is incorrect because the promise was made after the act had been completed; past consideration is no consideration.

102. /C/ The best answer is that the parties have compromised their differences and entered into an executory accord to settle a disputed obligation. **(A)** is not the best answer because promissory estoppel provides a substitute for consideration; here there is consideration in that the parties have changed their position in the executory accord. **(B)** is incorrect in that a novation usually means substituting a new party in place of an old; here the parties are the same. **(D)** is incorrect because

restitution is usually appropriate to compensate a victim of an economic crime where there is no contract.

103. /D/ Tony Trucker's promise and liability to pay for the trucks is subject to the express condition precedent that 10 trucks would be completed no later than June 30. Because this involved both the quantity and time of performance, Mary Manufacturer would probably interpret the quote as a promise. **(A)** is incorrect because Tony's statement to pay for the trucks if they are completed on time is both a promise and a condition. **(B)** is incorrect because Tony's statement to pay for the trucks if they are completed on time is both a promise and a condition. **(C)** is incorrect because Tony's statement to pay for the trucks if they are completed on time is both a promise and a condition.

104. /C/ If the contract contained an express condition precedent stating that "time is of the essence," this provision would be enforced. **(A)** is not the best answer because the truck contract would fall under the UCC. The UCC rejects the common law's substantial performance test in favor of the "perfect tender" rule. **(B)** is incorrect because a slight drop (10%) in market value does not seem to be sufficient to constitute UCC commercial impracticality. **(D)** is not the best answer because unless the flood destroyed the entire business operation making it impossible for Tony to accept delivering, it would not constitute an excuse for breach.

105. /D/ The UCC rule is that goods must be delivered in one entire lot unless the terms or circumstances indicate to the contrary. In this case, the contract was for 100 trucks in total but was to be delivered in 10 different lots. Thus the contract is partially divisible and partially whole. **(A)** is not the best answer because the contract is partially divisible and partially whole. **(B)** is not the best answer because the contract is partially divisible and partially whole. **(C)** is not the best answer because the contract is partially divisible and partially whole.

106. **/D/** The receipt of performance that is not in accordance with the contract terms allows the other contracting party to seek assurances of performance under the UCC. **(A)** is incorrect because deviation from the contract terms constitutes a breach. **(B)** is incorrect because the contract is likely divisible. **(C)** is incorrect because a court would require an equivalent payment for the 5 trucks unless they were returned to the seller.

107. **/C/** The offer was complete as to what would constitute a valid acceptance. **(A)** is incorrect because it is not required that there be a named offeree; reward offers may be accepted by anyone. **(B)** is incorrect because normally an advertisement merely specifies the goods to be sold and does not specify the means or manner of acceptance. **(D)** is incorrect because a gift does not require any consideration or performance by the recipient.

108. **/A/** A promise for an act constitutes a unilateral contract. **(B)** is incorrect because the offeree performance satisfied the acceptance requirement; a mere promise of performance would have been inadequate. **(C)** is incorrect because the offeree performance satisfied the acceptance requirement; a mere promise of performance would have been inadequate. **(D)** is incorrect because under the common law the offeror is the master of the bargain and determines if a return promise or performance is necessary to constitute acceptance.

109. **/B/** The student receiving discipline was not a condition of acceptance, only the student being reported to the law school administration. **(A)** is incorrect because public policy would not seem to be an issue. **(C)** is not the best answer because the facts do not state that there was a student code of ethics requiring reporting. **(D)** is incorrect because promissory estoppel is only necessary if the contract fails under the common law; here the contract is enforceable.

110. **/A/** Under the mailbox rule, acceptances are effective on dispatch; the revocation on April 15 was too late since the contract was formed on April 10. **(B)** is not the best answer because under the mailbox rule, acceptances are effective on dispatch. **(C)** is incorrect because the offeree's knowledge of an attempted revocation does not effect a previous acceptance. **(D)** is incorrect because in theory acceptance under the mailbox rule is effective on dispatch even if never received by the offeror.

111. **/C/** Rejections are only effective on receipt and the facts here state that the seller never received it. Therefore, the offer was not terminated but rather remained open. The rejection, however, does deny the offeree the ability to use the mailbox rule under which acceptance may have an effective date on dispatch. Therefore, the

effective date of acceptance goes back to the general rule of being effective on receipt by the other party. **(A)** is incorrect. Because of the rejection, the effective date of acceptance goes back to the general rule of being effective on receipt by the other party. **(B)** is incorrect. Because of the rejection, the effective date of acceptance goes back to the general rule of being effective on receipt by the other party. **(D)** is incorrect because while rejections do terminate offers such terminations are only effective upon receipt; here the facts state the rejection was never received.

112. /C/ A liquidated damage provision must be reasonably related to either the anticipated or actual damages; if so large as to constitute a penalty they will be struck and the non-breaching party is left with compensatory damages. **(A)** is incorrect because if the provision is deemed to be penalty it will be struck, even if bargained for. **(B)** is not the best answer; liquidated damages may be enforced if they are reasonable in light of the anticipated damages. **(D)** is not the best answer because substantial performance is not a prerequisite to the enforcement of a liquidated damage provision.

113. /A/ This alternative is the best answer because Harry has made a good faith offer to settle the disputed amount for a partial payment. By cashing the tendered check without reserving rights or otherwise objecting, Paul has accepted the offer of settlement creating an accord and satisfaction. **(B)** is not the best answer because the accord and satisfaction would include any amount for the deficiency in the work. **(C)** is not the best answer because this accord and satisfaction would include any reduction in price that would be allowed under the doctrine of substantial performance. **(D)** is not the best answer because this accord and satisfaction would include any reduction in price that would be allowed under the doctrine of substantial performance.

114. /C/ Whether the written agreement was a complete integration would determine if parol (or extrinsic) evidence could be introduced to prove that Paul agreed to pay the $30,000 to Bill. **(A)** is incorrect because the fact that the parties have not read a contract they signed is not usually a defense. **(B)** is incorrect because the fact that the parties have not read a contract they signed is not usually a defense. **(D)** is incorrect because a third party beneficiary has enforceable rights if they were so intended and specifically identified by the original contracting parties.

115. /D/ Neither I nor II is correct. **(A)** is incorrect because there was a written purchase and sale agreement so the statute of frauds is satisfied. The final written agreement cured the problem of the preliminary oral negotiations. **(B)** is incorrect because the Larry to Paul primary agreement was for the property purchase; this is a different contract than the subsequent agreement to pay a third party beneficiary. Further this second undertaking was an indemnity obligation because Paul agreed to pay Larry's past debt. This is different than a promise to pay upon another's default which is not yet certain to occur. **(C)** is incorrect because there was a written purchase and sale agreement so the statute of frauds is satisfied.

116. /B/ If the original parties modify or rescind the agreement to pay Bill before his rights vest, the modification is binding on the third party beneficiary who loses any rights. **(A)** is incorrect because the issue of whether Bill had enforceable rights against Larry on the underlying debt is not relevant since any such rights are not available to Paul. That is a different contract. **(C)** is incorrect because the issue of whether Bill had enforceable rights against Larry on the underlying debt is not relevant since any such rights are not available to Paul. That is a different contract. **(D)** is incorrect because it is not necessary for the third party beneficiary to notify the original parties of an acceptance of the new rights if there was reliance thereupon.

117. /B/ The remedy of specific performance is not generally available in a personal service contract such as the performance of a legal engagement. **(A)** is incorrect because a delegation of a duty that involves the personal skill of the obligor requires the approval of the obligee. **(C)** is incorrect because the fact that Laurie has begun performing does not mean specific performance would be granted. **(D)** is incorrect because the fact that Laurie has skills and unique services does not mean specific performance would be granted.

118. /D/ Exculpatory clauses that purport to relieve a professional from liability resulting from his own negligence or breach of contract are not enforceable. **(A)** is not the best answer because while Charlie may be partially at fault, this would not prohibit a suit by Charlie. **(B)** is incorrect because there was not a novation in which Charlie

substituted Nathan for Laurie. **(C)** is incorrect because exculpatory clauses that purport to relieve a professional from liability resulting from his own negligence or breach of contract are not enforceable.

119. /A/ Charlie was a third party beneficiary of the delegation contract between Laurie and Nathan. **(B)** is incorrect because the third party beneficiary status provides the standing to sue even though there may not be direct privity between Charlie and Nathan. **(C)** is incorrect because this clause is void as against public policy. **(D)** is incorrect because Charlie can sue for inadequate performance even if there was no payment for the services.

120. /D/ The landlord will not prevail in their contract action over either Jackie or her parents. Jackie was a minor and since she lived at home with her parents, the apartment can not be characterized as a necessity for which a minor may be liable. Parents are not usually liable for their infant's contracts for non-necessities where they lacked knowledge of the infant's agreement or otherwise had some fault. **(A)** is incorrect because Jackie was a minor and since she lived at home with her parents, the apartment can not be characterized as a necessity for which a minor may be liable. **(B)** is incorrect because Parents are not usually liable for their infant's contracts for non-necessities where they lacked knowledge of the infant's agreement or otherwise had some fault. **(C)** is incorrect because Jackie was a minor and cannot be held liable for a contract for anything but necessities, and parents are not liable for their infant's contracts for non-necessities where they lacked knowledge of the infant's agreement or otherwise had some fault.

121. /C/ There was a bilateral contract but there appears to be a mutual mistake of fact (which farm was to be optioned?). There clearly was no true meeting of the minds. While the factual mistake does affect the value of the option right that Wendy sought, it would be more likely to be characterized as factual to allow rescission. **(A)** would require a court to decide which farm should be imposed and perhaps the price; such an action would mean that one party's intentions would not be fulfilled. **(B)** would require a court to decide which farm should be imposed and perhaps the price; such an action would mean that one party's intentions would not be fulfilled. **(D)** is not the best answer because words or terms that are ambiguous are usually susceptible of more than one meaning. Here the term used – fruit farm – has only one meaning. The question of which farm was intended is one of fact.

122. /A/ Fred would have to prove the existence of a contemporaneous oral agreement to pay the $500. This would be an exception to the parol evidence rule if Wendy should assert it as a defense. Fred would also have to prove the consideration for which Wendy committed herself to pay the $500. Fred would also have to allege that payment of the $500 for the option was never made. **(B)** is incorrect because Fred would have to allege that payment of the $500 for the option was never made. **(C)** is incorrect because Fred would have to prove the existence of a contemporaneous oral agreement to pay the $500. **(D)** is not the best answer; Fred would have to allege that payment of the $500 for the

option was never made, prove that consideration was provided, and prove the existence of a contemporaneous oral agreement.

123. /C/ An illusory promise would be the best defense since if there were no detriment to the promisee, the promisor's agreement to pay the $500 would not be supported by consideration. **(A)** is incorrect because Fred had the right to sell the property to another. **(B)** is incorrect because Fred retained the right to sell to another. **(D)** is incorrect because promissory estoppel requires a change of position; here there is no change.

124. /D/ All three defenses would provide Fred with a viable defense. I is a correct choice because the facts do not state that there was an explicit acceptance of the commission offer. II is also a correct choice because the purchaser's interest in property predated the arrival of the broker so present consideration may be lacking – past consideration is no consideration. III is also a viable defense because a real estate commission agreement must be written under the statute of frauds in effect in most jurisdictions and the facts do not state the agreement was written. **(A)** is incorrect because all three would provide Fred with a viable defense. **(B)** is incorrect because all three would provide Fred with a viable defense. **(C)** is incorrect because all three would provide Fred with a viable defense.

125. /A/ The lawsuit was timely filed because the three year statute of limitations was tolled during the two years that Alice was outside the jurisdiction. **(B)** is incorrect because the statute of limitations is only triggered (begins to run) upon discovery of the malpractice. **(C)** is incorrect because attorneys' lawsuits are generally subject to the same statute of limitation period as other professional malpractice claims. **(D)** is incorrect because the three year statute of limitations was tolled during the two years that Alice was outside the jurisdiction.

126. /C/ When the subject matter of the contract is destroyed the court will usually excuse performance. Here Mike had no involvement in the theft of the automobile so his performance would be excused. The demand/request to install the motor in a different automobile is an offer to enter into a new contract and Mike apparently has not agreed. **(A)** is incorrect because (even if there were a new contract) courts will not usually order specific performance of a personal service contract. **(B)** is incorrect because it assumes Mike has to perform under either the old or proposed new contract. **(D)** is incorrect because it assumes Mike has to perform under either the old or proposed new contract.

127. /D/ When a contract to improve an existing house becomes unenforceable because of destruction of the subject matter, a court may allow an innocent party a recovery by using the contract rate and interpreting the contract as divisible; payment of an equivalent amount would be ordered. Here 80% of the siding was completed so the $2,400 would be the total equivalent amount Sarah would be entitled to. Since she has already received $2,000, she would be entitled to the $400 deficiency. **(A)** is not the best answer because this work is being performed on an existing house and the homeowner retains the sole risk of loss. This is contrary to a new home in which the general contractor normally has the sole risk of loss unless the contract specifies to the contrary or the property owner has insurance coverage. **(B)** is not the best answer because this work is being performed on an existing house and the homeowner retains the sole risk of loss. This is contrary to a new home in which the general contractor normally has the sole risk of loss unless the contract specifies to the contrary or the property owner has insurance coverage. **(C)** is not the best answer because this would give Sarah an unjust enrichment beyond the 80% she partially performed.

128. /C/ Reliance interest provides damages for out-of-pocket expenses where compensatory damages fail to provide the benefit of the bargain. Here the recovery of future business profit might be too uncertain and speculative since David has no prior Internet sales experience. The out-of-pocket expenses incurred in reliance on the expectation that the Bank would have made the loan seem the most certain and likely recovery. **(A)** is not the best answer because reliance interest could provide an equitable recovery even if the contract did not come into effect until the final loan documents were signed. **(B)** is incorrect because the profits for a business with no history are usually too speculative to be recovered. **(D)** is incorrect because the profits for a business with no history are usually too speculative to be recovered.

129. /D/ Bob revoked or withdrew the unilateral offer by making a statement to Patty that was clearly inconsistent with a continuing intent to enter into a contract. The basic contract law rule is that the offeror can revoke at will unless there is consideration to support a promise not to revoke. Here there was no consideration and Patty had not begun performance. The firm offer rule might apply since Bob appears to be a merchant who deals in those kind of goods but that requires a writing which is not present here. **(A)** is incorrect because there was no contract. **(B)** is incorrect because there was no contract. **(C)** is incorrect because while the newspaper advertisement was a mere invitation to deal, the oral promise to sell constituted a valid offer.

130. /D/ The right to receive payment from an executory personal service contract is not usually assignable. Performance by Alice must have occurred since the compensation is a substantial factor which promotes satisfactory performance. Another approach is to treat personal service contract rights as divisible; assignment of the payment would be allowed for the time period that Alice had already performed. **(A)** is not the best answer since it presupposes the assignment of the payment right is enforceable against the promisor. **(B)** is not the best answer since it presupposes the assignment of the payment right is enforceable against the promisor. **(C)** is not the best answer since it presupposes the assignment of the payment right is enforceable against the promisor. In addition, the right to receive a sum due in the future is an intangible property right which under Article 9 of the UCC can only be perfected by control or filing. There are no facts given here to suggest any filing or bank control arrangement occurred.

131. /D/ Whether the American Bar Association will accredit the new law school appears to be a condition precedent to the offer of employment. **(A)** is incorrect because only if the condition precedent is met is the promise enforceable. **(B)** is incorrect because an illusory promise is where the promisor has total control over whether or not they will perform; here a third party accrediting body has such control. **(C)** is incorrect because (if and when the condition is met) the law school is bound to hire Dorothy Dean and she is bound to serve; both parties thus gave consideration.

132. /C/ It would seem that this is the best defense the new law school can assert. It may not be sufficient to avoid responsibility for the contract, but it will at least go to mitigation and the appropriate measure of damages; the lack of any detrimental reliance may provide the new law school with an offset for the salary Dorothy was earning. **(A)** is incorrect because this contract is not subject to the statute of frauds. The term of Dorothy Dean-to-be employment is not by the contract terms expressly over one year in length. It is apparently a mere "at-will" term in which either the employer or the employee may terminate the employment agreement. **(B)** is incorrect because the contract was formed subject to an express condition precedent that was satisfied. **(D)** is nonsense because this is a common law contract, not a UCC contract.

133. /D/ The omission may qualify as a formation defect, since both parties intended the clause to be included. **(A)** is incorrect because the omission is probably a formation defect (remember the DUCAS exceptions to the parol evidence rule). **(B)** is incorrect because the omission is probably a formation defect (remember the DUCAS exceptions to the parol evidence rule). **(C)** is incorrect because the omission is probably a formation defect (remember the DUCAS exceptions to the parol evidence rule).

134. /A/ A waiver is where one party excuses the right to sue for breach; that is what has occurred here. **(B)** is incorrect because a cancellation usually refers to the physical destruction of the written contract by agreement of the parties. **(C)** is not the best answer because a release would suggest a termination of the contract; here only one condition was extinguished. **(D)** is incorrect because repudiation refers to an expression that one of the parties will not perform a duty required in the future.

135. /B/ Reformation is the desirable remedy since Teresa apparently desires to continue operating the yogurt shop. Therefore she wants a court to reform the lease contract by imposing the exclusive condition on Larry Landlord. Damages are also possible because her yogurt shop lost the profitability she enjoyed before McDaisey began to sell yogurt. **(A)** is not the best answer because damages are also possible. **(C)** is incorrect because the facts state that Teresa desires to continue operating the yogurt shop. **(D)** is incorrect because the facts state that Teresa desires to continue operating the yogurt shop. Rescission would undo the lease contract but this would not allow Teresa to continue operating.

136. /D/ The best answer. Although the contract calls the liquidated damage provision a "penalty" it seems to meet the test of being difficult to ascertain the actual damages. **(A)** is incorrect because it seems likely a court would interpret the "penalty" wording as merely descriptive and in substance a valid liquidated damage provision. **(B)** misstates the law; true penalties are not enforceable. Liquidated damages provisions are enforceable. **(C)** is incorrect because the inability to show damages is precisely what justifies having a liquidated damages provision in the contract.

137. /B/ The best answer because the provision was a condition subsequent which operated to terminate the contract. **(A)** is incorrect because the condition subsequent did not include a requirement concerning treatment of any coach to be hired. **(C)** is incorrect because the liquidated damage provision is between Bertha and Wally, not Slippery and Bertha. **(D)** is not as good an answer as B because the termination condition was express and any implied condition would not likely be effective if it was contrary to an express condition.

138. /D/ Performance without knowledge of the (unilateral) contract offer is not acceptance. Here the facts state that Frank only learned of the reward offer after he had performed the requested act. **(A)** is not the best answer because performance of a unilateral contract may provide the necessary consideration. **(B)** is not the best answer because the bar exam questions usually focus on legal remedies rather than equitable remedies. **(C)** is not the best answer because a reward offeree is not

required to notify the offerror that performance is beginning. (Note that notification might be necessary under the UCC but this is a common law personal service contract).

139. /A/ A bounty is a government grant payable merely upon the recipient apprehending the criminals; prior knowledge of the bounty is not required. A bounty classification is helpful because Frank can not prevail under a contract theory since he was unaware of the offer when he rendered performance. **(B)** is not the best answer because it is an equitable remedy, which is usually less certain than a legal recovery. **(C)** is not the best answer because it is an equitable remedy, which is usually less certain than a legal recovery. **(D)** is not the best answer because if the reward is interpreted as a bounty Frank could collect it in addition to any other compensation.

140. /B/ An effective revocation of a public offer such as a reward must be made with the same or comparable publicity as the offer. **(A)** is incorrect because an effective revocation of a public offer such as a reward must be made with the same or comparable publicity as the offer. **(C)** is incorrect because a governmental unit is held to the same standard as a private party in revoking an offer. **(D)** is not the best answer because comparable publicity would be sufficient; here two local radio station's public service announcements seem significantly inferior compared to the extent of the original newspaper publicity.

141. /B/ Acceptances must be made with knowledge of the offer. Here the facts state neither party was aware of the other parties' offer. This is

classic example of crossing offers without an acceptance; such does not create a contract. **(A)** is incorrect because usually only the seller must sign a land contract. **(C)** is incorrect because newspaper advertisements are not offers. **(D)** is incorrect because Debbie did not know of Nancy's offer when she posted her communication.

142. /A/ If the modification by the parties only intended to complete the original contract there would be a lack of consideration which would violate the pre-existing duty rule. **(B)** is more likely grounds to show there was new consideration of a detriment to the promise to support the promise to pay the extra $500. **(C)** is more likely grounds to show there was new consideration to support the new contract promise to pay the $2,500. **(D)** is more likely grounds to show there was new consideration to support the promise to pay the extra $500.

143. /B/ A subsequent modification is an exception to the parol evidence rule. Thus a subsequent modification could be enforceable. **(A)** is incorrect because the modification does not violate the parol evidence rule. **(C)** is incorrect because the modification does not violate the parol evidence rule. (C) is also incorrect because the question did not address the oral character of the modification. **(D)** is not the best answer because this alternative does not relate to the question, which is the parol evidence rule defense.

144. /C/ This is the worst argument because Paula was under a pre-existing duty to perform as per the original agreement. **(A)** is really Paula's best defense to the argument that Harriet would raise of economic

duress. **(B)** is a good argument because if the main reason for the contract was the paint (which is "goods"), the UCC provisions would apply; the UCC will allow a modification without consideration if made in good faith. **(D)** is a good defense because promissory estoppel could eliminate the necessity of new consideration to support the promise to pay the additional $500 if the promisor was aware of the reliance by the other party.

145. **/B/** Even a non-merchant buyer (who has taken physical possession of goods before a rightful rejection) is under a duty to hold the goods for a reasonable time sufficient to permit the seller to remove them. **(A)** is incorrect because even a non-merchant buyer has the duty to take reasonable care of the rejected goods. [UCC 2-602] **(C)** is incorrect because while it is true that all buyers may reship properly rejected goods to the seller at the seller's expense this is not a requirement (as "must" implies). **(D)** is incorrect because a non-merchant buyer is not required to bear the cost of redelivering properly rejected goods to the seller.

146. **/A/** Acceptance of an unambiguous unilateral offer demanding immediate shipment requires actual performance of the act requested. **(B)** is incorrect because this rule would only apply to a unilateral contract that is ambiguous. **(C)** is incorrect because notification is not an absolute requirement to acceptance. **(D)** is incorrect because acceptance can only result from the act requested, i.e., immediate shipment.

147. **/C/** While a UCC Article 2 goods contract modification does not require consideration, the change must be made "in good faith." The facts do not indicate any benefit to the promisor, Everystreet, since they had a vested right to their requirements. Futhermore, there was no detriment to the promisee such as the seller experiencing a price increase in the cost of their inputs. **(A)** is not the best answer because UCC 2.209 would allow oral modifications to be considered as evidence of waiver of the "written modifications only" provision. **(B)** is incorrect because the parol evidence rule only precludes the introduction of prior or contemporaneous extrinsic evidence; here we have evidence originating subsequent to the original agreement. **(D)** is not the best answer because the facts say that the original contract was written and the modification was not $500 or more.

148. **/D/** UCC contracts under $500 are without the statute of frauds and thus an oral agreement would be enforceable. **(A)** is incorrect because suretyship and land agreements are MOULS contracts and require a writing signed by the party to be charged. **(B)** is incorrect because suretyship and land agreements are MOULS contracts and require a writing signed by the party to be charged. **(C)** is not the best answer, while the contract length itself is only for nine months, the time from the execution (January 1) to the end of May the next year is 16 months.

149. **/D/** The best defense because the contract specified that Harriet was not obligated to pay if she was not personally satisfied with the windows. **(A)** is incorrect because

the agreement was bilateral in that Harriet made an offer and Wanda either accepted at the time or subsequently when she began work on the project. **(B)** is incorrect because the statute of frauds does not apply to goods specially manufactured for a particular buyer which are not suitable for sale to others in the ordinary course of business. **(C)** is incorrect because the possibility that Wanda's damages may be mitigated is not the best defense because it would only support a partial offset.

150. /D/ Upon a buyer's breach, an aggrieved seller is entitled to the profit if the market price is the same as the contract price. This $25,000 is increased by the reasonable overhead of $4,000 and incidental damages of $6,000 and reduced by the $10,000 deposit. **(A)** is incorrect because the seller could have sold the other buyer a different car so the effect is not to pile up damages. **(B)** is incorrect because it excludes the overhead and incidental damages of $10,000 and assumes the seller is limited to $500 damages. UCC 2.718 does authorize a seller to retain the lesser of 20% of the contract or $500 of the buyer's deposit, but this is not the sole and exclusive remedy. **(C)** is incorrect because it assumes that an aggrieved seller is not entitled to the $10,000 incidental damages.

151. /B/ UCC 2.704 allows an aggrieved seller to complete the production process (as opposed to selling the work-in-process immediately upon the buyer's repudiation) if such is commercially reasonable and thus will mitigate or not pile up damages. This would apply if the marginal cost of completion ($15,000) is less than the marginal revenue (X less $10,000). It would

then be commercially reasonable to complete the production. X, or the necessary sales price, would be a minimum of $25,000. **(A)** is incorrect because it disregards the duty of the seller to mitigate damages. **(C)** is incorrect because while a reliance interest is present, this measure is usually applied only where compensatory damages are inadequate. **(D)** is similarly incorrect because nominal damages are to be awarded when P can not prove actual damages. When Good Sounds either sells the components for scrap or completes production and sells the finished product, the market price will be established; nominal damages are not then available.

152. /C/ The seller must be aware the buyer is relying upon his expertise in selecting the appropriate good for the particular purpose. **(A)** is not the best answer because the warranty of fitness for a particular purpose is implied. **(B)** is not the best answer because the buyer may prevail; the term in question was not covered in the written sales contract. **(D)** is incorrect because the implied warranty of fitness for a particular purpose applies to non-merchant sellers as well as merchants.

153. /D/ The best answer because of the implied warranty of title and against infringement. **(A)** is incorrect because a blanket disclaimer of warranty is ineffective to override this implied warranty. **(B)** is incorrect because innocence is not a defense against enforcement of this implied warranty. **(C)** is incorrect because a thief cannot transfer valid title and thus the true owner of converted property is entitled to the car even from a transferee who took it for full consideration without notice.

154. /B/ Such a warranty is automatic because it is implied in a UCC Article 2 sales contract. **(A)** is incorrect because the parol evidence rule, if applicable, would only apply to prior or contemporaneous agreements that contradicted the final written integrated agreement. **(C)** is incorrect because the warranty is implied. **(D)** is incorrect because the UCC does not allow a general disclaimer to override the implied warranty of title.

155. /C/ As long as the exclusion is clear, conspicuous, conscionable and consistent, the implied warranty of merchantability is negated by the wording "with all faults." **(A)** is incorrect because implied warranties attach irrespective of the price. **(B)** is incorrect because the fact the defects were hidden does not effect the merchantability warranty. Upon discovery that the goods were not conforming, acceptance may be revoked. [UCC 2.608] **(D)** is incorrect because the fact the defects were hidden does not effect the merchantability warranty. Upon discovery that the goods were not conforming, acceptance may be revoked. [UCC 2.608]

156. /C/ The best answer because it appears the breach of contract was caused in substantial part by Harry. Thus, the general rule of "cost to completion" is not available. The court could create a constructive condition that would preclude unreasonable interference (negative cooperation); Harry's violation of this condition would excuse performance. **(A)** is incorrect because the P's interference caused the breach. **(B)** is not the best answer because the D's involvement violated the implied duty to cooperate; this is what excused performance. **(D)** is

incorrect because the original contract was excused so the excess costs of P were self-inflicted.

157. /D/ The contract was excused and thus the P's recovery would be in quantum meruit for the value of the benefit received by the D. Since P's work was valued at $4,000 and she had been paid $2,500, the net amount of her recovery would be $1,500. Note that had P been the sole wrongdoer causing the breach of contract she would be limited to $500 which is calculated under the "cost to complete" concept as $5,000 - [2,000 + 2,500]. **(A)** is incorrect because the contract was excused due to the D's non-cooperation. **(B)** is incorrect because a recovery for emotional distress (or outrage) is only available if extreme and it was foreseeable by D that serious physical or emotional damages would result; it seems here we only have a homeowner who wants to control the construction of his garden. **(C)** is incorrect because the P is entitled to the value of D's enrichment; normal damages are not sufficient to avoid unjust enrichment.

158. /C/ A negotiable warehouse receipt entitles the holder to demand the goods from the warehouseman or bailee. Therefore, upon negotiation (delivery of the document), Fast assumed ownership and risk of loss. **(A)** is incorrect because these events do not in and of themselves shift the risk of loss. **(B)** is incorrect because these events do not in and of themselves shift the risk of loss. **(D)** is incorrect because these events do not in and of themselves shift the risk of loss.

159. /A/ The parties' intent controls at least under UCC Article 2 contract questions. **(B)** is not the best answer because the parties may not clearly specify the shipping terms, and the shipping terms themselves may not control risk of loss. **(C)** is not the best answer because title and risk of loss are not the same under the UCC. **(D)** is not the best answer because risk of loss is not determined by the parties insurance coverage.

160. /B/ FAS / shipping point or free alongside means that the risk of loss transfers to the buyer when the seller delivers conforming goods alongside the transportation carrier; since the loss occurred after this delivery, the risk of loss has shifted to the buyer. **(A)** is incorrect because the buyer would be liable if the shipment term is FAS. **(C)** is incorrect because risk of loss depends on the shipment terms. **(D)** is incorrect because excusable non-performance only applies if the unforeseeable event was external to the parties not involving a person's negligence.

161. /D/ Risk of loss shifts to the buyer upon tender of delivery if the seller is a non-merchant/casual seller. For a merchant seller, tender of performance is inadequate to shift the risk of loss. **(A)** is incorrect because risk of loss is not shared. **(B)** is incorrect because the casual seller's tender of performance is adequate to shift risk of loss to the buyer. **(C)** is incorrect because the casual seller's tender of performance is adequate to shift risk of loss to the buyer.

162. /C/ "Sale on approval" retains title and risk of loss in the seller so the buyer's creditors could not levy on the inventory. **(A)** is incorrect

because "sale or return" transfers title to the buyer and therefore the goods become subject to the claims of the buyer's creditors. **(B)** is incorrect because an agreement by the buyer may not be binding on third party creditors. **(D)** is not the best answer; filing a financing statement within 20 days may not always be effective against a previous lien creditor or an aggressive creditor moving against collateral under the after-acquired clause.

163. /A/ A discovery of material defects subsequent to acceptance may justify rejection unless the goods have substantially changed. **(B)** is incorrect because an aggrieved buyer can revoke his acceptance upon discovery of the defect. **(C)** is incorrect because an aggrieved buyer may "cover" or sue for damages including incidental and consequential damages. **(D)** is incorrect because it appears the blazers' lining was expressly agreed upon in the sales contract.

164. /D/ If the parties have not specified who will bear the risk of loss, UCC Article 2 dictates the breaching party retains risk of loss at least until the non-breaching party has insurance coverage. **(A)** is not the best answer because title terms are not the most important factor. **(B)** is not the best answer because shipping terms are not the most important factor. **(C)** is not the best answer because credit terms are not the most important factor.

165. /B/ UCC Article 2 allows a seller to request assurances upon learning of the buyer's insolvency, but such a remedy does not allow the seller to deny the buyer the goods if the buyer tenders cash. Goods in transit may be stopped. **(A)** is incorrect because the stoppage was proper. **(C)** is incorrect because Barstow would have a duty to Flanagan to hold the goods for a reasonable time and allow Flanagan to pay C.O.D. **(D)** is incorrect because insolvency affects the party's rights and duties.

166. /C/ The acceptance created a contract and the subsequent non-confirming shipment constituted a breach of which Dey can accept all, none, or a commercially reasonable protion. **(A)** is incorrect because the contract was breached not canceled. **(B)** is not the best answer because the facts do not specify whether Dey intended to create a bilateral or unilateral contract. **(D)** is incorrect because the shipment of nonconforming goods is breach.

167. /B/ The statute of limitations will totally bar recovery unless suit is commenced within the time specified within the contract. **(A)** is incorrect because the statute can be reduced to one year by agreement of the parties. **(C)** is incorrect because the UCC allows the parties to agree to reduce the limitation period to one year, but they may not extend it beyond four years. **(D)** is incorrect because the UCC allows the parties to agree to reduce the limitation period to one year, but they may not extend it beyond four years.

168. /A/ The buyer unequivocally repudiated the future performance duty; this allows the seller to immediately resort to its remedy for breach. An aggrieved seller is entitled to recover the difference between the contract price and the market price received upon resale. **(B)** is incorrect because after anticipatory repudiation the contract is deemed breached. **(C)** is incorrect because a repudiation may only be retracted prior to any material change of

position by the non-breaching party Mazur. **(D)** is incorrect in that specific performance is not usually a seller's remedy.

169. /B/ The buyer is entitled to inspect the goods before acceptance and payment. **(A)** is incorrect because unless otherwise agreed, the place of delivery is the seller's place of business. **(C)** is incorrect because the taking of a seemingly solvent party's check is commercially normal and proper. **(D)** is incorrect because, unless otherwise agreed, payment is due at the time and place of delivery of conforming goods.

170. /A/ The only true statement. All personal property, regardless of price, is covered under the UCC Sales Article 2. **(B)** is incorrect in that the UCC specifies that all parties must perform in good faith. **(C)** is incorrect because there are other non-conditional sales, regardless of the merchant or non-merchant status of the parties. **(D)** is incorrect because the sale of personal property is subject to the Statute of Frauds if the value is $500 or more, and this provision does not depend upon the merchant or non-merchant status of the parties.

171. /D/ UCC 2.719 states that a disclaimer attempting to limit personal injury damages is prima facie unconscionable and thus not enforceable. **(A)** is incorrect because the seller had privity with the Oaks and the benefit of her portion of the contract would transfer to the estate and surviving spouse. **(B)** is incorrect because there is no requirement that the tortfeasor be given notice other than service of process within the time period specified in the state statute of limitations. **(C)** is incorrect because a disclaimer of all liability would still be unconscionable as it related to the personal injury portion.

172. **/D/** F.O.B. means free on board, so risk of loss during shipment has shifted to the buyer. **(A)** is incorrect because risk of loss passes when goods are placed on the seller's loading dock. **(B)** is incorrect because the merchant or non-merchant status of the parties does not affect risk of loss transfer provisions. **(C)** is not the best answer because risk of loss transferred when delivered to carrier on the loading dock, not when actually shipped.

173. **/B/** The measure of damages available to an aggrieved buyer for a seller's non-delivery or repudiation is the difference between the contract price and the market cover price as of the time the buyer learned of the breach. [UCC 2.712 and 2.713] **(A)** is incorrect because the damages and the difference between the contract price and market price (cover) at the time of the breach. **(C)** is incorrect because while the non-breaching party is entitled to seek adequate assurance of performance this does not affect the computation of damages. [UCC 2.609] **(D)** is incorrect because if the buyer does not immediately cover upon receiving an unequivocal repudiation and the price increases before cover is made, a buyer will collect only the difference between the contract price and the cover price as of the repudiation date.

174. **/A/** The UCC imposes a general standard of good faith (and reasonableness) on all the contracting parties. **(B)** is incorrect because merchants are often held to a higher standard than non-merchants under the UCC. **(C)** is incorrect because the UCC has no dollar limitation (except the statute of frauds may apply if the price is $500 or more). **(D)** is incorrect because most of the UCC provisions are default in nature and apply only if the parties have not specified the treatment of the matter in question. In addition, some of the mandatory provisions may be disclaimed under certain circumstances.

175. **/B/** UCC 2.718 specifies the seller is entitled to retain the smaller of 20% of the contract or $500. 20% of the $2,000 contract is $400. Since the buyer has made a deposit payment of $1,000, they are entitled to restitution of $600. The merchant status of the buyer or the seller does not influence this provision restricting the amount of a buyer's deposit payment a seller can retain. **(A)** is incorrect; the amount is wrong and the category of the buyer is irrelevant. **(C)** is incorrect because it only refers to the upper limit of the deposit payment a seller may retain; the other limit is 20% of the contract that prevails if the resulting calculated amount is less than $500. **(D)** is incorrect in that the category of either party is irrelevant to the operation of this UCC rule. [UCC 2.718]

176. **/A/** The best answer because specific performance is usually available if the subject of the contract is a unique item such as the lease of a particular portion of real property. **(B)** is incorrect; this is a common law, not a UCC contract in which specific performance will not lie if the buyer can cover from another source. **(C)** is incorrect in that the order would require the landlord to begin performing the contract, not cease from breaching it. **(D)** is not

the best answer; while the lease agreement is not a personal service contract, the better legal reasoning for issuing the order is that the subject of the lease was unique.

177. **/D/** It seems under these facts that the non-breaching lessee would recover all their incidental and consequential damages including the future profit. This business had a history of successfully operated pizza restaurants and the lost profits seem established with reasonable certainty. The other requirement is that the D must have been able to reasonably foresee that the resulting damages would occur. The costs of the architectural plans and hiring the restaurant were incurred in reasonable reliance on the landlord's commitment to the lease. **(A)** is incorrect because these damages were foreseeable (<u>Hadley v. Baxendale</u>). **(B)** is incorrect because a mere potential mitigation sometime in the future is not a present failure to mitigate. **(C)** is incorrect because there are no facts to indicate the manager was overpaid and standing by for two months does not seem unreasonable.

178. **/D/** "With reserve" means the goods may be withdrawn before the completion of the auction if the bids are insufficient in amount. **(A)** is incorrect because a successful bid must at least be at the stipulated reserve price. **(B)** is incorrect because once the auction has begun, the status of "with reserve" is fixed until the reserve price is reached. **(C)** is incorrect because a bid can be withdrawn until the fall of the hammer.

179. **/B/** This is both a requirement contract (as to Cider Bottling who promised to buy all the apples it would use) and an output contract (as to Apple Farms who promised to furnish up to all the customer's needs for the next year). **(A)** is not correct because there does not appear to be an exclusive dealings agreement as to Apple Farm; it would seem that Apple Farm could sell to others as long as they fulfill the requirements of Cider Bottling. **(C)** is not the best answer because this is both a requirement contract (as to Cider Bottling who promised to buy all the apples it would use) and an output contract (as to Apple Farms who promised to furnish up to all the customer's needs for the next year). **(D)** is not the best answer because this is both a requirement contract (as to Cider Bottling who promised to buy all the apples it would use) and an output contract (as to Apple Farms who promised to furnish up to all the customer's needs for the next year).

180. **/C/** If Cider Bottling actually fails to purchase all their requirements from Apple Farm, they would breach their requirement contract. **(A)** is incorrect because an injunction against Mega would not seem appropriate since courts do not usually issue orders to prevent breach of contract. **(B)** is incorrect because the facts do not indicate a present breach or even sufficient grounds to constitute anticipatory repudiation. If Cider Bottling does actually breach their agreement, Apple Farms could sell their output to another buyer and collect damages if the (then) market price is less than the contract price. **(D)** is not the best answer because the possible market sale is more basic reasoning to support the conclusion that the injunction will be denied.

181. **/C/** Bill Heavengates' February 15 communication seems to be reasonable grounds to bring into

question the ability to perform on a timely basis. This entitles the non-repudiating party to demand a written response containing assurances of performance. Failure to respond adequately within 30 days is treated as a repudiation of the contract, which suspends the duties of the requesting party. This would include Big Blue's duty to pay the $25,000 otherwise due on March 1. **(A)** is incorrect because the law treats anticipatory repudiation as a breach. **(B)** is incorrect because Bill Heavengates' February 15 statement is not an unequivocal and unambiguous intent to breach. **(D)** is incorrect because courts will not usually enjoin a breach of contract.

182. /B/ This is the least accurate statement because Big Blue can bring suit immediately upon Bill Heavengate's repudiation of March 10. **(A)** is a more accurate statement than B because an aggrieved party may always wait before exercising their rights. **(D)** is a more accurate statement than B because Big Blue could attempt rescission and the return of the money they had paid Bill Heavengates. **(C)** is an accurate statement in that the aggrieved buyer may cover their requirements by purchasing elsewhere and recover the difference between the cover price and the contract price.

183. /D/ The aggrieved buyer's damages are the difference between the contract price ($110,00) and the cover price. The cover price after a seller's anticipatory repudiation is limited to the market price at the time the buyer learned of the repudiation ($120,000). Here the increased price of $125,000 is not recoverable because Big Blue could have covered at $120,000. Failure to immediately cover will bar damages attributable to later price increases. Only $120,000 of the increased $125,000 cost is thus recoverable since this was the cover price at the time of repudiation. An aggrieved buyer is also entitled to recover both incidental ($10,000) and consequential ($7,500) damages. **(A)** is incorrect because it miscalculates the damages, which are the difference between the contract price and the market cover price when the buyer learned of the breach. **(B)** is incorrect because it miscalculates the damages, which are the difference between the contract price and the market cover price when the buyer learned of the breach. **(C)** is incorrect because it miscalculates the damages, which are the difference between the contract price and the market cover price when the buyer learned of the breach.

184. /A/ This question tests the different treatment under the common law and UCC Article 2 when the forms of the offeror and offeree contain conflicting and different terms. Under the common law, the offeror is "the master of the bargain" and therefore Charlie's term ($5,000) would control the price of the construction contract. Under the UCC, when a term on each parties' forms vary, it is assumed that both parties object to the other's terms. The UCC contract consists of the terms expressly agreed to and the "gap filling" provisions of Article 2. [UCC 2.207]. The order of "gap filling" priority is: course of performance in the present contract, past course of dealings, and usage of trade. The past course of dealings price ($625) would thus probably be used to fill in the gap in the second garden shed contract. **(B)** is not the best answer because

the past course of dealings price ($625) would probably be used to fill in the gap in the second garden shed contract. **(C)** is incorrect because the offeror is "the master of the bargain" and therefore Charlie's term ($5,000) would control the price of the construction contract. **(D)** is incorrect because the offeror is "the master of the bargain" and therefore Charlie's term ($5,000) would control the price of the construction contract.

185. /D/ Shipment terms of "ex ship" require the seller to deliver goods to the buyer at the named port of destination and pay for unloading. Risk of loss then transfers to the buyer. [UCC 2.322] Here, delivery was never made so the seller retained the risk of loss and breached the contract. **(A)** is not the best answer because the buyer only recommended a common carrier; this is far short of a binding condition of the purchase. **(B)** is not the best answer because delivery was never made to Betty. **(C)** is not the best answer because a common carrier vessel is not usually the agent of either the seller or buyer.

186. /C/ Alice was a mere assignee of the rights that Betty may have had under the contract. **(A)** is incorrect because Alice never received the goods and under "ex ship" the liability for the risk of loss (destruction of the television) remained with the seller. Therefore Betty has done nothing for which she should compensate Alice. **(B)** is not the best answer because the buyer is only entitled to these "cover" damages if performance is not excused because of a failure of a pre-supposed condition; the accident was unexpected. **(D)** is not the best answer because the prohibition on "assignment of this

contract" relates only to prohibit the delegation of duties unless circumstances indicate otherwise. [UCC 2-210(3)].

187. /B/ This is Sam's worst defense because Betty did not have any risk of loss under the shipment terms of "ex ship." **(A)** is a better defense since a failure of a presupposed condition – commercial impracticability – may be a good defense if the non-occurrence of the condition was a reasonable basic assumption of the contract. **(C)** is a better defense since a failure of a presupposed condition – commercial impracticability – may be a good defense if the non-occurrence of the condition was a reasonable basic assumption of the contract. D may be a partial defense under comparative negligence; this seems a better defense than B, which has no merit as a viable defense because the risk of loss did not pass to the buyer.

188. /C/ Statements II and III are correct. UCC 2-719(3) provides that "limitations of consequential damages for injury to the person ... is invalid unless it is proved that the limitation is not unconscionable." **(A)** is incorrect because Statement IV is erroneous—UCC 2.318 extends third party beneficiary status and thus UCC warranty protection to family members. **(B)** is incorrect because Statement I is erroneous—the confession of judgment clause will likely be declared unconscionable by the court. **(D)** is incorrect because Statement IV is erroneous—UCC 2.318 extends third party beneficiary status and thus UCC warranty protection to family members.

189./B/ A seller is allowed to cure a tender of nonconforming goods if the conforming goods are delivered before the original contract performance date. Here the August 10 shipment was conforming and delivered before the August 15 contract date. **(A)** is not the best answer because a seller is allowed to cure a tender of nonconforming goods if the conforming goods are delivered before the original contract performance date. **(C)** is incorrect because a nonconforming tender is not a breach if the deficiency is cured. **(D)** is incorrect because a merchant has a duty to return non-conforming goods only if the seller so requests. [UCC 2.603]

190./C/ UCC 2-206 specifies a merchant buyer is under a duty after rejection of perishable goods in their possession to follow any reasonable instructions received from the seller. Here the goods were perishable and the buyer was given specific direction to refrigerate. **(A)** is incorrect because the goods were perishable and the buyer was given specific direction to refrigerate. **(B)** is incorrect because the UCC only says advanced indemnity for expenses is required if demanded by the buyer. Here there was no demand by the buyer but that does not eliminate the duty. (The buyer would have later been entitled to reimbursement of the costs from the seller or out of the sale proceeds of the goods). **(D)** is not the best answer because the buyer's failure to prevent spoilage is the reason Betty will prevail.

191./A/ This tests whether an additional term included within an acceptance becomes part of a UCC Article 2 contract. As between merchants they become a part of the contract unless the other party objects to their inclusion within a reasonable period of time. An exception applies if the additional terms materially alter the original terms. The comments to UCC 2.207(2)(b) specify that additions that negate standard warranties are material alterations. **(B)** is not the best answer because contractual limitations between two merchants (a wholesaler and retailer) are more likely to be held enforceable than if one of the parties was a consumer. **(C)** is not the best answer because only if the limitation were an allowable addition to the contract, would she have a duty to object. **(D)** is not the best answer because contractual limitations between two merchants (a wholesaler and retailer) are more likely to be held enforceable than if one of the parties was a consumer.

192./B/ In order to raise the implied warranty of fitness for a particular purpose, the seller must know the buyer is relying upon their advice in selecting the appropriate good. Here there is no indication that the seller even knew of the particular purpose. **(A)** is incorrect because the implied warranty of fitness for a particular purpose does not have to be written. **(C)** is incorrect because the implied warranty of fitness for a particular purpose does not require the seller to be a merchant. **(D)** is incorrect because in order to raise the implied warranty of fitness for a particular purpose, the seller must know the buyer is relying upon their advice in selecting the appropriate good.

193./D/ UCC 2.719(1)(b) specifies that to exclude the UCC's many other remedies (so that repair and replace is imposed as the buyer's sole remedy), it must be expressly agreed in the contract that repair and replace is to be the exclusive remedy. Here there was not such an agreement by Roberta; Roberta did not respond to the additional term. This is far short of an express agreement to the limitation. **(A)** is incorrect because UCC 2.719(1)(b) specifies that to exclude the UCC's many other remedies (so that repair and replace is imposed as the buyer's sole remedy), it must be expressly agreed in the contract that repair and replace is to be the exclusive remedy. **(B)** is not the best answer because the question is not one of "any remedy" but rather whether the repair and replace limitation is enforceable as the sole remedy. **(C)** is incorrect because as between merchants such a limitation is not usually unconscionable.

194. **/D/** The UCC Article 2 firm offer irrevocability rule requires (1) a written offer, (2) by a merchant, (3) that gives assurances that the offer will be held open. All three of those requirements appear to be met here. Revocations are ineffective; if no time is stated a reasonable period is imposed. Unless Megabuck can prove acceptance on October 15 was unreasonable, the contract would be enforceable. **(A)** is incorrect because a firm offer can not be revoked. **(B)** is incorrect because consideration is not necessary for the firm offer rule. **(C)** is incorrect because UCC 2.205 specifies that the period of irrevocability may not exceed three months. This does not mean the irrevocability period is fixed at three months; if the offeror does not specify a period, the court will determine what a reasonable period of irrevocability should be in those circumstances.

195. **/C/** The court will probably permit the parties to introduce extrinsic UCC

parol evidence to explain whether the contract was divisible into lots. The offer did not specify that the contract could not be made in separate lots. Had the price been for a total price for a single lot (100 Nedsels for $1,200,000) UCC 2.307 probably would have supported Megabuck's position. (Delivery in one lot is the general rule.) Megabuck's omission created a latent ambiguity which would need to be resolved by the circumstances of past course of dealings (prior purchases by Debra from Megabucks) and usage of trade (reasonable industry standards of dealers purchasing automobiles from manufacturers). **(A)** is not the best answer because court will probably permit the parties to introduce extrinsic parol evidence to explain whether the contract was divisible into lots. **(B)** is not the best answer because court will probably permit the parties to introduce extrinsic parol evidence to explain whether the contract was divisible into lots. **(D)** is incorrect because the subject matter and unit price were agreed; the only term in disagreement is whether performance was to be in one or multiple lots. This term can be determined and imposed on the parties by the court.

196. **/C/** The UCC statute of frauds 2.201 requires "some writing" and is not enforceable beyond the quantity stated. Requirement (and output) contracts are exceptions to the quantity requirement. UCC 2.306 specifies the quantity of the buyer's requirement is any amount demanded as may occur in good faith. **(A)** is incorrect because UCC 2.201 validates a non-signed written confirmation between merchants not objected to within 10 days. **(B)** is incorrect because the absence of

these terms will not usually cause the contract to fail if the parties and subject matter are specified (see next three questions). **(D)** is not the best answer because past performance takes those goods out of the statute's application; here the question focuses on future purchases.

197. **/B/** UCC 2.308 specifies that the place for delivery of goods is the seller's place of business (unless otherwise agreed). **(A)** is incorrect because Don's customers are not a party to the Albert to Don contract. While Don and Albert could agree to make the designated delivery place at a third party's location, the third party would not control the negotiations. **(C)** is not the best answer because UCC 2.308 specifies that the place for delivery of goods is the seller's place of business (unless otherwise agreed). **(D)** is not the best answer because UCC 2.308 specifies that the place for delivery of goods is the seller's place of business (unless otherwise agreed).

198. **/C/** UCC 2.305 specifies that if the price term is left open it is to be a reasonable price at the time for delivery. The court will determine this "reasonable" price through (in order of priority) course of performance, past course of dealings, and usage of trade. **(A)** is incorrect because UCC 2.305 specifies that if the price term is left open it is to be a reasonable price at the time for delivery. **(B)** is incorrect because UCC 2.305 specifies that if the price term is left open it is to be a reasonable price at the time for delivery. **(D)** is incorrect because UCC 2.305 specifies that if the price term is left open it is to be a reasonable price at the time for delivery.

199. **/D/** If the parties do not agree on a term in the contract, the court will impose or "fill the gaps" with a reasonable term. An exception to this "gap-filling" rule applies if the Code has a relevant standard provision. UCC 2.310 specifies that unless otherwise agreed payment is due at the time and place at which the buyer is to receive the goods without any discount or payment period. This term would override industry standards. **(A)** is not the best answer because UCC 2.310 specifies that unless otherwise agreed payment is due at the time and place at which the buyer is to receive the goods without any discount or payment period. **(B)** is not the best answer because UCC 2.310 specifies that unless otherwise agreed payment is due at the time and place at which the buyer is to receive the goods without any discount or payment period. **(C)** is not the best answer because UCC 2.310 specifies that unless otherwise agreed payment is due at the time and place at which the buyer is to receive the goods without any discount or payment period.

200. **/D/** UCC 2.609 specifies a seller with reasonable grounds to question a buyer's ability to pay according to the contract terms may submit a written demand for assurances of future performance. If the other party does not respond in 30 days, the seller has a number of rights. Here no such written demand was made and thus the seller must continue performing at the contract price terms unless the buyer agrees to change the terms. **(A)** is incorrect because UCC 2.705 does allow a seller to stop goods in transit upon discovery that the buyer is insolvent. **(B)** is incorrect because UCC 2.705 does allow a seller to stop goods in transit upon the

discovery that buyer is insolvent. **(C)** is not the best answer because no written demand was made and the seller must continue at the contract price terms unless the buyer agrees to change the terms.

201. /C/ Upon a buyer's insolvency a seller may reclaim goods from an insolvent buyer up to 10 days after delivery. **(A)** is not the best answer because upon a buyer's insolvency a seller may reclaim goods from an insolvent buyer up to 10 days after delivery. **(B)** is not the best answer because upon a buyer's insolvency a seller may reclaim goods from an insolvent buyer up to 10 days after delivery. **(D)** is incorrect because reclamation is an exclusive remedy in lieu of suing for damages.

202. /D/ The insurance company has subrogation rights against Ace because it steps into the shoes of the insured. Jennifer Jones' rights against Ace would thus be available to the insurance company. **(A)** is not the best answer because Jones could put in a claim with her carrier for the loss. **(B)** is not the best answer because Jones' insurable interest arose when the goods were designated. **(C)** is incorrect because a buyer's insurable interest arises only when the goods are designated by the seller. They must be distinguishable from the other goods.

203. /A/ The issue here is whether a promise to ship is adequate to constitute acceptance in response to an offer specifying "ship at once." UCC 2.206(1)(b) specifies that a prompt promise to ship is adequate unless the offeror has made it unambiguously clear that a promise would not be acceptable. Rebecca's wording does not seem to meet this level in that the offer does not preclude a promise constituting acceptance. In addition, the comments to the UCC section specifically give "ship at once" as an example of insufficient wording. **(B)** is not the best answer because the issue here is whether a promise to ship is adequate to constitute acceptance in response to an offer specifying "ship at once." **(C)** is not the best answer because the issue here is whether a promise to ship is adequate to constitute acceptance in response to an offer specifying "ship at once." **(D)** is not the best answer because the issue here is whether a promise to ship is adequate to constitute acceptance in response to an offer specifying "ship at once."

204. /A/ The issue here is whether the mailbox rule would validate acceptance and thus create a contract on dispatch on July 10. Under the common law, the means and mode of communication of the acceptance must be "as fast or faster" than the offer; here the offer was by e-mail and the acceptance by regular mail which is slower. The UCC only requires that the means and mode used to communicate the acceptance be reasonable under the circumstances. This is a UCC goods contract and a mailed acceptance appears reasonable in response to an e-mailed offer; therefore acceptance occurred and a contract was effective on dispatch. **(B)** is not the best answer because a mailed acceptance appears reasonable in response to an e-mailed offer, therefore a contract was effective on dispatch. **(C)** is not the best answer because a mailed acceptance appears reasonable in response to an e-mailed offer, a contract was effective on dispatch. **(D)** is not the best answer because a mailed

acceptance appears reasonable in response to an e-mailed offer, a contract was effective on dispatch.

205. /D/ The issue here is what price will be imposed on the parties where their communications specify different price terms. The offer specified $29.00 per unit and the acceptance $32.00. Under the common law, the offeror's price designation controls. UCC 2.207 specifies a goods contract with different terms between the seller and buyer includes those terms that the parties agreed upon together with any supplementary terms incorporated under any other provisions of the Code. UCC 2.305 specifies a "reasonable price" at the time of delivery" is to be imposed if "the price is left to be agreed and they fail to agree." This appears to be the situation here and the reasonable market price would probably be imposed. **(A)** is incorrect because UCC 2.305 specifies a "reasonable price" at the time of delivery" is to be imposed if "the price is left to be agreed and they fail to agree." This appears to be the situation here and the reasonable market price would probably be imposed. **(B)** is incorrect because UCC 2.305 specifies a "reasonable price" at the time of delivery" is to be imposed if "the price is left to be agreed and they fail to agree." This appears to be the situation here and the reasonable market price would probably be imposed. **(C)** is incorrect because UCC 2.305 specifies a "reasonable price" at the time of delivery" is to be imposed if "the price is left to be agreed and they fail to agree." This appears to be the situation here and the reasonable market price would probably be imposed.

206. /B/ The best answer. Delivery and payment by the end of the month appear to be conditions concurrent which must be performed about the same time. **(A)** is incorrect because a condition subsequent is a pre-defined uncertain event that discharges a contract. Here the contract does not specify non-payment terminates the whole contract and it is clearly an installment contract. **(C)** is not the best answer because non-payment of one installment may not substantially impair the value of the whole contract [UCC 2.612]. **(D)** is not the best answer. While Betsy's nonpayment may be a breach of only one installment, Mary could require Betsy to pay C.O.D. for the future installments.

207. /B/ Specific performance of unique goods is available under UCC 2.716 if (1) the buyer is unable to cover, (2) the goods have been identified to the contract, and (3) the goods have not been transferred to a bona fide purchaser. Here all three of these conditions appear met since it does not appear Betsy can purchase the same unique widgets from another source and therefore "other proper circumstances" do not apply. **(A)** is not the best answer because specific performance is available under UCC 2.716 if (1) the buyer is unable to cover, (2) the goods have been identified to the contract, and (3) the goods have not been transferred to a bona fide purchaser. Therefore Betsy's detrimental reliance alone is not sufficient reason to warrant specific performance. **(C)** is incorrect because the facts say only that the goods might be sold to a third party, not that the transfer has occurred. **(D)** is incorrect because UCC 2.716 authorizes specific performance.

208./C/ This is an installment contract in which the buyer must accept a nonconforming installment if the seller gives adequate assurances of intent to cure seasonably. [UCC 2.612] **(A)** is incorrect because while the UCC general rule is that a perfect tender is required, a portion of an installment contract is an exception unless the nonconforming installment substantially impairs the value of the whole contract. **(B)** is incorrect because the order of specific performance or seller's agreement reversed any prior refusal to perform. The seller will be allowed to cure the defect. **(D)** is incorrect because the UCC does not specify notice of breach and contract cancellation must to be written.

209./C/ The best answer because if the defects in question were hidden the homeowner may have been under a duty to make disclosure. **(A)** is not the best answer because a reasonable contractor probably has a duty to inspect the actual building site before submitting a bid upon which they know the owner will rely. **(B)** is not the best answer; a homeowner may not have a duty to make disclosure to a contractor with experience in bidding on and building custom-made homes. In addition, the facts do not state that the homeowner knew of the defects since the plans came from the architect. **(D)** is incorrect because contracts that are freely entered into are usually enforced and a unilateral mistake is not usually grounds for excusing performance.

210./C/ A party who wrongfully prevents the occurring of a condition precedent creates a maturity of the duty that otherwise was conditional. **(A)** is incorrect because a waiver is a voluntary excusing or relinquishing of a right and the homeowner did neither. **(B)** is incorrect because the contractor might be excused if architect approval and homeowner payment were concurrent conditions; that is not our situation here. **(D)** is incorrect because the architect's refusal to certify would be measured by an objective standard of whether a reasonable architect would have certified the contractor's performance.

211./D/ To give Fred the benefit of the bargain requires that the buyer Dave be ordered to specifically perform on his purchase agreement. The two primary requirements for specific performance – that the remedy at law is inadequate and the contract subject is unique – are present. **(A)** is incorrect because keeping the option fee does not make Fred whole since he now owns the property which he purchased only because Dave decided to breach the contract. **(B)** is not the best answer because the two requirements for specific performance – that the remedy at law is inadequate and the contract subject is unique – are present. **(C)** is incorrect because this measures the profit that Fred would make on "flipping" the property, but Fred would still own the property and thus not provide him with the benefit of the bargain.

212./C/ The best defense that Brandy can assert is that she lacked capacity in that she was too intoxicated to be aware of the legal consequences of her action. **(A)** is incorrect because the UCC only requires a writing for goods contracts of $500 or more and no other MOULS subject applies here. **(B)** is incorrect because the test is not whether she would have entered into the contract if sober, but rather whether she understood the legal consequences of her agreement. This outcome applies even if the alcohol may have been a partial motivation for Brandy entering into the contract. **(D)** is not the best answer because this was not a gift; it was a bargained-for exchange.

213. **/D/** Rescission seems most likely where there was a mutual mistake of fact such as which item was purchased. **(A)** is incorrect because while a UCC contract for over $500 must be written, there are PAWS exceptions. Performance – in this case taking possession – removes an oral contract from the statute of frauds rule. **(B)** is incorrect because a minor must within a reasonable time period of reaching the age of majority; 13 months does not appear to be reasonable. **(C)** is incorrect because before rescission is allowed the seller must seasonably be given reasonable notice and a right to cure a specified, particularized defect [UCC 2.602 and 2.605].

214. **/C/** The correct answer because it is a false statement. All parties to a contract have a responsibility to cooperate in good faith and not prevent or frustrate performance; this duty is not usually waivable. **(A)** is an accurate statement and therefore an incorrect answer according to the call of the question. **(B)** is an accurate statement and therefore an incorrect answer according to the call of the question. **(D)** is an accurate statement and therefore an incorrect answer according to the call of the question.

215. **/A/** While a condition precedent to acceptance is more subjective where the subject of the contract is one of the personal taste and fancy there still must be some basis for rejection. If the painting were not an accurate reproduction of Betty's appearance, Paula's recovery chances would be reduced. **(B)** is a situation that would be helpful to Paula's recovery, and therefore an incorrect answer according to the call of the question. **(C)** is a situation that would be helpful to Paula's recovery, and therefore an incorrect answer according to the call of the question. **(D)** is a situation that would be helpful to Paula's recovery, and therefore an incorrect answer according to the call of the question.

216. **/A/** UCC 2.207 addresses the situation where the parties differ on a particular term. This section assumes both parties object to the other's expression of the term. The applicable UCC "gap filling" provisions apply; UCC 2.310 specifies that unless otherwise agreed, payment is due at the time and place of delivery of conforming goods. **(B)** is incorrect; the "last shot" rule may apply under the common law if there are conflicting terms involving the "battle of the forms;" however UCC 2.207 controls conflicting terms under the UCC. **(C)** is incorrect because before a court would impose an "equitable remedy" they would look to the UCC for guidance such as UCC 2.207. **(D)** is incorrect because the "master of the bargain" rule may apply to conflicting terms under the common law; UCC 2.207 treatment applies under the UCC where the contract involves the sale of goods.

217. **/D/** The best answer because UCC 2.209 specifies that the negotiations leading to the accord (of 50% of the increased cost) may

be considered as evidence of waiver of the "written modifications only" provision. **(A)** is not the best answer; while detrimental reliance and unjust enrichment may support the equitable estoppel exception to the statute of fraud, the UCC provision is more applicable to a "goods" contract. **(B)** is incorrect because under UCC 2.209 oral negotiations may be considered as evidence of waiver of the "written modifications only" provision. **(C)** is not the best answer because Mary might have been able to argue excusable non-performance due to a failure of a pre-supposed condition [UCC 2.615]. Robert entered into an accord with Mary that discharged the prior agreement.

218. **/D/** UCC 2.603 specifies that a buyer who undertakes a sale of the seller's non-conforming rejected goods to recover costs and advances is entitled to receive any cash proceeds for the goods paid by a buyer, reimbursement for reasonable sale expenses, and a selling commission not to exceed 10% of the gross proceeds. The net amount to be remitted to the seller would be calculated as follows:

Proceeds		$750
Less Payment	$500	
Less Expenses	100	
Less Commission	75	675
Net Remittance to Seller		$75

(A) is incorrect because another alternative has the proper amount. **(B)** is incorrect because another alternative has the proper amount. **(C)** is incorrect because another alternative has the proper amount.

219. **/B/** Contracts made in consideration of a promise to marry must be written under the statute of frauds in most states. An exception applies to mutual promises to marry without any reference to a property transfer. **(A)** is incorrect because the consideration for the promise to give a million dollars was a promise to marry. **(C)** is incorrect because the consideration for the promise to enter into a prenuptial agreement was a promise to marry. **(D)** is incorrect because the consideration for the promise to enter into the joint tenancy property agreement was a promise to marry.

220. **/B/** Fraud in the execution (or fraud in the factual under UCC Article 3 commercial paper) goes to the instrument itself and creates a void transaction because the P was tricked into unknowingly executing a contract. **(A)** is incorrect because fraud in the inducement requires all the FIRD elements, which are not present. **(C)** is not the best answer since there was an actual voluntary signature by a person with full legal capacity. Further this alternative suggests the legal consequence rather than the theory of defense which is the call of the question. **(D)** is not the best answer because there was not a concealment of fact in the execution.

221. **/C/** The recovery amount normally includes the excess of the market cover price as of the date of receiving notice of repudiation over the contract price. However, if the market price decreases before the buyer covers the lower price applies; the buyer does not receive a windfall. In addition to the $5,000 difference, there is $10,000 of incidental and $40,000 of

consequential damages for a total of $55,000. **(A)** is incorrect because it involves the wrong combination of numbers. **(B)** is incorrect because it involves the wrong combination of numbers. **(D)** is incorrect because it involves the wrong combination of numbers.

222./D/ While the mailbox rule generally applies to validate an acceptance on dispatch, this does not apply to an option contract; acceptance is effective only on receipt which was after both the option had expired and the offeror had made the sale to Betty. **(A)** is incorrect because even if Betty had knowledge of the prior option agreement, she would still take free and clear since the acceptance was too late. **(B)** is incorrect; the mailbox rule, which deems acceptance and thus a contract on dispatch, does not apply to the acceptance of an option contract. **(C)** is incorrect because Evone purchased an option, not a right of first refusal, and the option had expired.

223./D/ Since the provision has an equivalent pair of part performance – the child support and custody provisions – and the jointly owned property provision is not affected, the court will likely sever the illegal portion of the contract and enforce the remainder. **(A)** is incorrect because the court could interpret the contract as divisible. **(B)** is not the best answer because it does not contain legal rationale to support the conclusion and there are insufficient facts given in the question to speculate on the level of child support to be imposed. **(C)** is not the best answer because it does not contain legal rationale to support the conclusion and there are insufficient facts given in the question to speculate on the level of child support to be imposed.

224./C/ The lease contract became illegal because of an expansion of the law occurring subsequent to the contract formation; thus supervening illegality discharges the lease contract under the doctrine of excusable nonperformance. **(A)** is incorrect because the duties on the contract are discharged due to the supervening illegality. **(B)** is not the best answer; while knowledge of the landlord helps increase the equity in allowing the tenant to escape the contractual duty to pay rent, the supervening illegality provides a legal rationale. **(D)** is incorrect; the facts state that the lease specified that the premises were to be used only for conducting "judgment award" contests.

225./B/ While the personal service portion of the contract will likely be excused, incapacity does not usually discharge a non-personal service contract. Thus Carol could be required to perform the home purchase contract because her heart attack would not affect a non-personal service obligation. Carole could still purchase the home. **(A)** is incorrect because the personal service portion will likely be excused, but incapacity does not usually discharge a non-personal service contract. **(C)** is incorrect because the personal service portion will likely be excused, but incapacity does not usually discharge a non-personal service contract. **(D)** is incorrect because the personal service portion will likely be excused, but incapacity does not usually discharge a non-personal service contract.

226./D/ "As is" may be effective to preclude a seller's liability under the implied warranty of merchantability. However, "as is" is not effective to override an express warranty. It is not clear whether the picture constituted an express warranty, but certainly the date – 1964 – does. Therefore 1968 does not conform. **(A)** is not the best answer because it is not clear the picture rose to the level of an express warranty. **(B)** is not the best answer since the "as is" exclusion only applies to the implied merchantability warranty, not the express warranty of the automobile date. **(C)** is not the best answer because the facts do not provide enough information to evaluate the consequence of the picture mistake and what representations were made about the picture.

227./B/ The best answer because Susan's original letter would likely be characterized as an invitation seeking an offer; "I want to sell" and "above $20,000" are not sufficiently definite to constitute an offer. **(A)** is incorrect because Bobby's communication is likely deemed to be an offer and the mailbox rule only applies to acceptances. **(C)** is not the best answer because the mailbox rule does not apply. **(D)** is not the best answer because Bobby's communication is more likely to be deemed to be an offer than an acceptance.

228./A/ A modification of a UCC Article 2 goods contract that raises the price to $500 or more must be written; here the modified price was to be $550. **(B)** is incorrect because Sally is not attempting to avoid her performance duty through excusable nonperformance. **(C)** is incorrect because the fact that the good was available from another source at a lower price does not make the contract unconscionable; Betty was not procedurally forced to sign the agreement. **(D)** is incorrect because consideration is not necessary to support a contract modification under the UCC Article 2 if made in good faith; the seller's cost increase would qualify. [UCC 2.209]

229./C/ Liquidated damages are not the sole and exclusive remedy unless the contract explicitly so states. Here, the liquidated damages only redresses late performance, not the cost for repairs required by the contractor's poor performance. The P could recover both of the two measures of monetary damages and specific performance. **(A)** is incorrect because late performance, not the cost for repairs required by the contractor's poor performance. The P could recover both of the two measures of monetary damages and specific performance. **(B)** is incorrect because liquidated damages for late performance is designed to cover related costs resulting from the late performance such as hotel rent. **(D)** is incorrect because the non-breaching party is not put to an election between liquidated and other damages unless the contract so states.

230./C/ Absent a novation or release, the original obligor remains liable after a delegation. **(A)** is incorrect because an acknowledgement is not the same as a novation or release, which is necessary if the obligor is to be relieved of liability. **(B)** is incorrect because the obligee may demand assurances of performance from the delegatee and if a response is not received within 30 days, the non-response is treated as an anticipatory repudiation. [UCC 2.609] **(D)** is incorrect because the UCC has an exception to the quantity requirement for output and requirements contracts. [UCC 2.306]

231./A/ Both the daughter and Friendly Finance are third-party beneficiaries of the Betty to Generous George promise to pay the $10,000. However, the daughter is a donee beneficiary whose rights did not vest, and Friendly Finance is an incidental beneficiary to whom no promise to pay was made by anyone but the daughter. **(B)** is incorrect because the daughter's rights as a donee beneficiary against the promisor only vest when she assents or does something to indicate affirmative reliance upon the contract rights in question. Here, the daughter did not even know rights had been bestowed so the rights did not vest. **(C)** is incorrect because Friendly Finance is only an incidental beneficiary since Betty's performance was to run to the intended beneficiary's daughter not one of her creditors such as Friendly Finance. **(D)** is incorrect because the daughter's rights as a donee beneficiary never vested, and Friendly was only an incidental beneficiary to whom no promise to pay was made by Betty or George.

232./C/ The assignment only involved a change in the identity of the person making the monthly payment; as such the Restatement and most courts would not enforce a prohibition on assignment. If Paula could show damages from the assignment (this would seem unlikely), she could sue the promisor, Mary. **(A)** is incorrect because the payment of money is not a personal service. **(B)** is incorrect because a contract that prohibits assignment does not require a contracting party to agree to accept the assignment. **(D)** is not the best answer because the assignment is valid even though Mary may be liable for damages.

233./A/ The contract specified that the 7% commission would be paid only if the broker could produce a buyer who was ready, willing, and able to close the transaction. This condition precedent was not satisfied so the responsibility to pay the commission did not ripen into a contractual obligation. It is not necessary that the seller bring an action for specific performance. **(B)** is incorrect since the two conditions precedent were not satisfied so the responsibility to pay the commission did not ripen into a contractual obligation. **(C)** is incorrect since the two conditions precedent were not satisfied so the responsibility to pay the commission did not ripen into a contractual obligation. **(D)** is incorrect since the two conditions precedent were not satisfied so the responsibility to pay the commission did not ripen into a contractual obligation.

234./B/ The best answer. There is no mention of the minimum offering dollar amount in the final integrated agreement so evidence of a condition precedent (minimum sale proceeds of $50 million) that did not occur is admissible; the PER only excludes inconsistent extrinsic terms. **(A)** is incorrect; while the UCC would allow _course of performance_, _past course of dealings_, and _usage_ of trade to be introduced as an exception to the PER, this is not a UCC contract. **(C)** is not the best answer because the PER intends to finalize what the contracting parties understood about a written agreement that integrated all the prior negotiations. **(D)** is incorrect; while the UCC would allow <u>c</u>ourse of performance, <u>p</u>ast course of dealings, and <u>u</u>sage of trade to be introduced as an exception to the PER, this is not a UCC contract.

235. **/D/** The best answer because ambiguity interpretation may be a reason for the court to allow introduction of evidence of the meaning related to the interpretation of the ambiguous term (as a DUCAS exception to the parol evidence rule). **(A)** is not the best answer because the issue of whether the bill should have been $400,000, $500,000, or $900,000 does not involve a condition precedent. **(B)** is incorrect because it reaches the wrong conclusion and lacks a legal rationale. **(C)** is incorrect; while the UCC would allow <u>c</u>ourse of performance, <u>p</u>ast course of dealings, and <u>u</u>sage of trade to be introduced as an exception to the PER, this is not a UCC contract.

236. **/A/** The best answer because Sally Seller never agreed to the time of the essence condition. **(B)** is incorrect because Sally Seller did not agree to the condition. (Notice (B) is the same answer as alternative (A) except stated in reverse.) **(C)** is incorrect because a statute of frauds defense is only applicable if there is no writing; here, the first writing satisfies the statute of frauds since it contained the essential terms of the agreement. **(D)** is incorrect because there was no duty to respond to the letter under the common law.

237. **/C/** Since the contract for land must be in writing, the "equal dignity rule" requires that any related agency agreement must also be written. **(A)** is incorrect because even if the land contract is written, the question is whether the agency agreements necessary to establish valid authority were written. **(B)** is incorrect because Sally had successfully created agency authority in her agent Betty to sign on her behalf; it was thus not necessary that she sign herself. **(D)** is incorrect; while it is true that the seller entered into an enforceable agency agreement, the buyer did not and thus the seller's lawsuit against the buyer will not be successful.

238. **/B/** The owner, Park Place, had the risk of loss and thus the earthquake did not extinguish their legal responsibility (even though the executory portion of the contract might be discharged because of the unforeseeable destruction of the subject matter). The measure of restitution recovery is the value bestowed on the D because of the P's performance. **(A)** is incorrect because the owner, not the contractor, assumed the risk of destruction (the contractor usually assumes the risk of destruction if a new building is being constructed). **(C)** is incorrect since the contract was not completed and the equitable measure of recovery is the benefit to the owner. **(D)** is incorrect because the equitable measure is the benefit to the owner, not the detriment to the contractor.

239. **/D/** Mutual assent requires an offer, acceptance, and bargained for consideration. Consideration to support the promise not to compete appears absent. The promisor, Elmer Employee, did not receive a

concurrent benefit and the promisee, Heavy Handed Employer Inc. did not suffer a detriment – past consideration is no consideration. This is a more certain defense than being able to argue that the reasonable SAT standard (subject, area, time) test was not met. **(A)** is incorrect because the court would have to apply a reasonable standard test for the SAT (subject, geographical area, and time period of the restriction) test. **(B)** is incorrect because the court would have to apply a reasonable standard test for the SAT (subject, geographical area, and time period of the restriction) test. **(C)** is incorrect because the court would have to apply a reasonable standard test for the SAT (subject, geographical area, and time period of the restriction) test.

240./C/ A non-consumer purchaser such as National Steel Company is likely bound by a contractual limitation such as repair and replace. [UCC 2.719] In comparison, a consumer purchaser such a Nalph Rader is entitled to rescission and a refund under the Magnuson-Moss Act which is enforced by the Federal Trade Commission. **(A)** involves incorrect combinations of a purchaser's right to demand rescission under the anti-lemon provisions of the Magnuson-Moss Act. **(B)** involves incorrect combinations of a purchaser's right to demand rescission under the anti-lemon provisions of the Magnuson-Moss Act. **(D)** involves incorrect combinations of a purchaser's right to demand rescission under the anti-lemon provisions of the Magnuson-Moss Act.

241./B/ Estoppel is where the P deliberately said that they would not enforce an alleged breach of contract and this factual statement created a justifiable belief and movement by the other party. **(A)** is incorrect because this went beyond negotiations and culminating in a statement of fact that lead to a concession. **(C)** is incorrect because this is equitable, not promissory, estoppel since the P made an incorrect factual assertion and not a promise. **(D)** is incorrect because consideration in the form of a benefit is not necessary for estoppel. This is intended to create accountability for deliberate factual words or conduct that induces reliance and consequential injury.

242./C/ If the buyer, Sharp, knew the seller lacked cognitive capacity, the fairness of the transaction itself would be put at issue; this would seem to be the best reason for a court to rescind the transaction. **(A)** is incorrect because age and senility themselves do not necessarily mean the required cognitive standard is not met. **(B)** is incorrect; the burden of establishing mental incompetence is on the party claiming insanity. **(D)** is not the best answer; most courts would place more import on the fact that one party knew the other party lacked cognitive capacity than any particular argument that Ike lacked capacity.

243./B/ Minors can not void an insurance policy contract as they are considered "necessaries." **(A)** is incorrect because both the assignee and the sub-assignee may collect on the insurance policy contract settlement because minors can not void an insurance contract. **(C)** is incorrect because both the assignee and sub-assignee have the same rights as the assignor. The assignor had the right to assign the insurance proceeds since the minor may not void a contract for past necessaries. **(D)** is incorrect because Fly-by-Night Insurance does not need to waive Harry Hotroder's minority in order to allow the assignee and sub-assignee to collect.

244. **/D/** Under the UCC Article 2, an admission in open court that the contract in question was consummated is binding upon the declarant. **(A)** is not the best answer because while the whole contract is within the statute of frauds, the executed portion would be enforceable. **(B)** is not the best answer because part performance takes only the executed portion of the contract out of the statute's application. **(C)** is not the best answer because part performance takes only the executed portion of the contract out of the statute's application.

245. **/C/** The buyer is entitled to the difference between the contract price and the cost of cover as of the date the buyer learned of the breach. This would be $500 or 100 widgets times (20 - 15). **(A)** is incorrect because if the market cover price declined between the time the buyer learns of the breach and the cover date, the buyer does not get a windfall. The recovery would be $200 or 100 widgets times (17 - 15). **(B)** is incorrect because if the buyer does not immediately cover upon the seller's anticipatory repudiation and the cover price increases, the buyer is limited to the contract/cover price differential as of the repudiation date. This would be $500 or 100 times (20 - 15).

(D) is incorrect because there is no UCC requirement that the buyer must cover; only that if she elects to cover all aspects thereto must be commercially reasonable.

246. **/C/** This is the best answer because while gratuitous assignments are generally revocable at will, an exception applies if the assignee relies to her detriment and this reliance is reasonably foreseeable by the assignor. **(A)** is not the best answer because notice to the promisor would only permit the assignee to enforce the assignment against the promisor if not effectively revoked. **(B)** is incorrect; gratuitous assignments in which the assignor receives nothing of value are generally revocable. **(D)** is not the best answer; while an assignment without consideration may be revoked, the assignment may become irrevocable if the assignee relies to her detriment. This is also an application of the doctrine of promissory estoppel.

247. **/A/** Restatement 2d, §87(2) specifies "an offer which the offeror should reasonably expect to induce action…by the offeree before acceptance…is binding as an option contract." **(B)** is not the best answer since the facts do not indicate that Geneva gave consideration to induce Connie to submit the carpentry bid. **(C)** is incorrect in that acceptance by the general contractor of the subcontractor's bid would occur only after the general is awarded the contract from the house owner. **(D)** is incorrect because the UCC's firm offer rule does not apply; this is a common law contract involving services not the sale of goods. The common law does not

distinguish between a merchant and a casual party.

248./D/ The condition (requiring the architect's certificate of completion) must be satisfied or excused if Charlie is to recover. If the non-fulfillment of the condition is due to bad faith by the architect, the court will likely excuse the condition. **(A)** is incorrect in that the architect does not assume the liability of the owner. **(B)** is incorrect because most courts would prefer to excuse the condition rather than try to supervise specific performance involving artistic services. **(C)** is incorrect because a court will not order reformation, but rather merely excuse the condition involving the bad faith.

249./B/ George Gratitude's oral promise to act as a surety was unenforceable under the statute of frauds because an oral telephone conversation is not a writing. Note that while the Bank's promise was in writing, they are not the party to be charged in this question. **(A)** is incorrect because application of the main purpose rule exception requires an intention to substantially benefit the economic interests of the promisor. Had the surety been a majority corporate shareholder or major supplier of the debtor hoping to be paid, the exception might apply. **(C)** is not the best answer because the fact that Bank breached does not necessarily mean the surety would be discharged and George never legally became a surety in the first instance. **(D)** is incorrect; while the UCC might be authorized to allow a "merchant-to-merchant" oral confirmation as an exception to the statute of frauds, this is not a UCC contract.

250./D/ This is the worst argument because the claim between the law school and Peter Professor was liquidated, not unliquidated. Peter was under a certain contract that required the law school to pay him $10,000 per month. **(A)** would be a better argument because it might lead to an implied accord and satisfaction. **(B)** would be a better argument because it might lead to an implied accord and satisfaction. **(C)** would be a better argument because a tender of a partial payment in a check containing such a legend usually constitutes an acceptance of the tendered sum in full discharge of the contested debt.

251./C/ Even though both promises in a bilateral contract are separately enforceable, the court will likely construct a constructive condition of cooperation or non-hindrance so the seller must produce the deed at the same time the buyer's duty to pay matures. **(A)** is incorrect because the alternative reverses the parties' roles. **(B)** is incorrect because while the statement is generally true, the court may create a constructive condition in order to avoid an unjust result. **(D)** is incorrect because if there was a discharge due to impossibility, both sides of the contract would be discharged.

252./B/ The most general and high level statement of the controlling legal rule. This was a bilateral aleatory contract involving two promises so each party can normally sue the other for breach even though they themselves are in default. Thus the insurance company being under an independent duty to pay a claim is the best theory of recovery. The coverage had not been affirmatively cancelled by

Paynoclaims Insurance. (A) is not the best answer because it goes beyond the facts and cancellation is an exception to the general rule which goes beyond mere non-payment of premiums. (C) is incorrect because it is not the best theory of recovery or responsive to the central issue of independent promises in a bilateral aleatory contract. (D) is not the best theory of recovery because this would suggest that the duty to pay was dependent.

253. /D/ This is the only correct combination of the five statements of fact given in the question. A true-false analysis of all statements is required. I is true because five years seems an unreasonable period to prohibit a person from working in their chosen profession. II is false because the required consideration was the benefit to the promisor Elmer who received the job. III is likely to be false because one year does not seem like an unreasonable time period of restraint. IV is likely false because a contract that promotes or encourages tortious interference with a third party is generally unenforceable. V is probably true because working for a direct competitor within one year may not be unreasonable if Elmer's position made him privy to strategic company information. (A) is incorrect because another answer has the correct combination of alternatives. (B) is incorrect because another answer has the correct combination of alternatives. (C) is incorrect because another answer has the correct combination of alternatives.

254. /D/ The question is the extent of the required duty of a terminated employee to mitigate damages by accepting alternative employment. The duty requires only reasonable mitigation. Accepting a counter sales job at 40% of pay is not comparable and thus is not required. Changing professions from a store manager to a traveling auditor is not comparable and thus is not required. Similarly, moving across the country is not comparable and thus is not usually required. Therefore there was no comparable position reasonably available so the full compensation should be entered by the court. (A) is incorrect because another answer has the correct combination of alternatives. (B) is incorrect because another answer has the correct combination of alternatives. (C) is incorrect because another answer has the correct combination of alternatives.

255. /A/ Nancy agreed to the terms of the employment agreement to get the job and therefore Profitisall will argue she is not eligible for the doctrine of "in pari delicto." However she was a member of the "protected class" which the statute was intended to benefit. Thus she may be able to recover the minimum wage deficiency of $1,092. (If this most likely outcome did not result and the contract was held illegal, Nancy would still potentially recover in quasi-contract.) Nancy would also be awarded the $480 in unpaid wages. (B) is incorrect because another answer has the correct combination of alternatives. (C) is incorrect because another answer has the correct combination of alternatives. (D) is incorrect because another answer has the correct combination of alternatives.

256. /C/ If Paula's statement did in fact constituted a valid acceptance, a

later refusal to perform would be breach. Notice that although this was probably not a promise and it is uncertain if the words constitute sufficient acceptance intention, the call of the question states to assume the statement in the alternatives are true. **(A)** is not the best alternative because reliance only becomes important if there was a contract. This implies Paula's statement constituted a promise which is more directly addressed in alternative C. **(B)** is incorrect because the fact that Computer Lease could have dealt with another programmer is irrelevant to whether there was an enforceable contract with Paula. **(D)** is incorrect because this represented either a counteroffer or an attempt at an accord and Paula accepted neither.

257./C/ The best answer because if Loretta knew of the specific use of the lease contract, the subsequent frustration of purpose or impossibility of performance caused by illegality would have discharged the contract. Without knowledge of the use, the illegality was not reasonably in contemplation by the landlord at the contract date. **(A)** is an incorrect outcome because Sally will remain responsible for the lease balance unless disclosure of the lease use was made. **(B)** is not the best answer because while Loretta will prevail, the reasoning does not turn on the timing of the disabling legislation. **(D)** is incorrect in that the lease itself is not discharged; only the use the tenant chose to put the premises to has been declared illegal.

258./C/ Roberta's completed order form varied significantly from the catalog stipulated discount terms

and is therefore not an acceptance but rather a counteroffer. This was accepted by Southern on December 5 when they trucked the computers to Roberta. If there are contradictory terms within the same contract, handwritten terms prevail over typed or printed terms; therefore the discount terms in Roberta's communication prevail. **(A)** is incorrect because the order form was not a "mirror-image" acceptance since it varied from the offer. **(B)** is incorrect because the order form became a counteroffer so acceptance was not expressly tendered. **(D)** is incorrect because a contract had been previously formed when Southern accepted by performance.

259./B/ Southern accepted Roberta's counteroffer by shipping the six computers. **(A)** is incorrect because the order form itself is not deemed to be the offer, but rather a mere invitation to deal and Roberta changed a material term in the bargain. (Notice that there is not a general UCC provision involving a default treatment for discounts and terms of payment. Thus a court must usually adopt one of the parties' treatment of the conflicting term.) **(C)** is not the best answer because the prior treatment of a material term would only be applied by the court if the term in question was not subject to negotiation in the current contract. Silence as acceptance requires either a more extensive prior relationship or industry custom; neither circumstance seems to apply in this fact pattern. **(D)** is incorrect because if there are contradictory terms within the same contract, handwritten terms prevail over typed or printed terms.

260./D/ Substantial part performance by the offeree in an unilateral contract is considered sufficient to prohibit the offeror's revocation. This would include offer termination by death of the promisor. Nancy's extra efforts to earn the As thus entitled Nancy to receive the $2,500 for the five As. **(A)** is incorrect because Uncle Harry's promise occurred subsequent to Nancy's performance on East's essay contest; past consideration is no consideration. **(B)** is incorrect because there is no rule of law requiring best efforts by law students (although there may be an ethical obligation). **(C)** is incorrect because performance of the unilateral contract had already begun before the offeror's death.

261./B/ A contract which by its terms cannot be performed within a year must be in writing under the statute of frauds in most jurisdictions. Here the promise to pay the LL.M. tuition would occur two years after the promise was made. **(A)** is incorrect because consideration to support a "gift" promise in the form of a detriment to the promisee was present in that Nancy made extra efforts to earn high grades in undergraduate law school. **(C)** is not the best answer as it relates to the promise to pay the LL.M. tuition because that depended upon a single action of being accepted by a quality LL.M. graduate program. **(D)** is incorrect because the promise to pay the LL.M. program tuition became irrevocable when Nancy made extra efforts to improve her academic performance in an attempt to enhance her chances of admission to a quality LL.M. graduate program.

262./C/ The best answer because Bigger Bucks reasonably relied on Roger's prospective inability to perform thus discharging their obligations to Roger under the contract. **(A)** is incorrect because it was not necessary that Roger specifically repudiated the agreement if reliance on his prospective inability to perform was reasonable. **(B)** is not the best answer since Roger never expressly repudiated to Bigger Bucks his responsibility to perform the contract. **(D)** is incorrect since Bigger Bucks justifiably relied on Roger's prospective inability to perform in hiring a replacement associate.

263./A/ The equitable remedy of rescission is for the discretion of the court. If the banker and his brother, the party in interest here, were aware of and concealed the potentially very large increase in value, there may have been fraud in the inducement or a fraudulent concealment about a basic assumption of the contract. **(B)** is incorrect because the banker's relationship with his client created a fiduciary duty requiring disclosure. In addition, the reasonable P standard applicable to negligence does not apply here. Even if it did, it would not be grounds for rescission. **(C)** is incorrect because the fraudulent concealment was inconsistent with a mere mutual mistake. **(D)** is incorrect because reformation may be ordered by a court if the contract does not reflect the true intentions of the contracting parties and the court can determine what their true intentions were; that defect does not apply here.

264./D/ The best answer because a party may not willfully prevent the performance of a condition to his performance obligation. **(A)** is incorrect because the doctrine of frustration of purpose may excuse a party's failure to perform, but does not usually result in affirmative liability. **(B)** is incorrect because the commission liability was conditioned on the transfer of title to a buyer, not merely provide a ready, willing, and able buyer. **(C)** is incorrect because the commission liability was conditioned upon the transfer of title to a buyer whom Brian produced and Paula was not produced by Brian.

265./A/ Transfer of title was specified in the brokerage contract as a condition precedent to the right to a commission. Since title did not transfer, this is an effective argument. **(B)** is not the best answer because the failure of the condition precedent (transfer of title) the commission was not due irrespective of whether the broker produced the buyer. **(C)** is incorrect because Oscar accepted the lower price of $200,000 thereby waiving the $250,000 price condition. **(D)** is incorrect because the contract between Oscar and Denise was entered into within two months of the listing agreement.

266./B/ A promise to pay given in return for the other party's promise to forbear or abandon a claim is referred to as a compromise. The new agreement is an executory accord and promise to forbear is sufficient consideration if the claim could have been asserted in good faith. Even though the facts do not indicate if Penny believed in good faith that she had a colorable claim, this is still the best alternative. **(A)** is incorrect because the facts do not indicate the tenants' judgement exceeded their damages, and even if they did it would be at the expense of the landlord, not Penny.

(C) is incorrect because the tenants' promise was given in exchange for Penny's promise not to bring suit; a promise for a promise is a bilateral contract. **(D)** is incorrect because promissory estoppel requires detrimental reliance, and the facts do not indicate that Penny made any affirmative agreement based on the tenant's promise.

267./D/ There may be a legal responsibility to pay the reasonable value of services that are rendered with the reasonable expectation of payment. Here however, Penny specifically stated that she had no expectation of being paid. In addition, any such expectation on Penny's part would not have been reasonable since she had not been admitted to practice law. **(A)** is not the best answer because it is internally inconsistent, and if the tenants' compromise promise is repudiated, Penny could also sue on the original 1/3 obligation if it is valid. **(B)** is incorrect because a quantum meruit recovery is available only when the services were rendered with the reasonable expectation of payment. **(C)** is incorrect because a "Good Samaritan" statute applies (in many jurisdictions) to shield a professional from liability for negligence in rendering emergency aid, not for enforcing compensation to be paid to a professional.

268./A/ The UCC applies to contracts for "goods" that are movable, and "goods" includes animals. The status of the parties as consumer or merchant is irrelevant. **(B)** is incorrect because the UCC applies even if both parties do not deal in goods of the kind or have superior knowledge regarding the good in question. **(C)** is incorrect because animals are specifically included in the definition of "goods." **(D)** is incorrect because the UCC includes "the unborn young of animals" under its coverage.

269./B/ The best answer because a recovery under promissory estoppel requires an express or implied promise that creates a reasonably inferred payment expectation by the promisee. **(A)** is incorrect because a promise may be enforceable without consideration under the doctrine of promissory estoppel. **(C)** is not the best answer because the facts state Rescuer "volunteered" in response to Pat's cries for help and the defense of "no inferred promise of payment" is a better answer. **(D)** is incorrect because the doctrine of promissory estoppel does not assign value based on the value of the service conferred. Value is assigned based on the value stated /implied in the promise or the detriment incurred by the promisee in reliance on the promise.

270./D/ If tendered goods fail to conform to the contract specifications in any respect, an aggrieved buyer has multiple and alternative remedies. The buyer may (1) reject the whole amount; (2) accept the whole amount; or (3) accept some and reject some. In addition to one of the preceding specific remedies, an aggrieved buyer may usually pursue the breaching party for any other remedy including damages. **(A)** is an incorrect itemization of the remedies to an aggrieved buyer upon the receipt of non-conforming goods sent as an accommodation. **(B)** is an incorrect itemization of the remedies to an aggrieved buyer upon the receipt of non-conforming goods sent as an accommodation. **(C)** is an incorrect itemization of the remedies to an aggrieved buyer upon the receipt of non-conforming goods sent as an accommodation.

271./C/ If the court interpreted Greta's statement to be one of a guarantee/surety rather than a statement by the principal debtor, the oral statement would be unenforceable under the statute of frauds. **(A)** is incorrect because if the offer accepted by Carol was a promise to pay the debts of another, it would have to be written. **(B)** is not the best answer because a loan of money is not the sale of goods (which does have to be written if over $500). **(D)** is incorrect; while the check was likely a negotiable instrument, the writing requirement applies to the surety agreement. The fact that the payment of money was by a written instrument does not suffice.

272./C/ The non-breaching party should receive compensatory damages equal to the benefit of the bargain. Since the contract was $400,000 and Connie avoided paying $50,000 for completion, the net judgment amount should be $350,000. This would be increased by $42,000 of interest ($350,000 x 12%) since this liquidated amount is capable of being computed with exactness. **(A)** is incorrect because it disregards the interest which would be assessed since it can be computed with exactness. **(B)** is incorrect because while the fair market value of the services might be awarded if the contract had failed at law, here there was a valid contract which was not completed. **(D)** is incorrect because it would be a windfall to allow a recovery for the full contract amount, since the non-breaching party has avoided paying the additional $50,000 cost to complete.

273./B/ This is the best answer because an assignment usually extinguishes the assigned rights in the assignor. **(A)** is incorrect because the Restatement and many jurisdictions will not enforce a covenant prohibiting the assignment of the right to received payment of money. **(C)** is incorrect because Big Bucks was a creditor beneficiary since the facts say they were previously owed money by the promisee. Always Building and creditor beneficiaries have enforceable rights. **(D)** is not the best answer; while the assignee's rights are subject to all defenses and counterclaims that the promisor could have asserted against the promisee, there is nothing specific in the facts to suggest such defenses and a "belief" is far from a legal defense.

274./C/ The best answer because an option – which is a promise not to revoke an offer – requires the optionee to affirmatively provide separate consideration. **(A)** is incorrect because promissory estoppel is not usually sufficient consideration to provide the "quid pro quo" for the option to keep the promise open. There is an exception if the optionee knew of the specific reliance; the facts state that Legal Clinic did not tell the landlord that they had commissioned the new plans. **(B)** is not the best answer rationale because a detriment to the offeree (option holder) not flowing to the offeror (option grantor) is not usually sufficient consideration to support an option. **(D)** is incorrect because the performance of the pre-existing duty to pay rent does not constitute separate consideration for the option.

275./C/ The best answer because to satisfy the UCC Article 2's Statute of Frauds for goods over $500 the written memorandum must contain at least enough information to indicate that a contract was formed. Here, both the identity of the parties and subject matter in question were missing in the August 1 memorandum. Note that the prior negotiations were strictly oral. **(A)** is incorrect because the threshold question is whether the memorandum meets the minimal requirements of UCC 2.201(2). **(B)** is incorrect because the UCC test for specially manufactured goods as an exception to the statute of frauds attempts to give relief to an aggrieved seller when the buyer will not honor the contract, not the other way around. It is also incorrect because the specially manufactured goods exception may apply even if the amount is $500 or more. **(D)** is incorrect because even if the memorandum is deemed an attempted modification, there was not then in existence a valid contract to be modified.

276./D/ Conflicting terms in an acceptance do not automatically become a part of the contract if they materially alter the original terms. [UCC 2.207] **(A)** is a distractor because if Hummer's admission excuses the lack of a writing the terms of the oral agreement would control. **(B)** is incorrect because the "master of the bargain – last shot" rule applies to common law contracts; this is a UCC sale of goods contract. **(C)** is not the best answer because the language of the attempted discount was not for additional terms but rather conflicting terms.

277./C/ Acceptance is deemed to occur when the buyer fails to make a rejection upon discovering the goods as tendered are non-conforming [UCC 2.606]. While rejection does not have to be made at delivery if the defects are hidden, it must be made within a reasonable time after discovery. **(A)** is incorrect in that the central issue here is not whether 15 days was an unreasonable time to discover the non-conformity but rather the buyer's failure to notify the seller of the non-conformity upon discovery [UCC 2.607]. **(B)** is incorrect; while inspection at delivery may usually be commercially reasonable, the facts here suggest that the defect was hidden; a buyer is allowed to revoke acceptance upon discovery but prompt notification to the seller is required [UCC 2.608]. **(D)** is incorrect; to avoid acceptance (and the resulting contract) the buyers must notify the seller upon discovery of the non-conformity within a reasonable period of time. Knowledge of a non-conformity without notification to the seller is deemed to be acceptance.

278./D/ The best answer because if a covenant not-to-compete is a bargained-for component of a sale of a business it will usually be enforced. **(A)** is not the best answer; while the three reasonable SAT constraints (<u>s</u>ubject matter, <u>a</u>rea and <u>t</u>ime) are strictly interpreted in employment agreements, a non-compete is usually given a presumption of reasonableness if associated with a business sale. **(B)** is likely incorrect because the prohibition on "a restaurant" would likely be interpreted to include any type of restaurant. **(C)** is likely incorrect because the word "restaurant" is not subject to ambiguity. This usually means a seller of food and beverage to retail customers, which is not susceptible of more than one meaning.

279./C/ The most effective argument which Terri could raise as a defense is that there was an effective novation. A novation involves a new party being substituted in lieu of the original obligor and would include an express assumption of the lease contract obligation by Betty. This would release Terri. **(A)** is not an effective argument in defense because even after assignment, the assignor remains liable unless there is a release or novation. **(B)** is not an effective argument. Whether there was an effective assignment is not the issue; here the issue is whether the assignor remains liable. **(D)** is not the most effective argument in defense because while accepting rent might infer that approval to assignment had occurred there is no suggestion that the parties agreed to a compromise resulting in an accord and satisfaction.

280./B/ David was a third party beneficiary of the Alice law firm contract whose rights had vested. If he could show damages he would likely prevail against the Law Firm promisor; there would also be a duty to mitigate by accepting other comparable employment **(A)** is incorrect because the required consideration for the promise was provided by Alice reducing her accounting fee. In addition, David giving up his other job would constitute promissory estoppel thereby eliminating the need for consideration. **(C)** is not the best answer because the employment agreement was for a term of exactly one year – not over a year as would require a writing under the statute of frauds. **(D)** is incorrect because the original contracting parties may not modify or rescind the contract after the beneficiary's rights have vested.

281./D/ The best answer because gifts do not require consideration. While it is true that gifts may become irrevocable in the hands of a donee beneficiary upon completion (usually requiring intent, delivery and acceptance) that is not a consideration issue. Further, this is the only argument listed that could provide rebuttal to the failure of consideration defense. **(A)** is not an effective argument because Alice's contract with the law firm did not give her the right to be hired as an associate, so there was no enforceable right to assign. **(B)** is incorrect in that there is no special requirement related to the details of consideration between spouses. **(C)** is incorrect; while it does identify the consideration the law firm received for their promise it is not relevant to a rebuttal argument that there was no consideration for the Alice to David promise.

282./B/ This is the best defense because a contract for the transfer of land ordinarily requires a writing signed by the party to be changed; here the promise of Paul and Paula to convey the house was only oral. **(A)** is not the best defense because while promissory estoppel may excuse the lack of consideration it does not excuse the statute of frauds violation, absent a land possessor's valuable improvement which does not seem present here. **(C)** is not the best defense because while promissory estoppel may excuse the lack of consideration it does not excuse the statute of frauds violation, absent a land possessor's valuable improvement which does not seem present here. **(D)** is not the best defense because

promissory estoppel is clear here and that would prevail against a lack of consideration; the aborted sale and movement from New York City to Spokane would be a sufficient beginning of performance to make the offer irrevocable if there was no other issue at play.

283./B/ UCC Article 2 specifies that a party having made demand for assurances may suspend their own performance until assurances have been received. [UCC 2.609] **(A)** is incorrect because the UCC states that a delegation of the performance duty is reasonable grounds for demanding assurances; no additional showing of potential prejudice is required. [UCC 2.210(5)] **(C)** is incorrect since there is not a general prohibition on delegation of a performance duty even if the good in question is a "necessity." **(D)** is incorrect because upon soliciting a request for performance assurances the insecure party is allowed to suspend their own performance until they receive assurances. [UCC 2.705]

284./A/ Absent a contractual prohibition, assignment of rights and delegation of duties is allowed. The original delegator remains liable unless there is a release or novation, neither of which seems present here. **(B)** is incorrect because it is irrelevant as to the breach of contract claim whether the assignment-delegation included all rights or duties if the performance by the delegation was inadequate. **(C)** is incorrect; even if the obligee agrees to the delegation there must be a specific agreement to release the original obligor. **(D)** is incorrect; an objection to the delegation is not required to retain rights against the original obligor.

285./D/ The best answer because it is the only argument of those given which a court could use to find for Penny. Traditionally however, moral obligation is not considered as sufficient to provide the consideration necessary to support the $25,000 promise. **(A)** is incorrect because the mere intention to purchase a new car is not sufficient change of position to support promissory estoppel as a substitute for consideration. **(B)** is incorrect because written or not, consideration is necessary to support the promise. **(C)** is incorrect because to create an implied contract or in quantum merit recovery requires a reasonable expectation of payment at the time of performance which does not appear to be present.

286./C/ The manifest actions of both contracting parties must be sufficiently definite so as to indicate a clear willingness to enter into a present binding contract. Whether Sandra's December 25 writing met this standard is unclear but this is the only alternative of the four presented that would support the conclusion there was not a valid offer. **(A)** is incorrect because it is not necessary that the terms of payment be specified in a UCC contract; the default payment treatment is cash at the time and place of delivery. **(B)** is incorrect because a UCC contract not specifying a manner of acceptance implies that acceptance may be made by any reasonable means. **(D)** is incorrect since "are you still interested" did not intend to create a contract, even if the December 25 writing was to be considered an offer.

287./A/ Unless the offer specifies that acceptance may only be effective upon receipt by the offer or an unacceptable manner was used to communicate the acceptance, a contract is formed upon dispatch of the acceptance. The offer here did not address any required details of the acceptance and an e-mailed acceptance in response to a written offer is usually considered to be reasonable. **(B)** is incorrect because unless the offer specifies required acceptance details, acceptance is authorized using any reasonable manner. **(C)** is incorrect because a revocation of an offer is only effective on receipt by the offeree and the facts do not state there was any such communication prior to Debra's contract with Betty. **(D)** is incorrect because a merchant's "good faith" is defined as "honesty in fact and the observance of reasonable commercial standards of fair dealing in the trade." [UCC 2.103] There are no facts given indicating that Sandra did not meet this standard.

288./B/ An implied contract may result from the conduct and performance of the parties. Performance by delivering the goods in question will be implied because Debra intended to be bound or she would not have delivered the goods. **(A)** is not the best answer because past course of dealings would only be used for interpretation purposes if the meaning of the language used in the agreement or conduct was unclear. **(C)** is incorrect because there are other interpretations of the legal consequences of the January 16th communication that could also create a contract. **(D)** is incorrect because there are other interpretations of the legal consequences of the January 15 communication that could create a contract.

289./D/ Consideration is present in this bargained for exchange in the form of a detriment to the promisee. Since consideration is present it is not necessary to invoke the doctrine of promissory estoppel as a substitute for consideration. **(A)** is not the best answer even thought detrimental reference is here present. **(B)** is not the best answer because Oscar's refusal to close the restaurant sale discharged (or at least suspended) Clark's condition of paying for the restaurant. **(C)** is incorrect because the promise to sell the restaurant to Clark was given to induce Clark to move to Pleasantville and purchase the restaurant.

290./B/ The alleged contract in question was a mere "agreement to agree" and Carol did not manifest a present intention to be bound. **(A)** is incorrect because while a court may order specific performance and impose a price on the parties, the threshold issue is whether there was a contract to be enforced and interpreted. **(C)** is incorrect because specific performance is an allowed remedy if the item is unique such as a painting. The threshold question is whether there was a contract to be enforced. **(D)** is incorrect because while a court may order specific performance and impose a price on the parties the threshold issue in whether there was a contract to be enforced and interpreted.

291./A/ The contract was not illusory because Sammy's right to cancel was dependent upon an aleatory condition outside his control – a quicker substitute computer

becoming available. **(B)** is incorrect because the right to cancel was subject to an aleatory external condition. **(C)** is incorrect because the court could determine what a "reasonable fee" amount would be to fill-in the gap. **(D)** is incorrect; since there is consideration this is not an illusory promise and the court will not need to apply the doctrine of promissory estoppel.

292./A/ If performance has become objectively impossible the contractual duties may be excused and/or discharged. Racerstar's disease could be transmitted to the other horses thereby creating tortious liability. There is no suggestion there was any fault by the owner and the offered substitute is not comparable. **(B)** is incorrect because performance will be discharged. **(C)** is incorrect performance will be discharged. **(D)** is incorrect because performance will be discharged.

293./D/ An offer seeking performance of an unilateral contract becomes irrevocable once the offeree makes a substantial beginning to performance; here the offeree has purchased equipment and completed one-third of the performance. **(A)** is not the best answer because this option would at least require a court to create a divisible contract which seems contrary to the parties' intentions. **(B)** is not the best answer since intent is tested using an objective test and the fact that the offeree detrimentally relied would make this conclusion unreasonable. **(C)** is not the best answer because the beginning of performance of an unilateral contract merely renders the offer irrevocable; it does not complete the offeree's action nor convert the agreement to bilateral.

294./C/ The offeree must complete full performance to fulfill the condition precedent to the offeree's duty to pay compensatory damages. **(A)** is not the best answer because it would require the court to divide the contract but this would imply that there was a valid offer and acceptance. **(B)** is incorrect because the offeree must complete full performance of the condition precedent to the offeree's duty to pay the $3,000. **(D)** is incorrect because, lacking a fiduciary duty, punitive damages are not to be awarded in most jurisdictions for simple breach of contract.

295./B/ The general rule is that the shipment of non-conforming goods may be treated as both an acceptance and a breach. An exception applies if the seller delivers early and reasonably notifies the buyer that the shipment is being made as an accommodation. Here there was no acceptance because the goods which were delivered early did not conform so the buyer had the right to reject and there was no contract. **(A)** is incorrect because the June 10 communication from the seller was not an acceptance since it materially altered the bargain (but could be construed as a counter-offer.) **(C)** is incorrect because a buyer may reject if the goods fail in any respect to conform to the contract. [UCC 2.601] **(D)** is not the best answer because of the fact that the seller stated the shipment was made early as an accommodation. Some courts would interpret this as a new offer that overrides the general rule that both an acceptance and a breach results from the shipment of non-conforming goods.

296./D/ This is the best defense which Roberta may assert because a notification of intent to cure a non-conformity must be seasonably made. Notice of cure two days before the final specified date might have been too late (not seasonable) especially since the order specified that the delivery was to be made "preferably earlier." **(A)** is incorrect because the shipment of non-conforming goods as an accommodation is not acceptance or breach. **(B)** is incorrect. Purchasing the goods from another seller is not anticipatory repudiation because no contract existed. **(C)** is not the best answer because while Roberta was entitled to reject a non-conforming tender of goods, the alternative suggests there was a contract.

297./A/ The option holder should be able to obtain specific performance of the property in question because all parcels of land are deemed to be unique. **(B)** is incorrect because the new city ordinance may make the instant use of the property - the sale of liquor – illegal but the facts do not indicate that the use is related to the option to purchase the property. **(C)** is a nonsense theory; the examiners work hard to make the red herrings and distractions seem quite attractive. **(D)** is incorrect because Laura should be able to secure an order of specific performance.

298./B/ UCC 2.306 provides that a quantity demanded in a requirement contract may not be demanded if it is unreasonably disproportionate to a stated estimate or prior requirement quantities; here a 20% increase over the previous year would appear to be reasonable. **(A)** is incorrect because the increased demand appears to be covered by external factors so the good faith test appears to be met; the unconscionability rational does not seem likely. **(C)** is incorrect because it is too simple and the quantity demanded was unreasonably disproportionate to the prior requirements. **(D)** is incorrect because the test has two prongs – bad faith or unreasonably disproportionate. Both tests must be met and here the facts suggest, the latter test is violated.

299./B/ Under a requirement/output contract, both parties are under a general obligation of good faith [UCC 1.203] and specifically as it relates to performance. [UCC 2.306] The comments to 2.306 specify that "a shut down to curtail losses would not… acting in good faith." **(A)** is incorrect because it would seem to violate the good faith requirement by defeating the reasonable expectation of the buyer. **(C)** is not the best answer because this would allow a contracting party to escape the agreement and it does not focus on the section's escape rule of "unreasonably disproportionate to stated estimates or prior requirements." **(D)** is not the best answer because allowing a quantity reduction simply to avoid incurring a loss does not focus on the section's escape rule of "unreasonably disproportionate to stated estimates or prior requirements." "Commercial impracticality" may excuse performance but such a condition may not be self-created.

300./C/ A confirming memorandum sent between merchants sufficient to bind the sender is also binding on the recipient unless she objects within 10 days. Since Wanda would be bound so would Rosalind and the facts do not indicate she objected. **(A)** is incorrect because while the general rule is that the statute of frauds requires a writing signed by the party to be charged an exception applies to a memorandum between merchants not objected to. **(B)** is the right conclusion for the wrong reason and the question turns on the UCC's memorandum signature exception, not consideration. [UCC 2.201(2)] **(D)** is incorrect; a merchant is defined as one who deals in goods of that type or holds herself out as an expert having special knowledge and skill in those goods. It is not necessary they put goods into inventory. [UCC 2.104]

301./D/ The best answer because Ethyl successfully withdrew her bid before the drop of the hammer and the facts do not indicate that the auctioneer ever affirmatively accepted any lower bid. **(A)** is incorrect because bids exceeding the reserve price merely means the auctioneer must sell to the highest bidder; it does not change the bidder's power to revoke prior to acceptance or eliminate the need to formally accept a particular offer. **(B)** is incorrect because the effective withdrawal of the highest bid does not revive a lower bid that was never accepted by the auctioneer. **(C)** is incorrect because a reserve price merely allows the auctioneer to avoid the contract if that price is not met; once met the auctioneer must sell to the highest unrevoked bid they accept.

302./C/ This compelling MBE fact pattern is intended to raise the issue of whether moral obligation is a contractually enforceable substitute for consideration. Traditionally, the answer is no but some 21st century courts will enforce written promises made for consideration already received to the extent benefit was received. If so, the measure of recovery is to the extent that the discharged promise received prior benefits. Since Connie received $2,000 of the $10,000 debt, only $12,000 ($20,000 - $8,000) is due. **(A)** is incorrect because the exception to the rule that "past consideration is no consideration" is that the court may enforce a moral commitment to the extent of benefits received ($8,000 net discharged amount.) **(B)** is incorrect because if the court was to invoke the doctrine of moral obligation to avoid unjust enrichment it would only be to the value of the enrichment of $20,000 less $8,000. **(D)** is incorrect because the painting would not likely reactivate the discharged debt; this would take a new promise which does not appear to be present in the facts.

303./B/ The fire may have excused the builder's responsibility to complete the 10 houses under construction but the destroyed equipment is not unique and could be replaced. Thus this does not constitute excusable non-performance for the executory portion of the contract. **(A)** is incorrect because the facts do not indicate Betty personally suffered incapacity and construction tract homes would seem not to be unique. **(C)** is not the best answer because the conditional statement "only if" does not usually effect the application of excusable non-performance and shifts the burden to the other party. **(D)** is incorrect;

while the fire may be characterized as a frustration of purpose it does not excuse performance for the executory portion of the contract since the construction equipment may easily be replaced.

304./A/ Since the houses were new structures the risk of loss stays with the contractor until substantial completion and therefore no in quasi recovery is awarded. **(B)** is incorrect in that the reliance recovery measure does not apply because the contractor retained the risk of loss since this was a new structure. **(C)** is incorrect in that an in quasi contract recovery measure does not apply because the contractor retained the risk of loss since this was a new structure. **(D)** is incorrect because the contract was not complete, the architect did not approve the performance and the contractor retained the risk of loss since this was a new structure.

305./C/ If the owner commits a fatal breach by wrongfully barring the Contractor from finishing the project the component approach recovery in the contract prices less the cost to complete or $500,000 - $75,000. This is $425,000 less the $250,000 amount paid to the date of the breach or $175,000. **(A)** is incorrect because there would be some recovery at least in quasi contract since the facts indicate the builder added value. **(B)** is incorrect since this would only be a restitution amount of costs expended less payments to date; this would not apply if the owner breached. **(D)** is incorrect since this alternative suggests that the terminated contractor would share in the $100,000 market appreciation which would go only to the Owner.

306./B/ If the contractor commits a total breach the Owner may collect the difference between the unpaid balance of the contract price and the costs of hiring another contractor to complete the project. $250,000 of the $500,000 contract amount had been paid and the Owners cost to compete were $300,000. This totals $550,000 which is $50,000 above the original contract amount. **(A)** is incorrect because it implicitly assumes that the terminated Contractor should share in the inflation in the locale; perhaps if there was an in quasi recovery but here the Contractor breached. **(C)** is incorrect because it assumes that the owner is not entitled to collect an extra sum above the original contract if the Contractor breaches; this would not produce the benefit of the bargain. **(D)** is incorrect because it represents the amount due to the contractor if the owner breached.

307./D/ Denise's anticipatory repudiation of the executory portion of her dance contract prior to performance allows the promisee to treat the repudiation breach as material recession thereby discharging their responsibility to provide the future dance lessons and to sue at once for anticipatory breach. In addition, the promisor may retract her repudiation up to the time the promisee has elected any one of the above alternatives but not after. **(A)** is incorrect because it contains an incomplete itemization of the legal affects of the facts as given in this question. **(B)** is incorrect because it contains an incomplete itemization of the legal affects of the facts as given in this question. **(C)** is incorrect because it contains an incomplete itemization of the legal affects of the facts as given in this question.

308./A/ or /B/ While infrequent, the MBE may give credit for two answers where both are correct. **(A)** is correct because Denise's inability to dance would frustrate the essential purpose of the dancing contract since her ability to dance had been destroyed through no fault of her own. **(B)** is also correct because the agreement specifically stated that "all fees are non refundable." **(C)** is incorrect; while the payment of the second and third installment might be conditions precedent if the contract was deemed desirable by Denise, they would likely be excused under these facts. **(D)** is not one of the best answers; Denise could take the dance lesson with an ankle support so technically it is not objectively impossible to perform.

309./C/ A voluntary waiver may be accomplished without consideration only if the waived condition is not a material part of the agreed exchange. Here payment was more than incidental and the contract was partially executed so the change would likely be characterized as either a modification or accord both of which require consideration. **(A)** is incorrect because the breach here in question is present, not future anticipatory repudiation. **(B)** is incorrect because a waiver only applies to a non-material condition of the contract performance; the agreement to pay is material. **(D)** is not the best answer because any new implied contract would be a modification or accord of the existing contract.

310./A/ (I) is the only true statement. Normally a change in an executory contract (where no performance has been rendered by either party) is characterized as a modification rather than an accord or waiver. (II) is untrue because while an accord requires consideration, some cases do not require consideration to support a waiver of a non-material condition. Further, the UCC does not require consideration to support the modification of a sales contract if made in good faith. (III) is partially false; while the original contract responsibility remains potentially alive until satisfaction of an accord, a waiver of a non-material condition usually may not be revoked. **(B)** is incorrect because it contains a false answer option. **(C)** is incorrect because it contains a false answer option. **(D)** is incorrect because it contains a false answer option.

311./B/ The best argument because if the promises were truly independent of each other they would be seperately enforceable even if one is in default on their own promise. **(A)** is incorrect because the facts do not state that notice of delinquency and/or policy cancellation was necessary to suspend or cancel the insurance coverage. **(C)** is not the best answer because an "express" condition is not necessary since the court may constructively condition one promise as dependant on completion of the other. **(D)** is not the best answer because if the contract was held divisible it likely would be on the basis of time period, payment and coverage, not merely upon a basis that the recovery should be reduced.

312./B/ An assignment of future rights under a contract not yet in existence at the assignment date is

not enforceable. **(A)** is incorrect; while "first in time is first in right" is an accurate statement for rights associated with an existing contract, this contract was not then in existence. **(C)** is incorrect because as between the assignor and assignee any rights on an existing contract are assignable whether or not the original promisor receives notice. **(D)** is incorrect; while the disbursement of the $100,000 loan provided consideration in the form of a detriment to the promisee that consideration does not create an interest in a contract not yet in existence.

313./D/ An assignment of future rights to be derived from a contract in existence at the assignment date is enforceable. **(A)** is nonsense since Barbara was not named in the original All American contract as a third party beneficiary. **(B)** is not the best answer because once the promisor receives notice of assignment, payment must be made to the promisee; here there was at least six months of such notice. **(C)** is incorrect because only if the future rights are to come from a contract not in existence at the assignment date is the assignment not enforceable.

314./C/ The best answer because the advertisement by Lucky Store has sufficient specificity and detail to be characterized by most courts as an unilateral offer and therefore Sharon's performance constituted acceptance. **(A)** is incorrect because this was a unilateral mistake by Lucky Store, or their agent, the newspaper. **(B)** is incorrect because the offeree Sharon's acceptance consisted of the act requested, not merely a promise in the future to perform.

(D) is incorrect because promissory estoppel is an equitable remedy a court may impose if some contractual requirement, such as consideration, is missing. Here, all the contractual requirements appear present and the item is unique so the court will likely issue an order of specific performance.

315./A/ Since the offeror did not specify the contract was divisible the beginning of performance by the offeree implied a promise to complete. **(B)** is incorrect because even if the response "when should I start" could be interpreted as a mere inquiry not meeting the "mirror image rule," the beginning of performance created an implied contract binding both parties. **(C)** is incorrect because the beginning of performance of a unilateral contract by the offeree implies a promise to compete. **(D)** is incorrect because promissory estoppel applies when consideration to form a contract is missing and equitable estoppel applies when a contracting party promises not to enforce a previously vested contractual right; here there is a contract so an equitable remedy is not necessary.

316./C/ On the MBE the student must carefully analyze the parties' wording which may waive a non-conforming aspect of performance; here the delivery date may have been extended by Wanda but the right to claim for damages was specifically reserved. **(A)** is incorrect because Wanda made a specific reservation of rights to claim for delinquent delivery. **(B)** is incorrect because consideration may not be necessary to support the waiver of a minor contractual term. **(D)** is incorrect because this commercial impracticality may be rectified by hiring substitute wine grape pickers; there is nothing unique about wine grape pickers.

317./D/ The issue here concerns the right to cancel for failure to make timely delivery of goods. The party awaiting performance may agree to a commercially reasonable extension time. If the five day period (August 23 to 28) was a reasonable period, the cancellation would be enforced. **(A)** is incorrect because "reasonableness" is imposed on all contracting parties. [UCC 2.103] **(B)** is incorrect because a reasonable extension time would be imposed on Victoria's August 16 communications; she knew Wanda needed the grapes for the grape stomping event. **(C)** is incorrect because even if there was a waiver of a particular date there was still a requirement of reasonableness.

318./B/ This contract for $12,000 was made when the promisor had capacity and the condition precedent has been fulfilled. **(A)** is incorrect; while it is true that an infant may be liable in quasi-contract for the reasonable value of necessities, an automobile is not usually considered to be a necessity. **(C)** is incorrect because the promise was not a ratification of the $26,000 contract to purchase the Ford Mustang but rather a separate promise to pay $12,000 with the condition precedent "when I get a job." **(D)** is not the best answer since the $12,000 promise may have had some consideration in that Iota arguably received the benefit of not being badgered and threats to be sued.

319./C/ A private statute of frauds requirement that all modifications are to be in writing is enforceable under UCC 2.209. **(A)** is incorrect because the statute of frauds in most jurisdictions applies to any contract that by its terms extends more than one year. **(B)** is incorrect because under the UCC contract modifications made in good faith do not require consideration [UCC 2.209.] **(D)** is not the best answer because the agreement may be considered as evidence of waiver of the provision of the "no oral modifications" term, but it is not conclusive as to the outcome. [UCC 2.209(4)]

320./D/ This complicated MBE question turns on the concept that a bargained-for exchange requires that the promise seeking to be enforced must have been given in return for another promise, act, or forbearance. Alice was already required to return Betty's truck and the statute of limitations on the underlying claim against Connie had run so there was no legal right to forbear. **(A)** is not the best answer because the facts and the guarantor's "duty to repay" is not necessarily extinguished even if the statute of limitations has run on the underlying claim. **(B)** is not the best answer because illusory promises tend to be statements of non-commitment such as, "I will pay if it suits me;" here the promise is absolute on its face. **(C)** is incorrect because even if there was an express forbearance, the statute of limitations had run.

321./C/ There was no legal benefit to the promisor or detriment to the promisee to provide the necessary consideration for Betty's promise. Therefore, the promisee's strongest argument is that a substitute for consideration exists such as promissory estoppel. **(A)** is incorrect in that there is no

evidence of a waiver by Alice and a promisee accepting payments would not be effective to waive a right of the promisor. **(B)** is incorrect; the law tests for consideration at the time the contract is formed and at that time there was no express detriment assumed by the promisee. **(D)** is incorrect because while a suretyship undertaking must usually be in writing, consideration is also required.

322./B/ Past consideration is no consideration and most courts do not recognize a moral obligation as a substitute for consideration. **(A)** is incorrect because this is not a bargained-for exchange since the rescue was already completed before the promise was made. **(C)** is incorrect because while a contract for over one year must be written, a contract for life may be oral since the employee could die within a year. **(D)** is incorrect in that past consideration is no consideration and most courts do not recognize a moral obligation as a substitute for consideration.

323./B & C/ Infrequently the MBE gives credit for two alternatives. **(B)** is a strong argument because there was no current consideration provided to support the original certificate of award since past consideration is no consideration. **(C)** is a strong argument because the original parties can rescind a contract prior to a third party beneficiary's rights "vesting" and "vesting" requires at least that the beneficiary know that the rights have been bestowed; here the facts say there was no knowledge. **(A)** is incorrect in that privity is not necessary to create potential rights in an intended third party beneficiary. **(D)** is incorrect because the effective date of a revocation is upon receipt by the other party since the mailbox rule does not apply.

324./B/ The majority of jurisdictions require that a promise to pay all or part of a debt barred by the statute of limitations must be in writing and signed by the debtor. **(A)** is incorrect because on February 1, 2011, the $5,000 debt was not yet due. **(C)** is incorrect in that most jurisdictions will not reactivate a prior debt by a new promise made after the statute of limitations has run. **(D)** is incorrect because separate consideration to support a written promise to pay all or part of an antecedent debt barred by the statute of limitations is not required in the majority of jurisdictions.

325./D/ Ethyl's best argument is that the two-class absence does not constitute a material breach so that All-American's executory duties for the rest of the year are not discharged. **(A)** is not the strongest argument since normally one professor teaches all the classes in a course so the contract is not likely divisible. **(B)** is not the strongest argument since performance was not rendered impossible for the whole of the executory portion of the contract and Ethyl could have come to the next week's classes with a bandaged face. **(C)** is not the strongest argument because estoppel only allows an equitable remedy in an amount that justice requires and provides less legal argumentative strength than minor breach.

326./A/ The best defense because the difficulty in obtaining a replacement professor for one week goes directly to the materiality of Ethyl's breach. **(B)** is not a good defense because it is not a viable justification for breach since it was only after the new professor was hired that the law school determined that she was a better teacher. **(C)** is not the best defense because it goes to mitigation, not a justification for breach and the position offered was not the same as the original contract entailed. **(D)** is not the best defense because it goes to mitigation, not a justification for breach and the salary offered was not the same as the original contract entailed.

327./B/ Offers under the common law may be revoked or withdrawn at will despite promises to the contrary unless the offeror receives consideration which is not present here. **(A)** is incorrect because to be irrevocable Harriet would have to receive consideration to create an option contract. **(C)** is not the best answer; even though the second contract could be evidence of anticipatory repudiation of the previous Betty contract, it would not affect Greta's legal rights since she had no knowledge of the prior contract. **(D)** is not the best answer since Greta has no legal rights to assign prior to beginning performance with or without Harriet's approval.

328./A/ An offer to form a unilateral contract becomes irrevocable once a substantial beginning of performance has begun. The Restatement would create an offeree's option to complete for a reasonable time which temporarily suspends the offeror's power to revoke. **(B)** is incorrect because the facts do not indicate whether Harriet terminated Greta, but if she did, Greta would have recovered the full contract price less Greta's cost to complete the painting. **(C)** is incorrect because the facts do not indicate whether Harriet terminated Greta, but if she did, Greta would have recovered the full contract price less Greta's cost to complete the painting. **(D)** is not the best answer because Harriet did have the right to revoke, but the beginning of performance suspended that right.

Index

CHAPTER 2

TORTS

RIGOS BAR REVIEW SERIES

MULTISTATE BAR EXAM REVIEW (MBE)

CHAPTER 2

TORTS

Table of Contents

CHAPTER 2

TORTS

I. MBE EXAM COVERAGE

A. Weight

34 of the 200 MBE multiple-choice questions test topics from the subject of torts. All questions have the same four-stemmed multiple-choice format. Two, three and four string questions flowing from a common fact pattern are frequent. About 15 of the tort questions focus on negligence. Intentional torts and strict liability will have about 5 questions each. The remaining questions are spread out over the other topics fairly evenly.

B. Emphasis

The MBE question emphasis is on the candidate's ability to analyze the elements of the tort. This inquiry tends to turn on the black letter law elements and requirements that P must present in a "prima facie" case to get the claim to the jury. The MBE usually follows the prevailing general-rule authority of the Restatement of Torts. Up to half the questions include an understanding of the claim's applicable defenses.

MBE Tip: The difficulty level of the MBE Torts questions has increased since 2000.

C. The Call of The Question

Question requirements usually ask the candidate to determine "will P prevail?" "what is the likely result of the claim?" "what is the best defense?" "what is the worst defense?" "will P's claim survive the D's motion for a directed verdict?" "the most likely reason for the judgment is," and "under which theory is P most likely to prevail?" If the call of the question states that P is "asserting a claim," the first question to ask yourself is "under which tort theory?"

D. Claim/Defense Approach

1. Threshold Question: Two-thirds of the MBE questions cover the three liability theories of the various intentional torts, negligence, and strict liability. If they do not identify the claim theory, ask "was this intentional?" and/or "is there a basis for strict liability?" If both answers are no, apply a negligence theory of recovery. One of the alternatives will usually contain a statement of the required elements for the applicable claim.

2. Elements Focused: The correct alternative will usually focus on a required or non-required legal element of the claim upon which the P has the burden of proof. Examples include (1) a statement of a reasonable person standard for negligence, (2) the non-requirement to prove fault in strict liability claims, or (3) actual damages required for some intentional torts.

3. Defense Important: Usually it is best to analyze the P's required elements separately from the D's defenses/privileges/justifications. The facts in the question often suggest a defense associated with a certain type of claim. Examples include the defenses of necessity to trespass, privilege in defamation, or assumption of risk in negligence. Relevant defenses are presented right after the required P's elements in the Rigos text.

MBE Tip: The best approach in torts is, on a claim-by-claim basis, to focus on the black letter law elements required for P to establish a prima facie case and thus survive a motion for dismissal, summary judgment, or a directed verdict after the P rests. Then consider the relevant defenses. The MBE question's four alternatives tend to focus on these elements.

II. GENERAL CONCEPTS / DEFINITIONS

A. Imperfect Parties

1. Heightened Susceptibility of P: Frequently on the exam, the P is especially susceptible or sensitive to damage such as the "egg shell" P, a mentally disabled person, or a blind person falling into a hole with a warning sign but no barricade. Child Ps may be more likely to suffer embarrassment and humiliation than adults. The usual rule is that the D takes the P as she finds him, including any unusual physical, mental, or emotional conditions.

2. Children D: For conduct usually engaged in by children, the standard is that of a reasonable prudent child of the same age, education, experience, and intelligence. Children are always individually liable for their own torts; their parents are not necessarily liable (see Family Relationship below for details).

a. Adult Activities: Where children are engaged in adult activities, the standard is that of a reasonable adult engaging in the activity. An example is a child driving a car.

b. Statutory Limitations: The general rule today is that children are liable for the torts that they commit. While some jurisdictions still presume a child under 7 lacks sufficient cognitive ability to be at fault and a child from 7 to 14 is rebuttably presumed incapable of negligence, such rules are not universal. Almost all jurisdictions hold that very young children (under 4) are incapable of negligence.

3. Unusual Mental Attributes: Examples include a D who is hot-tempered, mentally retarded, careless, or uses poor judgment. The required standard is the reasonable conduct that would be exhibited by a ordinary prudent person.

4. Mental Development Handicap: If the D's mental understanding level is low (or even considered imbecilic or moronic), the standard usually remains that of a reasonable person of average mental ability. The majority rule is that only extreme mental deficiency (insanity) will relieve a person of negligence or the intention requirement for some torts.

5. Physical Impairment: This applies to blind, deaf, and physically handicapped parties; it would be unfair to require them to conform to a standard that for them is physically impossible. The jury will be directed to decide how a reasonable visually impaired or deaf person should have acted in those circumstances.

B. P or D Deceased

1. Survival of Actions: In most jurisdictions, a statute specifies that tort and contract claims survive the death of the P or D whether for or against the deceased. The personal representative (PR) acts on behalf of the estate. Any recovery is distributed to the heirs. Decedent's pre-death pain, suffering, mental anguish, medical expenses, and lost earnings are now recoverable in most states. Claims for defamation, invasion of privacy, and intentional infliction of emotional distress do not usually survive the death of the decedent.

2. Wrongful Death: The PR, decedent's spouse and children, or parent of a deceased child may bring suit for post-death damages in many states. Wrongful death claims may include the monetary loss of future earnings used for the economic support of the spouse and children. Non-monetary damages such as loss of the decedent's companionship and grief of family members are recoverable in many states.

3. Defenses: The D can assert against the PR any defenses that would be good against the decedent had they survived to file the claim.

┌───┐
│ **MBE Tip:** Frequently on the MBE are facts in which the P dies as a result of the tort. The │
│ action survives in the PR, spouse and children. Remember that viable defenses and offsets │
│ against the decedent remain available to the D. │
└───┘

C. Multiple Ds

In most jurisdictions the joint and several (proportionate) liability treatment depends upon whether P was at fault.

1. P Not at Fault:

a. Joint and Several Liability: Two or more wrongful tortfeasors may act in concert under the doctrine of joint venture (drag racing) or otherwise cause "indivisible" injury to P. Indivisibility means the harm is not capable of apportionment between Ds. All Ds are jointly and severally liable for the full amount of the damages. The "innocent" P can go against any or all Ds regardless of their relative percentage of fault. Settling with one D does not discharge the others.

b. Contribution Between Ds: The trier of fact is required to allocate percentages of fault for negligence between co-Ds. If a D pays more than their proportional share based upon their particular comparative fault percentage, they are entitled to contribution claim against the other co-Ds for the excess s/he paid the P. However, a willful or intentional tortfeasor has no right of contribution from her fellow wrongdoers.

c. Neither D Negligent: If neither D was individually negligent, but their combined actions create unforeseeable harm, there is no liability. An example is A releases an inert gas that explodes with an inert gas released by B thereby injuring P.

> **MBE Tip:** Joint and several liability and contributions between wrongful Ds are frequently questioned on the MBE. Non-negligent actors may not have liability.

2. P at Fault: Most states now have a pure comparative fault system. If the P was partially at fault, she can only recover against other tortfeasors to the extent that they were individually at fault.

a. Examples of Comparative Fault: Suppose P is 50% at fault, and D1 and D2 are both 25% at fault. Suppose further that P's indivisible damages are $100,000. First, P's damages are reduced by 50% (the amount of his fault) to $50,000. Then, judgment is entered against D1 for $25,000 and D2 for $25,000 – they are "severally" (not joint and severally) liable for their share. Neither can be compelled to pay more than $25,000 so they will have no contribution claim against one another.

> **MBE Tip:** Remember that joint and several liability – all Ds liable for the whole damages – applies only if (1) P is not at fault and (2) the harm is indivisible.

b. All Ds Must Be Named: For this reason, all Ds must be named and present in an action to determine fault for a single event.

> **MBE Tip:** On the exam, first identify and analyze the prima facie elements of all substantive torts that have been committed. If there are multiple Ds, consider any issues of joint and several liability. Finally look to P for comparative fault liability.

> **STOP!** Go to page 351 and work Learning Questions 1 to 8.

D. Immunities

1. Government: Federal, most states, and local governmental units have historically enjoyed sovereign immunity for "discretionary" public decisions and acts. Examples include planning functions, not issuing a license or permit to an applicant, and police and fire department activities. Many governmental units have waived immunity in some areas (such as the Federal Tort Claims Act), but this must be stated in the facts of the question.

a. Entity Liability: Many government entities are immune. Still potential entity liability remains for much "operational" negligence, such as a city's failure to repair a sidewalk after notice. Frequently, liability is imposed for "proprietary" (private) revenue producing activities such as operating utilities, hospitals, or airports. In many states, "discretionary" public functions performed with recklessness, malice, and/or bad faith are also excluded from immunity protection.

b. Officials' Personal Liability: Governmental officials are more likely to be personally immune than their public employers are. Still, officials may be held personally liable for their own malicious torts. Even if the immunity applies to an official's normal functions, liability attaches if it was a "frolic and detour" or it violated the rights of the P.

> **MBE Tip:** If the question involves a potential governmental entity D, look for proprietary functions or recklessness in performing discretionary public functions.

2. Charities/Education: At one time, charitable, educational, religious, and benevolent organizations that serve the public good were totally immune from tort liability. Beginning with non-profit hospitals, charitable entity immunity has been totally eliminated in most states. Directors and officers of nonprofit corporations usually enjoy immunity for non-proprietary functions. Even then, however, there is no immunity if the directors or officers were grossly negligent, exhibited bad faith, or breached their fiduciary duties.

3. Family Relationships:

    a. Can Sue Each Other: Spousal or intra-family tort immunity has been abrogated in most jurisdictions. Any family member can sue the other to the same extent as if they were unrelated. For example, wife and child passengers in a car operated negligently by the husband/father can recover just as if they were unrelated passengers. Pain and suffering are recoverable in full because these are the separate property of each spouse. Abrogation of parental liability to children is the rule in only a few jurisdictions unless the act was wanton or willful.

    b. Third Party Lawsuits: The torts of either spouse expose all jointly owned, tenancy by the entirety, and/or community property assets to potential liability. If the tortfeasor was acting for the benefit of the community, joint liability may result. There is no recovery against the separate property of the non-tortious spouse unless there would be joint responsibility if the marriage did not exist.

    c. Parent–Child: Parents are not subject to per se vicarious liability to third parties for their children's torts (although children are usually individually liable).

        (1) Three Areas: Parental liability may exist under three circumstances:

        (a) Agency: If the child was an agent for the parents pursuing a family economic matter such as driving a car for a family purpose.

        (b) Facilitator: The parents provided a dangerous instrumentality to the child knowing the child lacks sufficient maturity to appreciate and control the danger. This would include leaving car keys available to a child without a driver's license.

        (c) Supervision: The parents knew of the child's dangerous proclivity (e.g., playing with matches) and failed to supervise in a situation where a foreseeable harm could occur.

        (2) Monetary Limit: Often states have statutes making parents liable for their children's intentional torts up to a certain monetary limit, which is usually rather low.

    d. Child–Parent: A child may not sue their parents for injuries received because of negligent supervision unless the parent's negligence was "willful or wanton."

MBE Tip: Every MBE has at least one question testing a child tortfeasor producing potential liability to the parents. Remember the general rule – no per se vicarious liability – and the above three exceptions.

E. Remedies

1. Damages Requirement:

a. Proof Required: For most torts, P must prove actual damages as a part of their prima facie case. Both general and special damages are recoverable in the right circumstances. This includes property damage, economic loss, pain and suffering, mental distress, and loss of consortium.

(1) General Damages: These usually are considered to flow from the tort but may not be exactly quantifiable. They must be assigned a subjective value determined by the trier of fact. Pain and suffering are the primary examples.

(2) Special Damages: These are quantifiable economic losses that are in fact caused by the injury. They must have an ascertainable concrete monetary value, such as lost wages, medical expenses and property damage.

b. Proof Not Required – BAFTD: The **BAFTD** torts of <u>b</u>attery, <u>a</u>ssault, <u>f</u>alse imprisonment, <u>t</u>respass to land, and "per se" <u>d</u>efamation are considered inherently harmful. P is not required to establish specific monetary damages as a part of the prima facie case; the jury is allowed to presume injury and nominal damages may be awarded.

2. Future Damages:
Future damages, such as lost earnings, may be recovered if it was foreseeable they would occur as a consequence of the tortious conduct.

a. Details: Future economic loss is discounted to the present value but many courts also allow for an inflation allowance. Lost wages are usually awarded without netting for income tax liability.

b. Speculative Element: Still, damages cannot be too speculative such as a business's loss of future profits where there is no history of profitable operations.

3. Collateral Source:
The "collateral source rule" excludes from evidence at trial any other payments or consideration P received from other sources on account of the same injury. An example is an insurance recovery or reduction of debt. Collateral source evidence may not be presented to the jury.

4. Interest Award:
Unlike contracts involving liquidated damages (such as a promissory note), pre-judgment interest on a tort damage award is not usually allowed. The amount of liquidated damages must be capable of being exactly computed without being evaluated by a trier of fact. Such exactness is rare in tort actions where liability and the damage amount determination are usually left to the jury's discretion. Post-judgment interest on a successful tort verdict would begin to accrue as of the judgment date.

5. Attorney Fees:
Absent a D's breach of fiduciary duty, a specific statutory authorization, or a prevailing federal civil rights claim, attorney fees are not awarded in ordinary tort cases.

6. Punitive Damages:
Punitive damages (awarded as a penalty and for prophylactic purposes) are allowed in most jurisdictions. This usually requires tortious conduct

that is reckless, willful, or done with actual malice and a foreseeable high degree of harm. Punitive damages often are awarded in addition to actual damage in product liability claims.

7. Duty to Mitigate Damages: As in contract law, a P has a duty to mitigate damages after the tort occurred. A wrongfully discharged employee must accept other comparable employment and an injured P must promptly seek medical assistance. P's failure to mitigate damages results in a reduction of P's recovery by the amount that could have been reasonably avoided. In some states, a failure to wear seat belts may bar recovery.

8. Injunctive Relief: A court may issue an injunction in a case of continuing trespass, nuisance, conversion, or invasion of privacy. The P must show monetary damages are inadequate and that it is practical for the court to enforce the injunction it issues.

MBE Tip: The MBE focuses on imperfect parties (such as the egg shell skull rule), the collateral source rule, and identifying those claims (**BAFTD** intentional torts) that do not require P to prove actual damages as a part of the prima facie case.

F. Statute of Limitations (SOL) and Repose

1. Majority Time Periods: In the majority of states, the limiting time periods are:

a. Two Years: The state SOLs for short-lived injuries such as assault, battery, false imprisonment, libel, slander, and nuisance is often two (2) years.

b. Three Years: Other torts including negligence, fraud, and personal injury usually have a three (3) year limitation period.

2. Trigger Date: This date marks when the applicable time period begins to run.

a. Time of Injury: The general tort rule is that the statutory period is only triggered or begins to run against the P's claim at the time the injury occurs.

b. Accrual Over Time: If the injuries did not result from a single event, but rather accrued over time, the trigger date is the last exposure or when the injury has become sufficiently apparent to be subject to the discovery rule. An example is a latent injury such as exposure to an environmental pollutant.

c. Discovery Rule: The statute is only triggered or begins to run against the P's claim upon discovery in most states. This pertains to otherwise unknown injuries, such as leaving surgical instruments inside a patient. Discovery can be actual knowledge of the "injury" or constructive knowledge; this applies where a reasonable person in the exercise of due diligence would have discovered the "injury." "Injury" encompasses the four elements of duty, breach, causation, and damages.

3. Tolling: The statute is tolled (suspended) if the D is outside the state or the P has or develops a personal disability. Tolling also occurs until a child reaches the age of 18 in most states. Finally, active concealment by the D will also suspend the statute until there is a knowing and appreciative discovery by the P of the injury.

4. Statutes of Repose: Many states now have pre-defined maximum periods limited to specific classes of claims such as professional malpractice, a home builder's habitability warranty, and some strict liability claims. The difficulty is that memories fade over time, things wear out, and maintaining records and insurance coverage beyond some time period becomes too great a responsibility. Some state repose statutes have been declared unconstitutional since claims may be time barred before accrual under the discovery rule.

> **MBE Tip:** If the question gives numerous dates in years, look for an SOL issue.

> **STOP!** Go to page 352 and work Learning Questions 9 to 17.

III. INTENTIONAL TORTS

A. General Requirements

Intentional torts have unique characteristics. They start with a voluntary act by D.

> **MBE Tip:** The MBE often poses factual patterns combining related intentional torts. Examples include assault with battery, false imprisonment with intentional infliction of mental distress, or trespass to chattels with conversion.

1. Intent to Harm Not Required: Some intent is required. There must be desire by D to cause the consequences of his act, or the D must believe that the consequences are substantially certain to result from it. It is important to remember that intent or motive to actually inflict harm is not required, just intent to do the act that caused the harm.

a. Put Force Into Motion: The P must show only the D's intent to put in motion the force leading to the detrimental result. Even children and mental incompetents lacking capacity may have this minimal level of required intent and may potentially be liable.

b. Example: For example, D pulls a chair out from under P as P begins to sit down. She may not have intended to physically injure P, but this qualifies as intent because she knew to a substantial certainty what the detrimental result of the action would be. Similarly, if D shoots a gun into a room full of people he does not know or care about, there is knowledge of the detrimental result to a substantial certainty sufficient to constitute battery.

2. Transferred Intent Doctrine: Many torts require "intent" by the D to injure the P. Expansion of the tortfeasor to victim–intent relationship may be:

a. Between Parties: Intent may be transferred between victims or Ps if the intended consequence is the same. For example, if D intends to hit one person but actually hits another, the requisite intent for the tort of battery is present. This may make the D liable to the actual victim.

b. Between Torts – BAFTT: Intent may also be transferred among these five **BAFTT** torts: **b**attery, **a**ssault, **f**alse imprisonment, **t**respass to land, and **t**respass to chattels. The intent transfers from the intended tort to the resulting tort that creates the injury. The doctrine of transferred intent thus tends to expand the D's range of liability.

3. Ordinary Person P Standard: An offensive contact that an ordinary person would not object to, or be harmed by, is probably insufficient under intentional tort law.

a. Super Sensitive P: An example would be if D, intending to be friendly, intentionally touches P on the shoulder. Frequently tested is where a P is hypersensitive or has a phobia about casual touching. P's high sensitivity to D's contact will not satisfy the "harmful or offensive" element of the tort of battery.

b. Exception: An exception to this "ordinary standard" rule is if D was aware that P had the phobia or hypersensitivity. D should thus know P would be damaged or offended beyond the level of an ordinary person. If D acted anyway, the "harmful or offensive" element of intent would be satisfied, and D would be liable.

4. Negligence Claim Option: Below we cover the required elements P must prove to present a prima facie case to recover for an intentional tort. If some intentional tort element is lacking or there is an applicable defense or privilege, P may still be able to sue in negligence.

B. Battery

Battery is an intentional harmful or offensive contact with the dignity of the person of the P. The contact must be offensive to a reasonable person. Touching an object closely associated with that P (clothing, briefcase, purse) will qualify as a battery.

1. Contact Requirement: Contact must be made with P or close attachments such as pulling a chair out in which P is sitting or about to sit on. Mechanical devices, such as electric fences, spring guns or automobile security shock systems used to protect property may batter P. Excessive force used in defense may qualify as a battery.

2. Medical Operation: A non-emergency medical operation performed without patient consent is a battery. Watch also for original limited consent by the P patient, but the physician performs additional procedures for which consent was not obtained.

3. Apprehension of Injury Not Necessary: D kisses P while asleep or unconscious (Sleeping Beauty was battered when the prince kissed her).

4. Transferred Intent: Intention to batter anyone qualifies the victim's claim.

5. Nominal Damages: The P does not have to show damages as a part of their prima facie case. Nominal damages may be recovered even if no actual harm can be shown.

C. Assault

Assault is an intentional unprivileged act resulting in P's reasonable mental apprehension of imminent harmful or offensive contact to herself. An unwanted sexual advance such as an attempted kiss may qualify. The definition of civil assault differs from the criminal offense. The crime includes both apprehension and contact; the tort is apprehension before or without contact (as long as the apparent ability to accomplish the contact is present). See Criminal Law chapter for details on criminal assault.

1. Immediate Threat Required: The D must threaten imminent contact such as a raised fist, pointing a gun at P, or a threatening gesture. A threat of future contact that is not "right away" is not an imminent assault. Malice is not necessary; pointing a toy pistol as a practical joke may qualify. The P must be aware of the threat; a sleeping or unconscious P cannot be assaulted.

2. Words Typically Are Not Enough: Assault requires some overt act beyond mere words (like holding what appears to be a gun). However, it is not necessary that there be an actual ability if there is an apparent ability to inflict the assault. An example is a threat with a toy gun (that looks real).

3. P's Mental State: Usually P's apprehension must satisfy a reasonableness standard. However if P is extra-sensitive and D knows it, the standard is lowered.

D. False Imprisonment

False imprisonment is the intentional unprivileged confinement or restraint of P against their free will. D must have knowledge that she is confining P (not asleep). An example is if D locks the front door of a store not knowing the customer is in the bathroom; this would not meet the intent requirement.

1. Confinement Requirement: The D must intend to set definite physical boundaries, by either force or threat of force, confining P without any reasonable means of escape. This confinement could even occur in a moving car. P must have knowledge (not asleep) of the confinement. P voluntarily remaining in an area of an incident is not enough to create imprisonment. Similarly P may not prevail if he is only prevented from leaving a confinement via one particular mode of egress when another reasonable mode of escape is available and P is aware of it.

2. False Arrest: An arrest by police or private citizens is privileged if the crime was committed in the arrester's presence. If the crime was not observed, look to the status of the arrester.

a. Private Citizen: If no crime was committed and the arrest was made without a warrant, liability for false arrest may exist for a private citizen. A mistake, even if reasonable, negates the privilege for a private party D. A privilege would exist if a felony was committed in the citizen's presence.

b. Police: "Authority of law" provides a privilege to police and others who have legal authority to arrest in the event that they arrest the wrong person. While probable cause is necessary, a police officer has a privilege even if she is reasonably mistaken about the facts of the crime and the identity of the perpetrator.

> **MBE Tip:** The fine-line distinction of the status of the arrester is tested on every exam. Only police are allowed a reasonable mistake, and only if there was probable cause.

3. Shopkeeper Privilege: Most states by statute provide merchant shopkeepers a privilege to detain a suspected shoplifter. If the following requirements are all met, even a reasonable mistake is allowed (suspect was innocent of shoplifting):

a. Basis to Suspect: There must have been a reasonable basis to suspect that a theft has occurred.

b. Temporary Time: The detention may only be for a reasonable temporary period of time sufficient to conduct an investigation.

c. Restraint or Confinement: Any physical restraint or confinement must be reasonable.

> **MBE Tip:** Look for the P to be held or threatened within a specific geographical area and/or locked inside an automobile or room. Direct threats of force may also be sufficient. Facts may be police or private citizen arrest or the forceful reasonable detention of a store customer. unintentional containment is not false imprisonment, but may be negligence.

> **STOP!** Go to page 353 and work Learning Questions 18 to 22.

E. Trespass to Land

A trespass to land occurs when the D intentionally physically invades or wrongfully remains on P's possessory interest in real property (including below ground or low altitude air space above P's land) without privilege. Nominal damages are recoverable for intentional trespass; negligent trespass requires actual damages.

> **MBE Tip:** The distinction between intentional and negligent trespass is frequently tested.

1. Examples: This can be an actual physical entry, crossing over land, flooding from adjoining land, tunneling under land, low flying airplane, placing or throwing objects on the P's land, spreading fire, or a person's animal trespassing onto the land, etc.

2. Involuntary Act: No action lies for a totally involuntary trespass. Examples include a pushing of D onto land of P or D suffers a stroke while driving an automobile and crashes into P's property. Some intent by the D to do the trespassing act creating the damage is necessary.

3. Good Faith Irrelevant: Intention to trespass is not necessary. An example is if D relies on a surveyor's plans and mistakenly bulldozes P's land thinking it was her own. Unless P caused D's mistake, D is still liable in trespass to P. Other examples of trespass are D mistakenly building a fence over the lot line of a neighbor or escaping a danger by trespassing. If D trespasses to avoid a danger to herself greater than the trespass harm, she will usually have the privilege of private necessity (see below).

> **MBE Tip:** A good faith entry is frequently tetsed on the MBE.

4. Remaining on Land: Even though the original entry was lawful, a D's refusal to leave after the right to enter or remain on the land has expired is a trespass. (Tenant wrongfully holding over after the lease expires.)

5. Necessity and Emergency Privileges: See below discussion of these privileges.

> **MBE Tip:** Torts involving land are often combined with nuisance/trespass. See below coverage at page 321.

F. Trespass to Chattels

Trespass to chattels is the relatively minor use or intermeddling with personal property owned or possessed by P. Examples are D playing P's trumpet, "joy riding" P's car around the block, taking P's pet for a day, damaging P's sunglasses, etc.

1. Actual Damages Required: Unlike trespass to property, a harmless interference is not actionable. Actual monetary damages are necessary for P to prevail for trespass to chattels. Look for either damage to the chattel itself (dents on a car, etc.) or P being deprived of its use for a significant period. For example, leaning against P's car without permission but not causing any dents lacks damages.

2. Limited Intention Required: As in trespass to land, the intention requirement is minimal as long as there is some intent to do the physical act that resulted in the trespass. An example is picking up the wrong suitcase at the airport by mistake. The intent to pick up the suitcase is sufficient to create the tort. Good faith or even an innocent mistake is not a defense if there are damages.

3. Distinguished from Conversion: Trespass to chattel is an "intermeddling" with personal property without a purpose to exercise dominion over it. If the result is trivial, the tort is trespass to chattels and recovery is limited to the amount of actual injury or damage to the item or for deprivation of use. Mistake is no defense. If the damage is quite substantial (50% of value or more), the P's preferred remedy is conversion.

4. Privilege: The privilege of recapture of chattels allows P to use reasonable force to recover wrongfully taken chattels. This privilege is limited and usually is only available while the D is in "hot pursuit" immediately after the taking.

G. Conversion

Conversion is the big brother to trespass to chattels. It is defined as the wrongful exercise of dominion and control (a claim of ownership) over another person's property. The D may also be guilty of a criminal offense. This may include property theft, embezzlement, improper transfer or retention, damage or destruction, or transfer to a third party without the permission of the true owner.

1. Damages: Conversion goes beyond trespass of chattels and the P is entitled to the full fair market value of the converted asset. The Restatement would allow an innocent converter to promptly return an undamaged chattel and thus avoid paying full value to the true owner.

2. Intent Required: Transferred intent does not apply to this tort. The D must have actually intended to convert the item in question.

3. Stolen Goods: The thief did not have title to the stolen goods and thus cannot pass title to even a bona fide purchaser. The true owner is entitled to replevin of the converted goods from the transferee. The privilege of recapture of chattels applies here.

4. Distinguish from Trespass to Chattels: The tort of conversion involves more than just temporary "intermeddling" with personal property; conversion involves an intent to exercise permanent ownership dominion or control over the property. Where the motive is more culpable (theft) or the damages are substantial, the tort is conversion and P's recovery is for full value of the asset. Mistake as to ownership is not usually a defense.

> **MBE Tip:** Conversion of chattels is a more serious tort than trespass to chattels. The full chattel value may be recovered rather than having to prove actual trespass damages.

H. Infliction of Emotional Distress/Outrage

D's (1) extreme, outrageous, and reckless conduct (2) causing P to (3) suffer severe emotional or mental distress that is (4) manifested by objective symptoms (fainting spells, ulcers, heart attack, or other illness caused by the emotional distress) for which P usually seeks medical aid. Notice that actual physical harm is not required in most jurisdictions. The standard for outrageous conduct is it must "shock the conscience and exceed all possible bounds of common decency." The transferred intent doctrine does not apply to this tort.

1. Actual Damages Required: Actual damages must be proven as a part of P's prima facie case. Note also that the severe emotional distress must be a result of the D's outrageous conduct, not some other unrelated stimulus. The tort includes verbal behavior (extreme threats or verbal harassment by D to collect debt) and conduct (sexual harassment).

2. Mere Insults Not Enough: Words alone may be sufficient but simple insults or hurt feelings are not usually actionable, except in the case of common carriers/innkeepers. Examples include an airplane pilot insulting a passenger on a plane or a hotel manager berating a guest; these intentional acts might result in an actionable claim.

3. Third Party Ps: Transferred intent does not apply to intentional infliction of emotional distress. As discussed earlier, transferred intent only applies to the **BAFTT** torts. The D must have intended to inflict mental distress on the particular P. Still, third parties may recover if (1) they are family members of the injured person, (2) they were present in the zone of danger, and (3) their presence was known to the D who acted intentionally or recklessly (wife watches as her husband is brutally assaulted and battered).

4. P's Vulnerability/Sensitivity: Ordinary sensitivity and vulnerability of a reasonable person is the usual P's standard. However, if the D knows or should have known that the P is especially vulnerable or susceptible to emotional distress (such as a mentally retarded child), the duty level is raised. Similarly, Ds in a position of special trust (babysitter, sexual harassment by an employer, or outrageous bill collection actions) may aggravate the circumstances creating a higher duty level.

> **MBE Tip:** Frequently tested is distress suffered by a non-family member P. Usually a D takes the P as they find them including liability for super-sensitivity characteristics. This heightened standard does not usually apply in emotional distress.

5. Negligent Conduct: Even if D lacked actual intention, a P suffering emotional or mental damages may be able to sue in negligence. This requires more serious damages, i.e., a miscarriage or a nervous breakdown. Emotional harm or grief alone resulting from negligence is not sufficient to recover.

> **MBE Tip:** While intentional infliction of emotional distress may be asserted on a stand-alone basis, actual damages must be proven. It may be accompanied by a greater tort (assault, battery, or false imprisonment) which does not require proof of damages.

> **STOP!** Go to page 354 and work Learning Questions 23 to 26.

I. Defenses/Privileges to Intentional Torts

> **MBE Tip:** MBE questions often suggest the D committed the tort under a mistaken belief. An honest mistaken belief is not a valid defense or privilege unless it is also objectively reasonable under the circumstances. Remember that comparative negligence is not a defense to an intentional tort.

1. Consent: If P validly expressed a knowing willingness to accept the consequence of the tort, it may be a complete defense/privilege.

a. Express or Implied: P's consent to the tort may be express or implied by conduct or custom, such as participating in a sporting event. Valid consent by P requires an informed appreciation of the risks and dangers they assume. The test is objective. Would a reasonable person in D's position have believed the P knowingly consented to an invasion of their interests? Consent by mistake is still valid unless D knew of or caused P's mistake.

b. Exceptions: If D's fraud or duress induced consent or if the level, extent, and/or scope of P's consent was exceeded by D, consent is no longer a valid defense. Consent to a medical treatment must be informed as to all material medical risks and options. See also healthcare informed consent under negligence IV.A.3 below. Consent by one lacking capacity (a child, an intoxicated P, or an unconscious P) is invalid.

c. Criminal Act: Consent by P to participation in a criminal act may still be a defense (such as voluntary prize fighting). An exception applies if the law violated was intended to protect a class of persons that includes the P. For example, a minor who "consented" to acts that constitute rape of a child has not negated her battery claim).

MBE Tip: P's mistake does not vitiate consent as long as D had a reasonable belief (objective standard) that the consent was valid and informed.

---

2. Defense of Self: Use of reasonable force is justified to protect against threatened imminent, unprivileged harm to one's own person (battery, assault, or imprisonment). Self-defense is not justified while resisting a privileged lawful arrest.

a. Necessity Required: D must reasonably apprehend and believe that force is required for self-defense. A mistake as a defense may be allowed if objectively reasonable under the circumstances. Even a shooting may be privileged if D has a reasonable (but mistaken) belief that she was about to be put in jeopardy of life or limb.

b. Only Reasonable Force Allowed: The force used in defense cannot be beyond what is reasonably necessary. Unnecessary retaliation or significant escalation of force is not allowed and feasible escape or retreat may be required. However, there is no requirement to retreat in your own dwelling and deadly force is justified to prevent one's own death or serious bodily harm.

c. Third Party Injury: If the D was justified in defending herself, she is not usually liable for intended battery to a third party who is inadvertently injured in the affray. A third party batteree could still sue D for negligence if the self-defense was executed without the proper amount of care under the circumstances.

MBE Tip: Frequent on the MBE is the scenario of a mutual altercation (two parties voluntarily fighting). Consent may be a valid defense unless the P was fighting back in self-defense. Look for the D to be the first aggressor, or for a retreat and a change of position where the P becomes the aggressor.

---

3. Defense of Others: The intervening defender steps into the shoes of the victim as to self-defense rights. Under the common law, this defense was only available between family members; today, even a stranger coming to the aid of the victim has this defense.

a. Reasonable Belief: An intervenor coming to the aid of a third person victim must have a reasonable objective belief that the victim is not the initial aggressor and is being or is about to be attacked. A mistaken belief of imminent attack is still a defense if the belief was reasonable under the circumstances.

b. Only Reasonable Force Allowed: The acceptable level of force is the same as self-defense.

4. Defense of Property: Force may be used to prevent entry onto one's land or defend against the taking of one's chattels.

a. Before Occurrence: The force used must be for the purpose of preventing the tort. Force used after the occurrence is not protected (but note below that Recapture of Chattels during the period of "hot pursuit" is acceptable). A prior request/demand/warning to the intruder to depart or desist is usually necessary.

b. Reasonable Non-Deadly Force Allowed: The force level used to protect property must be no greater than necessary under the circumstances. Deadly force is not usually allowed to defend property alone (although it is available to defend persons present from threatened imminent death or serious bodily harm). Setting deadly spring-trigger guns or bear traps without warning to protect against trespassers would violate the "only reasonable force in defense" standard.

c. Deadly Force Exception: If the attacker uses deadly force, the level ratchets up so the victim may apply the rule of self-defense that allows deadly force as a defense.

> **MBE Tip:** Look for an issue as to whether the force used in the defense was reasonable. "Reasonable force" does not usually include deadly force; however, deadly force may be considered "reasonable" if the D acts in defense against P's imminent deadly force. A robbery victim may not use deadly force to defend her chattels from conversion, but may use deadly force to defend herself personally in the robbery.

5. Recapture of Chattels: An owner is privileged to recapture chattels from the thief by reasonable force, but a mistaken belief of ownership is no defense. Moreover the privilege applies only during the limited time period of "fresh" or "hot" pursuit.

a. Wrongful Taking: The chattel must be wrongfully taken from the owner.

b. Reasonable Non-Deadly Force Allowed: A D in "fresh" or "hot" pursuit of stolen chattels may use reasonable force. Deadly force is not allowed to protect chattels alone.

c. Trespass Defense: After demand to return the chattel, the owner may enter on the land of the wrongful taker to recover the owner's stolen chattel. If the landowner was innocent, the D will be liable for any actual damage caused by the entry.

> **MBE Tip:** Run the scenario in "slow motion." At any given point a D may become a P by virtue of a defense, or a P become a D by exceeding the scope of reasonable force.

6. Necessity: Interference with or trespass onto another's property, either real or personal, may be justified or "necessary" in order to avert threatened injury from another source. This privilege is only available when the apparent threatened injury is considerably more serious than the harm the D will inflict on the P's property. An example is that a D may trespass to avoid an approaching fire or an immediate threat of battery. A D who trespasses may be protected from a reasonable mistake of fact.

a. Public Necessity: When an individual acts reasonably to protect the public from a serious danger to the public's general interests, the privilege is absolute. The D asserting the privilege is not liable for the injury caused to P. An example is firefighters demolishing D's house in a fire path. Damages are not recoverable.

b. Private Necessity: When an individual acts to protect one's self, the privilege of necessity may still be available. A property owner in fresh pursuit of stolen chattels is usually allowed a privilege to trespass. Likewise, a drowning swimmer may trespass on to waterfront land.

c. Compensation Required: If private necessity is allowed as a defense, D must still pay for actual damages P has incurred.

> **MBE Tip:** When a person acts out of necessity, there is no liability unless actual damages can be proven (nominal damages are insufficient).

7. Under Color of Law: This is the major privilege asserted against battery and false imprisonment.

a. Police Officer: A police officer can arrest without a warrant if there is probable cause that a felony or a breach of the peace has occurred, and that P committed it. Later, a hearing must take place to establish that there was indeed probable cause.

b. Private Citizen: To qualify a "citizen's arrest" as a defense, the felony and breach of the peace must have been actually committed in the citizen's presence.

> **MBE Tip:** A police officer may arrest on the mere belief that a felony was committed, even if that belief turns out to be mistaken, the privilege will still apply. However, to constitute a privilege for a private citizen the crime must have actually occurred. If the crime was not committed, a private citizen cannot claim a privilege.

c. Shopkeeper's Privilege: Most states by statute provide merchant shopkeepers a privilege to detain a suspected shoplifter for a temporary period of time. The grounds for, means of, and period of detention must all be reasonable. A mistake defense may be allowed if based upon reasonable suspicion.

> **MBE Tip:** A favorite fact pattern of MBE testers involves a shoplifter. Such a question may include potential claims of battery, assault, false imprisonment, conversion, outrage, related defenses, privileges, and criminal law.

d. Arrest and Crime Prevention: Reasonable force is allowed. Deadly force may only be used to stop a fleeing suspect if the suspect poses a threat of death or has just engaged in a serious felonious crime such as an armed robbery.

8. Discipline Privilege: Parents, teachers, and military officials have a privilege to conduct reasonable discipline upon their charges which might otherwise constitute assault, battery, false imprisonment, or infliction of emotional distress.

a. Parents: Courts are reluctant to second-guess parents' discretion in applying force and restraint on their children. The test is whether the discipline was legitimately motivated (in good faith for a proper purpose without malice) and no more force or restraint/detention was used than appeared to be reasonably necessary.

b. Other Disciplinarians: Rules and regulations restrict those in authority. They must maintain discipline in a reasonable manner.

9. Justification: This is a general category that courts have used as a "catch-all" privilege allowing D to escape liability for an intentional tort that would have been administered by a reasonable person in a similar situation.

MBE Tip: In many intentional tort questions, there may be no defenses and/or the D appears to be operating reasonably. Even if no damages occur, a P may usually recover nominal damages from a D who has committed an intentional tort.

STOP! Go to page 355 and work learning questions 27 and 28.

IV. NEGLIGENCE – ABCD

Negligence is one-third to one-half of the MBE. Intent to cause harm is not required, so claims lacking this intentional torts requirement may be asserted under a negligence theory. Often the setting is a series or chain of events with multiple actors. The four negligence elements, abbreviated by the acronym **ABCD**, are heavily tested. In order for the P to make out a prima facie case of negligence, there must exist **a** D's legal duty to that P, a **b**reach of that duty, **c**ausation, and resulting **d**amages. Issues relating to defenses such as traditional contributory fault, comparative fault, or assumption of risk are also frequently tested.

MBE Tip: Follow the **ABCD** order of analysis discussed in detail below. Look for any missing element that would defeat P's prima facie claim. Only after all elements of the claim are met do potential defenses become of import.

A. A Legal Duty

The D has a legal duty and obligation to use reasonable "due" care to protect foreseeable parties within the zone of danger from foreseeable risks that are unreasonable (Judge Benjamin Cardozo in *Palsgraf*). This duty is met by adhering to recognized standards of care. The standards of care applied will depend upon the D's category. Picture a linear relationship like this:

A D's duty to P →	Breach of Duty →	Causes Harm →	Damages to P

| Foreseeable P → | What D did → | Cause in Fact → | Special/General |
| Foreseeable Risk → | Standard of Care → | Proximate Cause → | Comparative Fault |

1. General Duty Level: In most situations, the required due care standard is objective and measured by the conduct of a reasonably prudent person under similar circumstances. Negligence is a failure to meet this standard in the face of a foreseeable risk to a foreseeable P.

a. Balancing Test: The jury will be instructed to use a balancing test to weigh several factors including any social value created by D's activity. Judge Learned Hand would set the duty level standard by balancing the D's necessary precaution cost (PC) against the harm severity (HS) times the foreseeable probability that the harm (PH) would occur. (PC = HS x PH) Below we discuss particular classes of Ds.

MBE Tip: In a negligence question, an alternative which states, "Defendant operated reasonably," "Defendant did not operate unreasonably," "Defendant's action was unreasonable," or "Defendant could reasonably foresee," are attractive answers.

---

b. Expert Testimony May Be Helpful: If the incident or activity in question is one that ordinary people understand, the jury itself may decide the required standard of care. If the activity involves scientific, technical, or other specialized knowledge, experience, and skill, the judge may allow expert testimony to assist the jury. The question to be determined is "what would a reasonable specialist have done in the same circumstances?"

c. Establishing the Standard of Performance: Experts must be qualified by experience and training to render their opinion on how a reasonable D should be expected to perform. The court makes two relevant decisions. First, whether the jury's ultimate understanding of the issues to be decided would be assisted by the expert? Second, whether the proposed expert has the necessary qualifications and experience to be objectively helpful?

2. Legal Malpractice: Most states do not recognize a local legal performance standard; a sole practitioner in a small, rural community is held to the same performance standard as a partner in a large New York City firm. P must usually establish "but for" malpractice causation against an attorney. This requires a demonstration of near certain victory in the underlying case that has been called a "case within a case."

3. Health Care Professional D: The standard is that of an ordinary reasonably prudent medical professional or healthcare institution. If a specialist is involved, the standard is raised to a reasonably prudent specialist; for example, a reasonably prudent surgeon or radiologist.

a. Express Informed Consent: For a health care professional, the lack of informed consent by the patient is negligence. This requires D to make full disclosure of the treatment's particular risks and dangers, possible benefits, and any feasible alternatives including non-treatment. P must show that the patient would not have consented if they had fully appreciated the effects and/or risks. Usually this is accompanied by proof that a reasonable patient also would not have consented had they received full disclosure.

b. Implied Consent: Agreement to treatment in a life-threatening medical emergency may be imputed upon the patient if she is not capable of consenting. There must be a showing that a reasonable person would have consented if she had been capable.

c. Exceeding Scope: If a doctor exceeds the patient's scope of consent, it is a battery unless the matter is a life-threatening emergency. A non-emergency operation performed without consent is also a battery.

4. Rescuer: There is no common law duty of an uncompensated bystander to act or go to the rescue of a stranger. If a rescuer does voluntarily begin to provide assistance, she cannot be sued for negligently increasing the risk of harm or making the P's injury worse. The rescuer cannot abandon the rescue if an alternative rescuer forbears to go to the rescue because the original rescue was under way.

a. Tortfeasor Liability: Creating danger invites rescue under the "rescue doctrine." The original tort-feasor is liable for both injuries that are directly inflicted upon the victim and any additional injuries the victim suffers created by the rescuer. Moreover, the original tortfeasor is liable for any injuries the rescuer herself may suffer in attempting the rescue.

b. Good Samaritan: To avoid imposing liability on the well-intending rescuer who negligently makes the rescuee's injuries worse, most jurisdictions have "Good Samaritan" statutes. Such statutes will usually excuse ordinary negligence on the part of persons who, without compensation, render emergency care or transportation to the hospital from an accident scene. The P must show gross negligence or wanton misconduct to recover against an uncompensated rescuer D. Further, where a party has put someone in danger, it is usually foreseeable that a rescuer will subsequently come to his or her aid. Injuries to or caused by a Good Samaritan rescuer are thus also foreseeable.

MBE Tip: For healthcare Ds, consider the professional standard of care and the Good Samaritan excuse. Also be alert to the defenses of assumption of the risk and consent, including any excess treatment undertaken by the professional.

---

c. Harm Creator: Someone whose negligent conduct is responsible for putting another in danger is under a duty to rescue them, come to their aid, or summon help. The "Good Samaritan" lower duty of care standard does not apply to the original tortfeasor.

d. Co-Venturers: If D and victim are acting together in a common pursuit that creates danger, some courts impose a duty of assistance on both to rescue the other.

e. Special Duty: The "no duty to act" rule may not apply to common carriers and business premises open to customers and the public. A carrier or business that solicits public patronage has some duty to take actions to mitigate P's injuries suffered in their transportation vehicle or on their premises. Employers may have a similar duty to act to assist employees injured in workplace situations, and school personnel to assist their students.

f. Professional Rescue Doctrine: A rescuee (or original tortfeasor who caused the peril) is not usually liable to professional rescuers (police or fire fighters) if they injure themselves in the rescue. The regular compensation paid to the rescuer is usually considered to constitute a professional's assumption of the risk. Off-duty professional rescuers who are under no legal duty to rescue are not covered by this rule and may recover damages for their injuries.

g. Other Liability Issues: Some exam questions pose questions where the rescue itself increased the injury to the rescuee or the rescuer herself was injured during the process. The original tortfeasor is liable to both the rescuee and the rescuer (danger invites rescue). If the rescuer performs negligently, they may also be liable to the rescuee.

MBE Tip: Rescue rules and the duty to aid (or lack thereof) are on every MBE. Was there a duty to act? If so, and the rescuer created damages (to either the rescuer or rescuee), the original tortfeasor is likely liable. D's negligence that leads to a dangerous situation invites rescue.

---

5. Emergency Situation: The objective standard is one of a reasonable person in a similar emergency. The jury may consider the emergency situation in determining the reasonableness standard of care. Does the necessary immediate action leave little time for a deliberate, thoughtful weighing of options? Examples include emergency driving in a blinding snowstorm, extremely heavy fog, or a sudden sandstorm. This reduced duty standard is not available if the emergency occurred because of D's own negligence. Another exclusion from the lower care standard is if the injury should have been expected to occur because of forces D put in motion.

> **MBE Tip:** Frequently in MBE fact patterns, the rescuer P performed in an unforeseeable emergency situation thereby reducing the negligence "due care" standard.

6. Agency Vicarious Liability: Agents are always personally liable for torts they commit. Employers are also vicariously liable for damage caused by the negligence of their agents and employees operating within the course and scope of their employment relationship. This principle of law is termed "respondeat superior."

a. Frolic of Their Own: Vicarious liability to the employer will not apply if the employee was on an unauthorized frolic of her own, such as committing an intentional tort. If the employer makes payment to a third party because of an employee's tort, the employer may have a right of indemnification from the employee who caused the harm to a third party.

b. Not Independent Contractors: An agency relationship is necessary to support a recovery against the principal under respondeat superior. Torts committed by an independent contractor do not create vicarious liability for their customers.

(1) Safe Harbor: Independent contractors control the details used to accomplish the objective and usually work for multiple customers. Absent control of such details, the principal is not vicariously liable.

(2) Inherently Dangerous Activities: If the function was inherently dangerous, the responsibility for the legal duty may be non-delegable. This includes dynamite blasting and many governmental functions such as the maintenance and repair of streets and electric power lines (see Abnormally Dangerous Activities below).

c. Selection: Negligent selection liability may be imposed on employers who hire persons incapable of doing the duty assigned to them. Similarly, employer liability may exist for hiring persons with a history of violence or other dangerous behavior where a reasonable background check could have discovered the applicant's prior acts.

d. Supervision: Negligent supervision may also apply if there was a duty to supervise or control the employee.

e. Joint Enterprise: This involves a mutual right of control and community of economic interest between members involved in a joint venture. All such individuals are vicariously liable for torts committed by the others within the course and scope of the joint enterprise.

7. Automobile Use Liability: Automobile issues are very frequently tested on the MBE. They include:

a. Right-of-Way: At an intersection without traffic lights or signs, the automobile to the right is favored. The driver to the left must yield the right-of-way.

b. Rear-End Collision: The following driver is primarily liable to the leading driver.

c. Last Clear Chance Exception: The above rules may be overridden when the D had the last chance to avoid the accident. An example is the leading driver D suddenly stopping at a green light knowing that it would lead to a rear-end accident. This doctrine has been abolished in many jurisdictions that would prefer to consider both parties' negligent actions in determining the relative comparative fault.

d. Family Purpose Doctrine: Every MBE exam tests the situation of parents allowing a child to use a family automobile for the household's benefit. The parents (as well as the child) are liable to third parties for injuries sustained by the child's negligent driving.

e. Negligence Per Se: Violation of a statute prohibiting driving while intoxicated (under the influence of alcohol or drugs) is negligence per se in most states. This will usually create liability for the negligent party if the action causing the harm occurred because the actor was under the influence. In comparison, violation of a speeding statute is usually only some evidence of negligence for the jury to consider.

f. Owner Liability/Negligent Entrustment: The owner of a motor vehicle has a duty not to permit a known negligent, reckless, or drunken driver to use the vehicle. If she does, she may be liable for "negligent entrustment." Liability may also exist to third party Ps if D owner observed that the intended driver was visibly drunk or otherwise known to be very unreliable.

(1) Automobile Theft: Car owners are not liable if someone steals their vehicle unless they left the keys in the door or ignition.

(2) Vehicle Defect: An owner giving permission to another to drive their car does not usually have liability for an unknown vehicle defect.

g. Guest Statutes: A few states have "automobile guest statutes" that eliminate driver liability to non-paying passengers unless the driver was grossly negligent, reckless, or intoxicated. Car pooling passengers do not qualify for this exclusion.

h. Defenses: In addition to all the real negligence defenses (see IV.E below), claims arising from automobile accidents may be defended by proving some of P's injuries arose from avoidable circumstances. An example is P's physical injuries from a minor fender bender because of a failure to use the seat belts.

MBE Tip: Many MBE questions involve damages inflicted in an automobile accident. Look for the issues above, especially illegality – speeding or drunk driving usually – and causation. More details on statutory violations are discussed in item 12 below.

---

8. Common Carriers – Innkeepers: Transportation and hotel operators are held to a very high standard of care for their passengers and guests. This "slight negligence is enough" standard is very close to strict liability. However, this elevated standard of care does not apply to non-compensating passengers or guests. A hotel room is considered to be the temporary possessory property of the guest and unauthorized intrusion by the innkeeper is trespass. In addition, a hotel owner is not usually vicariously liable for torts committed by his or her guests.

STOP! Go to page 355 and work Learning Questions 29 to 35.

9. Land Owner/Possessor's Duty:

> **MBE Tip:** Every MBE has numerous questions covering a land owner's liability for injuries to third parties occurring on their property. Distinguish between naturally occurring dangers and artificially dangerous conditions and hazards created by the owners/possessors.

a. Outside the Premises: D is not liable for external injuries except:

(1) Damage from Controllable Items: An owner or possessor usually has strict liability to persons outside the premises for damages resulting from artificial falling objects they control in an urban environment. An example is bricks falling from a building.

(2) Falling Trees: In urban areas, the property owner is usually liable for damage caused by his own overgrown trees. In many jurisdictions, liability for falling trees and branches must be based on negligence such as when the owner knows the trees are rotten and nonetheless allows them to overgrow.

(3) External Pedestrians/Natural Conditions: A property owner normally has no duty to protect pedestrians from natural conditions. This includes water flowing from a natural spring or deposited snow/ice on adjoining public sidewalks.

b. On the Premises: An owner's or possessor's liability for damages suffered by a person coming on the premises depends in part on the nature of the hazard. The duty is higher for artificial (man-made) dangerous conditions created by the owner (such as a swimming pool) than for natural dangers (such as existing ponds and rivers). The status of the intruding P dictates the level of care required. There are four traditional categories.

> **MBE Tip:** Distinguish between the duty level owed a trespasser, licensee, invitee, and hazards attracting chldren.

(1) Adult Trespassers: Adult trespassers are those unknown to the landowner who enter the property without express or implied invitation or permission.

(a) General Rule: Uninvited unknown intruders usually trespass at their peril. The owner is not required to warn and is not liable for damages to trespassers resulting from dangerous conditions, whether natural or artificial. An exception applies if the owner gains knowledge that there is a constant trespass over a limited area such as a path across the property. (See also Children Trespassers below.)

(b) Willful Negligence and Excess Force: Even trespassers are owed a duty of not receiving injury because of an owner's willful or wanton negligence. Bear traps set by the owner without warning would create liability for battery. A related issue is that spring guns create strict liability in many jurisdictions. Unreasonable force cannot be used to defend property or evict trespassers. Most states justify the use of deadly force if the D was in his place of abode and threatened with imminent serious personal injury. The relevant privilege here is self-defense, not defense of property.

(c) Rescuers: The owner may have a duty to rescue if a trespasser has been imperiled by the owner or possessor's affirmative act. Liability may also exist for injuries sustained by a rescuer who is privileged to trespass. It must have been foreseeable someone would come to the rescue in an emergency caused by a hazard under the control of the owner.

(2) Licensee: A licensee, such as a personal social guest, has express or implied permission to be on the premises for non-business purposes.

(a) Examples: This category has been expanded to include uninvited canvassing salespersons, police officers, fire fighters, and emergency workers. Implied permission may apply to children if the landowner knows of their ongoing trespass.

(b) Liability: A possessor is liable to a licensee for damages from visible or known dangerous conditions. Liability requires that it could reasonably be anticipated that the licensee will not discover the hazard or realize its risks. The duty of care may usually be met by warning the licensee of the known hazard such as a sign on a rotten bridge or wood floor. Still, there is no duty to inspect for unknown dangers, and "a licensee takes the property as the possessor uses it."

(3) Invitee: Invitees fall into two categories. A public invitee enters the premises as a result of an express or implied invitation to come on to property. The facility is usually open to the public such as a retail store, church, or library. The invitee is encouraged to enter into transactions that will potentially benefit the host. A business invitee has express permission to be on the premises for business purposes to perform services.

(a) Examples: Included are employees, business customers, pay telephone users, mail carriers, building inspectors, utility meter readers, or garbage collectors.

(b) Inspection Duty: Invitee status creates a generalized duty for the property owner to inspect the property and remedy or warn of hazards that could reasonably have been discovered. An invitee is thus protected against latent or difficult-to-discover hidden dangers more than a licensee. The owner must use ordinary care to repair, make safe, or warn others of physical dangers such as "slip and fall" conditions.

(c) Unawareness Not a Defense: The fact that the owner is unaware of the defective condition is not usually a defense as against an invitee. If sufficient time passes without the owner discovering the dangerous condition, "constructive notice" will be inferred and liability imposed for failure to fix the defect.

(d) Exceeding Invitation: If the invitee wanders beyond the scope of the invited area, the duty of care level for the non-public area is reduced. Depending upon the circumstances, it would be that level of care due a licensee or trespasser.

(4) Attractive Nuisance: The "attractive nuisance" doctrine imposes near strict liability upon a property owner for damages to a child, even if a trespasser.

(a) Artificial Condition: The child must have been attracted to the artificial condition that is "dangerous in itself" and be young enough not to subjectively appreciate the risk and danger involved. The artificial condition must have been left exposed at a place where it is reasonable to expect children to play or satisfy natural youthful curiosity such as swimming in an unfenced swimming pool. Warning signs may not be enough to avoid liability if the cost of correcting the artificial hazard is slight compared to the risk to the children. [Restatement § 339] The effect is to elevate the status of a child from trespasser to invitee.

(b) Natural Condition: Natural dangerous conditions do not usually produce liability unless the owner could easily have avoided the injury by easy and simple precautions. The Restatement would impose on the owner a reasonable inspection duty for open natural hazardous conditions that should have been easily discoverable. Still, hidden natural conditions do not usually create owner liability, even if the injured party is a child.

MBE Tip: Distinguish between naturally dangerous conditions (natural pond or spring) and a landowner's active negligence including artificial attractive nuisances (failure to fence in a swimming pool). An owner's duty to inspect applies to invitees but not licensees. Children trespassers are a very heavily tested topic.

---

(5) Abolition of Categories: A growing number of jurisdictions (including California and New York) have combined the above categories into a generalized reasonable standard focusing on the foreseeability of P's presence, injury possibility, and D's reaction to that risk.

c. Dangerous Activities: A land possessor may be liable for dangerous conditions or activities even if outside the owner's property. This includes damages from D's vicious dog that attacks a neighbor. Strict liability for dog bites applies to licensees and business invitees, but not usually to trespassers. A landlord is not usually liable for a tenant's dog injuries to third parties.

d. Landlord's Liability: A lessor is not usually liable for personal injury to a P resulting from a hazard created after the lessee took possession. Exceptions exist if: (1) the latent hazard was known to the landlord but not the tenant; (2) the injury occurred in common tenant areas (hall, common stairway, or elevator); or (3) the landlord contracted for or made negligent repairs.

MBE Tip: The land owner/possessor's duty to intruders for injuries is heavily tested on the MBE. Lessors and tenant possessors may both be liable to guests.

---

e. Summary of Duty to Parties Entering Property:

Status of Entering Party	Duty of Land Owner/Possessor
Adult trespasser	No liability or duty to warn of any hazards
Child trespasser	Liable if "attractive nuisance" drew the child and the cost to correct the hazard was low
Licensee – social guests, police officers, firefighters, and emergency workers	Required to warn of known hazards unless obvious or adequate warnings are given.
Invitee – business customers, electrical meter readers, and garbage collectors	Must reasonably inspect for unknown hazards and correct or warn invitees of their existence.

f. Land Vendor: Under the common law, land sellers traditionally do not have liability under the doctrine of "caveat emptor" or "let the buyer beware." Most states now impose on sellers a duty to disclose latent hazards and dangerous conditions that the buyer would not discover on inspection. This includes termite infestation, significant drainage and sewage problems, and violation of fire resistance standards.

10. Animal Owners: The best approach for analyzing P's injury from an animal in negligence involves two steps: determine (1) whether the animal is wild or domestic, and (2) whether a trespass to the D's property is occurring.

a. Wild: Strict liability is imposed for personal injury and property damages caused by undomesticated animals owned by D. This includes dangerous animals normally kept in a zoo, such as tigers, lion cubs, leopards, monkeys, chimpanzees, wolves, elephants, skunks, killer bees, some snakes, and some vicious guard dogs. Even if the owner had the animal caged, de-clawed, or teeth removed, any damages by wild animals create strict liability.

b. Domestic: This domesticated animal category is divided into two parts in most states:

(1) Dogs: The majority rule is that strict liability is imposed against the owner only after she gains knowledge of the dog's vicious propensities. This is called the "one free bite" rule. This applies even to German Shepherd, Doberman and Pit Bull breeds, unless the facts say they are inherently vicious (in which case they are treated as wild). If a person is injured while lawfully present on the property (usually a business invitee), liability is also imposed.

(2) Everything Else: The owners of all other domestic animals (e.g. cats, horses, rabbits, cows, pigs, mice, hamsters, some snakes, and parrots) are subject to ordinary negligence liability. The inquiry is focused on what the D should reasonably have known about the animal's dangerous propensities and what precautions (if any) she took.

MBE Tip: Animal liability is a heavily tested topic on the MBE.

---

11. Vendors of Alcohol: Three categories of D are recognized and foreseeability is the touchstone.

a. Commercial Vendors: Commercial vendors of bottled liquor to-go usually have no control over the later consumption of their product. Thus, there is no vendor duty to adult patrons who suffer injuries as a result of their subsequent intoxication.

b. Commercial Hosts: For liquor served to an already intoxicated patron, the question of liability is one of foreseeability. There is usually no liability to the over-consuming adult patron who subsequently injures himself. Most jurisdictions have dram shop statutes specifying that injured third party eligible Ps include that class of P whom D should have reasonably foreseen would be subsequently injured by the adult drunk patron. The same standard usually applies to a "quasi-commercial" host such as employers who furnish alcohol at an office party. The protected class always includes children purchasers and other minors who might later share the liquor sold illegally.

c. Social Hosts: Traditionally, social hosts do not have to police adult consumption in non-business situations. The minority view would recognize tort liability where the D knowingly overserves their adult guests and actively assists the intoxicated person such as allowing the drunk to use the host's vehicle. Serving alcohol to children usually violates a statute and is negligence per se unless given by and consumed in the parent's presence.

> **MBE Tip:** Torts committed while under the influence of alcohol and other intoxicants are a favorite topic of MBE examiners. Foreseeability is the touchstone for liability.

12. Violation of Statute: The legislature of the jurisdiction may define unreasonable conduct by statute. If so, the court may adopt the violated statute/administrative regulation/local ordinance as the required standard of care. Note that this does not create strict liability unless the statute so states.

a. Criminal Statute: "Negligence per se" may result if the D violated a criminal statute and the conduct is defined by the statute as unreasonable as a matter of law. This is prima facie evidence of duty and breach; there must still be present causation and damages. Most states now consider driving while under the influence (of alcohol or drugs) to be in the category of negligence per se.

b. Civil Statute: In most states, violation of a civil statute is not conclusive as to liability but only evidence of negligence. The jury is to be instructed that the violation may be considered as some evidence of negligence. Two causal relationship conditions must be present:

(1) Intended Beneficiary Class? Is the P among the class of persons intended by the legislature to be protected by the statute? An example is that a statute intended to protect consumers may not cover business injury.

(2) Harm to be Prevented? Is the particular injury that P suffered among the class of harms or risks against which the statute was intended to prevent? A statute requiring a contractor to take out a construction permit is usually not dispositive of liability for an injury suffered in the construction process.

c. Causation Necessary: Many MBE questions have facts where the D's violation of the statute was not the "but for" or "proximate" cause of P's harm. The liability inference from a statutory violation is non-applicable unless there was also causation. An example is violation of licensing statutes such as D driving without a driver's license or without required insurance. A violation of the statute by D is not enough unless there is also a showing of operational negligence.

d. Excuses: Excuses for violations of a statute include inability by the D to comply after reasonable diligence (e.g., overgrown bushes cover a stop sign or driver becomes unconscious because of a stroke). Another excuse is that the consequences of a non-violation would be worse than the violation (e.g., child darts into the road, driver swerves into other lane to avoid killing the child and creates a fender bender collision).

MBE Tip: Every MBE has a few questions where the facts are that one of the parties violated a statute. Is P (1) a member the "protected class" that the statute intended to protect and (2) a victim of the same harm that the statute intended to prevent? Distinguish between strict liability, negligence per se, and a negligence inference that is akin to comparative fault. Always look for causation problems. Frequently the statutory violation does not cause the harm, so a "per se" or "inference" of negligence instruction is not warranted.

STOP! Go to page 356 and work Learning Questions 36 to 42.

B. Breach of Duty Proof

Breach of duty or proof of failure to conform to the required standard is the second negligence element. P has the burden of proof. This degree of carelessness determination is usually for the trier of fact.

1. Direct and Indirect Evidence:

a. Direct Evidence: This applies where there is direct factual proof of D's specific acts or omissions damaging the P. Normally what D did in fact is proved through direct eyewitness testimony. If reasonable people could not differ on a factual question, the judge may direct a verdict, thus taking this issue from the jury. Otherwise the jury decides what really happened and whether D breached her duty.

b. Indirect Evidence: Indirect or "circumstantial" evidence is occasionally used for proof. For example, if the P slips on an old banana peel that is black and covered in dirt, the condition of the peel is circumstantial evidence that it has been lying on the floor for a long time and the property owner thus had notice.

2. Res Ipsa Loquitur: Even if there is no direct evidence of negligence, circumstantial evidence may be used to infer "the thing speaks for itself." The jury is instructed that it may infer negligence from the fact that the damages occurred. The most famous example is a case in which a barrel fell from a second-story window and hit a pedestrian. No one witnessed the incident and there was no evidence that negligence occurred, but the court concluded that nothing short of negligence could have resulted in the accident occurring.

MBE Tip: Res ipsa loquitor is a rarely used principle that should not be confused with a case involving circumstantial evidence.

a. Required Elements: P must make two showings. First, that such an injury would not ordinarily occur in the absence of someone's negligence. The second requirement is that the operative instrumentality was under the D's exclusive control.

b. Example: For example, a patient awakes after an operation to find that a surgical sponge is inside of her body. This could be introduced to the jury as evidence of medical malpractice even though there is no direct or indirect evidence of how the sponge got there.

c. Not Conclusive: In most states application of res ipsa loquitur is not conclusive. It merely allows the P to meet the production requirements of a prima facie case. The case gets to the jury without proof of the breach and/or the causation elements. The D is allowed to rebut the inference of breach with evidence tending to show other causes for the damages or that the P voluntarily contributed to the injury.

MBE Tip: An answer on an MBE question stating "P prevails under the doctrine of res ipsa loquitur" is usually wrong.

C. Causation – "But-For" and "Proximate Cause"

MBE Tip: Many of the MBE negligence questions involve multiple or successive causes which contribute to the P's damages.

Causation examines the connecting relationship between the D's breach of the standard of care and the P's resulting injury and damages. The P must make two showings:

1. "But-For" Causation: First, that "but for" the D's lack of care, the damages would not have resulted. The negligent act must have been a cause-in-fact of P's injury. Ask whether the injury would have occurred anyway. If so, there is no causation. There may also be concurrent "but for" causation, perhaps creating multiple Ds. There need not be a sole cause.

a. Substantial Factor: "Substantial factor" causation arises in those rare cases where each of two Ds committed acts that were separately sufficient to cause P's harm. An example is where two negligently set fires merge to burn P's house where either one alone would have burned the structure. In such a case, both Ds are liable, and it will be said that their acts were both "substantial factors" causing P's harm.

b. Alternative Causes: If multiple Ds act negligently, but only one of their acts caused P's harm, P may have difficulty proving which act is responsible. An example is two Ds shoot guns towards P, but only one bullet strikes him. In such a case, the burden of proof shifts to the Ds to show that they did not cause the injury.

2. "Proximate" Causation: The second requirement is that the legal principle of "proximate or legal cause" is met. This is tested on every exam.

MBE Tip: Proximate causation is a MBE favorite issue.

---

a. Test: A proximate cause cannot be too improbable or remote from the D's act or omission. The causal chain cannot be broken by unforeseeable independent forces (or additional tortfeasors) that intervene unexpectedly. The question is whether the later intervening cause was reasonably connected with the risk that D's negligent conduct set in motion.

b. Examples: Normal reactions to D's negligence are included in the chain of causation. This includes subsequent medical malpractice, negligent rescuers (danger invites rescue), a new driver rear-ending automobile accident victims, or a subsequent disease caused by the P's weakened physical condition.

3. Foreseeability: If the D should have foreseen a significantly increased chance of the subsequent event occurring to P because of D's negligent conduct, proximate cause is present. An example is a security guard leaving a retail store's front door unlocked; it ordinarily is foreseeable that this omission would subsequently allow a burglar to illegally enter the premises.

> **MBE Tip:** Approach causation by looking for both the foreseeable P and whether it was foreseeable that the harm would occur. Usually the correct alternative on the MBE will include a statement containing the words "reasonably foreseeable."

4. Superseding Causes: To break the casual chain, a superseding cause must create results that are unforeseeable, thus removing them from the field of risk created by D's original act. This "zone of danger" limiting analysis was developed by Judge Benjamin Cardozo in *Palsgraf*. Judge Andrew's dissent argued the duty is properly expanded to include all harm that the D caused to society so a "but for" causation test is necessary.

a. Compelling Facts Help Break Chain: If subsequent unforeseeable intervening criminal behavior or willful wrongdoing is present, the chain of causation may be broken. The more unexpected and compelling the intervening act the better. This may relieve the original tortfeasor of liability for damages resulting from the intervening act.

> **MBE Tip:** Even if the intervening cause was unforceable, liability resulting from the original negligence is receoverable.

b. Example: An example is a painter leaving combustible material in a house that later was set on fire by a burglar smoking a cigarette after breaking into the house. The painter is probably not liable because foreseeability of such subsequent events is absent. But see paragraph 3 above; sometimes criminal wrongdoing is foreseeable, and hence does not constitute a superseding cause.

> **MBE Tip:** Look for a third party to come on the scene and make things substantially worse. This may include damages grossly disproportional to D's fault, or an unexpected chain of events or results occurring. More than one D may result but as to the original D, the most important consideration is always that of foreseeability.

D. Damages

Unlike nominal damages allowed P in the BAFTD intentional torts, negligence requires the P to prove actual material losses and/or damages.

1. Included: Property damage, economic loss, pain and suffering are all recoverable. A recovery for mental suffering usually requires accompanying physical symptoms. Future damages, such as lost earnings, may be recovered if it was foreseeable they would occur as a consequence of the negligent conduct. Future economic loss is discounted to the present value, but many courts also allow an inflation allowance. Lost wages are usually awarded at the gross amount not net after taxes.

2. Limitations: Still, damages cannot be too speculative. Examples of speculative losses are a business loss of hopeful future profits where there was no history of profitable operations or future earnings based on a college degree that has not been earned.

E. Defenses

If fault by the P is or may be relevant, the question will specify the jurisdiction's applicable contributory or comparative negligence rule.

1. Contributory Negligence: Under the common law, P's unreasonable conduct created a total defense to P's negligence claim. It was an all or nothing situation. This has also been called the "doctrine of avoidable consequences."

a. Standard of Care: The P is usually held to the same "reasonable" standard as D. Special knowledge or skill in a profession or occupation may raise the standard. Some decisions suggest reasonable care for others may be a higher standard than reasonable care for one's own safety. A lower standard may also apply for child, insane, and physical-attribute deficient Ps where the jury is usually allowed to apply a objective standard (a reasonable child, blind person, or deaf person). A mentally deficient D short of insanity is held to the ordinary reasonable person standard.

b. Last Clear Chance: An exception applied under the "last clear chance" doctrine; P's contributory negligence does not produce any offset if D subsequently had the last clear chance to avoid the accident by the exercise of ordinary care. Note that this helps the P, not the D. The P never loses a case solely because she had the "last clear chance" to avoid being injured.

c. Intentional or Reckless D: Contributory negligence is not a defense to intentional torts or willful, reckless, and wanton misconduct by D. The tortious activity must go beyond ordinary negligence. Courts usually find questions of P's sufficiency of care in contributory negligence to be a jury question.

2. Comparative Fault:

a. General Rule: The rule in most states today is that any fault by the P prior to the injury operates to diminish proportionally the amount awarded P for damages. An example would be a P who failed to wear a safety belt in an automobile accident and thereby aggravated the injury. This apportionment by relative comparative fault applies to all actions based on fault including negligence, strict liability, and product liability claims, and also includes any "last clear chance" element. Under "pure" comparative fault statutes a P may recover for any percentage of the damages. Jury finds P 80% at fault, so recovery is 20%.

b. Intentional Torts: Almost all states today do not employ comparative fault to reduce injury from intentional torts.

c. Exceptions: Most states have two exceptions to the comparative fault scheme, under which the P may not recover from any D.

(1) More than 50% at Fault: If the P's fault is more than 50%, no recovery is allowed in some states. This has been called "modified comparative negligence."

(2) Recklessness: Some states combine the "more than 50%" rule with unnecessary recklessness such as engaging in a risky activity while intoxicated.

(3) Felony Commission: Where the P was committing a felony that is a probable cause of the injury, the P is barred from seeking recovery against other actors.

> **MBE Tip:** The nuances and differences between contributory negligence and comparative fault are heavily tested on the MBE. Apply comparative fault unless the question specifies that "the jurisdiction follows contributory negligence."

3. Assumption of Risk: This may be express or implied and includes the consent doctrine that may be a defense to an intentional tort.

a. Express: One party may expressly and voluntarily consent that any claims are subject to an exculpatory clause insulating the D from liability resulting from existing negligence. This release includes informed medical consent or a car driver signing a release to enter a drag race at a racetrack. Similarly a merchant accepting goods "as is" with knowledge that the goods have defects after the seller reduced the price assumes the risk. Blanket exculpatory provisions are disfavored in most states if aimed at consumers. Such a provision must be separately negotiated for and particular as to the type of liability being disclaimed.

> **MBE Tip:** When evaluating express consent as a defense, be sure to evaluate whether or not the harm claimed by P was included within the scope of the release or waiver.

b. Implied: P has actual knowledge of the specific potential future risk involved, appreciates its magnitude, and voluntarily chooses to proceed or ignore warnings. The jury applies proportional fault to reduce P's recovery. Assumption of the risk may even apply to strict liability for abnormally dangerous activities or product liability. Examples include being struck by a baseball at a baseball game or trespassing on property after reading a warning sign clearly stating that serious potential injury could occur.

> **STOP!** Go to page 358 and work Learning Questions 43 to 49.

> **MBE Tip:** Up to 50% of all MBE tort questions focus on multiple aspects of negligence. You need to know it thoroughly, especially proximate causation and the various defenses against P's claim including the difference between contributory negligence, comparative fault, and express and implied assumption of the risk.

V. MISREPRESENTATION OR FRAUD – FIRD

Misrepresentation, deceit, or fraud in the inducement occurs when a false statement misleads P and this causes P to suffer foreseeable monetary damages. For MBE analytical purposes, the Restatement required elements can be condensed to four and abbreviated by the memory ladder/acronym **FIRD**.

A. False Statement of Fact

False statement of a material fact made by D with actual or constructive knowledge of its falsity. An action may also be sufficient such as turning back a car's odometer. The importance of the false fact to P determines the materiality.

1. Exceptions: Absent a fiduciary duty, opinions by non-experts, "puffing," sales talk, curbside subjective opinions, and general value or quality do not usually rise to the level of a misstatement of fact. Detailed, specific allegations are more likely to be considered material objective facts than general assertions such as "good value" and "great opportunity."

2. Future Promises: A promise to act in the future constitutes fraud only if made with a present intent not to perform.

MBE Tip: Often the false statement accompanies other tort actions. If D falsely represents to P that he is a policeman to induce P to agree to an arrest, false imprisonment has also occurred. If D falsely claims to be a physician to induce P to allow herself to be examined, a battery claim may also exist.

B. Intention/Scienter

Intention by D to induce that particular P to be misled and act upon the false statement. This culpable intention to deceive or defraud is frequently referred to as "scienter"; this must rise above mere innocent negligence. Scienter may be imputed in the right fact pattern on the basis that a person intends the natural and probable consequences of a reckless or wantonly negligent representation. This may apply where there is a reckless disregard for the truth.

MBE Tip: D's actual knowledge of the falsity of the representation is usual on the MBE exam. Often the P overheard the D make the false statement to another or heard it from a third party. Intention to defraud that P is lacking; a negligence claim may still lie.

C. Reliance

1. "In Fact": Did the P in fact rely upon the D's statement? Subjective reliance by P on the truthfulness of D's statement must be present.

2. Reasonable Person Test: Would a reasonable person under similar facts and circumstances have been justified in relying on the D's statement? This is an objective test. Reliance on mere sales talk, opinions, obvious falsity (I own this bridge and will sell it to you), or statements concerning the law made by non-lawyers are not usually justified. A P who acts unreasonably may have difficulty meeting this reliance element.

D. Damages

Damages recoverable are the "benefit of the bargain." This result should put P in the same position as if the representation were true. Punitive damages may also be awarded. Damages can't be too speculative and the burden is on P to prove the damage amount. Alternatively, P may attempt to rescind the transaction and recover money in restitution.

E. Negligent Misrepresentation

This cause of action is a blend of negligence and fraud. There is a false statement negligently made but D lacked the intention found in fraud. Still the D was careless in making the representation creating damages and thus potential liability.

1. D's Status: On the MBE, a professional or business D usually makes the negligent misrepresentation. An example is a CPA's audit report, an attorney's opinion letter, or a surveyor's title report.

2. Scienter Absent: Scienter is usually absent; the D may have believed the statement or report was true and accurate. Still, there was some carelessness or a failure to exercise reasonable care in gathering and/or presenting the facts.

3. Particular P: The P must have suffered monetary damages based upon justifiable reliance. D must usually have known that P was relying on the statement containing the representation. For a professional this class of potential Ps always includes the client. A fiduciary duty to P is usually required. There is usually no duty to third parties lacking privity. Liability may apply if the P was a part of a limited group of persons whom the D knew would rely upon the representations in the professional opinion.

F. Fraudulent Concealment

Unless the D has a fiduciary duty to P, nondisclosure does not usually constitute deceit. "Caveat emptor" or let the buyer beware is the traditional general rule. This result especially applies if the transaction is entered into under such terms as "as is," "with all faults," or similar terms indicating that the buyer knew the seller conveyed no assurance as to the items.

1. Active Concealment: Increasingly, state courts dislike active intentional non-disclosure. They may impose liability on a seller who conceals/fails to disclose a serious defective condition or facts basic to the transaction which materially affect the outcome. If P could not have readily discovered the defect, the law treats the seller D as representing the non-existence of the condition they concealed. An example is D seller's failure to disclose concealed termite infestation to a purchaser of a home.

2. Remedy: Rescission is the usual buyer's remedy. Damages in an amount of the actual cost less the value with the defect may apply if rescission is not possible.

VI. STRICT LIABILITY

A few MBE question areas will give rise to D's strict liability. There is an absolute duty of care so that P can recover without proving D was at fault.

> **MBE Tip:** Focus on the activity, not whether D was careless or intended to inflict damage.

A. Abnormally Dangerous Activity

If D is undertaking an abnormally dangerous (ultra-hazardous) activity, your answer choice should reflect the Restatement rules discussed below.

1. Elements: This applies to dangerous business activities involving a substantial risk of serious harm to Ps in their normal use. The activity must be of the type that cannot be conducted safely so that risk is eliminated. Liability is imposed even though reasonable care has been exercised to prevent harm. The responsibility for abnormally dangerous activities may not be delegated to independent contractors.

2. Typical Activity: This category includes the commercial storage and handling of explosives, nuclear reactors, toxic chemicals, aerial crop dusting, blasting and mining activities. Excluded are driving a car and firing a gun, which normally are able to be performed with minimal risk. Public firework displays conducted by commercial pyrotechnicians usually create strict liability. In comparison, an individual igniting personal fireworks is not usually classified as an ultra-hazardous activity; it requires some showing of negligence.

3. Defenses: Assumption of risk may be a viable defense such as P trespassing in a blasting area after reading a "this is a dangerous blasting area" sign. Public necessity and comparative fault may be partial defenses. Contributory negligence is not a defense to strict liability. Most states have merged these defenses into the doctrine of comparative fault.

B. Injury from Animals

Strict liability applies to injuries inflicted by all animals that have a wild nature and are not domesticated. This applies even though the owner has exercised utmost care.

1. One Free Bite Rule: The owner of a domestic animal with vicious or dangerous propensities who learns of the animal's past history of injuring people then assumes strict liability. Lacking knowledge, D may be eligible to defend against a victim's claim on the basis of "the one free bite rule." Look for injuries outside the scope of harm envisioned by the strict liability rule.

2. Non-Applicability: Note that in most states this "one free bite" rule does not apply to wild animals (even if domesticated such as a pet wolf, monkey, or snake); strict liability is always the rule for wild animals. Injury by a domestic cat might be an example of "the one free scratch rule." See above for Negligence rules.

C. Statute Applies

Strict liability may be imposed when a state statute so provides and there is causation. (See below discussion of Strict Liability causation.) The question will have to specify a jurisdictional strict liability statute for this to be tested on the MBE.

D. Product Liability

This is the big brother of abnormally dangerous activity discussed above. Defective products/goods are so heavily tested on the MBE, the topic is covered separately below.

E. Causation Problems

The causation element is more focused in strict liability than negligence. The harm must flow from the specific kind of risk used to justify the application of strict liability to the activity in question. An example is a truck carrying explosives that causes a typical vehicle accident.

The ultrahazardous activity used to justify strict liability must have caused the damage. Proximate causation and foreseeability of intervening causes must also be present.

F. Worker's Compensation

All states have some statute which compensates employees for on-the-job injuries.

1. Coverage: The damage must have occurred in the normal course of employment, but no showing of fault is necessary. Negligence is covered but not intentional self-infliction of harm or employee mutual altercation.

2. Employee's Claims: While liability is strict, the state's compensation schedule is the employee's sole claim against the employer. Compensation for a particular job-related injury is for a fixed amount based on a predetermined schedule. The employee may still sue a third party who caused the harm, but any recovery goes first to the employer for the benefits paid to the employee.

> **MBE Tip:** Be sure the risk created by the dangerous activity caused the strict liability injury. D exercising extraordinary caution – she did everything humanly possible – will not preclude strict liability. Look for wild animal injury or damages from abnormally dangerous activities like building demolition. Finally, if the strict liability claim fails, consider negligence as a fallback theory of recovery.

VII. PRODUCTS LIABILITY

> **MBE Tip:** Products liability applies only to personal injury or property damage of consumers. Economic loss providing contract expectation protection such as between two businesses remains covered under UCC Sales Article 2. That area is tested on the MBE in the contract questions. The exam focus here is on the safety-insurance policies contained in tort law to protect consumers.

A. In General

1. Theories of Recovery: The MBE recognizes three potential tort theories that a P buyer or user of defective products may use to sue for damages (1) negligence, (2) strict products liability, and (3) breach of warranty. These are discussed individually below.

> **MBE Tip:** A given MBE question tends to focus on only one of the product liability recovery theories. Usually, the requirements will state which cause of action to apply and sometimes the facts will support only one theory of recovery.

2. Types of Product Defects: There are three general categories of defects: design defects, manufacturing defects, and a failure to warn.

a. Design Defects: This is where the individual product is made according to the design, but the design itself is faulty.

(1) Included: This includes product structural defects such as a fuel tank that ruptures during low-speed accidents or tires made of such low-grade rubber that they are prone to exploding. Often such cases include a lack of reasonable safety features that could have been incorporated in the product. Usually only the manufacturer is liable unless a reasonable retailer would have tested the item before selling it to the consumer. (See below).

   (2) Balancing Test: Is there a public benefit? If so, the court may weigh the cost of implementing a safer reasonable alternative design (RAD) against the risk and extent of potential injury to consumers.

  b. Manufacturing Defects: This defect occurs because the individual product was not made or assembled according to the proper specifications. Three defects are possible.

   (1) Production Problems: The exam facts include problems in D's assembly, packaging, or handling where it was possible to produce the item correctly without the defect. An example is an automobile with only three of the four wheel nuts installed.

   (2) Inspection Duty: It is usually considered reasonable to inspect a product before shipping so any obvious manufacturing defects are discovered.

   (3) Testing Duty: In some industries, it is usual to test the product such as airplanes or large trucks (but probably not assembly line cars).

  c. Failure to Warn: This is present where the product is not capable of being made or sold in a safe condition for their intended and ordinary use, but the producer mitigates the danger through proper warnings as to its use. The warning itself must be reasonably descriptive so the P appreciates the danger.

   (1) Examples: Examples are prescription drug in-depth warnings to "learned intermediary" physicians and reasonable package label warnings to consumers. An instruction book containing adequate warnings of potential dangers usually accompanies the purchase of equipment such as a power lawn mower.

   (2) Obvious Danger: There is not usually a duty to warn of products which are well-known to be dangerous if consumed in excess over a long period. Examples are tobacco and alcoholic beverages.

   (3) Warnings of Non-Obvious Defects: Adequate warnings or instructions should be given for any non-obvious or hidden defect or danger.

   (4) "State of the Art" Defense: If the danger was not known at the time of manufacture, the "state of the art" defense may apply. In that case, the D is not responsible to warn against an unknown. This applies if all the industry manufacturers did the same.

  d. Subsequent Remedial Measures: This is where the D subsequently redesigned the product, corrected the manufacturing problem, or increased the warning. Such evidence is not normally admissible at trial to prove prior product defectiveness.

B. Negligence – Product Liability

  P's required elements of negligence covered above also apply to product liability. Use the **ABCD** acronym.

1. A Legal Duty: The big issue here is to whom is the duty of care owed? The traditional common law rule of privity between P and D is no longer required. The current standard includes all Ps within the foreseeable zone of danger. The Restatement calls this group of persons those located in "the stream of commerce." All D's in the chain of commerce (manufacturer, wholesaler, and retailer) should exercise reasonable care. But a retailer usually has no duty to inspect the goods they sell and a manufacturer's negligence is not usually imputed to a retailer.

2. Breach of Duty: P may use either direct evidence or res ipsa loquitur.

3. Causation: In fact and proximate causation are both required. P is usually entitled to a presumption that had a sufficient warning been made, they would have read it and thus avoided the harm warned of therein.

4. Damages: Included is personal injury and a consumer's property damage. See the details under negligence above. Pure economic loss not caused by the negligence is not usually recoverable. An example is where D's machine had a manufacturing defect leading to a company's production line being closed. The laid-off production workers would not have a claim against the D.

5. Defenses: Contributory negligence, comparative fault, and assumption of the risk are all available to D as potential defenses.

MBE Tip: The MBE questions may pose facts where strict liability could apply, but the P has decided to pursue a negligence claim often through the theory of failure to warn. P must prove all ABCD elements for a negligence claim. Here the standard of necessary proof P must meet is lower than strict liability.

C. Strict Products Liability

Products liability is the big brother to abnormally dangerous activity covered above.

1. Negligence Comparison: There are three basic differences between the recovery theories of strict product liability and negligence.

a. All Ds: Unlike negligence, all Ds in the chain of distribution are liable. Vertical privity is imposed on the manufacturer, wholesaler, and retailer. This strict liability applies even if the particular D acted reasonably in the circumstances.

b. Allowed Defenses: Contributory negligence is not a bar to recovery as in common law negligence. Instead, the court will apply comparative fault analysis.

c. Burden of Proof: The requirement to disprove some of the elements shift to the D in strict liability. Examples include whether D's actions were reasonable given the industry standards or knowledge of danger at the time the product left D's control.

2. Elements: The Restatement treatment controls.

a. Products Only: Real property and services are not covered. Automobiles, lawnmowers, and household appliances are frequently asked. Mixed contracts of products and services are categorized by the predominate purpose.

b. Merchant D: The D must be engaged in the commercial business of selling such products. This requirement excludes casual or occasional sellers, such as garage-sale sellers or a flea market organization. Some states extend this concept to exclude strict product liability for the sale of used items.

c. Defective Condition / Unreasonably Dangerous: Both of the conditions above must be met.

(1) Includes: Defective condition may include a manufacturing defect or design error. A failure to warn may qualify. P has the burden of proof.

(2) Ordinary Usage: The product must have been unreasonably dangerous in its normal usage by an ordinary consumer. Clothing is not inherently unreasonably dangerous so a buyer of defective clothing would have to prove negligence.

(3) Obvious Dangers: The P may not claim strict liability by disregarding general knowledge such as the fact that cigarettes are inherently dangerous. Instead, P must prove negligence.

d. Without Substantial Change: The good must be expected to and must in fact reach the user or consumer without substantial change. Some cases treat downstream alteration as a break in the causation element or allow it as a manufacturer's defense if the alteration was unforeseeable.

e. Degree of Care Irrelevant: D is liable even if he or she exercised all possible care.

f. Privity Abolished: All injured Ps in the zone of foreseeable danger have standing to sue. The requirement of vertical privity is abolished so a retailer may go against a remote manufacturer. Horizontal privity is eliminated so a non-purchaser P whose use or consumption of the product was foreseeable has standing to sue the seller D. Thieves are not considered to be in the class of reasonably foreseeable users.

MBE Tip: Many exam questions test a non-commercial seller or where the product was not in a defective condition and/or unreasonably dangerous when D sold it.

---

3. Damages: Personal injury of P and damage to the defective product itself are recoverable under strict liability. Damages to property other than the product itself are also recoverable. Economic losses beyond these amounts are not recoverable under strict products liability. An example of economic loss is consequential damages such as lost profits resulting from a critical component which fails thus closing down the whole manufacturing line. Such damages must be pursued under UCC Article 2.

4. Defenses – SCAAM:

a. State of the Art: If it was not possible to know of the danger at the time of sale or it was not then technically possible to design the product safely, there is a defense. All current manufacturers must be equally unaware of any danger. Compliance with a mandatory government rule also provides this defense. An example is an approved AIDS drug that had unavoidably unsafe side effects when first released.

b. <u>C</u>omparative Fault: Contributory negligence is replaced by comparative fault. P's failure to discover a latent or hidden defect is not a defense to a strict product liability action.

c. <u>A</u>ssumption of the Risk: This might apply if the P discovered the defect, appreciated the significance, and still proceeded in the face of the known danger. Some questions indicate the buyer knew that the price was reduced because of the defect. The P's going forward to encounter the danger must be both voluntary and unreasonable.

d. <u>A</u>lteration: If the P is a downstream retailer or some third party altered the product after it left the D's hands, the manufacturer may have a defense. Again the court may treat this as breaking the chain of causation if the alteration was not foreseeable.

e. <u>M</u>isuse or Overuse: The P might put the product to a different or more intense use than what was reasonably intended by the parties. Overuse may also be a defense if under normal, reasonable usage the malfunctioning would not have occurred. The misuse or overuse must also not have been reasonably foreseeable by the D.

MBE Tip: Over half the strict liability MBE questions test one or more of the above-described **SCAAM** defenses. Frequently the P assumed the risk/misused the item, or the D acted reasonably and the product was altered after it left the manufacturer.

---

5. Statute of Limitations: Strict products liability claims are governed by the general statute of limitations for torts, which is three (3) years in most states. The statute is triggered – begins to run – when the injury occurred or when the injury has become sufficiently apparent to be subject to the discovery rule.

D. <u>Breach of Warranty</u>

This UCC topic is not heavily tested on the tort section of the MBE. The contract-UCC section has an expanded treatment of the warranties of transfer and defenses. The few questions focus on situations where the D was not negligent according to the reasonable industry standards, but they made a representation creating a special or heightened duty.

1. Express Warranties: An affirmative statement of fact by the seller, such as an advertising or label description, usually qualifies if it is a basis of the bargain. This will have the effect of raising the reasonableness standard. If the stated quality is absent, the buyer may pursue a warranty claim. Intention to deceive is not necessary. [UCC 2.313]

2. Implied Warranty of Merchantability: All products sold by a merchant must be of average quality, fit for their ordinary purposes, and pass without objection in the trade. The merchantability standard imposed is the quality level that is reasonable and customary in the industry. This warranty does not apply to a casual seller. [UCC 2.316(3)]

3. Implied Warranty of Fitness for a Particular Purpose: This applies to a seller representing that the product is suitable for P's specific use and the P so relies. This may create liability even if the Ps use exceeded industry standards. [UCC 2-315]

4. Title and Against Infringement: This imposes on the seller the requirements of good title, the right to transfer, and that the item is free from undisclosed security interests, liens, encumbrances, or claims. If a merchant seller, the goods also must not infringe on any third party's patent or copyright. This last restriction does not apply if a buyer gives the seller the specifications for custom ordered goods. [UCC 2-312]

5. Advantages: It may be possible to recover under a warranty theory even if D was reasonable under the general negligence standard. Economic losses, such as lost profits, may also be recoverable. The UCC has a four-year statute of limitations, but it begins running as of the date of purchase of the good (not the date of discovery, as in most tort claims).

MBE Tip: MBE product liability questions focus on whether the seller is a merchant, whether the good was in a defective condition when it left the D's hands, and the defenses.

STOP! Go to page 359 and work Learning Questions 50 to 57.

VIII. NUISANCE

Nuisance involves an unreasonable interference with property, like trespass. However, trespass requires a physical invasion while this is not necessary for nuisance. The P need not allege or prove bad intentions on the part of the D.

A. Public or Private

1. Private Nuisance: Private nuisance is defined as substantial and unreasonable interference with an individual's or small group's significant use or enjoyment of their private real property. The D's conduct may be negligent, abnormally dangerous, or irrational.

a. Trespass Distinction: Distinguish nuisance from trespass, which involves interference with P's right of exclusive possession. Trespass requires a physical invasion, whereas private nuisance does not.

b. Examples: Nuisance would include a neighbor's loud noises, offensive odors, or starting a gun firing range next door. This tort has been extended to include persistent and unwanted telephone calls made to P's home and outrageous billboard ads in close proximity intended to create unreasonable visual interference to the neighboring P.

c. Reasonableness: The unreasonable test looks to use alternatives available to D and the effect the nuisance has upon the land enjoyment and value. Mere mental annoyance or slight physical discomfort without a decrease in land value is usually not sufficient. A nuisance can also amount to a trespass. The injured party may bring suit.

2. Public Nuisance: Public nuisance is defined as actions that interfere with the health, safety, public peace, or other rights of the entire community or neighborhood. Ultrahazardous activities, prostitution or drug houses, polluting municipal beaches, blocking roads, etc., are included in the public nuisance category. A government entity normally brings a public nuisance lawsuit. Private parties may also sue for a public nuisance if they can show special damages different in kind (not just amount) from those suffered by the general public at large.

MBE Tip: Many MBE torts questions turn on the requirement that in order to recover for a public nuisance, a P show damages different from those suffered by the general public.

B. Elements

1. Substantial Interference: This interference must be more than trivial, inconvenient, or a little irritating to the P. An example is a neighbor's son who practices his drumming musical skills 20 minutes a day. Is this more than a reasonable person should be expected to tolerate in a crowded city?

2. Balancing Test: If there is some usefulness to the D's nuisance, this must be balanced against the harm. This balancing test is often applied to a public nuisance such as a pulp mill (bad smell to the community v. jobs which would be lost) or oil refinery (pollution created v. need for automobile gasoline).

C. Damages

Actual harm to the property including diminution in value is recoverable. But the harm must be substantial, unlike intentional trespass to land where nominal damages may be awarded. Injunctive relief may be sought if money damages are inadequate or there is a continuing interference. However, the court will again balance the P's harm against the negative consequences to the D (and community if an essential product or jobs will be lost) if the injunction is issued.

D. Defenses

1. Coming to the Nuisance: If P knowingly purchases land next to an existing nuisance, there is an assumption of the risk. Damages may be limited or barred under this concept and injunctive relief denied. Such an assumption of the risk may be limited to a given level of interference. Can P argue there was a significant and unreasonable expansion of the original nuisance activity or level of interference?

2. Extra-Sensitive P: P's abnormal sensitivity is not a recoverable factor. An example is P with very sensitive hearing who is bothered by normal sounds. The nuisance must constitute a substantial and unreasonable interference to P's with normal sensibilities.

> **MBE Tip:** Nuisance is also frequent in real property questions. A nuisance may also be a trespass to adjoining land and intention is not required; strict liability applies.

IX. DEFAMATION

> **MBE Tip:** Defamation is closely connected to and often tested with invasion of privacy torts.

A. Definition – FPID

Defamation is (1) an unprivileged **f**alse statement of fact concerning P, (2) **p**ublicized to a third person (in understandable language) with (3) a wrongful **i**ntention or at least negligence in exposing the P to hatred, contempt, ridicule, or disgrace that (4) creates **d**amages to P's reputation and good name. Look for an outrageous and/or unsupported statement made by D damaging P.

> **MBE Tip:** Consider the four above **FPID** defamation elements as they vary (see below) in applying to the defaming of a public or private figure P.

B. Details

1. Defamatory Slander/Libel: "Slander" is oral "spoken" factual defamation. "Libel" is factual defamation written in "letters." A fact must rise above mere opinion, though opinion that implies the existence of fact is actionable. The defamatory statement must be more than unflattering, annoying, or embarrassing. Innuendo is where proof of extrinsic facts is required to show the defamatory meaning.

2. Falsity: Under the common law, falsity was assumed so the D had the burden to prove substantial truth. The current rule in most states is that P has the burden of showing falsity in cases involving public (non-private) Ds and issues. As to private P and issues, the states are divided whether P must prove falsity or D must prove truth.

3. Concerning P: The third party must interpret the false statement as referring to the P specifically. Statements targeted towards small groups may qualify; "all lawyers are crooks" would not suffice. Colloquium is when extrinsic facts are necessary to establish that P is the one defamed. A non-name reference to P is sufficient if P is easily understood to be the target ("our largest competitor").

4. Publication: The publication must have been made to a third party. If it was made only to P or P's agent there is no publication. A third party must understand the defamatory statement aimed at P. A defamatory statement made in a foreign language may not qualify unless the listener understood the language. Each primary publisher may be liable. Every repetition by each republisher may be a separate publication.

> **MBE Tip:** Many MBE defamation questions turn on whether there was an effective publication. Also whether the statement was false. The opinion (v. fact) exception from liability will ordinarily turn on the exact wording the D used.

C. Damages Requirement

The P must allege and prove special damages to reputation that resulted from a third party's reaction to the defamatory statements, especially if it is oral slander that is short lived.

1. Per Se Exceptions: The damage proof requirements have four "per se" **LUNI** exceptions categories of defamation. These "per se" violations entitle P to substantial damages without proof of special pecuniary loss.

2. Damage Categories – LUNI: Special pecuniary economic damages include the loss of a specific loan, sale, job, a prospective gift, or inheritance; non-pecuniary damages include humiliation, injury to one's reputation, or loss of friends.

a. Loathsome Disease: This would include accusations of leprosy, venereal diseases, and AIDS.

b. Unchastity or Other Serious Sexual Misconduct: Usually the allegation is made against a married person having adulterous relations outside his or her marriage.

c. Notorious Criminal Allegation: This must be a serious felonious offense. Falsely calling a P a "crook" is not defamation per se; an allegation of child molestation is.

d. Injury in Trade, Business, or Profession: The false allegation must go directly to the proper conduct of the business, trade, or profession.

> **MBE Tip:** The MBE frequently tests the issue that P does not have to prove special damages for the per se defamation **LUNI** categories.

D. Degree of Fault Required

The law distinguishes between private and public Ps and the nature of the matter being publicized.

1. Private Person / Private Matters: A mere showing of ordinary negligence is all a private person P needs to make for private matters; recklessness or malice is not required.

2. Public Figure / Private Matters: "Public Figures" include elected officials, candidates for office, celebrities, movie stars, sports figures, and police officers. If the matter involves only the P's personal or private life, P must show recklessness beyond ordinary negligence. Recklessness in the investigation means the D had either actual or constructive doubt as to the truth of her publication.

3. Public Figure / Public Matter: If the P is a public figure (or one who has voluntarily injected himself into a specific public controversy) and the publicized matter is "public" (non-personal or private life issue), the required showing is raised. P must show D's malice (knowing falsehood and usually an intention to harm the P) or extreme recklessness. The *New York Times v. Sullivan* case held that media fall into this category if reporting on public figures involved in the performance of their public function.

> **MBE Tip:** The degree of required fault – ordinary negligence, recklessness, or malice depending on the status of the P and the matter addressed – is frequently tested on the MBE.

E. Defenses – TEMPR

There are five major **TEMPR** defenses that may be asserted against a defamation claim.

1. Truth: Substantial truth is an absolute defense to defamation (but not invasion of privacy). While character evidence is not normally admissible, an exception exists when the P's character is put in issue. Similarly, fair comment or criticism is protected if based on true facts.

2. Express or Implied Consent: An example is P grants a reporter an interview and later objects to the resulting "story" which P alleges present a biased viewpoint because of the reporter's selection of contents.

3. Mere Subjective Opinion: An expression of pure subjective opinion rather than an objective statement of fact may be a defense. This usually depends upon the phrasing of the descriptive words used; the more precise and specific the language used by D, the more likely it is a fact. Statements of ridicule or verbal abuse are usually classified as opinions, such as "I think that Tom is an S.O.B." or "Jack is a jerk." But if opinion implies the D knows the underlying facts, it is actionable. An example is, "In my opinion, Bill must be a thief," which implies D knows facts justifying the opinion.

4. Privilege: A privilege may excuse what otherwise would have been a defamatory publication.

a. Absolute Privilege: Statements in the course of judicial proceedings, legislative proceedings/debates, statements by government officials, and political broadcasts are protected. This includes statements by governmental executive officers in the course of their duties. Communications between husband and wife are also privileged.

b. Qualified Privilege: This is where a statement is fairly made in the discharge of some public or private duty, or in the conduct of one's own affairs in matters where one's interest is concerned.

(1) Examples: Qualifying circumstances include self-defense, warnings for public protection or interest (identifying criminals) rather than a purely private import. Examples include a former boss warning a new employer that the employee was terminated for embezzlement. Fair criticism (book or film review), republishing official records or employment references enjoy a qualified privilege.

(2) Abuse of Privilege: Good faith must be shown and the fair comment standard is that of a reasonable person in the same or similar situation. Even false statements of fact may qualify for the privilege if made in good faith. If a qualified privilege is not exercised in a reasonable manner for a proper purpose, or the P can prove malice, this defense is lost (abuse it and you lose it).

5. Retraction: A few states provide a defense if D publishes a retraction within a certain period.

> **MBE Tip:** Defamation is a favorite tort on the MBE exam with a minimum of two questions. Know the **FPID** elements, degree of fault required and the applicable **TEMPR** defenses. Even if the statement was true, consider the tort of intentional infliction of emotional distress/outrage and the below invasion of privacy torts.

X. INVASION OF PRIVACY TORTS

Protection against unreasonable interference with a P's right of solitude includes four specific torts under the common law. Proof of intent is not required. The right to privacy is personal and does not extend to family members. No general damages are presumed. P must prove actual damages such as substantial mental anguish, humiliation, ridicule, or contempt.

> **MBE Tip:** Invasion of privacy torts are often combined with defamation and intentional infliction of emotional distress. The MBE will sometimes refer to a claim for "invasion" which requires you to decide which of the four sub-torts apply.

A. Publication in a False Light

1. Elements: This is a publication of false attribution about P by D that casts a false light on P in the public's view. The false light must be highly offensive to a reasonable person (beyond mere embarrassment) and result in actual damages.

2. Examples: Examples of a "false light" would be showing P's picture next to an article with the headline "Mobsters take over city" or "Child molesters found among City's elite." There may be no actual statement that P is a mobster or a child molester, but the P may suffer damages similar to a defamatory statement. Note the close connection to defamation. A key difference is that the tort of defamation protects one's reputation and good name, whereas the false light tort protects a person's emotional well-being. Also be sensitive to the First Amendment issues – see Constitutional Law chapter.

B. Public Disclosure of Private Matter

1. Elements: Disclosure to the public (broad publication) by D of private information regarding P that a reasonable person would expect to remain private. The subject of the matter disclosed must be objectionable to a reasonable person of ordinary sensibilities and therefore not be of legitimate public concern.

2. Examples: A clerical worker in a medical office makes a photocopy of P's medical records and gives it to P's ex-spouse. Another example is posting a notice in a grocery store that "H is an adulterer." However, the publication of the identities and addresses of sexual predators is not actionable in most states. Also, republishing matters from official public records also is usually privileged ("H was convicted of statutory rape").

> **MBE Tip:** Truth is a defense to the tort of defamation, but not to publication of private facts.

C. Intrusion Upon Seclusion

1. Elements: This invasion-of-privacy tort involves D's physical invasion into the private affairs of the P. The intrusion into the P's solitude, seclusion, or private affairs must be considered highly offensive to a reasonable person. Note the possible connection of intrusions to trespass.

2. Examples: Peeking through keyholes and windows, repeated unwanted telephone calls, tapping P's phone without permission or a court order, or placing a listening device in a wall of a neighbor's bedroom may all qualify. Even an outrageous billboard across the street has been held to be an intrusion on P's solitude. However, taking a photograph in a public place (even if by paparazzi) is not actionable as an intrusion.

D. Commercial Appropriation (Misappropriation) of Likeness

1. Elements: This is the unauthorized use by D of P's name, picture, likeness, or other similar item for D's commercial advantage or use to promote D's product or service. P is usually a celebrity on the MBE. The fact P used the D's product and was satisfied does not constitute P's consent to associate their identity as an endorsement. Damages may be royalties imposed on D or the reasonable value of the use of P's commercial identity.

2. Examples: This usually involves using P's name or picture without permission. Liability is generally limited to a commercial context such as marketing, promotion, or advertisement of a service or product implying the P endorsement. Even in an advertisement, merely reproducing a photograph of a celebrity at a public event may not be actionable.

E. Defenses

1. Traditional Defenses: Most jurisdictions recognize: (1) consent, (2) public figure activities which are newsworthy, (3) legitimate news story, and (4) the defamation privileges covered above. This includes publishing facts which are contained in an official public record.

2. Whistleblowing: In most states, whistleblowing is given an immunity from civil liability if the communication is made in good faith to any federal, state, or local government agency, or regulatory organization. Intimidation, retaliation, and workplace reprisals against a whistleblower are likewise illegal in most states. Again, truth and lack of malice are not defenses.

MBE Tip: A claim for invasion of privacy is personal to the P; other family members or third parties do not qualify.

XI. INTERFERENCE WITH ADVANTAGEOUS RELATIONS

A person has a right to enjoy valid contractual agreements and pursue business expectancies unmolested by wrongful and officious intermeddling.

A. Interference with Contract or Business Expectancy

If one induces another to disrupt or breach a contract with P, there may be a cause of action against the interferor. If the interference causes the other party to breach the contract with P, there may also be a claim against the other contracting party.

1. Contract or Expectancy: There must be a bona fide existing contract for a non-privity party to interfere with. A contracted business expectancy must be reasonably certain to qualify. A prospective advantage of a future contract that is merely possible is not protected.

2. Knowledge and Intention Required: The interferer must have knowledge of the contractual relationship or expectancy. Unintentional or indirect interference is not generally actionable.

3. Active Role: D must play an active role in bringing about the breach or defeating the prospective business advantage. Merely offering a better price or accepting an offer by a party that creates a breach with a third party is not usually sufficient (but may give the third party a breach of contract claim).

4. Damages: P must plead and prove actual pecuniary damages.

5. Factual Examples: A typical MBE exam fact pattern includes a competitor interfering with an employer/employee contract, interference with a principal/agent relationship, or a third person interfering between a business and its customers. One question involved an accountant who convinced the client to fire a retained attorney without justification. The accountant was likely responsible for interference and the attorney should receive an award of the fee that she would have earned in the representation.

B. Defenses – Privileges to Interference

The D's interference with a valid contractual relationship may have defenses or be privileged. Interference with a contract to marry, illegal contracts, and at-will contracts cannot give rise to this tort. The burden of showing privilege for interference rests with the D.

1. Justifiable Conduct: The basic test is whether, under the facts and circumstances of the particular case, the interferer's conduct is justifiable.

2. Examples: Some of the defenses/privileges that have been legally recognized include legitimate business competition, the public interest (consumer reports), an architect giving honest advice upon which a client terminated a contractor, and an interferor protecting their own financial interest in the contract. This privilege is lost if the P can prove the D acted out of sheer malice and not primarily for economic advantage.

3. Prospective Advantage: If the interference is with a prospective potential advantage (such as a future contract award), there is a greater scope of privilege to interfere. A D's desire to obtain business for herself justifies many aggressive competitive actions as long as they are not illegal such as price fixing, attempted monopolization, etc.

MBE Tip: Usually on the MBE, the interferor either lacked knowledge of the contract or business expectancy or had a viable defense or privilege.

C. Product Disparagement/Trade Libel/Injurious Falsehood

This is similar to defamation, except that it occurs in a commercial competitive environment.

1. Elements: This tort involves a publicized false statement to third parties that disparages or casts doubt about the reliability or quality of a competitor's business, product, or service. P must prove that D knew the statement was false or had a reckless disregard for the truth and acted out of spite. Examples include an advertisement that falsely claims a competitor has gone out of business or that an "independent" survey found P's product only 40% as efficient as D's.

2. Damages: Nominal damages are not usually recoverable. There must be a showing of special pecuniary loss such as a drop in sales volume where there is no other explanation for the decrease.

3. Privileges: A truthful factual comparison of products and mild "puffing" of D's own products are not actionable. Many of the privileges available in defamation apply.

XII. ABUSE OF LEGAL PROCEEDINGS

A. Malicious Criminal Prosecution

This is D's unjustifiable initiation of criminal proceedings (private arrest, warrant, indictment) which are terminated in P's favor.

1. Absence of Probable Cause: There must have been a lack of probable cause for initiating the prosecution, and P must be acquitted at trial on the merits. Termination of the prosecution of P based upon plea-bargaining, procedural defects, and prosecutorial discretion are not "on the merits."

2. Malice Required: Malice (a purpose other than to bring an offender to justice) is required. Examples include signing an affidavit for a baseless criminal warrant, wrongfully persuading a prosecutor to bring charges, or giving false information to the authorities with knowledge of its falsity. Filing a police report in good faith is usually not actionable, nor is a reasonable mistake in reporting to authorities.

3. Privilege: Judges, police, and prosecuting attorneys enjoy an absolute privilege.

B. Wrongful Civil Proceeding

This claim is similar to malicious criminal prosecution. Special damages, such as damages to reputation, must usually be shown because the absence of probable cause is more difficult to prove. Some decisions require D to show an arrest of the person or seizure of personal property such as wrongful attachment or wage garnishment. The victim may also assert a Rule 11 sanction motion with the trial court against the attorney signing the pleading if the lawsuit lacked a reasonable legal or factual basis.

C. Slander of Title

The D slanders the title of P's real property by using a legal process. This may occur if D wrongfully files a lis pendens, lien attachment, levy of execution, or similar property restraint against P's real property. D has a conditional privilege to assert a bona fide legal interest of her own. The privilege is lost if abused such as bad faith or a filing with malice intended merely to tie up P's property and thus extract an economic concession. If the slander on the title wrongfully blocks a pending sale or purchase of the property, P is entitled to damages and the attorney fees necessary to clear title in most states.

D. Abuse of Process

This is the wrongful use of the legal process to accomplish an ulterior purpose not reasonably related to the legal proceeding of that claim. An example is issuing a witness deposition notice in order to execute service of process against that person in a different proceeding.

MBE Tip: These abuse of proceedings torts may be combined with an evidence issues.

XIII. ALIENATION OF AFFECTION AND RELATED CLAIMS

At common law, the claims of alienation of affection, criminal conversation, and/or loss of continued affection and consortium were recognized.

A. Criminal Conversation

These were usually actions by a jilted spouse against a romantic rival D who interfered with a marriage by having adulterous sexual relations with P's spouse. Many states have abolished all such types of sexual adulterous events concerning husband and wife torts in this class even when denominated as an outrage claim.

B. Loss of Consortium

At common law, this claim was not available to a wife. Today, loss of consortium is usually recoverable by both spouses. Damages may result from D's tortious conduct against a spouse of P. An example is a battery by D that paralyzes a spouse thus depriving the P of love, affection, assistance, care, companionship, and loss of income or support. The spouse may also bring a claim for pre-death loss of consortium.

C. Child Recovery for Parental Abuse

A child usually has no claim for mere alienation of their parents' affections. But there is a claim against a tortfeasor who seriously injures or murders her parents. Recovery would be allowed for loss of support and consortium. The deceased parent's pain and suffering would also be recoverable as a portion of the survival action.

D. Parent Recovery for Child Abuse

Parents may have a claim against D for the death or abuse of their child if under 18. This may include a claim against a D who had sexual intercourse with a minor child. Also tested on the MBE is the parents' lawsuit against the members of a cult who induce their child to leave the family home.

> **STOP!**   Go to page 361 and work Learning Questions 58 to 66.

XIV. FINAL CHAPTER REVIEW INSTRUCTIONS

1. Completing the Chapter: Now that you have completed your study of the chapter's substantive text and the related Learning Questions, you need to button up this chapter. This includes your preparing your Magic Memory Outlines® and working all of the subject's practice questions.

2. Preparing Your Own Magic Memory Outline®: This is essential to your MBE success. We recommend that you use our software template in this process. Do not underestimate the learning and memory effectiveness derived from condensing the text chapter into your succinct summaries using your own words. This exercise is covered in much more detail in the preface and on the CD-ROM.

a. Summarize Knowledge: You need to prepare a summary of the chapter in your own words. This is best accomplished using the Rigos Bar Review Series Magic Memory Outlines® software. The words in the outline correspond to the bold headings in the text.

b. Capture the Essence: Your job is to summarize the substance of the text by capturing the essence of the rule and entering your summarized wording into your own outlines. Go to the text coverage and craft your own tight, concise, but yet comprehensive statements of the law. Take pride in your skills as an author; this is the best outline you have ever created.

c. Focus: Focus your attention and wording on the required technical elements necessary to prove the relevant legal principles and fine-line distinctions. Integrate any helpful "learning question" information into your outline.

3. Memorize Outline: After you have completed your own Magic Memory Outline® for the whole chapter, read it over carefully once or twice. They are the best book ever written. Refer back to your Outlines frequently.

4. Work Old Questions: The next step is to work all the final questions of each chapter. These vary in degree of difficulty, but the ones towards the end tend to concentrate on fact patterns and issues at the most difficult testing level. Consider using the Question Map on the CD-ROM. Click on the questions under the subject and topic you have just studied. This allows you to cross relate the subjects and related MBE testing.

a. Question Details: Again, it is usually worthwhile to review the explanatory answer rationales as they reinforce the relevant principles of law. If you are still unsure of the controlling rule, refer back to the related portion of the text. This will help you to appreciate the fine-line distinctions on which the MBE questions turn.

b. Do a Few Questions At a Time: Work the final chapter questions in sequence. Make sure you stop after no more than a few to check the answer rationales. Do this frequently so that the facts of the individual question are still in active memory.

c. Work Them All: We have tried to pick questions with an average or higher probability of reappearing on the MBE. You should at least read all the questions and ponder their answers. Every question and answer has some marginal learning and/or reinforcement value. On the MBE you will recognize many of the actual MBE questions as very similar to the ones in your Rigos Bar Review Series review books.

d. Learn From Mistakes: The objective is to learn from your mistakes by reviewing the explanatory rationales while you still remember the factual and legal details of the question. It is good to miss a few; they will help you become familiar with the MBE fine-line distinctions. The examiners' use of distracters, tricks, and red herrings is repetitive.

e. Flag Errors: Put a red star in the margin of the book along side every question you missed. Missed questions should be worked again the day right before the MBE. Do not make the same mistakes on the exam.

f. Essays: Candidates in jurisdictions that administer the Multistate Essay Exam should refer to the *Rigos Bar Review Series Multistate Essay Exam Review — MEE* for practice essay questions.

5. Practice Exam: After you complete the last chapter, you should take the 200 item practice exam. There is detailed information covering this simulated MBE test in both the preface and at the beginning of the exam in Volume 2. This is important because you need to build your concentrated attention time span. You also need to get intellectually used to jumping between unrelated topics and subjects.

6. Make Your Own Exam: The Rigos Bar Review Series software allows you to pick 5, 10, 20 or 100 questions at random from all six MBE subjects. This is an important feature because you must become comfortable with switching intellectual gears between different subjects. If you are not an early riser and/or get going slowly when you get up, try working 10 or 20 questions using the "Make Your Own Exam" software the first thing every morning.

7. Update Your Magic Memory Outline®: The fine-line distinctions in the question and answer rationales will improve your understanding of how the MBE tests the law. Consider updating your Magic Memory Outline® while the question testing environment is still fresh in your mind.

8. Next Chapter: It is now time to go to the beginning of the next subject. Begin by previewing the chapter. Scan the typical coverage.

RIGOS BAR REVIEW SERIES

MULTISTATE BAR EXAM REVIEW (MBE)

CHAPTER 2

TORTS

Magic Memory Outlines®

Question Distribution Map

> Numbers immediately following the topic are the chapter question numbers. The **boldface** numbers preceded by "F" are the final exam question numbers. For example, for the topic "II. A. 4. Mental Development Handicap" below, question 225 is in the chapter questions on page 2-408; question **F155** in the final exam on page 7-487 of Volume 2.

I. MBE EXAM COVERAGE

II. GENERAL CONCEPTS / DEFINITIONS
A. Imperfect Parties ....
   1. Heightened Susceptibility of P – 1, 68, 112, 254...
   2. Children D – 2, 102, 191, 192, 194, 199, 225, 231 ....
   3. Unusual Mental Attributes – 226 ....
   4. Mental Development Handicap – 225..**F155**
   5. Physical Impairment – 3, 226...**F155, F163**
B. P or D Deceased – 219 ....
   1. Survival of Actions – 76, 219 ....
   2. Wrongful Death – 76, 219 ....
   3. Defenses – 4 ....
C. Multiple Ds – 151, 72, 152...
   1. P Not at Fault ....
     a. Joint and Several Liability – 6, 7, 113, 134, 151, 152, 176, 191, 217 ....
     b. Contribution Between Ds – 5, 152, 176..**F19, F20**
     c. Neither D Negligent – 107 ....
   2. P at Fault ....
     a. Examples of Comparative Fault – 8, 150, 72, 217.......................................
     b. All Ds Must Be Named – 72 ....
D. Immunities...
   1. Government – 10, 95, 96, 224...
   2. Charities/Education – 206, 229 ....
   3. Family Relationships – 72..
     a. Can Sue Each Other – 72 ....
     b. Third Party Lawsuits – 72 ....
     c. Parent – Child – 9, 10, 88, 89, 110, 192, 199, 232 ....**F194**
E. Remedies..
   1. Damage Requirement – 69, 205 ....
     a. Proof Required – 11, 69 ....**F86**
     b. Proof Not Required – BAFTD – 69 ....
   2. Future Damages – 12, 214 ....**F86**
   3. Collateral Source – 205..

V. MISREPRESENTATION OR FRAUD – FIRD

MEE Candidates: If your jurisdiction administers the Multistate Essay Exam in addition to the MBE, please refer to the *Rigos Bar Review Series Multistate Essay Exam Review — MEE* for practice essay questions and sample answers covering torts.

Torts
Learning Questions

1. Plaintiff sues Defendant for physical damages due to Defendant's alleged negligence in hitting him while crossing a street. In which situation will the Plaintiff's damages be reduced or barred due to the condition of the Plaintiff?

(A) Plaintiff's injuries were more severe than would have occurred due to Osteogenesis Imperfecta, a bone density disorder.

(B) Plaintiff was on his way home from the hospital and was still recovering from previous injuries.

(C) Plaintiff was a hemophiliac (inability of the blood to clot) who bled to death from a minor injury.

(D) Plaintiff was intoxicated causing him to exercise poor judgment in crossing the street where he did.

2. In which situation would a ten-year old child be held to the standard of care of a reasonably prudent person?

(A) Discharging a firearm.
(B) Playing hopscotch.
(C) Riding a bicycle.
(D) Jumping rope.

3. In which situation would the Defendant not be held to the standard of care of a reasonable person?

(A) Defendant was deaf and is accused of being negligent in failing to heed a warning bell.
(B) Defendant has poor judgment.
(C) Defendant is hot tempered and damaged property in a tantrum.
(D) Defendant has an I.Q. of 85.

4. Which of the following is false?

(A) A personal representative may recover for the decedent's pain and suffering up to the point of death.
(B) A decedent's family may recover for decedent's lost earnings.
(C) A decedent's family may recover for their own loss of companionship.
(D) The Defendant cannot assert defenses against the personal representative.

Questions 5 and 6 are based on the following:

Pedestrian is crossing a street in a non-negligent manner. Driver A approaches from the West, and Driver B approaches from the East.

5. Both drivers negligently strike Pedestrian at the same time causing a broken leg. A jury determines the Pedestrian's damages at $10,000.00. Plaintiff's attorney will take $3,000.00 as attorney's fees. If Driver B has no assets and petitions for Bankruptcy, for how much is Driver A liable?

(A) $5,000.
(B) $8,000.
(C) $10,000.
(D) $13,000.

6. Assume the same circumstances as above except that Driver A causes the Pedestrian a broken leg and Driver B causes a broken arm. The jury finds Driver A is liable for the broken leg and Driver B liable for the broken arm. The jury awards damages of $6,000 for the broken leg and

$4,000 for the broken arm. How much is Driver A responsible for paying?

(A) $4,000.
(B) $6,000.
(C) $10,000.
(D) $13,000.

7. Driver negligently strikes Pedestrian causing a broken leg. Upon arrival at the hospital, Doctor negligently and unnecessarily amputates the leg. In a suit against both Driver and Doctor, the jury awards $500,000.00 in damages for the loss of the leg. What additional information must be known to determine a judgment amount against Driver?

(A) None
(B) The damages for the injury to the leg less damages for wrongful amputation.
(C) The damages only for the wrongfully amputated leg.
(D) The percentage apportionment of fault of each Defendant.

8. Plaintiff suffers one injury due to the negligence of both Defendants X and Y. The jury awards damages in the amount of $100,000.00. The jury also finds the Plaintiff 10% comparatively at fault. For how much in a judgment is Defendant X liable?

(A) $45,000.00
(B) $90,000.00
(C) $100,000.00
(D) More information is needed.

9. In which situation will a parent not be liable for the torts committed by a child?

(A) The child injures another while mowing the lawn at the parent's behest.
(B) The child injures another with a firearm given to him by the parent.
(C) The child injures another while speeding down the street on his bicycle after his parent had warned him to stop doing so.
(D) The child injures another while playing a pick-up game of football.

10. Which of the following is an incorrect statement regarding immunity?

(A) Governments are immune from suit unless such immunity is waived.
(B) Spouses are not immune from suit by each other.
(C) If immunity is waived, a government is still immune from suit due to a decision not to install a guardrail along a dangerous highway.
(D) If immunity is waived, a government is still immune from suit due to the negligence of the government in installing the guard rail along the dangerous highway.

11. Plaintiff sues Defendant for negligence. Plaintiff alleges only that Defendant breached a duty to exercise reasonable care. For what will Plaintiff recover?

(A) Nothing, because there is no allegation of damages.
(B) Present damages only.
(C) Future damages only.
(D) Both present and future damages.

12. In which situation will damages be allowed?

(A) Plaintiff is a new business and sues for loss of future profits due to delays in business licensing.
(B) Plaintiff is a ballet student, is injured, and sues for loss of earning capacity based on becoming a professional ballerina.
(C) Plaintiff demonstrates past earning capacity and his inability to earn that amount in the future due to injuries.
(D) Plaintiff sues a shipping company for past damages due to the shutdown of a factory resulting from delays in delivering a replacement part for a major machine.

13. For which damages will an award of pre-judgment interest be given?

(A) For past pain and suffering.

(B) For past medical bills.

(C) For future medical bills.

(D) For past mental anguish.

14. Plaintiff is injured by the negligence of D. Plaintiff does not seek medical attention until a week later. Because of this delay, the Plaintiff's medical expenses increased by $5,000 and his pain and suffering was prolonged by a week. For which damages will the Defendant be liable?

(A) All damages.

(B) All damages less $5,000.

(C) All pain and suffering only.

(D) All damages less $5,000 and one week of pain and suffering.

15. In jurisdiction X, the statute of limitations for medical malpractice is three years from the date of the negligent act or one year from the date of discovery whichever expires later. Plaintiff Patient has surgery in year 0. In year 1, Patient begins experiencing severe pain in the area where the surgery occurred, but does nothing about it. In year 4, Patient discovers that the surgeon left an instrument inside her. Patient then files suit. Which of the following actions is a court most likely to rule?

(A) Dismissal of the case because the three year statute of limitations expired.

(B) Dismissal of the case because in the exercise of reasonable diligence a reasonable person would have discovered the negligence in year 1.

(C) Dismissal will be denied because the suit was filed within one year of actual discovery of the negligence.

(D) Dismissal will be denied because the statute of limitations is four years.

16. Patient begins visiting doctor on day 1 of year 0 for treatment of depression. Doctor prescribes Addictol, a very powerful and addicting anti-depressant. The patient sees the doctor each month for 20 years. In year 21, another doctor advises the patient that the 20-year prescription has resulted in irreparable liver damage. Patient files suit in a jurisdiction with a three-year statute of limitations and a ten-year statute of repose. What result upon Doctor's motion to dismiss?

(A) Granted, because the statute of limitations has expired.

(B) Granted, because the statute of repose has expired.

(C) Denied, because the last act of a continuous tort is the start of the limitations period.

(D) Denied as to the last three years of treatment, granted as to the period prior to the last three years.

17. Plaintiff is born in year 0. During birth the Plaintiff is injured due to medical malpractice. At age 2, the child's parents discover the negligence. At age 18, Plaintiff brings suit against the doctor. The jurisdiction has a three-year statute of limitations. What result from Defendant's motion to dismiss?

(A) Denied, because the statute was tolled while Plaintiff was a minor.

(B) Denied, because the Plaintiff did not discovery the negligence until age 18.

(C) Granted, because the Plaintiff's parents discovered the negligence at age 2.

(D) Granted, because the statute of limitations period expired at the latest five years after birth.

18. Donny Defendant is intentionally swinging a baseball bat. Percy Plaintiff walks up behind Donny without Donny's knowledge. Donny swings the bat again thereby striking Percy. What cause of action will lie?

(A) Negligence.

(B) Battery.

(C) Assault.

(D) Trespass.

19. Donny Defendant needs to get Polly Plaintiff's attention. He gently taps her on the shoulder. Polly falls to the ground screaming in pain. It turns out that she had a latent infection at the very spot Donny touched her. As a result, bone exfoliation began causing more pain and a renewed infection. In order for Polly to succeed in a suit for an intentional tort, what at a minimum must she prove?

(A) That Donny intended to touch her.
(B) That Donny knew of the infection.
(C) That Donny intended to inflict pain.
(D) That Donny intended to inflict pain due to a prior grudge against Polly.

20. Polly Plaintiff is standing in the doorway of her ex-husband's house. From the living room the ex-husband shouts, "If you leave, you will regret it." What tort has the ex committed?

(A) Battery.
(B) Assault.
(C) False Imprisonment.
(D) None.

21. Donny points a pistol at Polly. What fact would exonerate Donny?

(A) Polly thought the pistol was unloaded.
(B) Donny intended it as a joke.
(C) The pistol was actually unloaded.
(D) Donny knew the pistol was unloaded.

22. Which set of circumstances does not establish a claim for false imprisonment?

(A) Defendant shoves Plaintiff into a closet and locks the door.
(B) Plaintiff is in a moving car and the doors are unlocked. Defendant refuses to stop and let Plaintiff out as Plaintiff has requested.
(C) Defendant steps into Plaintiff's path and grabs her arm refusing to allow her to leave.
(D) Defendant shoves Plaintiff into a closet and locks the door. There is an unlocked door on the other side of the closet.

23. Donny Defendant hates Paul Plaintiff. Donny sees Paul with his back turned to Donny. Donny picks up a stick and swings at Paul's head. Just before contact, Paul bends down to tie his shoe. Donny misses and runs away. Paul's companion tells him that Donny tried to beat him. Paul becomes very frightened and shaken and faints. What tort has Donny committed?

(A) Assault.
(B) Battery.
(C) Infliction of emotional distress.
(D) None.

24. For which of the following will Plaintiff need to prove actual damages in a trespass to land action?

(A) Defendant flies over Plaintiff's house at low altitude.
(B) Defendant chases several children onto Plaintiff's property.
(C) Defendant is walking along the property line on his side when a bear charges him. He jumps onto Plaintiff's property to escape.
(D) Defendant refuses to leave Plaintiff's property when ordered to do so.

25. For which of the following situations will the Defendant be liable for damages in trespass?

(A) Defendant cuts down trees believing the trees were on his side of the property line, but they were actually on Plaintiff's property.
(B) Defendant enters Plaintiff's property to rescue a child drowning in Plaintiff's pond.
(C) Defendant enters Plaintiff's property to dam a flooding creek that would have damaged a town downstream.
(D) Defendant is carried onto Plaintiff's property.

26. In which of the following situations is Defendant liable for damages?

(A) Defendant mistakenly picks up Plaintiff's suitcase. Defendant returns it to Plaintiff within two minutes after realizing the mistake. Plaintiff did not notice that the suitcase was missing.

(B) Defendant leans against Plaintiff's car causing scratches that cost only $20 to repair.

(C) Defendant is shoved into Plaintiff's car causing major dents costing $2,000 to repair.

(D) Defendant moves Plaintiff's personal property to one side to allow an ambulance access to an alley.

27. Sam Shopkeeper operated a retail store in Roughville. Sam ran a good operation and tried to provide his customers with quality products at a fair price. Carefree Capone worked for the local mob and had been trying to persuade Sam to make monthly cash payoffs for protection. Carefree came into the store just before closing and began to rough up Sam. Sam's young assistant, Ernest, had gone to the bank to make the daily deposit and in the money sack there was a pistol. As Ernest walked back into the store, he saw Carefree beating his boss's head. Ernest pulled the gun from the money sack and said, "Stop that or I will shoot you." If Carefree sues Ernest for assault, the claim will likely

(A) Prevail, unless Ernest is related to Sam.

(B) Prevail, because threatening to use a gun is excess force against fists.

(C) Not prevail, if Carefree was about to inflict serious bodily harm on Sam.

(D) Not prevail, since Carefree was the person who started the attack.

28. Terry Thief stole a diamond ring from Owner who left it on a shelf while washing her hands in a public restroom. Owner saw Terry leave and chased her yelling, "Stop, thief!" Terry ran into her house and Owner broke the door down to get in. If Terry sues Owner, the likely outcome is

(A) For Owner, if Terry used unreasonable force in defending

the chattel.

(B) For Terry, if Owner used reasonable force in recapturing the chattel.

(C) For Terry, because owner trespassed without permission or a valid license.

(D) For Owner, if non-deadly force was used in hot pursuit of the stolen chattel.

29. Defendant lived in Reasonable City, USA. One evening, she drove recklessly through town. To whom did Defendant not owe a duty to drive safely?

(A) Another driver on the road.

(B) The mayor of the city.

(C) A pedestrian crossing the street.

(D) A passenger in Defendant's car.

30. Plaintiff Patient sees Defendant Doctor concerning an enlarged prostate gland. The Doctor recommends removal of the prostate gland. A side effect of the recommended procedure is the Patient's possible impotence. Which option is the weakest argument the Doctor could make in response to an accusation of malpractice?

(A) The Patient would have undergone the procedure even if he knew impotence would result.

(B) The Doctor explained the procedure and all possible side effects including impotence.

(C) The Patient signed an informed consent form acknowledging that he had been counseled on the side effects of and alternatives to the procedure.

(D) The Doctor never counseled the Patient on the possible side effect of impotence because impotence was not foreseeable until the Doctor was operating and realized that due to Patient's peculiar anatomy impotence could result.

31. Patient is a member of a religion that believes it is sinful to administer or receive a blood transfusion. Patient is in a car accident and arrives at the hospital unconscious. A blood transfusion is needed to save his life. If the doctor administers a blood transfusion, is he liable for battery?

(A) Yes, because a reasonable person of Patient's religion would not have consented.

(B) Yes, but only if there are adverse consequences such as the patient acquiring Hepatitis.

(C) No, because a reasonable person would have consented to a blood transfusion.

(D) No, unless there was an alternative to saving the patient's life.

32. Plaintiff hires Attorney regarding a possible lawsuit against a Doctor for malpractice. Proof of causation of Plaintiff's injuries is very thin, but it does exist. The attorney fails to file the lawsuit prior to the statute of limitations. What must the Plaintiff prove in order to recover for malpractice?

(A) Nothing, because recovery is barred by the Statute of Limitations.

(B) That the Plaintiff would have recovered against the doctor.

(C) That the Doctor violated the local standard of care.

(D) That the attorney violated the local standard of care.

33. Doctor is driving down the road in his sports car when he happens upon an injury scene. He gratuitously renders aid to an injured person, but unfortunately the injured person's condition is made worse by the doctor. What result in most jurisdictions if the injured person sues the Doctor?

(A) If the Doctor was negligent, the injured person will recover for increase in injuries.

(B) No recovery, because the Doctor was uncompensated.

(C) No recovery, because the injured person was not the Doctor's patient.

(D) The injured person will recover, because a doctor is strictly liable for the result of negligence.

Questions 34 and 35 are based on the following:

Plaintiff is on board his private yacht "Peerless." Captain Hook comes by in his powerboat, the wake of which swamps the Peerless. Plaintiff puts out a mayday call.

34. Rescuer 1 responds by radio assuring Peerless that he will attempt rescue. Rescuer 2 hears Rescuer 1's response and decides not to attempt rescue since 1 is closer to Peerless. Rescuer 1 encounters engine trouble and abandons the rescue and puts out a radio call of that fact. Rescuer 2 is now the closest vessel, but decides not to rescue. Who is liable for Plaintiff's injuries?

(A) Capt. Hook only.

(B) Capt. Hook and Rescuer 1.

(C) Capt. Hook and Rescuer 2.

(D) Capt. Hook, Rescuer 1, and Rescuer 2.

35. Same facts as above except that Capt. Hook, seeing the danger which he has created, comes to the aid of the plaintiff. However, during the rescue Capt. Hook causes personal injury to Plaintiff. What result if Plaintiff sues Capt. Hook?

(A) Capt. Hook is liable for damages from the swamping of the Peerless, but not for personal injuries to Plaintiff because Capt. Hook was acting as a Good Samaritan.

(B) Capt. Hook is liable for both damages to Peerless and injury to Plaintiff.

(C) Capt. Hook is not liable for any damages because he was a Good Samaritan.

(D) Capt. Hook is liable for personal injuries to Plaintiff, but not damage to Peerless.

36. Plaintiff was injured on Defendant's property when she falls into a large, unguarded hole that Defendant has dug for a future well. No warning signs were posted. Under what circumstance will Defendant not be liable for Plaintiff's injuries?

    (A) Plaintiff is an adult who wandered onto Defendant's property by accident.

    (B) Plaintiff is an adult who ran onto Defendant's property to save a crying child who had previously fallen into the hole.

    (C) Plaintiff is a police officer called by Defendant to check for prowlers.

    (D) Plaintiff is a member of Defendant's gardening club, on the property for a monthly meeting.

37. In which situation would the Defendant not be liable for the Plaintiff's injuries?

    (A) Plaintiff is a child who drowns in a koi fishpond that Defendant had just finished constructing.

    (B) Plaintiff is a child who slips on some algae-covered rocks while attempting to cross a natural stream on Defendant's property.

    (C) Plaintiff is an adult friend of Defendant's on the premises with permission, who falls through a rotted floor in Defendant's home.

    (D) Plaintiff is an insurance salesman who falls down the porch stairs because of a missing step.

38. A small child trespasses onto Defendant's property and is injured when her leg is caught in a bear trap set by Defendant. In which situation will damages be allowed?

    (A) Defendant set the trap to "teach pesky trespassers a lesson."

    (B) Defendant lives in a fortress, and his entire property is surrounded by a 12 foot electrified fence.

    (C) The child is 16 years old and had been trying to trip the trap with a stick.

    (D) Defendant lives in the middle of 200 acres of wilderness and has

never seen another person enter his property.

39. Plaintiff is severely bitten by Defendant's pet bobcat. What result if Plaintiff sues Defendant?

    (A) No recovery, if Plaintiff antagonized the cat by chanting its name.

    (B) No recovery, if Defendant took every precaution to prevent the cat from harming anyone, including having its teeth and claws removed.

    (C) Plaintiff will recover, because Defendant is strictly liable for the injuries caused by his pet.

    (D) Plaintiff will recover only if he can prove that Defendant knew that the bobcat was unfriendly.

40. Defendant's dog bites Plaintiff. Which of the following is least correct?

    (A) Defendant will only be liable if his dog had previously actually bitten someone.

    (B) If Plaintiff is an adult trespasser onto Defendant's property, Defendant will not be liable even if his dog had previously bitten someone.

    (C) Defendant will not be strictly liable if he was unaware of his dog's dangerous propensities.

    (D) Defendant will not be liable if his dog had never before demonstrated dangerous propensities and Plaintiff was bitten after she had broken open the dog's kennel and let the dog out.

41. In which situation would Defendant be liable for the injuries caused by a drunk driver?

    (A) Defendant was a bartender who had served the drunk driver a beer eight hours earlier.

    (B) Defendant was a cashier at a convenience store who sold a six-pack of beer to the driver who later became drunk.

(C) The drunk driver became intoxicated after drinking vodka martinis at a friend's Superbowl party.

(D) Defendant was a bartender who served the drunk driver his 12th drink after witnessing the driver stumble over a bar stool and weave his way up to the bar.

42. In which scenario is the statutory violation the strongest evidence of negligence in a claim by Plaintiff?

(A) Plaintiff was a pedestrian in a crosswalk who was hit by Defendant's car after Defendant failed to properly stop at the crosswalk.

(B) Plaintiff was a person in a nearby coffee shop who suffered emotional distress after witnessing her daughter hit by Defendant in the crosswalk.

(C) Defendant lost control of his car after it blew one of its tires, hitting Plaintiff. At the time of the accident, Defendant had been driving with a suspended license.

(D) Defendant's car hit Plaintiff as Plaintiff was riding his bike on the sidewalk. Massive snow accumulation prevented Defendant from safely proceeding on the street as required by statute.

43. Which is a correct statement regarding proof of breach?

(A) Although a jury decides what really happened, it is ultimately up to a judge to decide whether a breach of duty occurred.

(B) Proof of breach need not be shown under the res ipsa loquitur doctrine.

(C) To establish res ipsa loquitur, Plaintiff must prove the injury was the type that would not occur in the absence of someone's negligence and that Defendant had notice that such an injury might occur.

(D) Res ipsa loquitur establishes Plaintiff's prima facie case for negligence against Defendant.

44. In which situation will Defendant be liable for Plaintiff's injuries?

(A) Defendant installed defective brakes on driver's car. Driver negligently fails to see Plaintiff and hits him without braking.

(B) Defendant sets off a firecracker at the same time that engineer detonates a bomb. A horse is frightened and hits Plaintiff. Either sound alone would have been sufficient to frighten the horse.

(C) Defendant negligently parks his car by a fire hydrant. An automobile later collides with it so that Plaintiff is injured.

(D) Defendant negligently fails to supply its plane with sufficient fuel. The pilot is forced to make an emergency landing. The plane is then hijacked and a passenger is killed.

45. Defendant was angry that motorcycles were speeding down the public road in front of his house, so he strung a rope across the public road. Plaintiff was later injured when he rode his bike into the rope after not paying attention to where he was going. What result if Plaintiff sues Defendant?

(A) No recovery if the accident occurred in a contributory fault state.

(B) No recovery if Defendant can prove that Plaintiff saw the rope and had an opportunity to avoid the accident.

(C) Plaintiff can recover 100% of his injuries if the accident occurred in a comparative fault state.

(D) Plaintiff can recover in a comparative fault state only if she can show that Defendant was reckless.

46. Under what circumstance would Plaintiff not be able to recover in most pure comparative fault jurisdictions?

- (A) If Plaintiff was 51% at fault in causing the accident.
- (B) If Plaintiff was more at fault than any one Defendant.
- (C) If Plaintiff failed to mitigate her damages.
- (D) If Plaintiff was driving drunk and 51% at fault in causing the accident.

47. Plaintiff falls into an 8-foot-deep hole dug by Defendant. The hole had been left uncovered and without warning signs. In which scenario will Defendant be able to invoke the defense of assumption of risk?

- (A) Plaintiff fell into the hole because she was not paying attention to where she was going.
- (B) Plaintiff saw the hole but thought it would be fun to jump over it.
- (C) The hole was filled with water and Plaintiff deliberately stepped into it thinking it was a shallow mud puddle.
- (D) Mentally handicapped Plaintiff saw the hole but deliberately attempted to jump over it.

48. Defendant negligently served patron a hamburger containing contaminated meat that had passed its expiration date. The patron became ill and was rushed to the hospital. Because he was in the hospital, patron was unable to pick his daughter up from school. The daughter was later hit by a bus as she attempted to walk home. What result if daughter sues Defendant?

- (A) Plaintiff will recover because the tainted meat was a cause-in-fact of her injuries.
- (B) Plaintiff will recover from Defendant in an amount proportionate to his fault.
- (C) Plaintiff will not recover because patron's consumption of the tainted meat was not a proximate cause of her injuries.

- (D) Plaintiff will recover but her recovery will be reduced by the amount of her comparative fault.

49. Defendant negligently causes an accident in which Plaintiff is injured. Defendant will be liable for Plaintiff's initial injuries as well as her enhanced injures in all but which of the following circumstances?

- (A) Plaintiff is taken to a hospital where the doctor mistakenly removes the wrong kidney.
- (B) A person comes to the scene of the accident and negligently pulls Plaintiff out of the car without securing her neck. Plaintiff is rendered paraplegic.
- (C) The accident aggravates Plaintiff's pre-existing heart condition and she suffers a heart attack and dies.
- (D) As Plaintiff is being loaded into the ambulance she is bitten by a mosquito and develops West Nile Virus. She later dies from complications from the disease.

50. Which set of circumstances establishes a claim for misrepresentation?

- (A) A car salesman tells Plaintiff that the car is the most reliable model that they sell. Plaintiff buys the car which soon after blows a head gasket.
- (B) Same facts as in A, but Plaintiff knew that the car was not reliable because he had just thoroughly reviewed the car in a buying guide.
- (C) Defendant is a pediatrician who is asked at a bus stop to look at Plaintiff's mole. He tells Plaintiff that it is nothing to worry about. Plaintiff is later diagnosed with skin cancer.
- (D) Defendant is a real estate agent who is desperate for a commission. She falsely tells Plaintiff that the house is already connected to the city sewer. Plaintiff buys the house and later has to pay $5,000 to connect the house to the sewer.

51. Which of the following is a correct statement regarding damages for misrepresentation?

(A) Plaintiff need not prove actual damages if he can demonstrate that Defendant intended to deceive him.

(B) The proper remedy for misrepresentation is the value of the benefit of the bargain.

(C) The burden is on Defendant to prove Plaintiff suffered no damages.

(D) If Plaintiff is unable to calculate actual damages the judge may make an assessment that she deems to be fair.

52. A driver comes to the crest of a hill and his car stalls. He signals to the driver behind that it is safe to pass. The passing driver is hit by an oncoming vehicle as he attempts to pass. What tort has Defendant committed?

(A) Negligent misrepresentation.

(B) Fraud in the inducement.

(C) Misrepresentation.

(D) Fraudulent concealment.

53. Which of the following activities will not give rise to strict liability for injuries?

(A) Imploding a skyscraper office building.

(B) Operating a wildlife safari.

(C) Designing a defective propane tank that is prone to exploding.

(D) Selling a defective propane tank at a garage sale.

54. In which situation is Defendant most likely to be held strictly liable for Plaintiff's injuries?

(A) Defendant's mongoose jumps from his moving vehicle. Plaintiff swerves to avoid it and collides with another vehicle.

(B) Defendant is driving a truck filled with toxic sludge. He falls asleep at the wheel and collides with Plaintiff, damaging the bumper on her car.

(C) Defendant is Plaintiff's employer. Plaintiff is injured at work when she slips on an oil spill.

(D) Plaintiff paints the interior walls of her business with paint that Defendant manufactured. The paint smells so bad that Plaintiff loses all of her customers to the competition. Plaintiff later files for bankruptcy and sues Defendant for damages.

55. The airbag in Plaintiff's car failed to inflate properly and Plaintiff suffered extensive injuries in an accident. Plaintiff sued the manufacturer under a strict liability standard for a manufacturing defect. Which of the following is the manufacturer's best defense?

(A) The manufacturer employed the best quality control standards in the industry and there was no way to have detected the particular defect.

(B) The defect was not present when the automobile left the plant, but rather was introduced sometime later by someone else.

(C) Plaintiff was traveling at an excessive rate of speed at the time of the collision, impairing the ability of the airbags to function.

(D) The manufacturer provided adequate warnings to consumers of the possibility of air bag failure.

56. Which one of the following constitutes a design defect?

(A) A hammer that is prone to smashing fingers.

(B) An automobile windshield that breaks into sharp shards of glass upon impact.

(C) A new AIDS drug that causes hair to fall out.

(D) A car roof that collapses when the car rolls.

57. Plaintiff is injured in an automobile accident when thrown from his vehicle due to a defective door latch. Plaintiff sues the automobile manufacturer. Which of the following is Defendant's best defense in a strict products liability action?

- (A) Plaintiff could have avoided the injury by locking the door.
- (B) Plaintiff operated a shuttle service using the car. For that reason, the car door was opened and closed far more often than is typical for that type of car.
- (C) Plaintiff could have discovered the defect had he performed an inspection of the door mechanism.
- (D) A recall was issued over a year ago notifying all purchasers of the defect. Plaintiff failed to have the door latch replaced.

58. Noise, smoke and odor from Defendant's factory seriously interfere with Plaintiff's use and enjoyment of a neighboring public park. In a nuisance suit, will neighbor recover?

- (A) Yes, for the diminution in value to the park.
- (B) No, if the value of the factory to the community far outweighs the inconvenience to Plaintiff.
- (C) No, because Plaintiff's harm is not substantial.
- (D) No, because Plaintiff's injuries are not different from those of the rest of the community.

59. Which of the following Plaintiffs is most likely to succeed in a nuisance suit?

- (A) Plaintiff cannot tolerate the noises of children playing in a new outdoor play yard due to her nervous condition.
- (B) Plaintiff's neighbor runs his loud lawn mower each afternoon for an hour.
- (C) Plaintiff's neighbor breeds outdoor cats who howl all day and all night long.
- (D) Plaintiff bought land next to a pig farm, not realizing how smelly they could be.

60. Which of the following statements are in themselves defamatory?

- (A) He picks his nose.
- (B) His face resembles an oyster.
- (C) He cheated on an exam.
- (D) He molested his children.

61. Defendant sends Plaintiff a letter accusing him of sexual misconduct. Plaintiff's spouse opens the letter and leaves Plaintiff as a result of the false facts in the communication. In a defamation suit, Plaintiff will

- (A) Prevail, because Defendant's accusation constitutes libel per se.
- (B) Not prevail, unless Defendant knew that Plaintiff's wife was in the habit of opening Plaintiff's mail.
- (C) Not prevail, unless Defendant made the accusation with knowledge of its falsity.
- (D) Not prevail, because there is an absolute interspousal immunity.

62. Defendant accuses Plaintiff of stealing from him. Plaintiff sues Defendant for defamation. Which of the following statements is false?

- (A) Plaintiff will not prevail, if Defendant can prove that Plaintiff did steal from him.
- (B) Plaintiff will not prevail, if Defendant made the statement in a criminal court proceeding.
- (C) Plaintiff will not prevail, if Defendant made the statement in an attempt to recover goods stolen from him.
- (D) Plaintiff will not prevail, if Defendant made the statement in an attempt to recover his stolen goods, knowing the statement was false.

63. Which of the following is false?

- (A) Truth is not a defense to the tort of publication of private facts.
- (B) Damages for the tort of commercial appropriation of likeness is determined by the actual commercial losses suffered by Plaintiff.

(C) The tort of publication in a false light requires that Defendant intentionally publicized a false attribution which cast a highly offensive false light on Plaintiff.

(D) The tort of intrusion requires that the intrusion be highly offensive to a reasonable person.

64. Under which circumstance will an action for interference with contract lie?

(A) Defendant was aware that Betty had signed a one-year contract to provide daycare services for Plaintiff. Defendant offers Betty twice the pay if she will care for Defendant's son instead. Betty breaks her contract with Plaintiff.

(B) Defendant was angry with Plaintiff for not coming to her party and for gossiping about her. Defendant tells Betty that Plaintiff is impossible to work for and probably won't be able to pay her. These comments induce Betty to break her contract with Plaintiff.

(C) Same facts as in B, but Betty and Plaintiff had not yet agreed to the terms of the one-year contract.

(D) Betty hears from a friend that Defendant is paying twice as much for daycare and breaks her contract with Plaintiff.

65. Under which circumstance will an action for product disparagement lie?

(A) Defendant runs a newspaper advertisement which falsely states that 90% of people taking the competitor's medication have severe side effects.

(B) Same facts as in A. Plaintiff goes out of business and Defendant sees a substantial increase in sales volume in the following year.

(C) Same facts as in A. Defendant establishes that indeed, 90% of people taking competitor's medication have severe side effects.

(D) Defendant runs a newspaper advertisement that accurately claims that 9 out of 10 people that tested the product preferred Defendant's product over the competition.

66. Which of the following is false?

(A) To succeed in a malicious criminal prosecution proceeding, Plaintiff must be acquitted at trial on the merits.

(B) A claim for wrongful civil proceeding will lie if the lawsuit lacked a reasonable factual basis.

(C) Defendant slanders the title of Plaintiff's real property where Defendant files a lien attachment because Plaintiff failed to pay back a secured loan.

(D) Defendant commits an abuse of process where he uses the legal process to accomplish a goal unrelated to the legal proceeding at issue.

Torts
Practice Questions

67. Perfect Beach was a popular seaside resort city whose economic viability depended upon tourists staying in the seaside hotels and condominiums. During a week in May, the beach experienced a perfect storm which deposited massive boulders on the sandy beach. The municipality hired Rock Crusher Inc. to grind up the boulders into sand and thereby recreate the pristine sand beach. Grinding started on July 1 at the height of the tourist season. Rock Crusher's grinding machine made very loud noises that the tourists found very disturbing.

The tourists staying at Perfect Beach left and new guests refused to check into the condominiums and hotels. A large hotel on the beach lost more money than the other businesses. If the hotel seeks to recover their financial losses from Rock Crusher

Inc. and the municipality, their best theory of recovery is likely
    (A) Negligence.
    (B) Public nuisance.
    (C) Private nuisance.
    (D) Abnormal and dangerous activity.

68. Frank Fister was drinking beer with a number of his fraternity brothers on a Friday evening. As the evening progressed, some of the group began to shadow box. This game involved real sparring, but the body and face blows were very light – little more than a touching. Timothy Timid, a new fraternity pledge, was sitting in the corner drinking his beer when they announced that the shadow boxing was going to begin and any non-participants should leave the room.

One of the brothers picked Timothy up and pushed him into the middle of the room. Frank was bouncing around the room and tapped Timothy lightly on the chin to annoy him. Frank did not intend to hurt him, but unknown to anyone, Timothy had just recovered from complicated facial surgery because of a serious automobile accident and had a "glass jaw." Frank's tap broke Timothy's jaw and he sued Frank for battery. Frank's best defense is that
    (A) He did not intend to injure Timothy.
    (B) If Timothy had a normal jaw, no damage would have resulted from the tap.
    (C) Timothy consented to the damage by not leaving the room when the fighting began.
    (D) Timothy assumed the risk by not leaving the room when the fighting began.

Questions 69 and 70 are based on the following:

Sharon Shannydresser was a Monday night customer in the local mall outlet of a 40,000 square foot retail store named Spectacular Outfits. Sharon started shopping at 8:30 P.M. The store closed at 9:00 P.M. Sharon took three full outfits into the dressing room at 8:40 P.M. At 8:55 P.M. the store manager decided to close a little early and locked all the doors at 8:59 P.M. The clerk who had waited on Sharon forgot she was still in the dressing room. Sharon took over 2 hours trying on every combination of all three full outfits. At 10:40 P.M. Sharon became very tired and laid down on a couch in the dressing room for a quick nap. She slept until 7:00 A.M. Tuesday morning when she was awakened by the sound of employees opening the store. Sharon then learned about her confinement and she decided to file a legal claim.

69. If Sharon sues Spectacular Outfits for false imprisonment seeking nominal damages, the Defendant's worst defense is
    (A) The store manager did not know he was confining Sharon.
    (B) Sharon had no knowledge of her confinement.
    (C) Sharon can show no actual damages.
    (D) The false imprisonment did not set physical boundaries since she could have walked around the store.

70. After a legal analysis, Sharon's lawyer advised her that the false imprisonment claim might be better pleaded under a theory of negligence using a claim called negligent containment. Spectacular's best defense is
    (A) Sharon was partially at fault under the state comparable negligence proportional statute.
    (B) Sharon assumed the risk by staying in the dressing room after 9:00 P.M.
    (C) The manager never saw or knew of Sharon's presence, so no harm was foreseeable.
    (D) It was not negligent to omit checking the dressing room before locking the door.

71. Carol Compass and Harriet Hikers were good friends who frequently went on mountain hiking trips together. One trip was a 10-mile backpacking exercise into a beautiful alpine lake named Packwood Lake. They hiked to the lake one hot day each carrying a 50-pound backpack. They were both very tired by the time they arrived at the lake. Carol took off her pack and jumped into the lake to cool off. She swam out into the middle of the lake where she experienced a severe leg cramp. She cried out for help; Harriet heard her but was tired herself and unsure of her ability to swim out there and back. As a result, she failed to act and Carol drowned. If Carol's heirs bring suit against Harriet, the likely outcome is the suit will

(A) Prevail, if Carol and Harriet are determined to have been engaged in a common pursuit so they are considered co-venturers.

(B) Not prevail, because an uncompensated party has no duty to rescue.

(C) Not prevail, because Harriet did not cause the risk.

(D) Prevail, unless Harriet told Carol that she thought it was a bad idea for her to go swimming.

72. Doug Dragger and his wife Sue were driving their fully restored 1932 Ford "duces" roadster convertible on a Sunday afternoon. Doug was very proud of his Ford restoration and he and his wife often dressed in 1950 style clothes when they attended antique car events in Boston. They were going west on Commonwealth Avenue and Doug was not paying careful attention. Sarah Speeder was going north to Cambridge on Backbay Avenue and because she was not paying attention, she failed to stop at a stop sign and collided with the Draggers' car, injuring Sue. Had Doug been more alert, he might have been able to swerve or stop in time to avoid the accident. If Sue Dragger brings suit against both her husband and Sarah for her injuries, Sue will

(A) Not prevail against her husband because of intra-family immunity.

(B) Prevail against her husband only if Sarah is determined to have no fault.

(C) Prevail against both her husband and Sarah in proportion to their relative fault.

(D) Prevail against her husband and Sarah for joint and several liability.

Questions 73 and 74 are based on the following:

Luke Landlord owned an apartment building with 12 individual apartments. The building had a common entrance containing a large common lobby with a fireplace that the tenants sometimes used for parties. Daniel Dogowner was one of the new tenants in the building. The lease contract did not address use of the lobby area, but did contain a clause requiring no noisy parties. There was also no mention of whether the tenants could have dogs as pets, but Luke was aware that another tenant had a small cat.

On December 31, 2004, three of the tenants decided to host a party in the lobby area. As the evening went on, a lot of alcohol was consumed and the party grew quite noisy. At 1:00 a.m., one of the tenants started a fight that escalated into a brawl. A guest partier was seriously injured by the brawl.

73. The injured guest brought suit against Luke Landlord for his injury. The least effective defense is

(A) The landlord did not know the tenants were going to hold a party on December 31, 2004.

(B) The landlord did not give the tenants permission to hold the party.

(C) The party was held in a common area of the apartment building.

(D) The party injured was not a tenant.

74. Daniel decided to buy a Rottweiler dog that he considered very cuddly. Unfortunately, the Rottweiler, who seemed to have a mean streak, attacked and seriously injured a neighbor boy. The neighbor boy who was injured by the Rottweiler dog sues Luke Landlord. The likely outcome is that the suit will

(A) Prevail because injuries from a Rottweiler dog is strict liability.

(B) Not prevail because a landlord is not usually liable for a tenant's dog injuries to third parties.

(C) Not prevail unless the injury occurred on Luke's property.

(D) Prevail because the Rottweiler dog was housed in Luke's property and thus is a latent defect.

75. Larry's Lawnmowers Inc. sold new and used lawnmowers to a variety of retail customers. Nancy New came into the store and purchased a new electric lawnmower. The store gave her a $50 trade-in on an old gasoline lawnmower she had in her garage that had not been used for years. Larry's mechanics inspected the machine and determined that the connector between the drive shaft and the rotary blade had worn out and that the blade could fly off if the mower was started. The store put a "for sale" sign on the mower and wrote on the sign "AS IS – may be dangerous if operated – $20."

Mike Motor paid $20 for the mower because he wanted to use the gasoline motor to power a home electrical generator. Before taking the motor off the mower, Mike started it up to see how it ran. The blade flipped out, seriously cutting Mike's ankle. If Mike sues Larry's Lawnmower Inc. for his injuries, the court will likely find for

(A) Mike, because the lawnmower was not fit for its ordinary purpose.

(B) Larry, because Mike purchased the title to the lawnmower "as is."

(C) Larry, if Mike had the last clear chance to avoid the injury.

(D) Mike, if it was unreasonable for Larry's to sell the lawnmower without a detailed warning of the drive shaft problem.

Questions 76 and 77 are based on the following:

Harry Homeowner was putting new tar and shingles on the roof of his house. Rather than hiring a roofing contractor, he decided to do all the work himself on the weekends. One Saturday morning, he was up on his roof and had just completed putting the tar on one side. The 50 pound heavy steel tar bucket was almost empty. Without looking, Harry threw it over the side of the house.

Nathan Neighbor was standing just inside Harry's property watching Harry's activities on the roof. Harry saw Nathan watching him on the roof. Unfortunately, the heavy steel tar bucket thrown by Harry hit Nathan on the head. Nathan cried out in pain as he fell to the ground. His head struck the sidewalk and he was rendered unconscious. Harry heard Nathan's cry, but since he did not particularly like Nathan anyway, decided to begin putting the shingles on that side of the roof even though he could have called 911 on his cell phone.

Rosalind Rescuer was a passing driver who saw the whole event. She immediately loaded Nathan into her car and began driving to the closest medical center. During the trip, Rosalind was distracted by the news she received in a cell phone call from her daughter and negligently ran into a highway concrete divider. In his weakened state, Nathan died in the crash.

76. The personal representative of Nathan's estate sued Harry Homeowner asserting that he was negligent in failing to lend assistance after he knew he had just created an injury was negligent. Which of the following is most correct?

(A) Nathan was an uninvited trespasser who trespassed at his own peril.

(B) A landowner owes no duty to assist a trespasser.

(C) By coming onto the land knowing that roofing operations were going on, Nathan assumed the risk of injury.

(D) Harry's refusal to call for assistance was not a factual cause of harm to Nathan.

77. The personal representative of Nathan's estate sues Rosalind Rescuer for wrongful death. The most likely outcome of the suit is that the suit will

(A) Prevail, if the jury finds that Rosalind acted unreasonably for a rescuer in the emergency situation.

(B) Not prevail, since Rosalind was a mere uncompensated bystander with no duty to rescue an injured party.

(C) Not prevail, since a rescuer in an emergency is not held to a reasonable care standard.

(D) Not prevail, since a normal uninjured victim would not have died in the accident.

78. Sharon Stampcollector and Ellen Expert were in New York's largest stamp shop one afternoon. The clerk laid out on the counter 50 premier stamps the store had just purchased in bulk. Sharon and Ellen immediately began looking through the 50 stamps for bargains. Ellen told the counter clerk that a US 1899 1¢ stamp was worth $1,000 because it was printed with a reverse waterpress. She then offered $750 for it. The clerk refused the offer and Ellen left. Sharon overheard the negotiations and had previously read about the expertise of Ellen Expert in valuing old U.S. stamps. She offered the clerk $900 for the 1899 1¢ stamp which was accepted. Later it was determined that the stamp was not the reverse waterpress, but rather just a normally printed 1899 stamp worth very little. If Sharon sues Ellen for misrepresentation or deceit, the best defense that Ellen could offer is

(A) The value of a rare stamp is an opinion, not a fact.

(B) There was no intention to deceive Sharon.

(C) There was no reliance upon the statements of Ellen.

(D) The Plaintiff did not suffer damages resulting from reliance on Ellen's statements.

79. Billy Boozer was out on the town for a party. He had been to a number of bars before he stopped in at Drift On Inn Bar & Grill at midnight. The jurisdiction had a statute which prohibited serving liquor to any intoxicated person. The bartender suspected Billy was intoxicated, but because Billy was a regular, he served him two beers anyway. Billy prided himself on being a responsible drunk driver.

The bottles of beer served Billy were from a new case. Unknown to the bartender, there had been a freak mistake at the bottler and the toxic solvent used to clean the bottling equipment had been put in one of the beer bottles Billy drank. The toxic solvent was colorless, had no smell or taste, and would have required a laboratory test to discover.

Billy left the bar and began driving carefully and reasonably home. Ten minutes later the toxic solvent ruptured his kidneys, causing Billy to pass out. Out of control, Billy's car ran into Phillip Pedestrian. If Phillip brings suit against Drift On Inn, the most effective argument Drift On Inn could make would be

(A) The two beers served Billy did not contain enough alcohol to make him intoxicated.

(B) Serving the two beers to Billy was not the cause-in-fact of Phillip Pedestrian's injury.

(C) The jurisdiction's statute was not intended to prevent injuries from people drinking beer that contained toxic poison.

(D) The mistake at the bottler was a superseding cause of the injury in question.

80. Sobriety Forever was a city with a statute which stated, "any business or individual who sells alcoholic beverages to a minor shall be liable to any party injured by that minor while intoxicated." Dick Drinker was only 17 but had a mature look and a beard, which allowed him to enter a few bars. He liked to go out on the town and get drunk. This evening he spent all night in two bars named Tuesday's and Friday's. After two drinks at Tuesday's, Dick became relaxed and one of his friends talked him into going to Friday's. Upon leaving Friday's, he got into an accident because of his intoxication. Tuesday's did not serve Dick enough alcohol to make him intoxicated and the alcohol that Friday's served Dick would have been enough to make him intoxicated even if Tuesday's had not served him at all. If the injured party sues, the court should hold that

(A) Tuesday's is liable under the statute even if their conduct did not cause Dick to become intoxicated.
(B) Tuesday's conduct was a cause of Dick's intoxication, but not a cause of the injury because his driving superseded their violation.
(C) Tuesday's conduct was not the cause of Dick's intoxication because Friday's conduct was a substantial factor in making him intoxicated.
(D) Tuesday's conduct was a cause of the injury because Dick would not have become intoxicated if Tuesday's did not sell him the alcohol.

81. Larry Lone Ranger, an off-duty police officer, was sitting in his pickup and observed a masked man, Ryan Robber, running out of a bank carrying money bags and a shotgun. Larry had just heard on his police radio that a robber had knocked off the bank and shot two tellers. Larry grabbed a rifle off his truck gun rack. As Ryan ran by, Larry yelled, "Stop or I'll shoot." Ryan heard him, crouched down and fired off a round at Larry. Larry took careful aim and shot Ryan at 20 paces. The bullet hit Ryan in the heart immediately killing him. If Ryan's personal representative brings suit for battery, the least effective defense is that Larry Lone Ranger believed the fleeing suspect

(A) Posed a threat of death to him.
(B) Had just committed a felony.
(C) Posed a threat of serious physical injury to others.
(D) Had evidenced significant "serious dangerousness" due to the weapon and shot aimed at him.

82. Billy Bully started a fist fight with another 10-year-old boy named Jack DeLong whom Billy thought was a weakling. Unknown to Billy, Jack had been working out with weights and had developed into a very good fighter. Ike Intervenor, a large 25-year-old was out for a walk. As Ike turned the corner of the block, he saw Jack strike Billy twice. Billy fell back and Jack stepped forward to strike him again. Ike thought Jack was the aggressor and to protect Billy, he stepped in and threw Jack into the bushes. Jack's arm was broken and he brought suit against Ike for his damages. Ike's best defense is

(A) He thought Jack was the initial aggressor.
(B) Billy had a valid defense if Jack sued him.
(C) The force Ike used was not excessive.
(D) He had no intention of injuring Jack, only to stop his beating of Billy.

83. Susan Swimmingpool lived in a house with a swimming pool in the back yard. The neighbor's 19-year-old son, Stan Swimmer, asked Susan if he could swim for free if he vacuumed the pool once a week. Susan agreed. Without mentioning it to Stan, Susan drained the pool in the morning so a tile worker could replace some cracked tiles. Stan came home at night after playing in a baseball game and wanted to cool off by going swimming. In the dark, Stan ran out to the end of the diving board and jumped in. Unfortunately, both of Stan's ankles were broken. The jurisdiction has a comparative fault (negligence) statute. If Stan asserts a claim against Susan, the likely outcome is that the claim should

(A) Prevail, because the pool was an artificial attractive nuisance.
(B) Not prevail, if a reasonable person in Stan's position would have known of the risk of diving into a swimming pool in the night in the dark.
(C) Not prevail, because Stan was a trespasser.
(D) Prevail, if it was unreasonable for Susan to drain the swimming pool without warning Stan.

84. Evan Experiment was a street person in Washington D.C. Evan saw a sign in a window of a medical clinic, seeking volunteers who would undergo a mild experimental surgical operation. The sign stated that volunteers would be paid $500 under a federal program. Evan walked in and volunteered for the surgery. Doctor Dave took Evan's application and made detailed disclosure of the medical risks involved. Evan signed a form consenting to experimental surgery. The surgery resulted in the medical complications that were explained to Evan. Unfortunately, the federal program funding had expired and Evan did not get paid. If Evan sues Doctor Dave and the medical clinic for battery, the likely outcome is

(A) Prevail if the doctor was negligent.
(B) Not prevail because Evan consented to the operation.
(C) Not prevail unless Doctor Dave knew the statement of $500 compensation was false.
(D) Prevail if Evan would not have consented to the operation if he knew the truth that the government program funding had run out.

85. Richard Realman was married to Louise Realman and they had a 16-year-old daughter named Denise Delinquent Realman. Richard's wife Louise met a romantic young man named Roger Ready at a Moonbuck's coffee store and fell hopelessly in love. Roger and Louise began to meet regularly, and Roger convinced Louise to leave Richard. Richard's daughter Denise reacted negatively to her parents' loss of affection for each other. She found solitude in a youth group called the Sunies. The Sunies convinced her to leave home, join their convent, and give the Sunie group all of her money. Richard hires a lawyer and brings suit against Roger Ready for criminal conversation and against the Sunies for alienation of his child's affection, a claim that is recognized in the jurisdiction. Richard's suit will probably

(A) Prevail against Roger for criminal conversation even if he cannot prove monetary damages.
(B) Prevail against Roger for criminal conversation only if he can prove monetary damages resulting from the loss from her earnings.
(C) Prevail against the Sunies for alienation of affection if he can prove they wrongfully caused his daughter to leave and not return home.
(D) Prevail against the Sunies for alienation of affection only if he can prove monetary damages.

Questions 86 and 87 are based on the following:

Waxford Manufacturing Company employed Frank Fairfax as a route salesman paid primarily on a commission basis. Frank was driving a company-owned car when a truck owned and operated by Red Van Lines collided with Frank's car. He was injured and applied for workers' compensation under state law. The state agency specified a certain dollar amount of damages for this type of injury.

86. Waxford receives notice from the State Worker's Compensation Fund regarding Frank's claim. Waxford realizes that if the state pays the claim, its assessed tax rate will increase, so Waxford wants to defeat Frank's claim. The best argument that Waxford can advance to deny Frank's claim is

(A) Any injuries suffered by Frank did not arise out of and in the course of employment.
(B) A route salesman paid on a commission basis is automatically deemed to be an independent contractor and therefore excluded from worker's compensation coverage.
(C) Frank himself was grossly negligent in driving, thus he assumed the risk of injury.
(D) The injury did not occur on the employer's premises and was due to the negligence of Red Van Lines.

87. Assume that the state worker's compensation department allowed Frank's claim. After receiving the benefits, Frank has asked your advice about suing Red Van Lines. Your advice is that Frank

(A) Must assign a negligence cause of action against Red Van Lines to Waxford Manufacturing pursuant to respondeat superior.
(B) Can recover in full against Red for any negligence that can be proven and retain the full amounts awarded him under worker's compensation.
(C) Can recover in full against Red for any negligence that can be proven but must return any duplication of the worker's compensation award.
(D) Is precluded from suing Red for negligence because of the worker's compensation award.

88. Robert Rifleman was a proud card-carrying member of the National Handguns Association. He was to receive an award from the Association for recruiting new members. The Association bought him a stun gun as an award, which he could use to chase crows out of his wife's garden. The stun gun he received emitted an electric pulsating charge that could paralyze an animal for up to five minutes. Robert's 15-year-old son, Robert Jr., begged his father to allow him to take the gun out with him on a Friday night. Robert finally agreed. Junior was hanging out with his friends when he spotted one of his schoolteachers. This teacher had just given Junior a D-grade in a civics class. Junior shot the teacher with the stun gun. He fell to the ground and received a serious concussion when his head hit a large rock. If the teacher brings suit against the father, the teacher's worst theory of recovering is

(A) The father facilitated the injury by providing a potentially dangerous instrumentality to the son.
(B) Respondeat Superior.
(C) The father knew of the son's dangerous propensities and failed to supervise them.
(D) The parents owned the instrumentality that created the damage.

89. Mountain Road Construction Co. specialized in building roads that required extensive blasting and explosives. Mountain had a warehouse containing large amounts of explosives. The warehouse was located close to an Alkada ranch where a "cell group" containing a large number of religious terrorists lived. On September 4, the terrorist cell members received a command that they were to begin to steal explosives because on September 11 there was to be massive attacks against American targets. One of the members of the terrorist cell was a counter agent for the U.S. government and he informed his supervisors that the cell members were going to break into Mountain's explosives warehouse that evening.

The local Police and Federal agents surrounded the warehouse and ordered the terrorist cell members to surrender. They refused, and instead committed mass suicide by detonating all the explosives in Mountain's warehouse. The explosion damaged a neighboring resident's building.

The resident asserted a claim for damages against Mountain. If the claim is based upon a theory that Mountain's storing of explosives was an abnormally dangerous activity, which of the following is Mountain's most effective argument in defense?

(A) The explosion creating the damages did not result from the failure to exercise reasonable care by Mountain.

(B) The damage to the building did not result from a physical invasion of the neighbor's property by Mountain.

(C) The conduct of the terrorists was an intervening cause of the harm.

(D) It was not reasonable foreseeable that terrorists would intentionally detonate explosives in Mountain's warehouse.

90. National Nuclear operated three nuclear power plants creating large amounts of electricity. The plant was located alongside Columbia River in what some scientists believed was an earthquake sensitive area. The nuclear plant's reactors generated a large amount of heat, which created a danger of explosion. To reduce this risk National pumped water from the Columbia and circulated it in the reactor equipment. After cooling, the water was highly radioactive and required extensive "cooling" to reduce the toxicity. The "hot" water was stored in large concrete holding tubs for a substantial time period before it was drained back into the Columbia River.

There was an unexpected earthquake and many of the concrete holding tubs cracked with massive amounts of water flooding Nancy Neighbor's adjoining farmland. If Nancy asserts a claim against National Nuclear for strict liability for an abnormally dangerous activity the court should find for

(A) National, because the unexpected earthquake was caused by an act of God.

(B) Nancy, because operating a nuclear power plant is an abnormally dangerous activity.

(C) Nancy, because it was unreasonable to operate a nuclear power plant in a geographic location where an earthquake could occur.

(D) Nancy, because "hot" water in a large quantity is an element that is foreseeably likely to create harm to neighbors if it should escape from its containers.

91. Sally Seller owned a two-story brick residence that she had listed for sale with a real estate firm. Betty Buyer made an offer on the house conditional upon inspection of the home. In a recent earthquake many of the bricks on the home became dangerously loose. Betty hired Iris Inspector to conduct an investigation of the house. Iris missed the hidden loose bricks. While Betty was unaware of the loose bricks, Sally knew of it from an investigation that the listing real estate firm conducted. After the sale closed and Betty moved in, a neighbor was walking alongside the house. There was a slight tremor and the neighbor was hit by falling bricks and was seriously injured. It was then that Betty discovered the loose bricks. If the neighbor brings suit against Sally and Betty, the likely outcome is that the neighbor will prevail against

(A) Sally, because she knew of the dangerously loose brick work.

(B) Betty, since a landowner is strictly liable for all harm neighbors suffer because of defects in the landowner's property.

(C) Both Sally and Betty.

(D) Neither Sally nor Betty.

92. David Driver was driving on an interstate to his home 200 miles away. At a road stop, Henry Hitchhiker came up to him and asked for a free ride. David agreed. Henry got in the driver's side back seat and promptly fell asleep. Unfortunately he did not fasten his seat belt. About 50 miles later, David also fell asleep and the car went off the road and ran into the ditch. The jurisdiction in question has a guest statute. If Henry sues David, the court will likely find for

(A) Henry if he can prove David failed to exercise ordinary care.
(B) David because Harry failed to fasten his seat belt.
(C) Henry only if he can prove David was grossly negligent or reckless.
(D) David because a hitchhiker assumes the risk.

93. Doug Dogman had a domesticated golden retriever named Retrieve. Retrieve was a good dog, friendly to the neighbors, but loved to run and chase. One evening when the sky was dark but the street lights had not yet come on, Retrieve began chasing cars going down the street. An 85-year-old woman named Ginny Grandmother was driving on the street. She spotted the dog and swerved to avoid hitting Retrieve. She hit a parked car and suffered injury. If Ginny brings suit against Doug Dogman under a strict liability theory, the court will likely find for

(A) Ginny, because Doug's dog was a cause in fact of Ginny's injuries.
(B) Doug, because Retriever is a domesticated animal.
(C) Doug, unless a statute or ordinance made it unlawful for an owner to permit a dog to be unleashed on a public street.
(D) Doug, because the strict liability rule for dogs would not include dogs not displaying vicious propensities.

94. Susan Shoplifter went into her local shopping mall wearing loose, baggy clothes. She entered a women's clothing store and began to try on numerous dress outfits for over two hours. The store clerk began to get suspicious and watched Susan closely. The last trying-on session began when Susan took three dresses into the dressing room. 10 minutes later, she came out and only put 2 dresses back on the store rack. The clerk noticed this and informed the store security guard. As Susan left the store the security guard arrested her. The guard then ordered her into the manager's office where many of her neighbors looked on her with ridicule. One hour later, a female security guard arrived and strip searched Susan discovering she did not hide the dress under her baggy clothes, but rather that the third dress was left in the dressing room. Susan was then released but later brought a false imprisonment claim against the store. If the jurisdiction has a typical shoplifter privilege statute, Susan's worst argument is

(A) The one-hour detention period was unreasonable.
(B) The clerk should have looked in the dressing room where she would have discovered the third dress.
(C) The detention should have been conducted in a room where she was not put up for public ridicule.
(D) She did not shoplift.

Questions 95 – 97 are based on the following:

Pleasant Town, USA operated a municipal utility department that provided water to all the homes and businesses in the city limits. One of the major water lines' inflow pipes ruptured underground thus decreasing the water pressure in that segment of the city. The Pleasant Town water department hired Fix It Inc. to repair the break. Fix It's repair crew located the break and excavated the ground around the break to repair the pipe. In doing this they had to dig a deep hole in the street and pedestrian sidewalk. The water department put up one warning sign but did not put any barriers around the hole.

Betty Blind was an elderly woman who lived in the neighborhood and had failing eyesight. For many years she had taken an early evening walk on the sidewalk down the street where the hole was located. This evening she took her usual walk. Due to her failing eyesight, she did not see the hole or the warning sign and fell in.

Ruth Rescuer happened to be walking by and heard Betty calling for help. Ruth stopped and tried to reach Betty in the hole but negligently failed to get a solid footing as she grabbed Betty's hand. She slipped and fell on top of Betty breaking Betty's arm. Both women were in the hole for many hours and the cold escaping water caused them both serious physical injuries. Pleasant Town does not recognize the "Good Samaritan" doctrine.

95. If both Betty and Ruth sue Pleasant Town, the likely outcome is a decision for

(A) Betty and Ruth, only if Fix It Inc. was negligent in failing to put barriers around the hole.

(B) Pleasant Town, because sovereign immunity applies.

(C) Pleasant Town, because any fault was caused by Fix It.

(D) Betty and Ruth, because sovereign immunity does not apply to such proprietary functions.

96. If Betty brings suit for her broken arm, she will likely prevail against

(A) Pleasant Town, Fix It Inc., and Ruth.

(B) Pleasant Town and Fix It Inc. only, because Ruth as a gratuitous rescuer is not liable.

(C) Fix It only, because they were the organization whose negligence caused all the subsequent damages.

(D) Ruth only, because she is personally responsible for her own negligence.

97. If Betty Blind sues Ruth Rescuer for the damages to her broken arm, the likely outcome is that her suit will

(A) Prevail only if Ruth had some relationship with the original tortfeasors.

(B) Not prevail unless Ruth was expecting compensation for the rescue.

(C) Not prevail unless Ruth was grossly negligent.

(D) Prevail.

98. Harry Healthcare held himself out as a "natural doctor" by listing this title on his business card, office door, and yellow page advertisements. Harry did not have a license to practice medicine or render chiropractic treatments. Nonetheless he gave Peter Patient chiropractic treatments and "prescribed" certain medicines for Peter's affliction. Peter became paralyzed from Harry's treatments and filed a lawsuit. The trial court instructed the jury that non-compliance with the mandatory medical doctor state licensing law could be considered as "clear evidence" of negligence. This instruction was

(A) Proper, because Harry Healthcare was practicing medicine without a license.

(B) Improper, because failure to obtain the required medical license did not cause Peter Patient's injury.

(C) Improper, because the lack of the required license here is negligence "per se" as contrasted to merely "clear evidence" of negligence.

(D) Proper, since practicing medicine without a license is conclusive evidence of malpractice.

99. Henry Homeowner lives in a small city with a centralized 911 emergency system. His home has a full basement that contains an old oil-heating unit. The stairway to the basement is made of wood and a few of the steps are loose. Henry has been meaning to nail these steps down securely to the supporting rails for many months, but has been unable to get to it.

Henry was in bed one night when he smelled excessive heating oil in the air. He opened the basement door and was hit with a blast of hot air. He ran out to the street and met Firery Fireman and Earl Emergency who were walking by having just left a local movie theatre. They agreed to help. Firery Fireman ran down the stairs and the unsecured steps slipped off the step supports injuring Firery. Earl Emergency got down to the basement floor intact but the furnace exploded in his face due to a defective ruptured oil input line of which Henry was unaware. If Firery and Earl sue Henry for their damages, the likely outcome under the general duty rules is a recovery for

(A) Neither Firery nor Earl.
(B) Firery but not Earl.
(C) Earl but not Firery.
(D) Both Firery and Earl.

100. Reliable Drug Company created an experimental drug intended to fight and/or slow down the HIV disease progression to AIDS. The company did as much testing prior to release as possible including requesting assistance from their competitors. Unfortunately, a number of patients died from cancer which was a consequence of the drug treatment that was unknown at the time of release. When these results became apparent, Reliable redesigned the drug components thereby correcting the previous cancer-causing side effect. A class action lawsuit was filed against Reliable. Reliable's defense strategy will least likely include which of the following?

(A) File a motion in limine to exclude at trial any evidence of the subsequent remedial measures.
(B) Defend on the basis that the drugs were state of the art at the time of release so it was not technically possible to design the HIV-AIDS drug with additional safety.
(C) Argue that strict products liability should not apply.
(D) Argue that the drug purchasers assumed the risk.

101. Mega Manufacturing produces a rodent grain poison called Rodent Rooter, and sells the product through a network of retail distributors. The distributors may market Rodent Rooter in package combination deals with other household products and add their own label with safety instructions. Distributor Acme Sales Co. sold three units to the Joneses, who have mice in their attic. Two units were opened and distributed in the home attic while the third was left intact and put in a kitchen cabinet. The Smith family is visiting the Jones family and Johnny Smith, a 4-year-old child who cannot read, finds the package of Rodent Rooter. Mistaking it for granola, Johnny eats some of it, thereby causing serious permanent damage to his liver and kidneys. The most viable defense that Mega can assert is

(A) Mega has exercised all possible care in the preparation of Rodent Rooter.
(B) Johnny Smith did not buy the product from or enter into any contractual relationship with Mega.
(C) Johnny Smith's parents should have supervised Johnny while in the Jones household.
(D) Acme Sales Co. put the Rodent Rooter poison in a new container that resembled a cereal box and substantially reduced the printed warnings on the container.

102. Stewart Soccer had played soccer in both high school and college. As an adult, he attended every soccer game in his hometown. His six-year-old son, Sonny Soccer, joined a public school team participating in a citywide junior soccer league. Stewart always accompanied Sonny to the game. One day, Stewart could not attend the game and during the game Sonny's arm was broken in a pile-up among his own players. Stewart believes the other team players were unnecessarily rough in the pile-up and has sued the public school on behalf of Sonny for personal injuries. Which of the following is most accurate?

(A) Sonny will recover because the public school coaching personnel are fiduciaries for the children on the team.
(B) Sonny will not recover because by joining the team he and Stewart impliedly assumed the risk of injury when they decided to join the team.

(C) Sonny will not recover unless he can show that the school soccer personnel failed to act reasonably in supervising the game.

(D) Sonny will recover because he is conclusively presumed to be incapable of contributory negligence until he reaches the age of 7.

Questions 103 – 106 are based on the following:

Better Boating manufactures medium-sized pleasure craft hulls complete with all structural hull and deck supports. It sells these boats through a national network of retailers who finish the interior of the boats and install the motor the retail customer orders. The range of motors is quite large from very small to large hydroplane power. All motors have a reverse feature that can be used to brake the boat. The larger the motor, the more likely that it will be dangerous in operation and that the reverse function fail.

Ole Bardell purchased a small Better Boating craft from Rapid Retailers and instructed them to put in the largest motor available. They did, but warned Ole that because the motor was so large, the reverse might not work well. On the first trip out, Ole was driving the boat on a lake at excessive speed. A small child was water skiing and fell right in the path of the boat. Ole threw the boat in reverse, but the reverse did not work. To avoid running over the child, Ole turned his craft hard to starboard, but ran into another boat that he did not see before initiating the turn. Skipper Safety was in that boat. The collision injured Skipper and sank both boats.

103. If Ole Bardell asserts a claim against Better Boating based only on strict liability, will Ole prevail?

(A) Yes, because the reverse that failed was in the boat Better manufactured.

(B) Yes, because Better should have insisted Rapid Retailer only install motors with adequate reverse features.

(C) No, because Ole did not purchase the boat from Better.

(D) No, because the boat's reverse gear feature was added after it left Better.

104. If Ole Bardell asserts a claim against Rapid Retailer based on strict liability and negligence, will Ole prevail?

(A) Yes, because the boat as delivered was negligently defective.

(B) No, because Ole was comparatively negligent.

(C) No, because the motor producing the inadequate reverse feature was installed pursuant to Ole's specifications.

(D) No, because the damages were not foreseeable.

105. If Skipper brings suit against Better Boating for negligence, the best defense Better Boating can assert is

(A) The damages were not reasonably foreseeable by Better.

(B) Skipper should sue Ole since he caused the harm.

(C) The vessel in question was not defective when it left their control.

(D) There is no privity of contract between Skipper and Better.

106. If Skipper brings suit against Ole Bardell for negligence, the worst defense Ole could assert is

(A) Skipper had the last clear chance to avoid the boat collision.

(B) Skipper should have sued Retailer since it was the defect in the motor and reverse gear they installed that caused the damage.

(C) Skipper's inattention was a partial cause of the accident.

(D) The water skier going down in front of Ole's boat was not foreseeable.

Questions 107 – 109 are based on the following:

Harry Hydrogen operates a refinery that allows raw hydrogen gas to escape into the air. The adjoining land contains a chemical plant owned by Oscar Oxygen. Oscar's plant releases raw oxygen into the air. Neither gas by itself is dangerous. Harry and Oscar are both major local employers and in full compliance with all environmental laws individually. However, the two gases unexpectedly combine creating H_2O or water on the property boundary. This sudden supply of water occasionally floods the neighbor Nancy Nice's land causing significant damages.

107. Nancy is quite upset and brings suit against both Harry and Oscar jointly and severally for negligence. Nancy will
- (A) Recover against Harry only.
- (B) Recover against Oscar only.
- (C) Recover against both Harry and Oscar.
- (D) Recover against neither Harry nor Oscar.

108. Assuming that both Harry and Oscar are sued under a theory of nuisance, which defense (if true) would be the best to assert?
- (A) Neither producer intended to create a dangerous condition or inflict damage to the neighbor.
- (B) The utility of the neighborhood benefits provided by both employers outweighs the gravity of harm suffered by the neighbor.
- (C) Nancy moved to the nuisance without knowledge of the potential risk.
- (D) Damages are preferred over specific performance.

109. The refinery and chemical plant increased their production, which also increased the amount of hydrogen and oxygen they released. This increased the quantity of water flooding into the neighborhood. Two blocks down the hill water flooded a public park and damaged the children's play area. The City has a local ordinance prohibiting the flooding of public parks. A neighborhood resident, Charlie Citizen, filed a lawsuit seeking an injunction based on public nuisance. The best defense that would be asserted against Citizen's lawsuit is
- (A) The violation of the city ordinance was minimal.
- (B) The city can show no damages.
- (C) Citizen did not allege any special damages.
- (D) The utility of the conduct of both employers outweighs the gravity of harm suffered by the city park.

110. Debra Driver was employed as a bus driver in the Pleasant Valley High School system. She was assigned to a suburban route. Debra picked up the students in the morning and delivered them home after school. On the last day of the fall quarter, the students had a holiday party beginning at noon. Unfortunately, many students consumed alcohol at the party. At 4:00 in the afternoon, the students staggered into the bus for the trip home. Shortly after Debra Driver left the school parking lot, the students began to trash the bus by ripping the leather on the seats and throwing bottles and cans at pedestrians through the windows. Debra decided to not continue the route and rather drove directly to the local police department. One student on the bus, Paul Perfect, was not involved in the drinking and vandalism. When Debra went by the regular stop by Paul's home, he went to the front of the bus and demanded Debra go back to his stop. Debra refused. If Paul brings suit against Debra for false imprisonment, Debra's best defense is
- (A) Self-defense.
- (B) Justification.
- (C) Private necessity.
- (D) Public necessity.

111. Harry Homeowner hired Pricilla Painter to paint the exterior of his home. The contract called for all painting to be completed in a workmanlike manner. Harry and his family moved out for the duration of the painting. Pricilla completed the painting and removed all the painting supplies from Harry's home on Friday except for a long ladder that she intended to pick up on Monday. Over the weekend while Harry was still away, a burglar used Pricilla's ladder to enter the house through an unlocked second floor window. Harry returned home, realized his favorite painting has been stolen by the burglar and brought a negligence lawsuit against Pricilla. Harry will

    (A) Prevail, because Pricilla was responsible for leaving the ladder on the premises as an unapproved holdover tenant.

    (B) Not prevail, because Harry should have sued for breach of contract.

    (C) Not prevail, because the burglary was a superseding cause.

    (D) Prevail, because Pricilla created the opportunity for the burglar to trespass and steal the owner's painting.

112. Charlie Careless is walking down the street not paying attention to his footsteps. He negligently bumps into Edwood Eggshell knocking him to the pavement. While this fall would normally only cause small bruises, Edwood has a rare form of calcium deficiency in his bones. The fall resulting from the collision shatters Edwood's hip, bones, and joints. If Edwood brings suit against Charlie for negligence seeking all the damages of the shattered hip, bones, and joints, he will likely

    (A) Prevail, because the shattering of Edwood's hip was reasonably foreseeable.

    (B) Prevail, because the Defendant takes the victim as they are found.

    (C) Not prevail, because the extent of the injury was unexpected.

    (D) Not prevail, because the damages are grossly disproportionate to the Defendant's fault.

113. Susan Sleepy was driving late at night on a narrow dirt road. She became increasingly tired and decided to stop and have a short nap to rest before continuing her drive home. She pulled over, but due to the narrow road, most of her car was still on the road. Hotrod Harry was driving on the same road with a passenger named Larry Lawsuit. Hotrod was distracted from his driving because he was talking on his cell phone. After passing the bend in the road, Hotrod rammed into Susan's car that was sticking out into the road. Larry was severely injured in the accident and Larry brings suit for his injuries. Larry will likely recover against

    (A) Hotrod Harry only.

    (B) Susan Sleepy only.

    (C) Both Hotrod and Susan.

    (D) Neither Hotrod nor Susan.

114. Bill Bearhunter had always wanted to shoot a bear, but had never been successful in the short hunting season in the lower 48 states. The bears always seemed to detect him first. He read about an organized hunting trip in Alaska that charged $10,000 for the week-long hunt. Bill flew up to Alaska and began the hunt. During the nine-day hunting excursion, he saw a number of bears, but could never get close enough to get off a shot. The guide suggested Bill dress up in a bear rug complete with a bear's head for a disguise. Bill agreed to try and put on the outfit. Bill went into the underbrush in an area known for bear grazing and sat down so only the head and upper chest of the bear outfit was visible.

Another hunter named Fred Ferocious was frustrated because he also was unable to shoot a bear. Fred had been at it for 30 days and was leaving for the lower 48 the next morning. He had been drinking heavily in Chillout Charlie's Tavern all day and was driving back to the Bear Camp in his pickup. He was legally drunk. As Fred slowed to make a sharp turn, he spotted Bill in the underbrush and thought he was a bear. Fred grabbed a double-barrel shotgun that was on the gun rack in the pickup and blasted away injuring Bill.

The jurisdiction in question has not adopted any form of comparative negligence. If Bill sues Fred for his injuries, the likely outcome is that he will

(A) Prevail, if Bill can show that Fred was negligent in hunting while intoxicated.
(B) Not prevail, unless Bill can prove he did not have the last clear chance to avoid being injured.
(C) Not prevail, because Fred did not have the required intent to justify imposing liability for an intentional tort.
(D) Prevail, if Bill can show that Fred's act of hunting while intoxicated was reckless and wanton behavior.

115. Patty Passenger went for an all-day plane ride with her friend Peter Pilot in his small two-seater airplane. Peter was a licensed pilot and the plane had been inspected and all instrumentation checked out by an aircraft maintenance company before the plane left. This same maintenance company had performed the plane maintenance for many years. The weather was good, but fifteen minutes after take off, the plane crashed killing both Patty and Peter. There were no eyewitnesses to the crash but witnesses had seen the plane take off and it was flying properly 10 minutes before the crash. The personal representative of Patty's estate has brought suit against Peter's estate and the maintenance company.

(A) Plaintiff will prevail under the doctrine of res ipsa loquitur.
(B) Defendant will prevail because the Plaintiff can produce no direct evidence of a breach of care by Peter.
(C) Plaintiff is entitled to a jury instruction that the jury may infer negligence through circumstantial evidence.
(D) Plaintiff will always prevail because the damages establish as a matter of law that Peter failed to exercise reasonable care.

116. Paul Pedestrian was walking on the sidewalk in the Upper East Side of New York City and minding his own business. Gallons of boiling hot water suddenly fell on his head. A large apartment house with hundreds of tenants was directly alongside him. Paul suffered extensive burns and brought suit against Leroy Landlord who owned the apartment house. If Paul offers the above facts, his claim will likely

(A) Prevail, because under res ipsa loquitur, the thing speaks for itself.
(B) Prevail, because such an injury would not ordinarily occur in the absence of someone's negligence.
(C) Not prevail, because there is no circumstantial evidence to support a reasonable inference that Leroy was negligent.
(D) Not prevail, because pedestrians assume the risk that foreign objects may fall on them.

Questions 117 and 118 are based on the following:

Douglas Driver was driving north on Park Place Road at 40 miles per hour. Fred Follower was driving behind Douglas in an old car with his prized laptop computer system on the passenger seat. Douglas braked quickly when a light turned yellow. To stop in time and avoid hitting Douglas' car, Fred had to jam on his brakes. In the process of the rapid braking, Fred's prized computer was thrown into the windshield and destroyed. Fred jumped out and he and Douglas got into a verbal argument. Douglas was particularly abusive in this argument.

After a few minutes, they both got back into their cars and continued down Park Place Road. This particular section of Park Place was alongside an elementary school and there was a posted sign that "speed limit is reduced from 40 to 25 mph during school hours." Neither driver slowed down. One block later, a schoolboy ran out in the road and Douglas slammed on his brakes. Fred was still upset about the previous incident and was not paying close attention. When he realized he had to stop quickly, he slammed on the breaks but was too late to avoid running into Douglas's car.

117. If Fred brings suit against Douglas for the damages to his computer, the most helpful fact supporting Fred's recovery would be that
   (A) Douglas had a history of stopping suddenly.
   (B) Fred will not recover the full amount since he was partially at fault.
   (C) Douglas could have probably gotten through the intersection before the light turned red.
   (D) Douglas was abusive in the discussion following the incident.

118. If Douglas brings suit against Fred for the damages to his car from the rear-end accident, the worst defense Fred can assert is
   (A) Douglas will not recover the full amount since he was partially at fault.
   (B) The schoolboy caused the accident so he should be responsible for the damages.
   (C) Douglas was going 40 mph in a school speed zone of 25 mph.
   (D) Douglas caused the prior incident, which resulted in Fred's inattention.

119. The New York Coal Company constructed a new coal-burning electricity producing plant in a farming community. The coal burning does emit a substantial amount of cancer-causing fumes. Florence Farmer purchased the farm next door intending to grow wine grapes. Two years later, New York Coal Company quadrupled their output due to the energy shortage. At the higher toxic level, Florence's grapevines died and Florence herself had a recurrence of the cancer she had 10 years ago which had been in remission. Her agricultural chemist expert at trial testified that the higher level of toxicity caused the wine grape failure and Florence's cancer recurrence. In Florence's claim against New York for damages, Florence will likely
   (A) Prevail, because New York's plant is a nuisance.
   (B) Not prevail, because she moved to the nuisance.
   (C) Not prevail, because her prior cancer made her extra-sensitive to toxic substances.
   (D) Not prevail, because the Plaintiff cannot prove that New York Coal intended to injure her.

120. Sam Speedy was driving with an expired driver's license on a two-lane road. Speedy negligently hit a parked car. After the collision both cars blocked the right lane of the road. Oscar Observer came along shortly thereafter and as he drove by he slowed down to look at the accident. At the slower speed, he was rear-ended by another driver. Oscar sustained substantial personal injury and physical damages. Oscar sues Speedy and Speedy files a motion for dismissal on summary judgment. With respect to the motion, a court will likely
   (A) Dismiss the case, since the Plaintiff could have passed the accident without slowing and was thus contributorily negligent.
   (B) Deny the motion, since a jury could reasonably conclude that Oscar's injury and damages arose from an event that was a continuing consequence of Speedy's negligence.
   (C) Deny the motion, because Speedy had violated the state law requiring a driver's license
   (D) Dismiss the case, since it was another driver who caused Oscar's injury and damage.

121. Susan Slander and Victoria Victim were adverse attorneys in a large business meeting in Tokyo, Japan negotiating the purchase of a business. All the other people in the meeting were Japanese. Susan got increasingly irritated at Victoria during the negotiation. Unable to control herself, Susan yelled out, "Victoria is a liar and convicted thief." This outraged Victoria who brought suit against Susan for defamation. Victoria will

(A) Prevail only if she can prove special damages.
(B) Not prevail unless some of the attendees at the business meeting understood English.
(C) Not prevail unless she can prove Susan intended to injure her reputation and had actual knowledge the statement was false.
(D) Not prevail even if the statement was true since a theft conviction is a personal matter.

122. Peter Pornography applied for a business license to operate a topless dancing establishment. The application process involved numerous public hearings and many in the community loudly complained. One neighbor, Patty Pure, who lived in the same block as the proposed establishment, was especially vocal. At a public hearing she stated, as her research indicated, that these types of establishments were run by organized crime. She further stated that they hire prostitutes, many of who are addicted to illegal narcotics. Furthermore, that some of the establishment's customers are rapists who often vandalize the community and attack single females. Based upon her complaints, the city license department denied Peter Pornography a business license. If Peter sues Patty for defamation, Peter will likely

(A) Recover, because he incurred monetary damages.
(B) Not recover, because Peter was a public figure.
(C) Not recover, because Patty reasonably believed her statements to be true.
(D) Not recover, because Patty's statements of fact did not refer to Peter.

Questions 123 – 127 are based on the following:

Cathy Consumer purchased an automobile on contract from Fly-By-Night Auto. The car proved to be an absolute lemon and Fly-By-Night was unable to repair the automobile. They also refused to rescind the sale or reduce the balance Cathy owed on the purchase contract. Cathy finally dropped off the car in their parking lot and wrote Fly-By-Night a letter in which she stated she would not make any more payments on the account. She also filed a written complaint with the Better Business Bureau. The letter stated that Fly-By-Night was unethical, dishonest, and would not repair the lemon automobiles they sold. The Better Business Bureau published Cathy's statements in the local newspaper, causing Fly-By-Night to lose sales.

Fly-By-Night wrote back to Cathy stating that they disagreed with her complaint and were going to begin collection action on her account. Their collection agent, named Tommy Thug, went out to Cathy's home. Cathy was holding a birthday party for her mother in the back yard and most of her family, friends and business associates were in attendance. Tommy went into the back yard screaming that Cathy was a deadbeat who did not pay her bills. Everyone present heard the statements.

Cathy was very embarrassed by the statements and fainted. When she regained consciousness, she was very distressed and ran into her house. Tommy followed closely behind Cathy continuing to yell the insults loudly. When Cathy saw Tommy was following her through the doorway, she became very angry and slammed the door in Tommy's face. The force of the door slamming into his face broke Tommy's nose.

123. If Fly-By-Night sues Cathy for libel in reporting the lemon car allegation to the Better Business Bureau, they will likely

(A) Recover because the untrue statements were publicized.

(B) Not recover because Cathy's statements were mere opinion.

(C) Not recover because Cathy had a qualified privilege.

(D) Recover because Fly-By-Night had real damages.

124. If Cathy sues Tommy for slander she will likely

(A) Recover, because the untrue statements were publicized.

(B) Not recover, unless she can prove special damages.

(C) Not recover, because Tommy had a qualified privilege and a first amendment right to speak.

(D) Not recover, because by not paying her legal obligation, she impliedly consented to become subject to such collection actions by her creditors.

125. Nancy Nosey was at the party and eavesdropped on Tommy's statements. She later told the story to her garden club. If Cathy sues Nancy Nosey for publication of private facts, Cathy will likely

(A) Prevail, because the facts were false.

(B) Not prevail, because truth is an absolute defense.

(C) Not prevail, because Cathy didn't pay off her account.

(D) Prevail, even if the facts were true.

126. If Cathy sues Tommy for outrage or the intentional infliction of emotional distress, Cathy will

(A) Prevail, because Tommy was trespassing on Cathy's property.

(B) Prevail, because Tommy's actions were extreme and outrageous.

(C) Not prevail, because words alone are never sufficient.

(D) Not prevail, because the statements were true since she did not pay the balance of her account.

127. If Tommy sues Cathy for battery, Tommy will

(A) Prevail, if Cathy intended the door to strike and injure Tommy.

(B) Not prevail, because Tommy was trespassing on Cathy's property.

(C) Not prevail, because Cathy did not order him to quit her property.

(D) Not prevail, because Tommy impliedly consented to physical contact by Cathy when he stepped into her doorway.

128. Her employer gave Susan Shifty a high ethics and honest employee award. She called a press conference to announce her award. One of the reporters asked her for an extended interview. During the interview, she told the reporter one of the reasons the company may have given her the award was because she had worked there for 10 years. The reporter asked her where she worked before. Susan identified her prior employer and reporter contacted them learning that she had been accused of embezzlement while working there. The reporter wrote up the amazing and contradictory story of an accused embezzler receiving a high ethics and honest employee award. The story appeared on the front page of the local paper. Susan was embarrassed by the story and brought suit against the reporter and newspaper for invasion of privacy. The newspaper and reporter file a motion for summary judgment of dismissal. The court will likely

(A) Grant the motion because the published facts were true.

(B) Deny the motion because the published story intruded on Susan's privacy.

(C) Grant the motion because Susan called a press conference and voluntarily gave the reporter her former employer's identity.

(D) Deny the motion because the published story was embarrassing to the Plaintiff.

Questions 129 and 130 are based on the following:

Gary worked at Horrid Hospital as a medical assistant.

129. The hospital was experiencing a decline in its number of patients and the administrator decided it was necessary to cut 15% of the staff. Gary received an advance notice of layoff and confronted the administrator in the hospital's lunchroom. An argument ensued between the two. The administrator yelled at Gary saying that "You are gay and have AIDS and it puts the patients at risk." Many heard the statement. While it was generally believed that Gary was gay, he did not have AIDS and the administrator had no basis for the statement. If Gary sues the administrator for defamation, he will

(A) Prevail, only if he can show special damages.
(B) Prevail, even if he cannot show special damages.
(C) Prevail, only if he can prove the administrator knew he did not have AIDS.
(D) Not prevail, because Gary was in fact gay.

130. Horrid Hospital subsequently terminated Gary. He then filed a lawsuit against Horrid Hospital alleging wrongful discharge. The hospital defended on the basis that Gary's poor work performance was the sole reason for the employment termination. Horrid's attorney took the deposition of one of Gary's former co-workers, who testified that he was present when the supervisor stated the Gary had AIDS. This portion of the printed deposition was published in the case and included within a motion for summary judgment. A newspaper reporter read these facts in the pleading in the court file. The reporter wrote an article specifying Gary had AIDS without verifying the fact with Gary. The next morning the front page of the Notorious News printed a story entitled "Horrid Hospital Fires Gay Employee For

Having AIDS." The article gave Gary's name, but did not disclose that Gary had denied the AIDS allegation. If a defamation lawsuit is brought against Notorious, their worst defense is

(A) By bringing the lawsuit, Gary impliedly agreed to waive any defamation claim.
(B) The facts presented in their front-page story in the morning paper were absolutely privileged.
(C) They exercised reasonable care in determining the overall truth of the article.
(D) Gary became a public figure by bringing the lawsuit and the newspaper lacked knowledge that the AIDS allegation was false.

Questions 131 and 132 are based on the following:

Larry Hawk was the highest scoring NBA basketball player in 2005. A web design company downloaded a color picture of him at the height of his best-ever slam dunk shot. This personal image of the player was superimposed over a pair of Low Quality sport shoes. A salesman for the web design company told Low Quality that Hawk had approved the sponsorship. Hawk was totally unaware that the image had been made. Low Quality made no verification to determine if the player had actually agreed to the advertisement. Because of this, Larry Hawk lost a similar product endorsement contract with High Quality.

131. If Hawk brings suit against Low Quality for defamation, will Hawk prevail?

(A) No, because the picture was not defamatory per se.
(B) No, if an employee of Low Quality actually believed the agent's statement that Hawk had given his permission to publish his image.
(C) Yes, because the objectionable image was in a printed format.
(D) Yes, if Low Quality was reckless in accepting the agent's statement of

permission without conducting an investigation.

132. If Larry Hawk brings suit against Low Quality for invasion of privacy, Larry will likely

(A) Prevail, because the Defendant used Plaintiff's picture for profit without permission.

(B) Prevail, because the Defendant intruded on Hawk's privacy.

(C) Prevail, because the Defendant published him in a false light.

(D) Not prevail, because the Defendant believed it had permission to use Hawk's picture in its advertisement and thus had no intent.

Questions 133 and 134 are based on the following:

Weekend Worker was in a storage area late Friday afternoon on an upper floor of an office building. She was so absorbed in her work that she failed to leave the storage area by 6:00 p.m. At that time, the company's security guard bolted the doors and disabled the elevator. The guard did not make a final inspection sweep of the storage area or the whole floor. When Weekend tried to leave at 7:30 p.m., she discovered the bolted door and realized she would have to spend the whole weekend locked up without water or food. She then broke out a window and tried to climb down a drainpipe. Twenty feet from the ground, the drain pipe broke throwing Weekend to the ground creating physical injury.

133. If Weekend sues the company for negligence, she would likely

(A) Not recover, because the security guard was an independent contractor rather than an employee.

(B) Recover, if a reasonable security guard in that position would have made a final sweep of the storage area.

(C) Recover, only if the security guard had actual knowledge he had

locked someone up for the weekend.

(D) Not recover, because by climbing out the window and down the drainpipe, she implicitly assumed the risk of damage.

134. If Weekend sues both the night watchman and the company for false imprisonment, she will likely

(A) Prevail against the employer, but not the night watchman since the night watchman was operating within the course and scope of employment.

(B) Prevail because she was confined and restrained against her will.

(C) Prevail because significant damage occurred because of the confinement.

(D) Not prevail unless the night watchman had actual knowledge that someone was still in the warehouse when he locked the door for the weekend.

135. A private neighborhood had a main road running through it that was used by residents of an adjoining neighborhood to get to the Interstate highway. A group of the neighbors got tired of the through traffic and barricaded the main road. Many of the drivers were forced to take a different route to and from the Interstate adding 20 minutes to their commute. A group of the irate commuters filed a lawsuit for false imprisonment against the group who had erected the barricade. Will the Plaintiffs prevail?

(A) Yes, because erecting the barricade on a public road was unlawful.

(B) No, because there was an alternate route available to commute to the Interstate.

(C) No, because the Defendants did not use force to restrain the Plaintiffs so the confinement was not unreasonable.

(D) Yes, because erecting the barricade was intentional.

136. Concerned Citizen saw Susan Shoplifter leave a retail store in a hurry and a person near her began to yell, "Stop, thief." Concerned jumped on Susan, holding her for 30 minutes until the police arrived. The police could not find any stolen items on Susan and released her. There was never a warrant issued. If Susan sues Concerned for false imprisonment, she will likely

(A) Prevail because Concerned is a private citizen, not a police officer and thus held to a lower standard.

(B) Prevail because there was no crime committed and the arrest was made without a warrant.

(C) Not prevail because Concerned had reasonable grounds for believing that Susan had committed a theft.

(D) Not prevail because the arrest was only for 30 minutes.

137. Sleazy Salesman had some raw land for sale that was polluted. While similar non-polluted acreage in the neighborhood was worth $250,000, the fair value of this polluted parcel was $100,000. Eager Edgar wanted the property and had read some comparable appraisals at around $260,000. While he had looked at the property, he was unaware of the pollution. He offered Sleazy $240,000 which was accepted. After the purchase had closed, Eager learned of the pollution and sued Sleazy for fraud or misrepresentation. Sleazy's least viable defense is

(A) He had not made a false statement.

(B) He had no intention to deceive Eager.

(C) Eager had no damages since the land could be used for some purposes even with the pollution.

(D) Eager had no right to rely.

Questions 138 and 139 are based on the following:

Tom Timid and his wife, Tracey, were walking in front of their home when physically large Ben Bully pulled up in a car. Tom owed a large sum of money to Ben, was delinquent in the payments, and did not have the money to pay. Ben stepped out of his car and tripped Tom. He then sat on Tom and punched him repeatedly. The beating was ferocious and Tom suffered both physically and mentally. When Ben left, Tom was close to death.

138. Unknown to Ben, Tom's wife, Tracey, had a pre-existing medical condition which was compounded when she visually observed the brutality to Tom. Tracy suffered a stroke while observing Ben attack Tom. Without this unusual medical condition, she would not have suffered any damage. If Tracey brings suit against Ben for outrage or the intentional infliction of emotional distress, Tracey will

(A) Not prevail, because she was not physically injured.

(B) Not prevail, because she was not threatened with physical injury.

(C) Prevail, only if Ben was aware of heightened sensitivity to emotional distress.

(D) Prevail, because a Defendant takes the Plaintiff as they find them.

139. Unknown to Ben, Tom's invalid mother Pricilla watched the whole incident from the second floor of their home. After seeing the brutal attack, she was very distressed and went into a long sickness. Pricilla then filed a lawsuit against Ben for outrage or the intentional infliction of emotional distress. Tom's mother will

(A) Prevail, because her distress was directly caused by Bully's acts and she was in the zone of danger.

(B) Not prevail, because she was not physically injured or even threatened with physical injury.

(C) Not prevail, because Bully did not know that she was watching the beating he gave Tom.

(D) Prevail, because Bully's conduct towards Tom was outrageous, shocks the conscience, and exceeds the bounds of common decency.

140. Wally Watchman has just left his warehouse guard job and was still wearing his uniform. He stopped by a low cost warehouse to purchase a case of wine. As he was leaving the store, he saw Betty Beautiful and immediately fell in love with her. Wally approached Betty in the parking lot and stated that he was a policeman and that she should come along with him. Betty, who had always been infatuated by men in uniforms, believed that Wally was actually a policeman as he had represented. She entered into Wally's custody, got into his car, and he drove to his house. At the home he took her by the hand into his house and locked the door. Betty pleaded with him to let her go to work. Four hours later, Wally passed out from drinking wine, thus allowing Betty to escape. Betty lost a day's wages because she could not get to work. If Betty sues Wally, she will

(A) Prevail for both fraud and false arrest.

(B) Prevail for false arrest because it is the highest level offense.

(C) Prevail for fraud, but not false arrest because Betty was not physically forced to accompany Wally.

(D) Prevail for false arrest, but not fraud because Betty should not have relied on Wally's statement that he was a policeman.

141. Debit & Credit, CPAs, is a firm of public auditors. One of their clients – Fast Eddie, Inc – hired the firm to audit their financial statements. Fast Eddie told Debit & Credit that they were going to submit their audited financial statements to a bank in the local area as the basis for a large loan. The auditors were negligent in performing their examination with the result that the audited financial statements submitted to Better Bank were materially misleading.

Better Bank made a large loan to Fast Eddie in reliance on the CPA firm's audit opinion. The CPA firm was unaware of the specific identity of the bank and did not have any communication with them. The loan subsequently went into default and the bank brought suit against the auditors, Debit & Credit. The auditor's best defense against the lawsuit is

(A) The bank was not their client and lacked privity of contract with the CPA firm.

(B) The bank did not rely upon the financial statements audited by the CPA firm.

(C) The bank made its own investigation and thus was contributorily negligent.

(D) The audit opinion was not a false statement of fact because there was not scienter or intent to deceive.

142. In order to establish a common law action for negligent representation, the aggrieved party must establish that

(A) Although the Defendant did not in fact know that his statements were false, he made the false statements with a reckless disregard for the truth.

(B) The contract entered into is within the Statute of Frauds.

(C) There was a written misrepresentation of fact by the Defendant.

(D) The Plaintiff acted as a reasonably prudent businessman would have in relying upon the misrepresentation.

143. Which of the following is not required in order for the Plaintiff to prevail in an action for fraud?

(A) That the misrepresentation was intended to induce reliance.

(B) That the misrepresentation amounted to gross negligence.

(C) That the Plaintiff timely filed the claim.

(D) That the Plaintiff relied upon the misrepresentation.

144. Naïve Nancy walked onto a used car lot. The salesman watched her admire a classic 1964 Mustang convertible. The salesman then approached Nancy, telling her, "This car is as good as new and was owned by a retired school teacher who kept it in the garage except to go to and from church once a week." Naïve said "I am glad the mileage is so low." The salesman knew the odometer had been turned back from 350,000 to 50,000 miles, but said nothing. Naïve would not have purchased the car had she known the mileage amount was that much understated. If Naïve brings suit, she will most likely prevail under the theory of

(A) Fraud, only if the agreement was written.
(B) Negligence, for failing to exercise due care.
(C) Nothing, because there is no duty to speak under caveat emptor.
(D) Fraudulent concealment, unless the purchase was "as is."

145. Robert Ripoff was an architect who owned a local architectural firm. He recently learned he would lose his major client due to a business merger. This client's billings had contributed 40% of gross revenue and 60% of net profits to his practice. Upon learning this bad news, he immediately listed his architectural practice for sale. The buyer asked him if he was aware of any significant change that could be expected in clientele base or revenues. Robert said no and did not mention the loss of the major client. If the buyer later sues Robert, she will

(A) Not prevail, because the rule of caveat emptor (let the buyer beware) applies to the sale of a business.
(B) Not prevail, unless the buyer can establish that Robert was under a duty to make disclosure of the loss of the major client.
(C) Prevail, if the seller expressly represented the non-existence of the undisclosed matter.
(D) Prevail, for the 40% of the gross business lost.

146. Jolly Manufacturing produces computer chips for sale to computer stores. The retail store uses the chips to repair customers' equipment experiencing operational problems. If the chips do not properly perform and the retail store brings an action against Jolly for negligence, the retail store will prevail if:

(A) Jolly cannot prove that it performed in a manner common to others in the computer chip industry.
(B) The retail store can prove that "but for" the Defendant's lack of care, the computer chips would have performed properly.
(C) The retail store can prove Jolly breached the industry's reasonable standard of production in manufacturing computer chips, causation and damages.
(D) Jolly cannot prove that no damages resulted from the breach of duty.

147. Charley Carseller was a used car salesman. He saw Georgina Gullible walk onto his car lot. He immediately walked out of the salesroom and met her in the middle of the lot. Georgina was looking at a used 1964 Volkswagen bug car. Charley immediately started in with his sales pitch. Which of the following statements, if incorrect, would least likely to be considered a fraudulent inducement to sell the car to Georgina?

(A) "I am sure that the insurance for this car would be half the regular rate."
(B) "We had this car appraised at $5,000 and are selling it for only $4,000.
(C) "This car will continue to increase in value $1,000 a year."
(D) "This car was owned by a retired law school professor."

148. Mighty Manufacturing produces a line of heart defibrillators, which it retails through a network of sales agents. Due to the many trade and customer secrets it protects, Mighty is quite concerned about its agents' loyalty. Each agent must agree to sell only Mighty's product and not to compete within a year of termination. A competitor approached one of Mighty's agents knowing the agent was under this legally enforceable agency contract. If

Mighty brings suit against the competitor, it will

(A) Not prevail, because there are no present damages.
(B) Prevail, even if a breach does not occur.
(C) Prevail, only if the competitor tried to bribe the agent.
(D) Prevail, against the competitor and also prevail against the agent even if no breach follows.

149. Which of the following does the Plaintiff not have to prove to recover for negligence?

(A) That the Defendant failed to exercise the degree of due care that was reasonable under the circumstances.
(B) That there was a close causal connection between the breach of duty and the resulting damages.
(C) That the Plaintiff was not comparatively negligent.
(D) That the claimed damages were more than nominal.

Questions 150 – 152 are based on the following:

David Drinker was a heavy partier who frequented nightclubs. One evening, he met Lois Looser in a bar. They partied and both drank heavily until the bar closed. David insisted that he was sufficiently sober to drive Lois to her home. Lois was sure David was drunk, but knew she herself was drunk too. Lois figured David had a better chance of getting her home than she did. Neither one of them considered taking a taxi and Lois neglected to fasten her seat belt. David began driving but collided with another moving vehicle driven by Larry Lush. The police arrived on the scene and determined that David, Lois, and Larry were all legally drunk and that both drivers had failed to stop at stop signs resulting in the collision. Lois was injured and sued David and Larry for negligence. The court determined that David and Larry were each 40% at fault, Lois was 20% at fault, and that Lois' damages were $25,000.

150. Will Lois be able to recover from David?

(A) Yes, because David's failure to stop at a stop sign was a substantial factor contributing to Lois' injuries.
(B) No, because Lois assumed the risk of an accident since she knew David was drunk and did not complain.
(C) No, because Lois' 20% fault and Larry's 40% fault together constitute over 50% of the total fault.
(D) Yes, unless the doctrine of last clear chance applies.

151. What amount will Lois likely recover from Larry?

(A) $10,000.
(B) $15,000.
(C) $20,000.
(D) $25,000.

152. Lois levies on her negligence judgment against both David and Larry. She is able to attach $15,000 from Larry's bank account. How much is Larry's right of contribution against David?

(A) $7,500.
(B) $5,000.
(C) $2,500.
(D) –0–

Questions 153 – 155 are based on the following:

Always Aluminum operated a large production facility producing aluminum. Its largest cost input was electricity, which they purchased from Regional Electric Company. Because of severe electrical power shortages in California, Regional Electric tripled its per-kilowatt charge to Always. This made it impossible to operate the production plant at a profit so the company closed its facility and laid off all its employees. It instructed all their utilities, including Regional Electric, to turn off the utilities. Regional turned off the meter generating the monthly bill to Always, but left open the electricity main leading to the equipment in the plant.

Angry Andrew was one of the laid-off employees. He knew the plant had closed and decided to jump over the fence and take some of the equipment to compensate himself for unpaid fringe benefits he claimed were due. Angry began dismantling some of the equipment, which had valuable electric generator components. Angry's steel wrench touched both the positive and negative electric poles of the generator at the same time. This severely shocked Angry causing him physical damages. The electrical component in the generator was destroyed thereby rendering valueless the equipment, which Always had intended to sell to a third party.

153. If Angry Andrew sues Always Aluminum for his physical injury, Angry will likely

(A) Prevail, because high voltage electricity is inherently dangerous.
(B) Prevail, because he reasonably assumed the power to the plant had been disconnected.
(C) Not prevail, because he was a trespasser on Always' property.
(D) Not prevail, because Angry was a common thief.

154. If Angry Andrew sues Regional Electric Company for his damages, Angry will likely

(A) Prevail, because high voltage electricity is inherently dangerous.
(B) Not prevail, because he was a trespasser who takes the land as he finds it.
(C) Not prevail, because Angry was attempting to steal.
(D) Prevail, because Always Aluminum directed Regional Electric to turn off the electricity.

155. If Always Aluminum sues Angry Andrew for trespass to chattels or conversion in destroying the electrical components, Angry

(A) Is not liable because Angry did not intend to cause damages.
(B) Is not liable for trespass to chattels but is liable for conversion.
(C) Is not liable for conversion but is liable for trespass to chattels.
(D) Is liable for either trespass to chattels or conversion at the election of Always.

156. Charlie Chicken and his elderly mother were walking along a city street alone at night. Up ahead, he saw a gang of teenage hoodlums. Charlie believed this was the gang he had read about in the local newspaper that had harassed and assaulted other neighborhood residents. To avoid having to walk through the gang, Charlie broke through a wooden fence in a privately owned lot. He then broke a house window to allow his mother and him to enter the abandoned residence owned by Harry Homeowner. Charlie and his mother went through the house and out the back door to the alley, thus avoiding becoming victims of the gang's attack. If Harry Homeowner sues Charlie for the cost of a new fence and window, Harry will likely

(A) Prevail, because Charlie intentionally crossed over Harry's property.
(B) Not prevail, because Charlie merely acted as a reasonably prudent person under the circumstances.
(C) Not prevail, because the action is justified by the defense of necessity, defense of others, and defense of one's self.
(D) Prevail, because Charlie knew the trespass would cause damages to the homeowner.

Toxic Repository Inc. became a national mid-level risk toxic reservation because it had a large desert location that was far away from any major population center and had almost no rain. Toxic received paints, batteries, and toxicants including chemical wastes such as arsenic. They dumped these toxicants into large pits that when full, were covered with five feet of soil. The whole reservation was fenced and large warning signs were posted every 50 feet that stated, "Do not trespass – this site contains very dangerous toxicants which may be hazardous to humans."

Edward Environment was a member of the board of directors of Save the Environment Inc. a nonprofit political action group. Based upon Board direction, Edward inquired of Toxic what amount of toxic matter was buried on the site. Toxic refused to answer Edward's questions. That night, Edward scaled the fence to make a personal investigation. In the darkness, Edward fell into one of the toxic pits receiving serious skin burns.

157. If Toxic Repository Inc. brings suit against Edward Environment and Save the Environment Inc. for trespass, they will

- **(A)** Prevail against Edward Environment, but not against Save the Environment Inc.
- **(B)** Prevail against Save the Environment Inc., but not against Edward Environment.
- **(C)** Prevail against both Edward Environment and Save the Environment Inc.
- **(D)** Not prevail, since there were no damages suffered because of the trespass.

158. If Edward Environment sues Toxic Repository Inc. for the skin burn damage he received from the toxic pit, he will likely

- **(A)** Prevail, because the pits should have been covered.

- **(B)** Not prevail, because he disregarded the signs and climbed over the fence.
- **(C)** Not prevail, because Toxic Repository was not negligent.
- **(D)** Prevail, because the storage of toxic waste is an abnormally dangerous activity creating strict liability.

159. The Rocking Riot was a very popular local band that was under a one year contract to perform every night in Delightful Disco. Since they started playing at Delightful Disco, the business had substantially increased. However, this came at the expense of Next Door Disco that was located in the next block of the neighborhood. Next Door hired Iola Interferor, a rock band agent, to hire away Rocking Riot. Iola approached the leader of Rocking Riot offering them $10,000 to quit Delightful Disco and go to work playing for Next Door Disco. If Delightful Disco sues Next Door Disco for interference, the best defense Next Door can assert is

- **(A)** The agent, Iola Interferor, was not authorized to offer Rocking Riot $10,000.
- **(B)** Neither Next Door Disco nor Iola Interferor was aware that Rocking Riot was under a binding contract with Delightful Disco.
- **(C)** Next door Disco has a justifiable competitive interest.
- **(D)** The offer was not made out of pure malice.

160. An attorney represents a patient in a medical malpractice claim that had questionable damages. In order to pressure a large cash settlement out of the physician, the attorney added a claim to the lawsuit that the doctor had sexually attacked the patient. The doctor's insurance policy was cancelled after the insurance company became aware of the sexual attack allegation. If the doctor initiates a claim of abuse of legal proceedings, the likely outcome is that the doctor will

(A) Prevail, if there were special damages and there was no basis in fact for the allegation of sexual misconduct.

(B) Prevail, only if the underlying claim of medical malpractice has no merit.

(C) Not prevail, if there is a finding that the underlying claim of medical malpractice has merit.

(D) Prevail, even if they can show no damages.

161. Captain Sailor was captaining his boat on Lake Lucious when a severe storm arose. As the waves and wind increased, Captain aimed for a private island in the middle of the lake, which was the closest piece of land he could see. As he got into shallow water, the boat went onto the rocks and began breaking up. Captain abandoned ship and successfully swam to shore. The storm created large waves that drove the boat into a private dock on the island creating significant damages. If the dock owner brings suit against Captain for damages, the likely outcome is

(A) No recovery because Captain acted reasonably as necessary in an emergency situation beyond his control.

(B) No recovery because the sudden storm was an act of God.

(C) Recovery for the damages even though Captain's actions were privileged.

(D) Recovery because a trespasser is always liable when they go onto another's land without permission.

Questions 162 – 165 are based on the following:

Charlie Cowboy operates Dude Ranch that advertises widely to attract weekend cowboys. The ranch provides lodging and horses to the dudes who pay a per diem charge to stay at the ranch. The ranch has developed a riding trail system and gives all the dudes a map of trails. This allows the guests to ride around the ranch in their own group at their own leisure. The horse trail has an old wooden bridge that crosses over a river. Unknown to anyone, the bridge supports were partially rotted. There was a large group of horse riders on the bridge resulting in a collapse.

162. A neighbor named Fisherman Fred had sneaked into the dude ranch and was fishing in the river below the bridge. As the bridge collapsed, the debris fell on Fisherman Fred forcing him under water resulting in his drowning. If Fisherman Fred's heirs bring a wrongful death action against Dude Ranch, the likely outcome is

(A) Verdict for Dude Ranch, because the drowning was the cause of Fisherman Fred's death.

(B) Verdict for Dude Ranch, because Fisherman Fred was on the property without permission or invitation.

(C) Verdict for Fisherman Fred, if Dude Ranch could have reasonably discovered the rotting bridge had they made an investigation.

(D) Verdict for Fisherman Fred, since Dude Ranch is responsible for any dangerous condition on the land.

163. The horse-riding group fell into the river when the wooden bridge collapsed. Many of the riders were injured and one drowned. They brought suit against Dude Ranch. The likely outcome is

(A) Verdict for Dude Ranch because the Dude Ranch owner did not know of the dangerous natural condition.

(B) Verdict for the horse riders because Dude Ranch is liable for any dangerous condition on its land which injures a guest.

(C) Verdict for Dude Ranch because the gradual rotting of the bridge supports is a natural condition of all wooden bridges.

(D) Verdict for the horse riders if Dude Ranch could reasonably have discovered the rotting supports by inspecting the bridge.

164. Sitting on the riverbank watching the scene were a group of guests and two staff members of Dude Ranch. This was the swimming group and they had just finished their afternoon swim and lunch. One of the guests was Loren Lifeguard, a trained lifeguard with experience rescuing swimmers in peril. With respect to the duty to go to the rescue,

  (A) Loren Lifeguard has a responsibility to go the rescue of the drowning guests.
  (B) The staff members of the dude ranch have a responsibility to go to the rescue of the drowning guests.
  (C) Both Loren Lifeguard and the staff members have a responsibility to go to the rescue of the drowning guests.
  (D) Neither Loren Lifeguard nor the staff members have a responsibility to go to the rescue of the drowning guests.

165. Loren Lifeguard jumped to his feet when he saw that the guests might drown. Without expectation of compensation, he waded into the river to try to save the guests. He had, however, drunk a full bottle of Dude Ranch red wine during his lunch. Because of this, he stumbled negligently and was unable to save the drowning dude ranch guests. If sued for wrongful death, the best defense that Loren Lifeguard can assert is

  (A) He was uncompensated and not guilty of gross negligence or wanton misconduct.
  (B) He was under no duty to come to the rescue.
  (C) If he had not gone to the rescue, the guests still would have drowned so there was no damages.
  (D) A drowning person assumes the risk of a negligent rescuer.

166. Peter Pure was a tenant in an apartment house in the unit next to Oscar Obnoxious. Peter developed a severe distaste for Oscar and tried to get the landlord to evict Oscar. After a few encounters and confrontations, the landlord decided to stay out of the controversy. Peter put a bag of marijuana in Oscar's mailbox and called the Police alleging that Oscar was a drug dealer. Peter also influenced the district attorney to bring charges by perpetuating the lie. A criminal indictment was filed. The prosecution was later terminated and Oscar brought suit against Peter for malicious prosecution. To prevail, Oscar does not have to show that

  (A) Peter instituted the criminal proceedings, which were terminated in favor of Oscar.
  (B) Actual pecuniary damages were inflicted.
  (C) There was an absence of probable cause.
  (D) Peter had a malicious purpose other than bringing a criminal to justice.

167. Paul Patient was very vain and desired to retain a mid-20s physical image. When he turned 40, he began going to a plastic surgeon named Stan Surgeon for on-going treatment. In 2000, Stan redid Paul's chin bone. In 2001, the new bone alignment became painful. When Paul asked Stan about the pain, Stan said it was normal and prescribed a pain pill. This went on for three more years to late 2004 when Paul decided to get a second opinion from another doctor. In early 2005, the new doctor informed Paul that he had been the victim of plastic surgery medical malpractice. Paul brings suit in 2007 in a jurisdiction that has a three-year statute of limitations for medical malpractice. Stan Surgeon files a Rule 12 motion for dismissal based on a statute of limitations defense. The motion will likely be

  (A) Denied since the statute of limitations will only expire in 2008.
  (B) Granted since the statute of limitations expired in 2003.
  (C) Granted since the statute of limitations expired in 2004.
  (D) Granted since the statute of limitations expired in 2005.

168. Lori Landlord owned a large apartment building containing a grass field. The residents of the apartment used this field for picnics and sports. In addition, residents of the surrounding neighborhood used the field. While the landlord never gave express permission to the non-apartment house residents to use the field, she knew of it and never objected. The grass field had an underground watering system with sprinkler heads that receded into the grass when the watering system was turned off.

Recently one pipe in the watering system had broken and the sprinkler heads in that part of the system would not lower into the grass. The landlord learned of the defective condition, but did not fix it. A group of boys from the apartment building and the neighborhood began a "pick-up" soccer game on the field. One of the neighborhood boys tripped over one of the non-receding sprinkler heads suffering a brain concussion when his head slammed into the ground. If a lawsuit for the boy's damages is asserted against Lori, the likely outcome is

(A) No recovery, because the boy was a trespasser who assumes the risk of damages.

(B) No recovery, because the landlord did not do any act of active negligence and a sprinkler head is not inherently dangerous.

(C) A recovery, because the soccer field was an alluring hazardous condition known to the landlord.

(D) A recovery, because Lori Landlord did not object to the non-apartment house neighborhood boys playing on her property.

Questions 169 and 170 are based on the following:

Everyproduct Store, Inc., was a large retailer-wholesaler. In this location, the retail store was connected to their large wholesale facility. The wholesale operation served as a warehouse and shipping facility for all Everyproduct stores. While store personnel moved between the two areas, the public was only allowed in the retail store. There were signs at the connecting door leading to the wholesale area which stated that "Only Everyproduct's employees and suppliers are allowed in this portion of the facility." The restrooms were located right at the intersection of the two areas.

Sharon and Sally Shoppers were sisters who spent most of their weekend afternoons browsing through merchandise at retail stores in their city. They considered themselves to be excellent shoppers with advanced expertise in quality-price decisions. On a Sunday afternoon, they were using their expertise in analyzing much of the inventory at Everyproduct Store.

The Everyproduct facility was heated by furnace oil, which was stored in a large fuel tank in the area near the door between the retail and wholesale areas. The fuel line broke flooding the floors in the area where the retail and wholesale portions adjoined with a clear, slippery oil film. Because the maintenance crew did not work on Sunday, it was close to closing time, and there were very few shoppers in the store, the store manager decided to leave the oil on the floor for the Monday morning crew to clean up. The manager did post a warning sign up at the front of the spill on the retail store side.

169. Sharon and Sally had entered the women's restroom right before this occurred and the warning sign was posted. Sharon left the restroom first and turned left to go back into the retail store. She slipped on the oil, fell, and broke her arm. If Sharon sues Everyproduct, the likely outcome is that she will

(A) Prevail, because Everyproduct is strictly liable for all harms that occur to its customers on its premises.

(B) Not prevail, because she was an expert shopper.

(C) Not prevail, if the signs the store personnel posted were a reasonable warning.

(D) Prevail, because she was a business invitee.

170. Sally was also in the restroom and left after Sharon. She had been shopping so hard that she got confused and turned right instead of left. This led her into the wholesale portion of Everyproduct and she disregarded the "employee only" sign. Twenty feet into the warehouse, she realized she was in the wrong area. She turned, slipped on the oil on the floor, fell, and broke her arm. If Sally brings suit against Everyproduct for her damages, she will

(A) Prevail, because Everyproduct is strictly liable for all harms that occur to its customers on its premises.

(B) Not prevail, because she was an expert shopper.

(C) Not prevail, because she went into the wholesale warehouse.

(D) Prevail, because she was a business invitee.

171. Marvin Monopoly was a very aggressive entrepreneur. He grew his Company by devising competitive strategies to damage the businesses of his competitors. Which of the following actions by Marvin are least likely to make Marvin liable for a viable lawsuit alleging interference with a prospective advantage?

(A) Predatory actions intended to create a sole monopoly.

(B) Questionable advertising practices that damage the Plaintiff in her business.

(C) Price fixing with another competitor to eliminate a third competitor.

(D) Malicious creation and coordination of a group boycott by potential customers of the targeted company.

172. Peter Pistol was a gun collector and had a very large collection of antique pistols. He was holding a party at his home and decided to show off some of the finest pieces in his collection to his party guests. He brought a large antique Colt 45 pistol into the living room and waived the gun at Tina Timid. Tina was quite disturbed by this and later filed suit against Peter. Peter's best defense is that

(A) This act would not create apprehension of an imminent battery in the mind of a reasonable person.

(B) Tina did not actually experience any mental apprehension.

(C) Tina knew the pistol was not loaded.

(D) Since the gun was unloaded, there was not an imminent threat of contact.

Questions 173 and 174 are based on the following:

Robert Runner was a long distance runner who practiced running every day. While he was running alone in a county park, he turned the bend in the trail and encountered a wolf. He was very frightened and scaled a high fence jumping into the adjacent property. The fence had large signs posted that stated, "No Trespassing."

The owner of the adjacent property, Archie Ambusher, was a member of the local property rights group and kept large German Shepherd dogs in a kennel at his house. Robert's entry onto the property triggered an alarm. Archie ran outside and put the most ferocious German Shepard dog on a leash. He then ran towards the fence intending to frighten the intruder.

Robert saw Archie and the large dog coming. The dog rushed at Robert, but was restrained by the leash. Archie only intended to frighten Robert so he would not trespass again. The dog retreated back to Archie's side and then took a second top-speed run at Robert. This time the dog broke the leash and took two large chunks out of Robert's leg.

173. If Robert sues Archie for assault, will he prevail?
- (A) Yes, if Robert Runner reasonably believed the dog would bite him.
- (B) No, because Archie was trying to protect his property.
- (C) No, because the dog did not come into contact with Robert on the first lunge.
- (D) Yes, because Archie did not have a privilege to use excessive force.

174. If Robert Runner sued Archie Ambusher for battery, the likely outcome is that Robert will
- (A) Prevail because the dog leash breaking establishes liability under the doctrine of res ipsa loquitur.
- (B) Prevail because Archie intended that the German Shepherd frighten Robert.
- (C) Not prevail because Robert was a trespasser without any rights.
- (D) Not prevail because Archie did not intend the German Shepherd to have any harmful contact with Robert.

175. Terry Traveler was a regular flyer out of Always Airport. The airport was spread out with different terminals. Terry was walking between the terminals in a tunnel. There was a sign on a post in the tunnel which stated, "Floor may be slippery, watch your step." Terry was pushing a luggage cart and did not see the sign. She slipped on a banana peel dropped by another traveler. She fell hard and severely injured her back. If Terry brings suit against Always Airport, the most favorable circumstantial evidence to support her case is
- (A) That the warning sign was very conspicuous.
- (B) That the banana peel was dirty.
- (C) That the banana peel was yellow.

- (D) That the banana peel was black indicating decay.

176. Able and Baker were two CPAs conducting a certified audit of Courageous Enterprises, Inc. They rendered an unqualified opinion on the fairness of the financial statements, but their examination failed to discover a massive embezzlement scheme by many of the internal accounting personnel. Courageous brings suit against Able and Baker seeking a joint and several judgment against them both. Able and Baker should cross claim against each other to protect their contribution right in the event that
- (A) The trial judge directs a verdict of dismissal in favor of only one Defendant.
- (B) The trial judge directs a verdict of dismissal in favor of both Defendants.
- (C) The trial judge directs a verdict for Courageous Enterprises.
- (D) The jury returns a verdict for Courageous Enterprises against both Defendants.

Questions 177 and 178 are based on the following:

Tommy Trucker was driving his pickup truck west on the interstate. He was a very careful driver and was always on the alert for accidents to be avoided. Debra Driver was driving east on the interstate with her children in her car. Tommy saw a stray kitten in the road and turned to avoid hitting the animal. Apparently Tommy turned the steering wheel too suddenly because the pickup truck began spinning end-to-end on the freeway. Tommy's pickup spun across the center divider and collided with Debra's automobile causing significant injury to one of her children in the back seat.

177. If Debra brings suit for battery on behalf of her child, the likely outcome is that the claim will
- (A) Prevail, only if Tommy trucker intended to cause the collision.

(B) Not prevail, because Tommy Trucker did not intend to cause the collision.

(C) Not prevail, because these damages were not foreseeable by Tommy to result from merely turning the wheel to avoid the cat.

(D) Prevail, because the doctrine of transferred intent applies to battery.

178. Debra, herself, was not injured in the accident. However, she personally suffered severe emotional distress including numerous physical symptoms from seeing her children injured in the collision. If Debra brings suit for outrage or emotional distress, the claim will likely

(A) Prevail, because she was present at the scene of the accident and saw the injury to her children.

(B) Not prevail, because she suffered no physical injuries in the collision.

(C) Not prevail, unless Tommy Trucker was driving at a unreasonably high speed which caused his pickup truck to spin out of control when he swerved to avoid hitting the cat.

(D) Prevail, because she suffered severe emotional distress with physical manifestations and she was herself within the zone of danger created by Tommy's act.

Questions 179 and 180 are based on the following:

Debbie Deadbeat purchased a deluxe television on credit from Charlie Creditor Televisions Co. for zero down payment. Debbie submitted a financial statement and credit application that materially overstated her assets and credit rating. As soon as Debbie left the store with the television, Charlie ran a credit check on her. The credit check result was so bad that it was clear that Debbie had fraudulently misrepresented her credit. Had Charlie known the truth, they never would have allowed her to take the television from the store. Charlie ran out of the store chasing Debbie as soon as he learned of the fraud. He jumped into his car and followed her to her home where she parked in the private driveway.

179. Charlie parked in the street and walked onto Debbie's property alongside the car in the driveway. If Debbie sues Charlie for trespass, the likely outcome is that the claim will

(A) Prevail, because there is never a privilege to trespass.

(B) Not prevail, because a driveway is considered public property.

(C) Not prevail, because the trespass was in fresh pursuit of personal property wrongfully taken from the property owner by fraud.

(D) Prevail, only if Charlie Creditor fails to make legal demand for replevin before initiating the trespass.

180. Debbie was looking out the window of her home and saw Charlie begin to walk up the driveway. She came out of the home and entered into a heated discussion with Charlie in which she refused to surrender the television that was sitting in plain view on her front porch. Charlie began to pick up the television and Debbie resisted. Charlie shoved Debbie away and picked up the television. Debbie was not hurt, but she sued Charlie for battery. The likely outcome is that the claim will

(A) Prevail, because Charlie's proper remedy was to bring a legal action to regain possession rather than use self-help.

(B) Not prevail, because Debbie attained possession of the chattel wrongfully and Charlie was in fresh pursuit.

(C) Not prevail, because Debbie's verbal refusal to recover the television provided reasonable grounds for Charlie's battery and there were no damages.

(D) Prevail, because Debbie did not attain the television through the use of force.

181. Larry Lastminute was a law student at Everyone Passes Law School. Larry had not attended most of his first year tort classes and was beginning to become quite nervous about how he was going to perform on the upcoming final exam. A week before the final exam, he walked into the law school library and left his books on a desk while he went to get a cup of coffee. When he returned he picked up a law book that he believed was his own. After highlighting a few pages with a yellow marker, he realized it was not his own. The true owner, Donna Diligent, then appeared and discovered Larry had marked up her book. Donna brings suit against Larry for trespass to chattels. As a part of her prima facie case, Donna will not have to prove

    (A) Intention by Larry to harm her book by using the yellow marker to highlight text.

    (B) That Larry has intermeddled with personal property.

    (C) That she had an ownership or possessory interest in the book.

    (D) Actual damages resulted from the trespass.

182. Expired Equipment Inc. operated a large equipment sale and repair shop. The facility had a retail store and office in the front and a large spare part and old equipment area in the rear. The company locked their store and office, but there was no fence around the old equipment area even though the company personnel knew neighborhood boys often played on the equipment. A group of neighborhood boys were playing on an old truck in the equipment area one Sunday afternoon when the company was closed. A 9-year-old boy named Tommy Trap got into the cab of a large truck and tried to turn the steering wheel. It snapped back causing the roof of the cab to collapse injuring Tommy. A guardian for Tommy filed suit and Expired pleaded contributory fault as a defense. Which of the following facts would likely be the most important in determining if Expired Equipment owed a duty to Tommy?

    (A) Whether the storage area constituted a public nuisance.

    (B) Whether the storage area constituted a private nuisance.

    (C) Whether the truck in which Tommy was injured could be seen from the street.

    (D) Whether Expired could have eliminated the risk of neighborhood boys trespassing by a fence at an insignificant cost.

Questions 183 – 185 are based on the following:

Oscar Owner operated an automobile repair garage containing, among other equipment, a gasoline tank and pump. Tracy and Tony Thief were driving in the neighborhood and ran out of gas. They saw the garage, which was closed at the time. They found a locked side door which they forced and entered the building. They located a large glass container and filled it with gasoline from the pump. Tracy turned suddenly and dropped the glass container, which broke and started a large fire. The fire trapped Tracy and Tony in the building. Ryan Rescuer saw the fire, called the fire department on his cell phone, ran into the building, and pulled Tracy to safety. He decided not to go back into the building to try to save Tony. In the process, Ryan received significant burn injuries, but the fire department saved the building.

183. If Ryan Rescuer sues Oscar Owner for personal injuries, the likely outcome of the claim is that it will

    (A) Prevail, because his call to the fire department saved Oscar's building.

    (B) Not prevail, because Oscar had no fault.

    (C) Not prevail, because a voluntary individual going to the rescue assumes the risk of suffering damages.

(D) Prevail, because gasoline is inherently dangerous, thus creating strict liability.

184. If Ryan Rescuer sues Tracy Thief for personal injuries, the likely outcome of the claim is
  (A) Prevail, because Tracy caused the fire.
  (B) Not prevail, because as a professional rescuer he knowingly assumed the risk of suffering damages.
  (C) Not prevail, because it was not reasonably foreseeable by Tracy that a third party would be injured if her theft did not go as planned.
  (D) Prevail, because he rescued her.

185. Tony died in the fire. His personal representative brought suit against Ryan Rescuer for wrongful death. The likely outcome of this lawsuit is that the personal representative will
  (A) Prevail, because once a rescuer begins the rescue, there is a full duty to complete.
  (B) Not prevail, because a trespasser assumes the risk of not being rescued.
  (C) Not prevail, because an uncompensated bystander has no duty to go to the rescue of a stranger.
  (D) Not prevail, because a thief assumes the risk of not being rescued.

Questions 186 – 188 are based on the following:

Peter Patient was experiencing some chest pains and went onto Daisy Doctor's office for a diagnosis. Daisy took numerous X-rays of Peter's chest area and forwarded them on an independent X-ray developing lab named Developer Inc. When the X-rays were returned, Daisy reviewed the accompanying X-ray report. She and Peter then had a second meeting in which the doctor made a diagnosis that there was malignant cancer in one of Peter's lungs and suggested an operation. The diagnosis was based on the X-ray report from the developing lab. Peter consented to the treatment.

186. In determining whether proper patient consent was obtained which is the least important component?
  (A) Whether the particular risks and possible benefits were disclosed.
  (B) Whether the consent was obtained in writing.
  (C) Whether any feasible available alternative course of treatment were disclosed.
  (D) Whether the disclosures were sufficient so that the patient appreciated the effect of the consent.

187. Daisy Doctor scheduled Peter Patient's surgical procedure at Heavenly Hospital. The procedure seemed normal and Daisy opened Peter's chest cavity and surgically removed a large portion of the lung that contained the malignant cancer. Toward the end of the removal, Daisy spotted what appeared to be cancerous growth in Peter's lower abdominal area. She removed the fat tissue in this area but in so doing lacerated Peter's upper colon. If Peter brings suit for battery against Daisy, the likely outcome of the claim is that it will
  (A) Prevail, because Daisy exceeded the scope of the consent.
  (B) Not prevail, because a patient impliedly consents to an extension of the procedure if the physician comes on unusual circumstance.
  (C) Not prevail, because a physician is always authorized to extend a procedure based upon unforeseen circumstances.
  (D) Prevail, because damages resulted from the procedure.

188. One month later, Daisy Doctor received a second set of X-rays for Peter Patient from Developer Inc. These X-rays showed no cancer in either lung. After research, it was concluded the second set of X-rays was accurate and the first set was of another patient sent to the wrong doctor. Thus the lung removal was performed under a mistake of fact. If Peter brings suit against Daisy for medical malpractice, the likely outcome is that the claim will

(A) Prevail, because a serious operation involves serious danger and therefore strict liability applies.

(B) Not prevail, because Peter consented.

(C) Not prevail, unless Daisy should have investigated beyond merely accepting the first X-ray Developer lab report.

(D) Prevail, because the doctor is always responsible for checking the work of their subordinates and a mistake of fact is not an excuse for a professional.

Questions 189 and 190 are based on the following:

David and Deloris Dwelling were in their home one evening peacefully watching television. Fugitive Fred was being chased by police in the neighborhood and ran into the Dwelling's home to escape arrest. Fred pulled a six-shooter handgun from his pocket aimed at David and Deloris. He fired 6 rounds at Deloris who was hit and injured.

189. Two of the shots missed Deloris, but went through the wall and hit the Dwelling's 4-year-old child, Innocent, who was asleep in the next room. If Innocent's guardian brings a suit for battery against Fred, the likely outcome is

(A) Prevail, because Fugitive injured Innocent.

(B) Not prevail, because Fred had no intent to injure Innocent.

(C) Not prevail, because Innocent was asleep so the Plaintiff lacked any mental apprehension of offensive contact.

(D) Prevail, because Fred intended to shoot Deloris.

190. After wounding Deloris, Fugitive Fred turned the handgun towards David Dwelling. All the rounds of ammunition in the gun had been used so it was impossible for Fugitive to fire the gun to injure David. David jumped up and ran into the kitchen. He grabbed a knife and stabbed Fugitive Fred. If Fred brings suit against David for battery, the result is that the lawsuit will likely

(A) Prevail, because David stabbed him.

(B) Not prevail, because he was a fugitive.

(C) Not prevail, because David was under a reasonable but mistaken belief that such force was necessary.

(D) Prevail, because David used excessive force.

Questions 191 and 192 are based on the following:

Prince and Paula Parents had an 11-year-old daughter, Caroline. The parents left their car keys lying on a table in the entryway of their home. They directed Caroline to go to the local store three blocks away and buy a loaf of bread for dinner. Caroline picked up the car keys off the table without her parents' permission and backed the car out of the Parents' driveway into the street. Caroline decided to go on a joy ride with two of her friends, Wendy and Julie. She drove down to the grocery store, purchased the bread, and then drove to the corner soda fountain where she picked up Wendy and Julie who joined her in the front seat of the car. As they drove down the strip, a car emerged from a cross street. The three girls were all talking which distracted Caroline who did not see that the green light had changed to red. Their car collided with the emerging car driven by Iola Innocent. Caroline did not have a driver's license.

191. If Iola brings suit against Caroline for her injuries, the probable outcome of the suit is Iola will

- (A) Prevail if the trier of fact determines that Caroline did not act as a reasonably prudent 11-year-old would have under similar circumstances.
- (B) Not prevail because an 11-year-old does not have the age, education, experience, and ability to properly operate a motor vehicle.
- (C) Not prevail because the chatter of Wendy and Julie distracted Caroline.
- (D) Prevail if the trier of fact determines that Caroline did not act as a reasonably prudent adult person would have under similar circumstances.

192. If Iola brings suit against Prince and Paula Parents, her worst theory of recovery would be that

- (A) The Parents are liable because they own the car, which was the dangerous instrumentality that inflicted the damage.
- (B) The Parents are liable because they sent Caroline on a family purpose to go to the store as their agent.
- (C) The Parents are liable because they gave Caroline express or implied permission to use the car.
- (D) The Parents are liable because Caroline had taken the car before without permission so leaving the keys on the table in the entryway was negligent.

193. Fast Freddie was proceeding north on the Expressway at a rate of 70 m.p.h. (miles per hour) in a speed zone where the posted maximum speed limit was 60 m.p.h. Sally Sidestreet pulled out on the northbound entrance and immediately went into the middle lane. Fast Freddie was in the middle lane and could not stop in time to avoid running into the rear of Sally's car. Expert testimony was introduced that Fast Freddie would not have been able to stop in

time even if he was only going 60 m.p.h. If Sally brings suit against Fast Freddie for her damages, the likely outcome of the lawsuit is

- (A) Prevail, since Fast Freddie's violation of law was negligence per se.
- (B) Not prevail, because she pulled out on the freeway in front of Fast Freddie.
- (C) Not prevail, because the violation of the law was not the cause "in fact" of Sally's damages.
- (D) Prevail, because Fast Freddie's driving was criminal.

Questions 194 – 196 are based on the following:

A junior-high school treated regular teachers as employees and the occasional substitute teachers as independent contractors. A substitute teacher named Shawn Stern was in charge of an eighth grade class. Stern had a history of violence in prior schools.

A 12-year-old boy in his class named David Delinquent began to horseplay with some of the other students at the back of the room. Mr. Stern told him to stop. When David continued to horseplay, Mr. Stern ran to the back of the room and began to violently hit David in the head. David suffered a rupture to his eardrum because of Mr. Stern's repeated blows.

194. If David's guardian brings suit against Mr. Stern, the least important factor for the court to consider is whether

- (A) David signed a waiver of any right to complain against discipline by any member of the school's faculty or staff.
- (B) The severity of David's misconduct and the age, strength, and maturity of David.
- (C) The degree of force used by Mr. Stern was reasonable.
- (D) The motive of Mr. Stern.

195. If David's guardian also brought suit against the school district, the school district's best defense would be that

(A) Mr. Stern was on a frolic or detour of his own.
(B) They did not have a duty to investigate the background of a substitute teacher.
(C) Mr. Stern was an independent contractor.
(D) They did not have a duty to supervise the classroom and the battery was unauthorized.

196. Assume that the school district was held liable and paid the damages Shawn Stern inflicted on David Delinquent. Which of the following is not a reason why the school district would be entitled to indemnity by Shawn Stern.

(A) Mr. Stern's conduct was more culpable than the school district's.
(B) Mr. Stern was following specific instructions from the school's principal to engage in such discipline.
(C) Mr. Stern agreed with the school district to pay the full amount of the damages.
(D) The school district was liable to David Delinquent because of respondeat superior.

197. Albert Attorney was a sole practitioner in Littletown who operated a general law practice. In 1990, Albert drafted a document for an estate plan that unfortunately violated the rule against perpetuities. Upon the testator's death in 2004, fourteen years later, the mistake was discovered. Because of the error, the estate plan was not admitted to probate so the distribution of the assets went under the state intestate statute. Gordon Greedy was to be a substantial taker under the estate plan, but did not take under the intestate statute since he was not a relative. The state statute of limitations for professional malpractice is three years. If Gordon sues Albert for professional malpractice in 2005, the best defense Albert can assert is

(A) The statute of limitations has run so Gordon's lawsuit is not timely.
(B) The legal fee for the original estate plan was never paid.
(C) The rule against perpetuities is too complicated for the average lawyer in the locality of Littletown to understand.
(D) Gordon was not an eligible taker under the estate plan.

Questions 198 and 199 are based on the following:

The Rat Hole Tavern sold beer for consumption on the premises and to go. The bartender server on that shift was gregarious and the customers were allowed to buy the bartender drinks. Peter Parties purchased two full cases of beer to go. David Drunkard entered the tavern at 5:00 pm after leaving work. He sat at the bar drinking heavily for 4 hours straight until 9:00 pm. During this time, David also bought the bartender at least three drinks.

198. David Drunkard then left the bar and got into his car, which was in the tavern's parking lot. He drove to the Interstate freeway and, due to his drunken state, entered the exit lane, emerging going north in the south bound lanes. His car hit Florence Family's car head-on thereby severely injuring Florence personally and demolishing her car. If Florence brings suit against the Rat Hole Tavern, the likely outcome is that she will

(A) Prevail since a commercial vendor of alcohol is strictly liable for any damages their customers inflict on third parties while under the influence of liquor they sold or dispensed.
(B) Not prevail unless Florence also sues David Drunkard.
(C) Not prevail since the tavern server did not know their customer would drive his car the wrong way on the freeway.

(D) Prevail if the tavern server knew or should have known that David Drunkard had over consumed.

199. Peter Parties took home the two cases of beer he purchased at the Rat Hole Tavern. Peter's 16-year-old son, Paul Parties was holding a party for three of his teenage friends at the Parties' family home. Peter believed it was all right to provide beer to his son and his friends at home since they could get it anyway and would drink in their cars if they were not allowed to drink at home. He told the boys to help themselves. After four hours of heavy partying, the four boys had consumed all of the 48 bottles of beer. Paul Parties got in his father's car and drove to a store to purchase some more beer. Due to his intoxicated state, he ran a red light colliding with Bob Bicyclist who was severely injured. If Bob brings suit, he will likely prevail against

(A) Paul Parties only.
(B) Peter Parties only.
(C) Paul Parties and Peter Parties only.
(D) Paul Parties, Peter Parties, and the Rat Hole Tavern.

Questions 200 – 202 are based on the following:

David Doglover had a german shepherd dog named Attack and a pet monkey named Playful. The German Shepherd was generally friendly, but had bitten people in the past and David kept him in a well-fenced area. The pet monkey was purchased from a traveling circus many years ago and had become almost totally domesticated when around adults, but still liked to jump on small children.

200. A child left the gate to the German Shepherd's fenced area open allowing Attack to get out. Attack spotted a cat across the street and ran to see if he could catch the cat. At this same time, two small children were crossing the same street in Attack's path. Attack was running at full speed when he hit the children knocking them down onto the concrete street. The children received substantial injuries from the fall and their guardian has brought suit against Attack's owner, David Doglover, alleging strict liability. The likely outcome of this suit is

(A) Prevail, under strict liability because Attack has a history of biting people.
(B) Not recover under strict liability, because David Doglover exercised extraordinary precaution to fence in the animal.
(C) Not recover under strict liability, because the Plaintiff's injury was not within the scope of the harm of biting people.
(D) Prevail under strict liability, because David Doglover owns the dog.

201. David Doglover took the monkey Playful to Victoria Veterinarian. Victoria represented to David that she could remove the gland that caused monkeys to jump on young children. Victoria performed the operation, but unknown to David it was not successful.

David was subsequently walking down the street with Playful when a 9-year-old child approached. Playful apparently wanted to play with a person closer to his size so he jumped on the child. The child was severely injured. If the child's guardian brought suit against David, the probable outcome is that the guardian will

(A) Prevail because the monkey was a private nuisance.
(B) Not prevail because the owner, David, thought the animal was safe in public.
(C) Not prevail because Victoria Veterinarian was the cause of the injury.
(D) Prevail because the monkey, Playful, was not a domestic animal.

202. If the child's guardian brought suit against Victoria Veterinarian, the likely outcome is that the Plaintiff will

(A) Prevail on the claim of negligence.

(B) Not prevail because David, not the child, hired the health care professional.

(C) Not prevail because proximate causation is absent.

(D) Prevail on the claim of strict liability.

203. Tom Terrible and Dick Destroyer were gang members out on the prowl for people to rob. They came upon Victor Victim in an alley coming out of the back door of his mercantile shop, which he had just closed for the night. Tom and Dick pulled large knives from their pockets and came at Victor. Victor pulled a handgun from his cash bag. Tom stabbed Victor in his right arm while Victor was holding the gun. The stab caused Victor's arm to move and the gun fired with the bullet missing Tom. Unfortunately, Iola Innocent was then passing by the alley and the bullet hit her. If Iola sues Victor for battery, the most likely outcome is that Iola will

(A) Prevail because shooting a gun is excessive force in defending against attackers with only knives.

(B) Not prevail unless she can show that Victor was negligent.

(C) Not prevail because the chance of her being unintentionally hit by the bullet was so remote as to be classified as an act of God.

(D) Prevail because Victor's intent to shoot Tom may be transferred to her battery.

204. Billy and Betty Briney spent their summers in an old farmhouse. When they left at the end of the summer, they boarded up the windows so burglars could not see they had valuable belongings in the house. After repeated break-ins, the Brineys decided to use a more aggressive defense. They set a spring trigger to a 20-guage shotgun that would fire if a thief opened the door. Killer Katko was seriously injured when he broke into the house to steal fruit jars. If Katko brings suit against the Brineys, the likely outcome is the suit will

(A) Prevail, because there was no fair warning.

(B) Not prevail, because Katko was an unauthorized trespasser who takes the land and dwelling as he finds it.

(C) Not prevail, because Katko impliedly assumed the risk of injury when he decided to steal the chattels of another.

(D) Prevail, if the Brineys would have not been allowed to use deadly force had they been in the house.

205. A negligent driver ran into the rear of a car at a red stoplight. The driver in the leading car, Wally Whiplash, was not wearing a seat belt, suffered substantial injuries and was taken to the hospital. Wally refused to undergo surgery to alleviate the injury thereby creating permanent injuries. The insurance company paid Wally a substantial sum for disability benefits. In the lawsuit Wally brings against the negligent driver to recover damages, Wally will likely

(A) Prevail, for damages including punitive damages.

(B) Not be able to block the negligent driver from introducing at trial evidence of the payments received from the insurance company.

(C) Prevail, for an extra award for the attorney fees he incurred

(D) Not be entitled to interest on the principal damage sum from the date of the accident to the date of judgment.

206. Martin and Mary Moving decided to relocate their family from Boston to Seattle. They had for years lived in a large Victorian house in Cambridge while Martin attended law school. To dispose of many of their possessions, they decided to contribute them to a needy community group. The community group held a garage-sale style of event to raise funds. At the event Nancy Neighbor purchased a flower arrangement made by Mary Moving. When Nancy grabbed the flower arrangement she was cut by a very sharp edge on the back of the arrangement's container. If Nancy sues the community group for her injuries, the likely outcome is that she will

(A) Prevail, against the community group since they are strictly liable for the defective product.
(B) Not prevail, against the local community group since they did not produce the product in question.
(C) Not prevail, against the community group unless they were negligent in not inspecting the flower arrangement prior to selling it.
(D) Not prevail, against the community group because they have a right of indemnification or reimbursement from the Movings.

Questions 207 and 208 are based on the following:

The Almighty Automobile Company manufactures a sports utility vehicle named Jump. The Company has recently received consumer complaints that the vehicle had traveled backwards in reverse gear when the gear shifter indicator was in park. A class action lawsuit has been started alleging that a poorly designed internal component part can allow the Jump's transmission to come to rest in an unstable position between park and reverse. A door slamming or air-conditioner cycling can cause it to slip into reverse, according to the expert engineers for the Plaintiffs.

Wally Wheeler read about this action with interest. He really liked the other features of the Jump and wanted to buy one. He went to the Jump dealer and purchased the vehicle after the salesman gave him a 25% discount on the price due to the transmission problem.

Wally was returning home from work the next afternoon in the new Jump. He was going bowling with his friends and he shifted to park and left the car running in his driveway and the driver's door open, while he ran into the house to get his bowling ball. Norman Neighbor had to get by the Jump in the driveway so he slammed the driver's door Wally had left open. 10 seconds later, the car began rolling in reverse and rammed into Norman who was walking back to his house.

207. If Norman sues Almighty Automobile Company, a verdict for the Defendant is most likely because

(A) Wally's knowing use of a defective product relieves the manufacturer of liability.
(B) Norman was contributorily negligent by slamming the door and then walking with his back to the truck.
(C) Norman was not a consumer or user of the product.
(D) Norman's use of the Jump vehicle gearshift without turning the engine off was an unforeseeable misuse of the product.

208. If Norman sues Wally Wheeler, the likely outcome is that the suit will

(A) Prevail, if Norman can prove the Jump vehicle's transmission was defective.
(B) Not prevail, because Norman, not Wally, caused the Jump to go into reverse.
(C) Not prevail, because Wally was not the manufacturer or retailer seller of the vehicle creating the damage.
(D) Prevail, because Wally knew the Jump vehicle was defective.

Questions 209 and 210 are based on the following:

Power Saws Inc. manufactured a soft wood power saw unit built into an aluminum table intended for the consumer market. The unit consisted of a table, electrical motor, pulleys, and a faceplate connector. The connector had four bolts to tighten over individual saw blades and sanding faces.

The manufacturer also sold a full line of recommended blades for use on this unit. There was a warning in the instruction booklet that read, "Use only Power Saws Inc. blades on this machine."

Charlie Carpenter purchased the basic table and related power saw unit for his own use. He wanted to saw extremely hard wood and since he could not find a hardwood blade made by Power Saws Inc he purchased a blade from another vendor. The blade he used was much larger than those sold by Power Saws and the hardwood he was cutting was much thicker and denser than ordinary soft wood putting heavy stress on the machine. The third time Charlie tried to cut the hardwood, the pulley snapped and the oversize blade flew off severely cutting his wrist.

Charlie sued Power Saws Inc. for his injuries based on strict product liability. At trial, Power Saws Inc. produced evidence that when used with the blades they sold, the unit was completely safe for cutting softer wood. There were neither design nor manufacturing defects if the unit was used as intended.

209. If the jury is properly instructed, the Plaintiff should

- (A) Prevail, since the manufacturer's liability was established by the failure of their product.
- (B) Not prevail, since the product had no design or manufacturing defect when it left the manufacturer.
- (C) Not prevail, since Charlie misused the product when he attached another manufacturer's blade to it.
- (D) Prevail, if it was foreseeable that consumers would buy and use other brands and sizes of saw blades than those sold by Power Saws, Inc.

210. The best argument that Power Saws Inc. could make to justify a lack of a warning label on the unit itself would be

- (A) Reasonable care in this circumstance does not require a warning be given since the danger of using other manufacturers' saw blades was obvious.
- (B) There was a proper written warning given to the purchaser.
- (C) It is up to the retailer to give the warning since they know their customers better than the manufacturer.
- (D) Power saws are unavoidably unsafe products and the costs of warning everyone outweighs the minimal risk of a few injuries.

Questions 211 – 214 are based on the following:

Green Thumb Gardening is a large retailer of garden equipment and supplies. The store sells, rents, and repairs a large selection of new and used power lawn mowers. Occasionally, they will take a used mower in on trade for a new mower. Every traded-in mower is then completely disassembled and either used for parts in the repair process or rebuilt for sale in the used mower inventory. During the rebuilding process all moving parts are thoroughly oiled and new bearings and bushing installed where the power drive train intersects with the rotary grass-cutting blade. Green Thumb prides themselves on their high-quality rebuilt mowers, guarantees they will "function as new" and promises a full refund for any reason within 90 days of purchase.

Glorious Golf Course operated a local 9-hole course and was in need of a new power mower. Being short on money, the course manager decided to purchase a reconditioned rather than a new mower. The power mower the manager picked out was manufactured by Safety First Lawnmowers. Green Thumb took the mower in on a trade-in from another customer. This model had a grass-cutting rotary blade, which had coarse teeth for mowing rough lawns. The golf course, in comparison, had very fine and thin grass sprouts which produced a tighter, more consistently level lawn that golfers preferred.

The golf course manager explained the particular golf course purpose to the lawn mower salesman. In response the salesman represented that a mower blade manufactured by Super Blade Company would be fit for the golf course's purpose. Relying on the salesman's skill and judgment, the golf course manager purchased the mower and Green Thumb installed the Super Blade.

A few days later when the golf course gardener was using the reconditioned mower, the shaft holding the cutting blade came loose when a bearing gave way. The blade flew out from under the mower, severely cutting the gardener's ankle. The golf course was forced to close down for two days while it hired a new gardener and had the lawn mower repaired.

211. If the golf course gardener asserts a claim for his injuries against Green Thumb Gardening, the theory upon which recovery is most likely is
- (A) Negligence because the lawn mower is an inherently dangerous product.
- (B) Express warranty.
- (C) Implied warranty.
- (D) Strict product liability.

212. If the golf course gardener asserts a strict product liability claim against Safety First Lawnmowers, the likely outcome is that the claim will
- (A) Prevail because Safety First Lawnmowers was in the business of manufacturing dangerous products.
- (B) Not prevail because the lawnmower had been rebuilt by Green Thumb Gardening.
- (C) Not prevail because the golf course gardener was not the purchaser of the lawn mower.
- (D) Prevail if the shaft holding the cutting blade that came loose was the original shaft when it was manufactured by Safety First Lawnmowers.

213. The golf course gardener asserts a strict product liability claim against both Green Thumb Gardening and Super Blade Company. In discovery, it is revealed that the gardener had just completed mowing the border of one of the fairways, which contained rocks, brush, and very high wild grass. The best defense that can be asserted is
- (A) The golf course gardener was contributorily negligent in failing to inspect the mowing blade shaft the morning of the accident.
- (B) Green Thumb used all possible care in the rebuilding process and Super Blades used every available means to inspect their blades for defects.
- (C) The gardener was putting the lawnmower to an unintended use.
- (D) The gardener assumed the risk by mowing off the border of the fairway.

214. Glorious Golf Course has a standard policy of paying all employees for employment related expenses. Pursuant to this policy, they paid the golf course gardener $6,500 which was a reasonable damage amount for the personal physical injuries he sustained from the blade injury in the lawnmower malfunction. In addition, the company lost $2,500 in profit because the course was closed for two days that it took to replace the gardener and repair the mower. The $2,500 damage amount was a reasonable amount of the lost profits according to the golf course's expert witness CPA. This expert opinion was not controverted. If Glorious Golf course brings suit against Green Thumb Gardening for strict product liability and prevails, the likely judgment amount will be

(A) – 0 –
(B) $2,500.
(C) $6,500.
(D) $9,000.

215. Mary Mountaineer was born and raised in a large US city, but always dreamed about living in the mountains. After she retired from a busy career with a large urban law firm, she built a very quaint cabin on the edge of a national forest in Great Woody County. Mary had not researched the history of the Great Woody area, which experienced major forest fires about every ten years. Two years after she moved into the cabin, the area had a very dry spring and summer with almost no rain. In August, a major forest fire began in the national forest adjoining her cabin. To create a firewall, the Forest Service used explosives to blast a firebreak in the forest that could contain the oncoming fire. Unfortunately, the blasting damaged Mary's cabin. If Mary brings suit against the Forest Service under a strict liability theory of recovery, the best defense that the Forest Service can assert is

    (A) Mary was contributorily negligent by not building a stronger, more fire resistant cabin.
    (B) This was a public necessity.
    (C) By moving to the fire-prone area, Mary assumed the risk.
    (D) By moving to the fire-prone area, Mary exercised comparative fault.

216. Daylight Manufacturing Co. manufactured, assembled, and marketed a steel cutting press designed to cut aluminum sheets into can covers. In 2002, Goodboy Beverages purchased a deluxe cutting press model for $20,000. In 2002 and 2003, Daylight received a few complaints that other customers had experienced malfunctions with the cutting presses. In response, Daylight created a safety device for the machine and offered it to all their customers for $5,000 each in a brochure that mentioned the fact that a few users had been injured using the machine without the safety device. Goodboy

received the brochure in the mail, but did not respond to the $5,000 safety device offer. In 2004, an employee of Goodboy was injured using the press. At trial, Daylight introduced evidence that had Goodboy purchased the safety device for $5,000, the injury probably would not have occurred and moved the court for a directed verdict. The court should

    (A) Grant the motion because the refusal to purchase the safety device was an effective assumption the risk.
    (B) Deny the motion because Goodboy's negligence in failing to purchase the safety device was less than Daylight's negligence in manufacturing the unsafe press initially.
    (C) Deny the motion because the jury could find that Daylight could reasonably foresee that Goodboy would be unwilling to pay $5,000 for a safety device.
    (D) Deny the motion because the press was inherently dangerous and therefore Daylight was strictly liable.

217. Sarah Solitude was carefully driving her car and stopped at a red stoplight. Ralph Reckless was the driver of the following car and negligently ran into the rear of Sarah's car. The collision pushed Sarah's car into the intersection. Sam Speeder, who was traveling through on a cross street, hit Sarah's car on the passenger side. Sam was going 30 mph over the speed limit at the time. Had Sam been driving at the speed limit, he could have easily stopped in time to avoid the collision. Sarah was not injured because her car was equipped with a high quality lap and shoulder seat belt. The injury to the rear of Sarah's car cost $7,000 to repair while the side damages cost $5,000. If Sarah is determined to be without fault and she brings suit against both Ralph and Sam, the likely outcome is judgment against

    (A) Ralph for $7,000 individually and Sam for $5,000 individually.

(B) Ralph and Sam jointly and severally for $12,000.

(C) Ralph individually for $12,000 since, but for his negligence, the second collision involving Sam would not have occurred.

(D) Ralph for $12,000 individually and Ralph and Sam jointly and severally for $5,000.

Questions 218 and 219 are based on the following:

Paul and Susan Property Owner owned a large tract of undeveloped forest between the Olympic National Park and a small city named Port Angeles. The area had a number of natural hot springs and two of the neighboring property owners had developed hot spring resorts, which attracted thousands of paying customers a year. Paul and Susan wanted to protect the non-developed natural beauty of their property and posted signs on their property "No Trespassing." Children from Port Angeles have in the past trespassed onto Paul and Susan's property and played in a large natural hot water spring pool located there. A young swimmer, while diving, got his feet caught in a submerged tree branch. This submerged branch was not visible from the pool's shore. He struggled, further tightening the grip the tree branch had on his foot, and after a few minutes drowned.

218. If the boy's personal representative brings suit for wrongful death against Paul and Susan Property Owner, the likely outcome is that the suit will

(A) Not prevail.

(B) Prevail if the danger of the pool was a foreseeable risk to children that they were unlikely to discover.

(C) Prevail if the danger of the pool was a foreseeable risk to children that they were unlikely to discover and the Defendants knew or should have known that children were trespassing on their property.

(D) Prevail if the danger of the pool was a foreseeable risk to children that they were unlikely to discover, the Defendants knew or should have known that children were trespassing on their property, and the Defendants could have undertaken reasonable measures to warn or protect against the danger.

219. Assume that in the above case the property owner is held to be potentially liable for the wrongful death of the child who drowned. Concerning this action, which of the below is an incorrect statement?

(A) In most states, a statute specifies that tort and contract claims survive the decedent's death and vest in the personal representative of the estate.

(B) The property owner may assert against the personal representative all defenses that would be good against the decedent had he survived.

(C) The decedent's claims for defamation, invasion of property, and intentional infliction of emotional distress usually survive the death.

(D) The decedent's claims for pre-death pain, suffering and mental anguish do not terminate with the decedent's death.

220. Francis Fearful was 65 years old. Her neighborhood has recently experienced a number of purse snatchings by a mugger. The police prepared a composition picture of the mugger from the identification descriptions given by four prior victims. This composition picture was printed on a poster and the local television station ran the picture as a public service. The warning told people to be on the lookout for this mugger and stated the mugger was dangerous and advised single women to carry mace pistols. Francis was walking home from the local drug store alone one night and encountered a street person that appeared to her to look very much like the publicized mugger. When they were about five feet apart, the street person raised his fist. Thinking the street person was the mugger and fearing an imminent physical attack, Francis maced him. The street person was not the mugger and the mace caused him injury including serious eye damages. If the street person filed suit against Francis who relies on the privilege of self-defense, the likely outcome is that Francis will

(A) Prevail only if a reasonable person under the circumstances would have believed that the street person was about to attack.
(B) Not prevail because the street person was not about to attack.
(C) Not prevail unless the street person intended his gesture as a threat.
(D) Prevail if Francis honestly believed that the street person was about to attack her.

Questions 221 – 223 are based on the following:

Hilly Home Owner's house is located on a point of land over a steep slope on a hill overlooking a waterway known as the Puget Sound. The hillsides in the area are known for sliding away after heavy rains in the Fall and Spring. A prior owner of Hilly's house installed steel and concrete reinforcing on both sides and the front of Hilly's property to stop any sliding.

Eight years later, Hilly's neighbor, Cathi Complainer, lost part of her property to a slide in the spring rains. This exposed the steel and concrete reinforcement on that side of Hilly's property. Cathi had a boundary line survey done showing that the Hilly's reinforcements were on her property and threatened Hilly with a lawsuit if the reinforcements were not removed.

Hilly hired Excavation Contractor Inc. to take the steel and concrete reinforcements out of her land adjoining Cathi's property. It was left to the contractor to decide how

to accomplish the removal. Hilly paid Excavation in full on completion. Five days after the contractor had completed the removal, a large portion of Hilly's property slipped away into the Puget Sound. The slide destroyed a sailboat owned by Sally Sailor that was legally moored at the base of the hill. Both Hilly and Excavation have stipulated that the removal of the reinforcing steel and concrete caused the hill to slide into Sally's boat.

221. If Sally brings suit against Excavation Contractor Inc. which defense, if true, would be the best to assert?

(A) Any liability he had was terminated when Hilly accepted and paid for the work.
(B) The contractor could not reasonably foresee that removing side supports on the property would cause a slide on the front of the property.
(C) The contractor removed the steel and concrete reinforcing at the direction of Hilly Home Owner.
(D) The sailboat owner had no privity with the contractor.

222. If Sally brings suit against Hilly Home Owner, the best theory to assert liability is that

(A) Liability is based on respondeat superior.
(B) Liability is strict because the damage came from her property.
(C) The principal is liable because payment to the contractor is accompanied by assumption of responsibility for any damages resulting from the work.
(D) The owner had knowledge that the contractor was engaged in an inherently hazardous activity of removing the reinforcements that could cause the hill to collapse.

223. If Cathi Complainer's lawsuit against Hilly Home Owner is successful, does Hilly have recourse against Excavation Contractor?

(A) Yes, if the verdict against Hilly was based on vicarious liability.

(B) No, if payment by Hilly did constitute an acceptance of the work.

(C) Yes, because Hilly's activities were not a cause in fact of the damage.

(D) No, because Hilly hired Excavation to accomplish the removal work.

224. A policeman was in his police car when he received an emergency dispatch call to go to a given address. When he arrived at the address he found a pregnant woman who had just gone into premature labor. The woman had experienced problems during the pregnancy and the decision was made to take her to the maternity ward at the nearest hospital. On the way the police car carrying the officer and woman drove north through a busy intersection against a red light at 45 miles per hour without using a siren. The speed limit was 30 miles per hour in the area. Ike Innocent was driving west through the same intersection and collided with the police car. If Ike brings suit against the police department, the likely outcome is that the suit will

(A) Prevail, if the police officer's actions were determined to be reckless.

(B) Not prevail, because he was a government employee performing a discretionary act within the scope of his official duties.

(C) Not prevail, unless a reasonable police officer under similar circumstances would have used the siren.

(D) Prevail, if the police officer failed to act as a reasonable person.

225. Larry Lynch was 14 years old but had a mental age under 6. Larry worked as a manual laborer on a farm. Frank Farmer was his employer and instructed Larry to walk behind a corn picker tractor. Larry got too close and his arm got caught in the machine creating serious injury. Larry

brings suit against Farmer for his damages; Farmer asserts Larry was contributory negligent and thus should be barred from any recovery. Disregarding any workers compensation rule and assuming the jurisdiction recognizes contributory negligence, the likely outcome is that Larry's claim will

(A) Prevail, if the jury finds Larry was not sufficiently intelligent to understand he might be injured if he got too close to the machine

(B) Not prevail, and the court should direct a verdict for Frank Farmer since a reasonable person would not have gotten too close to the machine.

(C) Not prevail, and the court should direct a verdict for Frank Farmer since mere carelessness or poor judgment does not absolve one of contributory negligence.

(D) Prevail, and the court should direct a verdict against Frank Farmer if a reasonable person would not have gotten too close to the machine.

226. Harry Hardofhearing, a 74 year old practicing lawyer, was rapidly losing his hearing and close to being totally deaf. His doctor fitted him with a hearing aid unit. One morning he left home to drive the two-hour trip to his office. After 90 minutes the batteries ran out on the hearing aid. A fire department vehicle was responding to a fire alarm call with its siren blazing. Harry was proceeding west on Yellow Brick Road at a reasonable speed. The fire department vehicle ran a red light going south and collided with Harry's car at the intersection. Harry sued the fire department for his damages. The fire department defends on the theory of contributory negligence. The affirmative defense alleged that had Harry been wearing a hearing aid with a functioning battery, he probably would have heard the siren and pulled over, thus avoiding the collision. The court should instruct the jury that it

(A) May consider Harry's deafness when it considers whether he acted as a reasonable person.

(B) May consider Harry's deafness when it considers whether he acted as a reasonable deaf person under the circumstances.

(C) Direct a verdict for Harry because physical impairments are never considered in the defense of contributory negligence.

(D) Direct a verdict for the fire department on the defense of contributory negligence because physical impairments can never be the basis for a bar to recovery.

Questions 227 and 228 are based on the following:

Cathy Careless was driving her car to the corner store in Everycity, USA to purchase a pack of cigarettes. Because the store was only two blocks from her home, she did not put on her seatbelt. She got into an accident in which her injuries would not have occurred had she fastened her seatbelt. The police officer that came to the scene advised Cathy to go into the hospital immediately and have her neck injury treated. Cathy was leaving on vacation that evening and did not want to change her vacation plans. As a result, she did not go into the hospital until her return two weeks later. Cathy ultimately brought suit against the other driver who was determined to be at fault. This occurred in a contributory negligence jurisdiction.

227. The court should instruct the jury that if they find the failure to wear the seatbelt

(A) Would have avoided the consequence of the physical injury, Cathy's recovery should be denied.

(B) Constitutes assumption of the risk, so recovery should be denied.

(C) Constitutes contributory negligence, so recovery should be denied.

(D) Constitutes a failure to mitigate damages, so the damages should be apportioned.

228. Assume that the jury found that Cathy's two-week delay in seeking medical assistance created $25,000 of extra damages. Of this amount, the jury should award Cathy

(A) $25,000 since the driver at fault should have foreseen that an accident victim would not promptly seek medical assistance.

(B) $12,500 since she shares equally in the fault.

(C) $-0- since her delay in seeking medical assistance constitutes an assumption of the risk.

(D) $-0- since her delay in seeking medical assistance constitutes a failure to mitigate damages.

Questions 229 – 232 are based on the following:

Phil Photographer was an 11 year-old boy in the sixth grade of Entrepreneur Grade School, which is operated as a non-profit educational organization. This elementary school was planning its annual spring fair in which the students teamed up and created commercial operations and competed for awards. Phil's father owned a commercial film developing company and he encouraged Phil to start a film developing operation for the fair. The business plan was to print up a flyer to distribute to all the school's parents and teachers encouraging them to have their personal film developed by Phil and his teammate Patty.

Phil and Patty built a little demonstration booth for the spring fair. Their idea was to demonstrate to the other students and fair judges how they develop film. To develop the film they had to combine three chemicals and dip the film into it. Phil's father was to provide all the chemicals in the appropriate amount for the demonstration. Unfortunately, Mr.

Photographer was away on business, so Phil went down to the local photography supply shop and asked to buy all three ingredients, including a toxic solvent called Acetone. Acetone was potentially explosive unless very slowly mixed with other photographic chemicals.

There was a state law and store policy prohibiting the sale of Acetone to other than a registered film processor but there was no age requirement. The clerk was aware of the state law and store policy, but Phil pleaded with him and the clerk finally sold him the chemicals. At the time, the clerk did warn Phil that Acetone was potentially dangerous and could explode if poured rapidly into the other chemicals.

The day of the school Fair over 300 parents and students paid $5.00 per person to attend the event. Phil's father could not attend the event because he was away on business again. Phil mixed all the chemicals except Acetone in one flask in the booth, but was called away at that point. His teammate Patty saw that the Acetone had not been added so she dumped the Acetone flask into the flask containing the other chemicals. Phil had forgotten to pass on to Patty the warning he had received from the clerk in the supply store. The combined chemicals exploded in Patty's face burning her skin. This necessitated $10,000 of medical treatment.

229. If Patty's parents bring suit on Patty's behalf for her personal injuries against Entrepreneur Grade School, the likely outcome is
(A) For the Plaintiff, if the school authority failed to supervise every student's booth.
(B) For the Defendant, unless the Plaintiff could show some staff member of the charity at the event knew the dangerous chemical Acetone would be used.
(C) For the Defendant, because Entrepreneur enjoys charitable immunity.

(D) For the Plaintiff, because the chemical Acetone was unreasonably dangerous.

230. If Patty's parents bring suit on Patty's behalf for her personal injuries against the local photography supply shop, the likely outcome is
(A) For the Defendant, because Phil's actions were an independent, intervening cause of the injuries.
(B) For the Defendant, because the supply store had an express policy not to sell the chemical Acetone to other than a registered film processor.
(C) For the Plaintiff, because the store's sales clerk violated the state statute when he sold the chemical Acetone to a non-registered film processor.
(D) For the Plaintiff, because a reasonably prudent sales clerk would not have sold Acetone to an 11 year-old child.

231. If Patty's parents bring suit on Patty's behalf for her personal injuries against Phil, the likely outcome is
(A) For the Plaintiff, if a reasonably prudent 11 year-old would not have used Acetone in a manner that injured Patty.
(B) For the Defendant, because an 11 year-old is presumed incapable of negligence.
(C) For the Defendant, if the sale of Acetone by the store clerk is determined to be the legal cause of Patty's injuries.
(D) For the Plaintiff, if a reasonably prudent adult would not have used Acetone in a manner that injured Patty.

232. If Patty's parents bring suit on Patty's behalf for her personal injuries against Phil's father, Mr. Photographer, the likely outcome is
(A) For the Plaintiff, because there is per se parent vicarious liability to

third parties for their children's torts.

(B) For the Defendant, because parents are never vicariously liable to third parties for their children's torts.

(C) For the Defendant, unless the jury finds that Phil was acting as an agent for his father's commercial film developing company.

(D) For the Plaintiff, only if a judgment against Phil Photographer is returned unsatisfied.

Questions 233 and 234 are based on the following:

Holly and Harry Host operated the Sleepytime Inn, a Bed and Breakfast. The Hosts built the Inn on one corner of an old orchard that Harry inherited. The Hosts did not commercially farm the orchard, but left an old rusting tractor among the trees on the top of the hill. They placed "No Trespassing" signs on the rundown fence around the orchard.

Each afternoon, the Hosts provided free wine to the guests in the Inn. Many of the guests would take two or three glasses of wine and go to the outdoor hot tub. There was a leak in one of the water pipes to the hot tub, which created a puddle on the walkway between the hot tub and the guestrooms. Harry intended to fix the leak, but was waiting for a part.

The Inn experienced a very unusual late August storm involving a cold snap with freezing temperatures and significant snowfall. Since the Inn was full, the Hosts continued to operate.

233. Ten inches of snow fell in one day. Looking out the window, Harry saw several of the neighborhood children heading towards the orchard pulling sleds. Harry knew that the children liked to play on the tractor and had previously warned them to stay off the hill and out of the orchard. He yelled out the window, "Stop trespassing," but the children continued. Thirty minutes later, one of the children ran to the Inn screaming for help. She reported that one of the children, a six-year-old boy, had fallen off the tractor after slipping on the snow-covered fender. The boy suffered a broken arm as he landed on the ground. If the boy's guardian sues the Inn, the likely outcome is that their claim will

(A) Prevail, because the tractor is inherently dangerous.

(B) Prevail, only if the tractor is deemed to be an attractive nuisance.

(C) Not prevail, because he ordered the children not to trespass.

(D) Not prevail, because it was the unexpected snow on the tractor that caused the boy to slip, not the tractor itself.

234. In the evening, the guests were enjoying the hot tub and their usual free wine. One guest named Louise Loose had consumed three glasses of wine and decided she wanted some more. She got out of the hot tub and began walking into the Inn. Due to the unusually cold weather, the puddle on the walkway had frozen. Louise was not paying enough attention, slipped and hit her head on the cement suffering a concussion. If Louise sues the Inn, the likely outcome is that her claim will

(A) Prevail, because the Hosts are strictly liable for any damages suffered by their rent-paying guests.

(B) Prevail, because of Harry Host's negligence.

(C) Not prevail, because Harry Host did not yet have the necessary part to make the correction so it was impossible then to stop the leak.

(D) Not prevail, because Louise was intoxicated and should have looked where she was going.

235. Justin Justice was a lawyer who had spent most of his professional life as a court of appeals judge. On Friday evening while at a social event, he over consumed alcohol.

While one of the other judges offered him a ride home, Justin decided to drive himself since he did not want to come back downtown the next morning to get his car. The police stopped him for DUI and he was quietly charged. When Justin appeared in court, he accepted a deferred sentence and agreed to attend DUI school. One night upon leaving the DUI school, Tracy Truthful, a reporter for the Sensation Unlimited newspaper, spotted Justin. She recognized him as a judge so she went to the County Clerk's office and read the file of the matter. She then wrote an article entitled, "Judge Justice drove while drunk" and put a recent photo of him in his robes in the article. The Judge read this and became incensed because he had hoped to keep this private incident a secret. If Justin sues Tracy and Sensation Unlimited for invasion of privacy, the likely result is a verdict for

- **(A)** Plaintiff, if a reasonable person would be upset at the publication of such facts.
- **(B)** Plaintiff, since Tracy and Sensation Unlimited did not ask him for input before running the story.
- **(C)** Defendant, because the facts reported were true.
- **(D)** Defendant, because Sensation Unlimited printed public facts.

236. Diane Driver was operating a vehicle on an expressway. The gas gauge was close to empty and Diane was feeling a little tired so she decided to stop at a turnout to get some coffee and fill the gas tank. While in the store, a woman named Harriet Hitchhiker approached Diane and asked for a ride to the next city. Diane agreed to transport Harriet and Harriet put her own suitcase in the trunk of the car. Diane asked the attendant to check the air pressure in her tires including the spare tire in the trunk. The attendant was in a hurry and mistakenly left a bottle of acid in the trunk that he had been using to clean oil off old automotive parts. When Diane stopped the car to let Harriet out, it was later in the evening after the sun had set. Harriet opened the trunk to get her suitcase out and knocked the bottle of acid over thereby seriously burning her hands. Harriet brings suit against Diane in a jurisdiction that has an all or nothing contributory negligence statute and no automobile guest statute. Diane's most persuasive defense is that

- **(A)** Diane had no knowledge of the acid or that it would cause injury to the passenger.
- **(B)** Harriet did not pay for the transportation so she, in effect, assumed the risk of damages.
- **(C)** It was not foreseeable that injury would result from the passenger opening the trunk to retrieve her suitcase.
- **(D)** Harriet was contributorily negligent in not using a flashlight to light the car's trunk before reaching into the trunk.

237. On Larry Landowner's farm, there is a natural spring on a hill that occasionally overflows onto the neighboring public park. In the summer when the spring was dry, the county built an asphalt walkway around the park. By December, the fall rains had caused the spring to overflow over the path in the park. The temperature dropped one night and the water on the path froze. There was also a light snow, which covered the ice caused by the spring water. Joyce Jogger was running around the path to enjoy the sight of the fresh snow in the park. She slipped on the ice on the snow-covered path suffering a broken leg. If Joyce brings suit against Larry for her damages, her claim will likely

- **(A)** Prevail, if Larry knew his spring was running over the path.
- **(B)** Prevail, if Joyce did not know of the ice.
- **(C)** Not prevail, unless Larry had dug a channel for the spring to get the flooding off his property.
- **(D)** Not prevail, because joggers who run on snow-covered walkways assume the risk of danger.

238. Pattee Patient underwent a serious surgical procedure performed by Dickey

Doctor. Dickey performed the procedure negligently. Pattee continued to use Dickey's medical services. Dickey told Pattee that the ongoing pain she was experiencing was normal. Eight and a half years went by and Pattee's condition continued to deteriorate. In the ninth year, Pattee died. The jurisdiction has a three year statute of limitations and an eight year statute of repose. If Pattee's personal representatives sue Dickey Doctor, the best argument they can make is

(A) Dickey Doctor's ongoing representations to Pattee suspended the statute of limitations.

(B) Pattee believed Dickey's assertions that the pain was normal.

(C) If the court enforces the statute of repose it will mean that the claim was time-barred before accrual under the discovery rule.

(D) The statute of limitations should only begin to run upon the death of the patient.

239. Sam Speedy and Doug Dragger were members of a car club named the Spades. The two members owned what were considered to be the fastest cars in the city. The two were friends and decided to start a drag race partnership at an abandoned airport in the city. They rented the airport on a Saturday afternoon and charged admission to all the high school students. After a big crowd had accumulated, Sam and Doug began the quarter-mile race. The race began as planned but as the cars got to the end of the track, Sam's car blew a front tire. Apparently, Sam had neglected to check his tires before the race. Doug checked his tires and his drag car finished the race without incident. Sam's car went off the track and injured two spectators. If the injured spectators sue Sam and Doug they will likely prevail against

(A) Sam.

(B) Doug.

(C) Both Sam and Doug.

(D) Neither Sam nor Doug.

240. Scott Seducer was a 23-year-old high school teacher. One of the girls in his class, Mary Minor, was 17 and Scott was attracted to her. Scott asked Mary to stay after class and discuss her test performance. When they were alone, Scott told Mary that he would raise her failing grade if she would consent to sexual intercourse. Mary agreed. There is a statute in the jurisdiction that states it is illegal for a person over the age of 21 to have sexual intercourse with a person who is 18 years or younger. If Mary later sues Scott for battery, the likely outcome is that her claim will

(A) Not prevail, because there was no offensive touching since Mary consented to the encounter.

(B) Not prevail, if a reasonable person in Scott's position would have concluded Mary's consent was not coerced.

(C) Prevail.

(D) Prevail, unless the jury determines that raising Mary's grade was full and fair consideration for consent to the sexual encounter.

241. Oscar Owner lives in New York. He owns a 2-year-old Puegott automobile manufactured in France. He drove the car to work every day for over a year before the car began shaking violently when driving over 35 kilometers per hour. A mechanic told Oscar this shaking was due to a defect in the foreign-made drive line between the transmission and the rear axle. Because using the Puegott was uncertain, Oscar began using his second car to commute to work. Oscar's next door neighbor, Rita, came home from college and asked Oscar if she could use the extra car. Oscar said, "sure, help yourself" but forgot to tell Rita about the car malfunctioning and related shaking. Rita took Oscar's Puegott car and while driving at a reasonable speed crashed into an oncoming car after the drive line broke. If Rita sues Oscar Owner the outcome will likely be for

(A) Rita because Oscar is strictly liable for any damages resulting from his lending the dangerous automobile.

(B) Oscar because he was not compensated for the use of his vehicle and thus should not be held to a commercial standard of care.

(C) Oscar because it was the faulty drive line that was the cause in fact of Rita's damages.

(D) Rita if Oscar knew the Puegott's drive line was seriously defective and failed to so inform Rita.

Questions 242 and 243 are based on the following:

Clearwater High School built a new main high school building. The school staff was responsible for purchasing the equipment their kitchen needed to serve student lunches. The school buyer went into a retail store named Kitchen Supply Emporium and purchased a brand new oven for $900. The label stated that the net price included a $100 discount because the oven line was being discontinued. The new oven was delivered and installed by Kitchen Supply. The first day of use a defective hidden wiring in the oven failed and the sparks ignited a fire. The cook on duty was seriously injured. A lawsuit was filed and during discovery it was learned that the defective oven had been made by Allright Manufacturing and distributed through a wholesaler named Allstate Distributing Co.

242. In a strict liability action, which of the below parties will be held liable?

   I. Allright Manufacturing Co.
   II. Allstate Distributing Co.
   III. Kitchen Supply Emporium
   IV. Clearwater High School

(A) I only
(B) I, II and III.
(C) I, II, III and IV
(D) I and IV

243. Assume that the strict liability lawsuit was filed only against Kitchen Supply Emporium. Which of the following

defenses, if made, should prevail in the lawsuit?

(A) Allright Manufacturing Co. was the only party involved in the assembly of the defective oven and should have sole responsibility.

(B) The $100 discount the buyer accepted constituted assumption of the risk.

(C) The school's failure to inspect the oven prior to use is a defense subject to comparative fault in most states.

(D) None of the above.

Questions 244 and 245 are based on the following:

Robert Railroad was a miniature railroad enthusiast, collector and rebuilder. The whole basement of his home was one big model railroad shop in which he rebuilt used pieces of equipment and various high-profile models. One evening he went with his 7-year old daughter Roberta to the parents evening at her school. During a break in the program he was approached by Paul Purchaser, the parent of one of Roberta's school friends who had learned that Robert sold used model railroad items. He asked if Robert had any pieces ready for sale and Robert said yes. Robert then invited Paul to come to the house to look at his inventory of model railroad items.

Two days later Paul Parent and his daughter Pattie arrived at Robert and Roberta's home. Pattie and Roberta went up to the attic to play with their dolls. Paul followed Robert down the basement steps to look over the model railroad pieces that were for sale. As Paul walked down the stairs he stepped on a miniature railroad car engine left on the stairs and fell. As Paul fell he screamed out. Hearing her father's scream, Paul's daughter Pattie ran down from the attic. As she turned to go down the basement steps she grabbed onto an electrical cord of a microwave oven on a shelf. As she swung around her weight pulled the microwave oven off the shelf and it fell on her.

244. The legal status of Paul and his daughter Pattie after they entered Robert's home was

	Paul	Pattie
(A)	Licensee	Licensee
(B)	Invitee	Attractive Nuisance
(C)	Invitee	Licensee
(D)	Licensee	Attractive Nuisance

245. Pattie broke her arm because of the falling microwave oven she pulled off the shelf. If a lawsuit was filed on Pattie's behalf seeking compensation for the physical injuries she suffered on Robert's premises, the court will likely find for

(A) Robert because there was no duty to Pattie

(B) Patty because Robert failed to warn Pattie about the microwave oven on the shelf.

(C) Patty because Robert is liable for damages resulting from a visible and known dangerous condition.

(D) Robert because Pattie assumed the risk and the hazard was not unreasonable.

Questions 246 and 247 are based on the following:

Albert Authority was a retired career marine who believed passionately in law and order. In retirement he took a job as a part-time security guard at Ceiling-Mart, a low quality discount store. Albert frequently dreamed of his days as an active marine and wore his old uniform to every civic event he attended. He also enjoyed perusing the Criminal Wanted posters published by the Police Departments in his area and prided himself on keeping current on the most wanted list.

On one of Albert's days off he went to a veteran's parade. He wore his old marine uniform including a belt holster containing his old marine-issue revolver. As he walked home after the parade he turned the corner and found he was facing a very large man with wild red hair and a full red beard. It took Albert only a moment to remember that he had seen a "wanted for murder" poster for a man meeting such a description. Albert pulled his marine-issue revolver and "arrested" the tall man with the wild red hair and beard.

The arrestee protested and pleaded that Albert got the wrong man. He affirmatively said that his name was Big Red and he was running late to catch an airplane. A passer-by called 911 on her cell phone and 15 minutes later the police arrived on the scene. They then ran a full identification check on Big Red. After 20 minutes the police announced that Albert indeed had arrested the wrong man and ordered Big Red released. Albert did as ordered and showed the police that his old marine-issue revolver was not loaded. He then explained that the seriousness of the murder allegation in the wanted poster justified his reasonable mistake. Big Red arrived at the airport late and missed his plane. He was very upset over the whole incident.

246. Big Red asserts a claim against Albert for false imprisonment. The court will likely find a

(A) Recovery unless Albert reasonably believed that Big Red was in fact the wanted murderer.

(B) No recovery because the period of time during which Albert restrained Big Red was not unreasonable for the police to establish his true identity.

(C) No recovery because Big Red did not suffer any physical injury.

(D) Recovery because Big Red did not agree to the confinement.

247. Big Red also asserts a claim against Albert for assault. The court will likely hold for

(A) Albert if his mistaken identity error was reasonable.

(B) Big Red only if he can prove monetary damages.

(C) Big Red if he saw Albert pointing the revolver at him.

(D) Albert because the revolver was unloaded so it was impossible to do any actual physical harm.

248. Alice Accountant was employed as the internal chief financial officer of Forever Inc. The outside auditor discovered a significant embezzlement had occurred when he performed their annual audit. The top management of Forever accused Alice of being involved in the embezzlement. Alice became outraged at the accusation and quit Forever Inc. Alice then applied for an accounting position at Next Employer, Inc. and received a conditional employment offer. The human resource director at Next Employer noticed Alice had previously worked at Forever and called them asking for their opinion on her prior work. Forever's President truthfully said, "well, she quit after we accused her of embezzlement. We think she did it." Based upon this report Next Employer revoked their job offer to Alice. Two months later another embezzlement occurred at Forever, Inc and subsequently it was determined Alice's assistant had committed all the embezzlements and that Alice was completely innocent. If Alice bring a defamation suit against Forever's President the court will likely find for

(A) Alice because Forever's President published false facts concerning the statement that Alice had embezzled.

(B) Forever's President because listing her former employer on the resume is consent to a defamatory report.

(C) Forever's President if there was a reasonable grounds for making the false statement and it was made in good faith.

(D) Alice because the special pecuniary monetary damages constituted "per se" defamation.

Questions 249 and 250 are based on the following :

Alice, Betty and Carol were sorority sisters in college and remained the best of friends. They all married and began to play golf once a week. They played alone but also with their spouses. During some of the golfing rounds, Betty's husband, Harley, developed an attraction to Carol. Carol was unhappy with her husband, Dullard, and Harley seemed very exciting. Harley and Carol began meeting secretly.

Alice, Betty and Carol were scheduled to play a threesome golf match one day. After they completed the first nine holes they stopped for lunch at the club house. Betty went into the restroom and overheard a conversation about the wild extra-marital affair her husband Harley was having with her friend Carol. Betty was deeply hurt and outraged that her friend Carol would be engaged in a secret affair with her husband.

The three women left the club house and started golfing holes 10 through 18. As the afternoon continued, Betty became more and more outraged at Carol. While Carol was teeing off at hole 16, Betty approached her from behind and raised a golf club with the intent to strike Carol on the head. Carol had her back turned and did not see Betty coming up to strike her. Alice clearly saw Betty approach Carol and raise the golf club in an apparent attempt to strike Carol. Nonetheless, Alice was shell-shocked and remained silent and Betty struck Carol injuring her quite seriously.

249. Assume for this question that Alice suffered significant nervous shock after witnessing Betty's attack on Carol. Alice was overcome by the thought that she might have been able to do something to avoid the attack on Carol and got more and more depressed. If Alice sues Betty for the intentional infliction of emotional distress, the court will likely hold for

(A) Alice because Betty's conduct in battering their mutual friend Carol was outrageous.

(B) Betty because Alice was not a member of Carol's family.

(C) Betty because Alice stood by and did nothing during Betty's attack.

(D) Alice because Betty knew she was present during her attack on Carol.

250. Carol hears of the above lawsuit between Alice and Betty. She suffered from on-going headaches because of Betty's battery. She wondered why her friend did not at least warn her of the impending attack. After considering the severity of her injuries, Carol asserts a claim against Alice. The court will likely hold for

(A) Carol because Alice failed to take any action to avoid the attack.

(B) Alice because she was under no duty to warn Carol of the attack nor go to her aid.

(C) Alice because Betty was responsible for the injuries.

(D) Carol because Alice was aware of the danger before Carol was.

Questions 251 – 253 are based on the following:

The Local Enquirer was a headline focused newsmagazine sold in grocery stores. They hired a new reporter named Alice Aggressive. Alice knew that if she was going to advance at the publication company she would have to create very high profile controversies that had a shock value. Her idea was to feature only spicy murder and sex stories. Her first two stories were featured on the front page of the paper.

The first story "reported" on an inmate in the state correctional facility who the story named as Peter Prisoner. The story stated that Peter had murdered his wife and two children to collect under their life insurance policies and was serving a life sentence for the murders. Alice copied the story from an out-of-state newspaper, but to disguise the plagiarism, she changed the name from Paul Prisoner to Peter Prisoner. A copy of the Local Enquirer found its way to the state correctional facility and was read by many of the prisoners. A gang of prisoners read Alice's story and castrated the only Peter Prisoner in their state's prison. Unfortunately, that Peter Prisoner was only serving time for a minor embezzlement charge.

The second story Alice wrote concerned the governor of the state in which the Local Enquirer's was printed, named Governor George. This story was also substantially copied from another publication. It accused Governor George of an extra-marital affair with his female campaign manager who was conducting the last few days of his re-election campaign. While the governor and his campaign manager had traveled together, they both were happily married and their relationship was purely platonic. The consequence of the story was that Governor George lost 5% of the vote and narrowly lost his re-election bid.

A great deal of complaints were received by the editors of the Local Enquirer from the public and their advertisers. In response, they fired Alice Aggressive and printed a short retraction of both stories. Unfortunately the retraction was too late to avoid Peter Prisoner's castration and Governor George's re-election failure.

251. If Governor George brings a defamation claim against Local Enquirer, the minimum showing of fault the plaintiff must present is

(A) Ordinary negligence by Local Enquirer.

(B) Recklessness in the factual investigation by Local Enquirer.

(C) Malice or extreme recklessness in the factual investigation by Local Enquirer.

(D) The fault is irrelevant since Local Inquirer retracted the story.

252. If Peter Prisoner brings a defamation claim against Local Enquirer, the minimum showing of fault the plaintiff must present is

(A) Ordinary negligence by Local Enquirer.
(B) Recklessness in the factual investigation by Local Enquirer.
(C) Malice or extreme recklessness in the factual investigation by Local Enquirer.
(D) Irrelevant since Local Inquirer retracted the story.

253. Peter Prisoner was released from prison shortly after the castration. His wife, Affectionate, grew despondent and filed a lawsuit against Local Enquirer alleging loss of consortium. The court will likely hold for

(A) Affectionate only if she is able to establish that Local Enquirer acted with malice in reporting the story.
(B) Local Enquirer because the other prisoners not Local Enquirer was the legal cause of Peter's castration leading to the loss of consortium.
(C) Local Enquirer because most courts still do not recognize a wife's right to sue for loss of consortium.
(D) Affectionate only if she can establish that her husband's castration was caused by Local Enquirer's improper investigation and reporting of the story.

Questions 254 and 255 are based on the following:

Children Stores International was opening a new location in Pleasantville. One of the promotional techniques which they used was an essay contest among local grade school students. The winner was to receive a prize and public award at the new store's grand opening. The topic of the essay contest was "What I have overcome."

10 year old Susan Sensitive submitted an essay for the contest. She wrote a three page essay covering her parents drug and alcohol addiction and how she had not let this background stop her active participation in school activities and academic success. The management of Children Stores read Susan's essay and awarded her the first place award. The store then hired a private detective to "research" her family background. They ascertained that Susan's parents had been in drug rehab and served time in prison. At the opening of the new store, Children Shoes International announced that Susan was the contest winner, and to gain newspaper reporter interest, proceeded to reveal her full family background, including her parent's prison history.

This information shocked the other children and parents in attendance but was so scandalous that it was widely reported. This resulted in Susan's friends shunning her which then led to her depression. Her school grades feel by a significant amount. Susan's father's employer read the story and decided to fire him because he did not want a "druggy felon" working for his company.

254. If Susan asserts a claim against Children Stores International for infliction of emotional distress, the court would likely find for

(A) Susan but only if she can prove the emotional depression was accompanied by physical damage consequences.
(B) Children Stores unless Susan can show the store management intended to emotionally depress her.
(C) Susan unless Children Stores can prove a reasonable award winner would not have been upset by their comments.
(D) Susan even if Children Stores agrees Susan impliedly consented by entering the contest knowing the essay results would be made public.

255. Children Stores also took pictures of Susan that they widely advertised as an endorsement of their stores. In the advertising many commercial statements were attributed to Susan. Susan never agreed to the publication. This and the damages Susan suffered from the statements about her parents prompted Susan to bring a lawsuit against Children Stores. She sued for publication of private life, intrusion and commercial misappropriation. The court will likely decide these actions by holding that the prevailing party is

	Publication of Private Life	Intrusion	Commercial Misappropriation
(A)	Susan	Susan	Susan
(B)	Children	Susan	Children
(C)	Children	Children	Susan
(D)	Children	Children	Children

Questions 256 and 257 are based on the following:

Nancy Nightclub opened a night club on the ground floor of a two story building she owned in Quiettown. Nancy herself lived on the second floor of the building. The nightclub was an immediate success. A religious neighbor, Perfect Pious, lived across the street from the nightclub and viewed the partying every night as sinful and believed it had to be stopped.

Perfect began a series of telephone calls to Nancy harassing her for the "evil thing" she brought to the neighborhood. This did not persuade Nancy to close the nightclub, so she called in "bomb threats" to the club during their busy hours. Upon receiving the calls, Nancy was forced to tell all the patrons to leave the nightclub. All this caused Nancy's business to decline.

256. If Nancy brings a lawsuit against Perfect, the best theory of recovery is:
(A) Intentional infliction of emotional distress.
(B) Private nuisance.
(C) Public nuisance.
(D) Negligence.

257. If Nancy brings a lawsuit against Perfect for invasion of privacy, the court will likely hold for
(A) Nancy because the telephone calls created monetary damages.
(B) Perfect because she honestly felt her actions were serving the community and public interest.
(C) Perfect because Nancy has other and better causes of action which may be asserted to recover her damages.
(D) Nancy since the telephone calls intruded upon Nancy's solitude and seclusion.

Questions 258 and 259 are based on the following:

All American City prided itself on its patriotic civic attitude. One of the many activities it performed annually was a very large firework display over the central city lake on the Fourth of July. The City contracted the pyrotechnic display planning, setup and execution to Always Careful Fireworks, Inc.

This July was very warm and a large group of citizens turned out to the various parks on the lake. When the sun went down the firework show began. One of the rockets shot off by Always Careful was apparently defective. When fired, it veered horizontally. The rocket landed on a shingle wood roof of a home on the other side of the lake causing a roof fire.

A motorist from another state driving through on an intestate above the lake began looking at the firework display. He became so excited with the display that he took his eyes off the road and failed to navigate the next turn in the road. A passenger in his car named Pattie was injured when the car went off the road.

258. If the homeowner files a claim against All American City, the best defense that can be asserted is

(A) Any responsibility for damages belongs to Always Careful Fireworks, Inc. not the City.

(B) The homeowner assumed the risk by using wood singles on the roof rather than tile or composition.

(C) The City could not reasonable foresee that a roof fire on the other side of the lake would result.

(D) The firework product was not inherently dangerous.

259. If the injured passenger in the automobile files a tort action against Always Careful Fireworks, Inc., the court will likely hold for

(A) Passenger because Always Careful Fireworks, Inc. is strictly liable.

(B) Always Careful Fireworks, Inc. because the motorist driver was negligent when he took his eyes off the road.

(C) Always Careful Fireworks, Inc. because passenger was not a resident of All American City and their product had no physical impact upon a remote car and passenger.

(D) Passenger if Always should have reasonable foreseen the zone of danger would include the risk that a motorist driving through the area would be distracted by the fireworks display.

260. Pattie Petlover was not able to bear children. As such, she developed strong relationships with a few of her pets. One of the pets was a chimpanzee named Christo who Pattie had domesticated. Christo learned how to play peacefully with children and had been trained to stay in Pattie's back yard. One day Christo escaped from the backyard even though Pattie exercised the utmost care.

The chimpanzee crossed the street to a grade school because she was trying to find children to play with. A first grade school teacher, named Terry, looked out her classroom window and saw Christo. Terry believed that the school's children were about to be attacked. She ran out of the school building and in her hurry, fell on the school steps spraining her ankle. If Terry brings a claim against Pattie the court will like hold for

(A) Pattie because the chimpanzee was tame and posed no risk to the school children.

(B) Terry because Pattie is strictly liable for damages flowing from the chimpanzee's escape.

(C) Terry because of the doctrine of res ipsa loquitur.

(D) Pattie because she exercised the utmost care.

261. PriceCo was a large wholesale warehouse club located in Everytown. PriceCo had experiences where thieves hid in cars waiting for individual customers to rob. These attacks usually occurred in the evening hours after the sun went down and the parking lot was dark. In response to the robberies, the store put up some warning signs and additional lights in the parking lot.

Two days later, Susan Shopper arrived at the store at 7:00 P.M. As she walked into the store she noticed one of the warning signs. She completed her shopping at around 8:00 P.M. and while walking back to her car she was robbed. At about the same time, a passing motorist, Charlie Changer, pulled into the parking lot. He went into the store to get a roll of quarters to play a pinball machine. He got the change but did not buy anything in the store. When he walked back to his car he also was robbed. If both Susan and Charlie file claims against PriceCo the court will likely hold for

(A) Both Susan and Charlie if PriceCo failed to exercise reasonable care.

(B) Susan but not Charlie because he was only a licensee.

(C) Charlie but not Susan because she saw the warning signs.

(D) Neither Charlie or Susan because the store is not liable for dangers resulting from intentional torts committed by third parties not under their control.

Questions 262 – 264 are based on the following:

Tracy Tenant had just passed the bar exam and decided to hang her shingle. She leased a building from Laurie Landlord for a 5 year term. The building had two stories and a full basement. There was an interior elevator that went to all three levels. There was also a run down outside wooden staircase at the back of the building next to the parking lot that led to the first and second floors. When they signed the lease Tracy asked Laurie if the back staircase was safe. Laurie replied she did not know but would have the handyman make any necessary repairs. Laurie immediately put up a sign on the first step of the back stairs which stated, "Under repair. Use the elevator on the street side of the building." Both Tracy and Laurie forgot about the rear staircase and it was never repaired.

Tracy rented the first floor of the building to a deli and used most of the second floor for her law firm. Tracy kept two of the upstairs rooms for her personal use; one as a kitchen-dining room and one as a bedroom. The basement was used as storage by the deli, Tracy's law firm and Tracy herself to store some of her personal possessions.

One evening Tracy was working on a legal brief at 7:30 P.M. She received a call from her old college friend, Victoria, who she had not seen in 6 years. Tracy invited her over to share a pizza she had just ordered out from a delivery store. Twenty minutes later the pizza arrived. Tracy waited a few minutes and called Victoria on the phone urging her to hurry up before the pizza got cold. Victoria pulled into the rear parking lot, saw Tracy in the second floor window and ran up the wooden back stairs. In the darkness Victoria did not see the unlighted warning sign and fell through a rotten step

at the top thereby receiving serious physical injury.

262. Concerning Victoria's legal status on the property owned by Laurie and leased by Tracy, Victoria is a
   (A) Public invitee.
   (B) Business invitee.
   (C) Gratuitous licensee.
   (D) Public licensee.

263. In most jurisdictions, Victoria would be due the following duty of care from Tracy
   (A) An absolute duty of care because defective wooden steps are abnormally dangerous.
   (B) Inspection of the property and either remedy or warn of hazards that could reasonably have been discovered.
   (C) Either remedy or warn of known hazards.
   (D) No duty because a warning sign was put on the back stairs.

264. If Victoria initiates a claim for negligence against both Tracy and Laurie a court would likely enter judgment against
   (A) Neither Tracy nor Laurie because they made sure there was a warning sign on the back steps.
   (B) Tracy only because she was the possessor of the premises and invited her friend Victoria to enter.
   (C) Laurie only because she owned the building and premises in which Victoria was injured.
   (D) Both Tracy and Laurie.

265. Teresa Teacher taught accelerated classes to preschool and grade school students in her proprietary Advanced Learning Center. She had been operating this private school for ten years and had invested substantial money in building and equipping the school. Her students would usually come to the Learning Center after their regular school was out and on the weekends.

It came to Teresa's attention that the building next to the Learning Center was to be converted into a city-wide drug rehabilitation house. Many of the students' parents told her that they would no longer allow their children to go to the Learning Center if a drug rehabilitation house opened because they do not want their children in an area of drug activity. The parents' fears were largely imaginary since the drug rehabilitation center was to be policed and was in compliance with all zoning laws. Still, the parents seemed quite serious about their intentions and Teresa realized she would suffer a significant decrease in her land values.

Teresa filed a lawsuit seeking an injunction claiming the drug rehabilitation house would constitute a nuisance. The rehabilitation house in turn filed a motion for summary judgment with the trial court on the basis that there was no credible factual basis for the lawsuit. The motion should be

(A) Granted because the use complies with the zoning laws.
(B) Denied because Teresa may suffer substantial damages even though the parents' fears are unreasonable.
(C) Denied if the court believes that the usefulness of the new drug rehabilitation home exceeds the harm to the Advanced Learning Center.
(D) Granted because the parents' fears are unreasonable and Teresa has not yet suffered any detriment.

Learning Question Answer Rationales

1. **/D/** A D usually does not get a reduction in damages due to the P's heightened susceptibility for damages. A D takes a P as he finds her. Intoxication in this case contributed to the D's own negligence, but does not exacerbate an injury once an injury occurs. Intoxication may very well have increased the likelihood of injury, but not the severity. **(A)** is an example of an "Eggshell Skull" P (a P with a heightened susceptibility to exacerbated injury greater than a "normal" person.) **(B)** is an example of an "Eggshell Skull" P (a P with a heightened susceptibility to exacerbated injury greater than a "normal" person.) **(C)** is an example of an "Eggshell Skull" P (a P with a heightened susceptibility to exacerbated injury greater than a "normal" person.)

2. **/A/** Children are held to the standard of a child of the same age, education, experience, and intelligence *unless* the child is engaging in an adult activity. Discharging a firearm is certainly an adult activity as is driving a car, flying an airplane, etc. **(B)** is incorrect because it involves a children's activity (playing hopscotch) and children are held to a child's standard when engaging in a child's activity. **(C)** is incorrect because it involves a children's activity (riding a bicycle) and children are held to a child's

standard when engaging in a child's activity. **(D)** is incorrect because it involves a children's activity (jumping rope) and children are held to a child's standard when engaging in a child's activity.

3. **/A/** A D will not be held to a standard, which is physically impossible for him to achieve. In this case, the D will be held to the standard of a reasonable deaf person. (Was failure to wear a hearing aid negligent, for example). **(B)** is incorrect because D will be held to the reasonable person standard despite any unusual mental attributes. Usually, only the insane will not be held to the reasonable person standard. **(C)** is incorrect because D will be held to the reasonable person standard despite the mental hot temper characteristic. **(D)** is incorrect because D will be held to the reasonable person standard despite any unusual mental attributes. Usually, only the insane will not be held to the reasonable person standard.

4. **/D/** Use a true-false approach to a negative question. The odd one out is almost always the correct answer. A D may assert any defense against the personal representative as if she were the P himself. A personal representative steps into the shoes of the decedent. **(A)** is incorrect because

it is an accurate statement of the legal aspect in a survival action. **(B)** is incorrect because it is an accurate statement of the family's rights in a survival action. **(C)** is incorrect because it is an accurate statement of the family's rights in a survival action.

5. **/C/** Both Ds are jointly and severally liable for damages from an indivisible injury when fault has not been apportioned, so Driver A will be liable for the entire amount. **(A)** is incorrect because both Ds are jointly and severally liable. **(B)** is incorrect because the question ignores contribution issues, and is moot because of Driver B's bankruptcy. **(D)** is incorrect because an attorney's contingency fee does not become part of the judgment, so neither D is liable for that amount.

6. **/B/** Because the damages have been apportioned, Driver A is responsible for only the amount of damage he caused. Under causation analysis, Driver A was not the proximate cause of the broken arm. **(A)** is incorrect as it is the liability amount of Driver B. **(C)** is incorrect because there is no joint and several liability. **(D)** is incorrect because attorney fees are not usually added onto the judgment amount.

7. **/A/** No other information is needed because two separate acts of negligence creating indivisible damages result in joint and several liability. Thus, Driver will be liable for the entire amount unless the jury apportions damages. Note that the call of the question asks what *must* be known to determine a judgment amount. **(B)** is incorrect because knowing this information would then allow for an apportionment of damages, but this is not necessary under the call of this question. **(C)** is incorrect because knowing this information would then allow for an apportionment of damages, but this is not necessary under the call of this question. **(D)** is incorrect because knowing this information would then allow for an apportionment of damages, but this is not necessary under the call of this question.

8. **/D/** More information is needed. If, as the facts imply, the jurisdiction is one of pure comparative fault, we need to know the percentage of fault determined by the jury for each D because each D is liable only for his own percentage. Furthermore, the facts do not specify whether joint and several liability is applicable, which would also affect the answer. **(A)** is incorrect because more information is needed to determine percentage of fault. **(B)** is incorrect because more information is needed to determine percentage of fault. **(C)** is incorrect because more information is needed to determine percentage of fault.

9. **/D/** A parent is not vicariously liable for the torts of a child except for the situations in A, B, or C. **(A)** is incorrect because parents are vicariously liable under the "family purpose" doctrine where a child performing a task for the benefit of the family. This will impute liability onto the parents. **(B)** is incorrect because parents are vicariously liable when the parents negligently furnish the child with a dangerous instrumentality when the child does not have sufficient maturity to control the danger. **(C)**

is incorrect because parents are vicariously liable when they are aware of a child's dangerous propensities.

10. /D/ If a government entity waives immunity, then it is liable for negligent operation of its functions. Remember if two of the four alternatives are opposite, one is likely the best answer. **(A)** is a correct statement of immunity, so incorrect under the negative call of the question. **(B)** is a correct statement of immunity, so incorrect under the negative call of the question. **(C)** is incorrect under the call of the question because a government is immune from liability resulting from discretionary decisions such as whether to fund or install safety devices.

11. /A/ There is no allegation of damages, so P will not recover. Note that actual damages need not be proved for an intentional tort. **(B)** is incorrect because negligence as such is not compensable; damages must be proved as part of a prima facie case. **(C)** is incorrect because negligence as such is not compensable; damages must be proved as part of a prima facie case. **(D)** is incorrect because negligence as such is not compensable; damages must be proved as part of a prima facie case.

12. /C/ This type of future damages are allowed because the damages are readily calculable. **(A)** is incorrect because the future damages are too speculative. The business is new with no history of profitable operations. **(B)** is incorrect because the future damages are too speculative since there is no guarantee a ballet student will become a professional ballerina. **(D)** is incorrect because damages must be foreseeable and a factory shutdown seems too remote. *Hadley v. Baxendale.*

13. /B/ An award of interest for past medical bills is a liquidated sum because it is not subject to jury discretion. **(A)** is incorrect because pain and suffering is an unliquidated amount (left to the discretion of the jury). Only liquidated amounts can receive an award of pre-judgment interest. **(C)** is incorrect because future bills are an unliquidated amount (left to the discretion of the jury). Only liquidated amounts can receive an award of pre-judgment interest. **(D)** is incorrect because pain and suffering is an unliquidated amount (left to the discretion of the jury). Only liquidated amounts can receive an award of pre-judgment interest.

14. /D/ A P has a duty to mitigate his damages. Here, the P delayed treatment incurring an additional $5,000 of damages and an extra week of pain and suffering. The D is not responsible for this amount. **(A)** is incorrect because it does not take mitigation into account. **(B)** is incorrect because it does not fully account for mitigation. **(C)** is incorrect because it does not fully account for mitigation.

15. /B/ Upon the onset of severe pain, a reasonable person would most likely begin to investigate the cause of the pain, thus the negligence should have been revealed in year 1; Patient then had constructive knowledge of the negligence. [The conditional wording following "because" is the only correct reasoning necessary to satisfy the legal condition.] **(A)** is

not the best answer because the one-year discovery period may be applicable. **(C)** is incorrect because a reasonable person would have discovered the negligence. **(D)** is an incorrect application of the three year/one year discovery provision. The one year discovery period ended in year two (one year after constructive discovery), and the three year limitation period ended in year three. If the negligence was discovered six months prior to the expiration of the three years, the one year period would extend to six months after the expiration of the three years.

16. **/C/** The limitations period begins upon the last act of a continuous tort. The course of treatment is a single, continuous act for the purpose of the statute of limitations or repose. **(A)** is incorrect because the course of treatment is a single, continuous act for the purpose of the statute of limitations or repose. **(B)** is incorrect because the course of treatment is a single, continuous act for the purpose of the statute of limitations or repose. **(D)** is incorrect because the course of treatment is a single, continuous act for the purpose of the statute of limitations or repose.

17. **/A/** Minors are incompetent to bring suit, so the limitations period is tolled until the incompetence is over, upon reaching the age of majority. **(B)** is incorrect because there are no facts in the question to support this conclusion. **(C)** is incorrect because even if discovered, it is the child who "owns" the cause of action and it is the child who is incompetent, so the period tolls regardless of P's knowledge. Also, many jurisdictions do not impute the parent's knowledge or comparative

fault onto the child. **(D)** is incorrect because the discovery rule does not apply to a minor.

18. **/A/** The only viable alternative is A – Donny could be negligent if it can be shown that he failed to act reasonably. **(B)** is incorrect because Donny lacked the intent for battery. **(C)** is incorrect because Donny lacked the intent for assault. **(D)** is incorrect because there are no facts given which would support trespass.

19. **/B/** When dealing with a hyper-sensitive victim, the reasonable person standard applies; would a reasonable person find the contact offensive? An exception applies if the D knew that the specific victim would find the contact offensive. In answer B, if Donny knew of the infection, one could conclude that he would be aware that the contact would be offensive. **(A)** is incorrect because an intended act is not always enough to prove the D committed an intentional tort. **(C)** is incorrect because the intentional infliction of pain is not required to prove an intentional tort. **(D)** is incorrect because motive is not required to prove an intentional tort.

20. **/D/** None of the required elements of the three listed torts are present. **(A)** is incorrect because battery requires contact. **(B)** is incorrect because assault requires Polly to fear an imminent harmful contact. This is not present due to the ex-husband being across the room. On the exam look for a raised fist or other threatening gesture; words are usually not enough. **(C)** is incorrect because false imprisonment requires confinement and Polly was not confined. If the ex-husband were in the doorway

preventing her escape, then a claim for false imprisonment would be present.

21. /A/ In this assault question, alternative A contains the only fact of the four that would negate Polly's apprehension of an imminent harmful contact. **(B)** is incorrect because the alternative does not indicate that Polly had knowledge that would negate her apprehension. Only if Polly knew Donny was only joking or that the pistol was unloaded would there be a lack of apprehension. **(C)** is incorrect because the alternative does not indicate that Polly had knowledge that would negate her apprehension. Only if Polly knew Donny was only joking or that the pistol was unloaded would there be a lack of apprehension. **(D)** is incorrect because the alternative does not indicate that Polly had knowledge that would negate her apprehension. Only if Polly knew Donny was only joking or that the pistol was unloaded would there be a lack of apprehension.

22. /D/ False imprisonment requires confinement in an area with no reasonable means of escape. Since another door was present there was a reasonable means of escape. **(A)** is incorrect because P is being confined by the D. **(B)** is incorrect because leaping from a moving car is not usually a reasonable means of escape. **(C)** is incorrect because P has been physically restrained thus preventing escape.

23. /C/ Paul suffered physical symptoms due to Donny's conduct that exceeded all bounds of decency. **(A)** is incorrect because Paul was never in fear of an imminent battery required for assault. **(B)** is incorrect because there was no

contact required for battery. **(D)** is incorrect because there is an applicable tort listed as one of the options.

24. /C/ When there is a trespass due to necessity, the trespasser is not liable for nominal damages. However, he will be liable for any actual damages, which P must prove in order to recover. **(A)** is incorrect because low flying over the property is a trespass without an excuse like necessity. **(B)** is incorrect because chasing children onto the property is a trespass without an excuse like necessity. **(D)** is incorrect because refusal to leave property is a trespass without an excuse like necessity and is a BAFTT tort so damages are presumed.

25. /A/ A good faith mistaken belief does not exonerate a trespasser. **(B)** is incorrect because emergency or necessity is a defense to trespass, though D would be liable for any actual damages caused by the trespasser. **(C)** is incorrect because this is a public necessity, which precludes even actual damages. **(D)** is incorrect because the entry onto P's property was not voluntary.

26. /B/ Actual damages must be proven for trespass against chattels even if de minimus. **(A)** is incorrect because there were no actual damages. The fact that D was mistaken is not a defense if actual damages occurred. **(C)** is incorrect because there was not an intentional act by D. **(D)** is incorrect because the defense of necessity is available and there were no actual damages.

27. /C/ Defense of others is a defense against battery and the intervening defender steps into the shoes of the

victim as to self defense rights. Here, the level of force was not excessive or unreasonable because the boy could not have possibly defended Sam with his fists. **(A)** is incorrect. Under the common law, this defense was only available between family members; today even a stranger coming to the aid of another has this defense. **(B)** is incorrect because reasonable force in defense is allowed and the boy could not possibly defend Sam with his fists. **(D)** is not the best answer since it does not discuss the legal justification supporting Earnest's intervention.

28. **/D/** The best alternative because an owner may use reasonable non-deadly force in recapturing stolen chattels if in hot pursuit. **(A)** is incorrect because if the thief used unreasonable force in defending, the true owner will prevail. **(B)** is incorrect because the true owner is allowed to use reasonable force in recapturing the chattel. **(C)** is incorrect because a true owner in hot pursuit of a stolen chattel is allowed a reasonable right to trespass without permission of a valid license.

29. **/B/** The mayor of the city is only person who is not foreseeably within the "zone of danger" created by the D's reckless act. **(A)** is not the best answer because D's reckless driving creates a "zone of danger" that another driver on the road is foreseeably within. Try not to equate the "zone of danger" with purely physical zones. **(C)** is incorrect because a pedestrian is within the "zone of danger" created by D's reckless driving. **(D)** is incorrect because a passenger in the car is within the "zone of danger" created by D's reckless driving. Try not to equate the "zone of danger" with purely physical zones.

30. **/D/** When the impotence became foreseeable, the doctor going forward with the procedure exceeded the scope of the patient's consent since the patient was not aware of this risk. There is no indication in these facts that the surgery was an emergency that might preclude the necessity for consent. **(A)** is incorrect because this fact would negate the necessity for informed consent and that would be contrary to the law. **(B)** is incorrect because explaining all possible side effects tends to show informed consent. **(C)** is incorrect because this is the best way to obtain informed consent.

31. **/C/** In an emergency situation, if the Patient is unable to consent, then consent is presumed if a reasonable person would have consented. Since his life was in jeopardy, a reasonable person would have consented. **(A)** is incorrect because it does not articulate the correct reasonable person standard. **(B)** is incorrect because battery need not cause actual harm. Whether the doctor is liable for the hepatitis damages turns on negligence not battery. **(D)** is not the best answer because the Doctor may use reasonable life saving measures if consent is presumed.

32. **/B/** This is the "case within the case" standard that the P must prove in order to recover against the attorney. To prove causation, the P must prove that "but-for" the attorney's negligence she would have recovered against the Doctor in the underlying malpractice action. **(A)** is incorrect because the P has a cause of action against the attorney. **(C)** is incorrect because

there is not usually a "local standard" for professional malpractice. **(D)** is incorrect because there is not usually a "local standard" for professional malpractice.

33. **/B/** Because the Doctor was uncompensated, the Good Samaritan defense applies in most states. **(A)** is incorrect because the doctor was compensated, therefore the Good Samaritan defense is unavailable. **(C)** is not the best answer because the Good Samaritan defense does not turn on that fact. **(D)** is incorrect because strict liability does not apply to the professions.

34. **/A/** Capt. Hook is liable since his act was the cause of the swamping and any subsequent injury or damage. **(B)** is incorrect because Rescuer 1 put out the call that he could not complete the rescue. Had he not put out his own abandonment call, then he may be liable for negligence as other vessels may have believed that he was still attempting rescue. **(C)** is incorrect because Rescuer 2 was under no duty to attempt a rescue. Only upon undertaking the rescue does the duty arise to do so non-negligently. **(D)** is incorrect because Rescuer 1 and 2 are not liable.

35. **/B/** A person who places another in danger has a duty to rescue them in a non-negligent manner. **(A)** is incorrect because the Good Samaritan doctrine does not apply to the tort-feasor who created the peril. **(C)** is incorrect because the Good Samaritan doctrine does not apply to the tort-feasor who created the peril. **(D)** is incorrect because the Good Samaritan doctrine does not apply to the tort-feasor who created the peril.

36. **/A/** A landowner has only limited liability toward adult trespassers. **(B)** is incorrect because D is liable to the trespasser because it was foreseeable that someone would enter his property to rescue a child who had fallen into the unguarded hole. **(C)** is incorrect because a landowner is liable for injuries to adult invitees and licensees who are on the property with permission. **(D)** is incorrect because a landowner is liable for injuries to adult invitees and licensees who are on the property with permission.

37. **/B/** Landowners are generally not liable for injuries caused by natural dangerous conditions, even to children. **(A)** is incorrect because landowners are liable for injuries to children caused by artificial conditions that rise to the level of an "attractive nuisance." **(C)** is incorrect because landowners are liable to adult invitees for hidden dangers. **(D)** is incorrect because landowners are liable to adult licensees for visible dangerous conditions.

38. **/A/** Landowners are liable to child trespassers for injuries caused by artificial conditions that rise to the level of an attractive nuisance. However, the condition must be exposed and at a place where it was reasonable to expect children to enter. The child must also be unable to appreciate the danger. D is liable because he knew that a child might enter and acted in a willful and wanton manner. **(B)** is incorrect because it was not reasonable to expect that children would enter the property. **(C)** is incorrect because the child was old enough to appreciate the danger and invited the damages she

received. **(D)** is incorrect because it was not reasonable to expect that children would enter the property.

39. /C/ Owners are strictly liable for personal injuries caused by their wild animal pets, even if they took all possible precautions to protect others from harm. **(A)** is incorrect because P's conduct will not relieve D from liability, although it may reduce P's ultimate recovery. **(B)** is incorrect because the imposition of strict liability removes from consideration D's knowledge and any precautions she undertook. **(D)** is incorrect because the imposition of strict liability removes from consideration D's actual knowledge and any precautions she undertook.

40. /A/ "Least incorrect" is a form of negative question and the best approach is a true-false method. Dog owners are strictly liable for injuries caused by their dogs only after they become aware of their dog's dangerous propensities. This alternative is false because D may still have had constructive knowledge that his dog was dangerous. Additionally, D may still be liable in ordinary negligence even if he was unaware that his dog was dangerous. **(B)** is true and therefore not the best answer. Use a true-false approach to questions with a negative call. **(C)** is true and therefore not the best answer. Use a true-false approach to questions with a negative call. **(D)** is true and therefore not the best answer. Use a true-false approach to questions with a negative call.

41. /D/ A bartender will be liable for injuries caused by a drunk patron if he furnished intoxicating drink to an obviously intoxicated customer. **(A)** is incorrect because there is no indication that the bartender knew the customer was drunk and the alcohol service is too remote in time from the accident. **(B)** is incorrect because commercial vendors and social hosts generally are not liable to third parties injured by drunk patrons/guests. **(C)** is incorrect because commercial vendors and social hosts generally are not liable to third parties injured by drunk patrons/guests.

42. /A/ The violation of a statute is evidence of negligence where P was the intended beneficiary of the statute and the harm that P suffered was the kind the statute sought to prevent. Causation is clearly present in scenario A. **(B)** is incorrect because causation is lacking. **(C)** is incorrect because causation is lacking even though D's driver's license was suspended. **(D)** is not the best answer because snow accumulation on the street may mitigate the violation of the statute.

43. /B/ P is not required to prove breach if res ipsa loquitur is properly established. **(A)** is incorrect because a jury generally decides whether a breach of duty occurred. **(C)** is incorrect because P must establish that the injury was one that would not ordinarily occur without someone's negligence and that the operative instrument was under D's exclusive control at the time of the incident. D's notice that injuries might occur is not a requirement for res ipsa loquitur. **(D)** is incorrect because res ipsa loquitur only removes the breach and causation elements from P's required showing to make a prima facie case.

44. **/B/** Both Ds are liable because each was a substantial factor in bringing about P's harm. **(A)** is incorrect because D is not liable due to a lack of causation. **(C)** is incorrect because D is not liable due to a lack of causation. **(D)** is incorrect because D is not liable due to a lack of causation.

45. **/C/** Neither comparative nor contributory fault is a defense against intentional torts or reckless, willful, or wanton misconduct by D. **(A)** is incorrect because neither comparative nor contributory fault is a defense against intentional torts or reckless, willful, or wanton misconduct by D. **(B)** is incorrect because the "last clear chance" doctrine does not apply to bar P's recovery; the last clear chance applies if the D could have avoided the accident so P's contributory negligence does not produce any offset. **(D)** is incorrect because P's negligence is not a bar to recovery in comparative fault jurisdictions. In a contributory fault jurisdiction, however, P's contributory negligence would act as a bar to recovery unless P could show that D had acted in a reckless or willful manner in bringing about the injury.

46. **/D/** In most pure comparative fault states, P's damages are reduced proportionately by his level of fault. P's comparative fault is not a bar to recovery unless he was more than 50% at fault and was engaged in a reckless activity, such as drunk driving. **(A)** is incorrect because P will recover even if more at fault than D. **(B)** is incorrect because P will recover even if more at fault than any one D. **(C)** is incorrect because failure to mitigate is not a bar to recovery, although it may reduce P's damage award.

47. **/B/** Assumption of risk applies if P had actual knowledge of the risk involved, appreciated its magnitude and voluntarily chose to proceed. **(A)** is incorrect because P was unaware of the risk. **(C)** is incorrect because P failed to appreciate the magnitude of the risk. **(D)** is incorrect because the D takes the P as he finds him including any mentally handicapped characteristics.

48. **/C/** P will not recover because her injures were not proximately caused by D's conduct. Although D's conduct was a cause-in-fact of the accident, proximate cause is lacking because the result was remote and unforeseeable. **(A)** is incorrect; proximate cause is lacking because the result was remote and unforeseeable. **(B)** is incorrect because P is not entitled to any recovery from D where proximate cause is lacking. **(D)** is incorrect because P is not entitled to any recovery from D where proximate cause is lacking.

49. **/D/** D is liable for the enhanced injures that are the normal, foreseeable result of his negligent conduct. D is not liable in scenario D because it was not possible to foresee that the West Nile disease would occur as a result of his conduct. **(A)** is incorrect because a medical mistake is a foreseeable result of D's conduct. **(B)** is incorrect because a rescuer's acts were a foreseeable result of D's conduct. **(C)** is incorrect because a worsening of a pre-existing heart condition is a foreseeable result of D's conduct.

50. **/D/** Misrepresentation requires FIRD (a false statement of material fact with the intent to deceive. P must rely on the misrepresentation and incur damages). **(A)** is incorrect because mere puffing and curbside opinions do not rise to the level of a misstatement of fact. **(B)** is incorrect because P did not rely on the false statement. **(C)** is incorrect because mere casual statements and curbside opinions do not rise to the level of a misstatement of fact.

51. **/B/** The correct statement of the fraud remedy. P is to be awarded the benefit of the bargain. **(A)** is incorrect because the burden is on P to prove damages as part of his prima facie case, including the valuation of such damages. **(C)** is incorrect because the burden is on P to prove damages as part of his prima facie case, including the valuation of such damages. **(D)** is incorrect because the burden is on P to prove damages as part of his prima facie case, including the valuation of such damages.

52. **/A/** Negligent misrepresentation occurs where D was careless in making a false statement to P that P relied upon to his detriment. **(B)** is incorrect because intent to deceive is not necessary for negligent misrepresentation. Intent is necessary, however, for fraud in the inducement, misrepresentation and fraudulent concealment. **(C)** is incorrect because intent to deceive is not necessary for negligent misrepresentation. Intent is necessary, however, for fraud in the inducement, misrepresentation and fraudulent concealment. **(D)** is incorrect because intent to deceive is not necessary for negligent misrepresentation. Intent is necessary, however, for fraud in the inducement, misrepresentation and fraudulent concealment.

53. **/D/** Strict product liability does not attach to casual sellers of used products, even if they are defective as in D. **(A)** is incorrect because strict liability will arise where D participates in abnormally dangerous activities. **(B)** is incorrect because strict liability will arise where D owns a wild animal. **(C)** is incorrect because strict liability will arise where D designs a defective product.

54. **/C/** The correct answer because employers are strictly liable for injuries to employees for on-the-job injuries. **(A)** is incorrect because causation is lacking. The specific risk that wild animals pose is not traffic accidents. **(B)** is incorrect because causation is lacking. For strict liability to attach, the injury must flow from the specific risk. The specific risk from toxic sludge is not fender benders. **(D)** is incorrect because strict product liability does not apply to mere economic damages.

55. **/B/** The best defense because if the defect was the result of an unforeseeable alteration after it left the manufacturer, the chain of causation would be broken. **(A)** is incorrect. While a manufacturer employing the best quality control standards may be a viable defense to a negligence claim, it is irrelevant under a strict liability theory. **(C)** is incorrect because it is foreseeable that people will drive their automobiles at high speeds. **(D)** is incorrect. The fact that the manufacturer warned of possible damages is not a defense to a strict liability claim when the manufacturer could have made the product safe.

56. /B/ The correct answer because an inexpensive, safer alternative exists. A design defect may exist where the product was capable of being made in a safer way and the cost of doing so was not unreasonably excessive relative to the risk involved. **(A)** is incorrect because a hammer would lose its utility if it was made incapable of smashing fingers. **(C)** is incorrect because it is likely that a safer alternative does not exist. **(D)** is incorrect because the cost of making car roofs totally collapse-proof is likely excessive relative to the low risk involved. D may be correct for automobiles more prone to rolling over, such as sports utility vehicles.

57. /D/ D's best defense is that P assumed the risk because he was aware of the danger by virtue of the recall. **(A)** is not a good defense because a person not locking the car door should be foreseeable to D. **(B)** is not a good defense because a car door opening was foreseeable to D. **(C)** is incorrect because P is not under an obligation to discover hidden defects.

58. /D/ P may not recover under nuisance because D's factory is a public, not a private, nuisance. To recover for a public nuisance, P must show that his injury is different in kind from that of the rest of the community, which the facts do not establish. **(A)** is incorrect because P may not recover under nuisance because D's factory is a public, not a private, nuisance. To recover for a public nuisance, P must show that his injury is different in kind from that of the rest of the community, which the facts do not establish. **(B)** is not the best answer because there are not enough facts given to establish this as a possibility, and is irrelevant if P cannot prove that his injury is different from that of the community. **(C)** is incorrect because there are not enough facts given to establish it as a possibility, and is irrelevant if P cannot prove that his injury from a public nuisance is different from that of the community.

59. /C/ The P is the most likely to prevail in this alternative because the howling of the cats would likely be considered excessive, and is likely to be characterized as a substantial and unreasonable interference with P's enjoyment of her property. **(A)** is incorrect because the noises would not bother a person with average sensibilities. **(B)** is incorrect because the neighbor's activity is not unreasonable. **(D)** is incorrect because P purchased the land knowing that the pigs were there (P came to the nuisance).

60. /D/ A notorious criminal allegation, such as child molestation, is defamation per se. However, the allegation must be a serious felonious offense. **(A)** is not defamatory because it is mere opinion and is at most only unflattering, annoying, or embarrassing to P. **(B)** is not defamatory because it is mere opinion and is at most only unflattering, annoying, or embarrassing to P. **(C)** is not defamatory because merely calling someone a cheater on an exam does not rise to the level of notorious criminal allegation.

61. /B/ In order to constitute defamation, the false statement concerning P must have been intended to be publicized to a third person. There is no publication if the statement is made only to P. However, there may have been publication if D knew that P's wife would read the letter. **(A)** is incorrect because there was likely no publication. **(C)** is incorrect because defamation requires only that a false statement be negligently made or with wrongful intent – knowledge of the statement's falsity is not required. **(D)** is incorrect because while there is an absolute interspousal immunity, this does not apply to a statement made by a third party.

62. **/D/** A true-false approach is useful in double negative questions. A qualified privilege attaches to statements made in matters where one's own interest is concerned, unless the statement was made in bad faith. Here, D's knowledge of the falsity of the statement vitiated the privilege. This alternative is a false statement and is thus the correct answer. **(A)** is true because substantial truth is an absolute defense. **(B)** is true because an absolute privilege attaches to statements made in the course of judicial proceedings. **(C)** is true because a qualified privilege attached to D's statement because he was attempting to protect his own interest.

63. **/B/** A true-false approach is useful in double negative questions. The proper amount of damages for the commercial appropriation of likeness is D's commercial advantage, not P's commercial disadvantage. The second alternative is false and is thus the correct answer. A true-false approach is useful in double negative questions. The proper amount of damages for the commercial appropriation of likeness is D's commercial advantage, not P's commercial disadvantage. **(A)** is a true

statement and therefore incorrect. A true-false approach is useful in double negative questions. The proper amount of damages for the commercial appropriation of likeness is D's commercial advantage, not P's commercial disadvantage. **(C)** is a true statement and therefore incorrect. A true-false approach is useful in double negative questions. The proper amount of damages for the commercial appropriation of likeness is D's commercial advantage, not P's commercial disadvantage. **(D)** is a true statement and therefore incorrect.

64. **/B/** Interference with contract requires that D induce another to breach a contract with P. The interferer must have knowledge of the contract. **(A)** is incorrect because merely offering a better price to a party is not usually sufficient to create an interference claim. **(C)** is incorrect because a contract did not yet exist. **(D)** is incorrect because D played no role in inducing Betty to break the contract.

65. **/B/** Product disparagement requires that D publicize a false statement about P's product that casts doubt on the reliability or quality of the product and creates damages. These elements are all met in B. **(A)** is incorrect because P must prove actual damages to recover under the theory. **(C)** is incorrect because truth is a defense to a product disparagement claim. **(D)** is incorrect because a truthful factual comparison of products will not support an action for product disparagement.

66. **/C/** A true-false approach is useful in a negative call of the question. Slander of title occurs where P's real property is attached in bad

faith. Here, it appears that D had a valid claim to P's property. This alternative is thus false and is the correct answer. **(A)** is a true statement and therefore incorrect. P's must be acquitted to succeed in a malicious criminal prosecution proceeding. **(B)** is a true statement and therefore incorrect. If the lawsuit lacked a reasonable factual basis, a claim for wrongful proceeding will lie. **(D)** is a true statement and therefore incorrect. Using the legal process to accomplish a goal unrelated to the proceeding is an abuse of process.

Torts
Practice Question Answer Rationales

67. /C/ This is probably more of a private nuisance than a public one. The harm is only suffered by the property owners on the beach. The effect of the loud grinding machine created a substantial interference with the use of their private property. **(A)** is incorrect because the facts do not indicate the grinding is being conducted in a negligent manner. **(B)** is not the best answer because a public nuisance is an interference with the health, safety, or related right of an entire community. While a private party may sue for a public nuisance, they must show special damages different in kind from those suffered by the general public; here, the hotel is not different in kind from the other businesses who are dependent on tourism which has dried up because of the nuisance. The fact they may have lost more money than the other businesses is a difference in amount, not in kind. **(D)** is incorrect because there is no indication on these facts that there

is a substantial risk of serious harm in operating the rock grinding machine.

68. /C/ While this is probably the best answer, it may not be sufficient to prevent liability. Consent needs to include an appreciation of the risks and it is not clear Timothy understood that those who remained agreed to participate in the boxing. **(A)** is incorrect; there was an intent to cause the contact which is sufficient. Specific motive to inflict the harm is not required if it results from the intended contact. **(B)** is incorrect; there was sufficient intent even though the consequence of the broken jaw was not intended. **(D)** is incorrect; assumption of the risk is a defense to negligence and the claim in this question is for an intentional tort.

69. /D/ This is the worst defense because the store's outer walls are still a technical confinement even if quite large. **(A)** is incorrect because this would mean D lacked intention, a very good defense to imprisonment. **(B)** is incorrect because the P must have knowledge they were confined; this is thus a good defense. **(C)** is incorrect because false imprisonment is one of those BAFTD torts (<u>b</u>attery, <u>a</u>ssault, <u>f</u>alse imprisonment, <u>t</u>respass to land and per se <u>d</u>efamation) that require P to show actual damages; here nominal damages are not sufficient so this is a good defense.

70. /D/ The best defense since it focuses on a required element P must prove. If P cannot meet her burden in establishing this D's duty element in her case in chief the court may dismiss the action on a motion for a directed verdict. **(A)** is not the best defense because comparable fault allows the trier of fact to allocate

fault among both P and D proportional to their degree of negligence. Since this outcome would result in some liability against the D it is not as good a defense as answer D which focuses on an element P has to prove in their prima facie case. **(B)** is not the best answer because assumption of the risk must be with knowledge and that was not present in the facts. **(C)** is not the best answer because the foreseeability of the specific P is not necessary if a person's false imprisonment could have been avoided by a dressing room inspection before closing.

71. **/A/** This is the best answer because one of the exceptions to the no duty to rescue rule is where the D and the victim are acting together in a common pursuit so that they are co-venturers. **(B)** is incorrect; the no duty to act rule is subject to the co-venturers (and other) exceptions. **(C)** is not the best answer; even though the facts are accurate, Harriet did not cause the harm; the conclusion is wrong due to the co-venturers exception. **(D)** is not the best answer; while the conclusion may be correct – the heirs prevail – the rationale is inadequate. A general warning is usually inadequate to satisfy the duty to rescue.

72. **/C/** The best answer since the recovery would be from both Ds in proportion to their relative fault. **(A)** is incorrect because interspousal tort immunity has been eliminated in most states. **(B)** is incorrect; interspousal tort recovery does not depend on sole causation. **(D)** is incorrect; this fact pattern does not state or imply that the two Ds were acting in concert, which would be necessary for joint and several liability. However, the contributory

negligence of the spouse may be asserted as a defense by the non-spouse D.

73. **/C/** While the landlord would not usually have a duty to supervise a tenant's apartment, there is a higher duty in the common areas open to the public; this is thus the least effective defense. **(A)** is incorrect because the lack of any knowledge of the party would mean it would be difficult to foresee any risk and thus create a landlord duty; this would be an effective defense. **(B)** is incorrect because the entryway was not an area over which the tenants had exclusive personal control, the use went beyond the use contemplated (to enter/exit the building). It might be reasonable for the landlord to expect the tenants to ask for prior permission to hold a party, so it would be easier to foresee any risk and thus create a landlord duty. This would be an effective defense. **(D)** is incorrect because if the injured party was not a tenant, there would be less likelihood of the foreseeability of harm to this P; this would be an effective defense.

74. **/B/** The general rule is that a landlord is not liable for a tenant's dog injuries to third parties. **(A)** is incorrect because the dog is not the responsibility of Luke Landlord. **(C)** is not the best answer because liability would not lie since the landlord did not invite the third party to the premise; therefore, if the injury occurred, it would be to a trespasser. **(D)** is incorrect; while the landlord may own the property housing the Rottweiler, he did not know of the animal, approve, or control him; liability stays with the dog's owner, the tenant.

75. /D/ The best answer because even "as is – may be dangerous if operated" may not be a reasonable warning given the foreseeable serious potential harm ("operated" might easily be taken to mean actual mowing of a lawn – "started" would be a more reasonable word). **(A)** is not the best answer because this refers to the implied warranty of merchantability; neither party intended the good to be used for its ordinary purpose. **(B)** is incorrect because while "as is" may disclaim the implied warranty of merchantability, this would not preclude a negligence claim. **(C)** is incorrect because "last clear chance" merely excuses any contributory negligence by P if the D had the last ability to avoid the harm.

76. /D/ Causation must meet the "but for" test. Here, the passing motorist made the call immediately so Harry's inaction was not the cause-in-fact of either the original injury or Nathan's death. **(A)** is incorrect because while a landowner may not be responsible for natural dangers, there may be liability if the danger is put in motion by the landowner with knowledge of the trespasser. **(B)** is incorrect because if a trespasser has been imperiled by a landowner's affirmative act, there may be a duty to go to the rescue. **(C)** is incorrect because implied assumption of the risk requires the P to have actual knowledge of the potential future specific risk involved, appreciate its magnitude, and voluntarily chose to proceed; here there was not an appreciation of the risk.

77. /A/ The best answer. The negligence standard for a rescuer in an emergency is still one of objective reasonableness, but the jury may consider the emergency situation in determining whether a rescuer operated reasonably. **(B)** reaches the incorrect result even though the rationale (uncompensated bystander has no duty to go to the rescue) is accurate. **(C)** is incorrect because the standard is still one of a rescuer's reasonableness even though the jury may consider the emergency situation. **(D)** is not the best answer. While it is true that a fort-feasor takes the victim as they find them, a non-compensated rescuer may be entitled to a jury instruction that they may consider the fact that a normal person would not have died in the accident. Still there would be some damages so even if Nathan was not previously injured, Rosalind would be subject to some liability.

78. /B/ The "I" in FIRD is D's intention to induce P's reliance. The facts do not indicate that the D intended that P rely on the value opinion stated to the clerk. **(A)** is not the best answer because an expert may have misrepresentation liability for an opinion. **(C)** is not the best answer because the P did rely on the opinion. **(D)** is incorrect because the P did incur damages resulting from her reliance.

79. /C/ The most effective defense argument since establishing liability under a statute requires that the P's particular injury be among the harms or risks which the statute was intended to prohibit. This injury occurred not because of alcohol, but rather because Billy's kidneys were ruptured by toxic solvents. **(A)** is incorrect (thus an ineffective defense) since the statute prohibited the sale of any liquor to a person already intoxicated and the facts say that Billy appeared intoxicated. **(B)** is incorrect because "but for" the D drinking the beers, the P's injury would not have occurred. **(D)** is not the best answer because the mistake at the bottler occurred before the beer was served to Billy; superseding causes which relieve the original D of liability must unforeseeably occur after the "in fact" cause so this is not an effective defense.

80. **/D/** The best answer because of the "but for" test. The injury would not have occurred without Dick's intoxication and he would not have become intoxicated at Friday's without Tuesday's serving him first so Tuesday's was a cause in fact of the injury. **(A)** is incorrect because the statute indicates that liability depends on the causal relationship between Tuesday's conduct and Dick's intoxication. **(B)** is not the best answer because the "but for" test and the driving while intoxicated may have been a foreseeable consequence of Tuesday's serving Dick. **(C)** is incorrect because it is uncertain whether Tuesday's serving of Dick was a substantial factor relaxing Dick and causing him to go into Friday's. Therefore it is unknown if Tuesday was a substantial factor in causing the harm.

81. **/B/** This is the least effective defense to the battery charge that the level of force used by D was reasonable; committing a felony, without more, is not a valid justification for the use of deadly force. **(A)** is incorrect because a threat of death does justify the use of deadly force; here, Larry was shot at by Ryan. **(C)** is incorrect because a threat of serious physical injury to others may justify the use of deadly force; here, Larry knew that Ryan had just shot two tellers. **(D)** is incorrect because evidence of significant "serious

dangerousness" may justify the use of deadly force; here, Larry knew Ryan was armed, had shot two bank tellers, had shot at him, and was fleeing – reasonable people would conclude that Ryan exhibited serious dangerousness.

82. **/B/** Under the defense of others, the intervenor steps into the shoes of the victim; therefore, if Billy had a valid defense, that same defense would be available to the intervenor D. **(A)** is incorrect because most courts would not allow this mistake since Ike did not observe the start of the confrontation. **(C)** is incorrect since it seems to be contrary to the facts; Ike throwing the P into the bushes seems excessive to defend against a punch. **(D)** is incorrect; the requisite intent was present because he intended to throw Jack; intention to injure is not necessary.

83. **/D/** P would likely receive a partial recovery under the pure comparative fault statute in proportion to the relative fault of the parties. Because a landowner owes a duty of reasonable care to an invitee, there is some liability if a reasonable owner would have warned P. **(A)** is not the best answer because attractive nuisance usually applies to children trespassers; here, we have an adult invitee. **(B)** is incorrect because in a pure comparative fault jurisdiction, negligence by P does not bar a partial recovery. **(C)** is incorrect because Stan had Susan's permission to come on the property and thus, was an invitee.

84. **/B/** For the payment mistake to invalidate P's consent, it must go to the essence of the battery or consent; here the fact that P may have to sue under a breach of contract to collect the $500 is

collateral to the medical consent. **(A)** is not the best answer because the requirement states the claim is for the intentional tort of battery, not negligence. **(C)** is not the best answer because even if Doctor knew the government program had run out it is possible the program would be refunded or payment made to Evan from another source. **(D)** is incorrect because the consent was made after detailed disclosure of the medical risks and the question of payment was collateral.

85. **/C/** In those states which recognize alienation of affections, a parent may recover against a D that induces a minor to leave home. **(A)** is incorrect in that most states have abolished criminal conversation claims by a spouse against a romantic rival. **(B)** is incorrect because the fact that the estranged husband no longer receives the wife's earnings does not create a claim against a third party for criminal conversation (although it might become an issue in the couple's subsequent divorce). **(D)** is not the best answer because monetary damages do not usually go to whether a parent's claim of alienation of affection would lie.

86. **/A/** To qualify under workman's compensation the claim for physical injury must arise within the course and scope of employment. **(B)** is not the best argument because there is not an automatic rule as to whether an agent is to be treated as an employee or an independent contractor. **(C)** is not the best argument because an employee's own negligence – even if gross – is not grounds to deny coverage. Also, assumption of the risk may not be asserted by the employer or state. **(D)** is not the best answer because the test is not the physical presence but rather whether the injury was within the course and scope of the employer's business.

87. **/C/** Accepting a worker's compensation award does not preclude an employee going against a third party tort feasor but any award cannot result in a double recovery. **(A)** is incorrect because the doctrine of respondent superior subjects a principal to potential liability for torts of the agent. **(B)** is incorrect because any award cannot result in a double recovery. **(D)** is incorrect because an injured victim may go against a third party tortfeasor; the preclusion is an employee claim being asserted against the employer.

88. **/B/** Respondent Superior is the worst theory of recovery; this doctrine creates employer vicarious liability for the torts of employees in the scope and course of their employment duties. **(A)** is not the best answer because it is a variety of a parent negligently allowing children access to a potentially dangerous instrumentality for which liability might be present. **(C)** is not the best answer because allowing children access to a dangerous instrumentality without supervision with knowledge of the child's dangerous propensities is negligence. **(D)** is not the best answer because it is a variety of a parent negligently allowing children access to a dangerous instrumentality for which liability might be present.

89. **/C/** Strict liability may apply to D's abnormally dangerous activity such as storing explosives. Here though the harm did not result from the risk used to justify the application of strict liability. Proximate causation is necessary and the intervening conduct by the terrorist was not

reasonably foreseeable (While a court might hold to the contrary, this causation alternative seems to represent the best defense). **(A)** is incorrect because strict liability may be imposed regardless of whether the D exercised reasonable care. **(B)** is incorrect because a physical invasion is not necessary to recover under a strict liability theory. **(D)** is not the best answer because it goes to a question of duty, which is one of fact. A more effective defense is one of law - that there was no causation.

90. **/D/** Strict liability may be imposed on a landowner who uses the land in a non-natural manner for the storage of radioactive "hot" water which may escape; the resulting damages to the neighbors are foreseeable. **(A)** is incorrect because the intervention of an act of God does not relieve the original wrongdoer of liability unless the intervening act was unforeseeable; here the plant was located in an earthquake sensitive area. **(B)** is not the best answer because Nancy's damages did not result from any of the aspects of operating a nuclear reactor, which made it an abnormally dangerous activity. **(C)** is not the best answer because an earthquake can occur anywhere in any frequency. The fact that some scientists believe the area was earthquake sensitive does not make an earthquake reasonably foreseeable.

91. **/C/** It seems likely that under these circumstances both the seller and the buyer will be liable to the third party. Sally engaged in active concealment of a known dangerous condition. It was foreseeable that a neighbor would be injured. Betty would be liable because an owner has potential liability to persons outside the premises for injuries suffered from falling objects on their premises. (Betty will prevail against Sally for concealment on a cross-claim.) **(A)** is incorrect because it involves the wrong combination of alternatives. **(B)** is incorrect because it involves the wrong combination of alternatives. **(D)** is incorrect because it involves the wrong combination of alternatives.

92. **/C/** A guest statute eliminates driver liability to non-paying passengers unless the driver was grossly negligent, reckless, or intoxicated. **(A)** is incorrect because simple negligence is an insufficient showing under the typical guest statute. **(B)** is incorrect because a failure to fasten a seat belt is usually to be treated as comparative fault requiring an apportionment of damages – this is not a total defense. **(D)** is incorrect because a fully effective implied assumption defense requires that P has actual knowledge of the specific potential future risk, appreciates its magnitude and voluntarily chooses to proceed. This degree of P's knowledge does not appear to be present here and the jury would apply proportional fault to reduce, but not eliminate, P's recovery.

93. **/D/** The best answer because in most states the owner of a domestic animal is not strictly liable unless the dog displayed vicious propensities in the past ("one free bite rule"). **(A)** is incorrect because the cause in fact is a negligence concept; the facts here say the claim was brought under a strict liability theory. **(B)** is incorrect; while "the one free bite rule" is limited to domestic animals, the better answer focuses on whether the dog displayed dangerous propensities so

the owner would have legal notice. **(C)** is not the best answer since even if Retriever was on a leash the same incident could have occurred had the dog escaped. This might be a viable negligence recovery theory however.

94. /D/ The worst argument because under most shopkeeper's privilege statutes innocence is not a defense if the three reasonable requirements are met by the shopkeeper (basis to suspect, temporary time of detention, and manner of restraint/confinement). **(A)** is incorrect because the detention period being unreasonable is a helpful argument. **(B)** is incorrect because the unreasonable grounds for the suspected shoplifter's detention is a helpful argument. **(C)** is incorrect because if some aspect of the restraint – here, the place – was unreasonable the P has a helpful argument.

95. /D/ Sovereign immunity does not apply to proprietary activities of a government entity which produce revenue as would a private business such as a utility department. Thus the original tortfeasor is liable to both the rescuer and the rescuee. **(A)** is not the best answer since this could be argued to be an abnormally dangerous activity in which the P does not have to prove negligence. **(B)** is incorrect because sovereign immunity does not apply to proprietary activities which produce revenue as would a private business. **(C)** is incorrect because the responsibility for dangerous activities may not be avoided by delegating the work to independent contractors.

96. /A/ The rescuee will likely prevail against all the parties named. Ruth is potentially liable because while a non-compensated bystander does not have a duty to rescue, they cannot negligently increase the risk of harm. Fix It Inc. is potentially liable because their failure to erect barriers was the "in fact" cause of Betty falling into the hole; creating danger invites rescue and any additional damages that might foreseeably result from the rescue. Pleasant Town is potentially liable because the liability for dangerous activities may not be avoided by delegating the work to independent contractors and immunity does not apply to such proprietary functions. **(B)** is incorrect because it involves the wrong combination of alternatives. **(C)** is incorrect because it involves the wrong combination of alternatives. **(D)** is incorrect because it involves the wrong combination of alternatives.

97. /D/ If a rescuer does voluntarily begin to provide assistance, she cannot negligently make the P's injury worse. It is to avoid imposing liability upon the rescuer that most jurisdictions have enacted "Good Samaritan" statutes that excuse ordinary negligence on the part of uncompensated rescuers. Here, the facts specify that this jurisdiction does not recognize this doctrine. **(A)** is incorrect because a relationship between the rescuer and the original tortfeasor is not necessary to hold the rescuer liable for the P's damages they caused. **(B)** is incorrect because an expectation of compensation is not necessary to hold a rescuer liable for the P's damages they caused. **(C)** is incorrect because absent a "Good Samaritan" statute ordinary negligence by a rescuer is actionable by an injured rescuee.

98. /B/ Failure to obtain a medical doctor license required of real doctors

under the civil licensing statute did not cause the P's injury so it was error to allow the jury to consider it to be "clear evidence" of negligence. **(A)** is incorrect because the license or lack of it did not go to the question of whether D's treatment of P was negligent. **(C)** is incorrect because the lack of a license does not prove negligence – either "per se" or "clear evidence." **(D)** is incorrect because the lack of a license is not conclusive as to malpractice.

99. /B/ Both Firery and Earl are to be categorized as licensees since they have express or implied permission to be on the premises for non-business purposes. (The professional rescue doctrine does not apply.) A property owner is liable to a licensee from known dangerous conditions (the loose steps on the stair) but not from unknown dangers (the defective ruptured oil input line). Since the owner knew the steps were in disrepair, he had a duty to the licensee Firery to at least warn him. To hold the owner liable to Earl would require knowledge of the defect, which is not present in this fact pattern. **(A)** is incorrect because Henry was aware of the loose steps and is liable to Firery as a licensee. **(C)** is incorrect because Henry was aware of the loose steps and is liable to Firery as a licensee, but was not aware of the rupture and is not liable to Earl. **(D)** is incorrect because Henry was not aware of the rupture and is not liable to Earl as a licensee.

100./D/ The least likely argument because it seems that the patients did not appreciate the side-effect danger of cancer. **(A)** is incorrect because subsequent remedial measures should not be admitted at trial; a

motion in limine should be granted. **(B)** is incorrect because if the D's drug was manufactured up to the then state of the art, it may not have then been possible to treat HIV safely; that would be a good defense. **(C)** is incorrect because if strict liability does not apply, the negligent standard would require foreseeability of the harm which may be absent in this circumstance.

101./D/ Restatement 402A imposes strict liability on a manufacturer without fault if the unreasonably dangerous product is expected to and has reached the user or consumer without substantial change in the condition in which it is sold. The product in this question was not defective when it left Mega's hands; the defect occurred in the change of container by the retailer, Acme Sales Co. Thus any damage was caused by Acme, not Mega. **(A)** is incorrect because strict liability does not require a showing of negligence. **(B)** is incorrect because neither vertical nor horizontal privity is necessary to create liability to the injured party. **(C)** is incorrect because this was not a known risk such as an unsupervised swimming pool that might put a reasonable parent on notice they should supervise their children.

102./C/ Recovery will require a showing of negligence by the school soccer personnel. **(A)** is incorrect because this relationship does not involve special expertise or a trust beneficiary status such as a lawyer-client fiduciary duty. **(B)** is not the best answer because such an assumption of risk would probably need to be accompanied by an appreciation of the specific danger that the P assumed. Merely joining the team would seem to be insufficient intention to constitute an express or implied agreement to assume the risk. **(D)** is incorrect because there is no magic age of contributory negligence and such a defense would only apply if there was negligence.

103./D/ The best answer. Strict liability under Restatement 402A requires that the product was in defective condition when it left the manufacturer's control and is not expected to undergo significant changes. Here, it is clear that the product was not defective when it left Better. It was also not complete. **(A)** is not the best answer because merely manufacturing a boat hull does not create either strict liability or negligence liability. **(B)** is not the best answer because whether it was negligent to allow a retailer to install the motor is not a strict liability issue. **(C)** is not the best answer since the conclusion – no is wrong and vertical privity is established by law.

104./C/ The best answer is one that totally defeats the claim. Since Retailer merely followed Ole's instructions and made an affirmative warning of potential danger, there should be no liability to the customer based on either strict liability or negligence. This is a form of assumption of the risk. **(A)** is incorrect because the negligence was in Ole ordering such a large motor for such a small boat and the excess speed of the boat. **(B)** is not the best answer because contributory fault would only allow a partial offset. **(D)** is incorrect because it contradicts the fact that Retailer had sufficient foresight and concern that it felt it was prudent to warn Ole.

105./A/ Given all the possible combinations of motor and reverse gears which could be installed by their chain of distributors and the speeding by the boat owner, the damage here suffered by Skipper does not appear to be reasonably foreseeable to the manufacturer. **(B)** is incorrect because tort law allows several liability; it is not necessary to name every party in the suit. **(C)** is incorrect because the facts state that the suit is for negligence, not strict liability. **(D)** is incorrect because neither horizontal nor vertical privity is a defense to suit for product liability negligence.

106./B/ This defense seems the worst of those given because it is not necessary that the damaged party sue every one who could conceivably be responsible for some portion of the injury. Tort liability is several. **(A)** is not the best answer since it may be a defense if Ole can prove Skipper did have the last clear chance to avoid the accident. **(C)** is not the best answer because it may be at least a partial defense since there might be an offset if Ole can prove Skipper had contributory fault. **(D)** is not the best answer because it is a better defense than B.

107./D/ The injured party will recover against neither party. This follows because neither party was negligent and thus causation in fact is not present. It was the unforeseeable combination of the two elements – hydrogen and oxygen – that produced the water which caused the damages. **(A)** is incorrect because the combination of elements was unforeseeable, therefore neither actor individually was negligent. **(B)** is incorrect because the combination of elements was unforeseeable, therefore neither actor individually was negligent. **(C)** is incorrect because the combination of elements was unforeseeable, therefore neither actor individually was negligent.

108./B/ A public nuisance's interference with the P's interest is unreasonable if the gravity of the harm of the nuisance outweighs the utility of the conduct engaged in by the Ds. Here, the employment loss and lack of intention would seem to outweigh the occasional water flooding. **(A)** is incorrect because the essence of a nuisance claim is usually the magnitude of the harm rather than the D's state of mind. **(C)** is not the best answer because the P moving to the nuisance would only be one factor to be considered and the P did not know of the nuisance when she moved there. **(D)** is incorrect because this is not a defense at all but rather the D's preferred remedy if the P's claim prevails.

109./C/ The best defense that the companies could assert against Citizen's lawsuit is that one of the required elements for a private citizen to sue for public nuisance is absent. Citizen has failed to allege special damages in addition to the ordinary damages a member of the public suffered. **(A)** is not the best answer because the flooding of the park could constitute a public nuisance even if there was not a relevant city ordinance. Still, the ordinance may be helpful in proving that the flooding water constitutes a nuisance. **(B)** is not the best answer because the city is not a party to this lawsuit, and this alternative contradicts the facts, which state the water destroyed the children's play area. **(D)** is not the best answer because while the

balancing test would be a defense against a lawsuit filed by the city that is not ripe. The better defense is that one of the required elements for a private citizen to sue for a public nuisance is absent.

110./B/ The best answer of those given. This restraint/detention seems to be justified for the purpose of preventing personal injury and damage to property. (Another related viable defense to the tort of false imprisonment would be discipline privilege.) The driver's confinement of the students was justified as a reasonable safety measure. **(A)** is incorrect because the facts do not indicate that Debra Driver was ever in danger of imminent personal harm which would be required for self-defense to be applicable. **(C)** is incorrect because necessity – private or public – applies as a defense to harm to P's property; here the D is not harming anyone's property. **(D)** is incorrect because necessity – private or public – applies as a defense to harm to P's property; here the D is not harming anyone's property.

111./C/ This intervening criminal behavior by a burglar does not seem to be reasonably foreseeable; thus it would constitute a superseding cause. **(A)** is not the best answer since the ladder was not responsible for the theft. The reference to a tenancy is a red herring. **(B)** is incorrect because the contractual provision requiring workmanlike manner refers to the quality of the painting. The facts do not state that the painting was inadequate or that Pricilla was specifically contractually required to remove the ladder from Harry's home. **(D)** is incorrect because Harry will not prevail against

Pricilla. Had Pricilla left the door unlocked, thus foreseeably inviting the burglar to trespass and steal, there might be a cause of action.

112./B/ Under the "eggshell skull rule," the negligent D takes the P as the victim is found even though the extent of the injury may be more than the D would have expected. **(A)** is not the best answer because the facts do not state the unusual physical condition of the victim was known to the tortfeasor. **(C)** is incorrect because the P will prevail even though the extent of the injury may have been unexpected. **(D)** is incorrect because the P will prevail even if the damages are grossly disproportionate to the D's fault.

113./C/ While neither wrongdoing (Susan's failure to pull completely off the road and Hotrod D's cell phone distraction) was sufficient to create the accident itself, both were acts of negligence and the two combined concurrent causes created the damages. Therefore, Susan and Hotrod are both jointly and severally liable for Larry's damages. **(A)** is incorrect because Susan was also negligent in failing to pull completely off the road. **(B)** is incorrect because Hotrod was also negligent in driving while being distracted by a cell phone. **(D)** is incorrect because both Hotrod and Susan were concurrently negligent.

114./D/ In a jurisdiction which has not adopted any form of comparative negligence or fault, contributory negligence is a complete defense to recovery. This result – a complete bar – applies to ordinary negligence, but does not apply to bar a recovery for reckless and wanton behavior beyond ordinary negligence. **(A)** is incorrect because the common law rule is that contributory negligence is a bar to recovery for ordinary negligence. **(B)** is incorrect for two reasons. First, because it puts the burden of proof on the P to disprove a defense which D could assert (that the P had the last clear chance to avoid the injury). Second, the last clear chance defense does not bar a recovery if the D's actions rise to the level of reckless and wanton. **(C)** is not the best answer because P's recovery is not dependent upon an intentional tort theory; reckless and wanton negligence is sufficient.

115./C/ Res ipsa loquitur allows the jury to infer from circumstantial evidence that the D failed to exercise reasonable care. A plane crash does not ordinarily occur in the absence of negligence. **(A)** is not the best answer because res ipsa loquitur provides only a jury instruction creating an inference; this is not a certainty of prevailing on the merits. **(B)** is incorrect because direct evidence of breach and causation is not necessary under res ipsa loquitur. **(D)** is incorrect because while the issue of a pilot's duty to a passenger may be a matter of law, breach of the duty and causation must be supported by circumstantial evidence. This is a jury question.

116./C/ To invoke the doctrine of res ipsa loquitur there must be a showing that the operative instrumentality was under the D's exclusive control. **(A)** is incorrect because res ipsa loquitur does not apply to these facts. **(B)** is incorrect because Paul will not prevail unless he can identify and sue the tenant who dropped the boiling water on his head. **(D)** is not the best answer because pedestrians do not normally assume the risk that foreign objects may fall on them.

117./C/ The most helpful fact of the four given is that Douglas could have probably avoided the incident because he could have cleared the intersection before the light turned red. This is the last clear chance doctrine and overrides any comparative fault on the P's part that would otherwise determine the relative allocated fault of the parties. **(A)** is not the best answer because a history does not indicate fault in the current dispute. **(B)** is incorrect because this alternative would allocate damages by relative fault; if Douglas could have avoided the accident, there may not be any reduction for P's relative fault. **(D)** is incorrect because what happened after the event does not determine fault or liability of the event itself.

118./B/ The schoolboy had no fault in the second accident since there was a sign which should have put both divers on notice to be on the alert for school children. **(A)** is incorrect because Douglas was speeding and a jury could thus find a high degree of comparative fault. **(C)** is not the worst defense since speeding in a school zone may be negligence per se and drivers following a speeder may be among the class of people and harms which the statute was intended to protect. **(D)** is not the worst defense since the inattention was caused at least in part by the prior incident and Douglas should have foreseen that the following driver would be upset and this might result in diminished attention.

119./A/ Florence will likely prevail on her claim of private nuisance. After the quadrupling of the emission

level, the nuisance created a substantial interference with Florence's use and enjoyment of her property. **(B)** is incorrect because she moved to a nuisance when the level was one quarter of the final emission level. She did not move to the expanded nuisance and such an expansion was not reasonably foreseeable. **(C)** is incorrect because a tortfeasor takes the victim as they find them including any extra-sensitive conditions. **(D)** is incorrect because it is not necessary to prove intent to recover for nuisance.

120./B/ There remain questions of fact whether the damaging event – the second accident – was a continuing consequence of Speedy's negligence. **(A)** is not the best answer since it was probably foreseeable that other drivers would slow down as they passed the accident scene. Some contributory fault is not a sufficient basis to dismiss the lawsuit. **(C)** is incorrect because Speedy's driving with an expired driver's license was not the proximate cause of the first or second accident. This is not a violation of a criminal statute that might produce negligence per se. **(D)** is incorrect because while the other driver may have been a concurrent cause, it does not excuse Speedy's negligence.

121./B/ The best answer because the false statement must be published to a third party. Publication requires that the third party understand the defamatory statement. **(A)** is incorrect because this is one of four categories of defamation – injury in her trade, business, or profession – creating liability per se. **(C)** is incorrect because a showing of actual intention to defame is not necessary – mere negligence is sufficient. **(D)** is incorrect since the facts do not state that the statement was true or false. In addition, since the publication was made in a business setting, the defamation could create damages.

122./C/ Patty was under a qualified privilege because she was a neighbor conducting her own affairs in a matter concerning her own interest. It appears as if she was speaking in good faith and the fair comment standard is that of a reasonable neighbor. This qualified privilege can be abrogated only by malice or D's knowledge that the statement was false. **(A)** is incorrect because Peter will lose and defamation damages must be to D's good name and reputation beyond monetary damages. **(B)** is incorrect because Peter was a mere businessman who does not become a public figure merely because he applies for a business license. **(D)** is incorrect because while Patty did not refer directly to Peter, statements targeted towards a small group of which P is a member will qualify.

123./C/ The best reason that the P will not recover for libel is that the D had a qualified privilege. These statements were made in the conduct of her own affairs in a matter where her own interest is concerned. The publication could also be considered to be a warning for public protection to people who act in the public interest. **(A)** is incorrect because the statements were substantially true; the P would have to show falsity as a part of their prima facie case. **(B)** is not the best answer because some of Cathy's statements probably went beyond opinion to become statements of fact. **(D)** is

incorrect because D will likely not recover.

124./B/ The best answer because proving special damages is required to recover for defamation unless the statement falls under one of our LUNI per se damage categories (loathsome disease, unchastity or other serious sexual misconduct, notorious criminal allegation, or injury in trade, business, or profession. Humiliation and diminution of respect by friends are not sufficient. **(A)** is not the best answer because P will not recover even if she proves untruthfulness unless she can prove special damages. **(C)** is not as good an answer as B because special damages are one of the requirements P must prove to prevail. Any qualified privilege was not exercised in a reasonable manner and the first amendment defense privilege protects media Ds against a public official. **(D)** is incorrect because any valid consent defense would require an express waiver of the publication itself; there is no indication in these facts that occurred.

125./D/ The best answer. The P should prevail even if the facts were true. The tort of publication of private facts looks to the reasonableness of the D's disclosure or lack of it. **(A)** is incorrect because the publication of even true facts may be actionable if a reasonable person would consider the "deadbeat" statement to be unreasonable. **(B)** is incorrect because truth is not an absolute defense. **(C)** is incorrect; Cathy will prevail because the "deadbeat" statement was unreasonable.

126./B/ The best answer because outrage requires that the D's extreme and outrageous conduct cause severe distress to the P. **(A)** is not the best answer since trespassing is a separate tort from outrage. **(C)** is incorrect because words may be sufficient if they create extreme and outrageous damages. **(D)** is incorrect because even if the P did not pay her account, it would not control if the outrageous conduct created extreme and outrageous damages. Truth may be a defense to defamation but not outrage.

127./A/ The best answer since this alternative addresses the most basic element required for P's case; that the harmful offensive conduct was made intending to offend P's dignity. **(B)** is incorrect because trespass, without more, is not usually a recognized defense to an intentional tort such as battery. **(C)** is incorrect because the defense of property, which may require an order to quit the property before eviction force may be used, is not at issue here. The major uncertainty in this case is whether the D intended the battery. **(D)** is incorrect because while consent may be a defense to battery, the facts do not provide any support that the P consented to this battery.

128./C/ This case involves the publication of private facts. Susan, however, was the person who called the press conference and granted the reporter an interview in which she voluntarily identified her former employer. This makes her a self-promoted public figure and her activities thus newsworthy. **(A)** is incorrect because truth is not a defense to invasion of privacy. **(B)** is incorrect because Susan opened the door thus impliedly consenting to the publication. **(D)** is incorrect because mere embarrassment is insufficient. Even if the

publication subjected Susan to extreme ridicule and contempt, there is a valid defense of consent.

129./B/ A showing of special damages is not necessary if the false statement involved a loathsome disease, unchastity, or injury to the P's business. There would thus be some recovery for non-pecuniary humiliation, injury to one's reputation, or loss of friends. **(A)** is incorrect because if a LUNI category of defamation is involved, special damages are not necessary. **(C)** is not the best answer because the P must only show negligence by the D in making the publication. Actual intention to injure the P's reputation is not necessary. **(D)** is not the best answer. While the portion of the publication about Gary's sexual orientation may be truthful, the allegation about Gary having AIDS was false.

130./C/ This seems to be the worst defense that Notorious News could assert. Reasonable care would imply the newspaper at least made some investigation such as calling Gary and asking if he denied having AIDS. Ordinarily a reporter would report more objectively by at least disclosing this was only one party's opinion. **(A)** is a better defense because a P who initiates a public lawsuit may implicitly agree to any and all aspects of the dispute becoming public. **(B)** is a better defense because statements made in the course of judicial proceedings are afforded an absolute privilege. **(D)** is a better defense because *New York Times v. Sullivan* held the 1st and 14th Amendments protected media Ds against public figure Ps unless the false publication was made with actual malice. The question will be whether the lack of any investigation occurred because the reporter had serious doubts about the veracity of the AIDS fact and was afraid that the P would deny the allegation. If so, this might impute the necessary malice.

131./D/ A false picture may be a statement of fact which meets all the FPID requirements of defamation. Larry Hawk is unquestionably a public figure. For non-media publishers, the P must prove knowledge by the publisher of the falsity or a reckless disregard for the truth. **(A)** is incorrect because Hawk will likely recover and the *Gertz* case held strict liability in defamation was unconstitutional. **(B)** is incorrect because whether there may have been "in fact" knowledge is not relevant to the issue of whether Low Quality was negligent in not making an investigation of the agent's representation. **(C)** is incorrect since actionable defamation may be either slander (spoken) or libel (written in letters).

132./A/ Larry Hawk will prevail and the best reason is that commercial appropriation of likeness without permission is one of the four invasion of privacy torts. **(B)** is not the best answer because while Hawk will prevail, the proper action in the invasion of privacy family of torts is not intrusion since no private affairs were involved. **(C)** is incorrect because Hawk will prevail, but publication in a false light requires a false attribution. **(D)** is incorrect because Hawk's right to protect the commercial use of his identity is not affected by a mistaken belief of permission. This is not a valid defense even if the D had not been negligent in forming their mistaken belief.

133./B/ The standard for negligence is whether a reasonable security guard would have swept the warehouse prior to locking it; expert testimony would establish this standard. **(A)** is incorrect because the P could recover under respondeat superior, which creates vicarious liability. The facts do not state the security guard was an independent contractor. **(C)** is incorrect because intention by the D is not necessary to recover for negligence. **(D)** is incorrect because the defense of assumption of the risk requires an actual subjective appreciation of the magnitude of the risk involved and a voluntary assumption. Merely trying to escape a danger created by D does not usually rise to that level.

134./D/ False imprisonment is an intentional tort so a part of the prima facie case is that the night watchman intended to confine or imprison some person in that warehouse when he locked the door. **(A)** is incorrect because if there was liability, the agent is usually personally liable for his or her own torts (along with the principal). **(B)** is not the best answer because it omits the essential element of intention. **(C)** is not the best answer since it omits the essential element of intention.

135./B/ False imprisonment requires that the D set definite physical boundaries. That requirement is not met here because there was an alternate route available to the drivers. **(A)** is incorrect because the use of the public road is not the issue; intentional confinement is the touchstone of false imprisonment. **(C)** is not the best answer because force is not required if the threat of force or other restraining element is present. **(D)** is incorrect; while it is true that false imprisonment is an intentional tort, it must also involve confinement within a boundary, which is not present here.

136./B/ False arrest does not apply if there was a crime committed and/or the arrest was made under color of a warrant. Here, neither of these two excusing factors applies, so Susan would prevail. **(A)** is not the best answer because a private citizen is not held to a lower standard than a police officer. In fact, a police officer may arrest without a warrant if there is probable cause. In comparison, a private citizen must have seen the crime to avoid having the detention considered a false arrest. **(C)** is incorrect because Susan will prevail and a reasonable but erroneous belief for an individual, non-merchant arrester does not provide a defense. **(D)** is incorrect because the time of the period of physical confinement is not controlling.

137./D/ The correct alternative because this is the least viable or worst defense since it implies that Sleazy made a statement that Eager could rely upon. **(A)** is incorrect because fraud or misrepresentation requires a false statement of fact; the lack of same would be a viable defense. **(B)** is incorrect because fraud or misrepresentation requires an intention to deceive (scienter). The lack of scienter would be a viable defense. **(C)** is incorrect because fraud or misrepresentation requires damages; the lack of scienter would be a viable defense.

138./C/ A victim's ordinary sensitivity and vulnerability is the usual standard for intentional infliction of mental distress or outrage. (This is contrary to the usual "super-sensitive P" tort rule in which the D takes the P as she finds her.) If the D knows the P is especially vulnerable or susceptible to emotional distress, the duty level is raised. **(A)** is incorrect because physical injury is not absolutely required if there is some physical manifestation. **(B)** is incorrect because it is the effect that matters, not whether P was threatened. **(D)** is incorrect because outrage or the intentional infliction of emotional distress is an intentional tort. While a D takes a P as she finds them in negligence, P's extra-sensitivity requires knowledge by D for outrage.

139./C/ The best answer because it focuses on an element necessary for a third party to recover for outrage or the intentional infliction of emotional distress – that the D must usually have knowledge of the presence of the P. This is a non-BAFTT intentional tort and thus transferred intent does not apply. **(A)** is not the best answer because it is not necessary that the third-party P's distress be caused directly; watching an outrageous attack on another is sufficient if the D is aware of P's presence. **(B)** is not the best answer because the tort of outrage or intentional infliction of emotional distress does not always require physical injury. **(D)** is not the best answer because such conduct may be sufficient as it relates to the actual victim, but as to third parties, knowledge of the P by the D is necessary.

140./A/ Wally's false statement that he was a policeman constitutes fraud and taking Betty into custody to his home constitutes a false arrest. The damages of her lost wages were foreseeable. **(B)** is incorrect because the highest level offense falls under criminal law and is not a tort concept. **(C)** is incorrect because P will prevail for false arrest and detention does not require physical force – only that P was restrained against their free will. **(D)** is incorrect because P will prevail for fraud because Betty believed Wally's statement that he was a policeman to be true and her reliance does not appear unreasonable.

141./B/ The best defense is one that defeats an element that the P must prove as a part of their prima facie case. Reliance on the financial statement is a necessary element for P to recover for negligent misrepresentation. **(A)** is incorrect; while privity of contract is usually required to establish the client relationship, there is an exception if the P was a part of a limited group of persons whom the D knew would relay upon the representations in the professional opinion. **(C)** is not the best answer because contributory negligence will allow an allocation of fault; in comparison, a lack of reliance will completely defeat the P's case. **(D)** is incorrect because scienter or intention is not necessary for negligent misrepresentation.

142./A/ A reckless disregard for the truth is the best answer. This tort is also frequently referred to as negligent misrepresentation. **(B)** is incorrect because a written representation is not required. **(C)** is incorrect because a written representation is not required. **(D)** is not the best answer because the test is one of a reasonable person and only if the P is a businessman would such a standard apply.

143./B/ Gross negligence is a lesser degree tort than fraud thus a showing of gross negligence is not required. **(A)** is incorrect because this element is required in the FIRD acronym if the P is to prevail in a fraud action. **(C)** is not the best answer because the P must act promptly before the statute of limitations runs. **(D)** is incorrect because this element is required in the FIRD acronym if the P is to prevail in a fraud action.

144./D/ Fraudulent concealment is the appropriate recovery theory. Because the P mentioned her belief in the accuracy of the mileage, the concealment by the D salesman was active. The mention of the purchase "as is" is a distractor; most courts today would not excuse active concealment in such a circumstance. **(A)** is incorrect because a writing is not required and the representation of "This car is as good as new, etc." could be mere puffing or "sales talk." **(B)** is not the best answer because, if the nondisclosure was significant, it goes beyond mere negligence. **(C)** is incorrect because the old rule of caveat emptor (let the buyer beware) is being replaced by a more enlightened view designed to curtail sharp and unethical business practices.

145./B/ It is P's burden to establish that the D had a duty to make disclosure of the concealed fact. **(A)** is not the best answer because "under no circumstance" is too broad and "caveat emptor" has been replaced by a more progressive doctrine that examines the materiality of the fact concealed. **(C)** is not the best answer because the law may impose the same liability on the seller as through he had represented the non-existence of the undisclosed matter. **(D)** is not the best answer because the measure of damages would be the lost profit if the buyer did not attempt to rescind the business sale.

146./C/ This alternative is the best correct statement of the four elements of negligence that P must prove. **(A)** is not the best answer because it is the P's burden to establish the standard of care reasonable in the industry. **(B)** is not the best answer because the P must meet both the "but for" and the "legal or proximate" causation tests; one alone is not adequate. **(D)** is not the best answer because it is the P's burden to show damages; nominal damages are not available in negligence.

147./D/ A fraudulent inducement requires the D to have made a false statement of a material fact; materiality is a measure of the import to the P. Who owned the car would not seem to be material or of any real import to the buyer's decision and thus not a fraudulent inducement. **(A)** is incorrect because this is a opinion by a car salesman; reasonable buyers would not usually expect a car salesman to be an expert in general insurance but might expect accuracy in car insurance. **(B)** is incorrect because this statement of appraised values was material and likely to have been made with the intention to induce the buyer to commit to purchase the vehicle. **(C)** is probably not as good an answer as D; while a car salesman is not necessarily an expert forecaster of future value, it would seem more material to a purchase decision than who previously owned the automobile.

148./B/ A breach does not have to follow the interference to permit a recovery for tortious interference; the interference itself is actionable. **(A)** is not the best answer because present damages are not a prerequisite to the tort action; the possibility of future damages may be adequate. **(C)** is incorrect because intentional torts do not require consideration to be actionable. Here, the facts say that the interferer was aware there was a valid contract between Mighty and its agent. **(D)** is not the best answer since the principal's action against the contractee-agent is certain only if the agent breaches the contract.

149./C/ The P does not have to prove such a negative. The D may attempt to prove the P was partially responsible for the damages. If this is successful, there may be an offset allowed. **(A)** is incorrect in that the P must prove both the required performance standard and that the performance standard was breached. **(B)** is incorrect because the P must prove the element of causation. **(D)** is incorrect because the P must prove damages are material or more than nominal to recover for negligence.

150./A/ This is the best alternaive because David D's 40% fault is clearly a substantial factor contributing to Lois' damages. **(B)** is incorrect in that any such assumption of risk would have to involve a clear, cogent waiver with full understanding of the risks. **(C)** is incorrect because most jurisdictions have abolished assumption of the risk for over 50% fault in favor of comparative fault. **(D)** is incorrect because the doctrine of last clear chance operates to shield P's contributory negligence from any offset if D had the last clear chance to avoid the injury.

151./A/ The facts state that Lois was 20% at fault. Therefore, her maximum recovery was 80% of her $25,000 damages or $20,000. David and Larry were equally at fault so Lois' recovery from Larry would be

$10,000 or one half the total. **(B)** is incorrect because it miscalculates the recovery amount. **(C)** is incorrect because there is no joint and several liability. **(D)** is incorrect because it miscalculates the recovery amount.

152./B/ In those states that recognize contribution between Ds, if Larry pays $15,000, he would have a right of contribution against David for $5,000. This would be the excess Larry paid over his proportional share. ($15,000 − [.5 x 20,000]). **(A)** is incorrect because it miscalculates Larry's right of contribution. **(C)** is incorrect because it miscalculates Larry's right of contribution. **(D)** is incorrect because it miscalculates Larry's right of contribution.

153./C/ Uninvited unknown intruders usually trespass at their peril including injuries suffered from a defect unless the landowner had actual knowledge of the defect. **(A)** is incorrect because the D in this alternative is the ex-employer Always Aluminum, not the electric company. **(B)** is incorrect because P is a mere trespasser and there is nothing in these facts that would allow a trespasser-thief to reasonably assume any condition. **(D)** is not the best answer. Angry may have intended theft, but he did have some justification – the employer owed him money.

154./D/ The best answer. Regional Electric was negligent in agreeing to turn off the electricity for Always and then not doing so. It was foreseeable that employees or former employees might dismantle the equipment in the plant. **(A)** is not the best answer since the damage was caused by touching the positive and negative poles not the inherent danger of

electricity. **(B)** is incorrect because Angry was a trespasser as to Always Aluminum, not the D in this question, Regional Electric. **(C)** is incorrect because any such defense might be viable against the property owner, but not against the D in this question, Regional Electric.

155./D/ The best alternative because if the damages are substantial (good rule of thumb is over 50% destroyed), the P has the election of recovering for either trespass or conversion. Conversion is the higher level tort and allows recovery of the full fair market value of the equipment. **(A)** is incorrect because the intent required for trespass to chattels (like trespass to land) is simply the intent to do the thing that results in the interference with the D's possessory interest. **(B)** is incorrect because the D in this situation is potentially liable for this tort. Since the damages are substantial, the P would likely elect the higher level cause of action producing a higher level of damages. **(C)** is incorrect because the D in this situation is potentially liable for this tort. Since the damages are substantial, the P would likely elect the higher level cause of action producing a higher level of damages.

156./D/ Liability will exist for the damages suffered by the homeowner even if the necessity of the situation excuses the trespass or provides a defense such as a privilege. **(A)** is not the best answer since the intention to escape or trespass is not the primary reason for the liability. The primary reason is the damages suffered by the homeowner. **(B)** is incorrect because the homeowner will prevail for the damages he can prove. **(C)** is incorrect because the homeowner will prevail for the damages he can prove.

157./C/ An agent is always liable for his own torts. A principal is also vicariously liable under the doctrine of respondeat superior if the act occurred within the course and scope of the employment. **(A)** is incorrect because both the agent and the principal are liable under respondeat superior. **(B)** is incorrect because both the agent and the principal are liable under respondeat superior. **(D)** is incorrect because even if no damages occur, a P may recover nominal damages from a D who has committed an intentional tort.

158./B/ The best answer. Even though storing toxic waste is probably an abnormally dangerous activity, the intentional trespass, the clear warning on the signs, and going in the dark of night constitute a clear implied knowing assumption of the risk. **(A)** is incorrect in that the fence and signs warning of the danger was probably sufficient exercise of due care. **(C)** is not the best answer since P assumed the risk regardless of any negligence by D. **(D)** is incorrect because even strict liability may be subject to the defense of the assumption of the risk.

159./B/ The D must have acted with intent to induce the third party to breach the contract with the P. **(A)** is a poor defense because torts committed in the course and scope of business are vicariously imputed to the principal under the doctrine of respondeat superior. **(C)** is not as good a defense as A because it goes to the reasonableness of the D's interference; lack of intent to interfere is a better defense. **(D)** is not as good a defense as A because it goes to subjective motivation; lack of intent to interfere is a better defense.

160./A/ To prevail for abuse of legal proceedings, it is necessary to prove both special damages and that there was no basis in fact for the allegation. Based on these facts it appears that the necessary showing could be made. **(B)** is not the best answer; the patient could prevail on the underlying claim and still be held liable for abuse of legal proceedings. **(C)** is incorrect because the conclusion in the medical malpractice case is not controlling on the abuse of legal proceedings claim. **(D)** is incorrect; most courts would require a showing of special damages. Here, the cancellation of the physician's insurance policy is sufficient.

161./C/ Trespass is an intentional tort that the Captain intended to do. There is a privilege if the trespass was necessary under the circumstances. While nominal damages are thus not recoverable, the actual damages suffered by the landowner's dock are recoverable. **(A)** is incorrect because there will be a recovery for the actual damages. **(B)** is incorrect because the damages to P's dock were not caused by the Act of God, but rather by the Captain's boat hitting the dock. **(D)** is not the best answer because the trespasser, in this case, has a privilege against trespass.

162./B/ A landlord is not liable to a trespasser who is not known to be on the premises and was not given permission or invitation. Uninvited unknown intruders usually trespass at their own peril. **(A)** is not the best answer because the issue is the status of P not causation. **(C)** is incorrect because the duty of a property owner to inspect the property only applies to a business invitee, not usually a trespasser. **(D)** is incorrect because the question of the liability of a landowner usually depends upon the status of the P trespasser.

163./D/ A property owner is liable to a business invitee for damages resulting from dangerous conditions which are know or could reasonably have been discovered by inspection. **(A)** is incorrect because actual knowledge of the dangerous natural condition is not necessary if a reasonable inspection would have discovered the hazard. **(B)** is not the best answer because a landowner is not subject to strict liability for dangerous natural conditions. **(C)** is incorrect because while the gradual rotting of the bridge supports may be a natural condition of all wooden bridges, it does not negate liability if a reasonable inspection would have discovered the danger.

164./B/ Only the staff members have a responsibility to go to the rescue of the drowning guests. Even though the trained lifeguard has a high degree of expertise in saving drowning people, this does not create a rescuer duty to strangers. There is no duty of a non-compensated bystander to take affirmative action to aid others. In comparison, the staff members were compensated by Dude Ranch. In addition, the accident was caused by a defective condition on their employer's property. **(A)** is an incorrect combination of the two groups' liability. **(C)** is an incorrect combination of the two groups' liability. **(D)** is an incorrect combination of the two groups' liability.

165./A/ There is no duty to come to the rescue, but if a D undertakes to act, a full duty of reasonable care arises. Still the P takes the rescuer as he comes on the scene. It would seem that the negligence standard would be that degree of care exercised by a reasonable drunk lifeguard. Further, most states have "Good Samaritan" statutes that excuse ordinary negligence for rescuers rendering emergence care or transportation at an accident scene. To recover under these statutes, the P must show gross negligence or wanton misconduct. **(B)** is incorrect because once a rescuer undertakes to act, a duty to act reasonably arises. **(C)** is not the best answer because this question turns on the issue of duty creation and the performance level of a rescuer. **(D)** is not the best answer because the facts do not indicate any assumption of the risk, and because the question turns on the issue of duty creation and the performance level of a rescuer.

166./B/ Like most intentional torts, nominal damages exist even if actual pecuniary damages can not be proven. **(A)** is incorrect because a P must show the proceedings were favorably terminated to make a prima facie case of malicious prosecution. **(C)** is incorrect because a P must show an absence of probable cause to make a prima facie case of malicious prosecution. **(D)** is incorrect because a P must show a wrongful purpose to make a prima facie case of malicious prosecution.

167./A/ The statute of limitations was tolled (suspended) until the fraudulent concealment was discovered. The second doctor informed Paul of the malpractice in 2005. This was then the trigger date to start the 3 year statute of limitations period. Therefore, if the lawsuit was filed by 2008, it was within the period of the statute of limitations. **(B)** is incorrect because the statute of limitations began to run when Paul was informed of the malpractice in 2005. **(C)** is incorrect because the statute of limitations began to run when Paul was informed of the malpractice in 2005. **(D)** is incorrect because the statute of limitations began to run when Paul was informed of the malpractice in 2005.

168./C/ The best answer. The neighborhood boys are classified as licensees; the landlord knew of their on-going trespass and thus gave them implied permission to be on the premises. An unfenced soccer field is arguably an attractive nuisance since it may be "dangerous in itself" and naturally attracts youthful soccer players. A landowner is liable to a licensee for damages from known dangerous artificial conditions. **(A)** is incorrect because the landlord's knowledge elevated the boy's legal status above that of a trespasser. **(B)** is incorrect because the sprinkler head was hazardous to the soccer players and not making the repairs to the dangerous condition was negligence. **(D)** is not the best answer because this alternative does not address the central liability issue in this question, which is the status of the P.

169./D/ Sharon was a business invitee. This status requires the property owner to remedy or warn customers of known hazards. Here, the store should have realized some customers in the restroom might not see the signs when they returned to the retail premises. **(A)** is incorrect because strict liability does not

apply. **(B)** is incorrect because shopping expertise does not constitute assumption of the risk. **(C)** is not the best answer because it reaches the wrong conclusion and the warning sign was not posted where Sharon could see them.

170./C/ Sally has exceeded the geographical scope of the invitation and became either a licensee or a trespasser. Because she disregarded the "employee only" signs, it seems more likely she would be characterized as a trespasser. The owner is not liable for damages to trespassers resulting from conditions not caused by their active willful negligence. Spilled oil in the public area may also create a higher duty level. **(A)** is incorrect because strict liability does not apply. **(B)** is incorrect because shopping expertise does not constitute assumption of the risk. **(D)** is incorrect; while she began her shopping spree as a business invitee, going into the warehouse converted her status to a licensee or trespasser.

171./B/ Because the interference is not with a present contract, but rather with a prospective or potential advantage, there is correspondingly greater scope of privilege to interfere. Questionable advertising practices are usually insufficient to create a cause of action. **(A)** is incorrect because predatory actions to create a monopoly may constitute interference with a prospective advantage; monopolies are disfavored under the law. **(C)** is incorrect because price fixing would violate federal or state antitrust laws. **(D)** is similarly incorrect because a conspiracy to create and coordinate a group boycott by potential customers of the targeted company may also violate a federal or state antitrust law.

172./B/ If the P did not actually experience any mental apprehension, Peter would have a wonderful defense since this is the interest the tort of assault seeks to prohibit. **(A)** is incorrect because only if there was apprehension in fact would the P have to show that the apprehension was objectively reasonable. **(C)** is incorrect because the apprehension was not necessarily limited to being shot; the D was waving the large instrument, which could have been used to hit the P. **(D)** is incorrect because the apprehension was not necessarily limited to being shot; the D was waving the large instrument, which could have been used to hit the P.

173./A/ Assault requires mental apprehension of offensive or harmful physical contact. The facts state that Archie intended to frighten Robert so a reasonable belief completes the required elements for assault. **(B)** is incorrect because a landowner is not allowed to use excessive force and there is nothing here suggesting that any force at all was necessary. **(C)** is incorrect; the tort of assault does not require actual contact, only that the P apprehended contact. **(D)** is not the best answer; even though a landowner is not allowed to use excess force to resist trespass, there are no facts presented here suggesting any force was necessary.

174./B/ The best answer because battery requires intent. While Archie did not intend the battery, he did intend the assault. The transferred intent doctrine applies between the BAFTT torts; this includes battery and assault. **(A)** is not the best answer because the doctrine of res ipsa loquitur applies to actions alleging a negligence theory of

recovery. Here, the tort is intentional. **(C)** is incorrect because Robert Runner's trespass was privileged by the necessity of the wolf encounter. **(D)** is incorrect because while Archie did not intend the battery, he did intend the assault. The transferred intent doctrine between BAFTT torts applies.

175./D/ The airport is not strictly liable for an injury caused by a third person. An exception applies if the airport was negligent in failing to remove the banana peel within a reasonable period of time. The most favorable circumstantial evidence of this negligence would be that the normally yellow banana skin coloring had turned black. This would indicate that the peel had been lying there for a long period of time. **(A)** is not the best answer because there was no express assumption of the risk. **(B)** is not the best answer because the fact that the banana peel was dirty is not strong evidence as the fact that the banana peel had been on the ground for a long period of time. **(C)** is not the best answer because the fact that the banana peel was yellow is not strong evidence as the fact that the banana peel had been on the ground for a long period of time.

176./A/ This is the only alternative where either D would be prejudiced in their right of contribution against the other D. If only one D is dismissed, the remaining D would be required to cross claim to bring the dismissed D into the action. **(B)** is incorrect because under this alternative, both Ds would be without liability, so there is no need for a contribution. **(C)** is incorrect because if the P prevails against both Ds, the relative fault and right of contribution would be decided in the same proceeding. **(D)** is incorrect because if the P prevails against both Ds, the relative fault and right of contribution would be decided in the same proceeding.

177./B/ The best answer because battery is an intentional tort and intention to cause the harmful contact is absent in this fact pattern. **(A)** is not the best answer because the doctrine of transferred intent might apply even if there was no actual intent to cause the injury in question. **(C)** is not the best answer because foreseeability of the exact nature or magnitude of the damages or direct contact with P is not necessary if D put in motion a chain of events creating the damages. **(D)** is incorrect; while assault is one of the BAFTT torts, there does not appear to be an intention to either batter another party or commit another tort.

178./C/ If liability exists for Debra's emotional distress, it would be under a theory of negligence because intention is lacking. This would require some unreasonable act on the part of the D; speeding might so qualify. **(A)** is incorrect because contemporaneous awareness must be accompanied by some showing of negligence. **(B)** is not the best answer because physical injury in the same accident is not required if the physical injury was later caused by the incident put into motion by the D. **(D)** is incorrect because while these elements may be necessary to recover, it is also necessary that there be a showing that D was negligent and that appears lacking under these facts.

179./C/ The general rule is that physical invasion of land constitutes a trespass. However, the majority of the states and UCC 9.609 allows the true property owner in fresh pursuit to enter the land of the taker to recover possession of the stolen chattel. **(A)** is incorrect because "never" is an absolute word. **(B)** is incorrect because a private driveway is not public property. **(D)** is incorrect because the law allows a true owner to recapture chattels as long as all aspects of the repossession are commercially reasonable.

180./B/ Reasonable force may be used by the true owner in fresh pursuit to recover a chattel from a possessor who obtained the item wrongfully. Here, Debbie's fraud would qualify as wrongful and a shove without damages does not appear to be excessive force. **(A)** is incorrect because the UCC allows non-judicial repossession as long as all aspects of the repossession are commercially reasonable. **(C)** is not the best answer since the doctrine focuses on the reasonableness of the force used, not whether it was provoked. C also omits the important requirement that possession of the chattel was originally obtained wrongfully. **(D)** is incorrect because the doctrine is whether the chattel was obtained wrongfully and using force is not the same question. In addition, damages are not necessary to make a prima facie case of battery.

181./A/ While trespass to chattels is an intentional tort, the intention requirement is minimal as long as there is some intention to do the act which resulted in the trespass. Here, D intended the physical act of picking up the book and marking the pages. **(B)** is incorrect; P must prove that D intermeddled with P's personal property. **(C)** is incorrect; P must prove an ownership or possessory interest in the personal property. **(D)** is incorrect because P must prove actual damages; here the yellow marking of P's book could constitute these damages.

182./D/ The best answer through the process of elimination. The doctrine of attractive nuisance applies to a child trespasser. Since the D knew that neighborhood boys played on the equipment, the risk of danger was foreseeable thus creating a duty if the cost of protecting the attraction was slight compared to the potential risk. **(A)** is incorrect because a nuisance applies if P is restricted in using or enjoying their own property; Tommy's property is not involved. **(B)** is incorrect because a nuisance applies if P is restricted in using or enjoying his own property; Tommy's property is not involved. **(C)** is incorrect because a visual allurement requirement – that the defective condition lured a child to the property – is not a requirement to recover under attractive nuisance.

183./B/ Liability for negligence requires D to exhibit some fault. There are no facts suggesting the gasoline tank and pump did not operate properly or safely, and the door through which Tracy entered had been locked. **(A)** is incorrect because the result of Rescuer's call does not, in and of, itself determine liability. **(C)** is incorrect in that there is no assumption of the risk by a rescuer at least so long as they do not perform the rescue negligently. **(D)** is incorrect because having a properly functioning gasoline tank and pump does not create strict liability.

184./A/ Tracy put herself in peril by trespassing, stealing the gasoline, and dropping the container. Thus she negligently caused the harm and is liable for the injuries suffered by her rescuer. **(B)** is incorrect since an uncompensated rescuer, who undertakes to help, is privileged to take necessary steps without assuming any risk. Ryan Rescuer is not a professional rescuer even though the fire fighters are. **(C)** is incorrect because the possibility of rescue and any resulting harm would be foreseeable. **(D)** is not the best answer because the mere fact the rescue was effective does not excuse the rescuer from the duty to use reasonable care.

185./C/ The best answer because it focuses on why the rescuer did not have a duty. **(A)** is incorrect because Tony's rescue is different from the one completed for Tracy. **(B)** is not the best answer since it focuses on potential defenses rather than the reason why D did not have a duty. **(D)** is not the best answer since it focuses on potential defenses rather than the reason why D did not have a duty.

186./B/ Consent does not turn on whether the disclosures and consent were made in writing (although if a patient fails to survive the operation a writing may be helpful to prove the other three requirements were made. **(A)** is incorrect because the particular risks and possible benefits of the treatment should be disclosed. **(C)** is incorrect because proper consent would require that the patient was aware of any feasible alternative course of treatment that was available. **(D)** is incorrect because the purpose of the disclosure is so the doctor is sure that the patient appreciates the effect of the consent.

187./A/ Exceeding the patient's scope of consent is a battery. **(B)** is not the best answer because it is normal for the physician to disclose in advance that an extension of the procedure may be necessary and obtain the patient's express consent to the extension. **(C)** is incorrect because "always" is an absolute word and a physician may be authorized to extend a procedure because of unforeseen circumstances. **(D)** is not the best answer because the mere fact that damages resulted from the procedure does not necessarily mean the physician is liable; some damages are the expected consequences of many successful procedures.

188./C/ It appears as if the surgeon was unknowingly operating under a reasonable mistake of fact that the first set of X-rays which the lab returned to her was that of her patient, Peter. There would thus be no liability unless the doctor should have reasonably investigated and not merely accepted the X-ray lab report. **(A)** is incorrect because strict liability (no showing of fault is necessary) does not apply. **(B)** is not the best answer because Peter's consent was based upon the doctor's faulty diagnosis. This alternative does not question whether the doctor failed to exercise reasonable care. **(D)** is incorrect because the doctor is not required to second-guess an independent contractor unless there was some history that suggests an investigation was necessary.

189./D/ While battery is an intentional tort, the necessary intent may be transferred between victims: Fred intended to batter Deloris which is sufficient intent to allow the actual victim, Innocent, to recover. **(A)** is not the best answer since mere injury does not satisfy the requirements of the intentional tort

battery. **(B)** is incorrect because the required intent may be transferred between parties. **(C)** is incorrect because apprehension is not required to recover for battery.

190./C/ Since David had just witnessed Fred shooting his family members and Fred had turned the gun towards him, David had a reasonable but mistaken belief he needed to defend himself and others. The fugitive could easily reload the handgun. The fact that David was mistaken does not negate the defense/privilege of defense of self and others. **(A)** is incorrect because David has a defense-privilege. **(B)** is incorrect; it is possible that even a fugitive could prevail for battery if the D did not have a defense-privilege or used excessive force. **(D)** is incorrect; David's stabbing Fred with a knife is not excessive force in defense of a shooting gun. In addition, there is no requirement to retreat in your own dwelling and deadly force is justified to prevent one's own death.

191./D/ The usual standard for a child is that performance is measured by a reasonable prudent child of the same age, education, experience, and ability. An exception applies if the child is involved in adult activities, such as driving a car. The standard to be thus applied is that of a reasonable prudent adult person. **(A)** is incorrect because the standard is that of a reasonable adult person. **(B)** is incorrect because the P will prevail. **(C)** is not the best answer because while there may be potential joint liability, the P could still collect from Caroline.

192./A/ This is the worst theory of recovery that the P could assert against the parents seeking to hold them responsible for the torts of their child. Mere ownership of the car does not indicate fault. **(B)** is incorrect because both the family purpose and agency theories may create vicarious liability to the parents for the torts of their children. **(C)** is incorrect because giving a non-licensed driver express or implied permission to use the car is negligence. **(D)** is incorrect because liability may exist if the parents knew of their children's dangerous propensities and failed to safeguard the car keys.

193./C/ Illegality may help to establish the standard of the legal duty to be imposed on D and that there was a breach of that duty. But causation is one of the requirements that P must prove to make out a prime facie case of negligence; causation "in fact" is not present here. **(A)** is a distracter because it goes to the question of the standard to the applied and on the MBE the facts will state that violation of the statute is negligence per se if that is the situation. **(B)** is incorrect because the ultimate question here is whether Fast could have stopped in time had he been driving the speed limit of 60 m.p.h. **(D)** is a distracter because it goes to the question of the standard to the applied and the statute did not apply.

194./A/ Because David was a minor lacking legal capacity, a waiver is likely ineffective. In addition, the agreement could be declared against public policy or unconscionable if asserted as a defense against the teacher's violence. **(B)** is a factor that the court would likely consider in determining whether the D is entitled to the discipline privilege against the intentional torts of assault and battery. **(C)** is a factor

that the court would likely consider in determining whether the D is entitled to the discipline privilege against the intentional torts of assault and battery. **(D)** is a factor that the court would likely consider in determining whether the D is entitled to the discipline privilege against the intentional torts of assault and battery.

195./C/ If Stern was an independent contractor, the school district would at least have a argument that they should not be vicariously liable for his torts since he was not an agent. **(A)** is incorrect because an agent on a frolic or detour of their own has departed from the course and scope of employment duties; here Stern was about the school's normal classroom teaching duties. **(B)** is incorrect because negligent selection liability may be imposed on employers who hire persons with a history of dangerous behavior that could have been discovered by a reasonable background check. **(D)** is incorrect because there may be some duty to supervise and the fact the battery was unauthorized, does not necessarily avoid the application of the doctrine of respondeat superior.

196./B/ As between the employer and the employee, indemnity would be required unless the employee was following the specific instructions of the employer. **(A)** is incorrect because Mr. Stern's conduct being more culpable than the school districts is a reason that the school district would be entitled to indemnity. **(C)** is incorrect because Mr. Stern's agreement with the school to pay the full amount of the damages would be a reason that the school district would be entitled to indemnity. **(D)** is incorrect because the school district's status under the respondeat superior theory refers to their liability exposure to third parties; they still would be entitled to indemnification by the wrongdoer, Mr. Stern.

197./D/ Under the "case within a case" standard for legal malpractice, the P must prove "but for" causation; if the P would not have been an eligible taker under the estate plan, he cannot show he otherwise would have prevailed had the estate plan been admitted to probate. **(A)** is incorrect because the malpractice tort statute of limitations is only triggered upon discovery; discovery was in 2004 so a lawsuit in 2005 is timely. **(B)** is incorrect because the legal duty to exercise due care exists independently of whether the fee was paid. **(C)** is incorrect because in most jurisdictions have replaced the locality rule with a "reasonable attorney" standard.

198./D/ The question is whether it was foreseeable to the server that D's intoxication would put third parties at risk. **(A)** is incorrect because serving beer is not per se dangerous and some showing of fault would be necessary. **(B)** is incorrect; while both the tavern and David have fault, the liability is joint and several and the P decides which D to sue. **(C)** is incorrect because it is not necessary that the tavern server know the details of the future tort as long as it was foreseeable that David would put others at risk because of his intoxication.

199./C/ Liability would lie against Paul because he was the driver of the vehicle that hit Bob Bicyclist. Since this child was involved in an adult activity, he would be held to the standard of a reasonable adult.

Reasonable adults do not consume 12 beers in 4 hours and then drive. Peter, Paul's father, would be liable because he provided the beer to the minors, failed to supervise the boys, and allowed him to drive the family car under circumstances that had a high degree of risk. **(A)** is not the best answer because Peter is also liable. **(B)** is not the best answer because Paul is also liable. **(D)** is incorrect because the Rat Hole Tavern would not be liable since the subsequent misfeasance by Peter in giving the beer to the boys was not foreseeable at the time they sold him the beer.

200./C/ Strict liability will be imposed only if the resultant harm flowed from the specific risk used to justify the application of strict liability to the activity in question; the risk was the dog biting people as opposed to knocking down small children. **(A)** is incorrect even though under the "one free bite rule", the history of biting people has escalated the negligence biting standard to one of strict liability; here the damage was not caused by biting. **(B)** is incorrect because D's exercising extraordinary precautions will not preclude liability under strict liability. **(D)** is incorrect because mere ownership of a domesticated pet without more does not create strict liability. The P could always bring a claim for negligence.

201./D/ This is the best answer since the monkey was a wild or non-domestic animal and this status creates strict liability for the owner. The fact that the owner, David, relied on a medical professional's opinion and lacked knowledge of the monkey's dangerous propensities, might affect the question had the animal been domesticated and the P sued under a recovery theory of negligence. **(A)** is incorrect because the monkey did not interfere with the use and enjoyment or anyone's property. **(B)** is incorrect because the lack of knowledge of an animal's harmful propensities might apply to the "one free bite" rule that only applies to domestic animals. The monkey is wild. **(C)** is incorrect because the unsuccessful operation would not be the cause of the injury. At best, Victoria Veterinarian is guilty of a failure to improve the strict liability status of the animal's owner.

202./A/ This is the best answer and the most likely successful claim. **(B)** is incorrect because privity of contract is not necessary to recover for negligence (and the claim is not made under negligent misrepresentation where privity might be an issue). **(C)** is incorrect because Victoria Veterinarian knew her professional charge was to eliminate the possibility that the monkey will injure members of the public specifically children. It was thus foreseeable by the D that this type of risk would occur if the health care professional failed to exercise reasonable care. **(D)** is incorrect because the medical professional is not strictly liable for failure to achieve improvement to an existing condition of the patient; P would have to prove negligence.

203./B/ The lack of intent to shoot the gun precludes the battery action assuming that D was justified in defending a knife attack with a gun. The P could still seek a recovery for negligence, however. **(A)** is incorrect because whether the defense was excessive in a question of fact; both a large knife and a gun may inflict deadly consequences and the P did not begin the affray.

(C) is not the best answer because the probability that damages will result from a force set in motion is not the conclusive factor in determining liability for an intentional tort. **(D)** is incorrect because the doctrine of transferred intent applies primarily to an affirmative intentional tort, not a mistaken inadvertent defense.

204./A/ The best answer. The absence of a fair warning would probably be the most compelling reason to conclude the force used was excessive. Not only were there no warning signs, but the boarded up windows suggest this intentionally set spring gun was in the nature of a booby trap which is not a valid defense to battery. **(B)** is incorrect because this was an artificial, not natural, defect created by the D. **(C)** is incorrect because the mere fact of breaking and entering does not create an assumption of the risk absent some explicit warning. **(D)** is not the best answer because had the D been in the house, the Ps might have been allowed to use deadly force to protect themselves. Here, the force level must be justified based upon defending chattels.

205./D/ Interest on the monetary amount of the damages that would have been earned from the date of the accident to the date of judgment (prejudgment interest) is not recoverable because it is not liquidated. **(A)** is incorrect because punitive damages are not usually awarded for ordinary negligence that was not oppressive, reckless, or done with actual malice. **(B)** is not the best answer because the "collateral source rule" usually excludes from evidence at trial any other payments P received from other sources. **(C)** is incorrect because attorney fees are not usually awarded for ordinary negligence.

206./C/ Any claim against the local community group would have to be based upon a showing that they were negligent and the likely act of negligence would be a failure to inspect if there was such a duty. **(A)** is incorrect because strict product liability only applies if the seller was in the business of selling such items and here the community group was a casual seller. **(B)** is not the best answer because even though Restatement §402A Strict Liability does not apply, the D could be liable in negligence. **(D)** is not the best answer because whether the P could recover from her immediate seller is not dependant upon any right of indemnification or reimbursement, which the D may have from a third party.

207./A/ The best answer by elimination and because a buyer who has actual notice of a potential defect rendering a product unreasonably dangerous and injures a third party may shift the liability from the manufacturer to himself. **(B)** is incorrect because it is not clear this constitutes negligence by Norman and contributory negligence is not a defense in strict product liability. **(C)** is incorrect because non-privity parties may recover in strict product liability for injuries if they were in the foreseeable zone of danger. **(D)** is incorrect because the manufacturer had at least constructive knowledge of the defect alleged in the class action lawsuit and foreseeable misuse of the product will not bar recovery.

208./D/ The D was negligent because he knew the vehicle had a potential defect if the motor was left running and the transmission shifted from park into reverse caused by some external force such as someone slamming the door if he left the door open. **(A)** is incorrect since the P would only have to prove that the D was negligent – not that the product itself was defective. **(B)** is incorrect because it should have been foreseeable to the D that he created a significantly increased chance of harm occurring. **(C)** is incorrect because it infers the P is pursuing a claim under strict product liability rather than negligence.

209./D/ The best answer because while misuse may be a defense, it requires that the misuse must not be reasonably foreseeable to occur. Using another brand of saw blade to attempting to saw something besides softer wood would seem foreseeable. **(A)** is not the best answer because it is too simplistic and it ignores the central issue of product misuse. **(B)** is incorrect because it also ignores the central issue of the P's misuse. **(C)** is likewise incorrect because it ignores the central issue of the foreseeability of P's misuse.

210./A/ This is probably the best defense argument under these facts although it would probably not be enough to carry the day under strict product liability. **(B)** is incorrect because the verbal warning is evidence the seller appreciated there was a risk present; verbal warnings are worth the paper they are written on since people forget them too easily. **(C)** is incorrect because usually the duty to warn is on the manufacturer. A retailer might have a duty to warn if they modified a safe product creating additional risk to that which existed when the product left the manufacturer. **(D)** is not the best answer because the risk-utility balancing test is usually applied to justify a manufacturing or design defect, not a failure to warn. In addition, most power saws, like power lawn mowers, have extensive written operating instructions with much detail about proper and improper usage.

211./D/ The best answer through a process of elimination and because a strict products liability claim does not require proof of fault. These facts do not indicate that the D did anything affirmatively negligent, but they did rebuild and reassemble the motor, install new bearings and a mowing blade, and oil the moving parts. Under strict product liability, the exercise of due care in the manufacturing or assembly of the product is not a defense. Further, even though the D did not make the faulty bearing, they did assemble it. **(A)** is incorrect because it would be quite difficult to prove that the D acted unreasonably unless they somehow knew that one of the bearings they installed was defective or prone to failure. **(B)** is incorrect because it does not appear that D made any express warranties of quality. The phrase "functions as new" means little because defective bearings in a new mower could also fail. **(C)** is incorrect because, in this question, the implied warranty of fitness for a particular purpose was not breached; it referred to the type of grass the mower was best for rather than any defects in the product.

212./B/ A requirement of a strict product liability claim is that the product was defective when it left the D's control and it did not undergo substantial change in the condition in which it was sold. **(A)** is incorrect because manufacturing dangerous products is not enough; the product must be defective when

sold. **(C)** is incorrect because strict product liability does not require privity and extends to anyone in the zone of danger of the defective product including foreseeable users. **(D)** is not the best answer because the central issue in this question is whether the defect was created before the product left the control of the manufacturer D. Since the lawn mower had apparently been previously used without failure, it seems that the retailer created the defects in the rebuilding process.

213./C/ Unintended use is the best answer because the Ds' best defense is that the P knew exactly what use the lawnmower was intended for since they requested a blade for fine and thin grass sprouts on a golf course. Therefore, the use on land containing rocks, brush, and very high wild grass was clearly unintended. **(A)** is not the best answer because contributory negligence (which is not a part of assumption of the risk) is not a valid defense to strict product liability. **(B)** is incorrect because any analysis of fault or Ds' attempt to avoid the defect fails; this is an absolute duty. Due care or even extraordinary care does not reduce the absolute duty. **(D)** is not the best answer; while assumption of the risk may be a defense, it must be made with a full appreciation of the magnitude of the risks assumed. It seems unlikely under the facts that the gardener would have so qualified.

214./C/ The best answer is that the D will be liable only for the personal physical damages caused by the defective product under the Restatement. Strict product liability does not allow for purely economic loss including such consequential damages as lost sales revenue or lost profits. Notice that had the P brought suit under a breach of sales contract theory (such as breach of implied warranty of fitness for a particular purpose), such consequential damages would have been recoverable. **(A)** is an incorrect award amounts because D will be liable only for the personal damage caused by the defective product under the Restatement. **(B)** is an incorrect award amounts because D will be liable only for the personal damage caused by the defective product under the Restatement. **(D)** is an incorrect award amounts because D will be liable only for the personal damage caused by the defective product under the Restatement.

215./B/ The best answer because if successful, it would be a total defense. Unlike a private necessity, a public necessity involving even abnormally dangerous activities may produce a complete defense if the activity is necessary to prevent severe harm to the public in an emergency situation. No compensation for property damage is necessary. **(A)** is not the best answer because contributory negligence is not a defense to strict liability. **(C)** is not the best answer because "assumption of the risk" under strict liability is converted to "comparative fault," in which a partial recovery is still possible. Public necessity is a full defense. **(D)** is not the best answer because comparative fault would produce a partial recovery while public necessity as a defense would be a complete defense.

216./C/ The best answer. The press was dangerous in its ordinary operation when it left the manufacturer. To accept the D's position, the jury would have to find: (1) this injury was proximately caused by the P

not spending an additional $5,000 for a machine that had performed properly for two years, and (2) that this decision was both unreasonable and not foreseen by the D who placed the dangerous product in the stream of commerce. **(A)** is incorrect because even if the refusal to subsequently purchase the safety device was deemed an assumption of the risk, it would only be partial to be measured by comparative fault. **(B)** is incorrect because the central issue is the foreseeability of the likelihood of the subsequent purchase of the safety device at such a high relative price. **(D)** is incorrect because it is too simplistic and it does not contain any mention of the central elements of the foreseeability of proximate cause or comparative fault, which would be a jury question.

217./D/ The original tortfeasor is individually liable for the damages he inflicted ($7,000) and the damages resulting from the increased risk of injury he caused ($5,000). It is usually reasonably foreseeable that a collision with another car will move that car into a different place where other traveling cars may create additional injuries. Since Sam was also speeding, he becomes jointly and severally liable for the portion of the damages caused by his own negligence with the original tortfeasor. Note that Sarah would be limited to a $12,000 recovery from both Ds. **(A)** misstates the recovery amount. **(B)** misstates the recovery amount. **(C)** misstates the recovery amount.

218./A/ The risk in this case was from a natural condition. Unlike the attractive nuisance doctrine, which applies to artificial conditions, a landowner usually has no duty to protect even child trespassers against injury from natural conditions. Notice that here the danger of a submerged tree branch was a hidden defect that even an inspection of the property from the shore of the pool would probably not reveal. **(B)** gives cumulative additional conditions that are intended to make the conclusion of property owner liability seem more attractive. **(C)** gives cumulative additional conditions that are intended to make the conclusion of property owner liability seem more attractive. **(D)** gives cumulative additional conditions that are intended to make the conclusion of property owner liability seem more attractive.

219./C/ The rule in most states is that claims for such torts as defamation, invasion of property, and intentional infliction of emotional distress do not survive the death of the decedent. **(A)** is a correct statement of the survival of action in a wrongful death action. **(B)** is a correct statement of the survival of action in a wrongful death action. **(D)** is a correct statement of the survival of action in a wrongful death action.

220./A/ The best answer because it focuses on whether the mistake in utilizing the self-defense privilege is objectively reasonable. This alternative includes both the clear mistake about the identity of the attacker and the unclear threat imposed on Francis from the raised fist. The "if" modifier means the rationale must only be possible under the facts – it is here. **(B)** is incorrect because the central issue is whether Francis could reasonably believe she was in danger of imminent attack and responded without using excessive force to avoid the attack. **(C)** is not the best

answer because the central issue in this question is whether the mistaken belief of the D was objectively reasonable. The street person's intention does not address the reasonableness of Francis' self-defense. The modifier "unless" implies the condition must be necessary to the application of the rule of law; here the rule of law is whether the self-defense action was objectively reasonable. **(D)** is incorrect because an honest mistaken belief is not a valid defense unless it is also objectively reasonable.

221./B/ The best answer because it focuses on the central issue in negligence of whether the damage was foreseeable. If not foreseeable, the contractor would be exonerated from liability. **(A)** is incorrect because whether the customer paid the contractor is not relevant to whether the contractor may be liable for negligence to a third party. **(C)** is not the best answer because an agent is always liable for torts they committed even if the principal is also liable. **(D)** is incorrect because privity is not required to sue in tort if it was foreseeable that P might be damaged because of the negligence of D.

222./D/ The best answer because it is the only alternative which will allow the negligence of the independent contractor to be vicariously imputed to the principal. The rule is that if the function was inherently dangerous, the responsibility for the legal duty may be nondelegable. **(A)** is not the best answer because respondeat superior applies to create liability to an employer for torts committed by an employee within the course and scope of business. The problem here is that respondeat superior does not apply to an independent contractor; here the contractor decided how to accomplish the result. **(B)** is incorrect because any strict liability claim would be against the independent contractor who created the abnormally dangerous condition. **(C)** is incorrect because paying an independent contractor is not equivalent to assuming liability, particularly since the damages were not then apparent so a knowledgeable assumption of the risk was impossible.

223./A/ The best answer because the modifier "if" is followed by a rationale that is possible under the facts. If the liability for the damage was vicariously imputed to Hilly Home Owner (based upon the nondelegation of the responsibility for inherently dangerous activities), indemnification from Excavation Contractor is possible. **(B)** is incorrect because payment and acceptance of the work does not extinguish a right to indemnification if such a right otherwise existed. **(C)** is incorrect because whether Hilly has recourse against the contractor depends on whether Contractor caused the damages, for which Cathi is responsible. **(D)** is incorrect because the hiring of the independent contractor does not necessarily mean that Owner is not entitled to indemnification if the contractor caused the damages.

224./C/ The best answer because the test for a professional employee would be a reasonable police person in a like circumstance. **(A)** is incorrect because it is not necessary for the P to prove reckless behavior; mere negligence is sufficient. **(B)** is incorrect because this act would probably be characterized as operational, not discretionary. Further, not using a siren to cross a

busy intersection in a city is arguably reckless behavior. **(D)** is incorrect because the standard to be applied would be that of a reasonable policeman under like circumstances.

225./A/ The best answer because this exception turns on factual questions involved that are properly to be decided by the jury. The general rule is that P's contributory negligence as a bar to recovery is to be judged by the objective reasonable person standard. Exceptions apply for children (a reasonable child standard) and physical impairment. The Restatement indicates mental deficiency may relieve the P from contributory negligence if the P is a child or completely insane. The modifier "if" is followed by a rationale which is possible under these facts. **(B)** is incorrect because most courts would not direct a verdict but rather instruct the jury to make this factual decision. **(C)** is incorrect because most courts would not direct a verdict but rather instruct the jury to make this factual decision. **(D)** is incorrect because most courts would not direct a verdict but rather instruct the jury to make this factual decision.

226./B/ The best answer because it is usually for the jury to decide the effect of physical impairments in determining whether Harry acted as would a reasonable deaf person in the circumstance. The question would be whether a reasonable deaf person would have brought along a replacement battery for the hearing aid? **(A)** is incorrect; while the jury may consider Harry's deafness, the standard would be that of a reasonable deaf person. **(C)** is incorrect; while the physical impairment would become a part of the reasonable person standard. The jury would probably decide this. **(D)** is incorrect; while the physical impairment would become a part of the reasonable person standard. The jury would probably decide this.

227. /A/ The best answer is that the doctrine of avoidable consequences would apply since the omission occurred prior to the accident. Since the facts state that the injuries would not have occurred had she fastened her seatbelt, all recovery should be denied. **(B)** is not the best answer since any assumption of the risk would be implied and usually this requires specific knowledge of the risk assumed. **(C)** is not the best answer because contributory negligence constitutes a total defense in this jurisdiction. Here the defense is total because the facts state that no injury would have occurred had the P been wearing her seatbelt. **(D)** is incorrect because failure to mitigate damages occurs after the accident, not before as in the doctrine of avoidable consequences.

228. /D/ The best answer because these damages could have been avoided and it is reasonable to expect P to mitigate damages by promptly seeking medical assistance after being so directed by a police officer. **(A)** is incorrect because the failure of P to seek recommended medical assistance is not usually foreseeable; reasonable people do seek medical treatment after an accident in which they were injured. **(B)** is incorrect; "sharing" may be an equitable outcome, but the facts say the $25,000 damages could have been avoided had the P mitigated damages. **(C)** is

incorrect because assumption of the risk occurs prior to the event, similar to the doctrine of avoidable consequences, while a failure to mitigate damages occurs after the event.

229. /B/ The best answer because the "unless" modifier has a rationale that addresses more of the required legal reasoning than the other alternatives; there had to be some knowledge of the potential danger to create the duty. **(A)** is incorrect because merely supervising the booths is not the same as knowing there was a danger that required restraining the activities in one of the student's booth. **(C)** is incorrect because most charitable and educational institutions do not today enjoy immunity from liability, especially since the $5.00 fair admission charge could imply that this was a proprietary private function. **(D)** is incorrect because the institution Entrepreneur Grade School was not a seller of the chemicals.

230. /D/ The correct answer because it focuses on the element necessary for a finding of negligence against the agent of the principal D. **(A)** is incorrect because Phil's action was not independent and would not be considered to be an intervening cause sufficient to relieve the store of liability. **(B)** is incorrect because the store would be liable under the doctrine of respondeat superior even if the employee did not follow the store's procedure. **(C)** is not the best answer because a violation of a statute does not create negligence per se unless the statute so states and the facts in this problem do not say it does. The jury may consider the violation of the statute as some evidence of negligence; however, this is not conclusive.

231./A/ The best answer because the standard for determining if an 11 year-old was negligent would be judged by the standard of a reasonable prudent child of the same age, education, experience, and intelligence. **(B)** is incorrect; in some jurisdictions a child from 7 to 14 is rebuttably presumed incapable of negligence, but this is no longer the general rule. In addition, a rebuttable presumption is different than a conclusive presumption. **(C)** is incorrect because Phil's actions were a concurrent cause of Patty's injuries even if the store clerk's action were also a cause. **(D)** is incorrect (but in second place) because mixing chemicals is not usually considered to be an adult activity such as driving a car or operating heavy equipment.

232./C/ The "unless" modifier has a following rationale that is one of the three necessary circumstances which would allow P to prevail. One of the three situations in which parents may be liable for their children's torts is the family purpose doctrine where the child is acting as an agent for the parents. Since Phil's father is in the same business, this is a possible rationale. **(A)** is incorrect because it involves an absolute and parent vicarious liability is not automatic; one of three situations must be present. **(B)** is incorrect because it involves an absolute and parent vicarious liability is possible under three circumstances. **(D)** is incorrect because parents' vicarious liability is not a functional equivalent of a conditional surety undertaking.

233./B/ The best answer because the "attractive nuisance" doctrine imposes near strict liability upon a property owner for damages to a child, even if a trespasser. The artificial condition was left exposed and D knew the children had in the past played on the tractor and were going in that direction on the day in question. **(A)** is not the best answer because a deserted tractor is not inherently dangerous since it was not in operation; the danger was D leaving it exposed and failing to take reasonable safety measures. **(C)** is incorrect since D failed to follow up by going outside to physically turn the children back. **(D)** is incorrect; while the snow on the fender may be argued a proximate cause, it was reasonably connect with the risk which D's negligent conduct set in motion.

234./A/ The best answer under these circumstances. While ordinary comparative fault or assumption of risk could apply, here the P was a paying customer, the hot tub was placed outside rather than inside the Inn, and the Hosts provided the wine free, thus encouraging negligent behavior and it was foreseeable that a guest could be injured. **(B)** is not the best answer because innkeepers are held to a very high standard of care for their guests akin to strict liability. **(C)** is incorrect; at a minimum, the D should have posted a warning sign since he knew that there was a dangerous icy path over which his guests would be walking after drinking alcohol he had provided. **(D)** is incorrect; while ordinary comparative fault or assumption of the risk could apply, these would not negate any liability so the guest would prevail.

235./D/ Invasion of privacy includes both publication of private facts and intrusion into the private affairs of the P. Here the facts in question were in the court records – a public domain – which are usually privileged. **(A)** is incorrect because if the facts reported were public, there is a privilege. **(B)** is incorrect; while a few jurisdictions allow checking with the subject before publication to be a mitigating factor in defamation, that is not necessary if it is a public fact. **(C)** is not the best answer because even truthful statements may be actionable under publication of private facts which is one of the four categories of invasion of privacy. Further, publishing a public photograph is not actionable.

236./A/ The most persuasive defense because if the D had no knowledge of the risk, it is hard to create a duty. **(B)** is incorrect because the facts state that the jurisdiction did not have an automobile guest statute (had such a statute been in existence there would be no driver liability to non-paying passengers for simple negligence). **(C)** is not the best answer because the foreseeability of harm only becomes an issue if there is a legal duty, which is not present under these facts. **(D)** is incorrect because contributory negligence is the P's unreasonable conduct. Since Harriet had no reason to think there was any change in the condition of the automobile's trunk, this defense would fail.

237./C/ A landowner is not liable to passers-by for injuries resulting from natural conditions with an artificial addition; here, the alternative includes that the D created an artificial condition that would create the liability. **(A)** is incorrect because it is doubtful that the landowner reasonably foresaw that a jogger would be running on a path in the snow. **(B)** is incorrect

because the P knew she was running on a snow-covered path under which some hazard might exist. **(D)** is not the best answer; while contributory or comparative negligence (depending on the jurisdiction) is a viable defense, this only becomes important if the P prevails in showing the D was liable at all.

238./C/ This is the best argument because the obstacle to recovery is the eight-year statute of repose, which fixes a maximum period of recovery. This is the argument that some courts have used as a basis for declaring the statute of limitations unconstitutional. **(A)** is incorrect because while ongoing misrepresentations may toll the statute of limitations, they would not toll the jurisdiction's statute of repose. **(B)** is incorrect because this might toll the statute of limitations, but it would not toll the statute of repose. **(D)** is incorrect because the statute of limitations normally begins to run upon discovery of the harm.

239./C/ The Ps will likely recover against both Sam and Doug. Sam would be liable for his negligence in failing to check the tires, and Sam's negligence will be imputed to Doug under a "joint enterprise" theory. A joint enterprise exists because they had a joint agreement and shared a common financial profit-making purpose and had a equal right of control over the enterprise. **(A)** is an incomplete answer. **(B)** is incorrect because on his own Doug was not negligent. **(D)** is incorrect because one of the other alternatives is correct.

240./C/ Mary is a member of the class of persons protected by the criminal statute. Because of this, Mary's consent is not effective. **(A)** is incorrect because Mary's consent is ineffective. **(B)** is incorrect because even if the consent was not coerced, Scott's violation of the criminal statute makes Mary's consent ineffective. **(D)** is incorrect because regardless of the adequacy of the consideration, the violation of the criminal statute negates consent.

241./D/ An owner with actual knowledge of a serious defect in an automobile entrusted to another must make disclosure of the defect. **(A)** is incorrect because strict liability would not apply; some showing of negligence is necessary. **(B)** is incorrect because this inherent hidden unreasonable danger may be characterized as an exception to the no duty rule for a gratuitous bailment. **(C)** is incorrect because while the damage was caused by the faulty drive line, the risk was put in play by the non-disclosure.

242./B/ In a strict liability action, all sellers are potentially liable if they sold a product in a defective condition or unreasonably dangerous condition. There are no facts given in the question indicating that the oven's conditions was substantially changed after leaving the manufacturer. This "all sellers are liable" rule applies even though the P did not have a contract directly with the manufacturer or wholesaler. Clearwater High School could not be held liable in strict liability but could be sued for negligence. **(A)** is incorrect because it contains the wrong combination of alternatives. **(C)** is incorrect because it contains the wrong combination of alternatives. **(D)** is incorrect because it contains the wrong combination of alternatives.

243./D/ None of the three listed defenses would prevail. **(A)** is incorrect because all sellers of a good in an unreasonably dangerous condition are liable and the retailer or wholesaler can seek indemnification from or bring in the manufacturer as a third party defendant. **(B)** is incorrect because assumption of the risk as a defense must involve an informed appreciation by P of the significance of the risk assumed; there are no facts in this question so indicating. **(C)** is incorrect because the defense of comparable fault for strict product liability requires much more than P's failure to discover a latent or hidden defect.

244./C/ The question is the status of the intruders. Paul came onto the premises for the potential business purposes of purchasing model railroad pieces. Even if the injury occurred in the upper floors of the house that was not used for the model railroad business the purpose of Paul entering the premises was for business at the invitation of Robert. Pattie, Paul's daughter came on the premises as a personal social guest to play with Roberta. She is thus to be characterized as a licensee and not an attractive nuisance child trespasser. **(A)** is incorrect because it involves the wrong combination of alternatives. **(B)** is incorrect because it involves the wrong combination of alternatives. **(D)** is incorrect because it involves the wrong combination of alternatives.

245./A/ A land possessor's duty of care for a licensee, such as a social guest, coming onto the premises is to warn of known dangerous hazards. While Robert probably knew the microwave oven was on the shelf and the electrical connection went into the wall below, this would not normally be considered an unreasonably dangerous condition or hazard so there would likely not be a duty to warn. **(B)** is incorrect because under these circumstances there is no duty to warn a licensee since the hazard was neither hidden nor unreasonably dangerous. **(C)** is incorrect because under these circumstances there is no duty to warn a licensee since the hazard was neither hidden nor unreasonably dangerous. **(D)** is not the best answer because an assumption of the risk as a defense only becomes of import if there was a legal duty of care that was breached.

246./D/ The best answer because absent agreement by the detainee this was false arrest. **(A)** is incorrect because a reasonable belief defense to false imprisonment only applies to a police officer. An ordinary citizen arrests at his peril and takes the risk that the arrest is mistaken. **(B)** is incorrect; the facts state Big Red missed his plane and a reasonable time period only applies to a mistake by a police officer or suspected shoplifter. **(C)** is incorrect because false imprisonment does not require physical injury.

247./C/ The best answer because it focuses on the requirement that P must have a mental apprehension of harmful contact. If P did not see the revolver the required apprehension would be missing. **(A)** is incorrect because a reasonable mistake for a non-policeman is not a defense to assault or false imprisonment. **(B)** is incorrect because monetary damages are not necessary for assault and the facts indicate there was reasonable apprehension of harmful offensive contact. **(D)** is incorrect because the actual ability to inflict the assault is not necessary

as long as there is the apparent ability; a man in a marine uniform threatening with a marine-issued revolver could easily create reasonable apprehension.

248./C/ The best answer. A qualified privilege exists for a prior employer to make false statements of warning to a prospective employer of misconduct of a prior employee. Even if the statement is false the privilege exists if the statement was made in good faith. **(A)** is incorrect because falsity is not controlling if the statement was made in good faith and there was a reasonable basis. **(B)** is not the best answer because the facts do not state the former employee consented to be defamed and the focus of the question is whether there was a reasonable basis for the statement. **(D)** is incorrect because the "per se" category of LUNI damages go to the requirement to prove special damages, not the qualified privilege.

249./B/ The best answer because intent does not transfer for intentional infliction of emotional distress and Alice was not a member of Carol's family. **(A)** is incorrect because the P is not Carol but rather a third party. **(C)** is incorrect because Betty had no responsibility to go to the rescue and the facts do not indicate such intervention would have been successful in averting the attack. **(D)** is incorrect because there is no showing that Betty intended to injure Alice.

250./B/ There is not usually a duty of an uncompensated bystander to act or go to the aid of another. While there may be a special duty for a co-venturer, professional rescuer (such as police person or fire fighter), common carriers and business enterprises none of these exceptions apply here to Alice. **(A)** is incorrect because Alice was under no duty to take any action to avoid the attack although the facts do not indicate there was sufficient time to take any action. **(C)** is incorrect because it is too simplistic. **(D)** is not the best answer because mere awareness does not create a duty to intervene.

251./B/ A public figure pursuing a private matter must at least show D's recklessness in their factual investigation such that there was actual or constructive doubts as to the truth of the publication. **(A)** is incorrect because D's ordinary negligence is the defamation required minimum standard for a private person involving a private matter. **(C)** is incorrect because D's actual malice is only required for a public figure P involving a public matter. Here, the P is a public person but the matter – an extra-marital affair – is private involving his personal or private life. **(D)** is not the best answer because there is no mention in the facts of an applicable state statute and the retraction was too late to avoid the harm.

252./A/ A private person P pursuing a private matter must at least show that the D failed to exercise an ordinary duty of care. **(B)** is incorrect because a showing of recklessness beyond ordinary negligence is only required for a private figure P pursuing a private matter; here we have a private person. **(C)** is incorrect because D's actual malice is only required for a public figure P pursuing a public matter; here we have a private person. **(D)** is not the best answer because there is no mention in the facts of an applicable state statute and the retraction was too late to avoid the harm.

253./D/ The best answer because it focuses on the P's necessary showing of causation in a negligent claim. **(A)** is incorrect because P only has to show ordinary negligence (and incorrect) in a loss of consortium claim. **(B)** is incorrect because the castration by the other prisoners was not an intervening cause but rather a foreseeable effect of the forces D set into motion. **(C)** is incorrect because the common law prohibition on a wife's ability to assert this claim has been abrogated in the majority of jurisdictions.

254./D/ The best answer to this difficult MBE question. The defense of consent does not defeat the claim unless there was informed appreciation of the risks and damages assumed. Here the facts do not indicate the store made full disclosure of the either the private detective's investigation or the extent of the publication. **(A)** is incorrect because many courts have upheld liability for emotional depression lacking accompanying physical damage consequences if the conduct was very outrageous. **(B)** is incorrect because only the intention to do the act creating the harm is required. **(C)** is not the best answer because while the conclusion is false in that a D takes the P as they find them and it is common knowledge that children P may be more likely to suffer extreme embarrassment and humiliation than adults.

255./C/ The only correct combination of alternatives. Susan will likely prevail for the commercial appropriation because the unauthorized pictures of Susan were used with other false statements promoting D's products and services. Susan will likely not prevail for publication of private life and intrusion for two reasons. First, these invasion of privacy torts are personal and do not extend to family members (perhaps her parents would have a viable claim). Second, the D has available the defense that the facts complained of were in the public record (a prison sentence and related drug rehabilitation are likely in the court files). **(A)** is incorrect because it involves an incorrect combination of alternatives. **(B)** is incorrect because it involves an incorrect combination of alternatives. **(D)** is incorrect because it involves an incorrect combination of alternatives.

256./B/ The best answer. This difficult MBE question turns on the rule that a private nuisance is an interference with the use and enjoyment of a person's property. The reported telephone calls qualify. **(A)** is not the best answer because there are no facts indicating sever emotional and/or mental distress was suffered by P and transferred intent does not apply to intentional infliction of emotional distress. **(C)** is incorrect because this nuisance does not affect the entire community. **(D)** is incorrect because there was no duty and the wrongdoing was intentional (Notice that the more likely tort claims of interference and fraud were not listed as options.)

257./D/ The best answer because repeated unwanted telephone calls have been held actionable under the tort of intrusion. Notice that the MBE may refer to "invasion" and you have to determine which of the four subtorts applies – here that is intrusion. **(A)** is not the best answer because while it is true that no general damages are presumed for invasion torts the better rationale for the correct outcome is the prerequisite elements

P must prove of unprivileged intrusion upon P's solitude and seclusion which are contained in alternative D. **(B)** is incorrect because Perfect intentionally did the acts leading to damages. **(C)** is incorrect because it is a distracter; candidates should focus only on the cause of action stated in the question.

258./D/ The best defense because if successful it would defeat the strict liability claim so any recovery would have to be for negligence allowing the possibility of some contributory negligence offset. **(A)** is incorrect because the liability for inherently dangerous activities is not delegable. **(B)** is not the best answer because pure assumption of risk could become a part of a comparable fault apportionment only if strict liability did not apply. Thus, the best answer should avoid the strict liability category. **(C)** is not the best answer because mishandled fireworks may foreseeably lead to fire damages; even if that particular house was not a foreseeable P they were part of a class foreseeably put at risk.

259./D/ The best answer because negligence for damages resulting from subsequent force put in effect by the original tortious act requires foreseeability. **(A)** is incorrect because the harm – a passenger in a car with a negligent driver – did not directly flow from the specific kind of risk used to justify the application of strict liability to firework displays conducted by commercial pryotechnicians. **(B)** is incorrect because this argument goes to the remoteness of damages and not foreseeability. **(C)** is not the best answer; while the court would perhaps use Ps residence and physical impact as two factors in determining the foreseeability and remoteness of causation, the better answer addresses the ultimate legal issue – foreseeability and zone of danger.

260./B/ A possessor of a wild animal is strictly liable for personal injury and property damages even though they exercised utmost care. **(A)** is incorrect because an animal can always revert and exhibit their wild propensities. **(C)** is incorrect because res ipsa loquitur allows a negligence inference from the fact the damages occurred; here there is strict liability. **(D)** is incorrect because strict liability applies even if the D exercised the utmost care.

261./A/ A land owner owes a duty to invitees to exercise reasonable care to eliminate unreasonable risks and to protect invitees against danger. It is a jury question as to the standard of care; PriceCo could have hired a security guard to patrol the parking lot. **(B)** is incorrect because Charlie was an invitee since members of the public entering a retail store are business invitees that could result in a potential pecuniary profit to the store. **(C)** is incorrect (but in second place) because the duty to avoid invitees being robbed in the parking lot could require more than a warning sign and the question of whether the level of care was adequate is for the jury. **(D)** is not the best answer because while the general rule is that a store is not usually responsible for unforeseeable acts of third parties the acts here may have been foreseeable. The D had knowledge of prior robberies in their parking lot and could have patrolled the area at closing.

262./C/ Victoria was invited to a business premises as a personal social guest. As between the categories of a "gratuitous licensee" and "public licensee" the former is probably more accurate because "public licensee" has been traditionally used to describe public emergency workers such as fire fighters who come on the property not as a social guest. **(A)** is incorrect because a public invitee enters as a result of an invitation to make transactions which will benefit the host. **(B)** is incorrect because a business invitee has permission to enter for business reasons to perform services for the possessor. **(D)** is incorrect because a public licensee is used to describe public emergency workers not a social guest.

263./C/ Victoria was a licensee and the related duty of a land possessor (tenant in this case) is to either remedy or warn the licensee of the known hazards. **(A)** is incorrect because premise liability is not the same as strict liability; some showing of negligence is required. **(B)** is incorrect in that inspection of the property is only required if the injured party is an invitee; here the P is a licensee. **(D)** is incorrect because Tracy knew or should have known that there was no light on the warning sign.

264./D/ Judgment should be entered against both Tracy – the tenant – and Laurie – the landlord – because they both had knowledge of the defective back stairs condition and the warning was ineffective at night without lights. Tracy encouraged her friend Victoria to hurry and it may have been foreseeable that Victoria – the visiting licensee – would try to save time by going up the back stairs. Laurie is liable both because she promised Tracy she would make the repairs (visitors are foreseeable third party beneficiaries of the promise) and her putting up the warning sign may be interpreted as the beginning of repairs that she failed to complete. **(A)** is incorrect because both D's are joint and severally liable. **(B)** is incorrect because both D's are joint and severally liable. **(C)** is incorrect because both D's are joint and severally liable.

265./B/ Even though the facts state the parents' fears were unfounded there will be economic damages suffered by the property owner. The fears and feeling of the parents are to be considered even though precautions in operating the drug rehabilitation house may mitigate the consequences. Thus the case should not be dismissed without a trial. **(A)** is incorrect because the drug rehabilitation house may comply with all zoning laws and still be a nuisance. **(C)** is incorrect because while a balancing test might be the conclusion at trial there is enough to get the matter beyond summary judgment. **(D)** is incorrect; even if the fears are unreasonable there will be substantial financial detriment suffered by P which makes the use a nuisance.

Index

CHAPTER 3

REAL PROPERTY AND FUTURE INTERESTS

RIGOS BAR REVIEW SERIES

MULTISTATE BAR EXAM REVIEW (MBE)

CHAPTER 3

REAL PROPERTY AND FUTURE INTERESTS

Table of Contents

CHAPTER 3

REAL PROPERTY AND FUTURE INTERESTS

I.   PROPERTY MBE COVERAGE

A.   Coverage Issues

33 of the 200 MBE objective questions will test topics from the subject of Real Property.

1.   Exam Topics: The five main topics tested on the Real Property portion of the MBE are (1) ownership interests, (2) rights in land, (3) titles, (4) real property contracts, and (5) real property mortgages.

2.   Weight: Approximately 75% of the questions (24 to 25 questions) will involve the first three topics of ownership interests, rights in land, and titles. Of this probably one-third (6 to 8 questions) will involve future interests and landlord-tenant topics. The other 25% (7 to 9 questions) will deal with real property contracts, recording, and mortgages.

3.   Controlling Law: Apply the traditional common law majority rule unless the question asks for the minority view, which is unlikely. If a particular state has modified the common law rule, the question will provide the exact wording of the controlling statute.

B.   Question Format

Real Property questions tend to involve very long, complicated fact patterns. The candidate can expect to encounter many series questions, in which a common fact pattern is followed by two to four questions arising under those facts.

C.   Emphasis

Real Property questions on the MBE frequently require careful analysis based on the candidate's general knowledge of the subject. For each of the five main topics set forth above, the Bar Examiners expect the candidate to understand (1) the nature and characteristics of that topic; (2) how such interests are created; (3) classification of such interests; (4) rights of possession and rights of the user; and (5) the available legal and equitable remedies.

D.   Question Approach

MBE property question facts are often relatively complex and often involve multiple sequential transactions among numerous parties. Frequently the question focuses on a party whose legal right at issue was determined by earlier party(ies). The MBE questions almost always present the factual interactions in chronological order. It is often helpful to create a chronological skeleton diagram of the participants and conveyancing events on scratch paper.

Circling the participants' names as you read the fact pattern will assist you in analyzing the parties at play in the question. Creating a sequential diagram may also be helpful in complicated fact patterns. An example of party A conveying different deeds to multiple parties B, C, and D is as follows:

Parties			Transaction/Event
A →		B	Warranty Deed / Did Not Record
↓		↓	
C		↓	Quit Claim / Recorded but Notice
↓		↓	
D		↓	Bargain and Sale / Recorded w/o Notice
		↓	
		E	Warranty Deed / Recorded

E. The Call of The Question

Real property questions require the candidate to determine "what is the nature of the interest?" "who should prevail?" "what is the best defense?" "who is the owner of the property?" "how will the court likely hold?" and "what principle of law controls the outcome?" Usually there are two reasons given to support the successful party and the best answer contains the most correct reason for the outcome. Future interest questions tend to ask, "what interest is created by the conveyance?" or "whether the interest the grantor intended is valid?"

II. REAL v. PERSONAL PROPERTY DISTINCTION

A. Real and Personal Property

Real property is land (including minerals), whatever is erected thereon (building shell), growing thereon (trees, crops), and air rights above the property. This includes all ordinary building materials such as lumber, cement, and bricks incorporated into the completed building. Personal property or "chattels" is all other property called "goods" and includes movable appliances, furniture, and fixtures.

B. Fixtures

1. Definition: "Fixtures" are chattels that have become so permanently affixed or annexed to the land or building structure that removal will cause substantial damage to the real property. Examples include a water dam built on real property, a building elevator, aluminum siding, furnace and air conditioning duct systems, and perhaps partitions and interior walls in a building.

2. Trade Fixtures: Trade fixtures are readily detachable chattels and removable business equipment such as a drill press bolted to the floor, ovens built into bakery walls, or heavy machinery hooked up by pipes or cords.

3. Determination: The objective intent of the parties and the degree of affixation govern. The longer the estate, the more likely the conclusion that the improvement provider intended to improve permanently the real property, thus converting chattels to fixtures. A tenant may not usually remove fixtures at lease termination.

a. Real Property Examples: If the improvement is essential to the normal use of the real property, the personal property has probably been converted into a fixture. Examples include an elevator in an office building or a furnace and hot water heater in a house. In addition, the personal property may be classified as a fixture if firmly imbedded and an integral part of the real property, such as brewery vats in a brewery or an organ in a church.

b. Chattel: If the removed property is characterized as a chattel rather than a fixture, the real property owner must still be compensated for any removal damages.

4. Importance: This distinction is also important because real and personal property additions may have different owners or be financed by different creditors. If there is a default on the property obligation, the question is which creditor gets the fixtures. The answer is the fixtures are usually subject to a real property mortgage. This includes fixtures added after the mortgage was recorded.

C. Exam Focus

Two areas seem to be frequently tested on the MBE.

1. Sale Problems: Does the sale of the real property include the building fixtures? The sale of a home would include the central heating furnace (because essential to the home), but not wall paintings and space heaters, or a movable refrigerator or stove.

2. Tenant Improvement Removal: If tenants (Ts) add improvements, may they take those improvements with them when they quit the premises? Ts may remove fixtures if it does not significantly damage the landlord's (LL's) structural reversion. The T must normally restore the premises to the condition it was in before the fixture was attached.

III. CONCURRENT ESTATES

Concurrent estates involve two or more people with undivided interests and concurrent possessory rights. The three types of concurrent ownership are: (1) joint tenancy; (2) tenancy in common, and (3) tenancy by the entirety.

A. Joint Tenancy (With Rights of Survivorship)

A joint tenancy gives an undivided right to each tenant (T) to possess the same entire estate, the right of survivorship, and the right to partition. The right of survivorship requires that the property pass to any remaining Ts upon the death of another outside of probate; the joint tenancy ownership interest cannot be transferred by will. This is the **PITS** for the decedent's heirs because all rights of ownership remain with the surviving joint T(s).

1. Four Unities Required – PITS: Joint tenancies are disfavored. To qualify, all tenants must have the same four **PITS** unities:

a. Possession: All of the Ts must possess the same right to access and use of the whole property.

b. Interest: Each T must have an undivided identical interest in the whole property both as to duration and fractional share. An example is "To A and B in joint tenancy."

        c. <u>**Time:**</u> The ownership interest of each joint T in the whole property must be acquired at the same time.

        d. <u>**Source of Title:**</u> All Ts must derive their interest from the same source of title – same deed or testamentary devise.

        2. Severance: Once any of the four unities have been disturbed, the joint tenancy is severed. A frequent MBE example is an inter vivos transfer by one T.

        a. Grantee Becomes T-in-Common:

        (1) Two Joint Ts: The lifetime grantee of a conveyance becomes a T-in-common. Therefore, the grantee does not have a right of survivorship with the remaining joint Ts.

        (2) Multiple Joint Ts: Where there are only two joint Ts, a lifetime conveyance by one would convert the entire interest into a tenancy in common. However, where there are three or more joint Ts, a conveyance by one would establish a tenancy in common between only the transferee and the other original joint Ts. The remaining original joint tenants would maintain their joint tenancy with right of survivorship.

        (3) Example: A, B, and C are joint tenants in a home. B transfers his interest to D. This transfer severs the joint tenancy between B's interest and that of A and C. A and C hold an undivided two-thirds interest as joint Ts, while D holds an undivided one-third interest as a T in common with A and C.

        b. Encumbrance by One Joint T Only: If one joint T mortgages her interest, a severance does not usually occur. But if the mortgage is formally foreclosed and the property sold, the creditor may attach the committing tenant's portion of the sale proceeds.

        c. Judgment Lien: Similarly, an unrelated judgment against only one joint T does not sever the property. But the proportionate interest of the judgment debtor may be executed upon in a foreclosure sale if the debtor is still alive.

MBE Tip: The exam tests two main creation and destruction concepts: a conveyance during life to a third party and the affect of a will or intestacy devise at the death of one of the joint tenants.

B. <u>Tenancy in Common</u>

        Ts in common have separate, undivided interests that are alienable inter vivos, by will, or by intestacy. Each cotenant (co-T) has an unrestricted right to possess the entire property.

        1. Ownership: The default assumed treatment in most states is equality of ownership for all co-Ts. However, by agreement, the ownership may be other than pro-rata.

        2. Conveyance During Life: Ts in common can only convey their individual interests in the whole property. The grantee becomes a T in common with the other Ts.

3. Death Succession: At death, the property interest passes to the decedent's heirs and not the other Ts, as there is no right of survivorship. It is not required that there be unity of time, source of title, or interest. There is still an in-common possession requirement.

MBE Tip: Tenancy in common is preferred by courts and will be construed instead of joint tenancy where the language creating the estate is ambiguous. The intent to create a joint tenancy must be clear.

C. Tenancy by the Entirety

Tenancy by the entirety is available only to married couples and is now recognized by statute in about 20 states. Community property ownership is similar in some western states. In those states, there is usually a rebuttable presumption that a conveyance to a husband and wife creates a tenancy by the entirety (community property). This form of ownership gives the husband and wife the right of survivorship over jointly owned property. The heirs of the deceased spouse receive nothing. Neither spouse alone can destroy the jointly owned property interest during marriage.

1. Conveyance/Encumbrance: Neither spouse can convey his/her interest or encumber the property without the other's consent.

2. Severance: Tenancy by the entirety can only be severed by: (1) the death of either spouse; (2) a legal divorce; (3) the mutual agreement of both spouses; or (4) a creditor of both spouses executing against the property.

D. Rights and Liabilities of Co-Ownership – FAPS

Co-ownership of property (either joint Ts or Ts in common) has four main areas of duties and rights. Mutual agreement determines management decisions over the jointly owned property. An exception is a co-T in sole possession who may exercise sole control short of transferring another T's interest or engaging in a tortious act.

1. Fair Dealing Duty: Because the co-T relationship is deemed a special relationship (such as between partners), a duty of fair dealing exists. Transactions between one T and the entity are to be scrutinized to be sure that all terms of the transaction were reasonable, at fair market value, and did not damage the other Ts.

2. Accountability: Co-Ts must usually share rents received from third parties and profits beyond the proportionate share that is specifically allocated to them. A T in exclusive possession is not obligated to pay any imputed rent for their use or share of farming profits to the other non-possessory Ts unless they have been "ousted."

3. Possession: Every co-T has the right to possess any and all portions of the property. No one co-T has the right to exclusive possession of any specific part of the property. In tenancy in common, the co-Ts have an equal right of possession even if they each have a disproportionate percentage interest reflected in the title instrument.

a. Ouster: If the occupying T refuses to permit the other Ts equal occupancy to the entire property, there may be an "ouster." If there is sole possession by one co-T, a possessory action may be brought by the other "ousted" Ts. Additionally, the ousting T is now sufficiently hostile to establish a potential adverse possession claim regarding the ousted T's share, and the statutory period clock is triggered and begins to run.

b. Constructive Ouster: Where the property is too small for all the owners to possess, or divorce results in one party's exclusive occupancy, the court may recognize a constructive ouster and award damages to the ousted T(s).

4. Share Contribution:

a. Carrying Charges: Each co-T is expected to pay a proportionate amount toward necessary carrying charges (e.g., mortgage, insurance, property taxes, necessary repairs). If one pays more than their share, they have a right of contribution from the co-T(s). A co-T in sole possession must offset the carrying charges paid against the value of any benefit from the occupation and use of the property.

b. Improvements: If one co-T makes improvements to the property without approval, there is no right to reimbursement from the other co-Ts unless and until (1) the improvements significantly increase the value of the property and (2) the property is later sold.

MBE Tip: The co-ownership **FAPS** rules are heavily tested on the MBE.

E. Partition

A co-ownership tenancy in common or joint tenancy may be partitioned voluntary such as sale of the property and distribution of the proceeds to the Ts. One T may petition for a judicially mandated partition-division of the property or sale if their **FAPS** rights have been violated. The court may order a division of the property to reflect each ownership interest. This is not usually applicable to a tenancy by the entirety between husband and wife.

F. Condominiums and Cooperatives

Special rules apply when a single building has multiple separate owner-occupiers.

1. Condominiums: Each owner owns her separate unit of the building, which is financed separately from the other units. In addition, she owns an undivided interest in the interior common areas, exterior gardens, and land. Title to the individual condominium units is held in fee simple by the owner. The unit owner is a T in common with the other owners for the common areas and land.

a. Transferability: Each unit is financed separately through individual mortgages. Property taxes are assessed against the unit's owner of record. Sales of the individual condominium units may not be prohibited, but a right of first refusal is allowed in many states.

b. Maintenance Costs: The owners are responsible for repairs and maintenance of the interior of their own units. Maintenance of the common property is the responsibility of the homeowners or condominium association. This is funded by required monthly fees and assessments.

c. Assessments: Homeowners' associations are usually empowered through covenants in the condominium declaration agreement to levy assessments under a contribution formula. All owners may be assessed charges for maintenance and improvement of exteriors and common areas.

2. Cooperatives: In comparison, a co-op is owned by an artificial legal entity, often a corporation or LLC. The entity owns all the interior and exterior property and leases a unit to the shareholder or member. Shareholders own an interest only in the legal entity. The financing is done through one mortgage, and the taxes are assessed on the entire building. This economic quasi-partnership in the whole allows more restrictions to be placed on transfers than in a condominium. While the entity may have a right of first refusal, a prohibition on sale is not enforceable because it is usually considered an unreasonable restraint on alienation.

MBE Tip: The most common ownership of a cooperative is through a corporation or LLC. The lessee of a unit must own a specified number of shares in the corporation in order to acquire the lease. This is known as a proprietary lease.

STOP! Go to page 567 and work Learning Questions 1 to 5.

IV. NON-POSSESSORY INTERESTS – ELP (EASEMENT, LICENSE, PROFIT)

A. Easement

An easement is a generally assignable, nonpossessory right to cross over or use the land of another such as a footpath. There are two categories:

1. Easement Appurtenant: An easement appurtenant involves two adjoining parcels of land. The right of use directly benefits the holder of the easement by allowing the physical use of another's land. The dominant tenement is the benefited parcel. The servient tenement is the burdened parcel.

2. Easement in Gross: An easement in gross involves only one parcel of land, the servient estate, such as an easement for a water utility line crossing the land. There is no dominant tenement. The owner of the easement acquires a right of use in the servient tenement, independent of the holder's ownership or possession of another tract of property. An example is an electric company that is the holder of the easement in gross and has the right to run electric wires over land.

MBE Tip: Easements, especially appurtenant, are heavily tested on the MBE. Where only one parcel of land is involved, the easement is in gross; where two parcels are involved, it is appurtenant.

---

3. Creation of Easements: Since the easement usually has value to the holder, it runs with the land. In absence of evidence to the contrary, easements may be created by any of the following four "**PINE**" methods.

a. Prescription (Similar to Adverse Possession): An easement by prescription requires ("**CHO**") **c**ontinual possession, **h**ostile to owner, and **o**pen and notorious. Examples include well-defined footpaths and driveways encroaching on a neighbor's property line.

(1) Continual Possession for Statutory Period: Common law traditionally requires use for 20 years. The use may be periodic, such as a regular seasonal summer foot path to a lake, and still satisfy the 20-year requirement as long as that is normal for the use in which the easement is claimed. Occasional trespass is not sufficient. Succeeding users may "tack" their time. A transfer of the encumbered property does not suspend the statute from running.

(2) Hostile to True Owner's Interest: Possession must be against the true owner's interest. Legal hostility is required so that it is clear that the use is not with the owner's consent or permission. However, hostility may occur by mistake or inadvertence such as crossing over for many years a dirt road that the user thought was a public road.

(3) Open and Notorious: The use cannot be secret or hidden. Underground sewers are an example. The servient landowner must have actual or constructive knowledge of the adverse use. Knowledge, and thus notice, may be inferred if the unauthorized use could have been visibly discovered through a reasonable inspection of the property.

MBE Tip: By allowing the public to use land continuously for the prescriptive statutory period, the owner is deemed to have granted the public the right to use the land.

---

b. Implication: This applies where the single owner of adjacent parcels divides the land and sells a portion that has been subject to a prior easement-like use (there was an established quasi-easement). The existence of the prior use may give rise to the inference that the parties intended an easement by implication. This may occur even though the deed does not refer to a continuation of that use, but it is clearly the parties' intent.

(1) Prior Use: The prior easement use must have: been (1) permanent or continuous; (2) apparent (visible or discoverable) upon reasonable inspection; (3) reasonably necessary for the use of the dominant parcel of land; and (4) had no practical alternative route to the parcel except over the servient estate.

(2) Implied Grant: An implied grant is where the grantor sells a portion of the estate, retains the servient parcel of land, and gives no express rights allowing the grantee to continue crossing over. Reasonable necessity is all that need be shown for a court to uphold an easement by implied grant.

(3) Implied Reservation: An easement by implied reservation is when the grantor sells the property she had been crossing over but retains the dominant estate. Without an express mention in the deed, most courts hold an easement by implied reservation can only arise out of strict necessity.

c. Necessity: Prior use is not required for an easement by necessity. Necessity requires (1) that both the dominant and servient estates were previously owned by one person and (2) there is a strict necessity for the dominant estate's use of an easement such as being surrounded by other property so that there is no access to a public road. Necessity must go beyond mere user inconvenience such as another but less convenient road which is available. There does not necessarily have to be a reference of the interest in the deed for an easement by necessity to be enforced. This type of easement interest terminates if the necessity terminates.

MBE Tip:	Implied (grant or reservation) and necessity easements require that both the dominant and servient estates were under common ownership in the past.

d. Express: The creation of an express easement involves a property transaction. An express easement may be by grant or reservation.

(1) Express Grant: "To A the right to cross Blackacre," or "to City to allow water line maintenance." If the easement is expressly created, the conveyance is subject to all the SADD deed formalities and SOF requirements (see infra). A grantor's oral permission to cross over land without a signature likely creates a license.

(2) Express Reservation: "Fee simple absolute to A, reserving to the grantor the right to cross Blackacre." Similar to the express grant, the express reservation creates an interest in land and must be written and signed under the SOF. This applies where the owner of Blackacre sells the land, but in the deed reserves the right to use the tract or a part of it for a particular purpose after the conveyance.

(3) Easement Holder's Duties: The easement holder must pay any agreed charges for the use. In addition, the easement holder has a duty to maintain the easement as necessary to avoid unreasonable interference with the servient tenement.

4. Negative Easement: The above are affirmative easements allowing the dominant tenement the use of the servient tenement. Occasionally, the exam will test a negative easement that restrains the servient tenement. Examples are prohibitions on building a structure that restricts access to sunlight, air, view, or subjacent or lateral support. This is a form of restrictive covenant discussed infra

5. Common Driveways and Support Walls: If not expressly created in writing, courts will find cross-easements by prescription, implication, or estoppel. An agreement to maintain a common driveway or support walls runs with the land. This is a form of real covenant discussed in detail infra.

6. Easement Transferability: "Transferability" refers to whether easements remain in effect once land is sold.

a. Easement Appurtenant: The easement privilege passes (runs) with the possession of the dominant tenement. It is not necessary to have references to the easement in the land deed.

b. Easement in Gross: Only one parcel of land is involved. If the easement is commercial, it is transferable (usually involving utilities or public works). If the easement is personal, it is not transferable. This includes the sale of the property reserving an easement in favor of a third party.

7. Overuse: The dominant tenement may not overburden the servient estate although reasonable modification and/or expansion of the easement may be allowed. Overuse, misuse, or surcharge does not terminate the easement, but the additional use may be subject to an injunction. An example is the dominant tenement of a driveway easement is changed from providing access to a single family residence to providing the only access to a whole shopping center. Overuse may also create a nuisance.

8. Easement Termination (Extinguishment): Termination is caused by "L RAMP."

a. Lack of Necessity: Lack of necessity may terminate an easement by necessity or implication. Examples include a new access over other land purchased by the owner or the county builds a new road or bridge to the property that was formerly landlocked. This reason for termination does not usually apply to an easement that was expressly created.

b. Release or Estoppel: The dominant tenement may agree to a release of the easement burdening the servient tenement. This is subject to the SOF. Estoppel may be a defense against the dominant tenement claim if there was detrimental reliance on an expressed oral intention of non-use by the easement holder.

c. Abandonment: Termination may result from physical abandonment. Simple non-use is usually not enough to constitute abandonment; there must also be an objective manifestation of the user's intent to abandon. The evidence suggesting abandonment of an easement must be unequivocal, decisive, and inconsistent with the continued existence of the easement.

d. Merger: An easement can be terminated by a transaction in which the servient and dominant estates both come under the same ownership.

e. Physical Blockage: If the property owner builds a fence over the footpath, the prescription time stops running. Physical blockage is not effective to terminate an express easement. Self-help is illegal; an injunction or damages should be sought in court. If the 20 year period has run but the easement was not made of record, physical blockage starts another 20 year prescriptive period in extinguishing the easement.

f. Severance: An easement, which is formed for the benefit of a piece of land cannot be transferred to another parcel of land or person. If such a transfer takes place, it can be held invalid and the original easement terminated.

g. Destruction: When the servient parcel of land is destroyed, the easement is terminated, unless it was intentionally destroyed.

h. Bona Fide Purchasers: When the servient estate is transferred to a bona fide purchaser, the easement will bind the purchaser only if she had notice (actual, inquiry, or constructive) of the easement. If the easement is in the officially recorded abstract of the property title, constructive notice has occurred. If there was no actual, inquiry, or constructive notice, the easement is terminated.

B. License

License is a nonexclusive, nonassignable, personal, permissive right to use or come onto the property of another. In other words, it is a revocable privilege (permission) to enter upon the land of the licensor. A writing is not required. Examples would be theater tickets, the right to stay in a hotel, or a writing intending to create an express easement that did not meet all the SOF requirements. Unlike an easement, a license may not usually be transferred and is terminable at will by the licensor.

MBE Tip: Look for license cross-over questions that involve torts. A license might give the licensee certain property rights, but it also gives the landowner a certain duty of care that if violated may lead to negligence actions. Unlike easements, licenses are terminable at will and are not binding on a succeeding property owner.

---

1. Violation: Contract remedies are available when a license is violated. An example is A buys a ticket to a movie or stage play, only to be turned away at the door. A can sue under a contract theory to recover her damages.

2. Irrevocable Licenses: This involves an exception to the general rule that licenses are a revocable privilege.

a. Coupled With An Interest: When a license is coupled with an interest, it is irrevocable. An example would be an excavation company clearing land – the company has an irrevocable license to enter the land to maintain or remove their equipment.

b. By Estoppel: An example is a landowner giving a revocable license to use her land and she does not discourage the licensee from exercising her rights under the license for a long period. The landowner cannot later revoke the license once the licensee has changed position based upon the continued use of the license. Say A grants a license for B, A's neighbor, to use A's private road. 10 years later, B builds a house, using the private road. After the house is built, A may be estopped from revoking the license.

c. Failed Easement: Similarly to above, an easement may have been intended but the conveyance failed such as non-compliance with the SOF. If the failed easement holder reasonably relied and made an investment, the court may construe necessary access as a irrevocable license.

MBE Tip: A failed attempt to create an easement usually creates a license.

C. Profit

A profit a prendre is the right to go upon the land of another and take some resource from the land (e.g., timber, minerals, firewood, oil, wild game, huckleberries, etc.). Unlike a license, a profit is not usually revocable. The SOF applies to the creation of a profit.

1. Types: A profit may be in gross (one parcel of land), which does not run with the land. A profit appurtenant (two parcels) runs with the land. On the MBE, almost all profits are in gross. The SOF applies to both categories.

2. Similar to Easements: A profit is very much like an easement, except overuse can terminate a profit easier than an easement where natural growth is usually allowed. Waste or excessive taking under a profit interest that adversely affects the property value may be subject to injunction or damages.

> **MBE Tip:** Profits are frequently combined with waste (excessive taking) on the exam.

> **STOP!** Go to page 568 and work Learning Questions 6 to 14.

D. Nuisance

On the exam, nuisance issues may arise in questions involving easements, licenses, and profits. See discussion infra Part VI.H.

V. PRIVATE USE RESTRICTIONS AND LIMITATIONS

This section of your MBE review course includes real covenants and equitable servitudes, which are various types of restraints on land.

A. Real Covenants

A covenant is a written promise, usually in a deed, restricting the owner's use of his property (burdened "servient" tenement) for the benefit of other property (benefited "dominant" tenement). Examples include an affirmative requirement to join a homeowners association and pay periodic dues. Other examples include a negative prohibition against selling liquor on the premises, building a structure over 35 feet in height or conducting commercial activities in a residential development. Money damages may be awarded for breach. A covenant requires initial consideration and may also be called a negative easement.

1. Requirements for the Benefit/Burden to Run: A benefit or burden may run to a successor owner of the servient estate so they benefit from or are bound by the covenants on the land. The following **WITP** requirements must be met.

a. Writing Required: Same **SADD** requirements as for a deed (writing and signed by the grantor). A poll deed is not signed by the grantee; the grantee is still bound by the covenants if she accepted the deed containing the restriction.

b. Intent to Bind Successors in Interest: The best evidence of an express intent to bind successors is use of the words "heirs," "successors," or "assigns" in describing the parties. An implied intent can be found if the burden and benefit touch and concern the land.

c. Touch and Concern the Land: Any effect on land use, utility, or value – positive benefit or negative detriment – will usually suffice. Examples include a requirement to build a structure, keep a fence in good repair, an option to purchase the property, or the requirement to pay periodic fees to a homeowners' association.

(1) Benefit Test: If the effect of the covenant enhances or increases the use or utility of the land or makes it more valuable to the covenantee, the requirement is met.

(2) Detriment Test: Negative covenants, which restrict the use of property not sell liquor or block view), will always touch and concern the land.

(3) Personal Covenants: However, personal covenants, which create only a personal obligation on the owner of the burdened land, may not touch and concern the land beyond the original owner. Examples include a covenant requiring B to take care of A's dog, some covenants not to compete, a promise to sell all crops to a third party, a promise to build a barn on the grantor's land, and a promise to pay taxes on land other than the leased premises.

d. Privity of Estate (Horizontal and Vertical):

(1) Horizontal: Horizontal privity is met if the covenant is contained in an actual land conveyance document; a promise between two neighbors not involving a land transfer would not qualify. Parties in a grantor-grantee or landlord-tenant relationship qualify.

If an original developer, A, sells land to B, with a covenant attached, A will be able to enforce the covenant against B because they are in a grantor-grantee relationship. But if A sells another parcel of property to C, B will not be able to enforce the covenant against C. There is no horizontal privity between B and C because B has no interest in C's land other than the covenant.

MBE Tip: To meet the horizontal privity requirement for the burden of a real covenant to run to a subsequent owner, look for common ownership of the property at one time with a conveyance made to a third party containing the covenant. The burden will not run to a successor when the facts state merely that just two neighbors made a covenant; the covenant must be in the property deed during a conveyance, not afterwards.

---

(2) Vertical: Vertical privity requires that a successor in interest of the burdened estate takes the same identical estate as the original owner. If B leased out land for 5 years or gave a life estate to C, and C violated the covenant, A would not have vertical privity with C because C's interest is not for the same duration as B's fee simple.

MBE Tip: To run with the land, the burden or benefit must touch and concern the land and cannot be personal to one of the original parties.

---

2. Notice: The successor to the covenantor must have notice of the burden of the covenant at the time of acquiring her interest. The burdened party's notice may be actual, constructive, or inquiry notice.

a. Actual: Successor in interest actually learns of the restrictions contained within the covenant.

b. Constructive: This includes restrictions contained in the public record.

c. Inquiry Notice: If a reasonable person inspecting the neighborhood would have checked to see if the apparent restriction was formal, inquiry notice is satisfied.

B. Equitable Servitudes

These are restrictions on the use of land that do not meet all the formal requirements of a covenant – usually privity is missing.

1. In General: Equitable servitudes are commonly used in residential subdivisions to maintain a "common scheme" by restricting a purchaser's use of their lot. The benefited party may not be entitled to damages but still may seek enforcement in a court of equity through an injunction or an order of specific performance. The equitable servitude is unlike a real covenant in that neither horizontal nor vertical privity is required for enforcement by and against successors in interest. The D must only have notice – actual or constructive – of the restriction.

MBE Tip: If a covenant is determined to be unenforceable, consider an equitable remedy under the theory of equitable servitudes. While damages are not possible, injunctive relief may be possible against an assignee of the original promisor who now owns the burdened land.

---

2. Requirements for Equitable Servitudes to Run: Many of the requirements are identical to that of a real covenant, with some variations.

a. Written: In many, but not all, states, the creation of an equitable servitude must satisfy the SOF, usually in a deed. An exception is a negative equitable servitude (which restricts use of land), which can be implied from a common scheme.

MBE Tip: Since there is a split of authority on whether the SOF applies to equitable servitudes, use the following tactic for MBE questions: If the question can be answered on grounds other than the SOF, take that approach first. If it cannot, then the safe approach is to assume paragraph (a) above applies thus requiring a writing.

---

b. Intent: There must be an intention to bind the land and not merely the persons. If the servitude is expressly created, look for the words "heirs," "successors," or "assignee" in describing the parties.

c. Touch and Concern the Land: For the burden of a covenant to run to successors of the servient estate, the burden must touch and concern the servient estate, and the benefit must touch and concern (enhance the value of) the dominant estate.

d. Notice: The successor of the covenantor must have notice of the equitable servitude at the time of acquiring her interest. The burdened party's notice may be actual, constructive, or inquiry notice.

(1) Actual: A successor in interest has actual notice of the covenantal restrictions.

(2) Constructive: This includes restrictions that are in the public record.

(3) Inquiry Notice: A person may have inspected the neighborhood and observed a general pattern or common scheme to the development. If it would have been reasonable to ascertain if the apparent restriction of the common scheme was formalized, inquiry notice is satisfied.

3. Privity Not Required: Unlike covenants, privity is not required for the benefit r burden of an equitable servitude to run. This gives the equitable servitude the ability to onstrain those not bound under a real covenant, such as a life estate T, a contract purchaser ithout title, or an adverse possessor. A neighbor can also enforce a negative servitude.

IBE Tip: A breach of a real covenant usually results in a claim for damages, while a breach f an equitable servitude usually prompts the injured party to seek an injunction or order of pecific performance. Privity is not required for equitable servitudes to run, only notice.

---

4. Reciprocal Negative Servitudes: Restrictions on the use of land may be nforced even if not stated in writing. In order for a residential subdivision to have a common lan or scheme, the equitable servitudes must be enforceable by and against all owners of the ubdivision. To be reciprocal or mutually enforceable, the requirements are:

a. Common Plan or Scheme: It must have been the grantor/developer's intent nat the burdens and benefits of the restrictions be mutually enforceable. When the first lot is old, the grantor must have intended each subsequent lot to be similarly restricted for the enefit of all in the subdivision. This is evidenced by a recorded plan, representations by the rantor, advertisements, and related indicators.

b. Notice: The purchaser of a lot must have actual, inquiry, or constructive otice of the restrictions in order to be bound by them. This may be implied by the character of he neighborhood such as uniform architecture, residential uses only, light industrial buildings, arkland, etc.

IBE Tip: Frequently tested are subdivision residents. Suppose that G1 took under a estriction and is trying to enforce it against G2, whose deed did not contain the restriction. ven though the G2 interest and restriction did not exist when G1 received their contractual ght, an injunction may issue against G2 under the theory of implied reciprocal servitude.

C. Defenses to Enforcement of Covenantal Servitudes

Enforcement of covenants and servitudes often involves equitable remedies. She who eeks equity must do equity.

1. Estoppel: Estoppel may bar an enforcement action if the benefited party had hrough statements or actions led the burdened party to rely reasonably on the apparent waiver their detriment.

2. Unclean Hands: A person engaged in a violation of a covenant has unclean ands. They may not bring any action to require another person, who is similarly in violation, come into compliance with the covenant.

3. Acquiescence: If the owner of the benefited land allows violations by the urdened party, it may constitute a waiver or acquiescence as to the actions of that party. The onger the owner allows the violations to continue before enforcing the restriction, the more the urdened party may argue laches.

D. Termination and Extinguishment of Equitable Servitudes and Real Covenants

1. Abandonment:

a. Express: The developer or residents in a subdivision may expressly release the burdened estate from the restriction.

b. Implied: Implied abandonment applies to a failure to carry out or enforce the restrictions on numerous occasions against numerous burdened parties. The real covenant or equitable servitudes terminate under the doctrine of implied abandonment.

c. Multiple Covenants: Note that if multiple restrictive covenants apply, abandonment of one covenant does not automatically terminate the others.

2. Merger: If the benefited land and the burdened land become under the same ownership, real covenants and equitable servitudes merge and therefore cease to exist. If the owner later resells a portion, the covenants and servitudes are not automatically renewed.

3. Change of Neighborhood Conditions: If a court finds there has been substantial change in the neighborhood, which makes impossible a full appreciation of the benefit of the covenant and/or restriction, it may terminate the servitude or refuse enforcement. However, the change must make all lots in the neighborhood unsuitable for the covenant. A change in zoning (such as a change from residential to commercial) is evidence of this.

> **MBE Tip:** A person can elect to enforce a covenant in equity, which is an equitable servitude, or at law, which is a real covenant. The below summary analysis of the two may be helpful:

Covenant at Law	Equitable Servitude
Common Elements – WIT	
Writing which satisfies the SOF	
Intention for the promise to run with the land	
Touch and Concern the land	
Differing Elements	
Privity Required	Notice Required – not Privity
Legal Remedy of Damages	Equitable Remedy Only

E. Nuisance

Questions concerning real covenants and equitable servitudes may involve nuisance issues. See discussion infra Part VI.H.

> **STOP!** Go to page 569 and work Learning Questions 15 to 24.

VI. GOVERNMENT LAND USE REGULATION

The government uses zoning as a means to regulate property use and control development. Examples include restricting uses such as residential, commercial, industrial, and setting building limitations such as minimum lot size, setback rules, or height limitations. The power to zone is found in the police power of the government to protect and promote public health, safety, morals, and general welfare of the public. Zoning is presumed to be valid if it reasonably relates to police power objectives.

A. Ordinance

Zoning ordinances are divided into two types: cumulative and noncumulative. A cumulative ordinance sets the "highest" use possible for an area, and then allows any "lower" use to also be included. In a single family community area, residences would be the "highest" use allowed, thus, commercial or industrial uses would be prohibited since they are "higher." But a developer could build a single family residence in a commercial zone because this would be a "lower" use. A noncumulative ordinance allows only for a particular use in the zone and no other.

B. Nonconforming Use

A nonconforming use was legal when built but does not meet the current zoning code. It is allowed to remain "grandfathered" as long as the nonconforming use is continuous.

1. Expansion or Use Change: The use cannot be substantially expanded or changed to a different nonconforming use. Disagreements arise concerning repairs of a structure as opposed to expansion, improvement, or extension. An intensification of the same use is usually allowed (if in existence when the zoning ordinance was adopted and it does not adversely impact the neighbors) as opposed to a different use (gravel mining to coal mining).

2. Abandonment: If the nonconforming use is abandoned, the grandfather protection lapses and may not be revived.

C. Variance

A variance is an allowed deviation from a zoning restriction that will be granted if the owner can show special circumstances and unique hardship. This usually involves denial of the same rights and privileges enjoyed by other properties in the vicinity. The variance may not unreasonably interfere with neighbors or be inconsistent with the general character of the neighborhood.

D. Zoning Changes

1. Rezoning: A change in zoning may be applied for if conditions in the neighborhood have substantially changed. This would change the regulation for the entire zone. A rezone requires the same due process considerations as the original process.

2. Down Zoning: A change from a higher use or density to a lower use. An example is changing apartment zoning to single family residential.

3. Spot Zoning: This occurs if one parcel or a group of parcels are singled out for use or density different from and inconsistent with the property character of the surrounding area. Spot zoning is illegal if it grants a discriminatory benefit to one owner to the detriment of their neighbors or community without adequate public advantage or justification. A variance may be, in effect, illegal spot zoning.

E. Fifth Amendment – Takings

A taking, which is an invalid exercise of police power, may occur when a zoning regulation severely restricts all viable economic use of the property. A taking can be full or partial. When a taking occurs, a landowner may sue for damages (value reduction) or an injunction (less likely than damages). Various tests have developed over the years to determine if a new regulation constitutes a taking.

1. Balancing Test: When balancing the private hardship against the public benefit, if the private hardship outweighs the public benefit, it is considered a taking. Compensation in an amount of the value reduction is to be paid to the property owner.

2. Harm Test: If a regulation is imposed to prevent significant harm to the public, it will be upheld, regardless of the hardship on the private landowner. This is not considered a taking and no compensation is due the property owner.

3. Economic Loss Test: The regulation is such that the landowner cannot thereafter obtain a reasonable return on the investment of the property. If the economic value of the land is destroyed, it is considered a taking and just compensation is required.

MBE Tip: Parties to be compensated potentially include anyone with an interest in the property, such as easement owners and profit a prendre resource holders.

F. Fourteenth Amendment – Substantive Due Process

Zoning regulations can be challenged on the basis of failure to meet the appearance of fairness doctrine. Neighboring property owners must receive actual notice so that they may have input into any changes. Publication and posting on the affected property may be sufficient as long as the specific contemplated action is disclosed.

G. Fourteenth Amendment – Equal Protection

Zoning laws that adversely affect the poor or minority communities may be subject to attack on the basis of equal protection.

H. Nuisance

Nuisance restrictions are calculated to prohibit unreasonable interference with the use or enjoyment of a person's property. The sensibilities of the ordinary person is the standard used to determine the degree of unreasonableness. The conduct must involve a significant and substantial interference with safety, peace, or comfort in the use of property or violate a statute or ordinance. A nuisance can either be public or private.

1. Private: A private nuisance occurs when there is unreasonable interference with an individual's right to enjoy his or her own property. Examples include blocking a view, or persistent discomforting trespass of noise, dust, barking dogs, or offensive odors. A court will balance the utility of the activity against the severity of the damages to the complaining party.

2. Public: A public nuisance occurs when there is unreasonable interference with the public's right to enjoy public facilities. Examples are blocking traffic, nauseous odors, exposure to disease, explosive plants, drugs, and prostitution. Standing to sue under a public nuisance theory is met by alleging an injury that is unique and not shared by the general public.

MBE Tip: A nuisance – private and/or public – may result from an overused easement or license or failure to comply with a covenant or servitude.

---

3. Remedies: Remedies available include an injunction to prohibit future interference or damages for past and future harm caused by the nuisance.

4. Defenses: The D may assert the P "came to the nuisance." The D may also claim that the use, while objectionable to the particular P, is not objectively unreasonable and/or conforms to zoning laws.

MBE Tip: Nuisance often is tested on the MBE in the context of overuse, overcharge, or misuse of an easement, covenant, or servitude.

STOP! Go to page 572 and work Learning Questions 25 through 29.

VII. AGREEMENTS TO TRANSFER

A. Listing Agreements

The relationship between the broker and his client is that of agent and principal. Accordingly, the common law rules regarding agency usually apply (utmost good faith and fidelity, due care, no self-dealing, etc.). A dual agency (representing both the seller and buyer) may be allowed if there is adequate disclosure. In most states, the SOF requires broker listing agreements to be in writing and the broker to be licensed to collect commissions. **DEWD** is the acronym for the formalities of the listing agreement:

1. Duration: The listing agreement must state the duration of the broker's contract.

2. "Earned" Conditions: The agreement must specify the terms, details as to any necessary condition, and when the commission is deemed to be earned. The majority rule is that the commission is earned when the broker provides the seller with a buyer who is "ready, willing, and able" to purchase the property. Other conditions include inspection, financing, conveying clear title, etc.

3. Writing: The agreement must be in writing in order to comply with the SOF because the listing agreement concerns land.

4. Description: There must be a sufficient description of the property to be sold (not necessarily a full legal description) so that the specific property may be identified.

5. Types of Listing Agreements:

    a. Nonexclusive or Open: Seller may hire as many brokers as she wishes without liability to any broker who does not sell the property.

    b. Exclusive Listing Agreements: Exclusive listing agreements involve only one broker. They come in two types, "broker exclusive" and "exclusive right to sell."

    (1) Broker Exclusive: Seller signs up with one broker at a time to sell the property. The seller incurs no liability to the broker if the owner sells the property herself to some buyer not provided by the broker during the duration of the listing agreement.

    (2) Exclusive Right to Sell: This prohibits owner from selling both personally and through another broker without incurring liability for a commission to the original broker. The homeowner relinquishes the right to sell the property herself.

MBE Tip: Carefully analyze the listing types and any specified conditions precedent to the broker's right to receive the commission on the sale.

B. Land Sale Contracts

The buyer and seller agree in the realty contract on a particular price and other terms for the transfer of a parcel of property. Depending on the state, this is also known as a "purchase and sale agreement," "earnest money receipt and agreement," or "earnest money agreement." All common law contract formation rules apply to the negotiation process. This agreement to sell precedes the formal deed at closing. The conveyance of a marketable title (free from unreasonable encumbrances) at closing of escrow is implied in the sales contract unless the agreement expressly states otherwise.

MBE Tip: The below **LIPP** essential terms of a purchase and sale agreement/earnest money agreement are **l**egal description, **i**dentification of closing entity, **p**rice, and **p**arties.

---

    1. Legal Description: The description of the land being conveyed must appear on the face of the agreement in the form of a "legal description" of the subject real property. The accuracy of the legal description may be critical. A court of equity will not order specific enforcement of a purchase and sales agreement if the description appearing in the agreement is vague, ambiguous, or otherwise fails to specifically identify the property to be transferred.

    a. Reasonable Certainty: A description of the property with reasonable precision is required so the property may be specifically identified. Thus, the lot number, block number, addition, city, county and state, will normally satisfy a court. "Our family home," "1234 Main St," or "my property in New York City" are usually insufficient without more.

MBE Tip: The required degree of specificity in the property description is higher for the seller to buyer purchase and sale agreement than in the listing agreement.

---

    b. Metes and Bounds: Where metes and bounds descriptions are utilized, careful attention must be paid to ensure that the legal description "closes." That is, the description's point of beginning and the point of ending must be the same.

c. Mistakes in Legal Description: Reformation of an inaccurate legal description is an available remedy only if a scrivener's error or a mutual mistake was the reason for the inaccuracy.

> **MBE Tip:**   Often on the MBE, the legal description in the listing agreement or purchase and sales agreement has errors. The instrument is not generally operative, but may create a "color of title" in the grantee triggering the ability to qualify under adverse possession.

d. Boundary Dispute Exception: A boundary established by a common grantor that was physically apparent to both grantees is enforceable even if in variance with the legal description of the deed.

e. Personal Property: Personal property is not included with commercial property unless the deed so specifies. If silent on the matter, basic residential fixtures such as the furnace and hot water heater are usually required if the property is a residence.

2. Identification of Closing Entity: The closing agent is usually specified in the agreement along with the method of delivering title.

3. Price: The price of the property should appear on the face of the sales contract and should specify "United States Dollars" or other currency the parties intend to use. The method of payment – cash, seller-provided financing, or mortgage proceeds – should be specified in the sales contract.

a. Deposits: An earnest money "deposit" is often employed in both residential and commercial real estate sales. Any related conditions should be described in detail within the purchase and sales agreement. The amount and form of the deposit is negotiable.

b. Return of Deposit: Earnest money deposits must usually be returned to the buyer if the transaction does not close because of the seller's non-performance.

c. Earnest Money as Liquidated Damages: Forfeiture of earnest money to the seller is generally a valid and enforceable contractual remedy for breach by the buyer.

4. Parties: Proper identification of the parties is necessary. To avoid multiple excise taxation of the transaction, a property purchaser may identify herself in the agreement with the phrase modifier "and/or assigns." If, during the course of closing, the purchaser then wishes to substitute another party to receive delivery of title, she may do so by designating to the closing agent the identity of the assignee. If there is written evidence of the assignment, the closing agent will deliver the deed to the assignee.

5. Financing and Contingencies: The face of the sales contract should state whether financing is conventional, VA, FHA, or seller financed. All financing contingencies (sale of purchaser's current home, procurement of a certain type of financing, etc.) and their accompanying deadlines should also appear on the face of the purchase and sales agreement.

a. Contingencies: The buyer and seller may each desire contingencies that they must approve before they are bound to close.

(1) Obtaining Loan: A condition making the buyer's purchase obligation contingent upon loan approval requires a reasonable effort by buyer to obtain a mortgage.

(2) Inspection: The financing source, such as a bank, may require the buyer to undertake a satisfactory physical inspection of the property to meet their lending requirements.

(3) Time Limits: Parties are allowed a reasonable time to satisfy all contingencies unless agreed to the contrary. If the contract specifies "time is of the essence," late performance is usually to be treated as a breach of contract.

b. Balloon Obligations: References to balloon payments or acceleration clauses may also be found in purchase-sale and earnest money agreements as features of seller financing arrangements. The purchaser usually undertakes to retire his obligation by means of installment payments amortized over several years at a stated interest rate. A balloon clause requires an extra sum to be paid on a particular date or the occurrence of a predefined condition. In addition, the entire amount of the unpaid balance may be required to be paid on a date certain in the future.

6. Remedies: The remedies for breach or nonperformance of a real property contract are more narrowly defined than in general contract law.

a. Seller's Remedies: If the buyer will not perform, two remedies are available.

(1) Compensatory Damages: The seller may seek compensatory damages in an amount of the difference between the contract price and the current market price. The market price is established by selling the property to a third party at fair market value.

(2) Liquidated Damages: A liquidated damage clause in an purchase and sale agreement usually specifies the buyer's earnest money may be forfeited if the buyer is unable to complete the purchase. The earnest money must bear a reasonable relationship to the probable loss. In most states, a seller is put to an election; earnest money forfeiture is usually the sole and exclusive remedy, thereby precluding other damages.

b. Buyer's Remedies:

(1) Specific Performance or Damages: If the seller will not perform, specific performance is the property buyer's usual remedy because all land is deemed to be unique. The court may order the seller to convey a marketable title into escrow. If specific performance is not possible due to no fault of the seller (such as an unintentional defect in the title), the buyer is entitled to the return of the earnest money and interest. If the seller was at fault, an award of compensatory damages is possible, but the buyer would have the burden to quantify the amount thereof.

(2) Defective Property – Rescission: If the sale has been completed, the buyer may seek the remedy of rescission.

c. Quiet Title Action: A quiet title action is used to clear the chain of a title to a described real property parcel. This may be necessary to remove liens, resolve multiple claimants' priority, or remove clouds and encumbrances over the land. The claims of easements, adverse possession, or boundary disputes may also be resolved through this remedy and become of record. The court will examine the underlying controversy and issue an order clearing and thus "quieting" the claims and clearing the title to the property. A quiet title action may be necessary for a property owner to secure a marketable title.

STOP! Go to page 573 and work Learning Questions 30 through 33.

VIII. CONVEYING DEEDS AND RELATED

Real property normally transfers by deed. A written term or condition in the deed controls over a contrary term in the purchase and sale agreement in case of a conflict.

A. Deed Requirements – SADD

There are four requirements for a deed in most states:

1. SOF: Compliance with the SOF is required. The written deed must at least be signed by the party to be bound (the seller or grantor). The grantee does not have to be specified. Delivery of a blank deed signed by the grantor implies authority to fill in the blank grantee designation. A deed to a deceased person is void; title stays with the seller.

2. Acknowledgement: Most states require every deed to be formally acknowledged (notarized) before a notary public.

3. Description: The full accurate legal description of the property is required under the recording statutes in most states if the land is platted. More precision is required in the deed than in the preceding purchase and sale agreement where the test is usually specific identity.

4. Delivery: Title to the property passes upon delivery of the deed; delivery is the objective evidence of the grantor's intent to presently transfer ownership. Delivery of the deed is usually made to escrow at closing. Recording the deed with the county recording office where the real property is located creates a presumption of effective delivery.

a. Non-Delivery: If the grantor retains possession of the deed, there is a rebuttable presumption that there was not a present intent to transfer title. Similarly, if the grantor delivers but retains control over the deed and is free to change her mind, delivery is not effective.

b. Oral Condition: The grantor may impose an oral condition on the transfer, but intend the transfer to be immediately effective. In most states, the oral condition will be disregarded and the grantee takes free and clear of the condition.

MBE Tip: The SADD requirements apply to all conveyances of property or property rights such as an express easement or a profit a pendre.

5. Part Performance Exceptions – PIP: If a conveyance fails to meet all the formalities required by the SOF, most states allow specific performance in equity. To invoke this exception the facts of the case must be so compelling that the occupant's situation can be explained only by the existence of a conveyance agreement. The requirements for this doctrine vary from state to state, but they tend to have the following **PIP** common elements:

      a. Possession: Possession of land delivered by the seller to the buyer.

      b. Improvements: Purchaser undertakes significant acts that are consistent with ownership. An example is making valuable and permanent improvements to the property. The improvements must be far beyond what a T would usually make to leased property.

      c. Payment: Payment – in full or in substantial part – of the purchase price was made by the buyer.

      6. Change of Position: If the purchaser has changed his or her position in reliance on an oral agreement, a few states invoke estoppel to enforce the part performance exception. Courts that enforce the contract because of reliance will also usually require the buyer to have taken possession.

      7. Oral Rescission (Split of Authority): In a slight majority of states, title transfer may be orally rescinded. In the remainder of jurisdictions, a writing is required, and some of those states require a totally new deed from the original grantee to the original grantor.

MBE Tip: Very frequently on the MBE there was only an oral promise to convey or the deed did not meet all the **SADD** (**S**OF, **A**cknowledgement, **D**escription, and **D**elivery) requirements. Consider the **PIP** equitable exceptions. Adverse possession under color of title also begins to run at that time.

---

      8. Deeds Conveying Title: In most instances, title is passed at closing of escrow by a "statutory warranty deed." Quitclaim deeds, and in some states, limited conveyance documents may also be used to transfer ownership. The purchase and sale contract should specify what type of deed will be tendered at closing.

      a. Statutory (Warranty) Deed: A full statutory warranty deed represents integration of the seller's duties into a marketable title. A warranty deed protects the buyer-grantee even if the seller lacked knowledge of the defect. Absent an express provision to the contrary, such a deed contains the following grantor's **TAFED** covenants:

      (1) Title of Seisin: Grantor warrants that she has title or ownership of the property.

      (2) Authority and Right to Convey: Grantor has the power, authority, and right to make the conveyance. There also can by no contrary agreements such as options or rights of first refusal held by other parties.

      (3) Free of Encumbrances – Marketable Title: At closing the grantor warrants a marketable title and that the property is free of significant defects in the chain of title. This includes restrictions and encumbrances of record that might lead to litigation. Restrictive covenants, undetermined adverse possessions, claims not yet decided by a court, easements, and significant encroachments usually violate a marketable title unless the defect is known and expressly accepted by the buyer. Zoning and land use regulations do not render the title unmarketable.

(4) Enjoyment Quiet: Buyer will realize quiet enjoyment without disturbance by a legal challenge from a third party asserting claims to the property.

(5) Defend Buyer: This is also called the warranty of "further assurances." Grantor will defend and indemnify vendee's title against adverse claims by third parties.

(6) Remote Grantee Protection: Under the common law, the first three TAF covenants cannot run with the land because they become personal choses in action at the time of deed delivery if they are breached. Thus a successor in interest may not enforce them.

MBE Tip: Unless the sales agreement states to the contrary, the seller must provide a marketable title containing the **TAFED** covenants to their grantee.

---

b. Limited Conveyance Documents: The seller may not always be willing to warrant title fully to the extent required by the state's statutory warranty deed rules. Virtually all states have the two options of warranty deed or quitclaim deed. Some states have a third option – a limited warranty.

(1) Quitclaim Deed: If the purchase and sale contract does not specify that a fuller interest is to be conveyed at closing, a quitclaim deed is imposed in most states. A quitclaim deed conveys all ownership interest that the grantor has in the property without any covenants or implied warranties. The seller warrants only that they are transferring all of their ownership interest. The buyer has no protection against property liens, judgments, or encumbrances such as mortgages and restrictive covenants or servitudes. The property may be subject to easements, restrictive covenants, or other third party interest.

(2) Limited Warranties: Generally, the requirements for a limited warranty (aka "bargain and sale" deed) fall between those of a statutory warranty and a quitclaim deed. An example would be a warranty that seller has no knowledge of **TAFED** defects in his conveyance, but does not warrant prior conveyances.

MBE Tip: Many MBE exam questions involve a property sale where the purchaser was unaware of an encroachment, easement, restrictive covenant or servitude, etc. If the seller conveyed title by use of a statutory warranty deed, she violated the marketable title requirement.

---

c. Other Warranties:

(1) New Home Quality: In most states, a commercial builder selling a new home makes a common law implied warranty of habitability in addition to the **TAFED** covenants above. The habitability defect must be substantial. The seller may also make express warranties which most builders provide new home purchasers.

(2) Used Home Quality: For a used dwelling or commercial property, there is traditionally no implied warranty. If the contract specifies "as is," the buyer assumes the risks of defects. In a growing number of states, there may be a seller's duty to disclose serious defects of which they have knowledge and which are not readily apparent. In most states, this applies to the undisclosed conditions of termite infestation and fire code resistance standards violations.

9. Merger Into Deed: Under the common law, the purchase and sale agreement merges into the deed at delivery. The deed is usually controlling if a provision therein conflicts with a term in the purchase and sale agreement. Through its equitable power, a court may include consistent provisions in the final conveyance that both parties agreed to in the purchase and sale agreement but were absent in the deed. As to inconsistent terms between the contract and deed, reformation of the deed is very rare. A few cases have allowed reformation for fraud, misrepresentation, or other extreme inequitable conduct. Rescission may still be available to the buyer if the court will not reform the deed.

> **MBE Tip:** If there is a disagreement between the terms of the deed and the terms of a prior purchase and sale contract, the deed terms prevail.

10. Estoppel By Deed: This applies in many states where the seller conveys title that she did not then own. If the seller later acquires title, it then passes to the grantee. This type of estoppel applies only for the original buyer's claim against the seller; if the seller subsequently conveys the after-acquired property to a bona fide purchaser, they may take free and clear of the original buyer.

11. Risk of Loss: This is usually questioned on the MBE when the non-insured loss occurs during the middle of the property conveyance transaction. An example is a fire burns down the building before closing.

  a. Equitable Conversion: The common law rule of equitable conversion places the risk of loss on the buyer if the property is destroyed between execution of the purchase and sale agreement and closing. The seller retains legal title until closing, but equitable title passes to the buyer upon contract execution.

  b. Minority View: A minority of states place the risk on the seller. The Uniform Vendor and Purchaser Act places the risk on the possessor of the land.

  c. Impact of Insurance: The majority of courts will require the seller to pay the buyer some portion of the proceeds from seller's insurance coverage as equitable relief. The buyer may, of course, also purchase her own insurance. In many states, the parties may specify the rights and obligations of loss insurance as part of the purchase and sale agreement.

  d. Impossibility of Performance: If the property is destroyed, the buyer may be excused.

B. Closing

Closing is the formal delivery of the executed deed to the buyer and the payment of the purchase money to the seller. Both parties deliver their required documents to a closing agent pursuant to escrow instructions. All back taxes are paid current. The closing agent normally functions as a dual agent with a fiduciary duty to both parties.

> **STOP!** Go to page 574 and work Learning Questions 34 through 40.

C. Recording Statutes

Delivery of a properly executed deed is effective to transfer equitable title between the seller and the buyer. To protect against a third party later acquiring a superior interest from the seller, the buyer must usually record the deed at the county recorder's office where the real property is located.

> **MBE Tip:** The objective is determining if a subsequent party who records first prevails over a prior interest who did not file. This area is heavily tested on the MBE. Note that it does not usually affect an action between the original buyer and seller of the property; their rights vest at their contract date. Similarly, an adverse possessor's accrual rights are not affected.

1. Record Notice: Recording imputes constructive notice to the whole world of the interests contained therein. Recording of title and related priorities are normally governed by statute in the state. In the absence of an applicable recording statute, the common law rule is "first in time – first in right." There are three major statutory categories that are heavily tested on the MBE:

> **MBE Tip:** Apply the common law rule "first in time – first in right" if no subsequent party meets the statutory priority requirements specified in the question. This rule also applies if the recording is made in the wrong place and a reasonable title search would not have discovered the interest.

2. Pure Race: Under pure race statutes, the first in time to record has a priority.

a. Characteristics: Whether the purchaser is bona fide or has notice of a prior interest is irrelevant in a race state. Good faith or taking for value are not required. Priority is determined entirely by who wins the race to the recording office.

b. Sample Statutory Language: "In determining priorities in land, the first interest to record prevails."

3. Pure Notice: Pure notice statutes give priority to subsequent bona fide purchasers for value who take without notice of any prior conveyances. The last bona fide purchaser gets the priority.

a. Characteristics: This priority is based on the status of the purchaser when the deed transferred. The time that the deed is filed is irrelevant if the subsequent party takes without notice. Note that this rule only applies if the first purchaser does not record; if there was a prior filing, there would be constructive notice. The second purchaser does not have to record to prevail in a pure notice state.

b. Sample Statutory Language: The usual statutory language is: "No conveyance of an interest in land is effective against a subsequent purchaser for value without notice unless first duly recorded."

4. Race-Notice: Under race-notice statutes, a subsequent grantee must be a bona fide purchaser taking for value without notice of a prior interest and be the first to record.

a. Characteristics: This type of recording statute is in effect in the majority of the states. It combines the elements of the previous two; the impact is that a second purchaser wins the race only if she is both a bona fide purchaser – see below – and recorded first.

b. Sample Statutory Language: The usual statutory language is: "Every conveyance of land not recorded is void as against any subsequent purchaser taking for value without notice whose conveyance is first duly recorded.

MBE Tip: Some MBE questions do not specify the type of recording statute but rather give the actual statutory language, some of which may be quite convoluted. Decide first which of the three categories applies in this question. Race-notice is the most popular. Then focus on the statutory treatment of a subsequent party's filing position and the effect of notice if any.

D. Bona Fide Purchaser

In order to be a bona fide purchaser (BFP) each of the **FINS** elements must be satisfied.

1. For Value: The BFP cannot take by gift or devise, and must pay more than nominal value for the conveyance. Debts or judgments that are unrelated to the property do not qualify. A cancellation of debt on the property will usually suffice.

2. In Good Faith: The BFP cannot have actual knowledge of the prior unrecorded conveyance. This is a subjective test. Actual knowledge does not meet the good faith standard.

3. No Record or Inquiry Notice: This is an objective test and determined at the time the purchaser received the conveyance. The burden is on the holder of the prior unrecorded instrument to prove the subsequent vendee had sufficient inquiry notice to prompt a reasonable person to make an investigation. The MBE tests this doctrine in two situations.

a. Record Notice: Proper recording is constructive notice to the whole world. A BFP has a duty to search the recorded instruments in their chain of title.

(1) Recording Indexes: There are two systems.

(a) Tract Indexes: A tract index identifies a parcel of property by number and a title search examines transactions referencing the parcel number. All recorded instruments affecting that property are listed in one place.

(b) Grantor To Grantee Index: Without a tract index, a title searcher must examine the grantor to grantee indexes. Such indexes are problematic because an unrecorded conveyance breaks the grantor-grantee chain. This means record notice is not imputed to the subsequent party claiming a priority.

(2) Recording Error: A conveyance using the wrong legal description will likely be entered into the wrong tract index. Similarly a party could record in the wrong county, record in the grantor-grantee index, or use a wrong name. These are outside the chain of title and treated as unrecorded transactions, and constructive record notice is not imputed to a BFP.

b. Inquiry Notice: The second purchaser cannot have information sufficient to put a reasonable person upon inquiry that, if followed, would lead to the discovery of defects in the title to the property. An example is discovering a third party living on the property, thus indicating a claim based on an unrecorded deed.

c. Reference to Unrecorded Transaction: If a recorded instrument makes reference to an unrecorded transaction, one has an inquiry duty to investigate and discover the nature (gain notice) of the prior unrecorded property right. An example is discovering a conveyance instrument from a party who took under a "wild deed" that was not recorded and thus would not appear in the grantor-grantee index.

> **MBE Tip:** Usually the MBE questions indicate that the state does not have a tract index, so a BFP must search the grantor-grantee index.

d. Deed From Common Grantor: Under the "collateral document rule," a grantee is charged with notice of the contents of deeds of adjacent properties coming from a common grantor. Some courts will enforce this rule and impose restrictions contained within the adjacent parcel's deed such as height limitations. Under this rule a grantee must examine the title record forward from the date the common grantor sold one of the adjacent parcels.

4. Shelter Rule: In some states, a non-BFP may take title from a BFP. Once a BFP holds a valid title, he shelters or "cleanses" it and may transfer to anyone, even a non-BFP. The rationale is that the test for BFP is made upon receipt of the deed. If later they (or their transferee) learn of a defect, it should not retroactively eliminate any priority they otherwise would enjoy. The shelter rule may not improve the original purchaser's position by allowing one to "wash" the title through a BFP.

5. Example and Answer: On Day 1, X gives a deed to A who does not record. On Day 2, X gives a deed to B who knows of the prior conveyance. On Day 3, X gives a third deed to C who immediately files and does not know of the prior conveyance to A or B. In a race-notice state, what are the priorities of the three vendees? Answer. C has priority. Even though C took last, he filed first and appears to meet all the required **FINS** elements. A would have a second priority. While B took subsequent to A and prior to C, he had notice of a prior interest and therefore cannot be a bona fide **FINS** purchaser.

> **MBE Tip:** Unrecorded deeds and transactions are favorite MBE facts.

6. Recording Statute Chart:

State	Prevailing Party	Recording	BFP
Pure Race	First Recorder	required	not required
Pure Notice	Subsequent BFP	not required	required
Race-Notice	Subsequent BFP	required	required

E. Title Insurance

Title insurance is the purchaser's protection against unknown defects of record in the abstract of the chain of title. The abstract contains the history of the series of conveyance between various grantors and grantees. An insurance company then insures the abstract of title. Such a policy is usually not required unless specified in the purchase and sale contract. While this does not negate liability for breach of **TAFED** warranties, it does provide a recovery fund.

1. Transferability: The title protection may not be transferred with the property to a new buyer and does not cover subsequent events.

2. Exclusions: The carrier may exclude coverage for any defects that are not of record in the title abstract as of the closing date. Examples of usual exclusions include unrecorded deeds and mortgages, potential easements, encroachments on adjoining property, boundary disputes, setback rule violations, adverse possession, errors in public records, or other defects that could be discovered by a physical inspection of the property.

STOP! Go to page 575 and work Learning Questions 41 through 45.

IX. ADVERSE POSSESSION

A. Adverse Possession

Adverse possession (or an easement by prescription) can ripen into a title of record through a quiet title action. Adverse possession state statutes typically require the four **ECHO** elements:

1. Exclusive: The physical possession must be exclusive to the world as a whole. Sharing the property with the owner or the public is not adverse possession, but Ts-in-common may all adversely possess the same property at the same time.

2. Continuous: Continuous actual physical possession and use for the entire statutory period, which varies by state. Usually the statutory period is 15 to 20 years. Many states recognize a shorter period for adverse possessors claiming "under color of title" such as a defective deed that fails to meet all the **SADD** requirements, but the grantee paid the property taxes. Seasonal use of the property may be enough to support adverse possession if it is continuous and such use is consistent with other properties in the area. Examples include a summer lake cabin or fall hunting cabin.

MBE Tip: Because the adverse possession period varies between states, look for either explicit mention of the statute or look for a time of adverse possession that would include most states (e.g., greater than 20 years).

a. Tack Time: Successive adverse possessors with privity can add together or "tack" time. Tacking is also allowed against succeeding property owners.

b. Tolling: The statute of limitations is tolled if the property owner becomes incapacitated, insane, or imprisoned. If the owner is possessed with "disabilities" the day the adverse possessor takes initial possession, the statute of limitations begins to run when the owner is rid of all disabilities. Tolling applies until the owner reaches the age of capacity.

3. **Hostile:** Hostility to the true owner's title and interest is necessary.

a. Not With Permission: The possessor must hold the land as adverse to the whole world. This is required so that it is clear the possession is not with the owner's consent and permission such as a LL and T. If the rightful owner knows of the adverse possession and does not object, it may be construed as permissive so the adverse possessor is not occupying with the required hostility. Payment of property taxes is strong evidence of hostility.

b. Boundary Disputes: Most courts hold the hostility requirement is met by an adjoining property owner who mistakenly believes that the land in question was within the boundary of her ownership. An example is a fence or water line that is actually over the property line.

c. Prior Agreement: Some MBE questions state that the boundary line at issue was previously raised in a dispute leading to an agreement between the adjacent owners. The court will likely enforce that agreed-upon boundary line in the future even if the parties were mistaken in their earlier agreement. This result – respecting the terms of the owners' prior agreement – may apply even if it was not in compliance with the SOF.

d. Defective Deed: Taking property possession under color of title, such as a defective deed, meets the "hostility" requirement in most states.

e. Squatter's Rights: A few minority states require the possessor to have a bona fide belief they have title to the property in question. A boundary line dispute would be eligible for adverse possession, but a squatter would not in these minority states.

4. **Open and Notorious:** The possession cannot be secret or hidden. Visible and known possession requirements are calculated to assure that the true owner has actual knowledge of the adverse possessor. Building a structure, fence, posting a sign, or openly planting and harvesting crops will usually qualify to impute knowledge. Therefore, there is a reasonable opportunity for the owner to bring an eviction action.

5. **Miscellaneous:**

a. Constructive Adverse Possession: The adverse possessor can claim ownership to all of a tract by merely possessing part of it only if (1) the entire tract is one parcel in the public record and (2) they have "color of title."

b. Co-Tenants: There is a special requirement that applies to adverse possession by a co-T in exclusive possession of property. Non-possessory co-Ts have the right to assume the possessing co-T is not adversely possessing against their ownership interest. An exception applies if the possessor gives notice of hostility to the non-possessors by "ousting" or refusing to admit them to the premises; the adverse possession statutory clock is triggered at this date.

c. Mineral Estates: For purposes of adverse possession, mineral estates are considered a separate estate from the parcel of real estate. In order to acquire a mineral estate through adverse possession, the claimant must trespass onto both the land and in taking of the minerals. An example is a 300 acre tract of land that is rich in coal. The successful adverse possessor must fulfill all of the **ECHO** requirements for both the land and the mining of the coal.

d. Future Interests: The adverse possessor can only acquire title to the extent that a true owner could possess the land (e.g., life estate or fee simple). To prevail as an adverse possessor over a future interest, the four **ECHO** requirements must all be satisfied. The statutory period does not begin to run against an existing future interest until the future interest becomes possessory. Similarly, this is the time when the future interest may file an eviction action against the adverse possessor.

e. Encroachment: An encroachment on another's property is a trespass, so the statutory period begins to run. Until a quiet title order is issued, the title to the property is unmarketable. The usual remedy is eviction. A few cases allow damages instead of ordering removal if the cost of removing the encroachment substantially exceeds the benefit to be gained by the true land owner. An example is an office building that is encroaching five feet upon a neighbor's property. A court may determine that the office building owner pay damages to the neighbor, as a "tear-down/re-build" or structural move may be economically impractical.

6. Termination:

a. File Eviction Suit or Re-enter: If the owner files suit to eject the trespassing adverse possessor and/or re-enters the property to regain possession, the adverse possession period terminates. The owner could also purchase the adverse possessor's interest thus creating a merger of both interests.

b. Abandonment: The adverse possession claim may be abandoned by the possessor thus terminating the time period. Temporary interruptions, such as not using a summer cabin during the winter, are not deemed an abandonment. Tacking is not allowed for future occupancy by the original adverse possessor or their assignee if they once abandoned the property. The period begins anew when the adverse possessor reenters the property.

MBE Tip: The **ECHO** requirement nuances of adverse possession are tested on every MBE.

B. Eminent Domain

Eminent domain is the power of the state and federal governments (and their regulatory agencies) to take private property for a public use. "Public use" is broadly interpreted if it is rationally related to a public purpose.

1. Condemnation: Condemnation is a judicial proceeding brought directly by the state to obtain title and compute the compensation due the owner. The owner must receive the fair market value of the property in compensation at its "highest and best" use in the owner's hands. LLs and Ts share the award as their interests lie.

2. Inverse Condemnation: The state may so substantially restrict an owner's use of the property that an effective taking has occurred. Imposing new zoning and historical landmark restrictions are usually not enough of a diminution in value to qualify as an inverse condemnation if a reasonable economic return on the property is still possible. For inverse condemnation, the landowner must initiate a lawsuit against the state.

C. Quiet Title Action

A quiet title action is used to clear the chain of title to a real property parcel. This may be necessary to remove liens, resolve multiple claimants' priority, or remove clouds and encumbrances over a parcel of land. The claims of easements, adverse possession, or boundary disputes may also be resolved through this remedy and become of record. The court will examine the underlying controversy and issue an order clearing and thus "quieting" title to the property. Such an order following a quiet title action may be necessary for the property owner to secure a marketable title.

D. Testamentary Devise

A transfer may be inter-vivos or testamentary. A will is ambulatory and may be revoked or modified prior to death. A transfer by will only occurs upon the death of the owner/testator.

1. In General: Most of the property rules apply whether the transfer is inter-vivos or testamentary as a part of a will disposition scheme.

2. Ademption: This occurs when the decedent specified that certain specific property was to go to a particular taker and that particular property was disposed of prior to death. A few states allow the trial court discretion to give the taker an equivalent amount from traceable funds, equivalent property, or the residue of the estate. Usually the specified taker of that particular piece of property takes nothing.

3. Accessions: This occurs when the specified property going to a particular taker increases in value or grows larger before the testator's death. An example is land along a river that increases because of a shift in the river's path. The beneficiary of the specified property usually takes the increase with the property, not the residue of the estate.

4. Related Encumbrance: This occurs when the specified property going to a particular taker becomes subject to a liability between the date of the will and the date of death. In the majority of states the taker receives the property subject to the liability. A few states allow the trial court discretion to require the residue of the estate to absorb an equitable portion of the encumbrance.

5. Lapsed Devise: If the named beneficiary predeceases the testator and their devise was specifically conditioned upon them surviving the testator, the devise normally lapses. The effect of this is that the property is added to the residue of the estate and does not go to the devisee's heirs. Many states now have anti-lapse statutes that would give the devise to the beneficiary's heirs at law.

> **STOP!**   Go to page 576 and work Learning Questions 46 and 47.

X. REAL PROPERTY FINANCING INSTRUMENTS

A. Mortgage

A mortgage is a form of conveyancing deed that encumbers real property as security for the payment of a debt. It is usually accompanied by a promissory note.

B. Types of Mortgages

There are two basic types of mortgage states: lien theory and title theory. Some states allow deeds of trust as a variation to the lien theory.

1. Lien Theory (Majority): In most states, a mortgage creates a lien on the land. Title stays with the buyer and the mortgage company has a lien.

2. Title Theory (Minority): In some states, as well as originally under the common law, the mortgagee (the creditor or bank) holds legal title to the property. The title then is subject to transfer to the mortgagor (buyer/debtor) upon full payment of the debt.

3. Practical Differences: In practice, there is little difference between the two theories. Even with a lien theory state, the debtor has right to possession of the land during the period of the mortgage, and foreclosure actions for default under the lien theory versus title theory are similar.

C. Other Real Estate Financing Instruments

1. Deed of Trust: Some lien theory states allow a "deed of trust" as the debt securing instrument rather than a traditional mortgage. With a deed of trust, legal title is held in trust by a third party trustee until the debt is paid. One advantage of a deed of trust for creditors is that most states allow private foreclosure actions rather than going through the courts (see standard mortgage foreclosures below).

2. Real Estate Installment Contracts: The buyer and seller may contractually agree to a direct sale of the property using a purchase money mortgage to secure the balance.

a. Payment and Title Transfer: Under these contracts, the buyer makes payments directly to the seller until the full balance of the debt is paid. Only then does the seller transfer the title to the buyer.

b. Forfeiture: If the buyer stops paying, the seller may declare the contract forfeited. In theory, the seller keeps all the payments received to date. Many states require a judicial foreclosure on contract defaults if the buyer has paid a substantial portion of the price. A deficiency judgment is not usually allowed in a contract foreclosure.

D. Instrument and Recording Requirements

1. SADD Requirements: In order to be valid as a conveyance, the mortgage instrument must be written and meet the following **SADD** requirements:

a. SOF: A mortgage must be signed by the party owning the property to be encumbered. If a mortgage for jointly owned property is involved, it may become a lien on the entire property, but the non-signing joint Ts are not responsible.

b. Acknowledgment: The signatures must be acknowledged before a notary.

c. Description: The instrument must contain such a description of the land that it can be properly and clearly identified.

d. Delivery: The mortgage must be delivered and accepted.

2. Recording: A mortgage is usually subject to the race-notice recording statute applicable to deeds. The theory is, "First in time is first in right."

a. Constructive Notice: Filing at the county seat where the real property is located establishes priority and constructive notice to any subsequent lender that there is a prior superior position against the property.

b. Subsequent Bona Fide Mortgagee: A subsequent bona fide (**FINS**) mortgagee who files first has a priority over an unrecorded prior interest. The student should review the three types of recording statute discussed above in the deed section.

MBE Tip: Recording of deeds and mortgages are heavily tested on the MBE.

E. Due on Sale Clause

Unless prohibited in the instrument, the mortgagor has the right to assign the indebtedness to a buyer of the property. A "due on sale" clause accelerates all the remaining principal due on the debt if the property is sold. This requires the immediate payment of the balance and/or a renegotiation of the interest rates.

F. Transfer of Mortgages

This occurs if the owner sells the property encumbered by a pre-existing mortgage (or other) liability. The question is whether the new buyer has direct liability to the previous mortgagee (bank). An example is where there is a subsequent default and the foreclosure sale brings less money than the mortgage note balance.

1. Express Assumption: If the new buyer-grantee "expressly assumes" the mortgage she, like the mortgagor, is liable for a deficiency judgment if the debt exceeds the property proceeds. The assignee has entered into a promise with the assignor to pay the debt. The mortgagee bank is thus a third party beneficiary of the assignee's new promise and may sue either the assignor or the assignee or both for any deficiency amount.

2. Subject To: A buyer who takes the land "subject to" the mortgage avoids the possibility of a suit from the mortgagee bank seeking a deficiency judgment against them. An example is a grantee of a quitclaim deed where there is not a new promise or the buyer takes without knowledge of a prior mortgage. The mortgagee bank would be limited to retrieving the property and any claims which could be asserted against the original mortgagor. No deficiency can be asserted against the buyer.

3. Novation: The original mortgagor remains liable to the mortgagee bank even after an express assumption by a new buyer-grantee. A release or novation would be necessary to terminate the mortgagor's potential liability to the mortgagee bank.

MBE Tip: The potential liability for covenants that run and the deficiency judgment are the major differences between subsequent parties taking under an assumption and taking subject to. Possessors taking subject to still have privity of estate, but the lack of privity of contract negates responsibility for personal covenants of the original obligor.

G. Negotiation of Mortgage Note

The mortgage follows the note. The note may be negotiated to a holder-in-due-course who takes clear of personal defenses such as a breach of warranty. If the mortgagor continues to pay the original mortgagee after receiving notice of the assignment (or refuses to pay the HDC based upon an allegation of fraud in the inducement or breach of warranty in the original purchase), the HDC may foreclose on the mortgage.

H. Equitable Mortgage

An equitable mortgage is defined as an instrument that fails to meet the formal requirements for a mortgage. An equitable mortgage arises from a transaction that is an attempt or offer to pledge land as security for a debt. The intention of the parties is controlling, and creates an equitable mortgage even though the conveyance lacks the formal requisites of a mortgage or is expressed in inept or non-technical language. A court of equity may regard the instrument, technically deficient as a mortgage, as binding between the parties to the same extent as if the instrument were a properly executed mortgage.

MBE Tip: Look for a fact pattern where (1) the intent of the parties was to create an interest in particular real property to secure the payment of a debt, (2) the secured parties transferred the property or made the loan, but (3) some of the mortgage formalities were overlooked.

I. Financing Instrument Remedies

1. Foreclosure: In case of default by the debtor, foreclosure is the means by which the creditor may reach the land to satisfy the debt. All parties with an interest in the property that the foreclosing party seeks to eliminate are necessary parties to the action. There are two main types:

a. Judicial Foreclosure: The creditor initiates this action by lawsuit, and the disposition sale of the property is typically ordered by the court. The actual sale is usually conducted by a sheriff or other government official.

b. Private Foreclosure: Some states that use deeds of trust or private real estate installment contracts permit private foreclosures if the borrower defaults. In such cases, the sale must be commercially reasonable. State rules often impose other limitations as compared to judicial foreclosures, such as requiring that the creditor accept the private foreclosure sale proceeds as full satisfaction of the debt (no deficiency judgment against debtor).

c. Deficiency Judgment: The deficiency is the difference between what the mortgage debtor owed the foreclosing creditor and the net proceeds received at the foreclosure sale. If there is an express agreement for the payment of the sum of money secured, a foreclosure decree may provide that the deficiency judgment will be entered against the mortgage debtor. If a mortgage deficiency is sought by the creditor, the redemption period is one year in most states (see discussion infra).

d. Homestead Exemptions: The federal bankruptcy laws allow a bankruptcy homestead exemption, which typically includes both the owner's dwelling and the land upon which it sits. It is the higher of the federal or state dollar amount and is protected against judgment attachment or forced sale. Generally, these homestead exemptions are subordinate to a mortgage or deed of trust, mechanics' liens, child support obligation, and spousal maintenance, but are effective against other creditors.

2. Second Mortgages: The process for obtaining and recording a second mortgage is the same as a first mortgage.

a. Priority: The difference is that the second mortgage is subordinate to the first; if the second mortgagee forecloses, forcing a sale of the property, the first mortgagee must be fully paid before the second mortgagee receives anything. If this does not occur, their senior position is not affected by the sale. The purchaser at the foreclosure sale initiated by the second mortgagee would take subject to any balance owed the senior interest. In turn, the second mortgagee proceeds have priority over subsequent mortgagees and general creditors.

b. First Position Foreclosure: In comparison, if the first position conducts the sale and the junior interests are joined as a party, the second interest is eliminated.

MBE Tip: On the MBE, unless the facts state to the contrary, assume a purchaser at a foreclosure sale takes free and clear title. This means the senior interest receives the balance of their obligation in full before the second position shares in the proceeds.

---

3. Redemption: States vary on whether the debtor may recover the property after a foreclosure proceeding has begun. Redemption usually has a basis in equity and/or is authorized by a statute of the state.

a. Equity: Some courts allow redemption in equity, meaning that the defaulting debtor may pay off all mortgages in full and recover the property. This right generally may be exercised up to the foreclosure sale.

b. State Statute: Some states have statutes that permit debtors to pay off defaulted mortgages up to, and often after the foreclosure sale and still recover the property. The length of time varies, but six months or one year is frequent. Only a few states would allow a debtor to reinstate the mortgage by bringing the delinquent payments current.

J. Impact of Mortgage Foreclosure on Lease

If property under lease is subject to a mortgage, the impact of the foreclosure on the lease depends upon which was first in time. If the lease was first in time, the foreclosing mortgage holder takes the property subject to the remaining lease term. If the lease was signed after the mortgage was executed, the lease is terminated.

XI. OWNER'S RIGHTS

A. Possession Rights

The owner or possessor of land has the right to possession and to exclude anyone else from trespassing thereupon. An eviction action is designed to oust a trespasser. This may be the remedy for a personal physical invasion without permission, a building encroachment over the property line, or to terminate an adverse possessor.

B. Support Rights

Adjacent landowners have a duty under common law not to diminish substantially lateral or subjacent support of their neighbor's property. This duty is absolute (strict liability) for land in its natural condition. Damage to artificial structures is not usually recoverable since the lateral property support requirement does not traditionally include improvements such as houses or other structures. Remedies for such damages are normally pursued through tort claims for negligence.

1. Lateral Support: An adjoining property owner cannot remove the natural lateral support of adjacent land. The owner has the burden to prove that the neighbor's excavation caused the damage.

2. Subjacent Support: The sub-surface rights (mineral, oil, gas, etc.) may be severed from the surface rights. A miner must frame the removed underground dirt with sufficient support so the surface does not fall into the tunnel. A few states extend this requirement to the foundations of existing adjacent buildings that sink.

MBE Tip: For questions involving the lateral or subjacent support rights of adjacent land, distinguish between recoverable damage to the land itself and non-recoverable damage to artificial improvements like houses.

C. Resource Rights

1. Air Rights:

a. Common Law: A landowner owns the surface land, the subterranean soil underneath, and the airspace above. The airspace right applies only up to a reasonable height, but an overhead electrical line would need an easement.

b. Reasonable Overflights: High uses, such as commercial aircraft, are not a trespass, but may be a nuisance. Also an inverse condemnation action may be the remedy for taking property without compensation. An example would be increased jet plane noise from additional traffic patterns when a major international airport adds more runways.

c. Construction Height: Absent a zoning or building code restriction, a property owner can build a structure to the heavens.

d. Access to Above-Ground Natural Resources: Neighbors do not usually acquire an implied or prescriptive easement to unrestricted wind, sunlight, or view access. In comparison, an express grant creating such rights would likely be enforceable. However, an adjacent property owner using wind power or sunlight as an energy source might argue that a new tall building constitutes a nuisance.

2. Below-Ground Natural Resources Rights: A purchaser of property receives the right to all the natural resources thereon and therein unless the grantor specifically reserves such rights. Examples would include gold, oil, natural gas, standing timber, etc. However, a holder of a life estate may not commit natural resource waste that materially lessens the value of the future reversion or remainder interest.

3. Water Rights: Water rights are of increased importance.

a. Underground Water: Under the common law, percolating spring water or underground aquifer water could be withdrawn from a well without limit by the property owner. At present, the majority US rule is that there is no limit on reasonable withdrawal for use on the owner's land even though it may lower the water table in the area or otherwise adversely affect the neighbors. However, if the owner withdraws unreasonable amounts such as using the water elsewhere or selling it commercially, it must not damage the reasonable needs of the neighboring property owners.

b. Surface Water:

(1) Riparian Rights:

(a) Reasonable Use: For owners adjoining a lake or river, the majority rule is that a reasonable riparian use is recognized. Reasonableness depends upon the purpose of the use, quantity withdrawn, and historical duration of the user's previous use.

(b) Use Priority: If there is insufficient supply, domestic and household needs prevail over agricultural use which prevails over commercial uses. Uses that require the water to be transported off the riparian land have the lowest priority. Upstream riparian users may not withdraw an unreasonable amount if it will deprive downstream users of a reasonable amount for their needs.

(c) Prior Appropriation System: In a minority of states, a "prior appropriation" system vests the future right to the same quantity of use. A claimant later establishing a higher priority need may take from the prior user's share, but is required to pay damages. Non-riparian water use rights are under a permit system. An example is a wheat farm not on a river, but needing access to local water for irrigation.

(2) Floods: Surface water from rain, springs, melting snow and ice following the natural contours of the land fall under the "common enemy" doctrine. Natural drainage patterns may be altered to control floods by use of dikes, blockages, diversions, artificial channels, etc., regardless of the effect on neighboring land. A few states require that diversion may not create unnecessary damage to other lands.

c. Public Rights: The public usually has access and recreational rights to lakes and navigable rivers, etc., and riparian owners may not do anything to interfere therewith.

MBE Tip: The real world water shortage dictates that water rights are increasingly likely to be tested on the MBE.

---

4. Emblements: Property rights include items such as crops growing thereon. There are two recognized categories:

a. Fructus Naturales: Included are trees, bushes, perennial shrubs, and grasses that grow continuously without human efforts. Fructus naturales remain real property until severed from the land. They pass with a conveyance of the land (unless expressly excluded) and are subject to a mortgagee's interest. A separate conveyance of these items must comply with the SOF.

b. Fructus Industriales: Included are crops that grow annually from cultivation, planting, and fertilizing such as citrus fruits, wheat, corn, and grapes. Fructus industriales are usually treated as personal property except they pass with the land unless expressly excluded. A T is entitled to the harvest of the annual crop during their tenancy and the subsequent harvest derived from the crops they planted during their tenancy. The future harvests thereafter from regenerative crops revert to the owner.

> **STOP!** Go to page 577 and work Learning Questions 48 through 52.

XII. LANDLORD AND TENANT

The lease gives the tenant/lessee (T) a nonfreehold possessory estate with the landlord/lessor (LL) retaining a reversionary interest at the end of the lease. It establishes a T's right to use property for a period of time in exchange for rent.

> **MBE Tip:** Expect 3 to 5 MBE questions covering a variety of LL-T topics. Apply the common law rules and principles unless directed otherwise by a statute described in the fact pattern.

A. Types of Tenancy and Their Requirements

Four types of tenancy are recognized in most states:

1. Term Tenancy: This is also known as a "tenancy for years." This tenancy is measured by a definite period of time, beginning and ending on specified dates. This may be 10 days, 90 days, or 5 years, but there is no right to repeat the term.

a. Termination: The tenancy automatically ends on the last day of the lease period, without any need for notice of termination. The death of either the LL or T will not terminate the lease, it will merely pass on to the respective heirs.

b. SOF: For a lease estate that lasts over one year, the majority state rule is that the agreement must be evidenced by a writing sufficient to satisfy the SOF. Some states require recording of the lease details. An oral lease exceeding one year will be treated as if it is a periodic tenancy.

c. End of Term Negotiations: If the tenancy term expires and the parties are negotiating, the court may treat the tenancy as periodic.

2. Periodic Tenancy: A periodic tenancy continues for a fixed time (such as a week or a month) that repeats until either the lessor or lessee gives notice of termination.

a. Duration: If the duration of the tenancy is not stated, the rent payments will imply the duration. For example, if rent is biweekly, it will be a two-week periodic tenancy.

b. Termination: Notice requirements to terminate a periodic tenancy are the same as the lease term itself. For a month-to-month tenancy, a month's termination notice is required. To terminate a year-to-year tenancy, the common law required six months notice; however, many states have adopted statutes that provide a different lead time, most typically 30 days. Notice must be timely given or the tenancy rights and duties will continue to repeat for another term. Either T or LL can terminate the tenancy with timely notice.

3. Tenancy at Will: The T is in possession by permission, but there is no stated duration and therefore, the lease is mutually terminable at will by either party. If the LL terminates, the T is allowed a reasonable time to vacate.

a. Invalid Provision: When there is an invalid lease (such as SOF violation for a lease over one year), a tenancy at will exists. However, as soon as the T makes a payment that the LL accepts, the tenancy is converted to a periodic tenancy.

b. Termination: Under the common law, no notice was necessary to terminate a tenancy at will; today notice as described above (equal to rent period) is usually required. This blurs the line of distinction between a tenancy at will and a periodic tenancy.

4. Tenancy at Sufferance: A T holding over after the lease has terminated is not a trespasser since the original possession was not wrongful. In such a situation, the LL is put to an election: (1) create a new periodic tenancy lease or; (2) bring an action for eviction and sue for damages. Exceptions to this election are when the LL consents to the holdover period or when the T holds over for extenuating circumstances beyond her control.

MBE Tip: Many questions deal with a T remaining on the premises beyond the term of the lease. Initially, a holdover T not evicted is treated as an at will T. If the LL accepts rent, the tenancy converts to a periodic tenancy.

B. Landlord Duties

1. Delivery Required: The majority rule today is that the LL must deliver actual possession of the premises to the T and give the T exclusive control.

a. Fitness of Premises: Under the common law, the LL made no implied warranties of habitability. The T had a duty to make a thorough inspection of the premises and took the premises as is. The LL was only liable if they had actual knowledge of serious hidden dangerous defects such as a violation of fire resistance standards, weakened stairs, or a termite/rat infestation and did not make disclosure to the T.

b. Implied Warranty of Residential Habitability: The implied warranty of habitability is usually limited to residential leases such as rental apartments. The ALI Restatement requires the LL to provide habitable premises throughout the duration of the lease such as electricity, heat, water services, and working toilets.

c. T Remedies for LL Breach: The implied warranty of habitability protects the T. Potential remedies available to the T include:

(1) Vacate and Terminate the Lease: This is the basic remedy and envisions rescission of the contract. The T may also sue for damages.

(2) Action for Damages: The T can elect to remain on the premises and seek the difference between the rent paid and the actual value of the premises in its current condition ("as is").

(3) Equitable Relief: The T may also bring an action to require the LL to comply with housing codes. Retaliatory evictions for reporting housing code violations is illegal and is to be presumed if the LL evicts the T within six months.

(4) Deduct Costs of Restoring Habitability from Rent: In almost all states, the T can do LL-required repairs and then deduct the cost from rent due. The standards vary among states, but housing code violations usually qualify; in comparison, ordinary maintenance and repairs may not. See infra discussion.

(5) Withhold Rent: In a few states, the T can withhold rent and then raise the implied warranty of habitability as a defense if the LL brings action. In many states, this rent must be paid into a court-administered escrow account.

2. Implied Covenant of Quiet Enjoyment: The LL promises to not interfere with the T's use and enjoyment of the premises. Breach of the covenant can be actual or constructive. An eviction can be a breach of the implied covenant of quiet enjoyment.

a. Eviction: An actual eviction is a physical ouster. A constructive eviction is one in which the LL interferes with the T's use of the property or where the LL fails to keep the premises in a condition that is required for the T's enjoyment of the property, making it uninhabitable. An example of constructive eviction would be shutting off the water, electricity, or heat.

b. Acts by Third Parties: Acts by third parties usually do not constitute a constructive eviction; it must be something that the LL is directly responsible for. However, a LL is usually responsible for acts of Ts that are a nuisance to other Ts on the property.

c. T Remedies for LL Breach: If the LL breaches quiet enjoyment, the T has the right to terminate the lease and vacate the premises, owing no further rents. This right to terminate must be exercised within a reasonable time after the LL's breach or else it is waived. Many states require the T to give the LL prior notice so there is an opportunity to cure. The T must vacate for constructive eviction; if she remains in the premise, the rent obligation continues, but there may be a claim for damages.

MBE Tip: Even though the LL breaches the covenant of quiet enjoyment or implied warranty of habitability, look for T waiver, no notice, or a failure to vacate.

---

3. Repairs: At common law, the LL was under no duty to repair and maintain the premises. Modern courts and the Restatement have changed this rule especially as it involves residential property. And a LL who negligently undertakes repairs – her responsibility or not – is liable in tort for damages caused by the repairs.

4. Deposits: Treatment of a deposit taken in by a LL from a T depends upon the label placed on the deposit. A "security deposit" can only be used to repair damage to the property; any unused portion must be returned to the T. "Last month's rent" can be retained by the LL. A "non-refundable fee" paid to the LL for preparing and accepting the lease can be retained by the LL.

5. Retaliatory Eviction: The Restatement and statutes in a majority of states deem an eviction retaliatory if the LL evicts a T within 90 to 180 days of certain T acts. They include reporting housing or building code violations or otherwise validly complaining to authorities or other Ts. The T may sue for damages or an injunction.

MBE Tip: If an act that causes a breach of the covenant of quiet enjoyment is not created by the LL, consider whether the LL is obligated to remedy the situation.

C. T Duties

The lease will normally contain many duties that the T covenants to perform. These requirements are for the LL's benefit and may not usually be enforced by third parties.

1. Payment of Rent: The T has the duty to pay rent timely including utilities unless agreed to the contrary. The T is not usually excused from paying the rent even if the LL breaches an obligation of the lease. The obligations of each are mutually exclusive, so breach by one does not usually excuse performance by the other.

a. Exceptions: The T does not have to pay rent if: (1) the T and LL agree to terminate the lease; (2) the LL has expressly accepted the T's offer of premise surrender or if there is an intent to accept surrender such as using the premises; (3) the LL actually or constructively evicts the T; or (4) T has made repairs (see Implied Warranty of Habitability discussion above).

MBE Tip: A T's surrender, and a LL's acceptance of surrender, must be in writing to satisfy the Statue of Frauds, if the lease also had to be in writing (usually over one year).

---

b. LL Provision: Since the obligation to pay rent and right to possess the property are exclusive of each other, it would seem the LL could not evict a T for non-payment of the rent. To protect themselves, most LLs put a clause in the lease allowing them the right to evict for non-payment. Most states also have a statute for unlawful detainer that gives the LL the right to evict and sue for any unpaid rent, after proper notice is given. A statute will specify the minimum required time period for notice in the state.

2. Use Restrictions: If the lease contains a use restriction, it is usually binding on the T. An example is "the premises shall be used for a school and no other use is allowed without the prior written approval of the LL." Any other use breaches the lease contract.

3. Maintain Premises: In addition to any express covenants in the lease, the below common law rules apply in most states.

a. Repair: Day-to-day ordinary repairs are the responsibility of the T. Most leases contain a T's covenant to repair including liability to persons injured from failure to repair or negligent repair.

b. Waste: A lease T has the duty not to damage the premises beyond ordinary wear and tear. Damage extending beyond the end of the lease term, done either intentionally or through negligence, may constitute waste similar to a life T's duty not to injure or deplete the LL's reversion.

c. Insure and Taxes: In the absence of any provision in the lease, the T is under no duty to insure the premises or to pay taxes.

d. Alteration and Restoration:

(1) T Liability: The T may be liable to the LL for any changes and alterations to the property, even improvements. The T is also normally responsible for the cost of restoring the property to its original condition.

(2) Chattel Removal: Chattels and trade fixtures may be removed by the T only if it does not cause damage to the LL's reversionary interest. See the detailed discussion at the beginning of the chapter.

(3) Ameliorative Waste: This results from the T changing the nature or use of the premises. An example is converting a commercial rental to residential uses.

(a) Negative Ameliorative Waste: The LL may seek an injunction to stop the conversion of the property's use. If the T's activity reduces the value of the premises, the T is liable for the cost of restoration to the original use.

(b) Positive Ameliorative Waste: Courts may deny the LL a recovery for ameliorative waste resulting from T improvements if they increase the value of the premises. The change must be consistent with an overall similar change in the character of the neighborhood. An example is a T who improved a personal residence to use the space for commercial purposes that commands a higher rental amount in the market.

e. T Property Removal: Ts may remove their own personal property (pictures and furniture). At common law, fixtures such as furnace and heat ducts could not be removed if they became affixed to the real property. Today, residential Ts may usually remove fixtures and appliances that they added unless the removal would damage the structure.

f. T Guests: Ts are responsible for any acts of their guests that create damages to the property.

MBE Tip: Many exam questions come from the topics of duty to repair, waste, alteration of the premises, restoration so not to injure the reversionary interest, and property removal by the T.

---

4. Non-Disturbance: The T is under a duty not to create a nuisance or otherwise unreasonably disturb the other Ts.

5. Tort Liability: The T is treated like an owner for injuries occurring in areas where the T has exclusive control. Ts are liable for damages that they or their guests and pets cause. The LL has tort liability for injuries occurring in common areas such as hallways, stairwells, elevators, and exterior parking lots and gardens. A LL is also responsible for injuries resulting from a hidden defect if she had knowledge of the defect or if she negligently made repairs.

> **MBE Tip:** Since possession and rent are independent obligations, a T may remain liable for payment of a lease when the property has been destroyed due to the T's negligence or intentional act. Under the common law, this rule applies in cases where the leased premises consist of land and all of a building. If the T only occupied part of a building and it was destroyed, the requirement to pay rent is terminated.

D. LL Remedies

1. T Abandons Property: If a T quits the premises and defaults on the lease, a LL may:

a. Take Possession: The LL may surrender her rights to future rents by re-entering the premises and taking possession; this usually relieves the T of all future obligations. Some states have LL-T statutes that prohibit the LL taking possession without a court order (self-help) or without involvement of a public official, such as a sheriff.

b. Hold T Responsible: The LL can hold the T to his contractual obligation and sue for each rent payment as it comes due. Many states though, require the LL to mitigate the damages by attempting to re-let the premises. If a LL fails to mitigate, his right to recover from the T is limited.

c. Re-Lease the Property: Following a T's surrender, the LL can re-lease the property and hold the T responsible for any deficiency in the rent. The LL must first give the T notice that the surrender was not accepted and that the T is liable for rent deficiencies.

2. Anticipatory Repudiation: In some states, once an unequivocal anticipatory repudiation is given by the T, the LL is allowed to terminate the lease. An example is the T surrenders the premises, returns the keys, and states that they are quitting the premises.

a. Past Due Rent: All states allow a LL's suit for any past rent due. Many states permit recovery of the total future rents owed to the end of the lease term, especially for commercial tenancies. This is called an acceleration clause.

b. Accrual Rule: Other states exclude damages for the executory portion of the contract until the time the rent actually accrues. The theory is that the LL must mitigate the damages by making a reasonable effort to re-lease the property to another T on an ongoing basis. Any rents received should be deducted from any damages owed by the original T.

3. Mitigation Duty: In many states – probably a slight majority today – a LL has a duty to mitigate damages and cannot just let the premises sit empty thereby piling up damages. Especially for a residential lease, there must be a reasonable attempt to re-let the space for the remainder of the rental term. But this does not mean that the LL must accept a new use or otherwise rent the premises to unacceptable Ts.

E. Assignment and Sublease

Ts have the right to assign or sublease any portion of their leasehold interest to a third party unless these rights are expressly prohibited by the lease. These are independent rights; a transfer prohibition on assignment does not automatically prohibit a sublease. If such a prohibition exists and the LL accepts a rent payment from either the assignee or sublessee, the LL's right to enforce the transfer prohibition may thereafter be waived. (*Dumpor* case.)

1. T Assignment: An assignment is a transfer of the T's entire space and time remaining interest to a third party. This terminates the physical estate of the original T.

a. Assignor Remains Liable: The original T assignor remains contractually liable to the LL unless the LL specifically releases the assignor of all responsibility.

b. Assignee Liability: An assignee comes into privity of estate and becomes directly liable to the LL. Under a third party beneficiary theory, the assignee is responsible for covenants that run with (touch and concern) the land. This includes the promise to pay rent, taxes, insure, repair, and maintain the premises. In comparison, a personal covenant by the T to baby-sit the LL's children does not touch and concern the land.

2. Sublease: In a sublease, the original T retains a reversion by not giving up all of the estate's space, time, or dollar rent to the sublessee. The original T transfers less than all the square footage or the sublease is not for the full executory term. A sublessee has no direct obligation to the LL on the lease if they abandon. Absent a release, the original lessee remains liable to the LL if the sublessee does not perform. The sublessee is only liable to the original T.

3. LL Assignment, Sale, or Encumbrance:

a. Rent Assignment: The LL may assign their right to receive the rents to a third party. After the Ts are given notice of the assignment, they must pay the assignee.

b. Sale of Premises: The right to receive rent and future reversions may be assigned by the LL upon sale of the property. After receiving notice, the T must recognize and pay the new owner. Sale of the premises by the LL or death of the LL has no affect upon the T's lease interest unless such a condition subsequent was specified in the lease contract.

c. Property Mortgage: The lessor may give a mortgage to a creditor containing an assignment of rents clause that takes effect if the lessor defaults on the mortgage. All Ts are bound by the assignment and after notice must pay the mortgagee. Lessees' rights in place before the LL-mortgagee creation date are not affected by the lessor's default on the mortgage. Junior lessees who execute their leases after the mortgage was recorded may be dispossessed and their leases cancelled by the mortgagee.

F. Frustration of Purpose

It may become impractical or impossible for the T to use the premises for the planned purpose. Examples include the sole specified premises use becoming illegal or governmental action. In such a case, the lease contract may be discharged.

G. Lease Termination

1. In General:

a. Surrender Before Term: Surrender includes a T abandoning a dwelling if they are behind in the rent coupled with some indication of an intention not to continue the tenancy. The T has rent liability for the full contract term even if the lease is surrendered.

b. Mitigation Necessary: A LL has a duty to mitigate damages and cannot let the premises sit empty thereby piling up damages. There must be a reasonable attempt made to re-rent the space for the remainder of the rental term. But this does not usually mean that a LL must accept a new T with a different use.

c. Non-Renewal: Most states require notice on or before a specified number of days before the lease's expiration if the T wishes to renew the lease.

2. Condemnation by Eminent Domain:
Condemnation of the entire property ownership by a government agency through eminent domain terminates the lease. If the taking is only partial, the T is not discharged from the entire rent obligation.

a. Award Distribution: Both the LL and T share in the award as their financial interests may lie. Typically a lump-sum award is given for the entire fee ownership including both the leasehold and the LL's reversion.

b. T Portion: The T is entitled to the difference between the value of the business lease estate less the present value of the lease obligation owed to the LL. This always results in an award if the lease was at a bargain rent rate or the T had a fixed dollar option to purchase that was less than the award. If the T can show substantial business goodwill which would be lost if the business is forced to move, there may be an award. The longer the lease term, the higher the financial interest which might be awarded.

3. Mortgage Foreclosure:
In most states, a tenancy legally ends with a foreclosure if the mortgage security interest in the property predated the T's lease. The new owner can force a T to surrender and quit the property.

4. Merger:
Termination may also be by merger where the T purchases the premises or the LL purchases the lease. If the property is taken by condemnation, both the leasehold and reversion interests merge in the taker.

STOP! Go to page 578 and work Learning Questions 53 through 60.

XIII. ESTATES IN LAND

Up to 20% of the MBE tests the various present and future interests. This is not the easiest of information to learn and understand, but try to get as much of the basics as possible.

A. Present Interests and Their Accompanying Future Interests in Land

The classification of an interest in land is determined by the granting language used to convey the property. With the exception of a fee simple absolute, all present interests in land are accompanied by future interests in the same land.

1. Fee Simple: A fee simple is a present estate of potentially infinite duration. Fee simples may be non-defeasible (absolute) or defeasible.

a. Fee Simple Absolute: The characteristics of a fee simple absolute are indefinite duration, freely inheritable, and transferable during life. The usual language is "to A" or "to A and his heirs." There is no future interest that may defease the fee. Every estate is presumed to be a fee simple absolute unless the language of the grant is clearly to the contrary; thus fee simple absolute is the default estate.

b. Defeasible Fee Simple: A defeasible fee simple is an estate that may terminate upon a certain event. All defeasible fee simples have an accompanying future interest in favor of either the grantor (reverter) or a third person (remainder).

> **MBE Tip:** Be sure the language creating the future interest requires that a certain event occur and that the objective is not just a motive or wish by the grantor ("to A who I hope will continue to use the land as a farm."). Also look for a mere covenant by the grantee ("to my son if he promises to continue the farm operation") that, if breached, may create damages but not a future interest.

(1) Fee Simple Determinable (Automatic Termination): This is used to prevent the property from being put to a predefined use that the grantor feels is undesirable.

(a) Present Estate: A fee simple determinable is defeasible (terminates) upon the occurrence of a triggering event. "To A so long as the property is used only as a school." If the property is ever used for a non-school purpose, the land automatically reverts to the grantor. A has a present fee simple determinable and the grantor has a future possibility of reverter.

> **MBE Tip:** The technical language of duration used to create a fee simple determinable includes words of duration such as "while," "so long as," or "until."

(b) Future Interest: A possibility of reverter always follows a fee simple determinable. As long as the triggering event does not occur, the grantee retains possession in fee simple. Because the land could possibly revert to the grantor, however, it is termed a "fee simple determinable with a possibility of reverter." The possibility of reverter is a property interest that may be transferred inter vivos, by will, or through intestacy.

(2) Fee Simple Subject to a Condition Subsequent (Termination Requires Reentry):

(a) Present Estate: A fee simple subject to a condition subsequent is defeasible (terminates) upon the occurrence of a specified event; however, the forfeiture is not automatic. The forfeiture requires some affirmative step by the grantor (or heirs) to retake the property. "To A, but if the property is used for the sale of liquor, then the grantor may enter and retake the premises." The occurrence of the defined condition triggers the right of reentry.

MBE Tip: The technical language of duration used to create a fee simple subject to a condition subsequent and right of reentry includes words of condition, such as "on condition that," "subject to the condition that," "provided that," or "but if...." There must also be some wording indicating that if the condition occurs, the grantor must then make some affirmative movement to reenter the premises.

(b) Future Interest: A right of entry always follows a fee simple subject to a condition subsequent. The grantee's fee simple is not automatically forfeited upon the happening of the triggering condition (as in a fee simple determinable). It will revert to the grantor only if the right of entry is exercised.

(1) Waiver of Right: Failure to exercise the right of entry within a reasonable period of time of the condition occurring may constitute waiver of the right. This will serve to bar the grantor (or heirs) from retaking the premises.

(2) Transfer Only Upon Death: In a majority of states, the future right of entry can be transferred only at death by will or by intestacy. Inter vivos transfers are not valid.

(3) Fee Simple Subject to an Executory Interest: If the potential future interest may pass to a third party, it is termed an executory interest.

(a) Present Estate: A fee simple subject to an executory interest is created when a conveyance automatically passes to a third party upon the occurrence of a triggering event. "To A as long as he farms the homestead, and if not, then to B." A has a fee simple subject to an executory interest, and B has a potential future executory interest.

MBE Tip: A fee simple subject to an executory interest is created when either words of duration ("so long as," "until," etc.) or words of condition ("on condition that," "but if," etc.) are used to convey title automatically to a third party upon the happening of a triggering event.

(b) Future Interest: A future interest in a third person (other than the grantor) follows a fee simple subject to an executory interest. This future interest is subject to the rule against perpetuities.

(1) Shifting Executory Interest: A shifting executory interest causes possession to cut short or shift from one grantee to another. "To A in fee simple, but if (or until) A sells liquor on the property, then to B." Note that in this example, the land immediately shifts to B when A sells liquor.

(2) Springing Executory Interest: The grantor has a reversion, but it springs to a third party at a later time. A springing executory interest divests the grantor on the happening of some event in the future. "To A in fee simple until A sells liquor on the property, then one day later to B." Note that in this example, the land reverts to the grantor when A sells the liquor and springs forth one day later from the grantor to B.

STOP! Go to page 579 and work Learning Questions 61 to 65.

---

2. Fee Tail: The fee tail was created at common law with the words "To A and the heirs of her body." The purpose of this estate was to keep possession of property in the family for generations.

a. Modern Rule: Modern property law favors a policy of free alienability of property rights. Consequently, the fee tail estate has been abolished by statute in most U.S. states. Words of purchase purporting to create a fee tail estate will have no limiting effect, and, in most states, the primary grantee takes in fee simple absolute.

b. Executory Interest: The granting language may specify an alternative taker if the life estate grantee dies without issue. "To A and the heirs of her body, but if A dies without issue, then to B." A minority of states would give A a fee simple subject to an executory limitation. In those states, B would get the property in fee simple absolute if A dies without issue.

3. Life Estate: A life estate is a noninheritable, transferable estate for the duration of a named person's life. Upon the death of the measuring life, the life estate terminates, and the remaining interest goes back to either the grantor (a "reversion") or to a third party (a "remainder").

a. Present Interest: The estate is the length of the named person's life.

(1) Grantee's Life: A life estate can be measured by the life of the grantee: "To A for life." A could transfer the estate to B, but A remains the measuring life.

(2) Pur Autre Vie: "Pur autre vie" is a life estate for the life of a third party: "To A for B's life." It is important to note that the life estate continues for the duration of the named person's life (B), even if the tenant (A) pre-deceases the third party. Upon A's death, A's heirs would take the pur autre vie estate until B's death.

(3) Dower and Curtesy: The life estate is created for the surviving spouse provided there were children from the marriage. Dower is the related estate for a widow and curtesy is for a widower. Almost all states have abolished an inchoate (unexpressed) right to such an estate, but it may be expressly created.

b. Doctrine of Waste: The holder of a life estate or other temporary or joint interest in land (such as a tenant) has a duty not to materially reduce the value of the future reversion or remainder.

(1) Physical Waste: Consuming or selling extracted non-renewable resources of the land such as coal, oil, or other minerals are examples of waste. Waste may also result from the possessor's allowing the property to deteriorate without taking appropriate steps to prevent or repair it. Using farmland to grow and harvest crops is not waste. It is also not waste for a life tenant to cut timber in a reasonable amount, especially if she replants.

(2) Economic Waste: A life tenant may encumber her interest in the property, but such may not adversely affect the future reversion or remainder. Examples include a mortgage given or lease entered into by the life tenant. The mortgage or lease is limited to whatever interest the life tenant possessed.

c. Future Interest: This commences at the death of the life tenant.

(1) Reversion, if the Land Goes Back to Grantor: If no provisions have been made for disposition of the estate upon termination of the present life estate, the land automatically "reverts" back to the grantor. "To A for life." The grantor has a future interest in the estate known as "reversion." A reversion may be transferred inter vivos, by will, or through intestacy.

> **MBE Tip:** As a general rule concerning the grantor's future interest: (1) a possibility of reverter only follows a fee simple determinable; (2) a right of entry only follows a fee simple subject to a condition subsequent; and (3) a reversion only follows a life estate.

(2) Remainder, if the Land Goes to a Third Person: Where provisions have been made in the grant for transfer of the estate to a third person upon termination of the present life estate, the third person has a future interest known as "remainder." Remainders may either be vested or contingent.

(a) Vested Remainder: A remainder will automatically vest at the creation of the life estate if (1) the granting language is unconditional and (2) the grantee of the remainder is ascertained. "To A for life, then to B." A has a life estate, and B has a vested remainder in fee simple. This vested remainder is certain to become possessory and thus is alienable inter vivos, is inheritable and is devisable.

(b) Vested Remainder Subject to Open (Divestment): This applies when a gift is created in a class of persons (usually children) and at least one member of the class takes a vested remainder at the time the gift is created. The vested remainder is subject to open if more people could later join the class. "To B for life, then to the children of A." At grantor's death, A has one child, D, who takes a vested remainder subject to open (partial divestment) if A has any more children.

(c) Contingent Remainder: A remainder will be contingent only if (1) the grantee of the remainder is unascertainable or (2) the potential future interest must satisfy some condition precedent before the interest will vest. "To A for life, remainder to B if B marries before A's death." A has a life estate, B has a contingent remainder. A contingent remainder is not alienable, inheritable, or devisable until it vests.

Another example is "To A for life, then to such of B's children who are alive at B's death." A has a life estate; B's unborn children have an open class contingent remainder in fee simple that will not vest (or close) until all B's surviving children are ascertained at B's death. A contingent remainder is not certain to become possessory and thus is not alienable, inheritable, or devisable until it vests; in this case, at B's death. Contingent remainders are potentially subject to the rule against perpetuities (RAP) (see discussion below).

(d) Power of Appointment: The grant may give the life tenant the future right to pick (appoint) the remainder person. "To A for life and upon her death to those whom she may designate." This potential remainder becomes a reversion if not exercised and is not subject to the RAP.

MBE Tip on Remainders:	1.	Remainders only follow life estates – never a fee interest.
	2.	Remainders never cut short a prior estate.
	3.	Remainders are always created at the same time and with the same instrument as the present interest that precedes it.
	4.	There is never a gap between a life estate and a remainder.
	5.	If there is a gap between a life estate and a future interest, the interest is executory (either springing or shifting), not a remainder.

STOP! Go to page 580 and work Learning Questions 66 to 70.

4. Common Law Rules Governing Remainders:

a. Destructibility of Contingent Remainders: This common law rule requires that any contingent remainder must vest prior to or upon termination of the preceding estate or else it is destroyed. In "to A for life, remainder to B's children alive at B's death," if all of B's children predecease him, the contingent remainder is destroyed and the property reverts to the grantor.

b. Doctrine of Merger: When the same person holds both the life estate and the reversion or a vested remainder, the life estate and the vested future interest merge to create a larger estate. "To Z for life." If the grantor subsequently conveys his reversion to Z, Z holds both the life estate and the reversion, and therefore holds the estate in fee simple absolute.

c. Rule in Shelley's Case (Abolished in Most States):

(1) Common Law Rule: If an instrument conveys a freehold estate, typically a life estate, to an individual, and a remainder to the heirs of the same individual, that individual takes both the freehold estate and the remainder; the heirs take nothing. "To A for life, then to A's heirs." According to the Rule in Shelley's Case, A has a fee simple absolute.

(2) Modern Rule: Most states have abolished the Rule in Shelley's Case by statute. Today, therefore, A would have a life estate and the heirs of A would have a contingent remainder.

d. Doctrine of Worthier Title: At common law, a person could not grant or devise to his or her own heirs the same estate that the heirs would have taken by inheritance. If A grants Greenacre "To B for life, remainder to A's heirs," B has a life estate, and A holds a reversion in fee simple absolute. The majority of states continue to follow this rule.

B. Rule Against Perpetuities (RAP)

The RAP is designed to prevent grantors from restricting the free transferability of property by tying it up with contingent future interests. A contingent future interest not reserved to the grantor is not valid unless it is certain to vest within 21 years of the death of some life in being at the time of the creation of the interest. The life in being is usually specified in the grant.

> **MBE Tip:** The only future interests subject to the RAP are executory interests, open class remainders, and contingent remainders. Thus, the Rule does not apply to reversions, possibilities of reverter, rights of entry, vested remainders, and charitable trusts.

1. Period Begins: The time period begins to run for an inter-vivos transfer when deed is delivered to the first designated grantee. For a testamentary transfer, the testator's death triggers the time period.

2. RAP Applied:

    a. Example: "Blackacre into trust for A and her heirs, but if liquor is ever sold on the property, then to B and her heirs." A is the measuring life (person alive at the time the interest is created who can affect vesting). B's contingent remainder is void for violating the RAP because A and B could die and 21 years later liquor could be sold on the property.

    b. Distinguish: The measuring life is the key. Compare granting language that stated, "To A and her heirs, but if A ever sells liquor on the property, then to B and her heirs." This conveyance would not violate the RAP because B's interest will necessarily vest or fail within A's lifetime.

3. Violating Portion: If you do determine that a RAP violation exists, merely strike the portion of the conveyance (and the related interest) that offends the rule.

4. Result: If the conveyance's conditional wording was "but if," the previous interest gets a fee simple absolute and the grantor has nothing. If the wording was "so long as" the previous interest gets a fee simple determinable and the grantor a possibility of reverter.

> **MBE Tip:** For each measuring life, ask yourself, "Is there any way that the interest might fail or not vest within 21 years of the death of this measuring life?" If you can answer "no" as to all measuring lives, the interest is good. Thus, you are looking for that one person about whom you can say that the interest may not vest within 21 years after such person's death.

5. Common RAP Problems:

    a. The Unborn Widow: This addresses a grant to a widow in the future. An example is "To X for life, remainder to X's widow for life, remainder to X's children who survive X's widow." The contingent remainder to X's surviving children is invalid under the RAP. The RAP presumes that X, even if he is an elderly man at the time of the conveyance, could remarry a woman who is not a life in being at the time the interest is created.

    b. The Fertile Octogenarian: This rule assumes that any person, regardless of physical condition or age, may parent children in the future, even if biologically impossible.

        (1) Example: An example is "To A for life, remainder to her children for their lives, remainder to her grandchildren who reach the age of 25." A is 80 years old and has two children, B and C, and no grandchildren alive at the time the interest is created. The contingent remainder in A's potential grandchildren is invalid under the RAP.

        (2) Problem: In the above example, B and C could die tomorrow. Next year, A could have an afterborn child, D, who could in turn have a child who reaches the age of 25 more than 21 years after the death of B and C. Thus, the interest is void.

c. Class Gifts: Watch for a class of "remainders subject to open" that might obtain new member after the grantor's death. This will violate the RAP. The gift will fail unless the interest of each class member vests within 21 years of a life in being. An example is "To A and then to A's children who attain 20 years of age." Since A is the measuring life and could have a child more than one year after they take, the RAP would strike down the remainder.

MBE Tip: Class gifts to the testator's grandchildren contained in a will ("devise") are usually valid because the measuring lives are established on the testator's death ("all my grandchildren" or "my daughter's children then alive"). If created in an inter-vivos transfer ("grant" or "conveyance") or to the spouse's children, the chances of a RAP violation increase because after-born children, unborn widow, and fertile octogenarian problems are more likely.

---

d. Gifts to Charities: The RAP does not apply to trusts in which all vested interests are charitable. Also, a shifting interest from one charity to another does not violate the RAP. But if the interest goes first to a non-charitable interest and the charity's contingent interest is a remainder, the RAP applies. An example is "To Betty so long as the land is used exclusively for farming, then to Land Conservatory." The contingent remainder to Land Conservancy fails. But if Betty were a charity, the contingent remainder would be good.

e. "Wait and See" Rule: Some states have adopted a "wait and see" statute. This approach uses the time of vesting rather than the time of creation of the interest and waits to see if the interest vest before 21 years after the interest is created. This is the opposite of the common law rule that finds the interest invalid if it might violate the rule during a life in being plus 21 years, regardless of the outcome.

C. Restraints on Alienation

There are three types of restraints on alienation of a fee simple that the law disfavors. All of them are void in most states. The three types of restraints on alienation are "disabling," "forfeiture," and "promissory."

1. Disabling: "To A, but A shall not have the power to transfer the land without my consent." The effect is that A has a fee simple absolute.

2. Forfeiture: "To A, but if A attempts to transfer without my consent, the land shall automatically revert to me." The effect is that A has a fee simple absolute.

3. Promissory: "To A, but A promises and covenants not to transfer the land without my consent." The effect is that A has a fee simple absolute.

4. Allowed Restrictions:

a. Use Restriction: This restriction addresses use, not alienation, and thus is usually valid. "To A but if not used for church purposes, the land shall revert to me." Another example is "To A and his heirs, but if liquor is ever sold on the premises, the grantor may reenter." (Notice this is a reversion, not a remainder.)

b. Right of First Refusal: A right of first refusal restriction allows the holder to meet a third party's offer for the property if the owner accepts the offer. In order to be enforceable, the holder must respond within a reasonable time and must pay the offered price.

D. Present and Future Interest Chart

Operative Wording	Estate Created	Possible Interest After Termination In:	
		Grantor	Named Third Party
"To A" or "To A and his heirs"	Fee Simple Absolute	None	None
"To A so long as" or "To A while" or "To A until"	Fee Simple Determinable	Possibility of Reverter	Shifting Executory Interest *
"To A but if" or "To A provided that"	Fee Simple Subject to a Condition Subsequent	Right of Re-entry (affirmative steps must be taken by Grantor to re-enter)	Executory Interest- Shifting or Springing *
"To A and the heirs of his body"	Fee Tail	Reversion	None
"To A for life"	Life Estate	Reversion	Vested, Open or Contingent Remainder *

*Future interests that are potentially subject to the Rule Against Perpetuities

STOP!   Go to page 581 and work Learning Questions 71 to 78.

XIV. FINAL CHAPTER REVIEW INSTRUCTIONS

1. Completing the Chapter: Now that you have completed your study of the chapter's substantive text and the related Learning Questions, you need to button up this chapter. This includes your preparing your Magic Memory Outlines® and working all of the subject's practice questions.

2. Preparing Your Own Magic Memory Outline®: This is essential to your MBE success. We recommend that you use our software template in this process. Do not underestimate the learning and memory effectiveness derived from condensing the text chapter into your succinct summaries using your own words. This exercise is covered in much more detail in the preface and on the CD-ROM.

a. Summarize Knowledge: You need to prepare a summary of the chapter in your own words. This is best accomplished using the Rigos Bar Review Series Magic Memory Outlines® software. The words in the outline correspond to the bold headings in the text.

b. Capture the Essence: Your job is to summarize the substance of the text by capturing the essence of the rule and entering your summarized wording into your own outlines. Go to the text coverage and craft your own tight, concise, but yet comprehensive statements of the law. Take pride in your skills as an author; this is the best outline you have ever created.

c. Focus: Focus your attention and wording on the required technical elements necessary to prove the relevant legal principles and fine-line distinctions. Integrate any helpful "learning question" information into your outline.

3. Memorize Outline: After you have completed your own Magic Memory Outline® for the whole chapter, read it over carefully once or twice. They are the best book ever written. Refer back to your Outlines frequently.

4. Work Old Questions: The next step is to work all the final questions of each chapter. These vary in degree of difficulty, but the ones towards the end tend to concentrate on fact patterns and issues at the most difficult testing level. Consider using the Question Map on the CD-ROM. Click on the questions under the subject and topic you have just studied. This allows you to cross relate the subjects and related MBE testing.

a. Question Details: Again, it is usually worthwhile to review the explanatory answer rationales as they reinforce the relevant principles of law. If you are still unsure of the controlling rule, refer back to the related portion of the text. This will help you to appreciate the fine-line distinctions on which the MBE questions turn.

b. Do a Few Questions At a Time: Work the final chapter questions in sequence. Make sure you stop after no more than a few to check the answer rationales. Do this frequently so that the facts of the individual question are still in active memory.

c. Work Them All: We have tried to pick questions with an average or higher probability of reappearing on the MBE. You should at least read all the questions and ponder their answers. Every question and answer has some marginal learning and/or reinforcement value. On the MBE you will recognize many of the actual MBE questions as very similar to the ones in your Rigos Bar Review Series review books.

d. Learn From Mistakes: The objective is to learn from your mistakes by reviewing the explanatory rationales while you still remember the factual and legal details of the question. It is good to miss a few; they will help you become familiar with the MBE fine-line distinctions. The examiners' use of distracters, tricks, and red herrings is repetitive.

e. Flag Errors: Put a red star in the margin of the book along side every question you missed. Missed questions should be worked again the day right before the MBE. Do not make the same mistakes on the exam.

f. Essays: Candidates in jurisdictions that administer the Multistate Essay Exam should refer to the *Rigos BAr Review Series Multistate Essay Exam Review — MEE* for practice essay questions.

5. Practice Exam: After you complete the last chapter, you should take the 200 item practice exam. There is detailed information covering this simulated MBE test in both the preface and at the beginning of the exam in Volume 2. This is important because you need to build your concentrated attention time span. You also need to get intellectually used to jumping between unrelated topics and subjects.

6. Make Your Own Exam: The Rigos Bar Review Series software allows you to pick 5, 10, 20 or 100 questions at random from all six MBE subjects. This is an important feature because you must become comfortable with switching intellectual gears between different subjects. If you are not an early riser and/or get going slowly when you get up, try working 10 or 20 questions using the "Make Your Own Exam" software the first thing every morning.

7. Update Your Magic Memory Outline®: The fine-line distinctions in the question and answer rationales will improve your understanding of how the MBE tests the law. Consider updating your Magic Memory Outline® while the question testing environment is still fresh in your mind.

8. Next Chapter: It is now time to go to the beginning of the next subject. Begin by previewing the chapter. Scan the typical coverage.

Question Distribution Map

Numbers immediately following the topic are the chapter question numbers. The **boldface** numbers preceded by "F" are the final exam question numbers. For example, for the topic "II. B. Fixtures" below, questions 225 and 236 are in the chapter questions on pages 3-615 and 3-618, respectively; question **F30** in the final exam on page 7-456 of Volume 2.

MEE Candidates: If your jurisdiction administers the Multistate Essay Exam in addition to the MBE, please refer to the *Rigos Bar Review Series Multistate Essay Exam Review — MEE* for practice essay questions and sample answers covering real property and future interests.

RIGOS BAR REVIEW SERIES

MULTISTATE BAR EXAM REVIEW (MBE)

CHAPTER 3

REAL PROPERTY AND FUTURE INTERESTS QUESTIONS

Questions

Real Property and Future Interests Learning Questions

Questions 1 - 3 share common facts.

1. Larry, Mo, and Curly bought a parcel of timber land together as joint tenants with right of survivorship. Curly decided to sell his share to Shemp. What result?
    (A) Shemp is a joint tenant with Larry and Mo.
    (B) Larry, Mo, and Shemp are now tenants in common.
    (C) Curly's action requires the entire parcel to be partitioned and sold, because each had an undivided interest in the whole.
    (D) Shemp is a tenant in common.

2. Instead of buying the land as joint tenants, Larry, Mo and Curly bought it as tenants in common. Larry on his own invests his own money to make major improvements to the property. What outcome?
    (A) Larry is owed a right of contribution from Mo and Curly.
    (B) Larry receives no compensation because he acted without authorization.
    (C) Larry receives no reimbursement until the property is sold.
    (D) Larry's expenditure constitutes a gift.

3. After purchasing the property as tenants in common, Larry and Mo go off to Africa on a safari with the Marx Brothers, leaving Curly in charge. When they return, Curly has fenced off the land and put a padlock on the gate, denying them entry. What result?
    (A) Larry and Mo may sue Curly and force a partition of the land.
    (B) Curly owes Larry and Mo damages if he harvested an entire grove of trees on the land without replanting.
    (C) Both A and B are correct.
    (D) Neither A nor B is correct.

4. Magic Manors is a condominium complex with 80 buildings, 4 units per building, plus a common playground and swimming pool. The covenants specify that all owners must pay a $135 monthly maintenance fee, and that the association or its members have a right of first refusal before units are offered to the public for general resale. Which of the following is true?
    (A) The restriction on resale is unenforceable because the owners' interest is a fee simple, and the transfer of units cannot be restricted.
    (B) The association is responsible for paying for the re-roofing of a building, not the owners of the four individual units in the building.
    (C) The individual unit owners are responsible for the payment of re-roofing of their building.
    (D) Bob Jones, an elderly property owner, is entitled to demand a deduction from his monthly dues because he never uses the swimming pool or playground.

5. ABC corporation purchased a building for $1.8 million and converted it into a co-op. Joan, a loyal employee for the past 20 years, was offered a unit in the building for a very reasonable price. Joan decided to move in. Which of the following is most accurate?

(A) A co-op cannot be owned by a corporation.
— (B) Joan will have to take out her own mortgage on her unit, and taxes will be assessed against her individual unit.
(C) Units in co-ops are easily transferable.
(D) The success of co-op depends on regular payments being made by each occupant of a unit.

Questions 6 and 7 are based on the following:

Tiffany has an undeveloped 2-acre lot bordering a lake, which passed to her in her aunt's will in 1982. Her aunt kept the property strictly as an investment and never visited the property after its purchase. The neighbors had for years crossed over a small trail to the lake. Tiffany plans to build a vacation home on the lot.

Matt, an avid boater, loves being out on the lake, but does not live on it. Back in 1969, he found a trail from the road to the lakefront across the parcel which now belongs to Tiffany. Matt uses the trail on Tiffany's property daily to gain access to the lake. In fact, he used the parcel so much, that he expanded the path from the road to the lake so he could launch his boat.

6. Which best describes Matt's situation?

(A) Matt has an easement by implication.
(B) Matt has an easement by necessity.
(C) Matt has an easement appurtenant.
(D) Matt has an easement by prescription.

7. Which of the following is true?

(A) Any easement Matt has does not apply to Tiffany, only her aunt.
(B) Tiffany may terminate the easement by blocking the path for 20 years.
(C) Tiffany can request Matt pay her a reasonable price for using the path.
(D) Tiffany can transfer the easement to her brother.

Questions 8 and 9 are based on the following:

Cindy owned all 5 acres of Venezuela Ranch. In 1995, she divided the ranch and sold it in four equal parcels, A, B, C, and D. To access the highway from parcel B, Cindy had always used the main road across parcel A, even though there was an old steep and dangerous road on parcel B that led directly to the highway. When showing the lots, Cindy used this main road to access the parcels.

When Cindy conveyed the lots, all the deeds were silent as to the existence of any easements.

8. If an easement were present, how was it created?

(A) Express grant.
(B) Prescription.
(C) Implication.
(D) Necessity.

9. Assuming an easement was granted, which lot is the servient estate and which lot is the dominant estate?

	Servient	Dominant
(A)	Parcel A.	Parcel B.
(B)	Parcel B.	Parcel A.
(C)	Parcel C.	Parcel A.
(D)	Parcel D.	Parcel B.

10. Edgar buys a lot from Carl, while Jane buys a neighboring lot from Marc. Jane has no access to any roads from her lot. Can Jane use the road on Edgar's lot to get to the main road?

(A) Yes, because she has an easement by necessity.

(B) Yes, because she has an easement by implication.

(C) No, because there is no express easement.

(D) No, because there was no express reservation.

11. Oscar, a religious man, lives next to a church. For 20 years he has allowed the neighboring church members to drive over his property to get to the church's rear parking lot on Sunday mornings. Oscar is getting older, and decides he needs to downsize to a smaller place and decides to sell his property. In the deed to the buyer, Oscar reserves the right for the church to continue to cross his property. Which of the following is correct?

(A) The easement is valid because the new buyer is a bona fide purchaser.

(B) The easement is invalid because the new buyer takes without notice.

(C) The easement is valid because Oscar made a reservation in a third party known to the grantee.

(D) The easement is invalid because Oscar made a reservation in a third party known to the grantee.

12. Busco Buggs subdivided his lakeshore property, selling the upslope parcel to Maryanne Burns. In the deed, he recorded an agreement not to allow the trees on his property to grow taller than 15 feet so as not to obstruct Maryanne's view. Each year he has planted his live Christmas tree in the back yard, and 6 years later, some of them are 18-20 feet tall. Which of the following is correct?

(A) Maryanne has no remedy, because there must be separate consideration for negative covenants.

(B) Maryanne has an enforceable right to an easement to use the lakeshore for recreational purposes, since the original undivided parcel had such access.

(C) Maryanne may seek injunctive relief to enforce the 15 foot limit.

(D) Busco may allow the trees to grow, since they are on his property and Maryanne has no enforceable right.

13. Aislinn, the owner of Sleepy Pines, has an easement across Hardcore Hemlocks. Aislinn purchases Sleepy Meadows, which is contiguous to Sleepy Pines. Aislinn will

(A) Not be able to use the easement for the benefit of Sleepy Meadows because the use goes beyond the original intended scope.

(B) Not be able to use the easement for the benefit of Sleepy Meadows because the easement cannot be divided.

(C) Be able to use the easement for the benefit of Sleepy Meadows because the use was foreseeable at the time the easement was granted.

(D) Be able to use the easement for the benefit of Sleepy Meadows because the easement can be divided.

14. Barry orally tells Arlene, his neighbor, she can use the path on his property to access the lake. Which best describes the interest Arlene holds?

(A) A profit in gross.

(B) An easement appurtenant.

(C) An easement in gross.

(D) A license.

15. Ben owned a large lot, which he subdivided into 2 lots. He kept one for himself and sold the other to Jerry. In the deed, Ben wrote that no building taller than 30 feet could be erected at any time in the future. Ten years later, Jerry sold his lot to Cheri, who commenced to build a 40 foot high home. Is the covenant binding upon Cheri?

(A) Yes, because the requirements for the burden to run have been met.

(B) Yes, because the requirements for the benefit to run have been met.

(C) No, because there was no intent to bind successors.

(D) No, because there is no horizontal privity.

16. Martha sold a small building lot to Jeremy, a prize horse trainer, at a reduced price because Jeremy covenanted to care for Martha's horses on the lot. Ten years later, Jeremy sold the same lot to his sister, Lois, who does not even like horses. Will Lois have to care for the horses?

(A) No, because Lois does not like horses.
(B) No, because the burden does not run to Lois.
(C) Yes, because there is a covenant in place.
(D) Yes, because the benefit runs to Lois.

Questions 17 and 18 are based on the following:

Betsy and Ross were long-time neighbors. Betsy purchased her parcel of land from Mack in 1960, while Ross purchased his from Jack in 1962. Ross's parcel was situated in front of Betsy's and contained a one-story house. Both homeowners enjoyed a lovely view of the lake. In 1969 Betsy asked Ross to enter into a covenant that he, his heirs, and his assigns would never add another story to the home that would destroy Betsy's view of the land. Ross agreed, and the covenant was put into writing and included with the deed.

17. For the purpose of this question only, assume Betsy sells her home to Joyce in 2000. In 2003, Ross decides to build another story to his home and blocks Joyce's view. Will Joyce be able to enforce the covenant against Ross?

(A) Yes, because there is horizontal privity.
(B) Yes, because there is vertical privity.
(C) No, because there is no horizontal privity.
(D) No, because there is no vertical privity.

18. For the purpose of this question only, assume Ross sold his parcel to Gill in 2000. In 2004, Gill decides to build another story to his home. Will Betsy be able to enforce the covenant against Gill?

(A) Yes, because there is vertical privity.
(B) Yes, because there is horizontal privity.
(C) No, because there is no vertical privity.
(D) No, because there is no horizontal privity.

19. A small residential development was established in 1985. The developer was a cedar shake fanatic and he placed them on all the roofs. He also entered a restriction that "all homes may only use cedar shakes on their roofs" as a clause in their deeds. The development was hence called Cedar Shake Park. When Laura and Jason bought a home in the Park in 2001, all the houses in the development still had cedar shake roofs, but there was no mention in their deed about having to keep a cedar shake roof. 3 years later when the roof needed to be replaced, Laura and Jason opted for a less expensive composite roof.

Before installation began, their neighbors, the Smiths, bring an action to try to force them to install another cedar shake roof. What result is most likely?

(A) The Smiths will win by enforcing an equitable servitude.
(B) The Smiths will lose because Laura and Jason never agreed in writing to keep cedar shake.
(C) Laura and Jason will win because there is no real covenant in place.
(D) Laura and Jason will lose because there is both vertical and horizontal privity.

20. David Developer purchased Myrvin Gardens to develop into a residential community on a mountainside. He intended to restrict all the buildings to a single story so as to retain all the views for at least five years. David had very little luck in selling any of the lots in Myrvin

Gardens to the public, but was approached by Bryan Bottomfeeder. He told Bryan that he was abandoning the one story requirement even though his extensive advertisement for the lots had contained the one story feature. Based on that representation, Bryan bought all of Myrvin Gardens from David. Bryan later sold Myrvin Gardens to Harry Highrise who filed a building permit intending to build four story townhouses on the land. David objected and stated he would insist on one story maximum height. If Harry brings a lawsuit for a declaratory judgment seeking to eliminate the one story requirement, his worst argument is

(A) Estoppel.
(B) Merger.
(C) Lack of a common scheme.
(D) The restriction had lapsed.

Questions 21 and 22 are based on the following:

The developer of the Sunnyside subdivision had a grand vision of a large residential neighborhood that was friendly to all types of families. She promised all new lot purchasers that the lots would be restricted to residential use only, however, nothing was ever put in writing. Jane bought lot number 45 in the subdivision. At the time of her purchase, the subdivision was surrounded by woods. Jane's lot was a 5-acre corner lot that bordered the woods. Ten years later, the entire wooded area had been developed into more residential neighborhoods.

Jane now plans to turn her lot into a small gas station and snack shop to serve the subdivision and neighboring communities, which have no nearby amenities.

21. If Jane's plans can be stopped, it would be by

(A) A person in the neighboring community seeking to enforce an equitable servitude.

(B) A person in the neighboring community seeking to enforce a real covenant.
(C) Another resident of Sunnyside seeking to enforce a negative equitable servitude.
(D) Another resident of Sunnyside seeking to enforce a real covenant.

22. Assume for this question only that the suit to block Jane is being brought by, Tex, the owner of a competitor gas station on the other side of the Sunnyside subdivision. Tex turned his lot into a gas station five years ago. Jane's best defense against the attempt to block her business plan would be under a theory of

(A) Estoppel.
(B) Merger.
(C) Change in the neighborhood.
(D) Unclean hands.

Questions 23 and 24 are based on the following:

Ward and June purchased a home in Dreamacres in 2003. Before closing on the purchase, they discovered covenants in the deed of the current owner that dated back to the founding of the subdevelopment in 1952. The covenants stated that there was a homeowner's association with $25 mandatory monthly dues, and that all homeowners were restricted from allowing trees to grow over fifteen feet tall to preserve the view for the community.

23. Ward asked several of the neighbors who he should contact for information on the monthly homeowner association dues. They all told him that the homeowner's association went "belly up" in 1976. Which of the following is correct?

(A) Ward and June are still responsible for the $25 monthly dues.
(B) Ward and June are not responsible for paying the dues because the covenant governing the homeowner's association has been abandoned.

(C) Ward and June are not responsible for the homeowner's association dues because the covenant does not meet the "touch and concern" requirement.

(D) None of the above.

---

24. After Ward and June closed on the property, neighbor Ned approaches them to tell them that he protested the height of their 30-foot-high Douglas fir trees that are blocking his view of the nearby lake. Ward notices Ned's yard has 40 foot pine trees, but Ned says they aren't blocking anyone's view. Ned is the only other owner in the neighborhood with trees over 15 feet. Which of the following is correct?

(A) Ned cannot sue because the homeowner's association is defunct.

(B) Ned has a valid claim – he can sue for damages or equitable relief (to have the trees chopped down).

(C) Ward and June will not be required to remove the trees.

(D) Ned cannot sue due to a lack of privity.

Questions 25 and 26 are based on the following:

The zoning committee for the city of Brenton recently passed a regulation that all buildings in the town square can be no taller than 4 stories. At present there is only one building, which is situated on the edge of the square that is over 4 stories tall.

25. What can be said for the regulation?

(A) The regulation is presumed to be invalid, until proven otherwise.

(B) The regulation is presumed to be valid.

(C) It is invalid spot zoning.

(D) It is valid spot zoning.

26. Concerning the one building that is currently over 4 stories, which of the below is correct?

(A) It will have to be removed for violating the regulation.

(B) It will be allowed to continue as a nonconforming use.

(C) It will be allowed under spot zoning.

(D) The owner can claim a taking has occurred.

---

27. The city council recently passed an ordinance regulating the type of businesses allowed in the University neighborhood. The new ordinance states that bookstores shall only be situated on the edges of the district. Joe, a book merchant, operates a bookstore in the middle of the district. Currently there are no open buildings on the edge of the district to which Joe can relocate. Which of the following is not an option for Joe?

(A) Joe could apply for a variance to allow his bookstore to remain in its current location.

(B) Joe could claim the ordinance results in a taking.

(C) Joe could claim his is a nonconforming use that should be allowed.

(D) Joe could challenge the ordinance under the Fourteenth Amendment Equal Protection Act.

---

28. Joan Jones is environmentally minded, so she dries her clothes on a line in her back yard rather than use electricity for a dryer. Robert Burns, the next-door neighbor and aspiring poet, disposes of all draft poems by incineration, despite city ordinances to the contrary. Unfortunately, Robert's paper burning causes an awful smell and spews ashes all over Joan's white linens on the clothes line. Joan's best cause of action would be to allege a claim under the theory of

(A) Equitable servitude because the burning is out of character with the character of the neighborhood because it violates an ordinance.

(B) Public nuisance, because Burns is violating a public ordinance.

(C) Private nuisance, because Burns is interfering with private property rights.

(D) Public nuisance, because Burns is probably bothering more than one neighbor.

29. The Sanford Corporation purchased a large parcel of land next to a cattle ranch and built a large residential area for families. The flies and the smells of the ranch are beginning to disrupt the use and enjoyment of the community areas. Which of the following is the best answer?
   (A) This is private nuisance, so any one of the community members can bring suit.
   (B) This is a public nuisance, so any person, regardless of whether they own land in the development or not, can bring suit if they have special harm.
   (C) Since the cattle ranch was in existence first, nothing can be done.
   (D) The cattle ranch will have no defenses to the nuisance it is causing.

30. Sarah Seller signed a purchase and sale agreement with Bobby Buyer to convey her home, lot number 123, block 29, addition 23H in Pleasantville, Queens County, Anystate. Bobby paid Sarah $5,000 in earnest money, which she accepted. Although the lot number typed into the document was 321, the rest of the information was correct. Before closing, Harry offered Sarah $75,000 more for the property than her contract with Bobby. She accepted. The legal consequence is that
   (A) Return of the earnest money to Bobby is the only relief available.
   (B) Bobby is not entitled to return of the money because he did not ensure the contract contained a valid legal description of the property.
   (C) Bobby may have relief if the address was a "typo" despite the legal description rule.
   (D) Harry has committed fraud by purchasing property already contracted to another buyer.

31. Mom decided to sell her home to Daughter, with whom she had a loving and close relationship. They agreed upon a price and a moving date, but since they had such a wonderful loving relationship, nothing was put in writing. In anticipation of the move, Daughter placed her home on the market, which sold within a few days. A week before the home sale was to close and after the daughter had moved into Mom's house, Mom had a change of heart and decided she did not want to move or sell her home to Daughter. If Daughter brings a suit for specific performance, the likely outcome is a holding that the contract
   (A) Is enforceable because there has been part performance.
   (B) Is enforceable because the Daughter has changed position.
   (C) Is not enforceable because it was oral.
   (D) Is not enforceable because Daughter did not pay for the house.

32. Scott advertised his home for sale by owner. He received two separate offers on the same day for the full asking price of $200,000, one from Dan and one from Pam. He researched their credit ratings, and decided to accept the offer from Pam because her rating was slightly stronger. They signed a purchase and sale agreement, and Pam put down $1,000 as earnest money. They agreed to close on December 1st.

On November 30th, Scott received a letter from Pam stating she had purchased a different house instead, and requested a refund of her earnest money. Scott contacted Dan, who had subsequently purchased a different house, so he was no longer interested. The stock market then fell abruptly, and the house sat on the market for six months. At that time, Scott finally accepted an offer for $150,000 and promptly closed. What can Scott successfully claim against Pam?
   (A) He could keep the earnest money as liquidated damages.

(B) He could claim $50,000, the difference between actual sale price and market price.

(C) A and B.

(D) A or B.

33. Aggie and Dewey entered into a purchase and sale agreement to purchase Margo's beachfront cabin and acreage. The prices of beachfront property were soaring in that state; the agreed price was $2.5 million. Three weeks later, before the deal closed, Margo notified Aggie and Dewey by certified mail that she was withdrawing from the contract. Aggie and Dewey then discovered that Margo had contracted to sell the property to Gus for $3.5 million. Assume that Aggie and Dewey's contract was not subject to any contingencies. Under what theory might Aggie and Dewey recover the property?

(A) Statutory warranty of title.

(B) Quiet title action.

(C) Punitive damages.

(D) Action for damages.

Questions 34 and 35 are based on the following:

34. Desmond sold his home to Sydney for $275,000. In the purchase and sale agreement, the house was described by its street address, Desmond was listed as the seller and Sydney as the buyer, the sales price was listed, and it was signed by Desmond. What's the possible problem with enforcing this contract?

(A) The house description was not adequate for a valid contract.

(B) The parties were not identified with enough accuracy.

(C) The contract was not signed by Sydney, the buyer.

(D) The contract was not notarized.

35. Assume the above sales contract is valid and enforceable. Three days before closing, a fire burned down the house. Under the common law majority rule, the result would likely be that

(A) If neither party had any hand in starting the fire, then the risk of loss is allocated to the buyer, unless stated otherwise.

(B) If neither party had any hand in starting the fire, then the risk of loss is allocated to the seller, unless stated otherwise.

(C) After a valid contract is executed, the doctrine of Equitable Conversion deems the seller to be the equitable owner, and the buyer to be the legal title holder.

(D) If the buyer has not taken possession of the land, then risk of loss remains with the seller.

36. Grandma Gertie orally promised in front of the whole family to give her grandson Johnny her house as a gift. Before he had a chance to move in, she had a change of heart, and contracted to sell it for $200,000 to a third party.

(A) Johnny is entitled to the property under promissory estoppel.

(B) Johnny may seek delivery of the deed through the doctrine of "estoppel by deed."

(C) Johnny has no enforceable property right because this was an oral agreement.

(D) Johnny has no enforceable right because he gave no consideration.

37. Which of the following conveyances of Sneezy Meadows from grantor to grantee violates the implied warranty of marketable title?

(A) Sneezy Meadows was an open field with a restrictive covenant that stated no buildings could ever be built on the lot. The grantee knew of the restrictive covenant, which was written in the contract, but bought the lot nonetheless.

(B) Sneezy Meadows was an open field, and a zoning restriction was in place that did not allow for any buildings to be built on the lot. The grantee had no knowledge of the restriction.

(C) Sneezy Meadows had a single building on the lot, a zoning restriction was in place that did not allow for any buildings to be built on the lot. The grantee had no knowledge of the restriction.

(D) Sneezy Meadows had a single building on the lot, an easement was in place that allowed the neighbor to cross the lot to get to her home and the grantee knew of the easement, but bought the lot nonetheless.

38. Zeke filed a law suit against Xavier for trespass because a survey indicated that Xavier's house extended three feet over the boundary onto Zeke's land. Xavier immediately listed his house for sale and conveniently forgot to mention this alleged encroachment when the property was sold to Yolanda. Yolanda later found out about the suit and was furious. What would be the basis of Yolanda's legal complaint against Xavier?

(A) Breach of implied warranty of habitability if the encroachment was intentional.

(B) Breach of warranty of title.

(C) She has no claim for breach of warranty, since a quitclaim deed conveyance is presumed.

(D) There is no claim available until Zeke's suit is final and a judgment is filed against Xavier.

39. Ronald was in dire straits financially, and he had missed mortgage payments on his house for four of the last six months. His home was worth $188,000, and he had a balance of $125,000 left on his mortgage. The state in which the property is located is a lien theory state. He conveyed the house to Daniel for $63,000 with a quitclaim deed. What best describes Daniel's interest?

(A) He has an interest in fee simple absolute, and it is subject to a warranty of title from Ronald's conveyance.

(B) He now possesses whatever interest Ronald had in the property, subject to Ronald's mortgage.

(C) If the bank forecloses on the property, he has a valid action against Ronald for breach of title warranty.

(D) Because the bank held the deed, Daniel has absolutely no interest in the property, since the bank already "owned" the property prior to the conveyance.

40. Bob and Lois purchased a home from Al and Linda that had been their personal residence for four years. Six months later, a pipe in a wall burst and flooded the entire basement, damaging the rest of the structure and destroying Bob and Lois' furniture. Upon inspection of the plumbing inside of the walls, they discover the entire house was originally plumbed improperly, and all of the walls must be opened up to replace all the pipes throughout the house. Bob and Lois sue Al and Linda. What results?

(A) Bob and Lois will prevail under implied warranty of habitability.

(B) Al and Linda are liable because they failed to disclose the defective plumbing.

(C) Al and Linda are liable under express warranty theory.

(D) Bob and Lois have no recourse against Al and Linda under these facts.

41. Buyer entered into a purchase and sale agreement with Seller. Closing was scheduled for one month later, contingent on Buyer obtaining financing. Assume a lien theory jurisdiction. Which of the following does not describe what happens at closing?

(A) The buyer receives equitable title.

(B) The mortgage bank now has a lien on the property.

(C) The buyer receives legal title.

(D) None of the above.

42. State X has a statute for filing deeds that reads in part: "An unrecorded conveyance is invalid as against a subsequent bona fide purchaser who takes without notice." This state is
- (A) A "race" state.
- (B) A "notice" state.
- (C) A "race-notice" state.
- (D) A "notice-race" state.

43. In State Y, Billy Jo purchases Greenacre from Bobby Jean. Billy files the deed at the county courthouse. One month later, Jack sues because he had previously purchased Greenacre, but failed to record the deed. The court decides that Billy Jo prevails, even though Billy Jo fully admits he had knowledge of Jack's prior purchase when he bought Greenacre. What kind of recording statute does State Y have?
- (A) A "race" statute.
- (B) A "notice" statute
- (C) A "race-notice" statute.
- (D) A "notice-race" statute.

44. Mary cannot make payments on her home anymore, and decides to "quitclaim" it to Jerry on December 25th. Jerry filed on December 26th. On January 2nd of the next year, Mary's bank commenced foreclosure actions because of a long-standing mortgage that they held on the property. This is a race-notice state. Who will prevail?
- (A) Jerry, because he filed first without notice of the mortgage.
- (B) Jerry, because of the title warranty.
- (C) The bank, because they held a prior interest that a quitclaim does not discharge.
- (D) Jerry, because his filing provides constructive notice to the bank of his ownership.

45. Sally Seller conveyed by deed property in Mason County to Betty Buyer who filed in Dixon county. Sally then conveyed the same property to Sarah Second who filed in Mason County which is a "race-notice" jurisdiction. Sarah had no knowledge of

Betty's interest in the property. The likely result is that
- (A) Sarah loses, because filing gave her constructive notice.
- (B) Sarah still wins even if she had constructive notice.
- (C) Sarah loses because Betty filed first.
- (D) Sarah loses if she had actual notice.

46. Barb and Ken purchase a summer cabin on the lake. Before closing, they buy standard title insurance with typical exclusions to protect the property investment they are about to make. One day later, Steve prevails in an adverse possession suit for that property. What result?
- (A) Barb and Ken are protected against adverse possession claims.
- (B) Barb and Ken are protected unless inquiry notice would have indicated there was a problem with adverse possession.
- (C) Barb and Ken are not protected because title insurance does not usually cover adverse possession.
- (D) Barb and Ken are only protected if the abstract of title included some notice of the adverse possession claim.

47. Art and Betty purchased a home from Charlie and Didi. Unbeknowst to any of them, neighbor Jeff's concrete driveway had been poured entirely on Art and Betty's side of the property line 26 years before. One month after closing, Art discovers the actual boundary lines while looking at papers at the local county courthouse. He confronts Jeff, who in turn sues to quiet title under adverse possession theory. The court would likely hold for
- (A) Jeff, because the adverse possession burden "tacks" from Charlie and Didi to Art and Betty.
- (B) Jeff, under adverse possession theory.
- (C) Art and Betty, because Jeff knowingly trespassed when he poured the concrete driveway.

(D) Art and Betty because Jeff cannot demonstrate the element of "open."

48. In a lien theory jurisdiction, Buyer takes out a mortgage to purchase a new home and the mortgage company files. Who owns what?

(A) Buyer owns legal title to the property; the bank has just a security interest.

(B) The bank owns legal title to the land, and Buyer has equitable title.

(C) Buyer owns legal title; bank owns equitable title.

(D) Bank owns legal and equitable titles until buyer pays off the mortgage, at which point both transfer to buyer.

49. Wilson sold his apartment house to Glenn. As part of the contract, Glenn expressly assumed the existing mortgage on the property that is held by Security Bank. Regarding the rights and duties of the parties, which of the following is correct?

(A) The promise by Glenn need not be in writing to be enforceable by security.

(B) Security is a creditor beneficiary of Glenn's promise and can recover against him personally in the event of default.

(C) Security is a mere incidental beneficiary since it was not a party to the assignment.

(D) Wilson has no further liability to Security.

50. Buyer purchases property from Seller using a real estate contract instead of a conventional mortgage. The terms of the contract require Buyer to pay monthly payments for 360 months, at which time Seller will convey title to Buyer. The contract also states that if Buyer defaults during the 360 months, Seller may privately foreclose. In most jurisdictions, which of the following is correct?

(A) Buyer defaults after 12 months. Seller may foreclose without a judicial proceeding.

(B) The private foreclosure clause is void in most jurisdictions because it is per se unconscionable.

(C) If Seller only recovers a portion of the outstanding debt on a foreclosure sale, he may go after the personal assets of Buyer.

(D) Judicial foreclosure is the only means of handling defaults on mortgages.

51. Delbert subdivided his two-acre property and sold Elton half. Elton built a small house 20 feet from the border of Delbert's land. After two years, the foundation began to buckle badly and finally collapsed into a six-foot sinkhole. A geophysical survey revealed that Delbert had dug an underground bomb shelter the previous year that extended under the entire width of Elton's property. A cave-in from weakened supports in the shelter caused the sinkhole to form. What is Elton's most likely cause of action?

(A) Public nuisance

(B) Private nuisance.

(C) Violation of subjacent support.

(D) Violation of lateral support.

52. Martha bought from George a 7th floor condo near the coast to use as a vacation getaway. George resides in the adjoining unit. George is upset that whenever Martha is in town, her little dog sits on the balcony and howls at the moon all night. After Martha's last vacation, George decided to change the locks on Martha's condo to "teach her a lesson." What action may Martha bring and why?

(A) This is a violation of Martha's ownership rights; therefore, she may bring a trespass action against George.

(B) This is an adverse possession; Martha needs to bring suit to quiet title.

(C) This is a violation of the sales contract; Martha needs to sue for breach.

(D) A nuisance action because Martha's dog is a nuisance to the whole condominium.

53. Tom has a month-to-month periodic tenancy. Tom has faithfully paid rent on the first of each month. On February 15th, Tom gives notice to Landlord that he is going to vacate the premises on February 28th. Tom vacates and pays no more rent. Which of the below alternatives best describes this situation under the majority rule?

(A) Tom has no further liability on the premises.

(B) Tom's notice of termination was not effective until March 31st.

(C) Landlord needed to give Tom notice before the tenancy was terminated.

(D) Tom's notice of termination was ineffective and new notice was required on the 1st of March.

54. Roberta Renter rented a two-bedroom apartment from Larry Landlord. The contract states that the lease was for 12 months, with rent due the first of each month. It had no provisions for extending the lease beyond the 12 months. Roberta did not provide notice as she approached the end of that year. At the end of 12 months, she remained in the apartment. Larry wants her to leave, but she submitted a monthly rent check for the same amount as each of the previous 12 months on the first day of the 13th month. Which is Larry's least desirable course of action?

(A) Cash the check.

(B) Begin unlawful detainer action.

(C) Sue for trespass because Roberta's right of possession expired even though she did not provide 30 days notice.

(D) Pay a moving company to move Roberta's belongings to storage while she is at work.

55. Trish is living in an apartment complex owned by Nancy, and is in year one of a three-year lease. Trish experiences a series of unexplained illnesses. Her doctor informs her that the illnesses are from exposure to toxic mold. She hires an inspector who determines that the walls and ceilings of her apartment are filled with high levels of the mold that is making her sick. She moves out her belongings, turns in her key to Nancy, and declares, "I'm outta here!" What are Nancy's remedies?

(A) She may sue for lost rent until she finds another tenant.

(B) She may sue Trish for waste for failure to maintain the premises.

(C) She may not sue for breach of contract because Trish failed to give proper notice, she may keep the security deposit.

(D) None of the above.

56. Larry Landlord rented a furnished apartment to Terrance Tenant in a term lease for 24 months, with rent payable the first of each month. After three months, the rent stopped coming. Larry sent notice to Terrance of the late rent, and after one week of no response, entered the apartment only to find Terrance and all the apartment's furnishings gone. Larry immediately filed a lawsuit seeking 21 months of rent plus the value of all the missing property. On his court date a year later, the apartment was still vacant because Larry wanted to await the outcome of the suit before re-renting the space. What is the court most likely to decide?

(A) Larry is entitled to no recovery due to Terrance's theft of the furnishings.

(B) Larry is entitled to 21 months of rent.

(C) Larry is entitled to some damages, but less than 21 months.

(D) Larry is entitled to 9 months of rent.

57. Nosey Norris was the landlord of a duplex. Tracy rented the other half of the duplex for $450 a month. Despite Tracy's complaints, Nosey would use his master key and let himself into her premises without notice to snoop through her personal papers and belongings. She caught him in the act several times, but he continued his offensive activity. What is Tracy's least viable remedy?

(A) Withhold rent.
(B) Vacate and terminate the lease.
(C) Injunctive relief.
(D) Sue for damages.

58. Tammy and Lou had a two-year tenancy in place. Towards the end of the two years, they began to negotiate another two-year lease. The negotiations extended beyond the end of the original lease and 15 days later the parties failed to agree. Tammy moved out. Lou

(A) Can elect to treat Tammy as having renewed the lease, creating a two-year periodic tenancy.
(B) Can elect to seek an ejectment and sue for damages.
(C) Impliedly consented to Tammy holding over on the property during negotiations, so he cannot pursue an immediate eviction action.
(D) Could not have consented to Tammy holding over on the property during negotiations and can seek either action.

Questions 59 and 60 are based on the following:

Libby Landlord entered into a lease with Tara Tenant for 2,000 square feet of space to be used as a law office. The lease stated that unapproved lease assignments were prohibited, and that the rent was $1,200 a month. Tara took possession and began making payments on the 1st of each month.

59. Which best describes the lease?
(A) This is a periodic tenancy.
(B) This is a tenancy at will.
(C) This is a term tenancy.
(D) This is a tenancy at sufferance.

60. Tara operated her solo law practice for six months and found that her legal practice did not grow as fast as she had predicted. She had a friend who had just passed the

bar exam to whom she signed a sublease for 1,000 square feet out of the 2,000 square feet contained within her lease. Libby objects and brings suit. The likely outcome is for

(A) Libby since she did not approve.
(B) Tara because restraints on alienation of land are strictly construed.
(C) Tara as long as her friend pays half the rent.
(D) Libby since assignment was expressly disallowed in the lease and that includes subleases.

61. Mother conveys her summer home "to Daughter, but if she does not graduate from law school and pass the bar exam at the first sitting, then the property goes to my Son."

(A) Daughter has a fee simple subject to a condition subsequent and Mother has a right of entry.
(B) Daughter has a fee simple subject to a condition subsequent and Son has a right of entry.
(C) Daughter has a fee simple subject to an executory interest and Son has a future executory interest.
(D) Daughter and Son's interests are merged giving Daughter a fee simple absolute.

62. Owen conveys Friendly Farm "to Adam, so long as the land is used as a farm." In Adam's will, he states, "any interest I may have in Friendly Farm is left to my son, Sam."

(A) Owen's future interest in Friendly Farm is a reversion of a life estate, and therefore, it may not be transferred by will.
(B) Owen has no future interest in Friendly Farm because the transfer to Adam was in fee simple absolute.
(C) Owen may not convey his future interest in his will.
(D) Owen's future interest is a possibility of reverter, and it is alienable by will.

63. Sister conveys Speedacres property "to Brother, so long as he does not get a speeding ticket."

    (A) Brother has a life estate and Sister, a reversion.

    (B) Brother has a fee simple determinable and Sister has a possibility of reverter.

    (C) Brother has a fee simple subject to condition subsequent and Sister has a right of entry.

    (D) Brother has a fee simple absolute and Sister has no future interest.

64. Sam conveys Whiteacres "to Bob until he finds a job."

    (A) Sam has given Bob a fee simple subject to an executory interest and retained a right of entry for himself.

    (B) Sam has given Bob a fee simple determinable and retained a possibility of reverter for himself.

    (C) Sam has given Bob a future interest in the suit.

    (D) Sam has given Bob a fee simple subject to a condition subsequent and retained a right of entry for himself.

65. Oscar owned Blackacre in fee simple absolute. He conveyed it "to Able, but if anyone uses alcohol on the premises, then to Bob and his heirs."

    (A) Able has a fee simple determinable, because of the "but if" language.

    (B) Able has a fee simple subject to a condition subsequent due to the "but if" language.

    (C) Able has a fee simple subject to an executory limitation.

    (D) Bob has a right of reverter.

66. Amanda conveys SurfAcres "to Scott for the life of Jackson."

    (A) If Amanda later conveys her possibility of reverter to Scott, Scott will have a fee simple absolute.

    (B) Scott has a life estate and Jackson has a reversion.

    (C) Scott has a life estate pur autre vie measured by Jackson's life.

    (D) When Scott dies, SurfAcres will automatically go to Amanda.

67. Terry Tycoon wants to keep his vast plantation in his family for several generations in the future, so he conveys it "to my son, Timmy, and to his heirs." The effect of this transfer is to create

    (A) A fee tail, which limits transfers out of the family.

    (B) An interest in fee absolute.

    (C) A life estate interest in Timmy, since that is the default interest in most jurisdictions.

    (D) A fee simple determinable, which has the possibility of reverter if Timmy conveys to other than his heirs.

68. Shy Sheila is a woman of few words. She conveyed her property by merely stating "To Zeke for life."

    (A) Zeke received an interest in fee simple absolute, because Shy did not specify what happened on Zeke's death.

    (B) The remainder passes as part of Zeke's estate upon his death.

    (C) The property returns to Shy upon Zeke's death.

    (D) Because the recipient of the remainder is not specified, the transfer is void under the rule against perpetuities.

69. G makes a conveyance of Blueacre "to A for life, then to B."

    (A) A has a life estate and B has a contingent remainder.

    (B) A has a fee simple and B has a vested remainder.

    (C) A has a life estate and G has a reversion.

    (D) A has a life estate and B has a vested remainder.

70. Grandpa George conveys Greenacre "to my son George W for life, remainder to any of his children living at his death."

George W currently has two daughters. The daughters' interests are:
- (A) Contingent remainders.
- (B) Tenants in common in fee simple absolute.
- (C) Reversions.
- (D) Vested remainders.

71. Scott conveys Goldacres containing a small house "to Suzy for life, then to Savannah." After several years, the pipes in the house developed some leaks, which Suzy does nothing about.
- (A) Suzy has a life estate pur autre vie and Savannah has a vested remainder interest which gives her the right to damages under the doctrine of waste.
- (B) Suzy has a life estate, Savannah has a reversion.
- (C) Savannah can claim damages under the doctrine of waste because she has a vested remainder.
- (D) Suzy has a life estate, Savannah has a remainder and Scott can step in and retake the land because of the waste Suzy is committing.

72. Robin conveys her property "to Drew for life, then upon Drew's death, to any of Drew's children who are living at the time of his death for their lives." Drew's children all predecease him. What happens to the estate when Drew dies?
- (A) It passes to the estates of Drew's children.
- (B) It is distributed as part of Drew's estate.
- (C) It comes back to Robin.
- (D) None of the above.

73. X conveys a small farm "to A for life, with the remainder to X's heirs."
- (A) A has a life estate, X has a reversion in fee simple and the heirs take nothing.
- (B) A has a life estate and X's heirs have a vested remainder.
- (C) A has a life estate and X's heirs have a contingent remainder.
- (D) A takes a fee simple.

74. Ralph conveys his home "to Wilbur, as long as the home remains in good condition, then to Zelda."
- (A) Ralph has given Wilbur a fee simple determinable and Zelda a vested remainder.
- (B) Wilbur has a fee simple determinable and Zelda has an executory interest.
- (C) Ralph has reserved the right of entry if the home is not kept in good condition.
- (D) Wilbur has a fee simple determinable and Zelda takes nothing.

75. Grantor conveys "to Zane for life, remainder to Zane's widow for her life, remainder to the children of Zane living at his widow's death."
- (A) The remainder to the widow's children is void.
- (B) The remainder to the widow's children is valid because they are an open class.
- (C) The remainder to widow's children is valid because the rule against perpetuities has been abolished in most jurisdictions.
- (D) The remainder to widow's children is valid under the Doctrine of Worthier Title.

76. State X is a "wait and see" jurisdiction in applying the rule against perpetuities. This means:
- (A) The rule against perpetuities is held in abeyance for charitable contributions only.
- (B) The rule against perpetuities applies even if the property interest might later violate the rule.
- (C) The rule against perpetuities does not cause automatic rejection if the property interest might later not violate the rule.
- (D) None of the above.

77. Harvey Homeowner conveys his house to his son, Brutus, on the condition that if

the son tries to sell the house without Harvey's consent, ownership returns to Harvey. Which of the below is correct?

(A) Brutus has a valid life estate in the house.
(B) Brutus owns the property in fee simple absolute.
(C) Harvey owns the future reversionary interest should Brutus try to sell.
(D) The rule against perpetuities makes Brutus's interest void.

78. Harvey Homeowner conveys his house to his son, Brutus, by stating "to Brutus, but if he decides to sell, I get the right of first refusal." Which of the below is correct?

(A) Brutus receives the property in fee simple absolute with no strings attached.
(B) Brutus forfeits the property to Harvey if he attempts to sell it.
(C) Harvey's restriction creating a right of first refusal is effective.
(D) Harvey may exercise his right of first refusal without any other limitations.

Real Property and Future Interests Practice Questions

79. Lyle Landlord advertised his apartment for rent as being in a "noise-free" zone, claiming all tenants were monitored for and prohibited from making excessive noise. Tim rented an apartment from Lyle. Tim's neighbor, Sam, had been renting from Lyle for 2 months. Sam was a professional drummer, who practiced his drums all night long. Tim moved out after two weeks because he could not sleep. What could Tim claim to relieve him of his obligation under the lease?

(A) Nuisance.
(B) Doctrine of Waste.
(C) Actual Eviction.
(D) Constructive eviction.

80. Louise Landlord leased a house to Terrance Tenant for two years, with rent due the first of each month. After 3 months, Terrance's mother fell ill and Terrance left to be with her. His friend, Tony, agreed to take over the lease for the next 4 months. The status of the lease is

(A) Terrance has assigned his lease to Tony.
(B) Terrance has sublet his lease to Tony.
(C) Terrance has no further liability on the lease.
(D) Tony is now fully liable to Louise.

81. In which of the following situations does a joint tenancy exist?

(A) Marla conveys her property to her son, Bob, as a joint tenant with her.
(B) Marla conveys her property to her three children, with 1/4 share going to Joan, 1/4 share to Bob, and 1/2 to Garth.
(C) Marla conveys her property to her three children. Because the children do not get along, Marla dictates that Joan shall possess and occupy the southern 1/3 portion of the land, Garth the northern 1/3, and Bob the central 1/3.
(D) Bob, Garth, and Joan own Brownacre as joint tenants. Joan dies devising all of her property to Mark.

82. Torel Tenant writes a letter to Lorrie Landlord telling her that he is unhappy in Lorrie's apartment house and wants to get out of his lease. Landlord writes back telling Torel that she will treat the lease as terminated. A few days later, Torel receives a bill in the mail for the rent due for the remainder of the lease term. Which of the following is correct?

(A) Torel need not pay rent because Landlord's letter constituted an acceptance of Torel's surrender.
(B) Torel must still pay rent because Landlord did not expressly waive this obligation in her acceptance letter.
(C) Torel must still pay rent because Landlord's letter was not an

acceptable acceptance of Torel's surrender.

(D) Torel must still pay rent because a surrender does not terminate a tenant's duty to pay rent.

83. Anne leases an apartment from Joe. The lease states that the tenant is responsible for "all repairs." In the middle of summer, Anne's air conditioner unit breaks and her apartment becomes extremely hot. Joe refuses to repair the unit. Anne vacates the apartment and refuses to pay rent. What result if Joe brings an action against Anne?

(A) Joe will be unable to enforce the lease because the air conditioner failure amounted to a constructive eviction.

(B) Joe will be unable to enforce the lease because the air conditioner failure amounted to a breach of the implied covenant of quiet enjoyment.

(C) Joe can enforce the lease because a tenant may not withhold rent as a remedy for a landlord's breach of the implied covenant of quiet enjoyment.

(D) Joe can enforce the lease because the air conditioner failure did not amount to a breach of any of his express or implied duties under the lease.

84. Which of the following restrictions does not constitute a negative easement?

(A) Landowner may not construct any building higher than one story on her property.

(B) Landowner may not operate a business on her property.

(C) Landowner may not build a 12-foot fence around her property.

(D) Landowner may not remove the retaining wall that surrounds her property.

85. Melinda lost her job and was unable to afford the rent due on her downtown penthouse apartment. The 5-year lease contained a prohibition on assignment and subleasing. She notified her landlord that she wanted out of her lease and that her friend would take the apartment. The landlord said no, but took four checks from the friend. The landlord then found another tenant willing to pay a higher rent. After notice, the landlord filed suit to evict friend. The court will likely find

(A) For landlord because the lease contained a prohibition on both assignment and sublease and he disapproved.

(B) For tenant because the friend's checks were accepted.

(C) For tenant because Melinda losing her job was unforeseeable and a condition subsequent to enforcement of the lease.

(D) For landlord because the acceptance of the rent checks was irrelevant since friend was a mere tenant at will.

86. Mortimer built a garage and driveway on his small lot. The driveway was against the boundary of the neighboring lot, owned by Gertrude. Because of the shape and size of his lot, each time Mortimer drove around the corner of his driveway into his garage, the back end of his car protruded over Gertrude's lot by about 5 inches. Which of the following is a correct statement?

(A) Mortimer likely has an easement by implication.

(B) Mortimer likely has an easement by necessity.

(C) Mortimer does not need an easement.

(D) None of the above.

87. Bart was seeking to rent a house for 24 months. Bart looked at the house Ben had for rent for $800 per month and told Ben that he would take it. Ben initially wanted a lease, but told Bart that he could rent it without a lease. Which of the following is a correct statement of Bart's position?

(A) Bart is a tenant at will and either he or Ben may terminate the tenancy at any time.

(B) Bart is a trespasser.

(C) Bart is a tenant at sufferance and has no right to possession.

(D) Bart is a term tenant and has the right to possession for 24 months.

88. Neighbors Barney and Melvin exchanged formal written covenants to use their lots only for residential purposes. Melvin later sold his lot to George who planned to build a bowling alley on his lot. What chance does Barney have to stop the bowling alley from being built?

(A) No chance unless the bowling alley is prohibited by the local zoning ordinance.

(B) Barney could enforce the restriction as an equitable servitude if George had notice of the restriction.

(C) Barney could not enforce the restriction because there was no horizontal privity of estate between Barney and Melvin.

(D) Barney could not enforce the restriction because it does not touch and concern the land.

89. In states which recognize tenancy by the entirety:

(A) Neither spouse can convey his/her interest without the other's consent.

(B) The right of survivorship cannot be broken during the marriage.

(C) Either spouse may sever the tenancy.

(D) The tenancy may be severed by either spouse's creditors.

90. Barkley conveys his property which he owns in fee simple absolute, "to Betty for life." Barkley then dies before Betty. Who takes the property at the end of Betty's life estate since Barkley is not alive to take?

(A) It escheats to the government.

(B) Betty's heirs.

(C) Barkley's heirs.

(D) The first to record the deed.

91. Annabelle dies leaving her estate "to Carter and his heirs, but if Carter should not

graduate from law school, to Belle and her heirs." What interest does Carter have?

(A) Fee simple absolute.

(B) Fee simple subject to a condition subsequent.

(C) Fee simple determinable.

(D) Fee simple subject to an executory interest.

92. Todd conveyed Wholeacre, which he owned in fee simple absolute, "to Robb for life, and the remainder to Robb's heirs." Assuming the jurisdiction applies the Rule in Shelley's Case, which of the following is true?

(A) Robb's heirs would have no interest in Wholeacre.

(B) Robb could immediately convey his entire interest in Wholeacre to a third party.

(C) Robb takes Wholeacre in fee simple absolute.

(D) All of the above.

93. In order for a covenant to run and be binding on the purchaser of the burdened land:

(A) The covenant must be intended to run with the land.

(B) The covenant must be stated in a deed.

(C) There must be a common plan or scheme of development.

(D) All of the above.

94. Harry bought season tickets to all of the home games of his local baseball team. His tickets indicated that he was able to sit in seat 323a for each game of the season. Which of the following accurately describes Harry's interest?

(A) A license.

(B) An easement.

(C) A profit in gross.

(D) An express reservation.

95. Mike, Connie, and Jamie were tenants in common owning an apartment building. The apartment was used as a rental property and Mike was in charge of collecting rents and making distributions to the other co-

enants. The roof started leaking and Mike made the necessary repairs. He also upgraded the flooring in all of the apartments to make the building more valuable. Mike then attempted to collect from Connie and Jamie their share of the repairs and improvements. Connie and Jamie refused to pay. Will Mike be successful if he sues Jamie and Connie for contribution?

(A) Mike may recover for the repairs but not the improvements.
(B) Mike may recover for the improvements but not the repairs.
(C) Mike may recover for the repairs and may recover for the improvements when the building is sold if the improvements enhanced the value of the building.
(D) Any recovery by Mike only applies if the property is sold at a profit.

96. Comic Book Guy owned and operated a comic book store. Bart barricaded the street running in front of Comic Book Guy's store so that he could have skate board races. May Comic Book Guy bring an action against Bart for public nuisance?

(A) No, because only government officials may bring actions for public nuisance.
(B) No, because Bart's activity is not illegal.
(C) No, because Comic Book Guy "came to the nuisance."
(D) Yes, because Comic Book Guy suffers a unique injury not shared by the general public.

97. Which one of the following likely constitutes a Fifth Amendment taking.

(A) The building of a prison next door to neighbor's property.
(B) Condemnation of neighbor's property due to chemical contamination.
(C) Rezoning of the area from residential to commercial.
(D) Physical blockage of access into and out of neighbor's gas station.

98. Which of the following is an allowable restriction?

(A) "To Bob, but Bob may not transfer the land without my consent."
(B) "To Bob, but Bob may not transfer the land without first allowing me to meet a third party's offer."
(C) "To Bob, but if Bob attempts to transfer without my consent, the land shall automatically revert to me."
(D) "To Bob, but Bob promises not to transfer the land without my consent."

99. George and Georgia Generous gave their farm Parkacre to the City of Pleasantville with a warranty deed. The conveyance language in the deed stated, "George and Georgia Generous hereby grant Parkacre to Pleasantville for the purpose of constructing a park thereon." Pleasantville did not need another park and after a few years sold it to Dorothy Developer who proceeded to build a strip mall on the property. Which of the following is true?

(A) Upon selling the property to Dorothy Developer, the property reverted to the Generouses.
(B) The gift to the City created a fee simple determinable and an automatic possibility of reverter in the Generouses.
(C) Dorothy Developer took Parkacre as a fee simple absolute.
(D) The gift to the city created a fee simple determinable and a right of re-entry in the Generouses.

100. Owen owned Greenacres in fee simple. He conveyed it "to Alma, but if Baker is living thirty years from the date of this deed, then to Baker." The limitation to Baker is

(A) Invalid.
(B) Valid, because Baker's interest is a reversion.
(C) Valid, because Baker's interest will vest, if at all, within a life in being.
(D) Valid, because Baker's interest is vested subject to divestment.

Questions 101 and 102 are based on the following:

Alison owned Camp Delight in fee simple. By her will she devised, "Camp Delight to my grandchildren who reach the age of 21; this includes all after born grandchildren as well." At the time of her death, Alison had 4 children and 3 grandchildren.

101. This devise is valid under the Rule Against Perpetuities because
  (A) There is a presumption that Alison intended only to include those grandchildren born before her death.
  (B) All of Alison's children are measuring lives.
  (C) Alison had 3 grandchildren born at the time of her death and they must turn 21 within 21 years of her death.
  (D) Alison could have had more children after the conveyance was made.

102. Which of the following would make the above gift invalid under the Rule Against Perpetuities?
  (A) Alison's will expressly stated the intention to include all after born grandchildren, whenever born.
  (B) Alison had only one grandchild at the time of her death.
  (C) The gift was made inter vivos rather than in a will.
  (D) One of Alison's children had died before she did.

103. Johnny, a widower, is owner of Apple Seed Farms in fee simple. Johnny has one son, Jr., who is married. Jr. has one daughter, Dawn, who is married but has no children. Dawn has requested for tax purposes that she be skipped over in any disposition of Apple Seed Farms. Johnny then makes the following conveyance, "To Jr. for life, then to Dawn's children in fee simple." What interest, if any, was created in Dawn's unborn children?

  (A) A springing use.
  (B) A vested remainder subject to divestment (open).
  (C) A contingent remainder.
  (D) None.

104. Marcus, a very sick elderly man, made the following conveyance before his death. "To my son, I give my little red corvette, so long as he does not get a speeding ticket, if he does, then to my grandson, Spike." What interest, if any, does Spike have?
  (A) A shifting executory interest.
  (B) A springing executory interest.
  (C) A vested remainder.
  (D) A contingent remainder.

105. Thelma's will devised all her property "to Aiden for life, remainder to Beth's children." At the time of Thelma's death she was survived by Aiden, Beth, and Beth's children, Claire and Donna. The interest to Beth's children, including those not yet born, can best be characterized as follows:
  (A) Claire and Donna have vested remainders, unborn children have executory interests.
  (B) Claire and Donna have vested remainders subject to condition subsequent, the unborn children have contingent remainders.
  (C) Claire and Donna have vested remainders subject to open, the unborn children have contingent remainders.
  (D) Claire and Donna have contingent remainders, the unborn children have executory interests.

106. Suzy agreed to sell her 100 acres of lakefront land, Sienna Ponds, to Kerry for about one-half of its actual market value based upon Kerry's stated intention to maintain the land in its natural condition for outdoor recreation. The deed recited that the land was transferred, "to Kerry in fee simple, who agrees that he will maintain the Sienna Ponds in its natural state so that all can enjoy its natural beauty." Three years

after the conveyance, Suzy died, leaving her entire estate and all her property to Lola. A year later, Kerry constructed a library on the tract filled with science and math literature. Upon learning of the library, Lola brought action against Kerry seeking a judicial declaration that ownership of Sienna Ponds had reverted back to her. Judgment should be for:

(A) Kerry, because Lola was not the grantor.
(B) Kerry, because no future interest was retained by Suzy when she made the land transfer.
(C) Lola, because the conveyance to Kerry created a fee simple determinable, and upon the occurrence of the specified event, the land reverted back to the grantor.
(D) Lola, because the conveyance to Kerry created a fee simple subject to condition subsequent, and upon occurrence of the specified event, the grantor obtained a right of entry.

107. In a validly executed will, Skipper devised his 10 acre parcel of land on a small island, Islandacre, "to Gilligan for life, remainder to Gilligan's children alive at his death, their heirs and assigns, so long as the land is used for residential purposes." At Skipper's death, he was survived by his daughter, Skipette, by Gilligan, Gilligan's son, Skip, and Gilligan's illegitimate daughter, Ginger. Three years later, Skipette sold "all my interest in Islandacre" to Ginger. The next year Gilligan died, leaving all his property to Ginger. This jurisdiction does not follow the merger doctrine, nor the Rule in Shelly's case. If, shortly after Gilligan's death, Skip sold Islandacre to the Professor who immediately began building a university, who has title to Islandacre?

(A) The Professor, because the restriction upon the use of Islandacre is an unreasonable restraint upon alienation.

(B) Ginger, because the devise from Skippette gave her a fee simple.
(C) Ginger, because the Professor ceased using Islandacre for residential purposes.
(D) Skippette, because the interest to Gilligan's children was void under the Rule Against Perpetuities.

108. Batguy devised his Cave "to Kit Woman, her heirs and assigns, so long as they fight injustice, then to Bobin, his heirs and assigns." Which best describes the various interests created?

(A) Kit Woman has a fee simple determinable, Bobin has no interest, and Batguy's heirs have a possibility of reverter.
(B) Kit Woman has no interest, Bobin has no interest and Batguy's heirs have a fee simple.
(C) Kit Woman has a fee simple determinable and Bobin has a contingent remainder.
(D) Kit Woman has a fee simple determinable and Bobin has a vested executory interest.

109. Ben, the owner of a large apple farm, decided it was time to downsize and subdivide his 500 acres into residential lots. He applied for and was granted all the necessary permits. His plan called for a small fruit farm in the center of the subdivision, in which he could supply the new residents with apples. Among the covenants, conditions, and restrictions, each new home owner, his/her heirs, and assigns agreed to purchase all their apples from Ben. Each deed reflected this covenant. Tom bought one of the new lots and began purchasing all his apple needs from Ben. Five years later, Tom sold his lot to Melinda. The deed to Melinda also contained the covenant. Melinda, a strictly organic fruit purchaser, refused to purchase from Ben, who did not farm organically. If Ben were to bring suit to enforce the covenant, verdict should be for:

(A) Ben, because the deed from Tom to Melinda referenced the covenant.

(B) Ben, because there was common scheme in place, which put Melinda on notice.

(C) Melinda, because the supplying of apples cannot be an enforced restriction.

(D) Melinda, because the covenant was personal to Ben and did not touch and concern his land.

110. Bill, a wealthy owner of an obscure computer software company, Megasoft, decided to sell two lots that surrounded his 24,000 square foot lakeside home, which he shared with his wife and 3 children. One lot was sold to his trustworthy antitrust lawyer, Brad. Bill, a very competitive businessman, took all sorts of measures to ensure the success of his company. In the deed to Brad was the covenant that Brad's heirs and assigns would not construct a competing software company on the lot. Brad, who recently became a well-reported media figure, had no problem in keeping with the covenant. Brad and his wife constructed a lovely English Tudor home with a mother-in-law cottage in the back.

While traveling from Washington DC, Brad and his wife Laura were tragically killed in a plane crash. Their only heir was their adult son, Paul. Paul took possession of the estate and moved in with his wife and child. Forty years later, after Paul had passed away, his child, Allen, took possession of the estate. Allen in need of cash, applied for and was granted all the appropriate permits to divide his lot into two. He sold one lot to his good friend, Bob, who had established a revolutionary internet browser. Allen kept the lot with the English Tudor and mother-in-law, while Bob constructed a small office on his parcel to market his internet browser. His company was a key competitor to Megasoft. Bill's great-great granddaughter, Melinda, just ran across the original deed. Can Melinda enforce the real covenant?

(A) Melinda will be able to enforce the real covenant against Bob, because there is horizontal and vertical privity.

(B) Melinda will be able to enforce the real covenant against Bob, because there was express intent for the covenant to run with the land.

(C) Melinda will not be able to enforce the real covenant against Bob, because Bob had no notice.

(D) Melinda will not be able to enforce the real covenant against Bob, because there is no privity.

111. Acme Corporation is developing an office building. It received a mortgage from Deep Mortgage Company for construction of the building and a loan from Friendly Financing Bank to purchase personal property for the building. Both creditors perfected their security interests by recording at the appropriate recording office. Acme later purchased an elevator which was installed in the office building. If there was a subsequent default on both the mortgage and the bank loan, the interest in the elevator

(A) Would go to Friendly Finance.

(B) Would be split equally between Deep and Friendly.

(C) Would go to Deep Mortgage Company even if the elevator was purchased after the mortgage was recorded.

(D) Would be a trade fixture.

112. A condition in a contract for the purchase of real property that makes the purchaser's obligation dependent upon his obtaining a given dollar amount of conventional mortgage financing

(A) Can be satisfied by the seller if the seller offers the buyer a demand loan for the amount.

(B) Is a condition subsequent.

(C) Is implied as a matter of law.

(D) Requires the purchaser to use reasonable efforts to obtain the financing.

113. Park purchased Marshall's department store property. At the closing, Park delivered a certified check for the balance due and Marshall gave Park a warranty deed with full covenants to the property. The deed

(A) Must be recorded to be valid between the parties.
(B) Must recite the actual consideration given by Park.
(C) Must be in writing and contain the signature of both parties duly witnessed.
(D) Usually represents an exclusive integration of the duties of the seller.

114. Fulcrum Enterprises, Inc., contracted to purchase a four-acre tract of land from Devlin as a site for its proposed factory. The contract of sale is silent on the type of deed to be received by Fulcrum and does not contain any title exceptions. The title search abstract revealed that there are 51 zoning laws which affect Fulcrum's use of the land and that back taxes are due. A survey revealed a stone wall encroaching upon a portion of the land Devlin is purporting to convey. A survey made 23 years ago also had revealed the encroachment. Regarding the rights and duties of Fulcrum, which of the following is correct?

(A) Fulcrum is entitled to a warranty deed with full covenants from Devlin at the closing.
(B) The existence of the zoning laws above will permit Fulcrum to avoid the contract.
(C) Fulcrum must take the land subject to the back taxes.
(D) The stone wall results in a potential breach of the implied warranty of marketability.

15. Linderman purchased a tract of land from Noteworthy for $250,000. Noteworthy revealed the fact that there was an existing first mortgage of $100,000 on the property, which would be satisfied out of the proceeds of the sale. Effective Title Company's title search and policy revealed only the first mortgage. Noteworthy did not reveal that there was a $50,000

unrecorded second mortgage on the property held by his father, Vincent. The first mortgage was satisfied at the closing and Linderman presumed he had clear title to the property. A month after the closing, Vincent appeared and claimed that Linderman was obligated to pay the principal and interest on the mortgage he held. Noteworthy has fled the jurisdiction. As among Linderman, Vincent, and Effective, which of the following is correct?

(A) Vincent will prevail since he had a valid second mortgage.
(B) Effective Title must pay on its title policy since it is an insurer.
(C) Linderman's failure to obtain an affidavit from Noteworthy representing that there was no other mortgage outstanding will result in his taking subject to the Vincent mortgage.
(D) Linderman will take free of the Vincent mortgage.

116. Gilgo has entered into a contract for the purchase of land from the Wicklow Land Company. A title search reveals certain defects in the title to the land to be conveyed by Wicklow. Wicklow has demanded that Gilgo accept the deed and pay the balance of the purchase price. Furthermore, Wicklow has informed Gilgo that unless Gilgo proceeds with the closing, Wicklow will hold Gilgo liable for breach of contract. Wicklow has pointed out to Gilgo that the contract says nothing about defects and that he must take the property "as is." Which of the following is correct?

(A) Gilgo can rely on the implied warranty of merchantability.
(B) Wicklow is right in that if there is no express warranty against title defects, none exists.
(C) Gilgo will prevail because he is entitled to a perfect title from Wicklow.
(D) Gilgo will win if the title is not marketable.

117. Glover Manufacturing, Inc., purchased a four-acre tract of commercially zoned land. A survey of the tract was made prior to the closing, and it revealed an unpaved road that passed across the northeast corner of the land. The title search revealed a mortgage held by Peoples National Bank, which was satisfied at the closing by the seller out of the funds received from Glover. The title search did not indicate the existence of any other adverse interest which would constitute a defect in title. There was no recordation made in connection with the unpaved road. Which of the following is correct regarding Glover's title and rights to the land against the claims of adverse parties?

(A) The unpaved road poses no potential problem if Glover promptly fences off the property and puts up "no trespassing" signs.

(B) Glover does not have to be concerned with the unpaved road since whatever rights the users might claim were negated by failing to record.

(C) The mere use of the unpaved road as contrasted with the occupancy of the land cannot create any interest adverse to Glover.

(D) The unpaved road revealed by the survey may prove to be a valid easement created by prescription.

118. Fosdick's land adjoins Tracy's land and Tracy has been using a trail across Fosdick's land for a number of years. The trail is the shortest route to a roadway which leads into town. Tracy is asserting a right to continue to use the trail despite Fosdick's objections. To establish an easement by prescription, Tracy must show

(A) Implied consent by Fosdick.

(B) Continuous use of the trail for the applicable statutory period.

(C) His use of the trail with an intent to assert ownership to the underlying land.

(D) Prompt recordation of the easement upon its coming into existence.

119. Smith purchased a tract of land. To protect himself, he ordered title insurance from Valor Title Insurance Company. The policy was the usual type issued by title companies. Accordingly

(A) Valor will not be permitted to take exceptions to its coverage if it agreed to prepare and insure the title abstract.

(B) The title policy is assignable in the event Smith subsequently sells the property.

(C) The title policy provides protection against any defects in title.

(D) Valor will be liable for any defects in the abstract of the chain of title which arises, even though the defect could not have been discovered through the exercise of reasonable care.

120. State X is a race-notice jurisdiction. Purdy purchased real property from Hart in State X and received a warranty deed with full covenants. Recordation of this deed is

(A) Not necessary if the deed provides that recordation is not required.

(B) Necessary to vest the purchaser's legal right to the property conveyed.

(C) Required primarily for the purpose of providing the local taxing authorities with the information necessary to assess taxes.

(D) Irrelevant if the subsequent party claiming superior title had actual notice of the unrecorded deed.

121. Recording of a real property mortgage

(A) Is required to validate the rights of the parties to the mortgage.

(B) Will not be effective if improperly filed even if the party claiming superior title had actual notice of its existence.

(C) Perfects the interest of the mortgagee against subsequent bona fide purchasers for value.

(D) Must be filed in the recordation office where the mortgagee' principal place of business is located.

122. Moch sold her farm to Watkins and took back a purchase money mortgage on the farm. Moch failed to record the mortgage. Moch's mortgage will be valid against all of the following parties except

(A) The heirs or estate of Watkins.
(B) A subsequent mortgagee who took a second mortgage since he had heard there was a prior mortgage and failed to record it.
(C) A subsequent bona fide purchaser from Watkins.
(D) A friend of Watkins to whom the farm was given as a gift and who took without knowledge of the mortgage.

123. Monroe purchased a ten-acre land site from Acme Land Developers, Inc. He paid 10% at the closing and gave his note for the balance secured by a 20-year mortgage. Three years later, Monroe found it increasingly difficult to make payments on the note and finally defaulted. Acme threatened to accelerate the loan and foreclose if he continued in default. It told him either to get the money or obtain an acceptable third party to assume the obligation. Monroe offered the land to Thompson for $1,000 less than the equity he had in the property. This was acceptable to Acme and at the closing Thompson paid the arrearage, executed a new mortgage and note, and had title transferred to his name. Acme surrendered Monroe's note and mortgage to him. The transaction in question is a (an)

(A) Assignment and delegation.
(B) Third party beneficiary contract.
(C) Novation.
(D) Purchase of land subject to a mortgage.

124. Golden sold his moving and warehouse business, including all the personal and real property used therein, to Clark Van Lines, Inc. The real property was encumbered by a duly recorded $300,000 first mortgage upon which Golden was personally liable. Clark acquired the property subject to the mortgage but did not assume the mortgage. Two years later, when the outstanding mortgage was $260,000, Clark decided to abandon the business location because it had become unprofitable and the value of the real property was less than the outstanding mortgage. Clark moved to another location and refused to pay the installments due on the mortgage. What is the legal status of the parties in regard to the mortgage?

(A) Clark took the real property free of the mortgage.
(B) Clark breached its contract with Golden when it abandoned the location and defaulted on the mortgage.
(C) Golden must satisfy the mortgage debt in the event that foreclosure yields an amount less than the unpaid balance.
(D) If Golden pays off the mortgage, he will be able to successfully sue Clark because Golden is subrogated to the mortgagee's rights against Clark.

125. Tremont Enterprises, Inc., needed some additional working capital to develop a new product line. It decided to obtain intermediate term financing by giving a second mortgage on its plant and warehouse. Which of the following is true with respect to the mortgages?

(A) If Tremont defaults on both mortgages and a bankruptcy proceeding is initiated, the second mortgagee has the status of general creditor.
(B) If the second mortgagee proceeds to foreclose on its mortgage and the buyer takes free and clear title, the first mortgagee must be satisfied completely before the second mortgagee is entitled to repayment.
(C) Default on payment to the second mortgagee will constitute default on the first mortgage.

(D) Tremont can not prepay the second mortgage prior to its maturity without the consent of the first mortgagee.

126. Wilson sold his factory to Glenn. As part of the contract, Glenn assumed the existing mortgage on the property which was held by Security Bank. Regarding the rights and duties of the parties, which of the following is correct?

(A) The promise by Glenn need not be in writing to be enforceable by Security.

(B) Security is a creditor beneficiary of Glenn's promise and can recover against him personally in the event of default.

(C) Security is a mere incidental beneficiary since it was not a party to the assignment.

(D) Wilson has no further liability to Security.

127. Which of the following is an incorrect statement regarding a real property mortgage?

(A) It transfers title of the real property to the mortgagee.

(B) It is usually accompanied by a negotiable promissory note that refers to the mortgage.

(C) It creates an interest in real property and is therefore subject to the Statute of Frauds.

(D) It creates a nonpossessory security interest in the mortgagee.

128. Marks is a commercial tenant of Tudor Buildings, Inc. The term of the lease is five years and two years have already elapsed. The lease prohibits subletting, but does not contain any provision relating to assignment. Marks approaches Tudor and askes whether Tudor could release him from the balance of the term of the lease for $500. Tudor refuses unless Marks would agree to pay $2,000. Marks locates Flint who is interested in renting in Tudor's building and transfers the entire balance of the lease to Flint in consideration of his

promise to pay Tudor the monthly rental and otherwise perform Marks' obligations under the lease. Tudor objects. Which of the following statements is correct?

(A) A prohibition of the right to sublet contained in the lease completely prohibits an assignment.

(B) The assignment need not be in writing.

(C) The assignment does not extinguish Marks' obligation to pay the rent if Flint defaults.

(D) The assignment is invalid without Tudor's consent.

129. Tom, Dick, and Harry purchased an office building as joint tenants with the right of survivorship. Tom sold his interest to John. Subsequently, Dick passed away. John, Dick's heirs, and Harry are trying to claim ownership to the property. Which of the following statements is correct?

(A) Tom's attempted conveyance to John was invalid because Dick and Harry did not approve.

(B) Tom's conveyance to John created a new joint tenancy between John, Dick and Harry.

(C) Dick's interest in the property goes to his heirs at law upon his death.

(D) John became a tenant in common with Dick and Harry when he received the conveyance from Tom.

130. Wilmont owned a tract of waterfront property on Big Lake. During Wilmont's ownership of the land, several frame bungalows were placed on the land by tenants who rented the land from Wilmont. In addition to paying rent, the tenants paid for the maintenance and insurance of the bungalows, repaired, altered and sold them without permission or hindrance from Wilmont. The bungalows rested on surface cinderblock and were not bolted to the ground. The buildings could be removed without injury to either the buildings or the land. Wilmont sold the land to Marsh. The deed to Marsh recited that Wilmont sold the land, with buildings thereon, "subject to th

rights of tenants, if any." When the tenants attempted to remove the bungalows, Marsh claimed ownership of them. In deciding who owns the bungalows, which of the following is least significant?

(A) The leasehold agreement itself, to the extent it manifested the intent of the parties.

(B) The mode and degree of annexation of the buildings to the land.

(C) The degree to which removal would cause injury to the buildings or the land.

(D) The fact that the deed included a general clause relating to the buildings.

131. Lorraine Lawstudent rented a flat in an apartment house while she was attending law school. The landlord experienced financial difficulty and did not pay the electric bill. The power company turned off the electricity. The least advisable action for Lorraine to take is

(A) Pay the electric bill and deduct the payment from her rent.

(B) Withhold paying rent.

(C) Vacate and terminate the lease.

(D) Sue for damages and seek the equitable remedy of specific performance.

132. Larry Landlord owned a strip mall which was located alongside a major highway. Terry Tenant rented the front unit in the strip mall for a pizza-to-go operation under a standard 25-year lease. Ten years into the lease, the state decided to expand the highway by adding two lanes. This required condemnation of the front half of Larry's strip mall. The state notified Larry and Terry of the condemnation proceeding. Larry insisted that Terry move to an empty space in the rear of the strip mall. The judge in the condemnation proceeding determined that Terry's leasehold was worth $75,000. The likely outcome is that Terry will

(A) Be forced to move to the rear of the strip mall, but will receive $75,000 from the condemnation award.

(B) Be liable for the balanced of the lease term, but will receive a $75,000 credit based on anticipatory repudiation.

(C) Receive $75,000 and have no obligation to Larry.

(D) Receive nothing because the lease violates the Rule Against Perpetuities.

133. Jones and Newton each own a one-half interest in certain real property as tenants in common. Jones' interest

(A) Will pass by operation of law to Newton on Jones' death.

(B) Will pass on Jones' death to Jones' heirs.

(C) May not be transferred during Jones' lifetime.

(D) Is considered a life estate.

134. Your client, Billy Buyer, has asked your opinion about purchasing property. He wants to buy property from Flaky Fred but is worried about rumors that there are liens on the property and that Fred may be insolvent. You advise him to purchase the property using a deed entitled

(A) Quitclaim.

(B) Bargain and sale.

(C) Limited warranty.

(D) General warranty.

135. Sklar Corp. owns a factory that has a fair market value of $90,000. Dall Bank holds an $80,000 first mortgage and Rice Finance holds a $20,000 second mortgage on the factory. Sklar has discontinued payments to Dall and Rice, who have foreclosed on their mortgages. If the factory is properly sold to Bond at a judicial sale for $90,000, after expenses,

(A) Rice will receive $10,000 out of the proceeds.

(B) Dall will receive $77,500 out of the proceeds.

(C) Bond will take the factory subject to the unsatisfied portion of any mortgage.

(D) Rice has a right of redemption after the judicial sale.

136. Jason owns a quarter section of property located in an area that was in transition from agricultural to industrial zoning. Jason wanted to keep the land agricultural because his cousin farmed the adjacent parcel. He listed one-half of the property for sale, but the listing agreement was silent as to the permissible uses. Buyer agreed to the price, but intended to use the property to build an industrial factory. The deed Jason signed at closing specified that the land could only be used for agricultural purposes. Buyer saw the condition in the deed and stated that he did not agree. Nonetheless, the closing agent filed the deed. Buyer will

(A) Be able to use the property for industrial purposes because the most recent expression of use controls.

(B) Be able to use the property for industrial purposes because the seller does not have the right to restrict a new owner.

(C) Not be able to use the property for industrial purposes because the terms of the deed would control over the purchase and sale agreement.

(D) Not be able to use the property for industrial purposes because the Buyer did not sign the deed.

Questions 137 – 139 are based on the following:

On February 1, Frost bought a building from Elgin, Inc. for $250,000. To complete the purchase, Frost: (1) borrowed $200,000 from Independent Bank (2) gave Independent a mortgage for that amount, (3) gave Elgin a second mortgage for $25,000, and (4) paid $25,000 in cash. Independent recorded its mortgage on February 2 and Elgin recorded its mortgage on March 12. The following transaction also took place:

On March 1, Frost gave Scott a $20,000 mortgage on the building to secure a personal loan Scott had previously made to Frost.

On March 10, Scott recorded this mortgage.

On March 15, Scott learned about the Elgin mortgage.

On June 1, Frost stopped making payments on all the mortgages.

On August 1, the mortgages were foreclosed. Frost, on that date, owed Independent $195,000, Elgin $24,000, and Scott $19,000.

A judicial sale of the building resulted in proceeds of $220,000 after expenses were deducted. The above transactions took place in a notice-race jurisdiction.

137. What amount of the proceeds will Scott receive?

(A) $0.
(B) $1,000.
(C) $12,500.
(D) $19,000.

138. Why would Scott receive this amount?

(A) Scott knew of the Elgin mortgage.
(B) Scott's mortgage was recorded before Elgin's.
(C) Elgin's mortgage was first in time.
(D) After Independent is fully paid, Elgin and Scott share the remaining proceeds equally.

139. Frost may redeem the property before the judicial sale only if

(A) There is a statutory right of redemption.
(B) It is probable that the sale price will result in a deficiency.
(C) All mortgages are paid in full.
(D) All mortgagees are paid a penalty.

140. Rich purchased property from Sklar for $200,000. Rich obtained a $150,000 loan from Marsh Bank to finance the purchase, executing a promissory note and a mortgage. Marsh did not file. Rich then borrowed $50,000 from Ace Financial who knew of the prior mortgage held by Marsh. By recording the mortgage, Ace Financial protects its

(A) Legal rights against Rich under the promissory note.
(B) Priority against the claims of subsequent bona fide purchasers for value.
(C) Priority against a previously filed real estate tax lien on the property.
(D) Priority against all parties having earlier claims to the property.

Questions 141 and 142 are based on the following:

Mary Beth contracted to buy an older home on a small lot in Ferndale. The previous deed had an easement recorded in it that said, "MUC (Midwest Utility Company) has the right to string four high voltage utility wires across the property along the eastern 20 feet of the lot at a height of 30-50 feet above the ground." Mary Beth visited the land and saw no wires there. She asked the sellers if they were aware of the easement, or if they knew of MUC plans to place the wires over the property. They had lived there for three years, and they knew nothing other than to have noticed the same wording in the deed when they took possession.

141. What is the legal effect of that clause in the deed?

(A) It has no legal effect because the easement has been abandoned.
(B) It is binding on the current owners but not upon her. Since it is their deed and not hers, the clause lacks "privity" with respect to her and the deed they will convey to her.
(C) It is binding because as an easement appurtenant, it binds all subsequent owners.
(D) It is binding because it is an easement in gross and binds all subsequent owners.

142. Assume Mary Beth closes the deal and the easement is binding upon her ownership. MUC sells their right to Raging River Utility Company (RRUC). RRUC begins to string the wires across her land as the easement specifies. Mary Beth files for an injunction to make them stop because she claims the MUC easement was not transferable. Who will likely win?

(A) Mary Beth: Easements in gross are not transferable.
(B) Mary Beth: Personal easements in gross are transferable, but not this because it is commercial.
(C) RRUC: Commercial easements are transferable, but not private ones.
(D) Mary Beth: She is only bound by what is in her deed, and her deed specifies MUC.

143. Mort bought a property with a small home on it. The next door neighbor, Tony, shared a concrete driveway that ran between their two houses. Mort was unaware of it, but the driveway was entirely on his side of the property line. Tony had been using the driveway for the past 25 years. During that time, the different three owners lived in Mort's house. Mort applied to refinance his loan due to lower mortgage rates, and the appraiser happened upon an old survey of the land that showed the accurate boundaries. When Mort found out, he was upset, and filed a suit against Tony for trespass. What is the likely result?

(A) Mort will prevail in an action for trespass, because Tony's use wasn't "hostile."
(B) Mort will prevail because Tony's use wasn't "open and notorious," since it was not widely known that he was on Mort's property.
(C) Tony will prevail if he used the driveway for the statutory period.
(D) Tony will prevail because the easement was due to necessity.

Questions 144 – 147 are based on the following:

Mick owned a plot of land that extended 500 feet up from the waterfront of a large lake. His house was on the uphill side of the lot, and because of the steep elevation, he had a commanding view of the water. He used a small foot path down the side of the lot to go to his lake front dock every day to fish and swim. When he sold the lower part of the lot to his friend, Eric, he and Eric agreed he would have future access over Eric's parcel to the waterfront. Eric built an expensive house on the water's edge.

144. Mick goes to his attorney for legal advice asking, "What do you call this agreement, and how is it handled?"
- (A) The agreement is an easement by express grant, and it is sufficient to describe it in the purchase and sale agreement.
- (B) The agreement is an easement by express reservation, and it is sufficient to describe it in the purchase and sale agreement.
- (C) The agreement is an easement by express reservation, and it is governed by the Statute of Frauds and recording statutes.
- (D) The agreement is an easement by express grant, and it is governed by the Statute of Frauds and recording statutes.

145. Mick later built a huge home on the uphill lot. In his will, he left his huge home to a non-profit foundation, which turned it into a boy's summer camp lodge. Each day in the summer, approximately 60 young screaming boys traversed Eric's property to access the beach for their swimming lessons. Eric wants to know what actions are available for his relief.
- (A) Because of overuse, Eric may seek an injunction.
- (B) Because the change of use from a home to a lodge constitutes an abandonment of use, Eric can sue

the current users for trespass.
- (C) Because of overuse, Eric can su[e] for any damages the boys hav[e] caused.
- (D) Both A and C above.

146. Eric decides to end the easement b[y] physically blocking it with a fence t[o] prevent his neighbors from crossin[g] through his yard. Will his tactic likely b[e] successful?
- (A) Yes, physically blocking a[n] easement is allowed to stop o[r] prevent an overuse.
- (B) Yes, physically blocking a[n] easement is appropriate to preven[t] these users from later claiming a[n] easement by prescription.
- (C) No, physically blocking is no[t] allowed for an express easement.
- (D) No, physically blocking is no[t] allowed because this easement i[s] due to necessity.

147. Assume that the parties originall[y] intended to create an easement down to th[e] lake, but they failed to meet the formalitie[s] required by the statute of frauds as well a[s] the deed formalities. Which of the followin[g] best states the legal situation?
- (A) The dominant estate may claim a[n] irrevocable license to use th[e] access to the lake.
- (B) The dominant estate may attempt t[o] claim access though necessity.
- (C) The dominant estate's only remed[y] is to attempt access throug[h] prescription.
- (D) The dominant estate may claim revocable license to use the lake.

148. Leif leased the right to Hagar to com[e] onto Blackforest. In the 10-year lease[,] Hagar was permitted to harvest timber in [a] reasonable manner. Leif left on a[n] extended vacation abroad. Every month h[e] received the full rent check from Hagar[.] After five years, Leif returned to find tha[t] Hagar had clear-cut the entire forest, pave[d] it, and had created a huge pay parking lo[t] for employees of the nearby hardwar[e]

orporation, Macrohard. What term best escribes Hagar's interest, and what is orrespondingly Leif's best claim?

(A) Easement/breach of contract.
(B) Profit a prendre/waste.
(C) License/waste.
(D) Easement/waste.

49. Harrison owned a two-acre plot of and on a peninsula overlooking a lake. His ext-door neighbor up the hill, Allison, wned a parallel parcel that was also two cres. Harrison subdivided his land and old half to Madison. In the sale, Harrison nd Madison agreed to a covenant that either lot owner could allow trees to grow aller than 15 feet on the land. The ovenants were properly filed both in Harrison's deed and Madison's deed. This ovenant would allow both Harrison and Madison to preserve the views across each ther's land to the water on the opposite ides.

welve years later, the fir trees on Madison's land had grown to 20 feet in eight. Harrison, who initially had wanted he tree heights limited, grew to appreciate he aesthetic view with the tall trees, and ecided not to enforce the covenant. However, Allison's view was now nearly otally blocked. She filed a lawsuit with the ourt seeking to require Madison to trim his rees to a height of no more than 15 feet. What is the likely result?

(A) Allison will prevail because the covenant touches and concerns the land.
(B) Allison will win because filing of the covenants with the deed made them a public record; therefore, there was constructive notice.
(C) Madison will prevail because a covenant for timber does not touch and concern the land.
(D) Madison will prevail because Allison lacks privity.

50. In real covenants, when comparing equirements for the burden to run versus a enefit, what is the main difference?

(A) For a benefit to run, it must have vertical privity, not so for a burden.
(B) For a burden to run, there must be horizontal privity, not so for a benefit.
(C) For a burden to run, there must be vertical privity, not so for a benefit.
(D) For a benefit to run, it must have horizontal privity, not so for a burden.

151. What is a major difference between covenants and equitable servitudes in both the majority and minority jurisdictions?

(A) Privity rules are relaxed with equitable servitudes.
(B) The Statute of Frauds need not be met with equitable servitudes.
(C) The requirements for benefits and burdens to run with the land are relaxed with equitable servitudes.
(D) None of the above.

Questions 152 – 155 are based on the following:

Helen and Menelaus lived a spartan existence in their tract home which was part of a major subdivision. The original developer built the homes in the subdivision with Greek stucco exteriors, and named the subdivision Athens Acres for its distinctive Mediterranean look and feel. All of the original homeowners signed purchase and sales agreements that required them to refrain from using any other kind of siding other than stucco to retain the character of the neighborhood.

These restrictions were recorded in the original deeds, but each of the homes in the area had changed hands several times, and none of the current deeds contained the restriction. Paris, an uncooperative neighbor, decided to put aluminum siding on his house because it was lower maintenance. Menelaus was upset because he thought aluminum looked tacky – that's why he had more expensive cedar shake siding installed on his home to replace the aging stucco.

152. Menelaus and Helen want to enforce the restriction on Paris. What is the best theory for enforcement?
- (A) Real covenant, because the restriction met the Statute of Frauds.
- (B) Equitable servitude, because there was an intent to bind successors in interest.
- (C) Real covenant, because the restriction touches and concerns the land.
- (D) Equitable servitude, because there was constructive notice to Paris.

153. Paris objects to Menelaus and Helen's action against him. What is his best defense?
- (A) No notice of the restriction.
- (B) The restriction is not in his deed.
- (C) Menelaus and Helen have unclean hands.
- (D) The restriction was abandoned since it is no longer in any of the current deeds.

154. Assume the 45% of the homes had changed from stucco to aluminum siding. Then what would Paris's best defense be?
- (A) Merger.
- (B) Lack of notice.
- (C) Abandonment.
- (D) None of the above.

155. The jurisdiction in which Athens Acres lies has had an excessive number of lawsuits over Greco-style stucco siding over homes deteriorating due to the damp weather of that area. Therefore, they passed a zoning restriction that prohibited Greco-style stucco siding as new or replacement siding, but grandfathered existing structures that had it. Paris found out about this change of events. Assume that his house and the Menelaus-Helen house are the only ones without stucco siding in Athens Acres. What could his additional defense be now?
- (A) Abandonment, because the city changed the zoning.

- (B) Change of neighborhood conditions.
- (C) Lack of common scheme or plan.
- (D) None of the above.

156. When Marty built his two story house the residential zoning ordinance required concrete foundation walls of 4 inch thickness or greater. Over the 20 years since his house was built, the city has experienced several earthquakes, and the zoning commission changed the requirements for concrete foundation walls to be 6 inches with steel rebar reinforcement and foundation "anchors." Marty cannot afford the expense of retrofitting his house at this time. His best argument for keeping it the way it is
- (A) The ordinance is a "taking" under the Fifth Amendment.
- (B) He has a variance because his house was built to old code before the new changes took effect.
- (C) His non-compliance with the current ordinance is permitted because it is "spot zoning."
- (D) He is allowed to keep his house as it is because of non-conforming use.

157. Tia owned a corner lot in the middle of an area zoned for residential use only. She wanted to open a "mom and pop" corner grocery and deli, because she felt that the older residents in the neighborhood needed access to food shopping within a very short walking distance. Which answer most closely describes the procedure and action she must apply for?
- (A) A non-conforming use.
- (B) Spot zoning.
- (C) A variance.
- (D) Rezoning to allow commercial enterprises.

158. Ted owned a house that was located exactly 10 feet from his side property line. This was in compliance with the city's old building codes, which required a minimum of 10 feet for buildings and 5 feet for porches and decks. Ted was restricted to a

wheel chair, and built an access ramp that was exactly five feet wide. When he was finished, the edge of the ramp was 5 feet from the property line.

Four years later, the city passed a new ordinance that required all structures, including decks and porches, to be 10 feet from the side property line. Existing structures were grandfathered. However, if they needed repair or replacement, the new ordinance required compliance with the 10 foot restriction. Ted's ramp was made of wood, and it was deteriorating after 15 years since its construction. Which answer provides the appropriate form of relief if he is contemplating replacing the ramp?

- (A) Non-conforming use
- (B) Spot-zoning
- (C) Variance.
- (D) Rezoning.

159. Ulysses and Penelope lived on a small island called Ithaca in King County. Their shorefront property was 120 feet wide, and was prime real estate for the area due to its water access and view. The county decided to build a walking path across the property of Ulysses and Penelope as well as several other neighbors in order to connect their neighborhood to a public walking path that circled the rest of the island. The path was to be maintained by the county parks department, and would be paved in asphalt to permit jogging, biking, and in-line skating on the 5 mile circuit around the island. Ulysses and Penelope are concerned for two reasons. First, it would ruin the privacy they now enjoy on their lot. Second, it would likely decrease the resale value of their home. What is the most likely relief for Ulysses and Penelope to be granted?

- (A) Claim it as a taking under the 5th Amendment; request an injunction against building the path.
- (B) Claim it as a taking under the 5th Amendment; request damages due to the decrease in property value.
- (C) Claim a violation of due process under the 14th Amendment; request damages due to the decrease in

property value.
- (D) Claim a violation of due process under the 14th Amendment; request an injunction against building the path.

160. Zeke owns a small parcel of land in an upscale portion of the city of Happyvale. The area is zoned for single and multi-family dwellings. Zeke filed for a building permit to build an apartment complex for low-income residents. One month later, the local zoning commission amended the zoning in that area to only permit single family homes "in order to keep the quality of the neighborhood high and maintain property values." Zeke was shocked, especially because he did not find out about the zoning change until after it took effect. Which of the following would be his least effective action?

- (A) Claim of violation of 14th Amendment (Due Process).
- (B) Claim of violation of 14th Amendment (Equal Protection).
- (C) Claim of violation of 5th Amendment (taking all economic value).
- (D) Claim of lack of actual notice.

161. Mike, Ed, Dan, and Bob started a rock band called "Oscar Thickfoot." They practiced in Mike's garage until the wee hours each morning. McMullen, the next-door neighbor, was not pleased. The loud bass vibrations cracked the plaster in some of his walls and shook his china cabinets so hard that some of the dishes fell out and broke on the floor. Additionally, he developed a nervous twitch and had to be treated for severe indigestion due to the anxiety and loss of sleep. What cause of action and remedy are likely?

- (A) Public nuisance for damages only.
- (B) Public nuisance for injunction only.
- (C) Private nuisance for damages only.
- (D) Private nuisance for injunction and damages.

162. Gail and Dale own a condo in Washita Forest Manors. The exterior

siding is deteriorating on their unit, and the association claims it has no money in the budget to fix the unit. Whose responsibility is it, and how can it get fixed?

(A) It is Gail and Dale's responsibility since it is their unit, and they must pay.

(B) It is Gail and Dale's responsibility since the association cannot afford it.

(C) It is the association's responsibility because it is on the outside of the unit; the association must pay.

(D) It is the association's responsibility because the association must do all maintenance on the condos.

Questions 163 and 164 are based on the following:

In the following two questions, the property is in a state that requires all broker listing agreements and property purchase and sale agreements to comply with the Statute of Frauds. Boris Broker and Sam Seller entered into an agreement that Boris would be the "exclusive agent for listing and sales of Sam's property for the next six months." Sam owned a number of properties but intended the agreement to mean the house in which he was currently residing. However, due to economic hardships that arose during the six months, he decided to sell his rental house also. He listed the rental and promptly entered a purchase and sale agreement with Billy Buyer through Alex Agent. Sam also sold his personal residence to his son and did not involve Boris in the sale.

163. Boris Broker was upset and sued for his commission. What is the likely result?

(A) Boris may collect the commission from Sam on the sale of the rental property.

(B) Boris may collect the commission from Sam on the sale of the primary residence only.

(C) Boris may collect commission on the sale of both properties.

(D) Boris will collect nothing.

164. The purchase and sale agreement between Billy and Sam specified that the rental property would be conveyed for $450,000 contingent upon an engineering inspection and conventional financing. The contract named the property as "Premier Apartments, Main Street, Pleasantville." Billy didn't realize it, but Sam's real estate management corporation was named "Premier," and Sam owned two other complexes a mile away on Main Street with the same name. Is the contract enforceable?

(A) No, it violates the Statute of Frauds.

(B) No, it is not enforceable until Billy successfully obtains conventional financing.

(C) Yes, it is enforceable if the apartments pass the engineering inspection.

(D) Yes, it is enforceable because there is a rebuttable presumption that Billy will obtain financing.

165. Frank divided his ten-acre lot into two parcels and sold the south one to his brother Joe. Their understanding was that the boundary line was the narrow stream that ran between the two properties. Joe later attempted to refinance the mortgage on his property, and in doing so, a routine search of the title turned up a survey that proved the actual property line was 20 feet on Frank's side of the stream, and his deed description agreed with the survey. It has been three years since the sale of the property. Joe wants to build a small picnic area and rope swing on what they both once believed was Frank's property on the north side of the stream. Frank protests and the dispute results in litigation. What is the likely result?

(A) Joe will prevail due to adverse possession.

(B) Joe will prevail due to the information in the recorded deed.

(C) Frank will prevail because Joe has not met the time period for adverse possession.

(D) Frank will prevail because the

stream will be enforced as the property line.

166. Laura and Fenton purchased a home in Bayport from their son's friend, Chet. They paid $4000 in earnest money and negotiated a mortgage through a local bank. When they closed the deal, they had the deed acknowledged by that bank. Fenton meant to record the deed, but forgot and left it in his desk drawer. Laura and Fenton moved into the house, and built a nice garage with a workshop upstairs. Chet subsequently died. Chet's records erroneously indicated that he still owned the property, and the executor for the estate researched the court records and did not find any recorded sales. He sued Laura and Fenton for his property on behalf of the estate. What is the likely result?

(A) Laura and Fenton will prevail because they had the deed acknowledged.

(B) Laura and Fenton will prevail despite not recording the deed.

(C) Chet's estate will prevail because the deed was never recorded.

(D) Chet's estate will prevail because Laura and Fenton do not have marketable title.

167. Sandy decided to give her 19-year old daughter Cindy title to her home, but wanted to live in it for the rest of her life. She communicated the gift by letter to Cindy, who was living in Europe. Sandy drew up the deed and left it in her desk drawer. Later, she became angry at Cindy for living a wild lifestyle, and decided to rescind the gift. She communicated the rescission to Cindy, then wrote a will that gave the home to Adolpho upon Sandy's death. Sandy then unexpectedly died before the letter was delivered to Cindy in Europe. When Cindy found out about the will, she made a claim against the estate for the home, and indicated she would litigate if her claim was refused. What is the likely outcome of her ownership claim in the property?

(A) The conveyance to Cindy was ineffective due to non-delivery of the deed.

(B) The conveyance to Cindy was enforceable because the letter indicating the gift satisfied the Statute of Frauds.

(C) The conveyance was unenforceable because it was later rescinded.

(D) The conveyance was enforceable because it is impossible to rescind a conveyance without a new deed.

Questions 168 and 169 are based on the following:

Bart and Homer were tenants in common of Blackacre. Homer was on an extended trip to Brazil, and Bart decided to sell the property while Homer was gone. He entered into a contract to sell the entire property to Brett. The contract specified that Bart would convey marketable title on closing. The title was conveyed with a standard warranty deed. Homer came back from Brazil and found Brett living on Blackacre.

168. When Brett found out about Homer's claim as a tenant in common, he sued Bart. What is the likely outcome?

(A) Brett will prevail because Bart breached the warranty of title.

(B) Brett will prevail because of the part performance exception.

(C) Bart will prevail because he actually only sold his half.

(D) Bart will prevail, because as a tenant in common, he had the right to sell the entire property.

169. Same situation as the prior question, but Bart only conveys his interest to Brett with a quitclaim deed. Now what is the likely outcome of the suit?

(A) Brett will prevail because Bart breached the warranty of title.

(B) Brett will prevail because of the part performance exception.

(C) Bart will prevail, because he actually sold only his half.

(D) Bart will prevail, because as a tenant in common, he had the right to sell the whole property.

Questions 170 and 171 are based on the following:

Cassandra purchased a new home from Hector. Six months later, the wiring in one of the walls overheated. This caused sparks, and the home burned down. The fire inspectors and insurance inspectors agreed that the cause was faulty wiring.

170. From just the facts above, what is Cassandra's best claim against the builder?
(A) Breach of title warranty.
(B) Breach of express warranty.
(C) Breach of implied warranty.
(D) Breach of merchantability warranty.

171. Same facts as the question above, except the house is one year old when Cassandra buys it from the first homeowner.
(A) Breach of title warranty.
(B) Breach of express warranty.
(C) Breach of implied warranty.
(D) None of the above.

172. Laura and Dick live in a jurisdiction that recognizes the traditional equitable conversion rule. They purchase a home from Rob with a standard purchase and sale agreement that has no explicit provisions for risk of loss. Between signing the contract and closing the deal, the home burns to the ground. Who does not bear any risk for this fire?
(A) Laura and Dick's insurance company, if they have insured the home.
(B) Rob's insurance company, if he has kept his insurance for the interim period.
(C) Laura and Dick personally.
(D) Rob personally.

Questions 173 – 175 are based on the following:

State "X" is a pure race jurisdiction. Stan deeded his property to Oliver, who was a bona fide purchaser for value. Oliver didn' immediately move to the property, and h put the deed in his safe deposit box. Abbot knew about the race filing statute. Abbot approached Stan and asked him to sell th property to him. Stan sold him the property with a quitclaim deed for what appeared t be a handsome discount. Abbot immediately filed the deed at the loca county courthouse. Three days later, Olive heard the rumor that Stan had resold th property. He raced to the courthouse an filed his deed.

173. As between Oliver and Abbott, wh will likely win the title dispute?
(A) Oliver, because he has a warranty deed, and Abbott only has quitclaim deed.
(B) Abbott, because he filed first.
(C) Oliver, because Abbott had notic of the prior sale.
(D) Oliver, because he was a bona fid purchaser for value.

174. Abbott is upset that Oliver brough legal action to quiet title. As a result, h brings an action against Stan. What woul be the likely result?
(A) Because Stan breached th statutory warranty of title by no ensuring quiet enjoyment, Abbot will prevail.
(B) Stan's sale with a quitclaim dee for a substantial discount is prim: facie evidence of his wrongdoin; therefore Abbott will prevail.
(C) Stan will prevail because he did no promise quiet enjoyment.
(D) Stan will prevail because in a pur race jurisdiction a seller has n responsibilities under warranty o title.

175. Now assume that the above transactio occurred in a race-notice jurisdiction. A: between Oliver and Abbott, who will likel win the title dispute?
(A) Oliver, because he has a warrant deed and Abbott only has quitclaim deed.

(B) Abbott, because he filed first.

(C) Oliver, if Abbott had notice of the prior sale.

(D) Oliver, because he was a bona fide purchaser for value.

Questions 176 – 178 are based on the following:

Mark entered into a purchase and sale agreement with Glenn to sell him his country home. Glenn purchased title insurance from Acme Title, Inc. The insurance disclaimed "any defect that is not of record in the attached abstract of title as of closing." Acme searched the court records, and found no defects in the title, and concluded that Mark held good title to the property. On January 6th at noon, Glenn closed. That afternoon at 1 p.m., Paul, recorded a prior deed he had received from Mark on that same property. At 9 a.m. the next morning, Glenn's attorney filed Glenn's deed.

176. Assuming a race-notice jurisdiction, in the later action between Paul and Glenn over title, who is the likely winner?

(A) Glenn, because he was the bona fide purchaser for value, and he filed within a reasonable time of closing.

(B) Glenn, because he had no notice of a prior conveyance to Paul.

(C) Paul, because he filed first.

(D) Paul, because Glenn's attorney committed malpractice by untimely filing.

177. What is the likely outcome of action involving the title insurance company?

(A) Glenn would prevail because he is insured against prior deeds like Paul's.

(B) Glenn would prevail because the disclaimer clause is void as a matter of policy; he is fully insured.

(C) Acme would prevail because of the disclaimer clause.

(D) Acme would prevail because until Glenn has title, he has no insurable

interest.

178. Assume that in the prior two questions, that Paul filed his deed before the property closing but Acme and Glenn never found out about it. Glenn decided two months later he really didn't want the property, and he decided to sell it to Jerry. In the contract, he also signed over his title insurance to Jerry. Now Paul commenced an action against Jerry to quiet title. What are the likely outcomes of the ensuing litigation?

(A) Jerry loses to Paul, but wins his insurance claim against Acme.

(B) Jerry loses to Paul, and then loses his insurance claim against Acme.

(C) Paul loses to Jerry because of the race-notice rule.

(D) Paul loses his claim against the insurance company.

Questions 179 and 180 are based on the following:

Jim and Maritza owned a small home in a subdivision in state X. That jurisdiction had a statute that specified adverse possession claims would be recognized after a specified period of time had elapsed. Their next-door neighbor Jan had a very unsightly ramshackle travel trailer sitting beside her house. The trailer was on cinder blocks and had not moved from that spot for 25 years. Jim and Maritza complained constantly that the trailer was an eyesore and needed to be moved. When Jan decided to build an additional room onto the back of her house, the local permitting rules required her to have her lot surveyed. At that time, she discovered that her trailer had extended 10 feet over onto Jim and Maritza's property the entire time it had been there. Jim and Maritza threatened to file a nuisance action against Jan.

179. Jan, who was fed up with the neighbors' complaining, filed a claim to gain title to the 10-foot strip of land under adverse possession theory. What are the likely results of Jan's action?

(A) Jan will prevail because she has

met the statutory period for adverse possession.

(B) Jan will not prevail because her possession was not "open" – both parties believed the land was Jan's to begin with.

(C) Jim and Maritza will prevail because the possession was without their permission: they had repeatedly asked Jan to move the trailer.

(D) Jan will not prevail because Jim and Maritza have a valid nuisance claim.

180. In the above question, now assume that Jan did not file the adverse possession claim but instead conveyed her property to her son, Jake. Not only did Jake keep the trailer where it was, he refurbished the inside and started holding loud parties in it. Now Jim and Maritza are hopping mad and complaining loudly. Jake consults an attorney and decides to make the adverse possession claim. He has been in possession of his property for only six months. What is the likely result of his adverse possession claim?

(A) Jake loses; he has not lived there for the statutory period.

(B) Jake loses; Jim and Maritza now have a valid nuisance claim.

(C) Jake wins; his mother's adverse possession period counts toward his claim.

(D) Jake loses because his possession was not exclusive.

181. When Rolf bought his ocean beachfront property, the area was zoned for residential use. He applied for his building permit one year later, only to find that in the interim, the state environmental agency had declared his property and the surrounding 150 acres "protected wetlands" and prohibited building. What is would Rolf's most likely legal claim?

(A) Claim unconstitutional "spot zoning."

(B) Request a variance.

(C) Claim damages under inverse condemnation.

(D) Claim "grandfather" status.

182. Fred the farmer owned a small pig farm in the Grant County, which is in a lien theory state. He needed to build a new barn in which to house the pigs in the wintertime. In order to finance it, he took out a $100,000 mortgage using the farm property as security. The note required monthly payments to Bagley's Bank. Two years later Fred, who could no longer farm due to age and failing health, sold the pig farm to Gregg. He conveyed the farm by a deed that stated "grantee expressly assumes the mortgage grantor previously made with Bagley's Bank." Gregg made payments for six months, then defaulted. Who is liable to Bagley Bank?

(A) Fred, because he signed the original note.

(B) Gregg, because he expressly assumed the mortgage.

(C) Both Fred and Gregg.

(D) Either Fred or Gregg.

183. Kaye contracted to sell Hodges a building for $300,000. The contract required Hodges to pay the entire amount at closing. Hodges put the $300,000 into escrow. Kaye changed his mind regarding the wisdom of selling the property and refused to close the sale of the building. Hodges sued Kaye. To what relief is Hodges entitled?

(A) Punitive damages and compensatory damages.

(B) Specific performance and compensatory damages.

(C) Consequential damages or punitive damages.

(D) Compensatory damages or specific performance.

184. John, Paul, and George own a large recreational property as joint tenants with a right of survivorship. George decides he wants to build his own home and occupy the northern one-third of the property. What is his best choice?

(A) Judicial partition.

(B) Dissolve the joint tenancy into tenants in common.

(C) Dissolve his third into a tenancy in common leaving John and Paul as joint tenants with respect to each other.

(D) Pay John and Paul to allow him exclusive use of the one third he desires.

185. Felix owns Lot A in fee simple absolute. Eddie owns the adjacent Lot B. They are in constant disagreement over where the property line is on their common boundary. Eddie wishes to sell his property to Gino, but he knows that due to the borderline dispute there will be issues with marketable title. Given these facts, how can he best resolve this issue?

(A) File an adverse possession claim.

(B) Sue Felix for trespass.

(C) Bring a quiet title action.

(D) Sue for specific performance.

186. Which of the following is the least appropriate situation in which to bring an unlawful detainer action?

(A) Trespass.

(B) Holdover tenant.

(C) Adverse possessor.

(D) Public nuisance.

187. Mary, Paul, and Peter own Blackacre as tenants in common. During a lengthy absence of Paul and Peter, Mary installed a cyclone fence around one third of the property and put a padlocked gate at the entrance. Paul and Peter returned and objected to her actions. Do they have ground for legal complaints?

(A) Yes, she is trespassing.

(B) Yes, she is violating their rights of possession.

(C) No, as part owner, she may use her third any way she sees fit.

(D) No, she still left them two-thirds of the property to use as they wish.

188. The boundary between Karl's and Rachel's residential lots was a 10-foot high concrete retaining wall. This was necessary because Karl was immediately uphill on a very steep slope from Rachel. Karl moved to the land and built a very large home on the uphill lot. Rachel decided to landscape her back yard. After placing many thousands of dollars of plants in the yard, the concrete retaining wall looked more and more like an eyesore, so Rachel had her landscaper remove it. The shift in land caused Karl's large house to collapse. The deprivation of the lateral support would not have resulted in damage to the land if Karl's new home were not so large. If Karl sues Rachel, the right/obligation involved in their dispute would be

(A) Against Rachel under theory of strict liability for damages to Karl's house.

(B) For Karl because his right of quiet enjoyment was breached.

(C) For Karl because his lateral support right is absolute.

(D) Against Rachel because she breached Karl's subjacent support right.

189. Georgette wanted to give her loyal companion-lover, George, one of her parcels of property to show her affection. George decided that he would prefer to receive property that could be used as a hunting lodge. George was certain he had to give Georgette some consideration for the conveyance to be valid, but Georgette would not take anything from him. Rather she gave him the deed to the hunting lodge with the oral condition that he never leave her for another female companion-lover. If the transaction is questioned, a court would likely find that

(A) The conveyance is not enforceable because no consideration was given.

(B) The conveyance is not valid because Georgette has placed a condition on the conveyance.

(C) If George later leaves Georgette, Georgette may introduce extrinsic evidence to prove the existence of the oral condition that he has breached.

    (D) The conveyance is valid because there was intent to deliver and the oral condition will be disregarded.

190. Horace owned a small farm. There was a stream that ran across his property. He decided to dam the stream to make a small private trout-fishing pond. Prior to his activity, there had never been any flooding problems. However, since building his dam, whenever it rained, the diverted water spilled over into his neighbor Ignatio's yard, causing crop damage. What is Ignatio's most likely action against Horace?

    (A) Violation of subjacent support.
    (B) Violation of lateral support.
    (C) Violation of riparian rights.
    (D) Flood damages.

191. Landlord rented a house to Buck pursuant to a one-year lease. After three months, he sent a letter to landlord stating that he was going to move out immediately, and then vacated. Enclosed in the letter was a check covering the following month's rent. Landlord made no attempt to re-rent the house and it remained vacant for the remainder of the lease. At the expiration of the lease, landlord asserted a claim against Buck for unpaid rent from the date that Buck vacated the premises until the end of the lease term. In deciding landlord's claim, the court should find for

    (A) Landlord, because Buck failed to pay the rent as agreed.
    (B) Landlord, because landlord had a right of re-entry.
    (C) Buck, because landlord had a right of re-entry.
    (D) Buck, because he essentially gave the landlord a month's notice of his intent to vacate.

192. Phil Pigfarmer came from a long line of pig farmers. When Phil died, his will specified that "I leave the family pig farm to my son Randy, but if he is not survived by children of Randy and his present wife Penny, then to my niece Lovely and her

heirs." Fifteen years went by and Penny turned 40 years of age without bearing children. Randy continued to take care of the family farm, but gradually became tired of the pigs. The neighbors around the pig farm began to mine coal. An engineering company Randy hired concluded there might be a viable coal deposit on the property. Based on their opinion, Randy decided to try mining for coal. He dug a cavern on the land and began excavating some coal to sell. Lovely learned of Randy's mining activities and asserted a claim against Randy for waste. The court's decision on the lawsuit will likely

    (A) Deny Lovely's claim because a life tenant may remove minerals from the land as long as the mining is reasonable and not excessive.
    (B) Deny Lovely's claim because a claim for waste does not exist at least until Penny's death.
    (C) Issue an injunction against further coal mining and order Randy to pay Lovely any profits derived from the mining operation.
    (D) Terminate the estate because Randy violated the terms of the life estate.

193. Arnie owned a large tract of land which he later divided into two separate parcels. Parcel A had access to a public road. However, Parcel B had access to the road only by virtue of a small gravel road that crossed over Parcel A. Arnie sold Parcel B to Bert, and included in the deed a right-of-way easement to use the gravel highway. Bert never occupied the parcel and never used the gravel highway that crossed Parcel A. A few years later, Bert sold the parcel to Charlie, never mentioning in the deed the right-of-way easement. If Charlie claims access by way of the gravel road, which of the following would be his best argument?

    (A) Because the gravel road was the only access to the public road, Charlie received an implied grant.
    (B) The right-of-way easement was a prescriptive easement.
    (C) Because the gravel road was the

only access to the public road, Charlie received an easement by necessity.

(D) Because the gravel road was the only access to the public road, Charlie received an easement by implied reservation.

194. Denise Developer found a near perfect piece of property zoned commercial in the downtown area of Pleasantville. She hired an architect to design a high tech office building with an objective of attracting dot.com tenants. She approached Microhard and secured a lease agreement for over half of the available square footage. The lease was not recorded but it allowed Denise to attract other dot.com tenants and apply for a construction loan of $1,500,000 from Maximum Mortgage Company. Maximum knew of Microhard's lease. Denise executed a mortgage and related promissory note in favor of Maximum. Maximum recorded their mortgage immediately.

The office building was completed and Denise had more demand than space so the building opened full. One year later, Denise ran into financial trouble and defaulted on the mortgage. Maximum took possession and immediately notified all the tenants that their leases were cancelled, that they were evicted, and that they must vacate immediately unless they were willing to sign a new lease at double the previous rent. The recording statute in the jurisdiction specified "every conveyance, encumbrance, or lease not recorded is void as against any subsequent party recording first." The tenants hired you as their attorney seeking to compel Maximum to honor the leases at the lower rents. Which of the following statements of advice is the most accurate?

(A) All the tenants will prevail unless otherwise in default on their leases because Maximum loaned money to Denise with actual knowledge that she intended to enter into binding leases.

(B) Microhard is entitled to continue their lease because Maximum had constructive notice of their prior lease.

(C) Microhard is entitled to continue their lease because Maximum had actual notice of their prior lease.

(D) All the tenants should renegotiate their leases with Maximum.

195. Bob and Mark who both own fee simple absolute estates in adjoining parcels of land enter into a restrictive covenant. Sara later acquires Mark's parcel. In which situation will there be vertical privity between Bob and Sara?

(A) Mark transfers to Sara a leasehold estate.
(B) Mark transfers to Sara a life estate.
(C) Mark transfers to Sara a defeasible fee.
(D) Mark transfers to Sara a fee simple absolute.

196. Billy owns a parcel of land in a residential area that is regulated by a local zoning ordinance. The ordinance prohibits any building from being less than 30 feet from the street. Billy seeks to build a home on his property, but the awkward shape of his parcel would prevent him from complying with the ordinance, and his home would have to be 15 feet from the street. In order to build his home, what should Billy seek from the city?

(A) Spot zoning.
(B) A variance.
(C) A nonconforming use allowance.
(D) Rezone.

197. Cecile, Eric, and Joan all inherited a single 144-acre parcel of land from their Uncle Buck as joint tenants. Joan later sold her share to her friend Tina. Which of the following describes the relationship between Cecile, Eric, and Tina?

(A) All three share an undivided interest in the property as joint tenants.
(B) All three share an undivided interest in the property as tenants in

common.

(C) Each owns a one-third fractional share of the 144 acres.

(D) All three share an undivided interest in the property – Cecile and Eric as joint tenants with each other and Tina as a tenant in common.

198. Ted owned a large piece of land which he divided into two parcels, A and B. He retained A and sold B to Ben. In the deed, the parties mutually agreed that, "Owners of A and B and all of their heirs and assigns promise to maintain a paved road between the two pieces of property, sharing the expenses equally in its upkeep." Over the next twenty years, several different people owned both parcels and the road fell into complete disrepair. David, the current owner of parcel A, wants to rebuild the road and wants the current owner of B, Jacob, to pay half of the expense. Jacob refuses. Can David successfully sue Jacob?

(A) Yes, because the covenant ran with the land.

(B) No, because the covenant was to maintain and here the road was completely destroyed.

(C) Yes, because the deed created an equitable servitude.

(D) No, because the covenant was void under the Rule Against Perpetuities.

199. Stan and Kyle negotiated and agreed over the phone that Stan would rent an apartment from Kyle for a period of five years. Kyle required neither prepayment of rent nor a deposit and Stan moved right in. Which type of tenancy was created?

(A) Term tenancy for five years.

(B) Periodic tenancy.

(C) Tenancy at will.

(D) Tenancy at sufferance.

200. Which of the following is a violation of the landlord's implied warranty of habitability?

(A) The landlord controls the heat and keeps it at 50 degrees.

(B) The neighbor's dog barks all night long.

(C) The carpet is worn so that it no longer provides cushioning.

(D) The apartment is not well insulated and is expensive to keep warm in the winter.

201. Which of the following scenarios will terminate an easement?

(A) Clarissa, the owner of lot 1, has a right-of-way easement across lot 2 owned by Baker. Baker purchases Clarissa's lot but later conveys it to Leroy.

(B) Clarissa has a driveway easement across Baker's property to a dirt road. The county constructed a new road that provided Clarissa with direct access from her property. Clarissa builds a paved driveway to the new road and stops using the driveway easement.

(C) Baker sells his lot to Bob but fails to tell him about the easement. Bob never asks about an easement and the access road is not clearly noticeable after a visible inspection of the property.

(D) All of the above.

Questions 202 – 204 are based on the following:

There are three different statutes to determine priorities between conflicting interests in land as follows:

1. "The priority of conflicting interests in land is determined by the first to have recorded."

2. "A conveyance of real property is ineffective against a subsequent purchaser for value and without notice unless recorded."

3. "All conveyances of real property are ineffective against a bona fide purchaser whose instrument is first recorded."

Adam sold Greenacres to Blake via a quit claim deed which Blake did not record. One month later, Adam experienced financial difficulty and was approached by Charlie who did not know of the prior conveyance to Blake. Adam conveyed to Charlie a full statutory warranty deed. Because Charlie's lawyer was on vacation, the deed did not get recorded for 10 days. Unfortunately, Adam sold the property via a bargain and sale deed to David. David knew of the Charlie's interest, but was able to record before Charlie's lawyer filed.

202. Blake will prevail

(A) Only if the jurisdiction has recording statute 1.

(B) Only if the jurisdiction has recording statute 2.

(C) Only if the jurisdiction has recording statute 3.

(D) Under none of three recording statutes.

203. Charlie will prevail

(A) Only if the jurisdiction has recording statute 1.

(B) Only if the jurisdiction has recording statute 2.

(C) Only if the jurisdiction has recording statute 3.

(D) Because his full statutory warranty deed is superior to both the quit claim deed and bargain and sale deed.

204. David will prevail

(A) Only if the jurisdiction has recording statute 1.

(B) Only if the jurisdiction has recording statute 2.

(C) Only if the jurisdiction has recording statute 3.

(D) Against Blake because a bargain and sale deed is superior to a quit claim deed.

205. Sarah Seller owned Whiteacre in fee simple in a race-notice state. On January 10th she conveyed a quit claim deed to Alice who forgot to record. Two months passed and Sarah was again in need of money so she conveyed a warranty deed to Barbara who also forgot to file. Barbara then conveyed a bargain and sale deed to Carol who filed. Carol did not know of Alice's deed. Alice learned of Carol's interest from a neighbor and immediately filed after Carol. Carol then learned that Barbara forgot to file so she went to Barbara, took the warranty deed Barbara had previously received from Sarah and filed it. As between Alice and Carol's claim to the property

(A) Alice will prevail because she was first in time.

(B) Alice will prevail because Carol had a "wild deed."

(C) Carol will prevail because she took under a bargain and sale deed that is superior to the quitclaim deed that Alice took under.

(D) Carol will prevail because she recorded first without actual knowledge of Alice's interest.

Questions 206 and 207 are based on the following:

Harriet Homeowner purchased a five-acre tract of land on an island to build her dream home. In order to provide water for her property, the county required that she agree to a fifteen-foot wide easement over her property. Harriet gave the county a deed, which the Water Department recorded. Forty years later, Harriet passed away and her children sold her home to Sally Second. The conveyance was by way of a quitclaim deed, which did not refer to the Water Department easement. Sally was unaware of the easement, because in forty years they had never come onto the property. Three years later, she built an expensive carriage-house style of garage over the area of the easement. Five years later, the Water Department announced that they needed to excavate the water main in the easement because the pipes were made of lead and there was a fear of lead poisoning.

206. Upon learning of the Water Department's plans, Sally hired a structural engineer. Because the carriage house was not built on a proper foundation, he believed it would be significantly damaged in the excavation process. Sally then went to her attorney and instructed him to request the court enter an order requiring the Water Department to either (1) pay for the damages to the carriage house or (2) be enjoined from coming onto her property and/or excavating her property. The likely outcome is that Sally's request will be

(A) Denied because the Water Department's need is paramount since there is a risk of lead in the pipes.

(B) Denied because the Water Department is within its rights.

(C) Granted because the deed under which Sally took her interest did not disclose the easement.

(D) Granted because 48 years have passed since the easement was given without the Water Department coming onto the property.

207. Assuming that Sally decided against filing a motion to stop the excavation and rather waited to see what damages she suffered. The engineers were able to use jacks to elevate the carriage house so the excavation did minimum harm. Sally's total costs were $7,500. If she brings suit against both the Water Department and the children of Harriet, the likely outcome is that she will

(A) Prevail against the children of Harriet because the deed she received did not mention the easement in gross restriction.

(B) Prevail against the Water Department because its excavation constituted overuse or misuse and it caused the $7,500 damages.

(C) Prevail against neither the children of Harriet nor the Water Department.

(D) Prevail against both the children of Harriet and the Water Department.

208. Sally Sobriety was an elderly recovering alcoholic. Her only heir, a daughter named Betty Bozer, was a heavy drinker. Sally decided she would convey the properties she owned to others so that her daughter would realize she might be disowned if she did not stop drinking. Sally conveyed Greenacre to "Friend and her heirs, but if liquor is ever consumed on the property, then to Betty." Sally also conveyed Blackacre to "Associate and her heirs, but if Associate ever consumes liquor on the property, then to Betty." One year later, Friend and Associate began to conduct drinking parties on their property and they both personally consumed alcohol. This so upset Sally that she had a stroke and died. The property interest should go to

	Greenacre	Blackacre
(A)	Betty	Betty
(B)	Friend	Betty
(C)	Betty	Associate
(D)	Friend	Associate

209. Albert Adam and Barbara Blake had lived together for ten years even though they were never officially married. The couple used the title "Mr. and Mrs. Adam" on a number of credit cards and retail store accounts. Albert decided to buy a house and the deed referred to "Albert Adam and Barbara Blake and their heirs." The jurisdiction does not recognize common law marriages, but does recognize tenancy by the entirety. Both parties signed the mortgage and promissory note as husband and wife. The couple made payments individually for about a year. Albert then fell in love with Carol Comfortable and left Barbara and the house. If Barbara brings a lawsuit for partition of the property, the likely outcome is that the request should be

(A) Granted because when Albert left Barbara for Carol, he severed the tenancy by the entirety.

(B) Granted because the deed did not create a tenancy by the entirety.

(C) Denied because Albert has absolute title to the home.

(D) Denied because one tenant in a tenancy by the entirety does not have the unilateral right to partition.

Questions 210 and 211 are based on the following:

Larry Landlord leased a 2,000 square foot store front rental space in his shopping center to Stucks Coffee Company under a 10 year lease. The agreement was a "bare bones" lease under which Stucks was to make all its own improvements. Stucks built out the space including equipment and a elevator and added furniture and coffee machines.

210. Assume that Stucks operated their store in Larry's shopping center for the full 10-year term of their lease. Their business continued to grow and Larry's premises were becoming too small. The store manager rented a new 5,000 square foot facility 1,000 feet to the north and began to move. Larry objected to them removing the fixtures and elevator. If Larry files a lawsuit seeking an injunction against removing these items, the court will likely

(A) Issue the injunction against removal of the elevator if it is firmly affixed to Larry's structure.

(B) Issue the injunction because the elevator's firm affixation to the structure converts the ownership to the reversionary interest.

(C) Not issue the injunction if Stucks can restore the premises to the condition it was in before the fixture was attached.

(D) Not issue the injunction if the elevator was paid for in full by Stucks.

211. Assume that Stucks was five years into their lease and doing a good business when the City decided that they wanted to expand the road in front of Larry Landlord's property. In order to add two additional lanes to the road, it was necessary to take all of Stucks' 2,000 square feet leasehold. The City held a condemnation proceeding and considered expert testimony on both sides. The experts determined that the amount and earning value of Stucks' leasehold was $200,000 and that the market value of all of Larry's property they were going to take was $350,000. Economists calculated the present value of the Stucks lease commitment to Larry at $75,000. If the City pays $500,000 for the total value of the taking, the likely distribution is as follows

	Stucks	**Larry**
(A)	-0-	$500,000
(B)	$125,000	$375,000
(C)	$150,000	$350,000
(D)	$200,000	$300,000

212. Pricilla Park loved green areas and parks in her hometown of Evergreen, USA. She gave a deed to three of her empty lots to Community Use Foundation. The deed stated "to Community Use Foundation subject to the understanding that the Foundation will establish a first class city park within two years." The Foundation thanked Pricilla, took title, and began tearing down the old buildings on the property. However, they ran out of funds, the project stalled, and three years later the Foundation Board decided to sell the property to WallShop, Inc. Pricilla was outraged that the property she intended for a park was going to be used for retail purposes. She filed a lawsuit seeking the return of her land. The court will likely

(A) Allow rescission of the conveyance because this grant was a defeasible fee.

(B) Deny rescission of the conveyance because this grant was a fee simple absolute.

(C) Deny rescission but require Community Use Foundation to pay damages to Pricilla.

(D) Allow rescission, but require Pricilla to honor the sale to WallShop.

213. Lorraine Landlord owns an older rental house on the main street of

Fairhaven. Tracy Tenant entered into a 10-year lease agreement with Lorraine. The lease stated the property was only to be used as a single-family residence. In year number 9, Tracy decided to convert the house to commercial use and start a Caffy's Coffee store on the premises. She made significant changes to the premises and installed commercial coffee and cooking equipment. Lorraine then stated that she would not renew the lease. Tracy was outraged and immediately filed suit to recover her costs in converting the premises to a coffee shop. Lorraine counter-claimed for the money to restore the house to a family residence. A court will likely decide for

(A) Lorraine, because Tracy committed ameliorative waste.
(B) Lorraine, because Tracy converted the house to commercial use.
(C) Tracy, if her use conversion of the property increased its value.
(D) Tracy, if Lorraine acted unreasonably.

214. Oscar Owner owns Greenacre in fee simple. He executed a testamentary devise conveying "Greenacres to my children for life and on their death to those of my grandchildren who reach 21 years of age." Oscar has two children and three grandchildren. The consequence of this conveyance is

(A) Oscar's children take in fee simple.
(B) Oscar's grandchildren take in fee simple, but only upon the death of their parents.
(C) Oscar's grandchildren take nothing since their interest may vest more than 21 years after the conveyancing document was executed.
(D) Oscar's grandchildren take because they would be the measuring lives for Rule Against Perpetuities purposes.

215. Gary Grantor owned a large lot on Lake Greenwaves in fee simple. He and his family had not been to the lakefront property for many years. For estate planning purposes, Gary decided to divide the lot into two equal parcels and give each of his two children one of the two new lots. Gary Junior was 22 and Gale was 18 at the time the property was conveyed to them. 14 years later, Gary Junior and Gale went to the property and discovered that Ike Intruder had built a summer cabin on the property. Ike had lived there every summer for 15 years. Two years later, Gary Junior and Gale filed an action to evict Ike. Ike counterclaimed to quiet title in his name. The jurisdiction specifies that the age of majority is 18 and that any action for recovery of land shall be commenced within 15 years after the right of action first occurred. The interests in Greenwaves will likely be awarded thus:

(A) To Ike, if his summer only occupancy is consistent with the usual use in the area.
(B) Gary Junior receives his one half and Ike receives the other half because the conveyance to new owners restarts the period for the statute of limitations.
(C) Gale receives her one half and Ike receives the other half.
(D) One half each to Gary Junior and Gale since the title transfer begins the adverse possession period anew.

216. Three neighbors had view homes on a steeply sloped hill above a picturesque lake. Able lived on the lakefront, Baker was directly up the hill from Able, and Charlie lived above both of them at the top of the hill. Their views were stunning because the trees and other vegetation was very green due to heavy annual rainfall. One fall day, there was a violent storm that dumped heavy rains on the property. Eventually the land at the top of the hill, where Charlie lived, got so saturated with water that it started a mudslide. This swept downhill into Baker's home pushing it into Able's house, which in turn was pushed into the lake. Able asserted a claim against Baker to recover damages to his house. The

majority jurisdiction view in the United States would decide the claim in favor of

(A) Baker because Able's proper cause of action should be against Charlie.

(B) Baker because Able may be able to recover for damage to the land in its natural condition, but not for injury to an artificial structure.

(C) Able because a landowner has an absolute right to lateral support by neighboring property owners.

(D) Able only if Baker was grossly negligent.

Questions 217 – 219 are based on the following:

Eunice Uphill owns an uphill farm acreage which grows wine grapes for sale to local wineries. Eunice's land is directly above and contiguous with Dorothy Downhill's wheat farm. Dorothy grows winter wheat on her land that does not require any water so her only water use is for personal household purposes. There is a medium-sized spring-fed stream that flows through Eunice's vineyards. While substantial volumes of water flow in the late fall, winter, and early spring, the flow decreases in the summer months. As the wine business has grown over the past few years, Eunice has increased her use of water. Still, during spring runoff the stream sometimes overflows its banks.

217. Dorothy's winter wheat does not use any water from the stream. Rather she depends on winter snow and the natural ingredients in the fertile topsoil to grow her wheat crop. When the stream overflows in the spring because of the melting snow and ice and heavy rain run off, it washes away the nutritious topsoil. In frustration, Dorothy built a four-foot concrete wall along the border of Eunice's land to stop the topsoil erosion. This causes the surface water to flood the lower part of Eunice's vineyard. The flood destroys some of the grapevines and Eunice brings suit to require removal of the wall. In applying traditional property rules, the court will likely

(A) Allow the wall to remain, but require Dorothy to pay Eunice for the damage to the grapevines lost.

(B) Allow the wall to remain without any damage award.

(C) Require removal of the wall because Dorothy may not obstruct or alter the flow of surface water.

(D) Require removal of the wall, but at Eunice's expense.

218. The rain supply in the area is somewhat uncertain and occasionally there is a drought. Still, as the demand for wine grapes increases, Eunice plants more and more grapevines on her property. Two years go by with minimal rainfall and in the second summer there is insufficient stream water to satisfy the use requirements of both Eunice and Dorothy. A court will likely hold the priority is to

(A) Eunice because she is the upstream user and thus her priority to the water is the first in time.

(B) Eunice as long as her use is not unreasonable.

(C) Dorothy because her use is for personal household purposes.

(D) Dorothy only if she is in an emergency and is unable to purchase water elsewhere, and there is a statuory prior appropriation law in effect.

219. Assume that the drought continues and Eunice becomes desperate for rainwater to sustain her grapevines. Eunice begins an experimental project of artificially seeding clouds. The experiment is a sporadic success, but the results are quite unpredictable. Some cloud seedings result in massive rainstorms and the rain creates damage to Dorothy's property. If Dorothy brings suit seeking an injunction to halt the cloud seeding, the court will likely

(A) Issue the injunction since no person has the right to create or interfere with natural rainfall.

(B) Issue the injunction because the cloud seeding constitutes an unreasonable interference with the air space above Dorothy's property.

(C) Not issue the injunction because Dorothy does not own the space above her land.

(D) Not issue the injunction unless the cloud seeding is necessary to save Eunice's vineyard.

220. Farmer Fred owned a large farm and decided to retire. Fred's only son, Wayward, had left the farm to become a city person, which Fred did not like. As an inducement for Wayward to move back, he conveyed his farm "to my son Wayward for life, but if he stops farming within 25 years, to the Ohop Grange Association." Wayward moved back to the farm in 2004 and planted a large crop of asparagus. In 2005, Wayward died before the asparagus could be harvested. Who is entitled to the harvest proceeds of the asparagus?

(A) Farmer Fred because the Rule Against Perpetuities is violated.

(B) Wayward's heirs.

(C) Ohop Grange Association since Wayward stopped farming within 25 years.

(D) One half for Wayward's heirs and one half to Farmer Fred.

Questions 221 – 223 are based on the following:

Lane Landlord owns in fee simple land upon which there was a building. Lane signed a five-year lease at $1,000 per month with Tom and Terry as co-tenants. The lease provided that the tenant(s) covenant and promise not to assign or sublet the premises without the consent of Lane. It also provided that the tenants were to keep the leased premises in good repair, including maintaining full fire insurance to be used exclusively for repairing and replacing any damage to the structure.

221. Tom and Terry took possession of the premises. One year later, Tom invited Teresa to move in and share the premises. Lane said that he "did not care as long as the full rent continued to be paid timely."

Terry, on the other hand, was outraged. When Teresa actually physically moved in, Terry filed a lawsuit seeking a declaratory judgment that Tom had no right to assign or sublease. Tom's defense was that he and Terry were tenants-in-common and that he had a right to assign a share of his undivided one-half interest. The court will likely find for

(A) Terry, because the lease contract contains a prohibition on assignment or subleasing.

(B) Tom, because Terry is not the beneficiary of the non-assignment/non-sublease provisions of the lease contract.

(C) Tom, unless Teresa fails to pay her share of the rent.

(D) Terry, because a co-tenant may not assign or sublease any part of the lease contract without the consent of all the co-tenants.

222. Tom, Terry, and Teresa resolved their differences and spent one year in Lane Landlord's building. The three of them decided to move and assigned their lease rights to Alice Assignee. Lane began to accept the rent checks from Alice and made no comment of approval or disapproval. Two years later, Alice assigned her entire remaining interest to Nancy Next. When Lane learned of the assignment to Nancy, he brought suit against Nancy to have the assignment declared invalid. Lane will likely

(A) Succeed because the lease contract prohibited assignment or sublease.

(B) Not succeed because Lane consented to the transfer to Alice.

(C) Not succeed because the privity of estate between Lane and Alice terminated when she assigned the leasehold to Nancy.

(D) Succeed because the covenant prohibiting assignment did not run with the land.

223. Lane made peace with Nancy. When Nancy took over the premises from Alice, the insurance company decided not to renew the fire policy and Nancy did not procure another policy. One year later, the building next to Lane (owned by Baker) was accidentally set on fire. The fire grew and spread to Lane's premises, then occupied by Nancy. When Lane learned that there was no fire insurance to cover the loss, Nancy defended on the basis that she never agreed to take out fire insurance. Lane then filed suit against Tom and Terry. The court will likely decide for

(A) Lane, because the covenant to provide fire insurance would touch and concern the land.
(B) Tom and Terry, because the covenant to provide fire insurance did not run with the land.
(C) Tom and Terry, because either Nancy or the neighbor would be liable for the fire loss to Lane's property.
(D) Lane, because Tom and Terry's covenant to provide fire insurance never terminated.

Questions 224 and 225 are based on the following:

Alice owned Blueacre, a five-acre tract of land, in fee simple. In 2000, Baker moved onto the property without Alice's knowledge. Baker built a large earth dam to create an artificial lake so that there would be a pond to water his flock of sheep. Baker stayed in possession of Blueacre until 2016. At that time, he sold his flock of sheep and other related assets to Charlie using a sale contract. The conveyance used was legally insufficient to transfer an interest in land although it was effective to transfer personal property. Charlie stayed in possession for 11 years and died. In the probate proceedings, all of Charlie's ownership interest passed to his heirs at law. None of his heirs moved to Blueacre.

In 2027, Alice entered into a lease with David for a period of 10 years and David left the property at the end of the lease. In 2038, Alice then sold the property to Edward by using a quitclaim deed. The jurisdiction in which Blueacre is located specifies that the time period to acquire property by adverse possession is 15 years or 10 years if possession is under a color of title claim.

224. In 2038, title to Blueacre was legally owned by
(A) Alice.
(B) Baker's heirs at law.
(C) Charlie's heirs at law.
(D) Edwards, since David quit the premises.

225. In 2038, title to the earth dam was legally owned by
(A) Alice since she owned the land.
(B) Baker since he owned the resources that built the dam.
(C) Charlie since he bought under a sale contract.
(D) Edward since Alice sold him the property in question.

226. Greenacre was a large tract of unimproved land located in Pleasantville, US, that was valued for tax purposes at $150,000. On April 1, Abby sold the land to Barbara for $145,000. Barbara recorded on April 4. Abby sold the same land to Carol on April 3 for $155,000, but Carol did not record until April 5. If there is a quiet title action filed, the court will likely award Greenacre to Carol under which of the following recording statutes?
(A) Pure notice recording statute.
(B) Race-notice recording statute.
(C) Pure race recording statute.
(D) Race-race recording statute.

Questions 227 and 228 are based on the following.

Magna Development purchased a large tract of desert land from Wherehouses, Inc. Magna decided to develop the area into a diversified neighborhood consisting of commercial areas, single family residences, and condominium units. The deeds from Magna expressly stated that "the grantee, heirs, and assigns" use was restricted to certain uses depending upon the location of the lot in the development and that they agreed to purchase all water from Magna Water Company. Magna developed about half the property and sold it to Mores Development. Mores, like Magna before it, operated the water company and all the units they sold contained the same covenants concerning use and water purchase.

227. Nancy Next purchased a large house site in the development from Patty Prior who had purchased from Mores. Nancy's house was alongside a river so she installed a pumping system and disconnected from Magna Water Company. If Mores brings suit to enforce the water purchase covenant against Nancy, the likely outcome is for

(A) Mores, because the water covenant runs with the land.
(B) Nancy, because privity of estate between Mores and Nancy is absent.
(C) Nancy, because the covenant does not touch and concern the land.
(D) Mores, since a reasonable homeowner would have investigated the area and learned everyone purchased their water from Magna Water Company.

228. Mores and Nancy resolved their dispute on the question of water source. But in the process of the dispute, Nancy became aware that starting a commercial marina on her river property would be quite profitable. She began to advertise for marina tenants who would rent the boat slips she intended to build. Mores learned of her plans and filed a lawsuit seeking a declaratory judgment and injunction that the marina violated the single family residence use which was required for her parcel. The court will likely find for

(A) Mores, because the use covenant runs with the land.
(B) Nancy, if the use restriction was not in writing.
(C) Nancy, unless she had actual

knowledge of the restriction.
(D) Mores, if they reserved all commercial activity to themselves.

229. Able owned Redacre in fee simple. The City Water and Sewer Department secured an underground right-of-way easement which was adequately contained in a deed signed by Able and immediately filed by the City. Able later sold Redacre to Brian who subsequently sold to Cory, but neither of the deeds contained any mention of the City's right-of-way.

Cory agreed to sell Redacre to Dennis in a purchase and sale agreement requiring a warranty deed and that Cory furnish an abstract of title. Cory purchased an abstract of title from Always Certain Abstract and Title Co. The abstract did not include the right-of-way and Dennis' lawyer gave an opinion that based on the abstract, the title to Redacre was marketable. Dennis built a large house without a basement. One year later, the Water and Sewer Department moved to condemn Dennis' house and Dennis brought suit against his vendor Cory. The court will likely hold for

(A) Cory because the buyer relied upon the abstract of title and not the seller.
(B) Dennis because Cory is responsible for misrepresentation.
(C) Dennis because Cory breached the covenants in a warranty deed.
(D) Cory because he had no knowledge of the defect of title.

230. Barbara and Carol entered into a purchase and sale agreement for the sale of Blueacre. Barbara agreed in writing to deliver at closing a full statutory warranty deed which contained a marketable title. The abstract of title which Carol ordered indicated that title was held by Adams, not Barbara. Carol did research and it appeared that Barbara had adversely possessed the property for a period of time which exceeded the statutory period required in the jurisdiction. Carol refused to close because Barbara could not deliver a marketable title. If Barbara brings an action against Carol for specific performance, the likely result is for

(A) Barbara, because the action seeking specific performance is an action in rem regardless of whether Adams is joined as a party.

(B) Carol, because Barbara's failure to disclose she did not hold title to the property is a fraud on the buyer.

(C) Carol, because she can not be required to take property which is subject to a lawsuit even if there is a high probability it would be successful.

(D) Barbara, because her rights to the property is the equivalent to a marketable title.

231. Albert owned Greyacre in fee simple. Brett conveyed a warranty deed to Chuck for the same property. Chuck immediately recorded the deed at the office of the County Recorder where Greyacre was located.

Subsequently, Albert conveyed a warranty deed for Greyacre to Brett which was promptly recorded. Chuck then conveyed a quitclaim deed to Edward who paid full value for the property and had no knowledge of the interest of Brett. In a dispute between Edward and Brett for Greyacre, the likely outcome is for

(A) Edward, because he paid full value for the property and had no knowledge of Brett's interest.

(B) Edward or Brett, depending upon whether a subsequent grantee is subordinate to the rule of estoppel by deed in the jurisdiction.

(C) Edward or Brett, depending upon whether Brett's deed is deemed to be recorded in Edward's chain of title.

(D) Brett, because his deed is superior to Edward's.

232. Geneiva Generous, an elderly widow without any children, had developed a very philanthropic philosophy over the years.

She had a favorite wayward nephew named Charlie. In her will, she left "Greenacre to Charlie and his heirs, but if drugs are ever used on the premises, then Greenacre should go to the Red Cross." She also left "Pleasant Farms to Greenpeace, but if the land is ever used for non-farm purposes, then to Nature Conservancy." Applying the standard Rule Against Perpetuities

I.   Charlie has a fee simple subject to an executory interest.
II. Red Cross has a valid shifting executory interest.
III. Red Cross's interest is stricken because it violates the Rule Against Perpetuities.
IV. Greenpeace has a fee simple subject to an executory interest.
V.   Nature Conservancy has a valid shifting executory interest.
VI. Nature Conservancy's interest is stricken because it violates the Rule Against Perpetuities.

Which of the below alternatives includes only true statements?

(A) I, II, IV, and V.
(B) I, III, IV, and VI.
(C) I, II, IV, and VI.
(D) I, III, IV, and V.

233. Active Andy was a wealthy entrepreneur who was married to Mary, an attractive 45-year-old woman who has had a hysterectomy. Andy dies and his will states, "I leave my entire property interest to my wife for life, and upon her death to her children at the time they reach 25." At the time of Andy's death, Mary has two children, Alice from a previous marriage and Betty who was Andy's daughter. The remainder to Alice and Betty

(A) Is valid, because they are lives in being.

(B) Is invalid, because it is possible for Andy's wife to acquire more children after Andy's death.

(C) Is invalid, unless Andy's wife acquires more children.

(D) Is valid as it relates to Alice and Betty, but potentially not to any after-born children of Andy's wife.

234. Toni Tenant, a second-year law student, rented a large apartment from Lorraine Landlord on a month-to-month basis. The rent was $500 per month payable in advance. Toni immediately convinced two of her classmates to move in with her and share the rent. The landlord became very upset even though the lease did not contain any restrictions on assignment, sublease, or maximum number to occupants in the apartment. The landlord wrote Toni and announced that she was imposing a rent increase on Toni and would no longer provide certain services. Toni and her two law school roommates drafted and filed a formal complaint of housing code violations with Pleasant Town Housing Department. Lorraine then gave notice of lease termination at the first of the month effective the first of the next month. If Toni sues Lorraine, the likely result is for

(A) Toni, if the doctrine prohibiting retaliatory eviction for reporting violations is in effect in Pleasant Town.

(B) Lorraine, since a month-to-month is a periodic tenancy that may be terminated at will.

(C) Lorraine, since Toni moving more tenants into the apartment violates the lease.

(D) Toni, only if she gave Lorraine prior notice that she was going to complain to the Pleasant Town Housing Department.

235. Francis Farmer and her family were a tenant farming family in Flatsburg County. Olivia Owner owned a 200-acre farm which she leased to the Farmer family for a fixed term of 20 years. 5 years into the lease, the Flatsburg County government condemned 100 acres of the farm. The total condemnation award was allocated between the Farmers and Olivia as their interests were determined. The Farmer family quit the remaining farm and Olivia brought suit to recover the rent from them. There is no applicable controlling statute for commercial farmland leases in the jurisdiction. The court will likely decide in favor of

(A) Olivia, because the tenant makes an implied warranty to return the land in the same condition as it was at the beginning of the lease.

(B) Farmer, because the landlord breached her implied warranty of quiet enjoyment since Olivia did not provide Farmer with the whole property for the full term of the lease.

(C) Farmer, because there was a frustration of purpose which excuses the tenant from future performance of the lease.

(D) Olivia, because the lease relationship was not terminated by the condemnation and the tenant was not discharged from the responsibility to pay rent.

236. Paul Plumber rented a house with a garage for a period of three years. Paul's day job was working as a journeyman plumber for Prestige Plumbing, Inc., which did all commercial work. Paul also moonlighted on the side plumbing for a few friends and single family residents he knew. In the rental house garage, he installed a workbench, electricity, and extended the natural gas line from the house to work on his moonlighting plumbing business.

The property owner subsequently experienced financial problems and took out a large mortgage with Easy Money on the house. Six months later, the property owner defaulted on the mortgage and Easy Money brought a foreclosure action. When Paul learned of this, his lease had only two months left and he began to remove the improvements he had made to the garage. Easy Money filed an action seeking an injunction against any removal. If the court refuses to issue the injunction, the best reason would be that

(A) Easy Money's mortgage did not specifically include the improvements Paul made so the mortgage holder takes a priority.

(B) The lease did not specify that Paul could not remove any personal property he brought to the premises.

(C) The evidence submitted indicated that the improvements were made exclusively for Paul's use.

(D) Paul had no knowledge of the Easy Money mortgage until they filed the lawsuit seeking an injunction.

237. Farmer Brown, who owned a large farm, was approached by Everycity Electric Company. Everycity planned to dam a river in the mountains and create a large electrogenerating plant. The plan was for large lines to carry the electricity 50 miles to tie into the Everycity electrical system. For a fat fee, Brown conveyed to Everycity the right to construct towers and overhead cables to transport the electricity over his land. The written agreement did not state who was responsible for maintenance or repair of the towers or cables. A large wind storm blew over one of the towers which apparently was not properly secured to a concrete foundation. The live electric power cables fell on Farmer Brown's barn starting a fire which burned down the barn, killing some of his cows. If Farmer Brown sues Everycity Electric for damages, the likely outcome is for

(A) Farmer Brown, because the holder of an easement in gross is absolutely liable for any and all damages inflicted upon the servient tenement.

(B) Everycity, because the owner of the servient tenement is under a duty to inform the easement holder of any defective position since they would have to trespass to make repairs.

(C) Everycity, because the owner of an easement in gross is only responsible for maintenance and repairs which benefit their economic interest.

(D) Farmer Brown, because the holder of an easement in gross is under a duty to maintain and repair the easement so there is not an unreasonable interference with the servient tenement.

238. Heavy Bucks, Inc., owned a large tract of land on the California coast. They subdivided it into four lots labeled A, B, C, and D as follows:

Heavy sold lots A and B to Mary and lots C and D to Nancy. Mary sold lot B to Oliver and agreed not to build any structure on lot A over 50 feet in height. Nancy sold lot D to Pattie who then bought lot B from Oliver. Pattie then started Beachbunnies, a private beach charging admission to sunbathers and wind surfers. After 12 years, Beachbunnies was so successful that Nancy and Mary decided to build high-rise hotels on lots A and C to service the guests coming into the area. Concerned that such large structures would cut off Beachbunnies' wind and sunlight, Pattie filed a lawsuit seeking an injunction to prohibit building of the high-rise buildings. There is a 10 year term for a prescriptive easement in the jurisdiction. The likely outcome is that Pattie will prevail against

(A) Nancy and Mary.

(B) Nancy, but not Mary.

(C) Mary, but not Nancy.

(D) Neither Nancy nor Mary.

Questions 239 and 240 are based on the following:

Adam and Eve were law students in their second year (2Ls). They had met as 1Ls and planned to marry so they decided to purchase a condominium together. Their offer on the unit was accepted contingent upon them securing financing. Because they had never held professional jobs, they were unable to secure credit. The seller became increasingly interested in making the deal because Adam and Eve were the only potential buyers to make an offer so he agreed to sell the unit on an installment contract if they could provide a guarantor.

239. Adam's father, Big Daddy, volunteered to provide the cash for the down payment and guarantee the debt. The seller filed the conveyancing documents to "Adam, Eve, and Big Daddy as joint tenants." Adam and Eve moved into the unit immediately. When they completed law school, Adam failed the bar exam because he did not study sufficiently. This so depressed him that he called off his engagement with Eve, conveyed his interest to a friend named Newton, and took a job as a bartender. Big Daddy died leaving his interest to his third wife. Eve continued to live in the unit. The ownership interest in the property was then

    (A) Eve, Newton, and Big Daddy's third wife as joint tenants with a one-third interest each.

    (B) Eve, Newton, and Big Daddy's third wife as tenants-in-common with a one-third interest each.

    (C) Eve and Newton as joint tenants with a two-thirds interest and Big Daddy's third wife as a tenant-in-common with a one-third interest.

    (D) Eve and Newton as tenants-in-common with a one-half interest each.

240. Eve became tired of the condominium unit because losing Adam broke her heart and living there reminded her of her loss. As a result, she moved out and stopped making the installment payments. The property seller waited for a few months and declared the contract forfeited. In most jurisdictions

    (A) Seller will be entitled to a deficiency judgment against Adam, Eve, and Big Daddy.

    (B) Seller will have to return any money they have received if they

are in excess of the appreciation in the property during the period of the installments.

    (C) Seller may be required to hold a formal disposition sale if the buyer had paid a substantial percentage of the total payments.

    (D) Seller's forfeited right of repossession is subject to a redemption right.

Questions 241 and 242 are based on the following:

Lucy Landlord owned a condominium unit in what was formerly a large apartment house. She purchased the unit when the building was converted. Lucy signed a condominium agreement containing numerous requirements including that she maintain her unit in good repair, pay a monthly fee to the association, not sell her unit without first offering it to the association, and not rent the unit unless the association approved the proposed tenant. The jurisdiction in question does not have a statute changing the common law landlord-tenant rules.

241. Lucy lived in the unit for two years, then her father passed away. Her aging widowed mother was in poor health and Lucy decided to go live with her in their family home. She found a tenant for her condominium unit who the homeowners association approved. The apartment was in good condition except an electrical outlet in the kitchen that shot out a large electrical charge if the kitchen circuit was overloaded. Lucy forgot to tell the tenant about the electrical circuit problem. Tenant moved in and unintentionally overloaded the kitchen circuit. The circuit shot out a large electrical charge, severely injuring the tenant. If the tenant brings suit against Lucy for damages, the likely outcome is a decision for

    (A) Tenant because a landlord is strictly liable for any injuries on the premises they could have avoided.

(B) Lucy because the tenant takes the premises as they are unless the landlord affirmatively represented that there are no defects.

(C) Lucy because the tenant had sufficient opportunity to inspect and failure to do so constitutes an assumption of the risk.

(D) Tenant because Lucy did not disclose the electrical defect.

242. Because of the dispute with the tenant, Lucy grew very tired of owning and maintaining the unit in the condominium. As a result, she listed it with a real estate broker for $500,000. A rock band member offered to buy at that price, but the other unit owners did not want him to move in because they felt he would be quite disruptive. They thus refused to approve the sale and filed suit against Lucy to enjoin the transfer. The likely consequence of the lawsuit is for

(A) The Condominium Association because Lucy knowingly agreed to this provision and they hold the right of first refusal.

(B) Lucy because the form of organization she voluntarily joined was a condominium rather than a cooperative.

(C) Lucy because the restraint is disabling.

(D) The Condominium Association because if Lucy had not agreed to this sale restriction provision, she never would have been allowed to take title.

Questions 243 and 244 are based on the following:

Florence Farmer owns a 1,000-acre ranch on which her personal residence is located. Her favorite daughter, Donna, wanted to move close to her and began to negotiate to purchase a portion of Florence's land.

243. Florence and Donna orally reached an agreement that Donna would buy a part of the land for $20,000. Donna gave Florence a check for $20,000, but Florence changed her mind and sent the check back. Donna sues seeking an order of specific performance. The court will likely find for

(A) Donna because a court of equity may enforce an oral agreement under the doctrine of part performance.

(B) Donna because she performed by giving $20,000 consideration.

(C) Florence if she did not sign any written agreement.

(D) Florence because she returned the purchase money.

244. Florence and Donna made peace in the $20,000 dispute and Donna dropped her lawsuit. They sat down and discussed in detail what Donna wanted to do with the ranch. They decided that Donna would buy Florence's house and some surrounding land to have a large lawn and garden. Florence was to move to a retirement condominium, but would keep ownership of most of the 1,000 acres. The parties signed the below agreement

> "Seller, Florence Farmer, agrees to sell to Donna for $25,000 my personal residence and a sufficient amount of surrounding land to have a large lawn and garden."

The next day, Florence again had second thoughts and refused to perform. If Donna sues for specific performance, the court will likely find for

(A) Donna because Florence signed the contract and she is the party to be charged.

(B) Donna only if she paid the purchase price.

(C) Florence if Donna did not pay the purchase price.

(D) Florence because the agreement is vague and ambiguous.

245. Betty Benefactor owned 500 acres of forest land. She had one estranged son, and in her later years, she became a member of the Total Faith Church. At the age of 85, the attorney for the Church convinced Betty to sign a deed stating "to Total Faith Church for Church use only for the life of my son and then to any of my then living grandchildren."

Total Faith Church began to conduct worship services on the land. Five years later, the Church granted to a church member the right to harvest the timber and mine gravel from the land in return for a share of the profits. The logging and mining increased and three years later, Betty's four grand children instituted a lawsuit against Total Faith seeking an injunction and damages for the timber harvest and the gravel removal. The court is likely to

    (A) Deny relief because the grant did not restrict Total Faith Church from any activity during the life of Betty's son.

    (B) Grant money damages, but deny an injunction.

    (C) Grant an injunction, but deny a monetary award for past damages because the grandchildren did not previously complain.

    (D) Grant an injunction and award damages with the damages impounded for future distribution.

246. Alice and Barbara bought side-by-side 5-acre tracts in Greenacre, which both backed up to a greenbelt where the City intended to build a public park. Both owners wanted to build their homes on the rear of their property to avoid the noise from the front street and get a better view of the park. When they realized they both had the same plans, they decided a common driveway would save both of them money. They thus built a 15-foot wide asphalt driveway straddling their property line and each gave the other a cross-easement to use the 7 ½ feet of their land. The document was recorded and for 15 years they both used the driveway.

After five years of study, the City decided it did not have the money to build the park

and sold the parkland to a developer. The developer then built a new road along the back border of the two properties owned by Alice and Barbara. Barbara decided to build a driveway from the new back road and informed Alice that she intended to terminate the cross-easement to the front street. If Alice refuses and Barbara brings suit to terminate, the likely outcome is for

    (A) Barbara, because the lack of necessity terminates the easements.

    (B) Alice, if she still wants to own the common driveway.

    (C) Alice, because a cross-easement is a partnership requiring both partners' agreement to continue.

    (D) Barbara, because Alice can not show an economic detriment if the easement is terminated.

Questions 247 and 248 are based on the following:

Mary and Nancy jointly owned Greenacre which included 20 acres of forest land in the suburbs. The closest city, Urban Sprawl, has been annexing property in the area. Dorothy Developer owned Blueacre, the land next door to Greenacre. Dorothy met with Mary and disclosed her plans to subdivide Blueacre and put in a water and sewer system which would cost $25,000. Mary decided that it was in her and Nancy's best interest to have the same water and sewer system contractor improve Greenacre when they improved Blueacre. While Mary was sure the property improvement would be very profitable, Nancy was reluctant and said no.

Mary then went to a property lawyer for advice. The lawyer said that she could bring a court action and petition for authority to mortgage Greenacre in order to raise the funds for the water and sewer system.

247. If Mary decides to go forward and files suit, the likely outcome is that the petition will be

    (A) Denied.

(B) Granted if Mary and Nancy are joint tenants with the right of survivorship, but not if they are mere tenants in common.

(C) Denied only if the increase in value is less than the cost of the improvements.

(D) Granted only if the land cannot be used economically in its present state.

248. Mary considers her options and concludes that the cost of the lawyer's fee to litigate may be more than the expected increase in value of Greenacre. Therefore, she borrows the necessary $25,000 from her parents. Assume that the improvements cost $25,000 and the property's value is increased by $40,000. If Mary sues Nancy for contribution, she likely will recover

(A) $20,000.

(B) $12,500.

(C) $7,500.

(D) -0-

249. Tracy Transferor owned 10 acres named Greenacre in fee simple upon which he and his family have lived for many years. Tracy signed a land sales contract with Denise Developer to sell to her 5 acres of Greenacre. Tracy knew that Denise hoped to use the property to develop a mini-shopping mall, but there was no reference to use in the sales contract. The deed tendered by Tracy at closing specified the subject property was to be limited to residential uses only. When Denise saw the condition in the deed, she orally objected, but still paid the purchase price and the closing agent recorded the deed at the county seat where Greenacres was located. Denise took possession and filed a permit application to build the mini-shopping mall. If Tracy files a lawsuit seeking an injunction against Denise building anything other than a residence, the court would likely decide for

(A) Denise because Tracy knew she hoped to use the property to develop a mini-shopping mall.

(B) Tracy only if Denise did not sign

the deed.

(C) Tracy since the deed specified the use was limited to residential uses.

(D) Denise because the only document she signed did not prohibit any use of the property.

250. Alice owns Appleacre and Barbara owns Bananaacre, the adjoining piece of property. Both parcels of land contained their personal residences. Alice began to construct a brick wall along the boundary line appurtenant to Bananaacre. Barbara complained when she saw the brick wall being constructed and told Alice she believed the new wall was protruding onto her property. Alice produced a study prepared by a surveyor which indicated the brick wall was right on the property line. Barbara disagreed but orally accepted the survey and both owners built gardens and ponds alongside their side of the new brick wall.

19 years later, Barbara sold her property to Carol. Carol had a survey done which conclusively proved that the brick wall extended 18 inches onto her property. The prescriptive period for adverse possession in the jurisdiction is 20 years. The court will most likely order that

(A) Alice must remove the wall at Carol's expense.

(B) The wall may stay, but Alice will be liable to Carol for damages.

(C) The wall may stay and Alice is not liable to Carol.

(D) Alice must remove the wall at her own expense.

Questions 251 and 252 are based on the following:

Alice owned in fee simple absolute Silveracre, a 500-acre tract that contained a substantial amount of silver which had been partially mined. Alice gave Betty Banker a first mortgage to secure the money necessary to reopen the silver mine. Betty immediately recorded. Unfortunately this did not yield enough money to open the mine and Alice found it necessary to take out a second mortgage with Caroline. The Caroline mortgage contained an express representation that there were no senior obligations against Silveracre. Caroline immediately recorded her mortgage.

The silver mine did not produce the revenue that was expected. Betty foreclosed on her first mortgage and named both Alice and Caroline party defendants in interest. At the foreclosure sale, Alice purchased the property, thereby extinguishing Betty Banker's interest. Alice then conveyed Silveracre to Doris using a statutory warranty deed. Doris paid full value and had no knowledge of the conveyances to Alice or Betty or the foreclosure sale. The jurisdiction has a race-notice recording statute.

251. If Caroline sues to foreclose her mortgage and names Alice and Doris as party defendants in interest, the court will likely find for
  (A) Caroline because when Alice acquired Silveracre at the foreclosure sale, Caroline would acquire a first mortgage through the doctrine of estoppel by deed.
  (B) Alice because when she purchased Silveracre at the foreclosure sale, the rights of all junior creditors were extinguished.
  (C) Doris because she will gain title to Silveracre since she paid full value and had no knowledge of the prior interests.
  (D) Caroline because the terms of her conveyance contained an express representation of no senior obligations against Silveracre.

252. The court determined that the 500-acre of Silveracre would go to the proper owner. This Owner realized that the silver mine might not be economically viable at the current market price of silver. She thus sold and conveyed the property to Ethel who intended to use the land to grow wheat. Two years later, the market price

for silver doubled. The Old Owner contacted Ethel and stated that she had only sold her the land, not the natural resource rights. If a lawsuit develops over who has the right to the silver resource, the likely outcome is for
  (A) Old Owner because she did not specifically convey the mineral rights.
  (B) Ethel only if she knew about the silver mine.
  (C) Ethel unless Old Owner specifically reserved the silver mine.
  (D) Old Owner because Ethel intended to use the land to grow wheat not mine silver.

Questions 253 and 254 are based on the following:

Adam conveyed Purpleacre to Bryan for $50,000 using a deed containing the warranties of title, authority and right to convey, and freedom of encumbrances. Bryan lived on the property for 10 years and then sold to Charlie by conveying a limited warranty deed, for which Charlie paid $60,000. Five years later, Charlie is evicted from Purpleacre by Daniel because he had a paramount title that predated Adam's interest.

253. If Charlie brings suit against Adam, the likely outcome is
  (A) For Charlie in an amount of $50,000.
  (B) For Charlie in an amount of $40,000.
  (C) For Adam because privity of estate did not exist between Charlie and Adam.
  (D) For Adam because the covenants which were breached do not run with the land.

254. Assume in the above facts that shortly before Charlie's lawsuit against Adam was scheduled for trial, Adam filed for bankruptcy. Charlie and his attorney conferred and concluded that the case should be abandoned because Adam was judgment-proof. Charlie decided to sue Bryan instead. If the case against Bryan goes to trial, the likely outcome is for

(A) Charlie since he has privity of contract with Bryan.
(B) Bryan unless he either had knowledge of the defects in the title or warranted prior conveyances.
(C) Bryan if the statute of limitations has run on the claim by the time Charlie decided to abandon the suit against Adam and go against Bryan.
(D) Charlie since he was evicted from Purpleacre and Bryan sold him the property.

255. Mary executed a full statutory warranty deed of Orangeacre "to Nancy for life, then to the heirs of Nancy." Nancy paid $250,000 and accepted the deed, but did not record it. Two years later, Mary developed Alzheimer's Disease and forgot about the conveyance to Nancy. She was pressured by her two children, Olivia and Patricia who did not know about the prior conveyance to Nancy, to gift to them Orangeacre. Mary thus conveyed Orangeacre by warranty deed to Olivia and Patricia as a gift. The deed was immediately recorded and two months later, Olivia and Patricia found Nancy on the property and threatened to evict her.

Nancy then filed the original deed and retained Louise Lawyer to file a quiet title action to determine the ownership of Orangeacre. The applicable recording statute in the jurisdiction provided "every conveyance or encumbrance of land not recorded is void against any subsequent purchaser who takes without notice and for value whose instrument is first recorded." If Nancy prevails, it will be because

(A) Nancy recorded her deed before Olivia and Patricia were able to file their eviction action.
(B) Olivia and Patricia are not shielded by the jurisdiction's recording statute.

(C) Mary's knowledge is imputed to her children even if she developed Alzheimers.
(D) Nancy paid $250,000 for the land which was sufficient consideration.

Questions 256 and 257 are based on the following:

On December 1, 2004, Ethel conveyed a full warranty deed for land known as Whiteacre to Florence for $250,000. Florence immediately recorded. Florence then sold Whiteacre to Gertrude and on December 5th, executed a properly drawn deed. Gertrude did not record the deed. On December 10th, Florence executed another deed to Harriet. Harriet recorded on December 15th, but knew that Gertrude had previously received a deed that was not recorded. Gertrude recorded on December 20th. On December 26th, Harriet sold Whiteacre to Iola who paid full value without notice of the conveyance to Gertrude. Iola immediately recorded. Iola decided not to purchase title insurance.

256. If Iola is to conduct a proper title search and the jurisdiction only has a grantor to grantee index, she should look in the

(A) Grantor Index under Harriet's name to determine if Harriet acquired title.
(B) Grantee Index under Gertrude's name and then to the Grantor's Index under Gertrude's name to see if she took any prior conveyance.
(C) Grantee Index under Harriet's name only.
(D) Grantor Index under Harriet's name then Grantee Index under Harriet's name and Grantee Index under Florence's name to see if Harriet acquired title.

257. Who would prevail if Whiteacre was located in a jurisdiction that has a recording statute which stated, "No interest in land is entitled to a priority unless it is recorded before a competing interest?"

(A) Florence.

(B) Gertrude.

(C) Harriet.

(D) Iola.

258. Jack was the owner in fee simple of Greyacre which he inherited from his father. His will left the property to Karen, his wife, in the devise "to Karen for the rest of her life, remainder to those whom Karen shall designate in her will." Karen subsequently married Lawrence and at his request conveyed the property to him by deed. That same afternoon, Karen died intestate survived only by Lawrence. Lawrence then contracted to sell Greyacre to Mary by a statutory deed containing a warranty of marketable title. Mary subsequently learned about the prior ownership history, refused to close the sale, and demanded a refund of her deposit. If a lawsuit is started between the parties, the court will likely find for

  (A) Lawrence because Karen's conveyance to Mary was a valid exercise of the power of appointment which she received under Jack's will.

  (B) Mary unless the deed tendered by Lawrence contained a covenant of general warranty.

  (C) Mary because at Karen's death, the property reverted to Jack's estate.

  (D) Lawrence if he was the only person qualified to inherit from Karen under the laws of intestacy.

Questions 259 – 261 are based on the following:

Absentminded Albert owned Greenacre which contained an old rental house. He orally promised his favorite niece Deserving Diane that he would leave her the fee simple interest in Greenacre if she would study hard in her bar review course. She complied with his request and when she passed the bar, she drafted a new will for Uncle Albert which would convey Greenacre to her upon his death. All the requirements of the statute of frauds were complied with in Albert's will.

Four years later, Albert forgot about his agreement with Diane and decided to sell Greenacre. He signed a standard exclusive listing agreement with Bobbie Broker at a 7% commission rate. In the property listing agreement, Albert promised to convey a full statutory deed with "full warranties as to the house" if a buyer would agree to a full price of $100,000 payable at $500 a month.

Albert's next door neighbor Nathan knew nothing about the above facts, but had heard of the property listing from his barber who had called Bobbie Broker's office in response to an advertisement in the local paper. Knowing Albert personally, he called him on the phone and inquired about the property. Albert sent him a copy of the purchase and sale agreement, but crossed out the portion containing the 7% commission payable to Bobbie Broker. Nathan and Albert both signed the purchase and sale agreement and hired Charlie Closer, a local attorney, to prepare the closing documents including the deed.

The lawyer's para-professional prepared a deed, but at Albert's direction, it stated that the conveyance of the house was "as is, with all faults" rather than with "full warranties as to the house." In addition, the para-professional mistyped $500 per month as $800 per month on the related promissory note. Unfortunately, Albert had a fatal stroke the morning of the day that he and Nathan were going to meet in Charlie Closer's office to sign the deed and promissory note that would later be recorded.

259. Diane claims she should get Greenacre according to Albert's will and that it should not go to Nathan pursuant to the real estate transaction. Her best argument is

  (A) She gave consideration for a contract by studying hard in the bar review class.

  (B) Her agreement with her Uncle predated any aspect of the property transaction with Nathan.

(C) Uncle Albert never delivered the deed to Nathan.

(D) The deed and note contained too many mistakes to be enforceable.

260. Assume that the court decided against Diane and awards Greenacre to Nathan. Nathan complains that the deed should be reformed to increase the warranties on the house from "as is, with all faults" to "full warranties as to the house." Nathan also wants the court to reduce the note payment amount of $800 per month to $500 per month to reflect the para-professional's typing mistake. The court would likely resolve the two questions by holding that the final transaction should include the following terms

	Warranty Question	Monthly Payment
(A)	Full Warranty	$500
(B)	"As is"	$500
(C)	Full Warranty	$800
(D)	"As is"	$800

261. Assume that the disagreement as to terms was satisfactorily resolved. Bobbie Broker demands that the estate pay her $7,000 to reflect the commission she believes is due her on the sale of Greenacre. The estate objects and in due course files an action seeking a declaratory judgment. In such an action, the best argument the estate can make to avoid paying the commission

(A) The transfer occurred after Albert's death so the commission agreement was terminated.

(B) The listing agreement was not exclusive.

(C) The purchaser was not procured by Bobbie Broker.

(D) The final agreement transferring Greenacre contained numerous changes which were not contained in the original listing agreement.

Questions 262 and 263 are based on the following:

Lenora owned Aquaacre in fee simple. In 2000, she executed a note secured by a mortgage in favor of Main Street Bank who did not record. In 2002, Lenora gave a second mortgage to Olive Mortgage who immediately recorded at the state capital. In 2004, Lenora's favorite niece, Nancy graduated from law school and passed the bar exam. Lenora gave her a deed to Aquaacre without disclosure of the prior Main Street Bank mortgage. Nancy immediately recorded. Lenora then stopped making the monthly mortgage payments and Main Street Bank initiated a foreclosure proceeding.

262. The jurisdiction's recording statute states, "No interest in real property is superior to a subsequent interest for value and without notice unless it is first recorded at the county where the property is located." The outcome of the dispute would be to award Aquaacre to

(A) Nancy because she recorded first.

(B) Olive because they were the first mortgage to record.

(C) Main because Lenora executed their documentation first.

(D) Nancy because a mortgage is not an interest in real property under the recording statute.

263. Assume for this question that the jurisdiction in which Aquaacre is located has a recording statute which states, "Every conveyance of an interest in real estate which is not recorded shall be ineffective against any subsequent grantee in good faith whose conveyance is first duly recorded at the county where the property is located." The outcome of the dispute would be to award Aquaacre to

(A) Nancy only if she gave full value.

(B) Nancy because she was the first deed to record.

(C) Olive because they were the first mortgage to record.

(D) Main because they were the first mortgage in time.

264. Tom Thirsty and Pete Plenty own adjacent pieces of real property in an area that does not have a public water supply system. Tom subdivided his property, constructing twelve townhouses. He also drilled a large well to tap the underground aquifer as the sole source of water for the townhouses. The sales market has been slow so Tom has been renting the units out to tenants. Five years later, Pete began construction of a large luxury house and has drilled a large well on his adjacent property.

Tom went to the county's building department and reviewed the plans Pete had submitted. He became quite alarmed when he discovered Pete planned a large swimming pool and 5 acres of grass. For all these uses, Pete intended to use water withdrawn from his new well. This well would draw water from the same underground aquifer as Tom's and will decrease the water available to Tom's tenants. If Tom sues and seeks an injunction requiring Pete to stop drilling the well, the likely outcome is for

(A) Pete if Pete's planned use of the water is found to be not unreasonable.

(B) Tom because his well supplies the water needs of more users than will Pete's.

(C) Tom only if Tom's use of the water is found to be reasonable.

(D) Pete because Tom is deriving a commercial profit from use of the water.

265. Francis Forlorn was a 35 year old single lady. Francis's mother had been encouraging her to marry for a decade. She was finally asked by Stuart Single and accepted. Francis's mother was ecstatic and decided to give them Foreveracre as a wedding gift. The deed was given to them at their wedding and it stated "to Francis and Stuart as joint tenants." They recorded the deed immediately. Three years later, Stuart left Francis, but neither party filed for divorce. Stuart began living with Gloria Golddigger, who demanded he show the abundance of his love by giving her his interest in Foreveracre. Stuart executed and delivered to Gloria a quitclaim deed purporting to convey all his interest to her. The jurisdiction where Foreveracre is located recognizes tenancy by the entirety. After the conveyance was recorded, the likely ownership status of Gloria was

(A) A joint tenant with Francis since the quitclaim deed conveyed all the title and interest which the grantor had.

(B) A tenant in common with Francis since a conveyance by a joint tenant severs the joint tenancy.

(C) A tenant by the entirety with Francis since the quitclaim deed conveys all the title and interest which the grantor had.

(D) No valid interest since conveyance by only one holder of a tenancy by the entirety is ineffective without conveyance by the other spouse.

266. George owned Aquaacre in fee simple having inherited the property from his favorite Uncle Frank. George's friend and neighbor, Harry wanted to build a larger house and connect to the main road by a new driveway over George's property. As a favor, George conveyed an easement to Harry. Unfortunately, Harry neglected to record the driveway easement George granted. Two years later, George sold Aquaacre to Iceman using a deed that referred to the easement. Three years after that, Iceman conveyed the property to John who paid full value and had no knowledge of the easement. The Iceman to John documents did not reveal any encumbrance for the easement. John and Harry got into a disagreement about the easement leading to a law suit. Regarding Harry's easement rights, the court will likely hold for

(A) Harry because Iceman should have known of the easement.

(B) John since he had no actual

knowledge of the easement.

(C) John if Harry did not give full value for the easement.

(D) Harry because John had notice of the easement.

67. Susan Seller owned a 10-acre tract named Violetacre in fee simple. She contracted to sell the property to Betty Buyer for $100,000 cash. The contract was legally valid to convey title except it did not specify the type or quality of title to be conveyed or specify any encumbrances. Betty found out that there was an easement over the property which Carol Crossover had been using continuously for 30 years and that zoning restrictions prohibited her from developing the property as she had intended. Susan says she is not responsible and that she never stated that any of these conditions did not exist. Is the contract enforceable?

(A) Yes, and Susan will be required to convey a marketable title.

(B) No, because there was never a meeting of the minds since too many material items were left unstated.

(C) No, because the title is not marketable due to the adverse possession and zoning restrictions.

(D) Yes, but Susan will only be required to convey whatever interest she has.

268. Farmer Fred was the owner of Grapeview Farm located in Grapeview County, State of Anywhere. Grapeview was the largest farm in the County. Fred was advised by his gift and estate attorney to begin making annual fractionalized gifts of the property to his children. Fred executed a conveyance instrument in 2005 stating the gifts as "one-thirtieth of my ownership interest in Grapeview County, the eastern one tenth of the western corner of the property to all my children per capita." This description of the land to be conveyed is

(A) Insufficient because it is too vague.

(B) Sufficient because it satisfies the

title of seisin.

(C) Sufficient because the property can be identified.

(D) Insufficient because the gifts to the children lacked consideration.

269. Alice owned Greyacre, a one-acre piece of property, in fee simple. Alice sold the property to Barbara who moved into the only residence on the land. Unfortunately, Barbara neglected to record the deed she had received from Alice. Three years later, Alice conveyed the same property to Charlene who immediately filed the deed received from Alice. The jurisdiction in question has a race-notice statute and a tract index system. If an action is filed for title to the property, the likely outcome would be for

(A) Alice since her ownership was first in time and she was of record.

(B) Barbara because Charlene had notice of the prior conveyance between Alice and Barbara.

(C) Barbara because she was the first to record her deed.

(D) Charlene because she was the first to record her deed.

270. Farmer Fred owned Farmacre in fee simple. He decided to make a contribution of Farmacre to his alma mater, Hilltop Agricultural College. The conveyance stated, "to Hilltop Agricultural College for so long as the College uses Farmacre for agricultural purposes, then to my sister Sally and her heirs." The jurisdiction has adopted the common law Rule Against Perpetuities. What is Farmer Fred's interest in Farmacre after the conveyance?

(A) No interest.

(B) A fee simple absolute.

(C) A reversion.

(D) A possibility of reverter.

Questions 271 and 272 are based on the following:

Albert owned Greatacre Farm in fee simple having inherited it from his parents. He and his son Charlie had worked the farm together for 20 years. He divided the property into two parcels named Firstacre and Secondacre. He conveyed Firstacre to his son Barry using the language, "to Barry but Barry promises and covenants not to transfer Firstacre without my consent."

Albert also signed and gave to Barry a fully executed, notarized, and delivered instrument which stated, "I may or may not sell Secondacre during my lifetime, but at my death or earlier if I decide to sell, Secondacre will be offered to my son Charlie at $1,000 per acre. Charlie should exercise this right if at all within 50 days of receipt of the offer to sell." Charlie immediately recorded the instrument.

271. Barry's right to sell Firstacre is
(A) Subject to Albert's consent.
(B) Subject to Albert's consent which may not be unreasonably withheld.
(C) Not subject to Albert's consent.
(D) Subject to Albert's consent during his life, but Barry achieves an unequivocal right to sell at Albert's death.

272. Is Charlie's right to purchase Secondacre valid under the instrument?
(A) No, because Charlie's right to purchase is an unreasonable restraint on alienation.
(B) Yes, because the instrument was recorded.
(C) Yes, because Charlie's right to purchase will vest or fail within the period prescribed by the Rule Against Perpetuities.
(D) No, because Charlie's right to purchase is a restraint on the owner's power to make a testamentary disposition.

Questions 273 and 274 are based on the following:

Lorraine Lawyer graduated from Summa Law School and passed the bar at the first sitting. Her legal practice was very successful. Later in life, the school

encouraged her to give back to the law school and she began to make cash and in kind contributions. Lorraine owned a piece of property called Greatacre and decided to contribute it to the law school for use as library. She conveyed an interest stating "to Summa Law School, but if Greatacre is ever used for non-library purposes, then to my son Ernest and his heirs."

Ten years later, Lorraine completed a deed for Magnum Acres naming the law school as the grantee. She placed it in an addressed envelope on a cabinet in the entryway to her home. The following morning, the housekeeper saw the envelope, affixed a stamp, and mailed it. Later in the day, it was discovered that Lorraine had passed away in her sleep the previous night.

273. Summa Law School built the library but found that increasingly legal publishers were using CD Roms and on-line data banks instead of library books. They also found the cost of running the library on Greatacre kept increasing. The school administration thus decided to convert the library on Greatacre to dormitory purposes six years after the gift from Lorraine. Two years later, Lorraine's son Ernest found out about the use change and demanded the property. If a lawsuit is filed in a jurisdiction that has adopted the common law Rule Against Perpetuities, the court will likely hold that Lorraine's interest in Greatacre during her life is
(A) No interest.
(B) A fee simple absolute upon Greatacre being converted to a dormitory.
(C) A reversion.
(D) A possibility of reverter.

274. Summa Law School received the deed to Magnum Acres after Lorraine's death which Lorraine had executed in their favor. They immediately recorded their property interest. Lorraine's heir at law, Ernest, also wanted Magnum Acre for his own. If litigation develops in a "race" recording statute jurisdiction, the court will likely find for

(A) Summa because they recorded the deed.
(B) Ernest because the deed remained under Lorraine's control until her death.
(C) Earnest because the deed only reached Summa after Lorraine's death.
(D) Summa because executing the deed was a testamentary substitute.

275. Lundy Landlord owned an industrial piece of property containing a factory in Benson, Texas. Lundy leased the factory to Terry for a period of four years at a rent of $10,000 per month. Two years later, Terry assigned the lease to Second for $15,000 a month. For 18 months, Second paid Terry $15,000 and Terry in turn paid $10,000 to Lundy. One weekend homeless people broke into the factory seeking relief from a heat wave. Overuse damaged the air conditioning system. Following the weekend, Second refused to pay Terry and moved out of the building because the air conditioning did not work. Terry now refuses to pay rent to Lundy. Under the common law, the duty to repair the air conditioning would likely be imposed on

(A) Lundy because he owned the building and the air conditioning equipment which had become a fixture.
(B) Terry only if the lease required him to make extraordinary repairs.
(C) Second because he had exclusive possession of the factory at the time of the damage.
(D) Lundy because the damage was caused by an act of God beyond the control of the tenant.

Questions 276 and 277 are based on the following:

Lorraine Landlord owned a number of income properties. One property was a small office building containing 12,000 square feet. Each of the floors had 6,000 square feet. Lorraine rented the whole first floor to Cost & Airhouse, a CPA firm. The rent was contracted to be $5,000 per month. The payment was due on the first of the month. When they moved in the tenants were required to put up a security lease deposit of three months rent. The three-year lease contract contained a provision that stated, "if tenant fails to pay the rent, landlord has the right to terminate the tenancy and re-enter the premises."

Thirty months later, the tenant CPAs lost a large lawsuit relating to their negligence in performing an audit and closed their office on April 30. The April rent had been paid timely.

276. The landlord brings suit against Cost & Airhouse, CPAs for unpaid rent to the end of the lease term. The best argument to support a judgment for the tenant is

(A) The landlord failed to mitigate damages.
(B) The landlord reserved the right to re-enter.
(C) Ten days after Cost & Airhouse vacated, Lorraine started using the first floor as a management office for all of her other rental properties.
(D) The landlord rented the first floor to Hard & Fast, a professional engineering firm for $4,000 per month.

277. Independent of your legal conclusion in the above question, may Lorraine Landlord keep the $15,000 lease security deposit?

(A) Yes, because the tenant abandoned.
(B) No, if Lorraine uses the first floor as a management office for her other rental property.
(C) No, if the landlord accepted a new tenant for the first floor.
(D) Yes, only if the lease states that the security deposit is non-refundable if the tenant abandons.

278. Sally Seller decided to sell her home with Betty Broker and executed a written

listing contract containing the exclusive right to sell. According to the terms of the agreement, Betty agreed to use reasonable efforts to locate and close a buyer at a price of $100,000. If the home were sold to a buyer who made an offer during the following 90 days, upon the title closing, Sally would pay to Betty a commission equal to 7% of the price actually paid.

The next week, Betty showed the house to Patricia Purchaser who fell in love with the quaint features at the first inspection. She made an immediate offer of $95,000 and put up a $15,000 non-refundable deposit. Two weeks later, Patricia communicated to Sally that she had located a house that she thought would better suit her needs and thus would not go forward with the purchase. 91 days after the listing agreement was signed, Sally personally sold the property to her neighbor for $85,000. If Betty initiates a lawsuit seeking judgment for commission due her, the likely outcome is for

(A) $7,000 (7% of 100,000).
(B) $6,650 (7% of 95,000).
(C) $5,950 (7% of 85,000).
(D) -0-

279. Betty Builder constructed a very large home on her lot adjacent to Nancy Neighbors' undeveloped lot. One month after completion, the house was sold to Connie Conner. Six months later, a survey of the property line between the two lots revealed that one of the eaves and gutter on Betty's home extended nine inches over the property line. Betty agreed with the result but claimed it was a good faith mistake on her part and that the non-intentional aspect was a defense. Further Betty proved that because the gutter system ran back to her house there would be no damage caused by water from the gutter falling on Nancy's land. Nancy was generally unhappy about the size of the new house and filed a lawsuit for an order of eviction and/or damages. The court will most likely decide the case for

(A) Nancy and issue an eviction order.

(B) Betty and Connie unless Nancy ca[n] show actual damages.
(C) Betty and Connie because Bett[y] and Connie made a reasonabl[e] mistake, acted in good faith, an[d] were unaware of the encroachmen[t] until after the building had bee[n] sold to a third party.
(D) Nancy for at least nomina[l] damages.

280. Denise Decedent executed a last wi[ll] and testament leaving Greenacre, wort[h] $100,000, to her son Terry Taker an[d] Brownacre, worth $250,000, to he[r] daughter Sally Second. The rest an[d] residue of Denise's estate was left to Hel[p] Everyone Charity. Between the time th[e] will was executed and the date that Denis[e] died, Denise experienced financia[l] difficulty. She sold Greenacre and mingle[d] the proceeds in her diversified portfolio o[f] other investments. She also took out [a] mortgage on Brownacre and the mortgage[e] filed at the County Recorder Office. At th[e] time of Denise's death the mortgag[e] balance was $200,000. Under the majorit[y] rule in most jurisdictions Terry and Sall[y] would receive from the estate probate

(A) Terry will receive nothing an[d] Sally will receive Brownacre fre[e] and clear with the residue of th[e] estate required to pay the $200,00[0] mortgage.
(B) The residue of the estate will b[e] ordered to pay Terry $100,000 an[d] the $200,000 mortgage due o[n] Brownacre.
(C) Terry will receive nothing an[d] Sally will receive Brownacr[e] subject to the $200,000 mortgage.
(D) The residue of the estate will b[e] ordered to pay Terry $100,000 an[d] Sally will receive Brownacr[e] subject to the $200,000 mortgage.

281. Betty Beauty was a 25 year ol[d] divorcee with a child from her firs[t] marriage named Edward Expectant. Sh[e] and Edward moved in with Generou[s] George who was 20 years her senior. Afte[r] ive years of living together, George refused to marry Betty. Betty then began to pressure George for a definite support provision for her and her child, which she would need after he passed. George executed a last will and testament which stated that on his death Greenacre was to go to Betty if she survived but that all his other property was to go to his children from his two prior marriages.

Ten years went by and Betty had a unexpected stroke and did not recover. Without Betty's love, care, and attention, George grew increasingly depressed and died of natural causes one year later. Edward Expectant, Betty's sole heir, put demand on the Executor of George's estate to deed Greenacre to him. George's children from his former marriages opposed conveying the property to Edward. Geroge's children's best argument in opposition to Edward's request is

- (A) There is not an applicable anti-lapse statue in their jurisdiction.
- (B) Betty and their father George were never married.
- (C) Betty's interest was a fee tail.
- (D) Betty's interest was a mere power of appointment.

282. Loretta Landlord owned a strip mall building containing two adjacent store fronts. On January 1, Loretta signed a 5-year lease with Terry Tenant for the front space. On February 15, Loretta signed a promissory note secured by a mortgage with Mary Mortgagee containing an acceleration provision and a rent assignment. Mary recorded the mortgage and related promissory note on March 1. On April 15, Loretta signed a 7-year lease with Sandra Second for the back space. On September 1, Loretta ran into financial problems and defaulted on the mortgage. On November 1, Mary gave both Terry and Sandra notice of the rent assignment default. The notice stated that all rents must now be paid directly to Mary and that both leases were to be cancelled as of December 31. Both Terry and Sandra

objected and filed a lawsuit. The court will likely hold in this case that

	Liability For Rent Assignment	Cancellation and Eviction Ordered
(A) Both tenants	Yes	Yes
(B) Terry Only	No	No
(C) Sandra Only	Yes	No
(D) Both tenants	No	No

283. Tom Tryagain was in a difficult marriage with Iola. He decided to obtain a divorce decree in a foreign country. The foreign divorce was legally invalid in Tom's home state although he did not know it at the time. One year later, Tom met Nancy Newlove. Six months later Tom and Nancy got married in his home state which had a statute specifying a marriage by an already married person is illegal. Tom and Nancy then sold their individual homes and together purchased a fancy lake front residence. They took title as "Tom and Nancy, husband and wife as tenants by the entirety, not as tenants in common."

For two years Tom and Nancy lived together in the lake front residence. One evening, Tom was riding home in a carpool and the driver of his van suffered a stroke. The vehicle went out of control and ran into a concrete post, killing all the occupants. Tom's will left all his assets to the children of his and Iola's marriage. Nancy claimed sole ownership of the lake front residence. If Tom's children bring a lawsuit claiming half the lake front residence, the best argument Nancy can raise is

- (A) She was a tenant by the entirety under the terms of the conveyance.
- (B) She was a tenant by the entirety due to her good faith belief that she and Tom were legally married.
- (C) She and Tom created a resulting joint tenancy by the terms of the conveyance because it sufficiently manifested an intent to create a tenancy with right of survivorship.
- (D) She can claim a right of survivorship under the principle of

estoppel by deed even if the law dictates she be treated as a tenant in common.

284. Francis Freeholder owned Greenacre in fee simple. Francis had one child named Wendy Wayward. Wendy was 35 years old and had failed to find direction in her life. Afraid that Wendy would fritter away any inheritance, Francis's will on her death conveyed Greenacre into trust. The trust instrument directed "Greenacre to my daughter Wendy for her life and remainder to the non-profit corporation Everything for the Environment, Inc."

Wendy took possession of Greenacre and within a year borrowed money from Friendly Finance to support her wild lifestyle. Every year she borrowed more money. In year 5, Friendly Finance demanded security for their loan to Wendy. Wendy executed and delivered to Friendly a mortgage on Greenacre. One year later, Wendy gave a 10-year lease on Greenacre to Tiffany Tenant.

Two years later, Wendy passed away. Friendly Finance began to execute on their mortgage. Both Friendly and an attorney for Everything for the Environment put demands on the tenant Tiffany to pay rent. When Everything found out that Friendly was trying to levy on the property, they filed a lawsuit to evict Tiffany and moved the court to determine Friendly's interest, if any. The court is likely to hold that

(A) Friendly takes nothing on their mortgage, but Tiffany may remain a tenant for the balance of the lease term.

(B) Friendly receives the right to levy on Greenacre for the balance due them on the mortgage, but Tiffany will have to leave the premises immediately.

(C) Friendly receives the right to levy on Greenacre for the balance due them and Tiffany may remain a tenant for the balance of the lease term.

(D) Friendly takes nothing on their mortgage and Tiffany will have to leave the premises immediately.

285. Adam purchased a large tract of home lots that had not been developed. For three years, he tried but was unable to finance the tract development. Adam was approached by Barbara Big Bucks to sell her the property. Adam and Barbara agreed upon a price and conveyed title via a full statutory warranty deed. Barbara developed one third of the property, but then ran into financial difficulty. She thus sold the remaining property to Carol Comelater via a quitclaim deed two years after her purchase from Adam. Three months after Carol took title, she was evicted from a portion of the property by Wendy Wildcome. Wendy had a superior title to a portion of the property and her ownership interest was wrongfully concealed by the person who sold the property to Adam. Adam lacked knowledge of Wendy's interest. Carol brought a lawsuit against Adam and Barbara for damages. The court is likely to award judgment against

(A) Adam only.

(B) Barbara only.

(C) Both Adam and Barbara.

(D) Neither Adam nor Barbara.

286. Felicia First owned Viewacre, a 20,000 square foot tract of land on the top of a hill with spectacular views. She subdivided the land into two 10,000 square foot lots A and B. Lot A was sold to Sarah Second with a deed specifying that "grantee hereby covenants she will not build any structure over 25 feet in height." Sarah recorded the deed and immediately built a 20 foot high home on the lot. Two years later, Felicia sold lot B to Tony Third with a deed that contained no restriction on structure height. Tony filed for a building permit which specified the house would be 40 feet in height. When Sarah learned about the planned height, she brought an action to require adherence to the 25 foot height limit. The jurisdiction maintains both grantor-grantee and tract indexes. The

ecording act specified "every conveyance
s void as against any subsequent purchaser
n good faith for value without notice
nless first duly recorded." Sarah's best
rgument to support the injunction is

(A) Tony was not a bona fide
purchaser.

(B) Tony was put on inquiry notice of
the height restriction by observing
the height of the building next
door.

(C) The jurisdiction follows the
collateral source rule and Tony
could have learned of the 25 foot
height limitation in his chain of
title by checking the tract index
containing all the other deeds
conveyed by Felicia.

(D) The equitable restriction runs with
the land independently of any
notice individual owners may
receive about it.

87. Susan Seller agreed in a written and
cknowledged contract to sell her home in
lorida to Betty Buyer for $400,000
ayable in cash at closing. The closing was
cheduled for two months hence. At the
nd of the month Susan's home insurance
olicy was up for renewal. She did not pay
he premium because of the pending sale on
he policy and received notice of lapse from
he insurance company. Hurricane Francis
it the neighborhood destroying the house.
he land without the house had a value of
100,000. Betty refused to proceed with
he closing. Susan filed a lawsuit seeking
pecific performance or a damage award. If
3etty prevails, it will likely because

(A) Susan remained in possession as of
the hurricane date.

(B) Susan negligently allowed
insurance on the home to lapse.

(C) The value of the land alone is
substantially below the $400,000
sale price.

(D) The doctrine of equitable
conversion applies.

**Questions 288 and 289 are based on the
following:**

Ethel Environment, a widow without
children, owned Greenacre in fee simple
and had a strong interest in maintaining the
natural setting of the land. Therefore she
sold the land in individual lots at a discount
to users who agreed they would only use
the property for camping and not develop
any permanent buildings. This equitable
restrictive covenant was contained in all the
deeds and enforceable against all the
grantees under local law.

Freda Fruit was not one of the grantees.
She took unauthorized possession of
Ethel's unsold lot 5 and improved it by
grading a campsite and clearing for walking
trails. She used the lot for enough time to
establish adverse possession in the state.

288. Assume for this question that one year
after Freda's adverse possession on lot 5
was established, Freda decided to sell her
lot. She thus signed a contract for sale and
full warranty deed in favor of Selina
Second that did not mention any equitable
servitude. Selina took possession of lot 5
and began to construct a large hunting
lodge. Neda Nextdoorneighbor owned lot 4
that she had purchased 25 years ago from
Ethel. She had maintained only a campsite
on lot and was extremely upset that anyone
would not adhere to the equitable restrictive
provision prohibiting development. Neda
thus filed a petition seeking an order
prohibiting any construction on Freda's lot
5. The best argument that Neda can use to
support her petition is

(A) The mutual use of their lots by
Freda and Neda created an
equitable restriction by implication
against developing any permanent
building between them which Neda
may enforce against Selina as
Freda's assignee.

(B) The sales contract and conveyance
deed by which Selina obtained the
property from Freda placed Selina
in privity with Neda.

(C) Freda occupation and use of lot 5 was not adverse to the rights of those entitled to enforce the equitable restriction.

(D) As a successor to Freda, Selina is bound by the equitable restriction that runs with the property.

289. Assume for this question that Ethel Environment was unaware of Freda's adverse possession or any of the subsequent transactions of lot 5. She sold the same lot 5 to Bee Bonafide for full value by way of a warranty deed. Bee recorded the deed immediately. The recording statute in the jurisdiction specified: "Every conveyance of land not recorded is void as against any subsequent purchaser for value without notice whose conveyance is first duly recorded." If Bee files an action to eject Freda, the court will likely hold for

(A) Freda because the recording act does not operate to give Bee a superior title to the property.

(B) Ethel because Freda's use was only seasonal and not fully continuous.

(C) Ethel because Freda did not document her acquisition of title in a method or manner at least equivalent to recording a deed.

(D) Freda because Freda's possessions should have put Bee on inquiry notice of the adverse possessor's interest in lot 5.

290. Mary Mother, a widow, had two children, Freda First and Selina Second. Mary owned two large apartment houses in Hicksville. The two girls had just started college when their mother Mary suffered a debilitating stroke. Freda and Selina talked about the situation and decided one of them would have to give up college and return home to care for their mother and the two apartment houses. Freda had her heart set on becoming a lawyer and was confident that her wealthy boyfriend was going to marry her. The two sisters orally agreed that if Selina returned to Hicksville and cared for their mother and managed the apartment houses, she would become the

sole owner of the apartment houses.

For the next six years, Selina cared for their mother and managed the apartment houses including merging her personal cash with the apartment house account. She used her own money to pay taxes and make improvements to the apartment house. During the sixth year, Mary died and in her will she left all her estate to Freda and Selina as tenants in common. Freda had lost her wealthy boyfriend, was short of cash, and demanded her half of the apartment houses. Selina objected. There is a five year time period required for adverse possession in Hicksville. If lawsuit is initiated, a court will likely decide the apartment houses are owned by

(A) Freda and Selina as co-tenants because an oral agreement for the conveyances of oral property ownership is not enforceable.

(B) Selina as sole owner because she completely performed her agreement with Freda.

(C) Selina as sole owner because she acquired ownership by adverse possession.

(D) Freda and Selina as co-tenants because one co-tenant cannot obtain ownership to oral property from another by adverse possession.

291. Alice and Barbara were co-tenants in ownership and they both lived on a tract of forest land located in Forestville. Barbara became increasingly tired of living in the forest so far away from city life. She began to argue with Alice and finally announced that she was leaving to move to New York City where she could find some culture. Alice stayed in Forestville and assumed complete management over the jointly owned forest land.

Alice was contacted two years later by Connie who owned the adjacent forest land. She explained that they should join together and put up a chain link fence on their joint boundary line because the boundary line was uncertain. Alice agreed and she, Connie and a fence builder walked off an agreeable and buildable fence line that reasonably separated the parcels. The fence builder constructed the chain link fence along the line they both had agreed upon.

Two years later, Alice died and her will devised all her assets to Barbara. Barbara moved back to Forestville and discovered the new chain link fence. She commissioned a formal survey of the boundary line discovering that the new chain link fence encroached on her property by up to 15 feet in various places. Barbara was outraged that Alice ever agreed to such a fence division and filed suit for trespass and damages against the neighbor, Connie. The court will likely find for

(A) Barbara because she did not receive notice of the fence agreement.
(B) Connie because Barbara was "ousted" from the tenancy in common thus terminating her right to participate in management.
(C) Connie because Alice had the right to establish the disputed property line between the two adjoining pieces of property.
(D) Barbara because the property line oral agreement entered into between Alice and Connie was not in writing.

Questions 292 – 295 are based on the following:

Frank and Florence Farmer operated a large vineyard in Nowhereville, which had been in the family for generations. The farm had been profitable for many years since Frank converted the Concord grapes to wine grapes. Frank and Florence had two children, Steadfast and Flighty. Both girls went through high school in Nowhereville. Steadfast enjoyed working on the farm and the local social life. Flighty, on the other hand, could hardly wait to get out of the farming community. She enrolled in college in Boston and after graduation, she married and took a job in Boston. Flighty

thoroughly enjoyed the pace and intellectual New England environment and had no plans to return to Nowhereville.

Frank and Florence were returning from a vacation in Mexico when their airplane crashed, killing all passengers. In their wills, they left the Farmer farm to their two daughters as tenants in common. Steadfast, who had been working as a manager on the farm, moved into the main home on the property, making all mortgage, property tax, and insurance payments. She also paid for all maintenance and repairs and built valuable and substantial improvements including new buildings for equipment storage and residences for workers with her own funds.

Twenty years went by and during that period Steadfast never asked Flighty for money nor offered her any share in the farm's operating profits. Flighty also did not mention an expectation of receiving any profits from the farm nor any responsibility to pay any part of the expenses or improvements. Flighty then filed a lawsuit seeking partition and sale of the farm. The jurisdiction has a 15 year period for adverse possession.

292 Flighty demanded that she be given an extra amount from Steadfast's half of the sales proceeds to make up for the farm's operating profits retained wholly by Steadfast over the past twenty years. Beyond splitting the property proceeds, the court will likely decide this issue

(A) Against Flighty on any additional amount beyond half the proceeds of the farm's sale because she did not participate in the farm's operations.
(B) Against Flighty on any additional amount beyond half the proceeds of the farm's sale because Steadfast was in exclusive possession of the property.
(C) For Flighty in an amount of half the farm's operating profits no matter how much or how little Steadfast paid for carrying charges.

(D) For Flighty in an additional amount of half the farm's operating profits that exceed one-half the carrying charges Steadfast paid.

293. For this question only, assume that Steadfast counterclaimed in the partition lawsuit brought by Flighty. She argued that she should be given an additional portion of the farm sales proceeds as compensation for the improvements she made. In deciding this issue, the court will likely hold for

(A) Flighty because the proceeds of the partition should be divided equally since a co-tenant not in possession who does not participate in the decision to spend money for property improvements has no responsibility to contribute to the expenditures.

(B) Flighty because the proceeds of the partition should be divided equally since Steadfast voluntarily made 100% of the property improvements without the knowledge or approval of any co-tenants and this is treated as a gift.

(C) Steadfast should be given an additional portion of the property sale proceeds for her improvements without setoff for any benefits she derived from the property.

(D) Steadfast should be given an additional amount of the sale proceeds for the property improvements she made with a setoff for any benefit she derived from the use of the property.

294. For this question only, assume that the farm brought $500,000 at the partition sale and that there was a $300,000 mortgage paid from the proceeds. Also assume that over the years Steadfast earned a net operating profit of $100,000 from the farm and a net rent of $50,000 from a second house on the farm that was leased to a third party. Flighty is entitled to how much in satisfaction of her co-tenant ownership interest?

(A) $100,000.

(B) $125,000.

(C) $150,000.

(D) $175,000.

295. For this question only, assume that when Flighty filed her petition for partition of the farm, Steadfast filed a quiet title action seeking sole ownership by adverse possession. Regarding the claim of adverse possession, the court will likely hold for

(A) Steadfast because she enjoyed sole occupancy for the statutory period.

(B) Steadfast because Flighty's filing her petition for partition is strong evidence that Steadfast's possession was adverse to Flighty's ownership interest.

(C) Flighty because a co-tenant may not adversely possess property as against her fellow co-tenant since i violates the duty of fair dealing.

(D) Flighty because Steadfast never ousted Flighty from possession of the farm.

Questions 296 and 297 are based on the following:

Denise Developer wanted to build a regional shopping center in Newtown Denise located a large farm in the area owned by Susan Seller that would be perfect for the development. They entered into a written agreement stating:

"Susan hereby agrees to sell my 50 acre farm to Denise for $500,000 and promises to convey unrestricted and marketable title at the closing of escrow in not more than 90 days. I Denise does not receive legal title in not more than 90 days, this agreement becomes null and void."

Forty days later, Town Title Company issued their abstract of title covering Susan's farm. It was then that Susan realized that the previous owner had conveyed an easement over the farm to the County government for construction of an electrical line for a proposed residential evelopment. Upon investigation, it was etermined that the development decided to urchase electricity from the adjoining ounty. Susan called Denise and explained .e situation, but said she believed she uld purchase the easement from the ounty since it was not being used.

orty days later, Denise called Susan to iquire about the negotiations with the ounty to purchase the easement. Susan ·ported that the negotiations were ompleted and that the County Executive ad agreed to a price of $10,000 to ·convey the easement. The ·commendation was to go to the County ouncil the next week. Denise stated, Please try to get this closed ASAP."

Infortunately, the County Council had a ıll docket of business at their next meeting nd delayed action on the easement sale ıatter. It was finally passed by the ·ouncil, but it was only completed 95 days ·om the date of the original agreement ntered into by Susan and Denise. The next ay, Susan paid the $10,000 to the County nd deposited a warranty deed into escrow ·r closing conveying marketable title to)enise. Denise then stated that Susan had ·reached the terms of the contract and she ·ould not close.

96. Susan filed a lawsuit against Denise lleging breach of contract and sought an ·rder of specific performance. If the court ·sues the order requiring Denise to accept ·e property and pay the $500,000 to Susan, ·e best reason would be

(A) Six days delay in the closing of the property transaction can never be deemed a total breach of contract.

(B) Denise's statement to Susan of "please try to get this closed as soon as possible" was a modification or waiver of the time is of the essence condition.

(C) Denise would be operating inequitably if she is allowed to escape her contract responsibility because of mere six day delay.

(D) Time was not of the essence in the contract between Denise and Susan.

297. Assume that 15 days before the date the contract specified as the closing date of the escrow, the buyer and seller talked. In this conversation, Susan reported to Denise that there had developed some opposition in the Council to her proposed purchase of the easement. Denise asked Susan what the chances were that the sale could go through and Susan stated, "I am not sure right now." Denise then stated that she had decided to rescind the contract. Susan then filed a lawsuit seeking damages or specific performance. Denise's strongest argument that she did not breach the contract is

(A) Susan was unlikely to deliver a marketable title within a reasonable period of time.

(B) Denise was entitled to rescind the contract because Susan repudiated the ability to perform.

(C) Susan did not have a marketable title when she entered into the agreement.

(D) Susan's agreement to sell property without marketable title was a constructive fraud upon Denise.

298. Francis First and Sarah Second were two friends who purchased Blueacres Farm as joint tenants with right of survivorship. They lived together on the farm in a residence that had been there for many years. They grew blueberries which they picked and sold at market.

Francis, on her own, made some bad investments and found herself owing a large balance to BigBank. She could not pay, so BigBank secured a judgment against Francis and all her assets. The Bank then forced a sheriff's sale of Francis' ownership interest in Blueacre. Theresa Third purchased Francis' interest in Blueacre at the sheriff's sale.

One year later, Francis died and Sarah felt too lonely living on Blueacre alone. She leased the farm to Fay Fourth who paid her 50% of the blueberry crop revenue as rent. Theresa sent Sarah letters demanding half of the rent paid by Fay. Sarah disregarded these demands, but continued to pay all the property taxes and insurance on Blueacre.

After six years, Theresa conveyed her interest to Felice Fifth via a quit claim deed. Felice then brought a quiet title action to determine the ownership interests of Blueacre. The statutory period for adverse possession in the jurisdiction is five years. The court will likely rule that

(A) Sarah and Felice own the property as tenants in common and no right of payment is due the other.

(B) Sarah and Felice own the property as tenants in common and Sarah must pay Felice one-half of the rents received from Fay Fourth.

(C) Sarah is the sole owner of Blueacre having obtained title to Francis' interest by adverse possession.

(D) Sarah is the sole owner of Blueacre because she succeeded to Francis' interest upon her death.

299. Sharon Stingy was the widow of a wealthy industrialist. She had two children, Pious and Prayerful, whom she adored. Prayerful never married, but Pious married Roundabout. They had one daughter named Playful. Roundabout died in a train accident leaving Pious a widow. Sharon was also an active member of the Women's Temperance Union, which believed alcohol was evil and should be prohibited. As she got older, Sharon became more and more involved with this anti-alcoholic group.

Playful married young and her husband Playboy was a heavy drinker. This outraged Playful's grandmother Sharon and she decided to disinherit Playful because she believed Playboy would squander the money on alcohol. Sharon's two children convinced her not to punish any children that Playful had because the bad habits of their father were not their fault.

Two years later, Sharon died and w[as] survived only by Pious, Prayerful, Playf[ul] and Playboy. When her attorney read h[er] will, the heirs learned that Sharon h[ad] established a testamentary trust as a part [of] her will. Sharon's devise placed all h[er] assets in trust with the income to be paid [to] her children, Pious and Prayerful durin[g] their lives and then the remaining corpus [is] to be distributed to Playful's children.

At the time of Sharon's death, the intere[st] of Sharon's great grandchildren in the tru[st] corpus was

(A) A springing executory interest.

(B) A contingent remainder.

(C) A vested remainder subject to ope[n]

(D) A power of appointment in the parents.

300. Gertrud Grantor owned tw[o] undeveloped tracts of land name[d] Greenacre and Blackacre. As she got olde[r] she became more and more concerne[d] about the environment and less and le[ss] concerned about the value of her propertie[s]. She joined a group named "Landsav[e] Foundation" and at one of their meeting[s] learned about how she could restri[ct] development on her lands after her death. Gertrud conveyed Greenacre to her frien[d] "Alice so long as the land is not develope[d] then to Landsave Foundation."

Two years went by and Gertrud conveye[d] Blackacre to her other friend with th[e] conveyance "to Betty but if developmen[t] should ever take place on Blackacre, th[e] property shall pass to Landsav[e] Foundation." One year later bot[h] properties were developed and two month[s] later Gertrud died leaving all her propert[y] to her friend Carolyn in a standard wil[l]. Alice, Betty, Landsave Foundation, an[d] Carolyn all claimed the properties. Th[e] court will likely decide the ownership as

	Greenacre	Blackacre
(A)	Alice	Betty
(B)	Carolyn	Betty
(C)	Landsave	Carolyn
(D)	Landsave	Landsave

Real Property and Future Interests Learning Question Answer Rationales

. **/D/** After the conveyance, Shemp is a tenant in common with Larry and Mo, but with respect to each other, Larry and Mo are still joint tenants with right of survivorship. **(A)** is incorrect because when a joint tenant conveys his interest to another outside the joint tenancy, the grantee becomes a tenant in common. **(B)** is incorrect because the original joint tenants who remain are still joint tenants, not tenants in common. **(C)** is incorrect because having an undivided interest in the whole does not require a sale; the tenancy in common can still exist between the grantee and the remaining joint tenants, and joint tenancy exists between the original joint tenants.

. **/C/** If a co-tenant improves the property without approval of the others, Mo and Curly do not owe reimbursement. However, if the improvement increases the value of the property, Larry may recover if they later sell the property. **(A)** is incorrect because immediate contribution is not applicable unless the expenditures were necessary or unless the others approved. **(B)** is incorrect because it ignores the possibility of a later sale. **(D)** is incorrect because it ignores the possibility of a later sale.

3. **/C/** This is the best response because (A) and (B) are both correct. While a co-tenant in exclusive possession may exercise sole management control this does not include the ouster of a co-tenant. In case of ouster, the ousted tenants may bring an action for a partition. Also, if Curly caused waste to the land by harvesting trees and not replanting, he could be liable for damages. **(A)** is not the best answer because it is incomplete; (B) is also correct. If Curly caused waste to the land by harvesting trees and not replanting, he could be liable for damages. **(B)** is not the best answer because it is incomplete; (A) is also correct. While a co-tenant in exclusive possession may exercise sole management control this does not include the ouster of a co-tenant. In case of ouster, the ousted tenants may bring an action for a partition. **(D)** is an incorrect alternative because (A) and (B) are both correct. While a co-tenant in exclusive possession may exercise sole management control this does not include the ouster of a co-tenant. In case of ouster, the ousted tenants may bring an action for a partition. Also, if Curly caused waste to the land by harvesting trees and not replanting, he could be liable for damages.

4. **/B/** The exteriors are normally considered part of the common property owned as a tenancy in

common, therefore, the association is responsible. **(A)** is incorrect; while restraints on alienation for titles in fee simple are generally unenforceable, rights of first refusal are exceptions and are usually enforced. **(C)** is incorrect because individuals are only responsible for maintaining their own individual property. **(D)** is incorrect because in joint tenancies, all the tenants in common are equally responsible for maintenance of the common areas. Additionally, maintenance fees are probably written into the condo covenants. Therefore, individual owners may not unilaterally opt out of paying such fees.

5. **/D/** Members of co-ops are economically intertwined. If one person does not pay his portion of the mortgage, the entire co-op will be in jeopardy. **(A)** is incorrect because a co-op is most commonly owned by a corporation. **(B)** is incorrect because with a co-op, there is only one mortgage on the entire building, not individual mortgages as with a condominium. **(C)** is incorrect because the individuals are so economically intertwined, more restrictions are allowed to be placed on the transfer of units.

6. **/D/** Matt has met all the CHO requirements for an easement by prescription; continual use for 20 years, hostile to the owner, and open and notorious. **(A)** is incorrect because there is only one tract of land and an easement by implication can only arise where there are at least two tracts of land that were at one time under common ownership. **(B)** is incorrect because there is only one tract of land and an easement by necessity can only arise where there are at least two tracts of land

that were at one time und[er] common ownership. **(C)** [is] incorrect because an appurtena[nt] easement benefits the holder in th[e] use of an adjoining piece of lan[d.] Matt's easement strictly benefi[ts] him, not another piece of land.

7. **/B/** An easement by prescription can b[e] terminated by Tiffany, the owner [of] the servient estate, taking the lan[d] back by way of prescriptio[n.] Tiffany can physically block th[e] path for 20 years as a means [of] terminating Matt's easement. A[ll] the CHO elements of prescriptio[n] must be met. **(A)** is incorre[ct] because the burden of the easeme[nt] will pass to the new owner of th[e] servient estate, unless the ne[w] owner is a bona fide purchaser an[d] takes without notice. Tiffany is n[ot] a bona fide purchaser since sh[e] took the land by a will, and ther[e] was notice – a path. **(C)** [is] incorrect because Matt is n[ot] required to pay Tiffany for th[e] easement. **(D)** is incorrect becaus[e] only the holder of an easement ca[n] transfer it, here that would be Mat[t.] Note that personal easements i[n] gross cannot be transferred even b[y] the holder.

8. **/C/** An easement by implication can b[e] claimed because Cindy owned a[ll] the land prior to the conveyance[s,] she continuously used the road, an[d] it is reasonably necessary for parce[l] B since the other road is dangerou[s.] **(A)** is incorrect because no writte[n] express grant was given. **(B)** i[s] incorrect because there would hav[e] to be continuous use for the perio[d] specified under state law, hostile t[o] the owners, and open and notoriou[s] for an easement by prescription t[o] arise. **(D)** is not the best answe[r] because no necessity exists sinc[e] parcel B is not absolute[ly] landlocked.

/A/ Here parcel A is the servient burdened estate and parcel B the dominant benefiting estate because the owner of parcel B has been benefited by gaining the right to pass over parcel A. This would be appurtenant because it benefits an adjoining parcel of land. **(B)** is incorrect because it specifies the incorrect servient and dominant estates. **(C)** is incorrect because it specifies the incorrect servient and dominant estates. **(D)** is incorrect because it specifies the incorrect servient and dominant estates.

0. **/C/** In order for Jane to have an easement, it must be expressly given by Edgar. **(A)** is incorrect because although there is a necessity, the facts did not state the land was ever owned by one person, so there can be no easement by necessity. **(B)** is incorrect because the facts did not state the land was ever owned by one person, so an easement by implication is not the best answer. **(D)** is incorrect because an express reservation can only be made by the grantor reserving the right to continue use for himself, not a third party.

1. **/D/** An easement by express reservation of the grantor can only be made in favor of the grantor, not a third party. So this easement is invalid because Oscar tried to create an easement in favor of the church. **(A)** is incorrect because the easement is invalid, regardless of whether the new buyer is a bona fide purchaser. **(B)** is incorrect because the new buyer had actual notice of the attempted easement (in the deed), but it is still invalid for the above reasons. **(C)** is incorrect because, as stated above, a grantor cannot reserve an easement for a third party even if known to the grantee.

12. **/C/** Maryanne has an enforceable negative easement, therefore she may obtain injunctive relief. **(A)** is incorrect because separate consideration is a distracting red herring; there is no such requirement. **(B)** is incorrect because none of the theories of easement allow Maryanne access to the lakeshore. **(D)** is incorrect because Busco transferred the right to limit a 15 foot tree height to Maryanne in the original property sale.

13. **/A/** The original use of the easement was intended solely for the use of Sleepy Pines. The attempted use to benefit Sleepy Meadows may be enjoined by the owner of Hardcore Hemlocks. **(B)** is incorrect because the easement may be divided. This is an easement appurtenant, which can be divided if Aislinn were to subdivide her lot, as long as the kind and extent of use could have been anticipated and does not excessively burden the servient estate. **(C)** is incorrect because at the time the easement was granted Aislinn did not own Sleepy Meadows, so the use could not have been foreseeable. Notice that this alternative contains facts going beyond those given in the question. **(D)** is incorrect because it is out of context. The use here is not a division, but rather an extension of the use, which goes beyond the scope of the easement.

14. **/D/** Barry gave Arlene an oral license. **(A)** is incorrect because Arlene is not taking anything off the land. **(B)** is incorrect because although it may have appeared to be an express easement, Barry did not comply with the statute of frauds, therefore,

it is a failed attempt at an easement, which is a license. **(C)** is incorrect because although it may have appeared to be an express easement, Barry did not comply with the statute of frauds, therefore, it is a failed attempt at an easement, which is a license.

15. **/A/** Here Ben is trying to enforce a burden on Cheri. Horizontal privity is met because Ben was the original grantor of the lot to Jerry, so his interest goes beyond just the covenant. Vertical privity is met because Cheri took the same estate that Jerry had. The covenant was in the deed, which satisfies the writing and notice requirement. There was an intent to bind successors since Ben stated buildings taller than 30 feet could never be erected. This touches and concerns the land. **(B)** is not the best answer because Ben is trying to enforce the burden on Cheri. The fact that the benefit runs only allows Ben to bring suit to enforce the burden upon Cheri, but it does not guarantee that the burden will be enforced. **(C)** is incorrect because there was an intent to bind the successors. **(D)** is incorrect because, as stated in the facts, horizontal privity of Ben to Jerry is present.

16. **/B/** The burden does not run to Lois because the covenant does not touch and concern the land. The benefit is personal to Martha, therefore, the burden cannot be enforced upon Lois. Only when the benefit touches and concerns the dominant estate will the burden run to servient estate successors. **(A)** is a distracter and not the best answer because it ignores the law. **(C)** is incorrect because although there may be a covenant in place with Jeremy, it does not pass to

Lois because the requirements fo the covenant to run are not me **(D)** is incorrect because Lois estate is the burdened estate, s there is no benefit that will run t Lois.

17. **/B/** Joyce needs to have the benefit ru to her in order to be able to enforc the covenant. For the benefit t run, there only needs to be vertica privity, which is met here becaus Joyce assumed the same estate tha Betsy once held (but even if sh took a lesser estate, such as tenancy, she would still be able t enforce the covenant). **(A)** i incorrect because horizontal privit is not required for the benefit t run. **(C)** is incorrect becaus although there is no horizont privity, Joyce will still be able t enforce the covenant. **(D)** i incorrect because there is vertica privity between Joyce and Ross.

18. **/D/** In this question we are looking t see if the burden of the covenan will run to Gill. Betsy will not b able to enforce the covenant agains Gill because there is no horizont privity between Gill and Betsy Betsy has no interest in Gill's lan besides the covenant. If Betsy ha sold the land originally to Ross an the covenant was made during tha transaction, then horizontal privit would be met. But since this was covenant made outside of a sal horizontal privity does not run. **(A** is incorrect because although ther is vertical privity, Betsy cann enforce with horizontal privity. **(B** is incorrect because there is n horizontal privity. **(C)** is incorrec because vertical privity does exis between Betsy and Gill becaus Gill took over Ross's estate for th same duration, a fee simple, a Ross.

19. **/A/** The best answer because all the elements of a negative equitable servitude are met. By placing cedar shake on all the homes and naming the development Cedar Shake Park, there was intent by the developer to have the restriction enforceable by future successors. The benefit touches and concerns the Smiths property, and the burden definitely touches and concerns Laura and Jason's property. Notice of a negative servitude can be met by a common plan or scheme - seeing all the houses still with Cedar Shake roofs and the name of the development would put Laura and Jason on notice of the restriction; no writing is therefore required. **(B)** is incorrect because there is no need for a signed agreement to enforce an equitable servitude. **(C)** is incorrect because even though there is no real covenant in place, an equitable servitude could still be enforced against them. **(D)** is incorrect because privity of estate is not required for an equitable servitude, only a real covenant.

20. **/C/** The lack of a common scheme is not a viable argument since the facts say that the one story restrictive covenant or equitable servitude was advertised for all of Myrvin Gardens. Thus there would be intent to impose a common scheme. **(A)** is incorrect because David's statement of abandonment to Bryan was the inducement for Bryan to purchase the property and thus a good defensive argument. **(B)** is incorrect because the purchase by Bryan of all of David's interest created a merger that would terminate the restriction and thus is a good defensive argument. **(D)** is incorrect since a lapse assumes there was only a set time period during which the developer

intended to enforce the restrictive covenant. It is thus a good defensive argument.

21. **/C/** The facts do not state that the residential restriction was ever put into the deeds, or that it was even put into writing. Therefore the best answer here is C, a negative servitude, which can be implied based upon a common scheme. The developer told each new lot owner of the scheme, so the requirement of notice is met. **(A)** is not the best answer because in most jurisdictions, an equitable servitude must be in writing in order to be enforced. A mutually enforceable negative servitude can only be enforced by a party who is similarly bound (i.e., another owner in the same subdivision). Here a person in the neighboring community may not be similarly bound. **(B)** is incorrect because there was no mention of a real covenant being in writing or in the deed, which is required for the creation of a real covenant. **(D)** is incorrect because there was no mention of a real covenant being in writing or in the deed, which is required for the creation of a real covenant.

22. **/D/** The theory of unclean hands would be the best defense for Jane since the person trying to enforce the servitude is similarly restricted to residential use and is engaged in the same type of violation that Jane is proposing to undertake. **(A)** is incorrect because estoppel could only be used as a defense when the person bringing the action acts in such a way as to create reliance that the servitude has been abandoned. Here the facts do not state that Tex acted in any way to make Jane rely. **(B)** is incorrect because merger can only take place when the burdened and benefited land come under common ownership. **(C)** is not the best answer because there has probably not been a sufficient enough change in the neighborhood to cause a court to conclude that the servitude is no longer beneficial to the subdivision.

23. **/B/** The best answer is that the beneficiary of the covenant, the homeowners' association, is no longer in existence. **(A)** is the incorrect conclusion because they are not responsible. **(C)** contains the correct conclusion – that they are not liable – but the reasoning is flawed in that the beneficiary is no longer in existence. **(D)** is incorrect because one of the above is the correct conclusion and to allow such an answer would reward mistakes.

24. **/C/** The covenant requiring a height limit on trees is still enforceable, but Ned will not prevail because of "unclean hands" doctrine. **(A)** is incorrect because covenants are independent: abandonment of one does not mean all are necessarily abandoned. **(B)** would be correct if it was any neighbor other than Ned suing. **(D)** is incorrect because both vertical and horizontal privity are present.

25. **/B/** A zoning regulation is presumed to be valid, as long as it is reasonably related to the police powers (health, public safety, morals, and the welfare) of the community. **(A)** is incorrect because the presumption is towards validity, not invalidity. **(C)** is incorrect because this is not spot zoning. Spot zoning is where one parcel is singled out for a use that is inconsistent with the surrounding area. **(D)** is incorrect because this is not spot zoning. Spot zoning is where one parcel is singled out for a use that is inconsistent with the surrounding area.

26. **/B/** The building will be allowed to continue as a nonconforming use, which is a use that was legal when built, but does not meet the current zoning regulations. **(A)** is incorrect because the building will not have to be removed, it will be allowed as a nonconforming use. **(C)** is incorrect because no spot zoning has taken place; the regulation is placed on future buildings and remodeling. **(D)** is incorrect because no taking has occurred. A taking is an invalid exercise of police powers, which severely limits the use of property.

27. **/D/** Generally, an ordinance can be challenged on the basis of Equal Protection when it involves illegal discrimination (normally based on religion, race, etc.). The facts here do not make this an option for Joe. **(A)** is an available option for Joe; a variance could be granted if unnecessary hardship was placed on Joe (i.e. having to close the business). **(B)** is also an available option; a taking occurs when an ordinance severely restricts the use of property. This is a factual question, but it is a legitimate option available to Joe. **(C)** is also an option available to Joe; nonconforming use is one that was legal when built, but later becomes illegal due to new zoning codes.

28. **/C/** Private nuisance is Joan's best theory because the neighbor's actions are interfering with Joan's private property rights. **(A)** is incorrect because the fact pattern lacks the elements of an equitable servitude. **(B)** is incorrect, because the use of public property or facilities is not at stake. **(D)** is no

the best answer because Joan could not show an injury that is unique and not shared by the general public.

29. **/B/** This situation describes a public nuisance since the use and enjoyment of public areas are being harmed. Any person that can show the nuisance is of greater harm to her than the general community will be able to bring a claim. **(A)** is not the best answer because the facts described the nuisance as harming the use of community areas, not a private lot. **(C)** is incorrect because, although the ranch was there first, some remedies can be sought, such as an injunction. **(D)** is incorrect because the community in fact "came to the nuisance" since the nuisance was there first. If the ranch is successful with this defense, the P may have to help pay for the D's relocation costs if that is the remedy granted.

30. **/C/** Note that the contract is unenforceable as it exists, because it does not contain a street address or a valid legal description of the property. However, Bobby may seek to have the contract reformed due to the scrivener's error. **(A)** is incorrect because in addition to return of earnest money, Bobby could seek relief through contract reformation. **(B)** is incorrect, because Bobby is entitled to return of the earnest money unless he is the cause of a breach of the contract. **(D)** is incorrect because the fact pattern does not give sufficient reason to support the elements of fraud by Harry.

31. **/B/** Although this contract violates the Statute of Frauds because it is not in writing, it may nonetheless be enforced based on the estoppel

theory. Daughter has changed her position (sold her home) based on the promise of Mom to sell her home to her, so serious injury can be proved if the contract is not enforced. **(A)** is incorrect because there is no evidence of part performance; Daughter does not possess the land and significant improvements were not made. **(C)** is incorrect because, although not in writing, an oral contract can be enforced based upon part performance or a detrimental change of position. **(D)** is incorrect because even if Daughter did not pay yet, the contract may be enforced because of her change in position (detrimental reliance) based on the promise.

32. **/D/** This is the best answer because both (A) and (B) are available remedies, but the seller must choose one. Most jurisdictions will allow the seller to keep the earnest money as liquidated damages if it bears a reasonable relationship to the amount of loss caused by the breach. In the alternative, the seller could claim actual damages; in this case that would be the difference between the actual sale price and the contract price. Because of the second offer from Dan, his case is strengthened by evidence that the market value of the land at the time of the contract actually was $50,000 more than when eventually sold. **(A)** is not the best answer because both (A) and (B) are possible options, but only one remedy is available to the seller. **(B)** is not the best answer because both (A) and (B) are possible options, but only one of these remedies is available to the seller. **(C)** is incorrect because the seller has a choice of liquidated or actual damages, but may not receive both.

33. **/D/** The remedy of a buyer when a seller of real property breaches is compensatory damages or specific performance. Normally, the buyer will petition a court to order the seller to convey a marketable title. But if specific performance is not possible, the buyer may sue for compensatory damages. **(A)** is incorrect because normally punitive damages are not available in a property transaction. **(B)** is incorrect because the buyer is never entitled to both specific performance and compensatory damages. **(C)** is incorrect because punitive damages are not normally available for simple breach of contract. But note that consequential damages, such as lost profits, might be available to an aggrieved buyer.

34. **/C/** According to the Statute of Frauds, a contract for land must be in writing and signed by the party to be charged. This means that each party must sign the contract for the other party to enforce it. Here the seller has signed, so the buyer can enforce the contract. But if the buyer refuses to close, the agreement may not be enforceable since the buyer did not sign. **(A)** is incorrect because a street address is usually adequate description for a sales contract. **(B)** is incorrect because there is apparently no doubt as to who the buyer and seller are. **(D)** is incorrect because this contract is not a deed, and for a contract to be enforceable it does not need to be notarized.

35. **/A/** According to the doctrine of equitable conversion, the risk of loss, prior to closing, rests with the buyer, unless other arrangements have been made in the contract. **(B)** is incorrect because the risk of loss is not automatically set with the seller, but rather, the buyer. The risk of loss is put on the seller only if it has been allocated to the seller in the contract. **(C)** is incorrect because after a valid contract is executed, the buyer is deemed to be the equitable owner and the seller the legal title holder under the doctrine of equitable conversion. **(D)** is incorrect because the doctrine of equitable conversion, which allocates risk of loss to the buyer, applies regardless of who has possession at the time the damage occurs.

36. **/C/** Johnny is out of luck because the gift did not comply with the Statute of Frauds, and the fact pattern does not support any of the exceptions to the Statute of Frauds doctrine. **(A)** is incorrect because the fact pattern does not support the theory of promissory estoppel; there was no detrimental reliance. **(B)** is incorrect because estoppel by deed refers to a grantor selling property they did not then own but later acquired. **(D)** is not the best answer because the lack of consideration is not as good a reason as a statute of frauds violation.

37. **/C/** A violation of a zoning restriction breaches the implied warranty of marketable title. Here there was a zoning restriction that did not allow buildings, but a building was put on the lot. This violation makes title unmarketable. **(A)** is incorrect because restrictive covenants, like this one, do not make a title unmarketable if the covenant is not violated and if it was expressly accepted by the seller in the contract. **(B)** is incorrect because a zoning restriction, by itself, does not make the title unmarketable; only if it is violated does it make a title unmarketable. **(D)** is incorrect

because an easement that does not reduce the land value does not make the title unmarketable. If there is an easement that significantly reduces land value, title is deemed unmarketable. If the buyer has knowledge of and agrees to the easement the marketable title rule is not violated.

8. /B/ The trespass and possible eviction or damages represent a breach of the warranty of title. **(A)** is incorrect because habitability is not stated in the fact pattern and even a good faith mistake is not a defense to trespass. **(C)** is incorrect because on the MBE assume that the TAFED statutory warranty applies in transactions as a default deed, unless there are indications that a quitclaim or limited warranty apply in the jurisdiction specified in the question. **(D)** is incorrect because of the "FED" elements in the TAFED of a statutory warranty are missing; the title is arguably not fully marketable with a pending lawsuit, the warranty of quiet enjoyment has been breached, and the buyer Yolanda will have to defend the suit.

9. /B/ A quitclaim deed only conveys whatever interest the grantor has. In this case, because it is a lien theory jurisdiction, Ronald held title to the property subject to the mortgage. Therefore, that is what Daniel holds after the conveyance. **(A)** is incorrect because there is no warranty of title with a quitclaim deed that runs to a mortgagee. **(C)** is incorrect because there is no warranty of title with a quitclaim deed. **(D)** is incorrect because it more closely describes a title theory jurisdiction.

0. /D/ P has no recourse because the implied warranty of habitability only applies to new homes. **(A)** is incorrect because the implied warranty of habitability only applies to new homes. **(B)** is incorrect because sellers are only liable for disclosures they knew about; there is nothing in the facts to indicate the sellers had actual or implied knowledge of the defect. **(C)** is incorrect because there was no express warranty made in this fact pattern.

41. /A/ The buyer does not receive equitable title at closing, because equitable title passed between the seller and buyer upon execution of the purchase and sale agreement. **(B)** is not the best answer because it describes what the bank's interest is in a lien theory jurisdiction. **(C)** is not the best answer because legal title transfers at closing. **(D)** is incorrect because **(A)** is a valid response.

42. /B/ This state is a notice jurisdiction. There is no element of "first to record" stated in the facts as found in race-notice statutes. Also, the priority is determined entirely by the status of the purchaser at the time of conveyance. **(A)** is incorrect because no time element is stated which would be necessary for a race state. **(C)** is incorrect because there is no time element stated, so it cannot be "race-notice." **(D)** is incorrect because notice-race is not a recognized type of recording statute.

43. /A/ The only kind of statute that would allow Billy Jo to take with knowledge of a prior unrecorded interest is a pure race statute. In such jurisdictions, constructive or actual knowledge of the prior interest has no bearing on the outcome; only who files first. **(B)** is incorrect because notice would

defeat Billy Jo's filing if a pure "notice" statute was in place in the jurisdiction. **(C)** is incorrect because notice would defeat Billy Jo's filing if a "race-notice" statute was in place in the jurisdiction. **(D)** is incorrect because while the recording statute of "notice-race" is not generally recognized, notice would likely defeat Billy Jo's filing if such a notice race statute was in place in the jurisdiction.

44. **/C/** A quitclaim deed does not override legitimate prior interests of other parties; it only conveys whatever interests the grantor had at time of conveyance. Because the bank had a prior interest to Jerry, the bank wins (note that if the bank had filed the mortgage, they would have won on both race and notice). **(A)** is incorrect because filing first without notice is only valid for good faith purchasers for value, not gift recipients. Also, since the bank likely filed the mortgage, (A) is incorrect because Jerry had constructive notice anyway. **(B)** is incorrect because there is no warranty with a quitclaim deed. **(D)** is incorrect because regardless of the filing, the bank still stands senior to Jerry in priority.

45. **/B/** Sarah wins because she had no notice, either actual or constructive, and because she was first to file in the proper county. **(A)** is incorrect because filing must normally be done in the county where the property is located. Otherwise, there is no reasonable means to hold another buyer responsible for "constructive notice" because she would not have been expected to search other county records. **(C)** is incorrect because filing first doesn't matter if it is in the wrong county. **(D)** is incorrect because the fact pattern specifies no actual notice.

46. **/C/** The fact pattern noted "typical" exclusions. Typically title insurance policies *exclude* adverse possession and several other possible legal problems that would not be discovered in a normal title search. **(A)** is incorrect because title insurance typically excludes adverse possession and several other possible legal problems that would not be discovered in a normal title search. **(B)** is incorrect because inquiry notice is not relevant to this title insurance coverage. **(D)** is incorrect because the insurance covers defects which are not recorded in the abstract of title.

47. **/B/** Jeff wins under the theory of adverse possession. He has met all of the ECHO elements, and it is likely that 26 years is more than enough time under any jurisdiction for the length of possession. **(A)** is incorrect because tacking applies to the adverse possessors if they should change over the years. Therefore, tacking has nothing to do with this problem. **(C)** is incorrect because knowledge of trespass is not a defense to adverse possession: in fact, it bolsters Jeff's case that his possession was open, notorious, and hostile to the true owners. **(D)** is incorrect because pouring a concrete driveway across someone else's property is about as blatant as "open" can be.

48. **/A/** In a lien theory jurisdiction, the buyer owns the property and the bank has a security interest in the form of a lien. **(B)** is incorrect because the bank does not own either a legal or equitable title. **(C)** is incorrect because the bank does not own either a legal or equitable

title. **(D)** is incorrect because the bank does not own either a legal or equitable title.

49. **/B/** An express assumption involves a new promise by the land vendee, Glenn. Because the mortgagee Security Bank was specifically identified and it was contemplated it would receive rights, the Bank is deemed to be a third party creditor beneficiary with rights directly against the vendee, Glenn. **(A)** is incorrect because the statute of frauds applies to such a promise involving land. **(C)** is incorrect because Security Bank is a third party creditor beneficiary. **(D)** is incorrect because the mortgagor always remains liable.

50. **/A/** In most jurisdictions, private foreclosures are available when they are provided for in the real estate contract. **(B)** is incorrect because private foreclosures are available when they are provided for in the real estate contract. **(C)** is incorrect because most jurisdictions limit relief on private foreclosures to the sale value of the foreclosed property; deficiency judgments are not allowed. **(D)** is incorrect because private foreclosure is an alternative means of handling defaults which is used in many jurisdictions.

51. **/C/** This is a classic example of violation of support rights, specifically subjacent support. There is an absolute duty to provide subjacent support for at least the natural land. Because the cabin was there when the bomb shelter was dug, damages to the structure were foreseeable and would probably be recoverable under a theory of negligence. The cause of action would most likely be negligence related to the failure to take proper precautions against the cave-in. **(A)** is incorrect because this does not involve the public. **(B)** is the second best answer, because it is technically an interference with the owner's enjoyment of his property, but the facts provide a more direct case of violation of subjacent support. **(D)** is incorrect, because lateral support violations would involve the sides of the property, such as when an adjacent owner removes a retaining wall that causes a landslide on the P's property.

52. **/A/** Violations of the ownership right of possession are resolved by an action for trespass. **(B)** is incorrect because the fact pattern does not indicate all the elements of adverse possession, especially the length of possession required. Additionally, the remedy to eject an adverse possessor is normally an action for trespass. **(C)** is incorrect because the sales contract is now irrelevant for issues of possession. If George had failed to allow possession upon closing of the sales contract, breach might be more appropriate. **(D)** is incorrect because a nuisance action might be available to George or the neighbors, but not to the owner, Martha.

53. **/B/** Here Tom has a month-to-month lease. In order to effectively terminate the lease, Tom must give one month's notice. The notice given on February 15th is effective to terminate the lease on the last day of March, not February since that would only be giving two weeks notice. **(A)** is incorrect because Tom will still owe the rent for the month of March. **(C)** is incorrect because a tenant can terminate the lease. **(D)** is incorrect because no new notice is needed;

the original notice will be effective on the 31st of March.

54. **/D/** Private evictions without court orders are prohibited by statute in most jurisdictions. **(A)** is not the correct answer because, while Larry has this option, if he takes it, he is most likely converting the status to a periodic tenancy. **(B)** is incorrect because an unlawful detainer action is his best option if he wants the tenant out. **(C)** is incorrect because it is the equivalent of B: a tenant who unlawfully detains is a trespasser. Note that if Larry takes option (A), he loses options (B) and (C) until one of the parties later gives proper notice.

55. **/D/** None of the above is the best answer. Trish may abandon the lease without notice because the premises are not habitable; therefore she has been constructively evicted. (Note that is only one of several possible options she had). (A), (B), and (C) are all incorrect because under these facts a tenant is within her rights to abandon the property and cease making payments. **(A)** is incorrect because suing for rent is a landlord's remedy if a tenant wrongfully terminates the lease. Here, the termination is not wrongful. **(B)** is incorrect because the tenant is not responsible for maintenance to the structure in a typical residential lease; the landlord is. Therefore, waste does not apply. **(C)** is incorrect because tenant notice is not required when the landlord breaches.

56. **/C/** Larry has a responsibility to mitigate damages. Therefore he is entitled to the amount remaining on the lease (21 months) minus the amount for which he could have reasonably re-rented the apartmen[t]. **(A)** is incorrect because th[e] landlord would be entitled to a[n] immediate judgment for the valu[e] of the converted furnishings. **(B)** [is] incorrect because it fails to includ[e] mitigation. **(D)** is not the be[st] answer because it fails to accoun[t] both for mitigation and the secon[d] year of rent. [Note that this MB[E] question ducks the issue of wheth[er] a court would make an award [of] future rent following the tenant['s] anticipatory repudiation.]

57. **/A/** Nosey is violating Tracy's right t[o] quiet enjoyment; therefore he is i[n] breach. Normally, the tenant ma[y] not withhold rent for landlor[d] breaches, with limited exception[s] usually related to significan[t] physical deficiency in the premise[s] rendering the premise[s] uninhabitable. This fact patter[n] does not fit the exceptions. **(B)** [is] incorrect because this is Tracy['s] best option if she wishes t[o] discontinue her residence ther[e.] **(C)** is incorrect, but an injunctiv[e] action is a viable option if sh[e] wishes to continue to live ther[e.] **(D)** is incorrect because this migh[t] be a viable remedy if Tracy ca[n] show damages.

58. **/C/** Lou has impliedly consented t[o] Tammy being a holdover tenant b[y] engaging in negotiations with he[r.] This consent stops him from bein[g] able to treat Tammy as a holdove[r.] **(A)** is incorrect because the implie[d] consent precludes other remedie[s] as least for a reasonable period o[f] time. **(B)** is incorrect because th[e] implied consent precludes othe[r] remedies as least for a reasonabl[e] period of time. **(D)** is incorrec[t] because the implied consen[t] precludes other remedies as leas[t] for a reasonable period of time.

9. **/A/** This is a periodic tenancy, month-to-month, established by the payment of rent. **(B)** is incorrect because, although this may have started as a tenancy at will (no duration was established), as soon as the first rent payment was accepted by Libby, it became a periodic tenancy. **(C)** is incorrect because no specific duration is stated which is necessary for a term tenancy. **(D)** is incorrect because Tara is not a holdover.

60. **/B/** A lease prohibition on assignment does not prohibit a sublease as these are separate rights of the tenant and are strictly construed. **(A)** is incorrect since approval is not the issue in this question. **(C)** is not the best answer since payment of the rent does not excuse the condition if it applies. **(D)** is incorrect because assignments and subleases are separate rights.

61. **/C/** Because the future interest is in a third party and not the grantor, the future interest is an executory interest. Therefore, Daughter has a fee simple subject to an executory interest and Son has a future executory interest. **(A)** is incorrect because the future grant is not in Mom, but in Son, a third, party. **(B)** is incorrect because Son is not the grantor and therefore cannot have a right of entry. **(D)** is incorrect because the doctrine of merger applies only to a single person having both the life estate and the future interest.

62. **/D/** Owen conveyed the farm in fee simple determinable, with a possibility of reverter. His possible future right may be transferred inter vivos, by will, or through intestacy. **(A)** is incorrect because a life estate must convey the estate to grantee for life, not until a triggering event.

(B) is incorrect because the transfer was fee simple determinable, not absolute. **(C)** is incorrect because future interests in a possibility of reverter are alienable.

63. **/B/** The granting language contains words of duration, "so long as," which make this a fee simple determinable. The future interest following the fee simple determinable goes to the grantor, S, and it is a possibility of reverter. Upon receiving the speeding ticket Speedacres will automatically revert back to S. **(A)** is incorrect because B does not have a life estate and therefore S does not have a reversion. **(C)** is incorrect because words of duration and not condition were used in the grant. **(D)** is incorrect because B does not have a fee simple.

64. **/B/** Sam used words of a triggering event, "until," in the conveyance of the property to Bob, therefore Bob has a fee simple determinable. The future interest was not given to a third party but was retained by Sam, which is implied because no other party was named. No action is required by Sam to exercise the reversion to the property ownership. **(A)** is incorrect because a third party was not given the future interest. **(C)** is incorrect because Bob has a present interest in the suit. **(D)** is incorrect because the "until" language indicates the property is subject to a possibility of reverter to the grantor.

65. **/C/** This is a fee simple subject to an executory limitation with a shifting executory interest in fee simple to Bob. **(A)** is incorrect because the conditional interest does not shift back to the grantor, but to a third party. **(B)** is incorrect because the conditional interest does not shift back to the grantor, but to a third party. **(D)** is incorrect because only the grantor may have a right of reverter.

66. **/C/** Scott was given a life estate that is measured by the life of another (Jackson) and not his own. He thus has a life estate "pur autre vie." **(A)** is incorrect because Amanda has a future interest following a life estate which is a reversion, not a possibility of reverter. If Amanda gave her reversion to Scott, then the doctrine of merger would apply. **(B)** is incorrect because Jackson has no future interest, even though he is the measuring life. **(D)** is incorrect because if Scott dies before Jackson, Surfacres will go to Scott's heirs until Jackson's death, then it will go back to Amanda or Amanda's estate.

67. **/B/** This conveyance is an attempt to create a fee tail, which is abolished in most jurisdictions, therefore the interest defaults to fee simple absolute. **(A)** is incorrect for the reason that a fee tail is generally abolished. **(C)** is incorrect because there is no indication of conveying an interest for life, nor is the life estate interest a default – a fee simple absolute generally is. **(D)** is incorrect because there is no language providing for a triggering event and possibility of reverter.

68. **/C/** If the conveying language does not specify otherwise, the default of a life estate is a reversion back to grantor after the death of the grantee. **(A)** is incorrect because the default treatment is a reversion back to the grantor. **(B)** is incorrect because Zeke's interest terminates upon his death. **(D)** is incorrect because the transfer is not related to the Rule Against Perpetuities – it

is simply a life estate wit[h] reversion to grantor upon Zeke[']s death.

69. **/D/** The conveyance gave A a li[fe] estate and B a vested remainde[r]. The remainder is vested because [B] is ascertainable at the time th[e] interest was created and there is n[o] condition on the vesting. **(A)** i[s] incorrect because B does not have [a] contingent remainder. **(B)** i[s] incorrect because A was not give[n] a fee simple. **(C)** is incorre[ct] because G does not have [a] reversion. If B were to die, th[e] interest would pass on to B's heirs.

70. **/A/** The daughters have continge[nt] remainders because their intere[st] does not vest until Grandpa die[s]. **(B)** is incorrect because Grandp[a] conveyed a life estate with [a] remainder, not a fee simple. **(C)** i[s] incorrect because a reversio[n] would return the property t[o] Grandpa, not give it to th[e] daughters. **(D)** is incorrect becaus[e] the remainders do not vest unti[l] Grandpa dies.

71. **/C/** Here Savannah has a remainde[r] because she is not the grantor; he[r] interest is vested because at th[e] time of creation of the life estat[e] she was ascertainable and th[e] granting language is unconditiona[l]. Under the doctrine of waste, Suz[y] is required to make repairs to th[e] land. Here she would have t[o] maintain the pipes, though no[t] replace them. **(A)** is incorre[ct] because the life estate is no[t] measured by the life of another, bu[t] rather, by Suzy's life. **(B)** i[s] incorrect because reversions ca[n] only revert to the original grantor – here Scott - and not a third party. **(D)** is incorrect because Scott doe[s] not have the right to retake the land under the doctrine of waste

2. /C/ The interest reverts back to Robin because the contingent remainder was destroyed when all of Drew's children predeceased him. Therefore, it is the equivalent of Robin having written the life estate "to Robin for life," which provides a reversion to her on Drew's death. **(A)** is incorrect, because Drew's children never had a vested interest, therefore, neither do Drew's heirs. **(B)** is incorrect because a life estate terminates upon death; therefore, nothing passes through Drew's estate. **(D)** is almost always incorrect on the MBE because this alternative (none of the above) would reward candidate's mistakes or lack of knowledge.

3. /A/ A clearly has a life estate. Under the doctrine of worthier title, X cannot grant to his heirs that which they would receive by inheritance. The farm would be inheritable by X's heirs therefore X has a reversion in fee simple and the heirs take nothing. **(B)** is incorrect because X's heirs do not have a vested remainder. **(C)** is incorrect because X's heirs do not have a contingent remainder. **(D)** is incorrect because A takes a life estate and not a fee simple.

4. /D/ The Rule Against Perpetuities applies here since there is an executory interest to other than the grantor. Zelda's interest could vest more than 21 years after Wilbur's death (measuring life); Wilbur's heirs may maintain the house in good condition for 30 years after he dies in which case Zelda's interest would then vest. Since it could vest 21 years beyond the death of Wilbur, the interest is invalid and stricken, leaving Wilbur with a fee simple determinable. **(A)** is

incorrect because Zelda does not have a vested remainder, it is conditional. **(B)** is incorrect because under RAP Zelda's interest is invalid and she is left with nothing. **(C)** is incorrect because with a fee simple determinable the grantor has a possibility of reverter, not a right of entry.

75. /A/ The remainder to the children is void because they must survive the widow, who might be unborn at the date of transfer. The RAP assumes that Zane could remarry a woman who is not a life in being at the time the interest is created. **(B)** is incorrect because the Rule Against Perpetuities would be violated. **(C)** is incorrect because the Rule Against Perpetuities has not been abolished, although statutory changes to the common law have been passed in many jurisdictions. **(D)** is incorrect because the Doctrine of Worthier Title does not apply to this fact pattern.

76. /C/ This alternative best restates the "wait and see" rule. **(A)** is incorrect because the Rule Against Perpetuities does not apply to charitable contributions. **(B)** is incorrect because it represents the common law rule that the "wait and see" doctrine replaced. **(D)** is incorrect on the MBE because this alternative would reward candidate's mistakes or lack of knowledge.

77. /B/ This is forfeiture, a void restraint on alienation. Therefore, Brutus receives the property in fee simple absolute. **(A)** is incorrect because a restraint on alienation defaults to a fee simple, not a life estate. **(C)** is incorrect because the transfer does not involve a reversionary interest. **(D)** is incorrect because there is no indication in the fact pattern that

the Rule Against Perpetuities cannot be complied with.

78. /C/ Reserving a right of first refusal is an allowable exception to the restraints on alienation prohibition. **(A)** is incorrect because the "string" of the right of first refusal is effective. **(B)** is incorrect because the rule does not require forfeiture. **(D)** is incorrect, because the right of first refusal must be exercised within a reasonable time and at the offered price.

Real Property and Future Interests Practice Question Answer Rationales

79. /D/ As long as Lyle had the right to prohibit excessive noise, the acts of Sam can be attributed to Lyle, and therefore Tim was constructively evicted. **(A)** is not the best answer because a nuisance, not under the direct control of Lyle, would not relieve Tim of his obligations. **(B)** is incorrect because the doctrine of waste cannot be used by a tenant to terminate the lease obligation. **(C)** is incorrect because Tim was not actually evicted.

80. /B/ Since Terrance has only given up 4 months of his lease (and retained a reversionary interest) he has sublet (and not assigned) the premises to Tony. **(A)** is incorrect because an assignment consists of the lessee's entire estate. **(C)** is incorrect because Terrance, as the original tenant is still liable on the lease. **(D)** is incorrect because in a sublet, the sublessee is only liable to the sublessor and not the landlord.

81. /D/ An interest in a joint tenancy cannot be devised by will. When Joan died, Bob and Garth continued as joint tenants with one another. The other answers are incorrect

because a joint tenancy is create only when all of the tenants hav the same four PITS unities possession, interest, time, an source of title. **(A)** is incorre because the interests were n created from the same source title. **(B)** is incorrect because for joint tenancy, each child mu possess an undivided identic interest in the whole property. **(C** is incorrect because each chi must possess the same right access and use of the who property for a joint tenancy to exis

82. /A/ A tenant is relieved of his duty pay rent if the landlord accepts th tenants offer of surrender. Her the letters constituted effectiv termination and acceptance of th surrender, relieving Torel of th obligation to pay rent. **(B)** incorrect because an acceptance surrender is all that is necessary relieve a tenant of the obligation pay rent. **(C)** is incorrect becaus Landlord's written acceptance wa a satisfactory acceptance of th surrender and complies with th statute of frauds. **(D)** is incorrec because an effective surrender an acceptance relieves a tenant of th duty to pay rent.

83. /D/ Anne may only withhold rent if th failure of the air conditione amounted to a constructive evictio under the implied covenant of qui enjoyment. There is no indicatio that the lack of air conditionin made the apartment uninhabitabl Because the landlord was n obligated under the lease to repai the air conditioner, his failure to d so did not amount to a constructiv eviction. Therefore, Anne wa obligated to pay rent and continu the lease. **(A)** is incorrect becaus there was no constructive evictio because Joe was not obligate

under the lease to repair the air conditioner. **(B)** is incorrect because Joe had no obligation under the lease to repair the air conditioner. **(C)** is incorrect because a tenant may withhold rent for a landlord's breach of the implied covenant of quiet enjoyment.

84. /B/ A negative easement restrains the servient tenement from building a structure that restricts access to light, air, or support. (B) is not a negative easement because it does not prohibit the building of structures that restrict access to light, air, or support. **(A)** is incorrect because it constitutes a negative easement designed to restrain the servient tenement from building structures that restrict access to light, air, or support. **(C)** is incorrect because it constitutes a negative easement designed to restrain the servient tenement from building structures that restrict access to light, air, or support. **(D)** is incorrect because it constitutes a negative easement designed to restrain the servient tenement from building structures that restrict access to light, air, or support.

85. /B/ If the landlord accepts a check from either the assignee or subleasee, the landlord's right to enforce the prohibition is likely waived. **(A)** is incorrect; while the landlord disapproved, his subsequent acceptance of the check waived the condition. **(C)** is incorrect; impossibility of performance (such as destruction of the premises) may excuse performance, but the tenant losing a particular employment position would not rise to that level. **(D)** is incorrect since friend appears to be an assignee of the remaining term of the lease, not a termination followed by a tenancy at will.

86. /D/ None of the choices given is the correct answer. **(A)** is incorrect because the facts do not support an easement by implication, which requires that a single owner divide the land and sell a parcel that had been subject to a prior use. **(B)** is incorrect because an easement by necessity requires that the necessity exist at the time the land is divided. **(C)** is incorrect because Mortimer is trespassing when the backend of his car enters the airspace over Gertrude's property.

87. /A/ Bart is a tenant at will because the statute of frauds requires a writing for leases lasting for over one year. The tenancy is at will and the lease is mutually terminable at will. **(B)** is incorrect because Bart entered into the tenancy with permission of the landlord. **(C)** is incorrect because Bart entered into the tenancy with permission of the landlord. **(D)** is incorrect because the statute of frauds requires a writing for leases lasting over one year.

88. /B/ A covenant may be enforced as an equitable servitude against a purchaser who had notice of the restriction. **(A)** is incorrect because the covenant can be enforced as an equitable servitude. **(C)** is incorrect because privity is not required for equitable servitudes to run. **(D)** is incorrect because a land use restriction does touch and concern the land.

89. /A/ Neither spouse may transfer his/her interest in or sever the tenancy by the entirety without the other's consent. **(B)** is incorrect because both spouses acting together can extinguish the right of survivorship. **(C)** is incorrect because the tenancy

may only be severed through mutual agreement. **(D)** is incorrect because only mutual creditors have the power to sever the tenancy.

90. **/C/** A life estate is not inheritable. At the end of Betty's life, the estate reverts back to the grantor. Because the grantor, Barkley, is no longer alive, it goes to his heirs. **(A)** is incorrect because the life estate reverts to the grantor or the grantor's heirs. **(B)** is incorrect because the life estate reverts to the grantor or the grantor's heirs. **(D)** is incorrect because the life estate reverts to the grantor or the grantor's heirs.

91. **/D/** This is a fee simple subject to an executory interest because there is a condition subsequent to Carter's interest and the future interest is held by a third party. **(A)** is incorrect because Carter's interest is subject to a condition subsequent. **(B)** is incorrect because the future interest is held by a grantee rather than the testator's estate. **(C)** is incorrect because fee simple determinable interests contain durational limitations such as "so long as" and "while."

92. **/D/** All of the above are correct. **(A)** is a correct answer because the Rule in Shelley's Case dictates that if an instrument conveys a life estate to an individual with the remainder to his heirs, that individual takes both the estate and the remainder and the heirs take nothing. **(B)** is a correct answer because Robb obtained a fee simple absolute and he may immediately convey his interest to a third party. **(C)** is a correct answer because Robb obtained a fee simple absolute and he may immediately convey his interest to a third party.

93. **/A/** In order to bind a subsequent purchaser, there must have been an intent to bind successors in interest. **(B)** is incorrect because the deed need not state that the burden runs with the land in order to bind successors. **(C)** is incorrect because real covenants do not require common schemes or plans. **(D)** is incorrect because not all three alternatives are correct.

94. **/A/** Harry has a license because he has a revocable right to enter upon the land of the licensor. **(B)** is incorrect because Harry does not have a right in land. **(C)** is incorrect because Harry does not have the right to go upon land and take resources. **(D)** is incorrect because Harry does not have a right to use property in some specific manner.

95. **/C/** The best answer because one co-tenant has the right to a shared contribution for necessary repairs. There may be the right to contribution for improvements made without the other tenants permission if the improvements enhance the value of the property and the property is later sold. **(A)** is incorrect because Mike may have a right to contribution for the improvements. **(B)** is incorrect because Mike likely has a right to contribution for the repairs to the roof. **(D)** is incorrect because Mike will at least recover contribution for the necessary repairs.

96. **/D/** An action for public nuisance may be brought by a private individual if his injury is unique from that of the general public. Here, the damage to Comic Book Guy's business is a unique injury. **(A)** is incorrect because a private individual has standing to sue if he

suffers a unique injury. **(B)** is incorrect because an activity need not be illegal to constitute a nuisance. **(C)** is incorrect because the facts do not indicate that Comic Book Guy "came to the nuisance."

7. **/D/** Blockage of access to neighbor's gas station likely constitutes a taking because the economic value of the land is completely destroyed. **(A)** is incorrect and likely does not result in a taking because although neighbor's property will suffer a loss in value, it still has economic value. **(B)** is incorrect because the regulation is imposed to prevent harm to the public. **(C)** is incorrect because the economic value of the neighbor's land is not completely destroyed.

8. **/B/** The language in B constitutes an allowable right of first refusal that allows the holder to meet a third party's offer for the property. (A), (C), and (D) are all void restraints on alienation. **(A)** is incorrect and constitutes a disabling restraint on alienation. **(C)** is incorrect and constitutes a forfeiture restraint on alienation. **(D)** is incorrect and constitutes a promissory restraint on alienation.

9. **/C/** Dorothy Developer took Parkacre as a fee simple absolute because her grantor, the city, had a fee simple absolute. The indication the grantor would like the land to be used as a park was only an expression of a wish or motivation without a future interest. **(A)** is incorrect because a future interest was not created. **(B)** is incorrect because a future interest was not created. **(D)** is incorrect because a future interest was not created.

100./C/ Baker has a potential shifting executory interest and is thus subject to the rules against perpetuities. The interest is valid because it must vest within a life in being (Baker's) plus twenty-one years; the interest will vest or fail during his lifetime. **(A)** is incorrect because the interest is valid. **(B)** is incorrect because Baker has an executory interest and not a reversion. **(D)** is incorrect because Baker's interest is not a vested remainder since there is a condition on his taking possession; he must be alive to take.

101./B/ This is the best answer because all of Alison's children will be measuring lives and Alison cannot have more children once the conveyance is effective because the class gift was conveyed by her will, (after her death). The gift must vest within twenty-one years of the deaths of Alison's children, and since their children can turn twenty-one after no more than twenty-one years of their death, it is valid. A key factor here is that the class gift was set up in her will; so it will not take effect until she dies. **(A)** is incorrect because it misconstrues the facts. Alison specifically said it was to include after born grandchildren. **(C)** is incorrect because Alison is not the measuring life since the gift was made in her will; her four children are. **(D)** is incorrect because Alison could not have had more children after the conveyance was effective because she would then be dead.

102./C/ If this gift had been made inter vivos rather than by a will, the gift would have been invalid because Alison could have had a child after she made the conveyance; that child would not be a life in being and therefore not a measuring life. It would then be possible that a grandchild could turn twenty-one beyond the perpetuities period, violating RAP. **(A)** is incorrect because Alison did expressly state her intention to include all after born grandchildren. **(B)** is incorrect because even if Alison had only one grandchild living at the time of her death, it would not violate RAP. **(D)** is incorrect because as long as one child is still living, that child is the measuring life and the interests must vest or fail within twenty-one years of that child's death

103./C/ The unborn children have a contingent remainder in the farm. A contingent remainder is either subject to a condition precedent or is made in favor of an unascertainable person. **(A)** is incorrect because this is not an executory interest. An executory interest will follow a defeasible estate – upon occurrence of a specified event. A life estate has a natural ending, the death of the measuring life, and therefore an executory interest cannot follow. **(B)** is incorrect because the unborn children are not ascertainable and hence cannot have a vested remainder. **(D)** is incorrect because the unborn children do have an interest in the farm.

104./A/ Spike has a shifting executory interest because upon the occurrence of the specified event, a speeding ticket, Son's interest in the car will be forfeited in favor of Spike. **(B)** is incorrect because the interest is not going from the grantor to Spike, but from one grantee to another. **(C)** is incorrect because Spike does not have any type of a remainder. A remainder only follows an estate that will naturally end, such as a life estate. An executory interest follows a

defeasible estate. **(D)** is incorrec because Spike does not have an type of a remainder. A remainde only follows an estate that wi naturally end, such as a life estate An executory interest follows defeasible estate.

105./C/ Claire and Donna have veste remainders subject to open becaus they are ascertainable, there is n condition on their grant, and th devise is subject to open becaus there are possible other remainde takers to come. The unbor children have continger remainders because they ar unascertainable at Thelma's deatl **(A)** is incorrect because the unbor children do not have an executor interest; executory interests onl follow a defeasible estate, not a lif estate. **(B)** is incorrect becaus there is not a condition subsequen the birth of additional children wi not divest Claire and Donna o their remainder. **(D)** is incorrec because Claire and Donna hav vested, not contingent remainders and the unborn do not have a executory interest.

106./B/ The language here is ambiguous a to creating any future interest s the courts will likely construe thi as a fee simple with a covenant The grant to Kerry did no specifically retain a future interes for Suzy, the breach would simpl entitle her to damages. **(A)** i incorrect because if there wa actually a reversion, all rights o Suzy would be bestowed upon he heir, Lola. **(C)** is incorrect becaus there is no future interest. **(D)** i incorrect because there is no futur interest

107./C/ The sale of Skippette's interest t Ginger passed the possibility o reverter Skippette owned as an hei of Skipper. When Islandacre was no longer used for residential purposes, the original interest given by Skipper was forfeited and the property reverted to Ginger via the purchase of Skippette's interest. **(A)** is incorrect because a restriction of residential use is not usually an unreasonable restraint upon alienation. **(B)** is incorrect because Skippette only had a possibility of reverter. **(D)** is incorrect because the interest is valid under RAP. The children have a contingent remainder, which must vest or fail upon Gilligan's death, and no later.

08./A/ The future gift to Bobin is void under RAP because the heirs may stop fighting injustice long after a life in being plus 21 years. **(B)** is incorrect because Kit Woman's interest remains valid even though Bobin's interest is void. **(C)** is incorrect because Bobin has no interest due to the violation of the RAP. **(D)** is incorrect because Bobin has no interest due to the violation of the RAP.

09./D/ In order for the burden of a covenant to run with the land, it must touch and concern the burdened land. Here the covenant to purchase apples does not concern Melinda's land. **(A)** is incorrect because although Melinda had notice of the covenant, it did not touch and concern the land. **(B)** is incorrect because it does not touch and concern the land and the requirement of notice to a common scheme applies to equitable servitudes. **(C)** is incorrect because depending on the facts, the supplying of apples may be enforced if it touched and concerned the land.

110./A/ In order for Melinda to be able to enforce the burden of the real covenant against Bob, a successor, there must be horizontal and vertical privity. Here horizontal privity is met because the covenant was contained in a conveyance from Bill to Brad. If Bill had not previously owned the land, and just made a covenant with Brad, then horizontal privity would not exist between Melinda and Bob. But since it was in a conveyance, there is horizontal privity. Vertical privity is met, because Bob took the parcel for the same duration as Allen; a fee simple. **(B)** is not the best answer because implied intent can also be used to show the intent for a burden to run. So although **(B)** is partially correct because there was express intent, implied intent could also be used, making this not the best answer. **(C)** is incorrect because Bob will be found to have notice because a reasonable search of the deeds would have shown the real covenant. **(D)** is incorrect because privity does exist between Melinda and Bob.

111./C/ The elevator has become so permanently affixed to the real property that removal would cause substantial damages. Thus, the real property mortgage would receive the fixture. This is true even if the elevator was purchased after the mortgage was recorded. **(A)** is incorrect because Friendly Finance would only be entitled to the personal property. **(B)** is incorrect because Friendly Finance would only be entitled to the personal property. **(D)** is incorrect because trade fixtures are readily detachable.

112./D/ A usual condition in a purchase and sale or earnest money receipt and agreement is that the buyer obtains satisfactory financing. The purchaser must use reasonable efforts to obtain the financing. **(A)** is not the best answer because a seller's demand loan does not provide the term repayment advantage of a conventional mortgage. **(B)** is incorrect because such a condition is a condition precedent to the conveyance contract which is entered into at closing. **(C)** is incorrect because, unless stated to the contrary, all cash is assumed.

113./D/ A full warranty deed usually represents the final integrated agreement and the parole evidence rule would prohibit the introduction of prior or contemporaneous agreements that contradict the deed. **(A)** is incorrect because, upon execution, the rights between the immediate parties attach. **(B)** is incorrect because most states do not require the exact consideration given by the buyer to be specified. **(C)** is incorrect because only the seller must sign the deed.

114./D/ The grantor implicitly warrants the property to be free of unusual encumbrances not specified in the deed. **(A)** is incorrect because courts often impose a limited warranty or bargain and sale deed if a full warranty deed is not specified in the contract. **(B)** is incorrect because the fact zoning laws may affect a property's use is not usually grounds to avoid the conveyance contract. **(C)** is not the best answer because back taxes are usually paid at closing.

115./D/ An unrecorded mortgage is not effective against third parties without notice. **(A)** is incorrect because Vincent failed to record h[...] interest. **(B)** is incorrect becaus[...] only if the mortgage was of recor[...] would the title insurance polic[...] cover same. **(C)** is incorre[...] because the real propert[...] conveyance statutes in most state[...] do not require an affidavit.

116./D/ The seller must provide marketable title free fro[...] encumbrances which might lead t[...] litigation unless the purchase an[...] sale agreement (or earnest mone[...] receipt and agreement) stated to th[...] contrary. **(A)** is incorrect becaus[...] the implied warranty o[...] merchantability is an UCC person[...] property concept and does n[...] apply to real property transaction[...] **(B)** is incorrect because there is a[...] implied warranty against titl[...] defects. **(C)** is incorrect becaus[...] even a warranty deed does n[...] guarantee a "perfect" title.

117./D/ An easement by prescriptio[...] requires at least the CHO part o[...] the adverse possession ECHO elements. This includes that th[...] usage be continuous, hostile an[...] open and notorious. **(A)** i[...] incorrect because such actions ma[...] not defeat a valid easement. **(B)** i[...] incorrect because the recordin[...] rules do not apply to an easemen[...] by prescription or possession. **(C**[...] is incorrect because the mere use o[...] a road can create an easement.

118./B/ The statute in the jurisdictio[...] dictates the necessary easemen[...] period which is often 20 years. **(A**[...] is incorrect because the crossin[...] must be hostile to the owner o[...] without permission. **(C)** i[...] incorrect because an easement wil[...] never convey ownership of th[...] property, but rather only the righ[...] to cross. **(D)** is incorrect becaus[...] recordation is not initiall[...]

necessary, unless an express grant of easement is the only means of claiming easement (in this case, it is not). If it is the only means asserted by the person claiming an easement, compliance with the Statute of Frauds (writing and signature by D) is required.

119./D/ The purpose of title insurance is the buyer's protection against any chain of title defects not specified as exceptions in the policy. **(A)** is incorrect because property title insurance policies normally contain a number of exceptions against which there is no coverage. **(B)** is incorrect because the title policy is personal to Smith and his vendee must purchase another policy. **(C)** is incorrect because generally a title policy protects only against defects that are of record in the title abstract.

120./D/ In a race-notice jurisdiction actual notice of a prior superior interest will defeat a subsequent party filing first. **(A)** is incorrect because recording is necessary to provide a subsequent vendee with constructive notice of the prior interest. **(B)** is incorrect because delivery of a properly executed deed is adequate to vest ownership rights in the purchaser (but may not be binding on third parties). **(C)** is incorrect because recordation is primarily designed to protect the vendee from subsequent vendees acquiring a superior interest.

121./C/ The mortgagee's security interest is perfected by filing. **(A)** is incorrect because the mortgagor and mortgagee's rights as to each other attach upon execution and delivery of the mortgage document. **(B)** is incorrect because a prevailing subsequent party cannot have actual or constructive notice of the

prior interest. **(D)** is incorrect because filing is at the county seat where the real property is located.

122./C/ The basic rule is that a subsequent bona fide purchaser without notice takes free and clear. **(A)** is not the best answer as Watkin's heirs and estate are obligated to satisfy the mortgage if they come into title. **(B)** is incorrect because an unrecorded second mortgage is junior to an unrecorded first mortgage. **(D)** is incorrect because a gratuitous vendee does not acquire the rights of a bona fide purchaser for value.

123./C/ A novation involves a new party replacing an old party. **(A)** is incorrect because assignment and delegation would only involve the rights and duties of the old mortgage. **(B)** is incorrect because third party beneficiary contracts would only include the rights and duties of the old mortgage. **(D)** is not the best answer because the facts state that Thompson executed a new mortgage.

124./C/ The original mortgagor is always potentially liable for a deficiency judgment in a purchase "subject to" the original mortgage. **(A)** is incorrect because a recorded mortgage runs with the land. **(B)** is not the best answer because the facts state Clark did not assume the mortgage but rather took subject to the mortgage. **(D)** is incorrect because the mortgagee has no right against Clark.

125./B/ If the buyer at the foreclosure sale takes free and clear title, the sale proceeds are to be applied to the first mortgage with any excess going to the second mortgage. **(A)** is incorrect because the second mortgage has a priority over subsequent mortgagees and unsecured creditors. **(C)** is incorrect because the first and second mortgages are independent. **(D)** is incorrect because the first and second mortgages are independent.

126./B/ An express assumption involves a new promise by the land vendee. Because the mortgagee Security Bank was specifically identified and it was contemplated it would receive rights, the Bank is deemed to be a third party creditor beneficiary with rights directly against the vendee, Glenn. **(A)** is incorrect because the statute of frauds applies to such a promise. **(C)** is incorrect because Security is a third party creditor beneficiary. **(D)** is incorrect because the mortgagor always remains liable unless there is a release by the mortgagee.

127./A/ In a lien theory jurisdiction (majority view) a mortgage becomes a lien on property but legal title stays with the mortgagor, it does not transfer to the mortgagee. Therefore (A) is an *incorrect* statement (per the call of the question). **(B)** is not the best answer because it is a correct statement. **(C)** is not the best answer because it is a correct statement. **(D)** is not the best answer because it is a correct statement.

128./C/ The original tenant remains liable unless the landlord executed a release. **(A)** is incorrect because the rights to sublet or assign are separate rights. **(B)** is incorrect because a lease is an interest in land requiring statute of frauds compliance. **(D)** is incorrect because the facts do not state Tudor reserved the right to require consent to an assignment.

129./D/ The grantee of a lifetime conveyance by a joint tenant becomes a tenant in common with the remaining joint tenants. **(A)** is incorrect because a joint tenant can convey their interest during lifetime without approval of the other joint tenants. **(B)** is incorrect because the grantee becomes a tenant-in-common with the remaining joint tenants. **(C)** is incorrect because Dick was a joint tenant at his death; thus his interest goes to the remaining joint tenants not his heirs at law.

130./D/ The general clause in the deed is not very significant because it is ambiguous as to the ownership of the bungalows. **(A)** is not the best answer because such an agreement might clarify the parties' intent. **(B)** is incorrect because it describes one of the two criteria normally applied by a court to determine if the property is a fixture when the parties' intent is unclear. **(C)** is incorrect because it describes one of the two criteria normally applied by a court to determine if the property is a fixture when the parties' intent is unclear.

131./B/ While allowed in a few states, many states interpret the parties' obligations as mutually exclusive, so breach by one party does not usually excuse performance by the other. **(A)** is incorrect because most states allow a tenant to pay for necessary repairs (and the like) and deduct the cost from the rent. **(C)** is incorrect because upon the landlord's violation of the implied warranty of habitability or a constructive eviction, a tenant is usually allowed to vacate and terminate the lease. **(D)** is incorrect because the tenant can always sue the landlord for damages and seek the equitable remedy of specific performance requiring the landlord to cure the implied breach of habitability.

132./C/ The lessee is entitled to a condemnation award for eminent domain from the state; the facts say this valuation is $75,000. In addition, the lease is terminated under both the theory of impossibility and the theory of merger since the state will own both the property's leasehold and reversionary interest after the eminent domain proceedings. **(A)** is incorrect because the lease is terminated and standard leases do not require the tenant to move to another property owned by the lessor. **(B)** is incorrect because the lease is terminated including the future interest and the tenant has no future liability to the landlord. **(D)** is incorrect because a lease vests when executed and the Rule Against Perpetuities only applies to unvested future interests.

133./B/ A tenants in common property interest passes to his/her heirs at law. **(A)** is incorrect because this is not a joint tenancy with the right of survivorship. **(C)** is incorrect because a tenant in common may transfer their interest during lifetime. **(D)** is incorrect because a tenant in common ownership interest survives death.

134./D/ A general warranty deed gives a property purchaser all the TAFED covenants. This is the highest level of protection possible. **(A)** is incorrect because a general warranty deed provides all the TAFED covenants and is a higher level of protection. **(B)** is incorrect because a general warranty deed provides all the TAFED covenants

and is a higher level of protection. **(C)** is incorrect because a general warranty deed provides all the TAFED covenants and is a higher level of protection.

135./A/ The proceeds of a judicial foreclosure sale are applied first to the senior first mortgage. Any excess proceeds are to be applied to second mortgagee. Rice thus receives $90,000 less $80,000. **(B)** is incorrect because Rice receives $90,000 less $80,000, the amount of the excess proceeds after the senior mortgage is satisfied. **(C)** is incorrect because Rice receives $90,000 less $80,000, the amount of the excess proceeds after the senior mortgage is satisfied. **(D)** is incorrect because Rice receives $90,000 less $80,000, the amount of the excess proceeds after the senior mortgage is satisfied.

136./C/ In the case of a conflict, the terms of the deed control the terms of the purchase and sale agreement. **(A)** is incorrect because the statute of frauds applies and the buyer's oral statement of protest does not matter since it is not a part of the writing. **(B)** is incorrect because the seller has a significant reason to restrict the use of the land and the buyer knew of the restriction at closing. **(D)** is incorrect because it is not necessary the buyer sign the deed at closing; only the seller needs to sign.

137./D/ The $220,000 of proceeds are first applied to satisfy Independent's $195,000 senior interest. Scott's mortgage was recorded on March 10 before Elgin recorded on March 12. Thus Scott's $19,000 is to be paid in full. **(A)** is incorrect because Scott recorded before Elgin, so his $19,000 is to be paid in full. **(B)** is incorrect because

Scott recorded before Elgin, so his $19,000 is to be paid in full. **(C)** is incorrect because Scott recorded before Elgin, so his $19,000 is to be paid in full.

138./B/ Under the race-notice statute in effect in most jurisdictions, the first bona fide mortgagee to record prevails. Because Scott recorded first without knowledge of the prior interest, he prevails over Elgin. **(A)** is incorrect because Scott did not know of Elgin's interest when he recorded. **(C)** is incorrect because the first to record prevails. **(D)** is incorrect because the proceeds distribution depends upon the date of filing.

139./C/ The mortgagor can usually redeem the property before the judicial sale by paying all mortgages in full. **(A)** is incorrect because if there is a statutory right of redemption in the jurisdiction it may be available to the defaulting party even after the judicial sale. **(B)** is incorrect because a probable deficiency does not justify redemption. **(D)** is incorrect because a penalty fee is usually only required if the right of redemption is exercised after foreclosure.

140./B/ Recording a mortgage protects the mortgagee against subsequent bona fide purchasers for value. Recording constitutes constructive notice of the prior interest. **(A)** is incorrect because the mortgagee's right against the mortgagor does not require recording – only delivery of the mortgage. **(C)** is incorrect because a lien filed previously would have priority. **(D)** is incorrect because the mortgagee Rich would not prevail against those mortgages of which Rich had actual or constructive knowledge of the earlier claims to

the property such as Marsh.

141./D/ This is an easement in gross, not appurtenant, and it is binding on the buyer when she closes the purchase. **(A)** is incorrect because there is no evidence in the fact pattern it has been abandoned. An easement need not be used constantly to remain valid. Simple non-use is not enough to claim abandonment; there must be a manifestation of intent to abandon. **(B)** is incorrect because it will bind her as soon as she receives a valid deed. Don't confuse privity in covenants with easements. **(C)** is incorrect because it only involves one parcel of land and thus is an easement in gross, not appurtenant.

142./C/ Commercial easements may be sold. Private ones may not. **(A)** is incorrect because as stated above, commercial easements are transferable. **(B)** is incorrect because it states the opposite of the correct rule. **(D)** is incorrect because commercial easements are transferrable.

143./C/ Tony has met the CHO elements of prescription, so he would prevail. **(A)** is incorrect because the use was hostile, which is defined as against the true owner's interest. **(B)** is incorrect because his use was open – it doesn't matter if Mort knew it was a trespass or not. **(D)** is incorrect because there are no facts given in the question that infer necessity.

144./C/ This is an easement by express reservation because the seller is reserving a future right for himself. It is subject to the Statute of Frauds and the recording statutes, otherwise it is ineffective. **(A)** is incorrect because an easement by express grant is where the buyer receives a right from the owner, which is the opposite of this case. It must also be recorded. **(B)** is incorrect because the easement must be recorded. **(D)** is incorrect because it is an easement by express reservation.

145./D/ Eric can seek the remedies in both (A) and (C). Because of overuse, he may sue for damages, or he may seek an injunction. **(B)** is incorrect because this does not fit the definition of abandonment; the easement right passes with the property to the subsequent owner. **(A)** is incomplete since Eric can also sue for damages (answer (C)). **(C)** is incorrect because it is incomplete. Eric can also seek and injunction (option (A)).

146./C/ This is an express easement, therefore, physically blocking it is not permitted. **(A)** is incorrect because the remedies for overuse are either an action for nuisance or injunction. **(B)** is nonsense because blocking an easement by prescription is irrelevant – an express easement already exists. **(D)** is incorrect because there are no facts in the question supporting the notion that this easement is due to necessity.

147./A/ If the Statute of Frauds or deed formalities are not complied with, the dominant estate can claim "license" if the parties intended to enter an agreement for access. In this case, because Mick built an expensive house on the upper lot in reliance on the license, it is irrevocable by estoppel. **(B)** is incorrect because necessity does not apply to access to the lake; it normally is used for ingress and egress to one's property. **(C)** is incorrect because prescription is not the only remedy. **(D)** is

incorrect because the license is irrevocable due to Mick's position change in reliance upon the promise.

148./B/ Hagar's interest in the timber is best described as a profit a prendre, and his unreasonable cutting of all the trees is best described as waste. As a tip, when you see abuse of a profit a prendre, think "waste." **(A)** is incorrect because profit is a better description than easement for this interest and the facts do not indicate the entering was unreasonable, only the number of trees which were cut. Also, breach of contract may be a valid claim, but together the combination of easement/breach is weaker than profit/waste. **(C)** is incorrect because the interest is not a license since it involved the right to take from the land. **(D)** is incorrect for the same reason as A: the combination of easement/waste is not as strong as profit/waste.

149./D/ There is a lack of privity of estate; Allison does not have the right to enforce the covenant since she was not one of the contracting parties. **(A)** is incorrect even though the covenant runs with the land. That factor alone is insufficient: the other requirements must be met, and privity is lacking. **(B)** is also incorrect because constructive notice has no bearing on a party who has no privity. It is relevant only for a party against whom a covenant may be enforced. **(C)** is incorrect because this is not a covenant for timber, it is a restrictive covenant that enforces the ability to preserve views.

150./B/ All of the requirements for burden and benefit are identical except horizontal privity: a burden requires horizontal privity and a benefit does not. **(A)** is incorrect because it deals with vertical privity. **(C)** is incorrect because it also deals with vertical privity. **(D)** is incorrect because it states the opposite of the horizontal privity rule.

151./A/ Horizontal and vertical privity are not required for equitable servitudes. **(B)** is incorrect because some jurisdictions require compliance with the Statute of Frauds to enforce equitable servitudes. **(C)** is incorrect because equitable servitudes and covenants have the same rules regarding benefits and burdens running with the land. **(D)** is incorrect because one of the other alternatives contains the correct answer.

152./B/ The best answer is equitable servitude, because the failure to record the covenant in the current deeds makes privity questionable. Also, there was strong intent to bind successors in interest by several means: initial notice, naming of the development, a common scheme, 100% initial compliance with the restriction, etc. **(A)** is not the best answer because an equitable servitude also may meet the requirements of the Statute of Frauds. **(C)** is not the best answer because touching and concerning the land is a requirement of both covenants and equitable servitudes. **(D)** is incorrect because there is doubt as to whether Paris had constructive notice through the chain of deeds.

153./C/ The best defense is that Menelaus and Helen are estopped from their action because they are in violation of the restriction. **(A)** is incorrect, because Paris had at least inquiry notice of the restriction. **(B)** is incorrect because a writing

containing the restriction is not a universal requirement for enforcing equitable servitudes. **(D)** is incorrect because there is no evidence of an intent to abandon the restriction. Only one other house that is not in compliance is probably insufficient to show abandonment.

154./C/ If such a large number of homes had changed siding, abandonment is the best answer because there is no longer an intent to enforce the restriction. **(A)** is incorrect because termination of servitudes and covenants by merger are when the same party gains title to both the dominant and servient estates, which is not present in this fact pattern. **(B)** could be valid, because the ability to show actual, or inquiry notice becomes increasingly difficult as more neighbors change their siding. However, **(C)** is a better answer because it is a more clear-cut case of abandonment than it is lack of notice. **(D)** is incorrect because abandonment correctly describes this situation.

155./B/ When a city or county changes zoning rules that override previous covenants or equitable servitudes, it is an indication that neighborhood conditions have changed and the restriction will no longer be enforced. **(A)** is incorrect because although the city changed the zoning, it does not fit the definition of abandonment; this alternative is thus internally inconsistent. **(C)** is incorrect; the Athens Acres subdivision still has a common scheme or plan, but it is no longer enforceable due to zoning changes **(D)** is incorrect because another alternative is correct.

156./D/ Normally, unless the zoning changes state otherwise, non-conforming uses that were legal when built are "grandfathered" after the requirements become more restrictive. **(A)** is incorrect because changing zoning rules is not normally considered a Fifth Amendment "taking." **(B)** is incorrect because a variance requires action by the property owner to obtain relief from zoning. **(C)** is incorrect because, as with a variance, spot zoning requires an approval before the use is allowed. There is no evidence of such an approval in this fact pattern.

157./B/ Spot zoning is the best answer because she is attempting to begin a use that is inconsistent with the current character of the surrounding area. **(A)** is incorrect because a non-conforming use is one that exists prior to the zoning change. **(C)** is the second best answer. Owners can apply for variances if zoning rules create hardships and the requested use is not inconsistent with the current uses of the neighborhood. However, this is really not a hardship case and the use is inconsistent with the neighborhood. **(D)** is incorrect because rezoning is not normally the correct tool to grant permission to one owner for an exception to zoning.

158./C/ A variance is an allowed deviation from a zoning restriction that will be granted if unnecessary hardship results and such grant is not inconsistent with the general welfare and character of the neighborhood. The only argument against a variance in this instance is if the ordinance was passed for some purpose such as fire department accessibility, in which case, there must be a balancing between the owner's needs and the needs of the community. **(A)** is incorrect because the ordinance grandfathers non-conforming use until repair or replacement is needed; therefore, rebuilding the ramp without some sort of formal relief would be prohibited. **(B)** is the second best answer, but is a less precise fit to these facts than variance. Spot zoning would indeed give the relief sought. However, in practice, the variance generally is easier to obtain and tends to be used for the types of circumstances in this problem. **(D)** would provide legal relief, but again in practice, this type of relief is harder to obtain than a variance (and even spot zoning), and like spot-zoning, it may be viewed as "overkill" for the problem at hand.

159./B/ This is a taking under the 5th Amendment, the relief they may seek may either be either injunction or damages. In this case, the relief actually granted would more likely be damages if the county was determined to take the land under eminent domain. **(A)** is not the best answer because the most likely relief would be damages since there is a public benefit. **(C)** is incorrect because there is no evidence in the fact pattern that due process was violated. **(D)** is incorrect because there is no evidence in the fact pattern that due process was violated.

160./C/ This is likely the least effective claim because he would have difficulty proving a "taking" from which he suffered economic loss. **(A)** is incorrect because it would be a valid claim: a property owner must receive actual notice of a pending zoning change impacting his property. **(B)** is incorrect because this is a blatant Equal

Protection violation. The restriction deliberately discriminates against the poor. **(D)** is incorrect because it is essentially the same as A: lack of notice gives rise to a 14th Amendment Due Process claim.

161./D/ This is a private nuisance, for which damages and/or injunction may be sought. **(A)** is incorrect because it is not a public nuisance. A public nuisance occurs when there is unreasonable interference with the public's right to enjoy public facilities. **(B)** is incorrect because this is not a public nuisance. **(C)** is incorrect because both an injunction and damages seem available.

162./C/ This is the association's responsibility because the individual homeowner is responsible for the interior maintenance; the association for the exterior. **(A)** is incorrect because homeowner's are generally responsible individually only for interior repairs; exteriors are considered part of the common responsibility. **(B)** is incorrect because the association still has responsibility even though it may have current financial inability to pay. **(D)** is incorrect because it overstates the association's responsibility: the association is responsible only for exteriors and common areas. The individual homeowner is responsible for the maintenance of the interior of their unit.

163./D/ Boris may not collect commission for the sale of either property, because when a jurisdiction requires that listing agreements comply with the Statute of Frauds, they normally require all the DEWD requirements: Duration of

contract, "earned" (amount and terms of commission), a writing and a sufficient description of the property to be sold. This contract fails on the description element: it only stated "property" and not which one. **(A)** is incorrect because the contract did not sufficiently identify the property. **(B)** is incorrect because the contract did not specify that property. **(C)** is incorrect because Boris will not collect a commission on either sale.

164./A/ A court will not enforce a purchase and sale agreement if the description appearing in the agreement is vague, ambiguous, or otherwise fails to specifically identify the property in question. Here, it is ambiguous because of the other properties with the same name. It also fails because it does not meet the requirements of a "legal description." **(B)** is probably incorrect (or less correct than A) because even with financing, the agreement still violates the Statute of Frauds. **(C)** is incorrect because even if the apartments pass the inspection, the agreement still violated the Statute of Frauds. **(D)** is incorrect because there is no such presumption in property law.

165./D/ The stream is the property line the court will enforce under the boundary dispute exception rule: A boundary established by a common grantor that was physically apparent to both grantees is enforceable even if in variance with the legal description of the deed. **(A)** is incorrect because even if adverse possession applied, the time element has not been met. **(B)** is incorrect because of the boundary dispute exception. **(C)** is not the best answer because Joe would prevail under the boundary dispute exception. Frank might later meet all of the elements of adverse possession, but three years is not enough time under that rule.

166./B/ The buyers will prevail under the part performance exception. They paid the seller the purchase price, changed their position (took out a mortgage), took possession, and made valuable and permanent improvements. **(A)** is incorrect because an acknowledgement is necessary, but not sufficient, to meet the conveyance formalities. **(C)** is incorrect because lack of recording may be overcome by the part performance exception. **(D)** is incorrect because a marketable title is not an issue in this question.

167./A/ The conveyance is ineffective because she never delivered the deed. **(B)** is incorrect because a mere letter is insufficient to meet all the formalities of the Statute of Frauds. **(C)** is the second best answer. Had the conveyance been valid, most jurisdictions would recognize an informal rescission without a new deed. However, this point is moot under these facts because there was not a valid conveyance to rescind. **(D)** is incorrect because rescission is moot in this case because there was not a valid conveyance. Also, if the conveyance had been valid, rescission is possible in some jurisdictions without a new deed.

168./A/ This is a breach of warranty of title. Seller did not have title or permission to convey the entire property, and the buyer did not receive quiet enjoyment free from potential litigation. **(B)** is incorrect because the part performance exception applies to failures to meet the Statute of Frauds; it has nothing to do with title warranty.

(C) is incorrect because the facts say Bart sold the entire property, not only his portion. **(D)** is incorrect because a tenant in common, lacking permission to convey the other tenant's interest, may only sell his own interest.

169./C/ With a quitclaim deed, a person is only giving whatever interests he or she has in the property. In this case, it is his interest as a tenant in common. **(A)** is incorrect, because Bart did not warrant the title. **(B)** is incorrect because the part performance exception applies to failures to meet the Statute of Frauds; it has nothing to do with title warranty. **(D)** is incorrect because a tenant in common is only free to convey his own interest, not ownership in the entire property.

170./C/ This is a case of breach of implied warranty of habitability, which is applicable only to new homes. **(A)** is incorrect because title warranty is unrelated to this fact pattern. **(B)** is incorrect because the facts do not specify any express warranty was made. **(D)** is incorrect because the merchantability warranty applies to UCC goods, not real property.

171./D/ In this instance, there are no warranties. **(A)** is incorrect because title warranty is unrelated to this fact pattern. **(B)** is incorrect because the facts do not specify any express warranty. **(C)** is incorrect because implied warranty of habitability normally only applies to new homes. Note that at least one jurisdiction has found the implied warranty of habitability applicable to a second owner when the home is still very new as in this case. However, that is still a minority opinion. If you get this question on the MBE, the majority still holds that implied warranty of habitability applies only to new homes.

172./D/ In an equitable conversion jurisdiction, the rule is that between the purchase and sale contract and closing, the buyer bears the risk. Therefore, lacking insurance proceeds, Rob cannot bear the risk of the loss. **(A)** is incorrect, because if the buyers purchased insurance, their insurance company would bear the loss. **(B)** is incorrect, because if the seller had insurance, even though he bears no risk, most courts would require the seller to pay the buyer the proceeds of the insurance in equity. **(C)** is incorrect because Laura and Dick are the primary bearers of risk under the equitable conversion doctrine.

173./B/ Abbott prevails because in a pure race jurisdiction, the first to file wins. **(A)** is incorrect, because the type of deed is not impacted by whether the jurisdiction is race, race-notice, or notice. **(C)** is incorrect because in a pure race jurisdiction, notice is not a factor. Also, the fact pattern says that Abbott had notice of the statute, not the prior sale. **(D)** is incorrect because the pure race statute would override this factor.

174./C/ A quitclaim deed means that the seller only conveys whatever property interests he has. It provides none of the protections of warranty of title, including quiet enjoyment. **(A)** is incorrect because the statutory warranty of title does not apply to a quitclaim deed. Quiet enjoyment is merely one element of a statutory warranty of title. **(B)** is incorrect because selling with a quitclaim deed for a discount is not unusual: in fact, because there is higher risk with

quitclaim deeds, it would be normal to expect the purchase would be at a discount over normal market prices. **(D)** is incorrect because the pure race jurisdiction has no bearing on whether the seller has responsibilities under the warranty of title.

175./C/ In a race-notice jurisdiction, a subsequent purchaser must be a bona-fide purchaser without notice of a prior interest and be the first to record. If Abbott has notice, his filing before Oliver has no effect. **(A)** is incorrect, because the type of deed is not impacted by whether the jurisdiction is race, race-notice or notice. **(B)** is incorrect in a race notice jurisdiction, because a purchaser must also be without notice to prevail against a bona fide purchaser for value. **(D)** is incorrect because it is only a partial answer: the purchaser must be a bona fide purchaser for value, and the subsequent buyer must be without notice. **(C)** is a better answer than **(D)**, because it is the defect in Abbott's situation – he had knowledge of the prior interest – that allows Oliver to prevail.

176./C/ In a race-notice jurisdiction without notice of a prior purchase by a bona fide buyer for value, the first to file wins. **(A)** is incorrect because Paul filed first and therefore won. **(B)** is incorrect because the notice aspect of race-notice only protects against the other party who may have filed first but with notice. **(D)** is incorrect because the possibility of malpractice has nothing to do with the competing validity of title.

177./C/ A disclaimer clause can protect an insurance company against unrecorded deeds or defects not in the abstract of title. **(A)** is incorrect because Mark is insured only up until closing, and then only against recorded defects. **(B)** is incorrect because such disclaimer clauses are both very common and enforceable. **(D)** is incorrect because Glenn had an insurable interest in the title as soon as he signed the purchase and sale agreement.

178./B/ Jerry loses to Paul because of the race-notice statute. He then loses to the insurance company because the insurance is not transferable, therefore he had no title insurance. **(A)** is incorrect because Jerry had no valid title insurance. **(C)** is incorrect because Paul won due to the race-notice rule in this jurisdiction. **(D)** is incorrect because it is a nonsense answer: Paul had no connection with the insurance company, therefore, there was no valid claim.

179./A/ Jan has met all the ECHO elements of adverse possession, and although statutory periods differ between jurisdictions, 25 years would meet virtually every jurisdiction's requirements. **(B)** is incorrect because her possession was open. It had to have been open in at least Jim and Maritza's view – they were complaining the entire time about it. **(C)** is incorrect because "without permission" is the equivalent of "hostile" – one of the required elements of adverse possession. **(D)** is incorrect because the nuisance claim is not part of the adverse possession claim.

180./C/ Because there is privity, Jake's period of possession tacks onto his mother's adverse possession to give him the requisite time under the statute. **(A)** is incorrect because under the concept of tacking he has sufficient time to satisfy the statute.

(B) is incorrect because the nuisance claim is irrelevant. **(D)** is incorrect because the exclusive requirement tacks since there is privity between Jake and his mother.

181./C/ Inverse condemnation is an appropriate claim when the state's action destroys the owner's property economic value. **(A)** is incorrect because an inverse condemnation is broader than spot zoning. **(B)** is incorrect because a variance will be granted if unnecessary hardship results and such grant is not inconsistent with the general welfare and character of the neighborhood. Here, if the area is now a protected wetland, his variance would be inconsistent with that character. **(D)** is incorrect because there was not a structure to be "grandfathered."

182./C/ Gregg is liable because he expressly assumed the loan. Fred is still liable because an express assumption does not release the original obligor; this would take a release from the mortgagee. **(A)** is incorrect because it does not mention Gregg's liability. **(B)** is incorrect because it does not mention Fred's liability. **(D)** is not the best answer because both Fred and Gregg are liable.

183./C/ Since land is unique, the normal buyer remedy for seller's breach is specific performance. **(A)** is incorrect because warranty of title deals with the quality of title that is passed at closing. **(B)** is incorrect because the plaintiffs are not asking for title to be corrected, but rather for a contract to be enforced. **(D)** is incorrect because an action for damages would not recover the property.

184./A/ The means of breaking up a joint tenancy to give one tenant exclusive ownership of one portion of the land is through judicial partition. **(B)** is incorrect because once they became tenants in common, he would still need a partition, because a tenancy in common allows all tenants access to all portions of the property. **(C)** is incorrect because he would still need a partition, because a tenancy in common allows all tenants access to all portions of the property. **(D)** is incorrect because Paul and George would still have an undivided interest in his one third until a partition occurs.

185./C/ Quiet title actions are used to resolve boundary disputes, title disputes, adverse possession claims, and several other real property issues. **(A)** is incorrect because if Eddie claims adverse possession, the proper remedy is actually a quiet title action. **(B)** is incorrect, because there is no evidence of trespass in the fact pattern. **(D)** is incorrect because specific performance is a buyer's remedy.

186./D/ Unlawful detainer is not appropriate to resolve a nuisance problem; a nuisance is a separate tort action. **(A)** is incorrect because it represents a typical problem for which an unlawful detainer action is appropriate. **(B)** is incorrect because it represents a typical problem for which an unlawful detainer action is appropriate. **(C)** is incorrect because it represents a typical problem for which an unlawful detainer action is appropriate.

187./B/ As tenants in common, each of the three has a right to an undivided interest in the whole property.

Mary has no right to fence off third. **(A)** is incorrect because she has a right to be where she is, but she just doesn't have the right to exclude other co-tenants. **(C)** is incorrect because she may use the property as she wishes as long as she doesn't interfere with the property rights of the other owners. **(D)** is incorrect because she is excluding them from one-third of the property.

188./C/ Removal of the retaining wall between adjacent properties by the Rachel violated Karl's lateral support rights and results in strict liability. **(A)** is not the best answer because lateral support strict liability only applies to damage to land in its natural state. Rachel would have to prove negligence to recover for damages to the house. **(B)** is incorrect because quiet enjoyment usually refers to matters involving title defect challenges. **(D)** is not the best answer because subjacent support applies to the ground beneath property, not the removal of lateral support.

189./D/ When delivery of the deed is made to a grantee, any oral condition placed on the conveyance will usually be disregarded and delivery will be deemed complete in most jurisdictions. Here, Georgette gave George the deed, this is sufficient evidence to prove her intent to deliver the deed. The condition of him not leaving her for another woman will be disregarded. **(A)** is incorrect because no consideration is needed for conveyance by deed. Remember, a deed is not a contract; a contract requires consideration, but a transfer by deed does not. **(B)** is incorrect because an oral condition will not make a conveyance by deed invalid. If the delivery is directly to the grantee, the condition will be disregarded. **(C)** is incorrect since the delivery was made directly to George, the grantee, and no extrinsic evidence is allowed to prove the existence of any oral conditions. If Georgette had made delivery to George through a third party, and placed a condition on the delivery, then extrinsic evidence would be allowed. (Note that any future interest would be a reversion so the RAP does not apply.)

190./D/ Natural drainage patterns may be altered to control floods (dikes, diversions, etc.) under the "common enemy" doctrine as long as it does not create unnecessary damage to the land of another. **(A)** is incorrect because subjacent support is under the surface of the land. **(B)** is incorrect because lateral support refers to support of the land itself, not what occurs with water running across it. **(C)** is the next best answer to D because they both deal with water, but it is incorrect since riparian rights deal with the priority of uses allowed access to the water, not to the right not to be flooded by another's actions.

191./A/ Normally, a tenant who abandons property before the expiration of a lease is liable for the rent due for the remainder of the term. However, many states have statutes requiring the landlord to mitigate the damages, and attempt to re-rent the premises. **(B)** is incorrect because landlord re-entry terminates the landlord's right to collect rent. **(C)** is incorrect because landlord re-entry terminates the landlord's right to collect rent. **(D)** is incorrect because Buck may not avoid his obligation under the lease merely by giving the landlord notice.

192./B/ Even though Randy's estate may terminate with his life it is still a fee (simple subject to an executory limitation) and waste does not apply to fee interests. It is still possible that Randy and Penny could conceive or adopt children. The interesting question is whether waste lies at Penny's death or only at Randy's death when the fee terminates. **(A)** is incorrect because non-renewable resources may not be consumed in any manner by a holder of a life estate. (Note that some jurisdictions make an exception under the "open mines" doctrine if there previously was an operating mine on the property.) **(C)** is incorrect because although the holder of a mere life estate has a duty to not materially lessen the value of the future interest, here Randy has a defeasible fee simple. **(D)** is incorrect because termination of the tenancy is not a proper remedy for waste.

193./C/ Charlie received an easement by necessity. An easement by necessity requires that the dominant and servient estates were both originally owned by one person and that there is a strict necessity for the use. However, no prior use is required. **(A)** is incorrect because only a grantee can receive an easement by implied grant. **(B)** is incorrect because a prescriptive easement requires continual possession that is hostile to owner, and open and notorious use. **(D)** is incorrect because only a grantor can receive an easement by reservation.

194./D/ The best answer because Microhard did not record and the other tenants stand junior to Maximum. **(A)** is incorrect because Microhard did not record before Maximum did so they are junior under the jurisdiction's pure race recording statutes. All the other tenants will not prevail because they have no greater right than Denise and had at least constructive knowledge of the prior Maximum's mortgage. **(B)** is incorrect because the jurisdiction has a pure race notice recording statute under which the first to file prevails. In addition, the facts state that the Microhard lease was not recorded so even constructive notice is absent. **(C)** is incorrect because the jurisdiction has a pure race recording statute under which even actual notice of the prior interest is insufficient to override a subsequent party who files first.

195./D/ Vertical privity requires that the successor in interest takes for the same duration as the original owner. **(D)** is the correct answer because Mark transferred his entire interest to Sara. **(A)** is incorrect because Mark transferred less than his full interest in the parcel. **(B)** is incorrect because Mark transferred less than his full interest in the parcel. **(C)** is incorrect because Mark transferred less than his full interest in the parcel.

196./B/ Variance is the best answer of the four alternatives presented. A variance will often be granted where a landowner suffers a hardship as a result of the zoning law. **(A)** is incorrect because spot zoning applies where a parcel is singled out for an inconsistent use unrelated to the hardships of the particular owner. **(C)** is incorrect because a nonconforming use requires that the use was legal when built but does not meet the current zoning code. Here, the house has not yet been built. **(D)** is

incorrect because a rezone changes the use of the property and is usually more difficult to achieve than a variance.

197./D/ Cecile, Eric, and Joan started out as joint tenants, but the joint tenancy was severed when Joan transferred her interest to Tina. Severance results in the new party becoming a tenant in common. The remaining parties, as long as there is more than one, continue as joint tenants. **(A)** is incorrect because the joint tenancy was severed by the transfer. **(B)** is incorrect because Cecile and Eric continue as joint tenants as to each other. **(C)** is incorrect because each owns an undivided interest in the entire property.

198./B/ Real covenants and equitable servitudes terminate if abandoned; the facts say that the residents failed to carry out or enforce the restrictions. Here, failure of the residents to repair the road over a 20-year period likely constituted an abandonment. **(A)** is incorrect because a court would likely find that the covenant had been abandoned. **(C)** is incorrect because a court would likely find that the covenant had been abandoned. **(D)** is incorrect because the Rule Against Perpetuities applies only to non-vested interests in land and does not apply here.

199./C/ A tenancy at will was created rather than a term tenancy for years because the parties failed to comply with the statute of frauds. **(A)** is incorrect because a term tenancy for years of more than one year requires a writing to satisfy the statute of frauds. **(B)** is incorrect because a failure to comply with the statute of frauds creates a periodic tenancy only after the landlord accepts a payment from the tenant. **(D)** is incorrect because a tenancy at sufferance is created where a tenant wrongfully holds over, which did not happen here.

200./A/ A violation of the implied warranty of habitability occurs where the landlord fails to provide habitable premises. Keeping the temperature at 50 degrees likely qualifies as a violation. **(B)** is incorrect because a barking dog does not affect the habitability of the premises. **(C)** is incorrect because a cushiony carpet is not required for the apartment to be habitable. **(D)** is incorrect because a lack of heavy insulation does not make the apartment uninhabitable.

201./D/ All of the scenarios can terminate an easement. **(A)** may act to terminate the easement because of merger. An easement terminates where the dominant and servient estates come to be held by one party, even if one parcel is later re-sold. **(B)** constitutes an easement termination by abandonment. **(C)** constitutes an easement termination because a bona fide purchaser took the land without notice of the easement.

202./D/ Blake did not record and none of the subsequent parties knew of him; therefore none of the recording statutes stated protect his interest. **(A)** is incorrect because a pure race statute gives a priority to the first to record. **(B)** is incorrect because a pure notice statute gives a priority to bona fide subsequent purchasers without notice of a prior conveyance regardless of when they filed. Blake was not subsequent to either Charlie or David. **(C)** is incorrect because a race notice statute requires both a

lack of notice and that the subsequent purchaser be the first to record; Blake did not record.

203./B/ While David recorded first, he had notice of Charlie's prior interest and thus was not a bona fide purchaser; since Charlie also filed, he will prevail over Blake who did not record at all. Both pure notice and race notice statutes require that the successful claimant may not have notice of the prior interest. **(A)** is incorrect because a priority under a pure race statute requires the successful claimant to record first and the facts state that David filed first. **(C)** is incorrect because priority under a race notice statute requires the successful claimant to be a bona fide purchaser with actual or inquiry notice. **(D)** is incorrect because the type of deed instrument conveyed is not relevant as to the priority between competing interests.

204./A/ **(A)** is the best answer because under a pure race recording statute, the first to record has a priority and the claimant does not have to be bona fide or without notice. **(B)** is incorrect because to prevail under a pure notice statute requires no notice of the prior interest (regardless of when they filed) and the facts state that David knew of the prior unrecorded interest. **(C)** is incorrect because a race notice statute requires no notice of the prior interest and the facts state that David knew of the prior unrecorded interest. **(D)** is incorrect because the type of deed instrument conveyed is not relevant to the priority between competing interests.

205./B/ Alice will prevail; Carol had a "wild deed" that was not in the chain of title when she filed. She cured the lack of chain of title, but only after Alice filed. In a race notice jurisdiction, filing a "wild deed" loses the protection given to a bona fide purchaser until such time as the chain of title is complete. **(A)** is not the best answer because it is simplistic and the better reason is that Carol took under a "wild deed" not in the chain of title. **(C)** is incorrect because the type of deed the parties took under is not relevant to their priority. **(D)** is incorrect because while Carol recorded first, her recording was ineffective since it was not in the chain of title.

206./B/ The Water Department properly filed the deed containing its easement in gross and this was constructive notice to the world, including Sally. **(A)** is not the best answer because it is not legally relevant to the easement in gross question. Lacking a legal easement, the Water Department could be liable for damages even if there was a paramount need. **(C)** is not the best answer because Sally has constructive notice of the easement in gross since it would appear in a title search as being in the chain of title. **(D)** is incorrect because simple non-use of an easement in gross is usually not enough to constitute abandonment and/or estoppel since there was no objective manifestation of intent to abandon.

207./C/ Neither defendant will be held liable. The children of Harriet conveyed by way of a quit claim deed which transferred all ownership interest without any covenants or implies warranties which might be imposed in a warranty or bargain and sale deed. The Water Department is not liable because its easement in gross was

of record and there are not fact given to suggest it was negligen Further a Water Departmen excavating piping once in 48 year does not seem to be overuse o misuse of the easement in gros **(A)** is incorrect because the conveyed by way of a quit clair deed. **(B)** is incorrect because ha the owner not built the garage ove the burdened portion of the servien estate, no damage would hav occurred. **(D)** is incorrect becaus neither the children of Harriet nc the Water Department are liable.

208./B/ The conveyance of Greenacre ha the measuring life of Friend an Betty's remainder is void as violates the Rule Agains Perpetuities (RAP). This resul because the condition could occu more than 21 years from Friend' death. Thus the future interest i stricken and Friend gets a fe simple. The conveyance o Blackacre to Associate will nc violate the RAP because Betty' contingent remainder wil necessarily vest within Associate' lifetime. Thus the future interest i respected and goes to the remainde person, Betty. **(A)** involve interests going to the wron; combination of parties. **(C** involves interests going to th wrong combination of parties. **(D** involves interests going to th wrong combination of parties.

209./B/ Because the two tenants were no officially married, a tenancy by th entirety never existed. Rather th couple were tenants in commo and either tenant in common ca; petition a court to partition th property. **(A)** is incorrect becaus it states the property was held as ; tenancy by the entirety, rather tha a tenancy in common. **(C)** i: incorrect because both Albert and

Barbara were listed on the deed and treated as tenants in common since they were not officially married and that is required in the jurisdiction. **(D)** is incorrect because while the statement in the alternative is accurate, this was not a tenancy by the entirety.

210./C/ Regardless of the status of the fixtures, degree of affixation, and question of damage to the landlord's reversionary interest, the landlord has no claim if the tenant can return the premises to the condition it was in before the fixture was attached. **(A)** is incorrect because if the tenant can restore the premises to the condition it was in before the fixture was attached, the degree of affixation is irrelevant. **(B)** is incorrect because the ownership does not transfer if the tenant can restore the premises to the condition it was in before the fixture was attached. **(D)** is incorrect because even if the tenant paid for the fixture, it may not be removed if it would damage the landlord's reversion.

211./B/ The total award was $500,000 for all the property including both the leasehold and landlord's reversion. The owner is entitled to receive the full value of the property less the value of the conveyed lease interest. Stucks is entitled to the $200,000 value of the leased premises less the $75,000 present value of the lease payments due to the landlord for a net of $125,000. The balance of the $500,000 award goes to the property owner, Larry. **(A)** is incorrect because the tenant shares in a condemnation award as their interest lies. **(C)** is incorrect because any surplus received above the net value of the tenant's interest goes to the property owner. **(D)** is incorrect because the tenant's interest in the lease must be reduced by the present value of the lease payments that would have to be paid to the landlord had there not been a condemnation.

212./C/ The best answer. Courts dislike restraints on alienation and would likely interpret the conveyance as a fee simple absolute with the "understanding" condition as a contractual obligation of the grantee. This would allow Pricilla to seek damages but not rescission. **(A)** is incorrect; had the grantor more clearly indicated a defeasible fee, rescission might have been ordered. **(B)** is not the best answer because it disregards the damage award that would lie for the donee's breach of the contractual obligation. **(D)** is incorrect because the court would likely not allow rescission and the characterization of a fee simple absolute would give Community Use Foundation the right to convey the property to a third party.

213./B/ The best answer. The lease contained a use restriction that is binding on the tenant; thus the tenant breached the lease contract and Lorraine's statement that she did not intend to renew is within her rights. **(A)** is not the best answer because while courts may deny recovery for ameliorative waste that increases the value of the property, the change in the use of the property was prohibited in the lease. **(C)** is incorrect because the improvements changed the use of the property in a violation of the lease. **(D)** is incorrect because the use restriction in the lease does not state, "unless landlord consents, such consent may not be unreasonable."

214./D/ Class gifts to grandchildren are valid if they are the measuring lives once the class closes as of the death of the testator, here, the grandchildren are the measuring lives for Rule Against Perpetuities purposes. **(A)** is incorrect because the testamentary grandchildren's interest is valid under this fact pattern. **(B)** is incorrect because the devise does not state that the grantor's two children receive any permanent interest and the facts do not discuss the children's mother. **(C)** is incorrect because the date that a testamentary devise vests for Rule Against Perpetuities purposes is the date of death of the testator, not the date the testamentary instrument was created and executed.

215./A/ The continuous possession requirement of adverse possession may still be met if the seasonal interruptions are consistent with the normal use of the property in the area; this is an area of summer cabins so Ike's possession likely qualifies. To suspend the period of limitations, the owner must have been under a legal disability at the time the adverse possession began. While Gary Junior and Gale lacked capacity at the time adverse possession began, they were not then the owners of record. **(B)** is incorrect because the time period tacks against succeeding property owners. **(C)** is incorrect because the adverse possessor prevails. **(D)** is incorrect because the 15 year statutory period begins when the adverse possession begins and is not usually affected by a title transfer.

216./B/ An adjoining property owner is absolutely liable for damages to land in its natural condition if lateral support is removed. Here, however, the land has been artificially improved with a house and the question refers to damages to the house. Under the majority American view, the recovery is limited to lateral support damages to the land and may not include any damages to any artificial structure unless negligence is shown which doesn't apply here. **(A)** is not the best answer because the question of who else may be named as a D is not relevant to the claim between Able and Baker. **(C)** is incorrect because this alternative fails to distinguish between damages to the land itself and damages to artificial structures. **(D)** is not the best answer because this is a property, not a tort question and there are no facts given to conclude Baker was grossly negligent.

217./B/ Surface waters are subject to the "common enemy rule"; the lower parcel of land is not burdened with any servitude in favor of the uphill estate and has the right to protect their property from the enemy water. **(A)** is incorrect because compensation to an adjoining property owner resulting from self protection from the common enemy is not required. **(C)** is incorrect because a court will likely not order removal of the wall. **(D)** is incorrect because a court will likely not order removal of the wall.

218./C/ While the general rule in water allocation between riparian owners for the same use is one of reasonableness of withdrawal, the use here is different. Domestic or household use is considered to be a higher use than agricultural so Dorothy will have the priority. **(A)** is incorrect because upstream and uphill users do not have a priority as such. **(B)** is incorrect; had both uses been the same – say both parties were grape growers – the allocation standard would be one of reasonableness, but here the uses were different. **(D)** is incorrect in that the personal downstream domestic user does not have to be in an emergency or unable to purchase the water elsewhere and the reference to a statutory prior appropriation law is a typical MBE distractor because the facts do not state which user was there first or that the jurisdiction had such a statute.

219./B/ The owner of property has the exclusive right to the airspace above their property and any unreasonable use of this air space which interferes with the use and enjoyment of the surface will constitute a trespass. **(A)** is not the best answer because "no person" is too broad and interference with natural rainfall may be allowed if it does not affect other's property rights. **(C)** is incorrect because a landowner does "own" the space above their land, at least up to a reasonable height. **(D)** is incorrect because this is not a public necessity, such as saving a city from flooding, but rather a mere potential benefit to an individual property owner.

220./B/ Growing annual crops such as asparagus are emblements (or fructus industriales) and treated as personal property. The proceeds would therefore pass to the life tenant's (Wayward's) heirs since the crop was planted by the life tenant. **(A)** is incorrect because any application of RAP would not apply to the life tenant's personal property proceeds. **(C)** is incorrect because any interest going to the remainder interest would not include the life tenant's personal property proceeds. **(D)** is incorrect

because the life tenant's personal property interest would not be shared but rather go to the life tenant's heirs.

221./B/ The beneficiary of the contract provision not to assign or sublease was Lane Landlord who has a legitimate interest in the identity of the tenants to whom they entrust their property. There is no intention to benefit the tenants from such restrictions so at best, Terry is a mere incidental beneficiary with no right to enforce the conditions. **(A)** is incorrect because Terry, as an incidental beneficiary, has no standing to enforce the restriction. **(C)** is not the best answer since Tom has the responsibility to pay one half of the rent if Teresa fails and the facts do not specify the rent allocation between Tom and Teresa. **(D)** is incorrect because the lease contract only requires the consent of Lane Landlord, not all parties who might be interested.

222./B/ If a landlord consents – expressly or impliedly – to a transfer, the right to enforce the covenant against later assignees is waived. **(A)** is incorrect because the provision against assignment or sublease was waived. **(C)** is incorrect because privity of estate is always present between the landlord and any tenant; in comparison, privity of contract only exists if the assignee makes an express assumption of the duties in the original lease. **(D)** is incorrect because the conclusion is wrong because a prohibition on assignment runs with the land if there was privity of estate.

223./D/ Absent a novation or a release by Lane, privity of contract continues between the original parties; thus the obligation to provide fire insurance did not terminate merely because the lease was assigned. **(A)** is not the best answer; while the covenant to provide fire insurance generally touches and concerns at least the building, the claim being asserted is against the original tenant, not an assignee. **(B)** is incorrect because the covenant to provide insurance does run with the land. **(C)** is incorrect because while Tom and Terry may have a claim against the assignees or the neighbor, this does not relieve them of their primary contractual responsibility to Lane.

224./C/ Baker adversely possessed Blueacre for 16 years which exceeded the 15 year required in the jurisdiction to acquire land by adverse possession. Charlie took under color of title from the then proper owner – Baker – and his 11 years of possession exceeds the 10 year requirement to acquire under color of title such as a defective deed. Therefore his heirs at law would have a priority claim to Blueacre. **(A)** is incorrect because Alice lost the property to Baker's adverse possession. **(B)** is incorrect because Baker sold his interest to Charlie and even though the deed was defective, he acquired the title by adverse possession. **(D)** is incorrect because Alice lost ownership because Baker prevailed under adverse possession and thus had no interest to convey.

225./C/ The best answer because the dam became so permanently affixed to the land that it would be characterized as real property. Thus, even though the dam was added as personal property, it goes to the owner of the real property. **(A)** is incorrect because Alice lost the property to adverse possession. **(B)** is incorrect; although Baker

built the dam, he lost ownership t[o] Charlie who prevailed as a[n] adverse possessor who took unde[r] color of title. **(D)** is incorrec[t] because Alice lost ownership o[f] Blueacre to an adverse possessor s[o] she had no interest to convey.

226./A/ Under pure notice statutes, the firs[t] bona fide purchaser (BFP) fo[r] value without notice of any prio[r] conveyance will prevail. Thi[s] result follows in a pure notic[e] jurisdiction even though the firs[t] grantee subsequently recorded[.] Notice is based on the status of the purchaser when the deed transferred; on April 3, Carol di[d] not have constructive notice sinc[e] Barbara had not filed at that tim[e] and there are no facts give[n] suggesting there was actual notice[.] **(B)** is incorrect because to procee[d] under a race-notice would protec[t] Carol only if she recorded firs[t] which she did not. **(C)** is incorrec[t] because a pure race statute woul[d] protect Carol only if she recorde[d] first which she did not. **(D)** is [a] distractor since there is no race[-] race statute.

227./C/ The correct answer because th[e] covenant to purchase water doe[s] not "touch and concern" the lan[d] since it does not change the use[,] utility, or value of the land. **(A)** i[s] incorrect because "run with th[e] land" is the conclusion of a rea[l] covenant that is binding on [a] subsequent owner; this is not a[s] focused a rationale as the on[e] requirement – "touch and concern" – which is necessary to get to the conclusion. **(B)** is incorrec[t] because there is privity of estate[.] **(D)** is not the best answer; while [a] common plan or scheme ma[y] provide inquiry notice (o[r] constructive if filed), this is usuall[y] applied to uniform architecture residential uses only, or other characteristics that are visible unlike water sources which are buried in the ground.

228./A/ The best answer because the covenant in question meets all the requirements of at least a reciprocal negative servitude (and an equitable servitude if the use restriction was not in writing) including the requirement to "touch and concern" the land because it affects the value. **(B)** is incorrect because the restraint could be upheld as a reciprocal negative servitude since the common plan or scheme conveyed at least inquiry notice to Nancy. **(C)** is incorrect because actual knowledge is not required if there is inquiry or constructive notice; here the common plan should have put a reasonable person on notice that there was a recorded plan restricting the use of Nancy's property. **(D)** is not the best answer; a reservation is not as strong a deterrent as an affirmative covenant that touches and concerns the land.

229./C/ The best answer because it recognizes that the seller is liable for breach of marketable title since there is an encumbrance. Notice that the encumbrance did appear in the chain of title so the seller had constructive notice and could not properly convey a warranty deed containing a covenant against encumbrances. **(A)** is incorrect because the fact that Cory may have relied upon a third party does not negate his liability for breach of warranty. (Notice that the facts do not state that the company issued an actual insurance policy; only an abstract of title.) **(B)** is incorrect because misrepresentation requires some degree of intention to

defraud; here that is missing and the tort in question would be negligent misrepresentation. **(D)** is incorrect because actual knowledge of the defect is not necessary; a seller executing a warranty deed is charged with constructive knowledge of all encumbrances in the chain of title.

230./C/ The warranty TAFED requirements include a marketable title which is free of restrictions and encumbrances that would lead to litigation; here an order of specific performance would require Carol to litigate and seek a quiet title action for Barbara's adverse possession claim. **(A)** is incorrect because it does not address a property issue, but rather a civil procedure issue of jurisdiction; civil procedure is not tested on the MBE. **(B)** is incorrect because there are no facts given in the question indicating that Barbara intended to defraud; her claim to the property appears valid and at worst, it might constitute negligent misrepresentation. **(D)** is incorrect; the seller promised a marketable title free of restrictions and encumbrances that would lead to litigation; here an order of specific performance would require Carol to litigate and seek a quiet title order for Barbara's adverse possession claim.

231./C/ The primary issue would be whether the first deed from Brett to Chuck is deemed to be in Edward's chain of title. If it was, then Edward would have constructive notice of the prior interest and thus can not qualify as a BFP to override the doctrine of estoppel by deed. **(A)** is incorrect because it depends on the statement that Edward had no knowledge of Brett's interest; if Brett was of record, Edward would have constructive notice. **(B)** is incorrect because it gives as a reason a fact which is at issue in the question. **(D)** is incorrect because the fact it gives will not determine who will prevail; Edward would not be bound if Brett's deed is deemed recorded in Edward's chain of title.

232./D/ Both interests to the first grantees are valid as fee simples subject to an executory interest for both Greenacre and Pleasant Farms. III is correct (and thus II is incorrect) because a contingent remainder following a devise to a non-charity is to be struck as violating the RAP since the condition of the grantee's drug use may vest more than 21 years after Charlie's life. V is correct (and thus VI is incorrect) because a contingent remainder is valid under the charity to charity exception to the RAP. **(A)** is not the best answer because II is incorrect. A contingent remainder following a devise to a non-charity is to be struck as violating the RAP since the condition of the grantee's drug use may vest more than 21 years after Charlie's life. **(B)** is not the best answer because VI is incorrect. A contingent remainder is valid under the charity to charity exception to the RAP. **(C)** is not the best answer because VI is incorrect. A contingent remainder is valid under the charity to charity exception to the RAP.

233./B/ It is conceivable that Andy's wife could adopt or even have a fertile implant that might produce more children later who would only take (at age 25) more than 21 years after Andy's death. Andy is the measuring life in this case. **(A)** is incorrect because while a true statement, the fertile octogenarian rule strikes the future remainder of

all the takers if there is a violation. **(C)** is incorrect because the remainder violates the RAP based merely on the possibility the rule may be violated. **(D)** is incorrect because the remainder violates the RAP based merely on the possibility the rule may be violated.

234./A/ The best answer because the rationale in alternative (A) controls "if" the doctrine of retaliatory eviction applies. Note that this alternative does not contradict the facts – only supplements the facts given. **(B)** is not the best answer because while a partially true statement as far as it goes, it does not address the required 30-day notice of a periodic tenancy and the central doctrine of retaliatory eviction. **(C)** is incorrect because the rationale – moving more tenants into the unit is a violation – goes beyond the facts and in most jurisdictions is not a violation unless these rights are specifically prohibited in the lease contract. (Had the modifier been "if" this alternative would be more attractive.) **(D)** is not the best answer because the "only if" condition is not necessary to support the outcome of the tenant prevailing and it does not address the central issue of retaliatory eviction.

235./D/ The correct answer because the taking was only partial and the tenant was compensated for their interest in the fee. **(A)** is incorrect because the tenant's only responsibility is not to commit waste on the property and condemnation by the county is not the fault of the tenant. **(B)** is incorrect because the landlord is not interfering with the tenant's use of the premises resulting in ouster the landlord is not responsible for acts of the government and the tenant has not been totally ousted from the premises. **(C)** is incorrect because a frustration of purpose would involve total or near total destruction of the premises; here, there was only a 50% reduction and the tenant has been compensated for their interest in renting the fee.

36./C/ Whether chattels sufficiently attach to the realty is a question of intention; here the intention of the improver was only to benefit his own interest and there is no factual suggestion that removal will cause substantial damage to the real property. **(A)** is incorrect because it is not necessary that permanent fixtures be described with particularity in the mortgage; improvements usually go with the land. Further, since the lease was first in time, the mortgage holder takes subject to the lease. **(B)** is incorrect because "any personal property" is too broad, contains an absolute word, and would include chattels. **(D)** is incorrect because knowledge by the tenant of an obligation of the owner is not a condition precedent to the mortgage company's ability to protect their rights in the land and fixtures.

37./D/ If the easement was expressly created, the owner of the easement in gross has a duty to maintain the easement unless otherwise agreed. **(A)** is incorrect because the easement owner is not subject to strict liability. **(B)** is incorrect because the conclusion is wrong and the easement holder has the right to enter the servient estate in a reasonable manner to perform maintenance and repairs. **(C)** is incorrect because the owner of the easement in gross has a duty to protect both their own and the

interest of the burdened tenement.

238./C/ The general rule is that neighbors do not acquire an implied or prescriptive negative easement to wind, sunlight, or view. An express grant is an exception and usually enforced as a contractual responsibility. Notice that lot A is still in the hand of the promisor, Mary, so the promise would be enforced against her. Had Mary sold the lot, the question would be raised whether the negative covenant would run with the land. The answer is probably yes because the restriction would "touch and concern" the land. But Nancy did not have privity with the promisor, Mary, so the easement burden would not run against her. **(A)** is incorrect because some other combination of alternatives is correct. **(B)** is incorrect because some other combination of alternatives is correct. **(D)** is incorrect because some other combination of alternatives is correct.

239./D/ When Big Daddy died, his one-third interest in the joint tenancy passes to the surviving joint tenants – Adam and Eve – not according to the decedent's will. The subsequent conveyance by Adam to Newton converted the joint tenancy to a tenancy in common since there were only two joint tenants remaining. **(A)** is incorrect because a testamentary devise by a joint tenant is ineffective; Big Daddy's interest thus went to Adam and Eve on his death. **(B)** is incorrect because a testamentary devise by a joint tenant is ineffective; Big Daddy's interest thus went to Adam and Eve on his death. **(C)** is incorrect because a testamentary devise by a joint tenant is ineffective; Big Daddy's interest thus went to Adam and Eve on his death.

240./C/ In many, if not most, jurisdictions, a formal disposition sale is required if the contract buyer has paid a substantial percentage of the total payments. **(A)** is incorrect because the installment contract forfeiture is the sole remedy; if the sale was by mortgage, a deficiency judgment is possible. **(B)** is incorrect because no such rule applies. **(D)** is incorrect because a mortgage repossession sale is subject to a redemption right, but not usually an installment sale forfeiture.

241./D/ Even under the common law, a landlord is liable if they had actual knowledge of serious hidden defects that could not be discovered in a reasonable inspection and that defect injures the tenant. **(A)** is not the best answer because strict liability is too high a standard and "any injuries" is too broad and absolute in scope. **(B)** is incorrect; while a tenant generally takes the premises as they find them, the landlord is under an affirmative duty to make disclosure of serious hidden defects they knew of that could not be discovered in a reasonable inspection. **(C)** is incorrect because any duty to inspect and resulting waiver or assumption of the risk would not apply to serious hidden defects of which the landlord had notice.

242./C/ A provision requiring consent to sell property is a disabling restraint on alienation which is void in most jurisdictions. **(A)** is incorrect; the right of first refusal to meet another's purchase offer is not a restraint on alienation since the seller can still make the sale (to either the outside offeror or the association exercising their right to

match the offer). **(B)** is not the b[est] answer because while a cooperati[ve] is allowed more restrictions [on] transfers than a condominium, ev[en] a cooperative can not outrig[ht] prohibit a sale. **(D)** is incorre[ct] even an agreement by a memb[er] will not be enforced if it is [a] disabling restraint on alienation.

243./C/ The statute of frauds requires t[he] seller to sign a written agreeme[nt] and the facts do not say Floren[ce] signed anything. **(A)** is incorre[ct] because the doctrine of pa[rt] performance requires more th[an] naked payment. Part performan[ce] usually requires possession of t[he] land by the buyer who mak[es] significant valuable and permane[nt] improvements which are [not] present here. **(B)** is incorre[ct] because the party to be charg[ed] must sign the sales contract a[nd] here there was no signature. **(D)** [is] incorrect because to be enforceab[le] against her, Florence must ha[ve] signed the sales contract.

244./D/ While the court may reform a me[re] scrivener's error or mutual mistak[e,] the amount and specific location [of] the land for a "large lawn a[nd] garden" lacks reasonable precisi[on] and is vague and ambiguou[s.] Indeed, the court may assume th[is] is at least one of the reasons t[he] transaction did not close. **(A)** [is] incorrect in that the description [of] the land to be conveyed must [be] specified even if the seller signs t[he] contract. **(B)** is incorrect becau[se] the consideration for the contract [is] mutual promises; payment is n[ot] necessary. **(C)** is incorrect becau[se] the consideration for the contract [is] mutual promises; payment is n[ot] necessary.

245./D/ The injunction would be grant[ed] since a life estate (even a pur aut[re] vie) may not commit waste if it materially reduces the value of the future interest – here a remainder. The provision "for church use only" would probably be construed as a covenant, not a condition that would terminate the life estate. Since the facts do not state that Betty's son has died, the past damages would be impounded for future distribution when the remainder class closes. **(A)** is incorrect because there is a general duty not to materially reduce the value of the future interest; the duty not to commit waste does not have to be expressly stated. **(B)** is incorrect because an injunction will issue to protect the future interest. **(C)** is incorrect; the duty not to commit waste exists even if the future interests do not complain.

246./B/ An express easement created by grant may only be terminated by abandonment, merger, or an instrument releasing the easement. **(A)** is incorrect because a lack of necessity is insufficient to terminate an express easement. **(C)** is incorrect because while a partnership may be terminated by any partner in many states, cross-easements are not a partnership. **(D)** is incorrect because there is not a negative burden of persuasion imposed on the non-moving party in an action to terminate an easement.

247./A/ Both tenants must agree to encumber the property to pay for non-required improvements; since Nancy would not agree, the petition will likely be denied even though Mary could seek partition. **(B)** is incorrect since the rule on unilateral improvements applies to both joint tenants with the right of survivorship and tenants in common. **(C)** is incorrect because

the marginal cost/marginal increase in value analysis is irrelevant. **(D)** is not the best answer; while inability to use the land economically would be grounds for partition or a judicial sale, this fact pattern suggests neither.

248./D/ A co-tenant who unilaterally makes non-required improvements without the approval of the other tenant(s) may not prevail in an action for contribution. Mary's remedy is to bring a petition to partition or sell the property; a court would probably at least allow her a claim against the proceeds for her $25,000 investment. **(A)** is incorrect because one-half of the value of the improvements would not be awarded. **(B)** is incorrect because one-half of the investment would not be awarded. **(C)** is incorrect because one-half of the profit would not be awarded.

249./C/ Merger by deed dictates that a provision in the deed controls if inconsistent with provisions in prior negotiations or preliminary agreements such as the sales agreement. **(A)** is incorrect because merger by deed would negate the effectiveness of any prior inconsistent agreement. **(B)** is incorrect because it is not necessary that the grantee sign the deed to qualify under the statute of frauds. **(D)** is incorrect because the grantee's signature is not necessary on the deed and under the merger by deed doctrine, provisions in the deed control contrary terms or omissions in the previous sales contract.

250./C/ An oral agreement between adjoining property owners to settle a dispute about an uncertain common property boundary line is binding if relied upon even though it does not comply with the statute of frauds. Barbara acquiesced to Alice and in effect gave her permission to erect the brick wall in that place and both parties built gardens and ponds in conformity with the agreement. Carol may still recover damages from her vendor, Barbara, however. **(A)** is incorrect because the wall will not have to be removed. **(B)** is incorrect because there will not be a damage award. **(D)** is incorrect because the court will not likely order the wall removed.

251./A/ Caroline would prevail over the other parties under the doctrine of estoppel by deed. Since Alice reacquired Silveracre by purchasing the property at the foreclosure sale, she came into the full unencumbered title which inured to Caroline. **(B)** is incorrect because Alice represented to the second mortgagee, Caroline, that there were no interests senior to hers and when this factual situation subsequently came about, Caroline's interest was re-established under the doctrine of estoppel by deed. **(C)** is incorrect because Doris does not meet the N requirement in FINS; the interest of Caroline was recorded so there was constructive notice. **(D)** is not the best answer because the misrepresentation by Alice would most likely support a mere action for damages.

252./C/ The rule in most jurisdiction is that a purchaser of property receives the right to all the natural resources therein unless the grantor specifically reserves same. **(A)** is incorrect because it is not necessary to specifically convey the mineral rights; they are included unless specifically reserved to the grantor. **(B)** is not the best answer because

knowledge of every aspect of the land is not necessary to acquire the rights thereto. **(D)** is incorrect because a land purchaser's intention of use does not usually determine the interest they take in the acquisition.

253./D/ The covenants of title (seisin), authority and right to convey are personal and therefore do not run with the land. If there was a breach, it became a personal chose in action upon Adam's delivery of the deed to Bryan. **(A)** is incorrect because Charlie does not have a valid claim against Adam. **(B)** is incorrect because Charlie does not have a valid claim against Adam. **(C)** is not the best answer because the personal covenants breached by Adam do not run with the land and they therefore are not available to a subsequent grantee.

254./B/ A seller conveying property using a limited warranty or a bargain and sale deed only warrants that he has no knowledge of TAFED defects in his conveyance and does not warrant prior conveyances. **(A)** is incorrect because while privity exists between Charlie and Bryan some breach of contract is necessary to support the lawsuit. **(C)** is not the best answer because it does not address the central issue of the question and the statute of limitations discovery rule may apply to some of the claim only if otherwise had a legal basis. **(D)** is incorrect because it merely states the facts underlying the lawsuit, not a legal rationale which would defeat the lawsuit.

255./B/ While a bona fide purchaser who files first may prevail, they must take for value which is more than nominal value. Gifts do not qualify. The "for value requirement applies even if they do not have knowledge or notice of the prior unrecorded interest. **(A)** is incorrect because the eviction action date is irrelevant to the priority question. **(C)** is incorrect because there is no imputed knowledge and the facts state that the children lacked knowledge. **(D)** is incorrect because it is the value of the consideration of the bona fide purchaser that is at issue here, not the first grantee, Nancy.

256./D/ Since Iola took from Harriet, she would begin the title search with her grantor, Harriet, to see if Harriet herself was a grantee. Since the search would show that Harriet took from Florence, Iola should then look to see if Florence took proper title (from Ethel). **(A)** is incomplete since all this would tell was whether the Harriet to Iola deed was recorded which Iola already knows. **(B)** is incorrect since Iola would have no way of knowing if Gertrude was even in the chain of title since she did not have privity with her. **(C)** is incorrect and incomplete because all this would indicate is if Harriet had received a conveyance from someone. Iola already knew this and what she needs to know is whether her grantor, Harriet, was herself a proper grantee in a previous transaction.

257./D/ This jurisdiction has a pure race-notice recording statute. The first in the race to record wins and notice of prior irregularities is irrelevant. **(A)** is incorrect because while Florence recorded first, she sold the property to both Gertrude and Harriet so Florence will not prevail. Iola paid full value and recorded **(B)** is incorrect because Gertrude did not record. **(C)** is incorrect because Harriet sold her

interest to Iola.

258./C/ Jack gave Karen a power of appointment to designate the subsequent transferees of Greyacre in her will. Since the property was not conveyed by Karen's will, it reverts to the estate of the donor. Therefore, Lawrence had no interest in Greyacre to convey to Mary so Mary is entitled to a return of her deposit. **(A)** is incorrect because Lawrence had no legal interest to convey. **(B)** is incorrect because even if the deed contained a covenant of general warranty, it would not make the title marketable. **(D)** is incorrect because the land did not pass to Karen's heirs under her will which was a requirement of the grantor.

259./C/ Lack of delivery is the best argument since it is a requirement for an effective deed conveyance in most jurisdictions. While recording creates a presumption of effective delivery, the facts state the vendor died before delivery. **(A)** is incorrect because the contract argument fails since a will is ambulatory until the death of the testator. **(B)** is incorrect because the breached agreement might lead to damages but not the property itself. **(D)** is incorrect because variances in terms is the deed and note do not automatically invalidate the documents in question.

260./B/ Courts may be reluctant to enforce the Merger Into Deed equitable doctrine because there could easily have been negotiations subsequent to the purchase and sale agreement that were incorporated into the final deed. Therefore, it is not likely that the court would disturb the "as is, with all faults" warranty designation in the deed. In comparison, the court would likely reform the dollar mistake from $800 to $500 made by the scrivener's drafting or typing mistake. **(A)** is incorrect because it contains a wrong combination of the alternatives. **(C)** is incorrect because it contains a wrong combination of the alternatives. **(D)** is incorrect because it contains a wrong combination of the alternatives.

261./B/ The best argument because a broker exclusive agreement only means the property owner will not sign up with another broker. This may not create a liability for the commission if the owner sells the property elsewhere without the broker's involvement. **(A)** is incorrect because a bilateral contract does usually survive the death of either party. **(C)** is incorrect since the majority rule is that the broker must "provide a buyer." The facts state Nathan learned of the property availability from a party who had contact with Bobbie Broker. **(D)** is incorrect because variances in terms between the deed and note do not automatically invalidate the documents in question.

262./C/ The recording statute in the jurisdiction applies only where the subsequent interest holder takes for value or files with the county recorder. Since Nancy did not take for value but by gift and Olive did not file at the county where the property is located, the recording statute thus does not apply. The common law rule of "first in time – first in right" thus prevails. **(A)** is incorrect because Nancy received her interest as a gift and thus cannot meet the "for value" requirement. **(B)** is incorrect because they filed at the state

capital rather than the county seat as required by the recording statute. **(D)** is incorrect because a mortgage is treated as an interest in real property similar to a deed.

263./B/ The "race-notice" statute here makes both good faith and prior recording (but not for value) necessary for a subsequent grantee to prevail. Nancy meets both requirements and therefore prevails. **(A)** is incorrect because Nancy does not have to give value to prevail under the recording statute specified in the question. **(C)** is incorrect because Olive recorded at the wrong location; a reasonable title search would not have discovered the interest so it is outside the chain of title. **(D)** is incorrect because there was a subsequent grantee, Nancy, who did file and the recording statute applies to both deeds and mortgages.

264./A/ The majority of jurisdictions apply the "reasonable use" standard to adjacent property owner's competing use of underground percolating waters. Thus as long as Pete's planned use of water withdrawn from the aquifer is found to be not unreasonable, the court will not enjoin that level of use. **(B)** is incorrect; the number of users of the aquifer is not the test applied. **(C)** is incorrect because both parties are entitled to reasonable use and the focus in this proceeding would be on whether the injunction's target's – Pete – use was or was not reasonable. **(D)** is incorrect because the commercial use is on Pete's own property and it would only be one factor in determining the relative reasonableness of the use.

265./B/ In those jurisdictions which recognize tenancy by the entirety, the presumption or inference that any conveyance to a husband and wife creates a tenancy by the entirety is rebuttable. Here, the conveyance specified Francis and Stuart were to take as joint tenants thus effectively rebutting the presumption. A joint tenant may convey their individual interest without the consent of the other joint tenant, but it severs the joint tenancy and makes the grantee a tenant in common. **(A)** is incorrect because the joint tenancy was severed and Gloria became a tenant in common. **(C)** is incorrect because only a husband and wife may hold title as tenants by the entirety. **(D)** is incorrect because Francis and Stuart held their interest as joint tenants since the presumption of tenancy by the entirety was rebutted.

266./D/ A subsequent purchaser is required to search the record which would have contained the George to Iceman deed. Since this recorded instrument makes reference to an unrecorded interest, one has an inquiry duty to investigate and gain notice of the prior unrecorded easement. **(A)** is not the best answer because Iceman's knowledge or lack of same has no effect upon the duty of John to investigate. **(B)** is incorrect because actual knowledge is not necessary if there is an inquiry duty that would lead to constructive record notice. **(C)** is incorrect because the lack of consideration in the original grant of the easement would not affect the question of subsequent parties and the facts do not say consideration was absent.

267./A/ The best answer because if the contract for sale does not specify

the quality of title to be conveyed, delivery of a marketable title is usually implied. Note that this may also mean that Susan breached the duty to convey marketable title. **(B)** is incorrect because there was a meeting of the minds on the property to be conveyed sufficient for a court to order specific performance. **(C)** is incorrect because the lack of marketability does not excuse performance and zoning and land use regulations do not usually render the title unmarketable. **(D)** is not the best answer because imposition of a mere quit claim deed would deprive the buyer of the benefit of her bargain – a marketable title.

268./C/ There appears to be a sufficient description in the conveyance instrument so that the property in question can be specifically identified. Although the description is not stated in metes and bounds, the prominence of the farm in the county would create sufficient identification and the facts do not state that anyone is questioning the identity of the property. Further, the facts do not state that this description was used in the final deed – only in the conveyance agreement. **(A)** is incorrect because the property can be specifically identified. **(B)** is incorrect because it is a distractor; title of seisin is the grantor's warranty that they have title and that issue is not raised in this fact pattern. **(D)** is incorrect because the presence or absence of consideration is not relevant to the question of the certainty of the property's identification.

269./B/ Under a race-notice statute, a subsequent bona fide purchaser will prevail over a prior unrecorded interest if they meet all the FINN requirements. The issue here is whether Charlene had inquiry notice, which would result from a diligent title search. If the record does not explain who is in possession of the property, the purchaser must inquire further. Thus Charlene had inquiry notice that Barbara owned the property. **(A)** is incorrect because Alice sold the property twice. **(C)** is not the best answer because the reason Barbara prevails is that Charlene had inquiry notice and thus cannot meet the FINN requirement not that Barbara was first in time. **(D)** is incorrect because under a race notice statute, filing first is not sufficient unless accompanied by no notice.

270./D/ Farmer Fred's conveyance of a potential shifting executory interest to his sister Sally fails because it violates the Rule Against Perpetuities. The College has a fee simple on the condition that the land be used for agricultural purposes. If not used for agriculture, the fee divests to Farmer Fred since there are no other directions stated in the conveyance. This is called a possibility of reverter. **(A)** is incorrect because Farmer Fred has a possibility of reverter. **(B)** is incorrect because Farmer Fred has a possibility of reverter. **(C)** is incorrect because Farmer Fred has a possibility of reverter.

271./C/ In most jurisdictions, promissory restraints on alienation of a fee simple are void. **(A)** is not the best answer because promissory restraints on alienation of a fee simple interest are void. **(B)** is not the best answer because promissory restraints on alienation of a fee simple interest are void. **(D)** is not the best answer because promissory

restraints on alienation of a fee simple interest are void.

272./C/ The correct alternative because the right of first refusal is valid and the Rule Against Perpetuities does not apply since no future interest violates the 21 year rule. **(A)** is incorrect because there is not a transfer of property presently involved – only a right of first refusal if Albert decides to sell Secondacre. **(B)** is not the best answer because recording an instrument only creates a position of priority. The question here is concerned with the validity of Charlie's rights, not the priority of the right. **(D)** is incorrect because Albert is restraining only his own power to convey or devise Secondacre by giving a right of first refusal. Restraints on alienation are only suspect if the grantor or testator tries to convey or dispose of property and subsequently retain control over a future transfer.

273./A/ The future executory interest to Ernest and his heirs violates the common law Rule Against Perpetuities. This interest fails and because the wording "but if" creates a fee simple subject to a condition subsequent there is no reversion. Summa Law School has a fee simple absolute. **(B)** is incorrect because Lorraine has no interest after the conveyance and Summa has a fee simple absolute since the executory interest violates the RAP. **(C)** is incorrect because the operative conditional words of "but if" extinguishes any potential future interest of reverter in the grantor. (Note if the wording had been "as long as" creating a fee simple determinable a reversion to the grantor would be the correct answer.) **(D)** is incorrect because the grantor has no future interest.

274./B/ The best answer because the other alternatives offered are less correct and delivery by the grantor was not completed prior to her death. The facts are not clear that Lorraine unequivocally intended to deliver the deed. Further, if she did initially have intent, she could have changed her mind since she did not mail the deed. **(A)** is incorrect because the recording statute may determine the priority of interests vis-à-vis multiple deed grantees, but it does not determine the validity of such interests. **(C)** is incorrect; while normally a deed conveyance is not effective until acceptance by the grantee, such acceptance is assumed if the grant is to a charity or non-profit organization such as a law school. **(D)** is not the best answer because the facts do not indicate that the deed was intended as a testamentary devise. Further, had delivery been accomplished before Lorraine's death, it would have been effective immediately as an intervivos transfer rather than a testamentary disposition.

275./C/ The best answer because under the common law, the landlord was under no duty to repair and maintain the premises. This was non-residential property, the landlord had no fault or role in the destruction of the air conditioning equipment, and Second had exclusive control over the premises. **(A)** is not the best answer because the status of a chattel v. fixture is not determinant of the duty to repair under a common law lease. **(B)** is incorrect because if the lease assignee does not perform the duty to repair, the lease assignor would have a higher

duty under the common law than the landlord. **(D)** is incorrect because over use is not an act of God and under the common law, the landlord has no duty to repair a commercial rental facility.

276./C/ If the landlord surrenders their right by re-entering the premises and taking possession, the tenant is usually relieved of all future obligations. **(A)** is incorrect because it contradicts the facts and mitigation does not require the new rent be the same as the rent of the abandoning tenant. **(B)** is not the best answer because the right of re-entry is not as compelling a reason as actual re-entry which is expressed in alternative C. **(D)** is incorrect because the deficiency of $1,000 ($5,000 lease amount less $4,000 mitigated rent) would still be the liability of the original tenant.

277./B/ By re-entering the premises and taking possession for her own purposes, the landlord also effectively terminated her right to keep the security deposit. **(A)** is incorrect because the landlord's re-entry for her own purposes effectively terminates her right to keep the security deposit. **(C)** is incorrect because if the mitigation resulted in a deficiency, the tenant's security deposit could be used for this purpose. **(D)** is not the best answer because "only if" means that there could be no other common law reason that would justify the landlord retaining the tenant's security deposit.

278./D/ On the MBE candidates should examine very closely the condition(s) precedent that must be satisfied before the property owner is required to pay a commission to an agent. Here, there was a condition that the agent must produce the buyer and also that the closing must actually occur. Although Betty found a buyer within the 90-day period, the sale was not closed with that buyer and Sally sold the property herself. Since all the prerequisite conditions were not satisfied, the obligation to pay the commission never matured into a liability. **(A)** is incorrect because the broker never produced a buyer who would close at the price of $100,000. **(B)** is incorrect because the $95,000 offer did not close. **(C)** is incorrect because the purchase at a price of $85,000 was not procured by Betty Broker.

279./D/ The best answer because even if built unintentionally the overhang invades the airspace owned by Nancy and this constitutes actionable trespass. While the usual remedy is eviction, a court could allow damages instead of ordering removal since the cost of removable would substantially exceed the benefit to be gained by Nancy. **(A)** is not the best answer because the remedy of eviction seems less likely than damages under these circumstances. **(B)** is incorrect because Nancy is entitled to at least nominal damages even if actual harm cannot be shown. **(C)** is incorrect because neither a good faith mistake nor the sale to a bona fide purchaser is a defense to trespass.

280./C/ Ademption applies when a specific property devised in a will is disposed of prior to the decedent's death; the testamentary taker receives nothing under the majority rule. Bequested property is taken subject to any related mortgage unless the will makes other specific provisions. **(A)** is incorrect; the majority rule is that the intended

taker of adeemed property does n[...] receive equivalent value from t[...] residue of the estate and the residu[...] of the estate is not responsible for mortgage attaching to proper[...] going to another beneficiary. **(B)** incorrect; the majority rule is th[...] the intended taker of adeeme[...] property does not receiv[...] equivalent value from the residu[...] of the estate and the residue of th[...] estate is not responsible for mortgage attaching to proper[...] going to another beneficiary. **(D)** incorrect; the majority rule is th[...] the intended taker of adeeme[...] property does not receiv[...] equivalent value from the residu[...] of the estate and the residue of th[...] estate is not responsible for mortgage attaching to proper[...] going to another beneficiary.

281./A/ If a named beneficiary predeceas[...] the testator and their devise w[...] specifically conditioned on the[...] surviving the testator, the devi[...] normally lapses. The property [...] thus added to the residual of th[...] estate and does not go to th[...] devisee's heirs. If the jurisdicti[...] has an anti-lapse statute in effe[...] the property goes to th[...] beneficiary's heirs at law. **(B)** [...] incorrect and a distractor sin[...] even if the grantor and grant[...] were married almost a[...] jurisdictions have abolished a[...] inchoate (unexpressed) right [...] dower and curtesy; here there w[...] not an expressed right. **(C)** [...] incorrect because modernly a fe[...] tail estate has been abolished b[...] statute in most jurisdiction and th[...] primary grantee takes a fee simp[...] absolute; this theory might favo[...] Edward, Betty's sole beneficiar[...] **(D)** is incorrect because a power o[...] appointment gives the non-fe[...] owner the future right to appoi[...] the remainder person; this theor[...]

might favor Edward, Betty's sole beneficiary.

82./C/ The only correct combination of the two sets of variables stated in the requirements. Both tenants are bound by the landlord's assignment of the right to receive the rental payments. Tenant's rights that pre-date receiving notice (actual or by notice through mortgage filing) of a default lose any lease contract rights and become in effect a tenancy at will. Junior leases executing after notice of default may be dispossessed and their leases cancelled by the mortgagee. **(A)** is incorrect because it contains the wrong combination of the two variables in the question. **(B)** is incorrect because it contains the wrong combination of the two variables in the question. **(D)** is incorrect because it contains the wrong combination of the two variables in the question.

83./C/ Under the common law, a conveyance of property to two non-married people was presumed to create a joint tenancy with right of survivorship. Most jurisdictions today would rebuttably presume that a conveyance to an unmarried couple creates a tenancy in common unless there was a showing of sufficient intent to create some other form of tenancy. The wording of the conveyance here clearly intended to create a right of survivorship rather than the default estate of a tenancy in common. The only other tenancy possible is a joint tenancy with the right of survivorship. This would avoid the ownership interest going to the joint tenant Iola's children so it is her best argument. **(A)** is not the best argument that Nancy could raise because the facts of the question state that only married

couples are eligible for tenancy by the entirety. **(B)** is not the best argument because the controlling statue states only legally married people may be tenants by the entirety and there is not an exception for a good faith mistake about their marital status. **(D)** is incorrect because the principle of estoppel by deed refers to a conveyance of property not presently owned but subsequently acquired; this rule is contained in this question as a red herring.

284./D/ A life tenant may encumber property with a mortgage or lease but any conveyance beyond the life tenant's estate is a form of waste. The life estate may be mortgaged but the mortgagee has no rights against the remainder interests. Similarly a life tenant may lease the premises to a third party but any such lease terminates at the death of the life tenant (pur autre vie). To allow to these parties rights against the remainder interest would constitute waste. **(A)** is incorrect because it involves a combination of wrong conditions. **(B)** is incorrect because it involves a combination of wrong conditions. **(C)** is incorrect because it involves a combination of wrong conditions.

285./D/ Carol is a remote grantee as it relates to Adam. The covenant of free of encumbrances and lack of significant defects in the chain of title that Adam breached does not run with the land to Carol. Rather it became a personal choses in action at the time the deed was delivered to Barbara. Carol is an immediate grantee as it relates to Barbara, but Barbara conveyed title via a quiet claim deed that does not contain any covenants of title. **(A)** is incorrect because it involves the wrong combination of alternatives.

(B) is incorrect because it involves the wrong combination of alternatives. **(C)** is incorrect because it involves the wrong combination of alternatives.

286./C/ The best answer to this convoluted question is that the Felicia to Sarah deed was within Tony's chain of title and thus Tony is charged with record notice of the restriction. **(A)** is not the best answer since the emphasis in the question is on the equitable height restriction not the priority of recording. **(B)** is not the best answer because the fact of one low house height is not sufficiently compelling to lead a reasonable person to conclude there is a neighborhood-wide height restriction. **(D)** is not the best answer since a better answer exists and the clear emphasis of the facts is on notice of the restriction that may be gained through the chain of titles not whether the burden of the restrictions run.

287./A/ The buyer will avoid liability of the equitable conversion doctrine does not apply and the seller retains possession of the property. This is also the growing preference of sellers absent insurance proceeds availability. **(B)** is not the best answer because the fact there may have been negligence does not necessarily avoid the transaction since damages could be awarded. **(C)** is not the best answer because if the possessory theory applies Betty can avoid all liability. **(D)** is incorrect because if the doctrine of equitable conversion applies, the risk of loss would shift to Betty upon execution of the sales contract.

288./B/ The best argument is that the adverse possessor, Freda First, acquired her owner's interest in lots

bound by the equitable restriction. Even though it is not clear this i[s] the law, this is the only alternativ[e] that would allow the neighbor t[o] enforce the equitable restriction[s]. **(A)** is incorrect because a[n] equitable restriction is an expres[s] promise and does not arise b[y] implication simply from the wa[y] neighbors use their property. **(B)** i[s] incorrect because privity of estat[e] requires succession to the sam[e] physical estate in land; neither i[s] present between Selina and Freda[.] **(D)** is incorrect because Selina i[s] not an assignee of Freda; rather [a] mere purchaser and the contrac[t] and deed did not mention an[y] equitable servitude.

289./A/ Acquiring title by advers[e] possession is not a "conveyance[e]" within the control of the recordin[g] act so a subsequent purchaser is n[o]t protected. Therefore th[e] determining priority sequence wil[l] default to the common law "first i[n] time, first in right." **(B)** is incorre[ct] because the sufficiency of the us[e] of the property for advers[e] possession varies and seasonal us[e] may be enough if continuous an[d] consistent with the use of propert[y] in the area. **(C)** is incorre[ct] because adverse possession doe[s] not have to be recorded in order t[o] avoid operation of the recordin[g] statute. **(D)** is not the best answe[r] since the various types of notic[e] only become important if [a] subsequent purchaser may gain [a] priority under the recording statut[e] here the recording statute does n[ot] apply to the adverse possessio[n] claim of ownership.

290./B/ The oral contract attempted t[o] transfer ownership of real propert[y] without compliance with th[e] writing requirements of the statut[e] of frauds. However the "pas[t] performance" exceptions appears satisfied since Selina took possession and made substantial improvements including paying property taxes. While Freda and Selina did not own the property at the contract date they subsequently received ownership and the estoppel by deed doctrine would require Freda to convey her later-acquired interest to Selina. **(A)** is incorrect because while the general rule it disregards the exception for past performance. **(C)** is incorrect because during the period in question the true owner was their mother, Mary, not Freda and thus Selina was not "hostile" as to Freda. **(D)** is incorrect because both the result and theory are wrong. One co-tenant can obtain shared property if the claiming tenant previously "ousted" the other tenant and this ouster continued for the statutory period.

291./C/ A co-tenant in exclusive possession of the real property may exercise reasonable discretion in making and executing regular management decisions. Barbara was not ousted by Alice and the law will respect an oral agreement fixing a boundary line between adjoining neighbors that was previously in dispute. **(A)** is incorrect because there is no general requirement that co-tenants who have voluntarily quit the premises must receive notice of proper management acts. **(B)** is incorrect because a co-tenant is only ousted if the tenant in possession physically evicts the co-tenant or attempts to convey sole ownership of the property to a third party; neither of these occurred in this fact pattern. **(D)** is incorrect because the statute of frauds has an exception validating an oral agreement establishing a disputed boundary line between adjoining property owners.

292./B/ A co-tenant in exclusive possession of jointly owned property is not accountable to the other co-tenants for shares of profits unless they ousted the other tenants. **(A)** is not the best answer because it is the exclusive possession, not the lack of participation, that best explains why Flighty does not receive any portion of the operating profits. **(C)** is incorrect because co-tenants in exclusive possession do not share operating profits with co-tenants unless they were previously ousted. **(D)** is incorrect because a tenant in exclusive possession does not share operating profits with co-tenants unless they were previously ousted. (Note: the distractor here is the rule in some states that if a tenant in possession seeks contributions from co-tenants not in possession, there may be an offset for the reasonable rental value and any profits realized.)

293./C/ A co-tenant in exclusive possession making valuable property improvements from her own funds is entitled to an additional amount from the partition sale proceeds without offset for any benefits derived from use of the property. **(A)** is incorrect because this alternative would result in a windfall profit to the tenant not in possession. **(B)** is incorrect because there is not a presumption of a gift when a co-tenant in exclusive possession makes improvements to property. **(D)** is incorrect because a co-tenant in exclusive possession of jointly owned property is not subject to a setoff for benefit from the use of the property.

294./B/ The best answer because this is the amount that Flighty is entitled to; she receives one-half of the net proceeds of the sale of the property, no share of the net profits from the farm operation (since she had not been ousted), but one half of the net rents received from a third party or

One half of property
sale proceeds
($200,000 ÷ 2) = $100,000
Share of farm profits = -0-
One half of
third party
rental proceeds
($50,000 ÷ 2) = $25,000
 $125,000

(A) is incorrect because a co-tenant not in possession does share rentals received from third parties. **(C)** is incorrect because a co-tenant not in possession does not share in operating profits earned by a co-tenant in exclusive possession. **(D)** is incorrect because a co-tenant not in possession does not share in profits earned by a co-tenant in exclusive possession.

295./D/ Acquiring title by adverse possession between co-tenants requires notice of hostility which usually includes an "ousting" by the co-tenant in possession; there is no suggestion that an "ousting" occurred. **(A)** is incorrect because it is too simplistic and does not refer to the necessary notice of hostility. **(B)** is incorrect because the necessary notice of hostility must be given to trigger the statutory period, not at the end. **(C)** is not the best answer because a co-tenant in exclusive possession may acquire sole ownership by adverse possession if notice of hostility is given. To not give such notice to the co-tenant may violate the duty of fair dealing which is why the requirement must be met to trigger the statutory period.

296./B/ The express time of the essence condition could be waived or have been converted to an accord since Denise led Susan to believe the condition was being modified. This alternative is reinforced by the fact that Susan paid $10,000 in reliance expecting that the contract date for performance was extended. **(A)** is incorrect because it contains the absolute modifier "never" and there may be circumstances when a failure to timely perform may be a breach. **(C)** is incorrect because insisting on enforcement of conditions in a contract is not inequitable. **(D)** is incorrect because the facts expressly indicate that time was of the essence in the original contract.

297./A/ This is the strongest argument because Susan has expressed an inability to purchase the easement and thus may not be able to deliver a marketable title at closing. **(B)** is not a strong argument because Susan's statement, "I am not sure right now" is not sufficiently unequivocal to qualify as anticipatory repudiation. **(C)** is not a strong argument because a marketable title is only necessary at closing. **(D)** is not a strong argument because any fraud would require knowledge of falsity by the seller at the contract date and the facts indicate that Susan did not know of the defect at the contract date.

298./C/ Severance of the joint tenancy with right of survivorship occurs when a tenant, voluntarily or involuntarily, transfers her interest to a third party. In addition, Sarah's refusal to pay her then co-tenant in common Theresa one-half of the rent received from a third party constitutes a hostile "ouster" which triggers the statutory period for adverse possession. Since more than five years have passed, Sarah has acquired title by adverse possession. **(A)** is incorrect because Felice would only have an ownership interest if her vendor Theresa had such an interest. However, that interest was lost to adverse possession. **(B)** is incorrect because it reaches the wrong conclusion about ownership. **(D)** is incorrect because the sheriff's sale severed the joint tenancy and a tenancy in common was created. Thus the survivor does not take.

299./D/ Since the future interest does not revert to the grantor, it is a remainder. Since the grantee of the remainder is unascertainable, the interests of the now unborn great grandchildren are contingent remainders because it is subject to the condition of being born to the grantor's granddaughter, Playful. **(A)** is incorrect because a "springing" executory interest is where the grantor has a reversion, but it springs to a third party later. **(B)** is incorrect because a power of appointment gives the designee the future right to pick (appoint) the remainder person(s). Here all the children of Playful take so there is no decision left. **(C)** is incorrect because none of the grantor's great grandchildren within the class are alive at the first vesting so that partial divestment may follow.

300./B/ The issue is whether the future interests are invalid under the Rule Against Perpetuities (RAP) thus reverting to the grantor so it is subject to testamentary direction. The grant of Greenacre used the conditional wording "so long as" to create an executory interest in Landsave Foundation. But since the condition could vest more than 21 years from a life in being, Alice, it is void under the RAP. What is left is the creation of a fee simple determinable with automatic reversion to the grantor Gertrud. On her death, this interest thus goes to her heir Carolyn. The grant of Blackacre used the conditional wording "but if" which also violates the RAP. But striking the offensive executory interest here leaves no wording of reentry and the wording "shall pass to" indicates no intention that the grantor intended a reversion. Thus this interest becomes a fee simple absolute in the grantee Betty and the grantor's heir takes nothing. **(A)** is incorrect because Alice's interest terminated when she violated the limiting condition of no development on Greenacre. **(C)** is incorrect because the executory interest to Landsave Foundation is void under the RAP. **(D)** is incorrect because the executory interest to Landsave Foundation is void under the RAP.

Index

RIGOS BAR REVIEW SERIES

MULTISTATE BAR EXAM REVIEW (MBE)

Volume 1 Index

Torts

Property